MOON

PACIFIC NORTHWEST HIKING

CRAIG HILL & MATT WASTRADOWSKI

CONTENTS

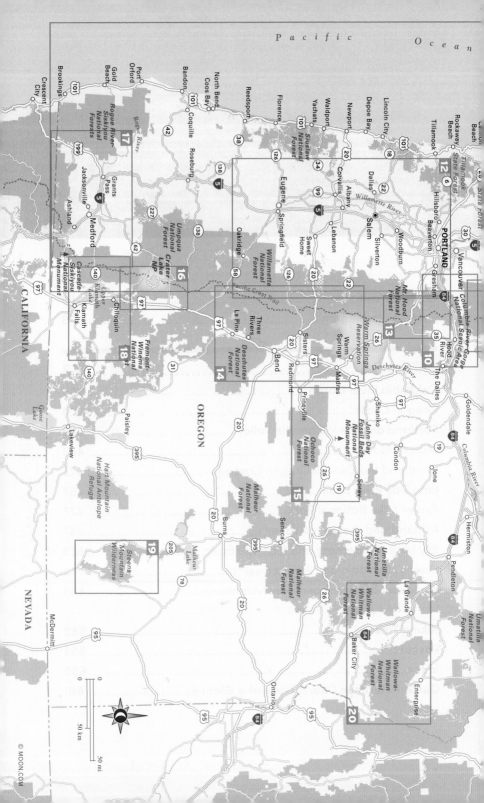

PACIFIC NORTHWEST HIKING REGIONS

1. Washington Coast
2. Olympic National Park
3. Seattle and Vicinity
4. North Cascades
5. Central Cascades

6. Mount Rainier
7. South Cascades
8. Central Washington
9. Eastern Washington
10. Columbia River Gorge

11. Oregon Coast
12. Portland and the Willamette Valley
13. Mount Hood
14. Bend and the Central Oregon Cascades
15. John Day River Basin

16. Crater Lake National Park
17. Ashland and the Rogue Valley
18. Sky Lakes Wilderness and Klamath Basin
19. Steens Mountain and Alvord Desert
20. Wallowa Mountains and Blue Mountains

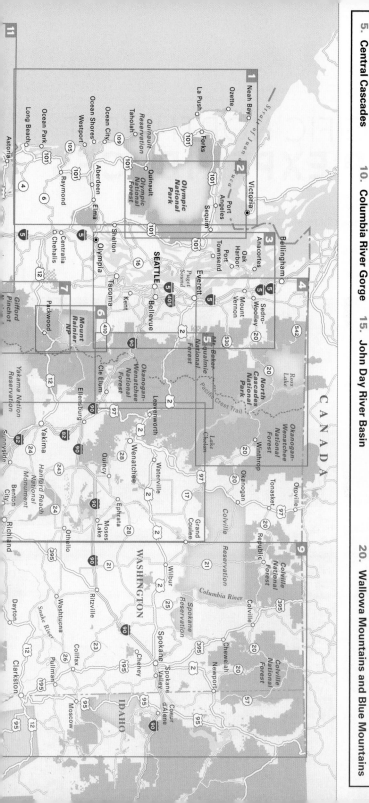

PACIFIC NORTHWEST
TOP EXPERIENCES

1 Explore the Columbia River Gorge (page 295).

2 Take in Pacific Ocean views and spot marinelife (pages 34, 37, 337, and 346).

3 Hike around volcanic landscapes on Mount Rainier (page 197) and Mount Hood (page 403).

4 Wander through fields of wildflowers (page 22).

5 Chase waterfalls (page 18).

6 Walk beneath curtains of moss and towering trees in Olympic National Park's Quinault (page 72) and Hoh Rain Forests (page 63).

7 Swim in mountain lakes (pages 133, 179, 532, and 535).

8 Follow trails through the urban forests of Seattle (page 97) and Portland (page 372).

9 Gaze into Crater Lake's dramatic blue depths (page 477).

10 Kick back with a post-hike beer (page 20).

HIT THE TRAIL

W hether leaving footprints on an ocean beach, wandering through lush Douglas fir forests, traipsing across landscapes shaped by ice age floods and volcanic eruptions, or climbing Cascade peaks, every step in the Pacific Northwest reveals anew why this is one of the world's most captivating hiking destinations.

Washington and Oregon collectively encompass four national parks, 42 national wildlife refuges, more than 350 state parks, nearly seven million acres of protected wilderness, and roughly 1,000 miles of the Pacific Crest Trail. The volume can keep hikers busy for a lifetime, but it's the variety that makes this region so special.

In Washington, adventures await on the snowy slopes of Mount Rainier, around the maritime playground of Puget Sound, and in the Olympic Peninsula's temperate rain forests, made lush by more than 10 feet of rain per year. In Oregon, the rugged, compelling coast is marked by crags, peaks, and lighthouses; Crater Lake shines like a sapphire gem; and the dusty high desert expanses around Bend beckon. You can walk through a retired railroad tunnel on Washington's Snoqualmie Pass and see Oregon Trail wagon tracks in the Blue Mountains. The states converge dramatically at the awe-inspiring Columbia River Gorge, a National Scenic Area that marks the border between them.

The Pacific Northwest gives generously to outdoors explorers. Each step takes you a little farther from the stress of everyday life, a little closer to tranquility. This is what we hope this book gives you. We'll show you the paths to take. Nature will take care of the rest.

▼ LOWER MACLEAY TRAIL, OREGON

Camping the Coast

With a mix of sea stacks, lighthouses, towering capes, tide pools, and beaches, the Pacific Northwest's coast offers classic adventure. Pick a hike and then pitch a tent nearby for the night, or string these suggestions together—they're listed north to south—to hop your way down the coast on a hiking-camping trip. Driving time between successive campgrounds is typically between 1 and 3.5 hours.

WASHINGTON
Makah Indian Reservation, Neah Bay

Start your day with an easy walk to **Cape Flattery,** the northwesternmost point in the contiguous United States. Then make the longer hike to **Point of Arches via Shi Shi Beach** to catch sunset. Spend the night at **Hobuck Beach Resort,** an oceanside campground on Makah tribal land, conveniently situated between the trailheads.

Olympic National Park, Ozette

Two legs of the **Ozette Triangle** are boardwalks cutting through the forest to and from the middle leg, a walk on Washington's wild coast. Nearby you can spend the night camping on the shore of Ozette Lake at **Ozette Campground,** and learn about the homesteads that once occupied this area.

Olympic National Park, Rialto Beach

Time your visit for low tide and examine tide pools as you stroll along **Rialto Beach** to the sea arch known as **Hole-in-the-Wall.** Spend a night sleeping in the forest less than 1.5 miles from the Pacific Ocean at nearby **Mora Campground.**

Olympic National Park, Kalaloch

Head about 30 miles inland from the coast to hike through rain forest on the **Quinault Loop.** Then head back to the coast for a night at **Kalaloch Campground,** one of the most popular campgrounds on the Olympic Peninsula; sites are close enough to hear the ocean surf.

Ilwaco

Spend a night near where the Lewis and Clark expedition camped at **Cape Disappointment State Park** and take a walk on the **North Head Trail.** After a short side trip to an old military battery, the trail leads through the forest to a lighthouse with sweeping views of the Pacific.

OREGON
Cannon Beach

The tent sites at **Saddle Mountain State Natural Area** promise a quiet respite from some of the region's more crowded campgrounds. Situated early along

▲ SHI SHI BEACH

the **Saddle Mountain Trail,** you'll appreciate the proximity after climbing nearly 1,500 feet up the mountain's slopes.

Tillamook
Sitting on a sand spit between Netarts Bay and the Pacific Ocean, **Cape Lookout State Park** has a developed campground nestled in the heart of the Tillamook coast. Just a few miles south, you can hike to the tip of **Cape Lookout,** one of the best whale-watching spots on the entire Oregon Coast.

Yachats
The **Cape Perpetua Campground** makes a great base for exploring the area's natural beauty. Thor's Well, Spouting Horn, and "the best view on the Oregon Coast"—according to the U.S. Forest Service—are some of the many highlights along **Cape Perpetua's** network of trails.

Florence
Embark on a magical hike to one of the coast's most iconic lighthouses—plus a beach—on the **Heceta Head to Hobbit Trail.** Less than a 30-minute drive south on U.S. 101 brings you to the campground at **Jessie M. Honeyman Memorial State Park,** set amid the Oregon Dunes.

Brookings
You don't have to go far to see one of the northernmost redwood groves on Earth—in fact, it's a short walk from your campsite at **Alfred A. Loeb State Park.** On the **River View Trail to Redwood Nature Trail,** you'll pass through a forest of Oregon myrtle before reaching the towering trees.

Day-Hiking the Pacific Crest Trail

The 2,650-mile Pacific Crest Trail (PCT) stretches from Mexico to Canada and is a dream trip for many backpackers. While thru-hikers take months to walk the entire trail, such an adventure isn't realistic for many. This doesn't mean you can't enjoy the famous route: Oregon and Washington are home to about 1,000 miles of it and offer numerous opportunities for day hikes, as well as nearby camping options.

WASHINGTON
Mount Rainier
Hike the scenic **Naches Peak Loop.** Not only does this classic wildflower hike have views of Mount Rainier, but you'll split time between the PCT and the national park's trails. Camp 13 miles northwest of the trailhead at **White River Campground.**

OREGON
Columbia River Gorge
The hike to **Dry Creek Falls** follows the PCT through patches of burned forest—damage done by the 2017 Eagle Creek Fire—before an offshoot trail detours to the base of the namesake falls. Camp about 8 miles east of the trailhead at **Wyeth Campground.**

Mount Hood
Ramona Falls, which tumbles over columns of basalt in a shady forest, is a popular destination, and on the hike you'll hop on and off the PCT. Spend the night about 10 miles southwest at **Tollgate Campground;** you're not far from U.S. 26, but the Zigzag River—which butts up against the campground's western edge—drowns out highway noise.

Bend and the Central Oregon Cascades
Hike part of the PCT on the way to **Little Belknap Crater.** You'll travel through a forest and emerge at the foot of a massive lava field with views of Cascade peaks. Camp 17 miles east at **Creekside Campground,** near downtown Sisters.

Ashland and the Rogue Valley
Hike the PCT through wildflower meadows and gain views of nearby peaks on **Mount Ashland.** Camp overnight just a few miles away at the **Mount Ashland Campground.**

Sky Lakes Wilderness and Klamath Basin
Follow the PCT on the **Brown Mountain Lava Flow** hike, which darts between verdant forests and eerie lava flows, all while delivering photo-worthy views of Mount McLoughlin. Sitting in the shadow of Mount McLoughlin about 5 miles north of the trailhead, **Fourmile Lake Campground** makes an ideal place to spend the night.

BEST BY SEASON

Spring
WASHINGTON

- **Hall of Mosses and Hoh River Trail:** This is the best season to see wildlife at this popular Olympic National Park destination (page 63).

- **Kamiak Butte:** The rolling hills of the Palouse are most green in spring (page 285).

- **Dog Mountain:** In spring this peak is capped with vivid wildflower fields (page 317).

OREGON

- **Tom McCall Point Trail:** Each spring, wildflowers dot the meadows leading to the summit of McCall Point, which affords views of Mount Hood and Mount Adams (page 326).

- **Cape Lookout:** Spy migrating gray whales from one of the best whale-watching spots along the Oregon Coast (page 346).

- **Lower Table Rock:** Hike to the pancake-flat summit of Lower Table Rock and admire its seasonal vernal pools and colorful wildflower displays before the summer heat arrives (page 506).

Summer
WASHINGTON

- **Chain Lakes Loop:** Visit lakes on a North Cascades trail with views of Mount Baker and Mount Shuksan (page 133).

- **Second Burroughs Loop:** Alpine tundra, wildflowers, glacier views, and the rumble of rock and ice careening down Mount Rainier make this an epic summer hike (page 206).

- **Steamboat Rock:** Start the day with a hike up a basalt butte in the Grand Coulee, and then spend the warmest hours playing on Banks Lake (page 256).

OREGON

- **Opal Pool and Jawbone Flats Loop:** Follow this trail to a popular swimming hole and an old mining camp (page 390).

- **Cleetwood Cove and Wizard Island:** This two-parter is only accessible in summer, when you can take a trail down to Crater Lake's shore and then boat to a volcanic cinder cone for a hike to its summit (page 483).

- **Sky Lakes Basin via Cold Springs Trail:** Hike to some of the region's most popular swimming holes (page 532).

Fall

WASHINGTON

- **Maple Pass Loop:** For fall colors, it's hard to beat this North Cascades loop (page 142).
- **Granite Mountain:** This scenic climb is awash in reds, oranges, and yellows in autumn (page 182).
- **Lake Ingalls:** October is the time to see mountain goats wandering among golden larches (page 191).

OREGON

- **Trail of Ten Falls:** This trail's 10 waterfalls are even more impressive alongside vivid fall foliage displays (page 381).
- **Bagby Hot Springs:** With temperatures cooling and crowds dissipating, early fall is an ideal time to hike through old-growth forest to enjoy a soak in Oregon's most popular hot springs (page 387).
- **Misery Ridge-River Trail Loop:** After the summer crowds have simmered down at Smith Rock, enjoy a sunny hike up to one of the best viewpoints in Central Oregon (page 441).

▼ FALL COLOR ON MAPLE PASS LOOP

▲ VIEW FROM THE PITTOCK MANSION IN WINTER

Winter

WASHINGTON

- **Point of Arches via Shi Shi Beach:** A worthy trip any time of year, you won't have to share the beach with as many visitors in colder months (page 37).

- **Oyster Dome:** This popular trail is open year-round and sees fewer visitors in winter (page 88).

- **Nisqually Estuary Boardwalk Trail:** In winter, bald eagles fish for chum salmon at the refuge. In late January, hunting season ends and the final 700 feet of the estuary boardwalk reopens to hikers (page 116).

OREGON

- **Mosier Plateau:** The Mosier Plateau's low elevation makes it a good winter hiking destination, and you also have a solid chance of spotting bald eagles overhead (page 323).

- **Cape Falcon:** Hike out to a windswept bluff overlooking the Pacific Ocean, where you might see migrating gray whales (page 337).

- **Lower Macleay Trail to Pittock Mansion:** When the region's most popular hikes are socked in with snow and ice, this hike remains accessible, delivers a hearty workout, and offers stellar views of the downtown Portland skyline (page 372).

BEST WATERFALL HIKES

WASHINGTON

- **Quinault Loop:** Pass multiple waterfalls on this loop through lush rain forest greenery (page 72).

- **Twin Falls:** View this dynamic cascade in the forest from several vantage points (page 109).

- **Cedar Falls:** Make this easy hike early in the spring when the falls are at their most powerful (page 145).

- **Wallace Falls:** The trail to these falls is one of Washington's most popular hikes (page 164).

- **Lake Serene and Bridal Veil Falls:** This stack of waterfalls is so tall you can't fit it all into one view (page 167).

OREGON

- **Latourell Falls Loop:** These scenic falls in the Columbia River Gorge cascade amid lichen-colored columnar basalt pillars (page 298).

- **Wahkeena Falls-Multnomah Falls Loop:** Bookend a hike with two of the most popular waterfalls in the Gorge (page 304).

- **Drift Creek Falls:** Cross a dramatic suspension bridge to this waterfall in the Oregon Coast Range (page 352).

- **Trail of Ten Falls:** On this iconic hike you'll pass 10 waterfalls in less than 10 miles (page 381).

- **Ramona Falls:** Hike to one of the most photographed waterfalls in the state, set in the shadow of Mount Hood (page 412).

BEST BREW HIKES

In the Pacific Northwest, you're never too far from a brewery. One of the joys of hiking is kicking back with a beer afterward. Here are some of the best trail-brewery pairings.

WASHINGTON

- **Discover Park Loop, Seattle and Vicinity:** This gentle trail offers a taste of Seattle history, forested trails, and sweeping views of Puget Sound, Mount Rainier, and the Olympics. It's also just minutes from several Seattle breweries, including **Fremont Brewing Company,** one of the state's fastest-growing breweries thanks to its broad selection of award-winning beers (page 97). To try: Dark Star (imperial oatmeal stout) and Session Pale Ale.

- **Rattlesnake Ledges, Seattle and Vicinity:** Ham it up for a few family photos against a spectacular backdrop from a rock outcropping high above Rattlesnake Lake. Then head to the **Snoqualmie Brewery and Taproom,** where kids can enjoy freshly brewed root beer floats while parents savor an adult version, or some of the brewery's award-winning offerings (page 103). To try: Black Frog Nitro Stout Float, Haystack Hefeweizen, and Copperhead Nitro Pale Ale.

- **Colchuck Lake, Central Cascades:** Work up a thirst on this hike to a stunning lake and then head into the Bavarian-themed village of Leavenworth. The Icicle River, which you'll drive alongside on the way to town, is used to produce the beer at **Icicle Brewing Company** (page 176). To try: Bootjack IPA and Priebe Porter.

- **Yakima Skyline Trail, Central Washington:** Admire views of the city of Yakima and the Yakima River canyon, then head to **Bale Breaker Brewing Company,** located on one of the area's commercial hop farms (page 262). To try: Field 41 (pale ale) and Topcutter (IPA).

- **Coyote Wall (Labyrinth Loop), Columbia River Gorge:** Every step of this trail offers picturesque views, and you can keep the views coming just five miles down the road in White Salmon, where you can sample the selection of session beers at **Everybody's Brewing** in view of Mount Hood (page 320). To try: Local Logger (lager) and The Cryo-Chronic (IPA).

ˈICICLE BREWING COMPANY

ˈEVERYBODY'S BREWING

OREGON

- **Cape Perpetua, Oregon Coast:** Hike a network of scenic trails and then refresh yourself afterward just a few miles north with a beer at **Yachats Brewing,** whose ales and lagers are named for local landmarks and incorporate locally and regionally sourced ingredients (page 355). To try: Thor's Well (IPA) and Log Dog Lager.

- **Lower Macleay Trail to Pittock Mansion, Portland and the Willamette Valley:** Pair some of Portland's best skyline views with one of the city's best breweries. After a hike up this trail inside city limits, head just a mile away to **Breakside Brewery,** which boasts a variety of hop-forward ales and crisp lagers (page 372). To try: Breakside IPA and Breakside Pilsner.

- **Tumalo Mountain, Bend and the Central Oregon Cascades:** This hike affords views of Mount Bachelor and its surroundings, and in nearby Bend you can unwind on the lawn at **Crux Fermentation Project** while soaking in more views of Cascade peaks, including the Three Sisters (page 444). To try: Cast Out (IPA) and PCT Porter.

- **Grizzly Peak, Ashland and the Rogue Valley:** Enjoy sweeping Rogue Valley views, Cascade peaks, and seasonal wildflowers, and then head into Ashland's **Caldera Brewing Company,** which boasts a tap list of 40 house-brewed beers (page 509). To try: Lawn Mower Lager and Pilot Rock Porter.

- **Hurricane Creek to Slick Rock Gorge, Wallowa Mountains and Blue Mointains:** Hike into the heart of the Wallowas amid a bucolic blend of alpine forests, crystal-clear rivers, and towering peaks. Afterward, in nearby Enterprise, enjoy sweeping views of the Wallowas from the outdoor bar at **Terminal Gravity Brewing** (page 566). To try: Terminal Gravity IPA and Terminal Gravity ESG.

▾ CRUX FERMENTATION PROJECT'S PCT PORTER

BEST WILDFLOWER HIKES

⌃ WILDFLOWERS

WASHINGTON

- **Grand Valley:** Look for scarlet paintbrush, bluebells-of-Scotland, and more on this hike (page 66).

- **Skyline Divide:** Heather, aster, daisies, and lupine add a kaleidoscope of color to a ridge with up-close views of Mount Baker and Mount Shuksan (page 127).

- **Skyline Trail Loop:** Conservationist John Muir's words are carved into the steps at the beginning of this hike and let visitors know what lies ahead: "the most luxuriant and the most extravagantly beautiful of all the alpine gardens" (page 216).

- **Cowiche Canyon:** Golden balsamroot and pink bitterroot add spring color to the arid terrain near Yakima (page 265).

- **Dog Mountain:** Colorful lupine, columbine, balsamroot, and other wildflowers attract so many visitors that you need a permit to visit in spring (page 317).

OREGON

- **Tom McCall Point Trail:** Among the most popular wildflower hikes in the Columbia River Gorge, this trail hosts yellow balsamroot, purple grasswidow, and red paintbrush, plus views of Cascade peaks (page 326).

- **Tryon Creek State Natural Area Loop:** Trillium, tiger lily, and fireweed dot this trail in spring (page 378).

- **Elk Meadows:** Host to everything from purple lupine to white-fringed grass of Parnassus, this is one of the best wildflower-viewing spots on Mount Hood (page 418).

- **Lower Table Rock:** The flat summit of Lower Table Rock hosts numerous rare wildflowers, including the dwarf woolly meadowfoam—a plant found nowhere else on Earth (page 506).

- **Mount Ashland (via the Pacific Crest Trail):** Find some of the Rogue Valley's most breathtaking wildflower displays along this hike through hillside meadows (page 515).

BEST DOG-FRIENDLY HIKES

WASHINGTON

- **Mount Ellinor:** Young, fit dogs will love this short but steep hike, and you'll love the views (page 78).
- **Lake Twenty-Two:** This climb past waterfalls, giant cedars, and a serene lake is a lovely treat for both you and your pet (page 154).
- **High Rock Lookout:** Dogs aren't allowed on trails at Mount Rainier, but this hike just outside the park is the next best thing (page 223).
- **Badger Mountain:** Leashes are available to borrow at the trailhead (page 268).
- **Coyote Wall (Labyrinth Loop):** This is the rare hiking trail with an off-leash season (page 320).

OREGON

- **Cape Falcon:** What dog doesn't love a day at the beach? Pair your hike with off-leash fun at Short Sand Beach (page 337).
- **Lower Macleay Trail to Pittock Mansion:** Fido will appreciate the well-graded, well-maintained paths en route to Pittock Mansion, where you'll enjoy skyline views (page 372).
- **Lost Lake Butte:** Fit dogs and their owners will enjoy the steady ascent to postcard-worthy views of Mount Hood (page 406).
- **West Metolius River:** Horseback riders and mountain bikers aren't allowed on this mostly flat path, which means you and your four-legged friend have it all to yourselves (page 432).
- **Misery Ridge-River Trail Loop:** Pick up a cleanup bag near the Crooked River bridge and wander fascinating terrain with your pup (page 441).

▼ HIKING AT HIGH ROCK LOOKOUT

EASY WATERFALL WALKS

The Pacific Northwest's renowned precipitation makes it quintessential waterfall country, and many don't demand a thigh-burning workout to appreciate. Visit in the spring to see them flowing at full force.

WASHINGTON
MARYMERE FALLS
Distance/Duration: 1.9 miles round-trip, 1 hour
Trailhead: Storm King Ranger Station, Olympic National Park
Depart from the ranger station and pass beach access to Crescent Lake before using a narrow tunnel to travel under U.S. 101. From here, the wide, smooth Marymere Falls Nature Trail passes two trails over a 0.5-mile stretch leading to the intersection with the Barnes Creek Trail. Turn right, cross bridges spanning Barnes and Falls Creeks, and climb 39 steps to a loop with two viewing areas (separated by 51 steps) of the 90-foot cascade splashing down a mossy cliff. After finishing the loop, return the way you came or explore other trails in the area.

SOL DUC FALLS
Distance/Duration: 1.8 miles round-trip, 45 minutes
Trailhead: end of Sol Duc Hot Springs Road, Olympic National Park
Sol Duc Creek splits into three falls, plummeting nearly 50 feet into a narrow canyon. A bridge and viewing platform overlook the falls, located next to the Canyon Creek Shelter. Built in 1939, the shelter is a year younger than Olympic National Park.

FRANKLIN FALLS

SNOQUALMIE FALLS
Distance/Duration: 1.4 miles round-trip, 45 minutes
Trailhead: Salish Lodge, Snoqualmie

You can see Snoqualmie Falls' dramatic 270-foot plunge just a few steps beyond the Salish Lodge, but the 0.7-mile walk from this upper viewing area to the Snoqualmie River greatly enhances your visit. The trail is wide, steep, and lined with salmonberries, elderberries, sword ferns, vine maple, and other flora. At the bottom of the trail hikers pass a massive turbine and sections of pipe from hydroelectric plants that have harnessed the river's energy since 1898. The falls' significance to the Snoqualmie Indian Tribe predates the power plants; the tribe considered the falls to be the birthplace of their people. Follow a boardwalk along the river to the lower viewing area. If the trail seems too steep, you can drive to the lower parking lot.

FRANKLIN FALLS
Distance/Duration: 2 miles round-trip, 1 hour
Trailhead: Forest Road 5830 north of Denny Creek Campground, Mount Baker-Snoqualmie National Forest

Wander a family-friendly trail along the South Fork Snoqualmie River and stand at the foot of a 70-foot cascade. Just beyond the intersection with the Wagon Road Trail (an option for the return trip), descend to the base of the falls. Be careful: The rocks can be slippery and debris sometimes washes over the falls or drops from surrounding cliffs. In wintertime when the falls freeze (and closed roads might make this trip longer), there is the risk of avalanche from the steep slopes of Denny Mountain. With an elevated stretch of I-90 passing above, the area is a striking intersection of nature and civilization.

PALOUSE FALLS
Distance/Duration: 1.4 miles round-trip, 45 minutes
Trailhead: Palouse Falls State Park parking lot

Visible just a few steps beyond the parking lot, this stunning, nearly 200-foot plunge in the Palouse River takes almost no effort to view. However, a path at the north end of the parking lot takes hikers to the less-visited upper falls. You'll follow a path right along the edge of the canyon and gaze down at the massive falls, then make a steep descent through a hillside slit to active railroad tracks. Follow the trail along the tracks before descending the talus slope to the canyon floor and the upper falls.

OREGON
BRIDAL VEIL FALLS
Distance/Duration: 1.4 miles round-trip, 45 minutes
Trailhead: between mileposts 28 and 29 on the Historic Columbia River Highway, Bridal Veil Falls State Scenic Viewpoint, Columbia River Gorge National Scenic Area

A pair of trails from the parking area showcase the best of the Columbia River Gorge without requiring much effort. The two-tiered falls here come from a creek that begins on nearby Larch Mountain. The upper loop trail shows off Gorge cliffs, along with springtime wildflowers, while the lower out-and-back trail descends to the base of Bridal Veil Falls. Keep an eye out for poison oak along this path.

HENLINE FALLS

Distance/Duration: 1.8 miles round-trip, 1 hour
Trailhead: roughly 18 miles northeast of Mehama on Forest Road 2209, Willamette National Forest

The path to Henline Falls starts in a forest of Douglas fir and hemlock, its undergrowth thick with ferns and, in spring, colorful wildflower displays. The out-and-back trail follows an old roadbed to a long-abandoned mine and climbs gently before ending at a small viewing area of the seemingly sheer wall of water. Keep left at two junctions along the way; the user-created trails off to the right don't head anywhere worthwhile.

PROXY FALLS

Distance/Duration: 1.5 miles round-trip, 45 minutes
Trailhead: roughly 10 miles southeast of Belknap Springs on Highway 242 (typically closed Nov.-June depending on snow; call 541/822-3381 for road info), Willamette National Forest

Just east of the McKenzie River, one stream cascades into two separate curtains of water—each dropping more than 200 feet—to form Proxy Falls. In turn, the water seeps into the porous lava rock at its base. This family-friendly loop affords views of both the upper and lower sections of Proxy Falls.

TOKETEE FALLS

Distance/Duration: 0.8 mile round-trip, 30 minutes
Trailhead: roughly 21 miles northwest of Diamond Lake on Forest Road 34, Willamette National Forest

Hike through an old-growth forest of Douglas fir and western red cedar alongside the North Umpqua River to a platform overlooking Toketee Falls, flanked by columnar basalt. The out-and-back trail includes nearly 200 steps.

WATSON FALLS

Distance/Duration: 0.8 mile round-trip, 30 minutes
Trailhead: roughly 19 miles northwest of Diamond Lake on Forest Road 37, Willamette National Forest

The path to Watson Falls—the third-highest waterfall in Oregon and the highest in southern Oregon—climbs through a forest of salal, Douglas fir, and vine maple before crossing a wooden bridge over Watson Creek. Just past the bridge, which affords spectacular views of the falls, a T-shaped junction offers two choices: Head left for a quick climb to the base of Watson Falls, or head right to complete a loop back to the trailhead.

▲ MOUNT RAINIER FROM HIGH ROCK LOOKOUT

WASHINGTON

WASHINGTON COAST

The Pacific Ocean is the artist responsible for much of the beauty on Washington's coast. With the help of constant wind, it carved the sea stacks adorning Point of Arches and chiseled the famous hole into the rocky wall at Rialto Beach. It reflects radiant sunsets and, for a few hours each day, it retreats to unveil tide pools teeming with life. Whether visitors come to watch birds wheeling in the sky, skip rocks, or wander long, secluded beaches, the wild coast is one of Washington's most-loved wonders.

▲ BANANA SLUG

▲ GULLS ON RIALTO BEACH

1 Cape Flattery

DISTANCE: 1.5 miles round-trip
DURATION: 1 hour
EFFORT: Easy

2 Point of Arches via Shi Shi Beach

DISTANCE: 9 miles round-trip
DURATION: 4.5 hours
EFFORT: Moderate

3 Ozette Triangle

DISTANCE: 9.3 miles round-trip
DURATION: 4.5 hours
EFFORT: Moderate/strenuous

4 Hole-in-the-Wall

DISTANCE: 3 miles round-trip
DURATION: 1.5 hours
EFFORT: Easy

5 North Head Trail

DISTANCE: 3.8 miles round-trip
DURATION: 2 hours
EFFORT: Easy

▼ SEA STACKS AT OZETTE TRIANGLE

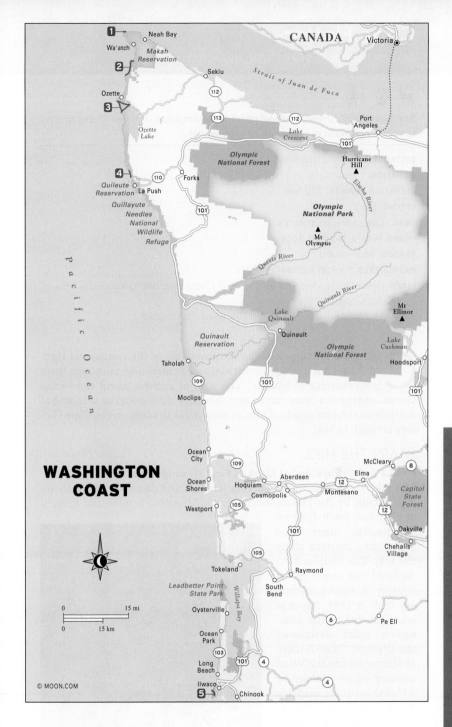

WASHINGTON COAST

1

Cape Flattery

MAKAH INDIAN RESERVATION, NEAH BAY

Stand on the northwesternmost point of the contiguous United States and try to catch a glimpse of a sea lion or gray whale.

DISTANCE: 1.5 miles round-trip

DURATION: 1 hour

ELEVATION CHANGE: 200 feet

EFFORT: Easy

TRAIL: Dirt, stairs, boardwalk

USERS: Hikers, leashed dogs

SEASON: Year-round

PASSES/FEES: Makah Recreation Pass

MAPS: Green Trails Map 99S for Olympic Coast Beaches, Green Trails Map 98S for Cape Flattery

CONTACT: Makah Tribe, 360/645-2201, www.makah.com

Cape Flattery comprises the northwest tip of the contiguous United States, but it is not a contrived tourist attraction (although there is no shortage of tourists). The view of Tatoosh Island, the Pacific Ocean, and the sea caves carved into the rocky cliffs would be stunning at any latitude and longitude. As far as easy walks to scenic spots, Cape Flattery is tough to beat.

START THE HIKE

▶ **MILE 0-0.5: Parking Lot Kiosk to First Viewing Area**

The hike starts next to the **parking lot kiosk** and descends gradually on a path built by the Makah Indian Nation. The trail is wide and smooth at first but you'll hike on boardwalks, steps, and some rooty sections along the way. The Makahs have declared this corner of the country a nature sanctuary and, in 1994, the cape was included in the 3,300 square miles designated the Olympic Coast National Marine Sanctuary. Wood walking sticks whittled by a Makah artist are available at the trailhead. They're free to borrow or $5 to keep.

TREE ON CAPE FLATTERY ▶

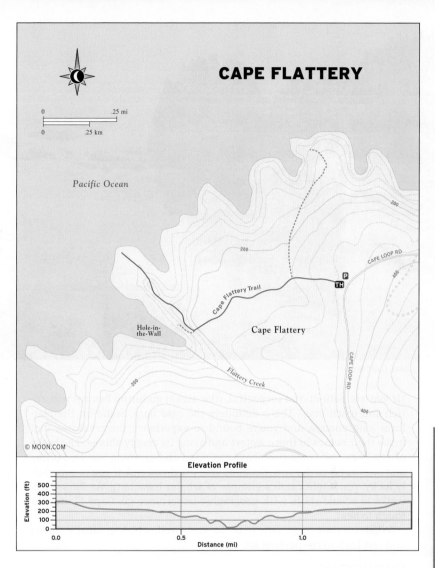

CAPE FLATTERY

Pacific Ocean

CAPE LOOP RD

Cape Flattery Trail

Hole-in-the-Wall

Cape Flattery

Flattery Creek

© MOON.COM

Elevation Profile

On the left about 0.5 mile down the trail, a boardwalk leads about 20 yards to a **platform** overlooking a rugged beach and sea stacks to the south.

▶ **MILE 0.5-0.75: First Viewing Area to Third Viewing Area**
Continue a few steps straight beyond the intersection to reach the **second viewing area**. Step down to a **perch** with views of caves notched into the cliffs.

The third and final viewing area is 0.25 mile farther. Climb a two-step ladder onto an **elevated wooden deck** and gaze west toward Tatoosh Island and a deactivated lighthouse that once directed ships to the entrance of the Strait of Juan de Fuca. At various times, tribal fishermen, whale and seal hunters, and the U.S. Coast Guard and Navy used the island, named for a former Makah chief. A sign at a nearby trailhead says,

▲ CAPE FLATTERY

"If you are patient and respectful, (the area's) enduring beauty will enrich and teach you." That's definitely the case here. Stand on the platform long enough and you're bound to experience the creatures that make their homes in these waters and along its craggy shores. The barks of sea lions and seals rise above the wind and crashing waves. Puffins and otters play in the surf. Seabirds soar overhead and, if you're especially lucky, you might catch a glimpse of whales breaching. As far as easy walks to scenic spots with geographic importance go, Cape Flattery is tough to beat.

When it's time to go, return on the same trail, which gradually climbs 200 feet back to the parking lot.

DIRECTIONS

From Neah Bay, follow Highway 112/Bayview Avenue until it bends left and becomes Fort Street. Turn right on 3rd Street after 0.1 mile, then left on Cape Flattery Road after less than 0.1 mile. Drive 7.8 miles (the road becomes Cape Loop Road after 3.2 miles) to the parking lot. Toilets are located at the trailhead.

GPS COORDINATES: 48.384880, –124.715790 / N48° 23.0928' W124° 42.9474'

2

Point of Arches via Shi Shi Beach

MAKAH INDIAN RESERVATION, OLYMPIC NATIONAL PARK

Explore the tide pools and towering sea stacks of what might be Washington's most striking beach.

BEST: Winter Hikes

DISTANCE: 9 miles round-trip

DURATION: 4.5 hours

ELEVATION CHANGE: 200 feet

EFFORT: Moderate

TRAIL: Dirt trail, beach

USERS: Hikers

SEASON: Year-round

PASSES/FEES: Makah Recreation Pass

MAPS: Green Trails Map 99S for Olympic Coast Beaches, Green Trails Map 98S for Cape Flattery

CONTACT: Olympic National Park, Wilderness Information Center, 360/565-3100, www.nps.gov/olym

Part of the longest stretch of wild coastline in the contiguous United States, the trek to Point of Arches on the south end of Shi Shi Beach (pronounced "Shy Shy") is a bucket list trip for many hikers, especially those with a passion for nature photography. Time your visit for low tide or sunset, and you'll see why.

START THE HIKE

Be aware that reaching Shi Shi requires walking an often-muddy trail through the woods and making a short but steep descent. While easiest to walk at low tide when there is wet, hard-packed sand at the edge of the surf, Shi Shi is passable at high tide. Always pay attention to the tide, so you don't find yourself stranded beyond the point.

▶ **MILE 0-2.1: Makah Tribal Land to Olympic National Park**
The walk starts on Makah tribal land. At 0.3 mile from the parking lot, you'll cross an A-frame **bridge.** The next 1.8 miles are along a wide, flat, and well-marked path under Sitka spruce and Douglas fir. You can skirt huge puddles in drier months, but for much of the year you should expect to get your boots muddy.

▶ **MILE 2.1-2.2: Olympic National Park to Shi Shi Beach**
At 2.1 miles, a sign welcomes you to **Olympic National Park.** Here, the trail drops more than 100 feet in 0.1 mile before emerging from the trees onto the sandy **Shi Shi Beach.** To the south, the sea stack skyline of Point of Arches rises in the distance, but it's still a ways before you get there. Pass

Point of Arches via Shi Shi Beach

WASHINGTON COAST

patches of green and brown kelp washed ashore by the sea. Watch herons and sea lions wade in the surf and coyotes, deer, raccoons, and other animals skitter across the tree line.

▶ MILE 2.2–3.5: Shi Shi Beach to Petroleum Creek

After 1.3 miles, step over **Petroleum Creek.** You'll see tents dotting the beach by the dozens. If you want to join them, you'll need to pay for overnight parking and a backcountry permit, and pack your food in a required bear canister. Contact Olympic National Park's Wilderness Information Center (www.nps.gov/olym) for more information.

▶ MILE 3.5–4.5: Petroleum Creek to Point of Arches

After 1 mile along the beach, you'll reach the **Point of Arches.** At low tide, walk around the point (designated a National Natural Landmark in 1971) and explore tide pools teeming with colorful starfish and sea anemones. Admire the towering sea stacks and arches, the handiwork of the pounding surf and perpetual wind. Stay for one of the most awe-inspiring (and most photographed) sunsets in Washington.

When you're ready, retrace your steps.

DIRECTIONS

From Neah Bay, follow Highway 112/Bayview Avenue until it bends left and becomes Fort Street. Turn right on 3rd Street after 0.1 mile, then left on Cape Flattery Road after less than 0.1 mile. Drive 2.4 miles and turn left on Hobuck Road. After about a mile, bear right following the signs to the fish hatchery. Drive 0.3 mile and then turn left on Makah Passage. Drive 0.8 mile and then turn right on Tsoo-Yess Beach Road. Drive 2 miles and turn left on Fish Hatchery Road. Drive 0.2 mile and find the trailhead on the right. A restroom with a comically loud foot-pump sink is located at the trailhead.

GPS COORDINATES: 48.29375, –124.66524 / N48° 17.625′ W124° 39.9144′

SHI SHI BEACH ▶

BEST NEARBY BITES

Cap off a day of seaside play by retracing your driving route about 7 miles (15 minutes) northeast to Neah Bay, where you can enjoy a thin-crust, smoked-on-site salmon pizza and a slice of pie at **Linda's Wood Fired Kitchen** (1110 Bayview Ave., 360/640-2192, hours vary).

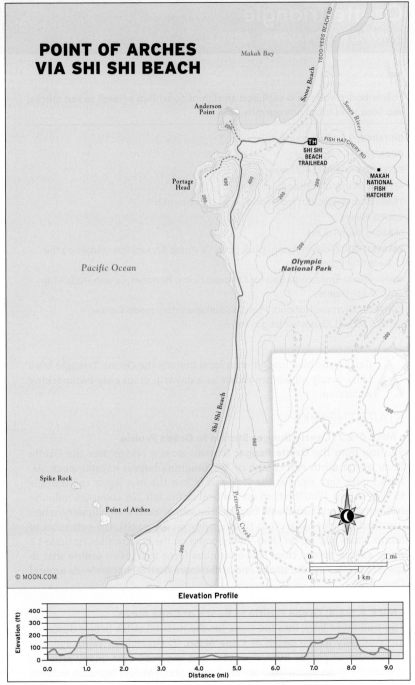

POINT OF ARCHES
VIA SHI SHI BEACH

Makah Bay

TSOO-YESS BEACH RD

Sooes Beach

Sooes River

Anderson
Point

FISH HATCHERY RD

TH SHI SHI
BEACH
TRAILHEAD

MAKAH
NATIONAL
FISH
HATCHERY

Portage
Head

Olympic
National Park

Pacific Ocean

Shi Shi Beach

Spike Rock

Petroleum Creek

Point of Arches

0   1 mi
0   1 km

© MOON.COM

Elevation Profile

Elevation (ft)
400
300
200
100
0

0.0   1.0   2.0   3.0   4.0   5.0   6.0   7.0   8.0   9.0
Distance (mi)

Follow boardwalks to a secluded stretch of coast that's home to sea stacks, sea lions, and tribal petroglyphs.

DISTANCE: 9.3 miles round-trip

DURATION: 4.5 hours

ELEVATION CHANGE: 400 feet

EFFORT: Moderate/strenuous

TRAIL: Boardwalk, dirt trail, sandy and rocky beach

USERS: Hikers

SEASON: Year-round

PASSES/FEES: 7-day national park pass, Olympic Annual Pass, America the Beautiful Passes

MAPS: Green Trails Map 99S for Olympic Coast Beaches, Green Trails Map 130S for Ozette

CONTACT: Olympic National Park, Wilderness Information Center, 360/565-3130, www.nps.gov/olym

A flat, scenic hike loaded with local history, the Ozette Triangle is an ideal family adventure either as a day trip or an easy backpacking excursion.

START THE HIKE

▸ **MILE 0-2.2: Ozette Ranger Station to Green Prairie**

Starting from the **Ozette Ranger Station,** cross a bridge over the Ozette River at the north end of one of Washington's largest natural lakes. After 0.1 mile, turn right at the fork and follow the first leg of the triangle to Cape Alava. (You'll return on the trail to the left.) In about 0.3 mile the trail's trademark **boardwalk** begins. The cedar planks are slippery when wet (and it's wet more often than it's dry on the coast); the soft soles of tennis shoes grip better than hiking boots on the boardwalk. Continue 1.8 miles among spruce trees and enormous ferns to a green **prairie** that in the late 1800s was the site of one of the more than 30 homesteads around Ozette Lake.

▸ **MILE 2.2-3.4: Green Prairie to Beach at Cape Alava**

The trail dives back into the trees for the next 1.2 miles before descending gradually to the beach at **Cape Alava.** Thousands of years ago, the Ozette Makah people hunted whales and sea lions here; many artifacts unearthed by archaeologists are on display at the Makah Museum in Neah Bay. Camping is allowed here with a permit and bear canister (visit www.nps.gov/olym for more information).

Turn left and walk south on the **rocky beach.** Look for starfish in the tide pools and watch your step on rocks covered with slippery algae and

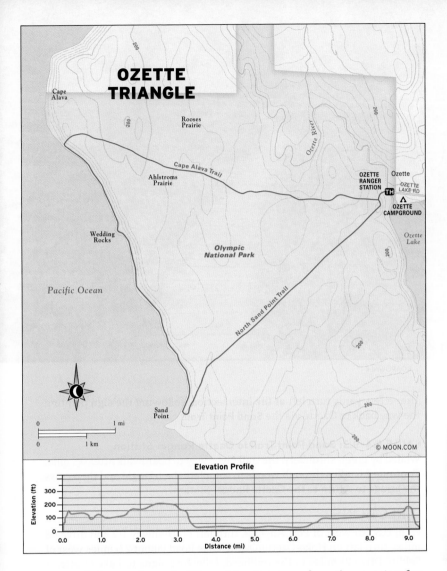

OZETTE TRIANGLE

Cape Alava

Rooses Prairie

Cape Alava Trail

Ahlstroms Prairie

OZETTE RANGER STATION

Ozette

OZETTE LAKE RD

TH

OZETTE CAMPGROUND

Ozette Lake

Wedding Rocks

Olympic National Park

Pacific Ocean

North Sand Point Trail

Sand Point

0   1 mi

0   1 km

Ozette River

© MOON.COM

Elevation Profile

Elevation (ft): 300, 200, 100, 0

Distance (mi): 0.0, 1.0, 2.0, 3.0, 4.0, 5.0, 6.0, 7.0, 8.0, 9.0

seaweed. Sea stacks and offshore islands appear from the morning fog and are home to cormorants, puffins, and gulls. Seals, bald eagles, and peregrine falcons make frequent appearances.

▶ MILE 3.4–6.4: Beach at Cape Alava to Sand Point

The beach leg of the triangle is 3 miles. About halfway is an area known as the **Wedding Rocks**. Take time to examine the large boulders for petroglyphs. You can find an orca, seal, and face etched in the rocks, but they're easy to miss if you don't look for them.

At **Sand Point** (another camping spot) it's clear how this place got its name: the rocky beach gives way to soft, barefoot-inviting sand. Look for a black and red disc mounted to a tree. Find the trail under the disc and

▲ BOARDWALK

after a few yards turn left at the intersection, following the sign pointing the way back to Ozette via the **Sand Point Trail.**

▶ **MILE 6.4–9.3: Sand Point Trail to Ozette Ranger Station**
Walled by green shrubbery, the trail gives way to boardwalk after 0.3 mile. Continue 2.6 miles through woods to complete the triangle and then cross the bridge to return to the Ozette Ranger Station.

DIRECTIONS

From U.S. 101 west of Port Angeles, turn left on Highway 112 and drive 48 miles; turn left on Hoko-Ozette/Ozette Lake Road (about 2.5 miles west of Sekiu). Drive 21 miles to the trailhead, following signs to Lake Ozette. A ranger station, campground, lake access, and toilets are located near the trailhead.

GPS COORDINATES: 48.153633, –124.668654 / N48° 9.218′ W124° 40.1192′

4

Hole-in-the-Wall
OLYMPIC NATIONAL PARK, RIALTO BEACH

Take a short, easy walk along the Pacific Ocean to a sea arch that allows you to walk through a bluff at low tide.

DISTANCE: 3 miles round-trip

DURATION: 1.5 hours

ELEVATION CHANGE: Negligible

EFFORT: Easy

TRAIL: Beach

USERS: Hikers, leashed dogs (only to Ellen Creek)

SEASON: Year-round

PASSES/FEES: 7-day national park pass, Olympic Annual Pass, America the Beautiful Passes

MAPS: Green Trails Map 99S for Olympic Coast Beaches, Green Trails Map 130S for Ozette

CONTACT: Olympic National Park, Wilderness Information Center, 360/565-3100, www.nps.gov/olym

START THE HIKE

▶ MILE 0-0.7: Rialto Beach to Ellen Creek

The magic of **Rialto Beach** is obvious as soon as you step foot the sand at the end of the short path at the north end of the parking lot. James Island is visible to the south at the mouth of the Quillayute River. Your journey, however, will take you north on a beach lined with sea stacks and enormous driftwood logs.

After 0.7 mile, cross **Ellen Creek.** While Rialto Beach is one of the few places in Olympic National Park where dogs are allowed, they aren't allowed beyond the creek. A permit (www.nps.gov/olym) is needed to use one of the campsites scattered along the tree line between Ellen Creek and Hole-in-the-Wall.

▶ MILE 0.7-1.5: Ellen Creek to Hole-in-the-Wall

On a clear day, the rocky bulkhead that is your destination is visible for the 0.8 mile beyond the creek. When sea stacks appear from the fog and the ocean subsides, revealing a secret passageway, it seems appropriate that Rialto Beach was named by a famous magician. In the early 1900s, Claude Alexander Conlin, "The Crystal Seer," had a home in the area. He is frequently credited with coining the beach's name, which was often used by theaters of that era.

Pause to skip flat, smooth rocks and to snap pictures of the towering sea stacks and explore the tide pools and enjoy the relaxing sound of waves lapping at the shore. Gulls and bald eagles soar overhead, while

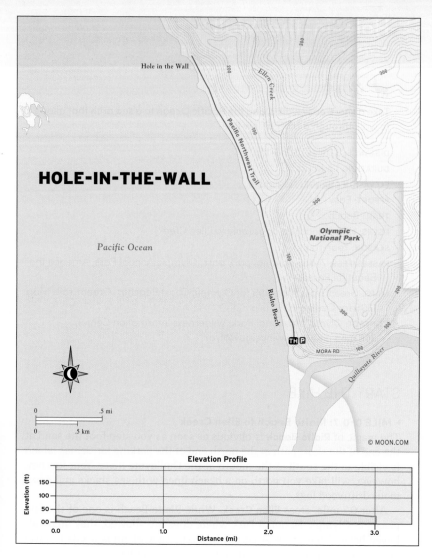

HOLE-IN-THE-WALL

Hole in the Wall

Ellen Creek

Pacific Northwest Trail

Pacific Ocean

Olympic
National Park

Rialto Beach

TH P

MORA RD

Quillayute River

| 0 | .5 mi |
| 0 | .5 km |

© MOON.COM

Elevation Profile

guillemots and scoters play in the surf. Just south of Hole-in-the-Wall, a pit toilet is located near what the park service calls the "split rock."

Ideally, you timed your hike to arrive at low tide when the **Hole-in-the-Wall** is usually exposed enough for you to scamper through. The sea arch, chiseled by wind and the sea, is one of the jewels of Washington's wild coast. Even at high tide, you can scramble atop the bluff on a short but steep trail. Find the trail under a black and red disc mounted to a tree.

Follow the beach south to your vehicle when you're ready to return.

▲ SEA STACKS NEAR HOLE-IN-THE-WALL

DIRECTIONS

From Forks, drive north 1.5 miles on U.S. 101 and turn left on Highway 110. Drive 7.8 miles and turn right on Mora Road. After another 5 miles, arrive at the Rialto Beach parking lot. A toilet is located at the parking lot.

GPS COORDINATES: 47.920983, -124.637986 / N47° 55.259' W124° 38.2792'

BEST NEARBY BITES

La Push is less than a mile south of the trailhead, but you'll have to make an 11-mile (18-minute) drive on Mora and La Push Roads to cross the Quillayute River and reach **River's Edge Restaurant** (41 Main St., 360/374-0777, 8am-8pm daily). Try the fresh salmon or a burger while enjoying the coastal view through enormous picture windows.

🦌 🐾 🚶

Take a hike brimming with history to a sweeping view of the Pacific and a century-old lighthouse.

DISTANCE: 3.8 miles round-trip
DURATION: 2 hours
ELEVATION CHANGE: 300 feet
EFFORT: Easy
TRAIL: Wide and single-track dirt sections, wooden steps, roots, pavement
USERS: Hikers, leashed dogs.
SEASON: Year-round
PASSES/FEES: Discover Pass
MAPS: USGS topographic map for Cape Disappointment
PARK HOURS: 6:30am-dusk daily
CONTACT: Cape Disappointment State Park, 360/642-3078,
http://parks.state.wa.us

START THE HIKE

▶ **MILE 0-0.2: North Head Trail to Railroad Tie Steps**
Start your exploration on the north side of the road where a sign welcomes you to the **North Head Trail.** With Sitka spruce towering overhead and the Pacific nowhere to be seen, you might be surprised that this hike starts within feet of a Corps of Discovery oceanside campsite. The dirt trail is flat for the first 0.2 mile as it cuts through the forested wetland to steps fashioned from railroad ties.

Marvel at giant trees as you wander the old-growth forest, but don't spend too much time looking up: Big trees mean big, gnarly roots, and there are plenty of these tripping hazards along the way. The trail can also be quite muddy at times.

▶ **MILE 0.2-1.6: Railroad Tie Steps to Parking Lot**
In another 0.9 mile, steps descend to a **bridge** crossing a creek and then ascend the opposite side. A few hundred yards farther, look for the Pacific through the trees. You aren't likely to regret walking even as the trail brings you to a **parking lot** in 0.5 mile that would have shaved a couple miles off the trip.

▶ **MILE 1.6-1.9: Parking Lot to Lighthouse**
From the lot, pass the **lighthouse keepers' residences** ($154-437/night, www.washington.goingtocamp.com) and follow a wide service road 0.3 mile to the **North Head Lighthouse** and a dramatic coastal view. Built in 1898, the beacon is still active. The lighthouse was deemed necessary when ship captains approaching from the north complained the rocky

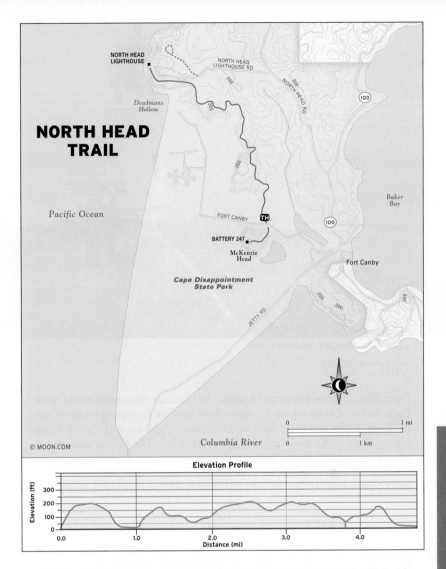

NORTH HEAD TRAIL

NORTH HEAD LIGHTHOUSE

NORTH HEAD LIGHTHOUSE RD

Deadmans Hollow

NORTH HEAD RD

Pacific Ocean

FORT CANBY TH

BATTERY 247

McKenzie Head

Baker Bay

Fort Canby

Cape Disappointment State Park

JETTY RD

© MOON.COM

Columbia River

0   1 mi

0   1 km

Elevation Profile

Elevation (ft)

300
200
100
0

0.0   1.0   2.0   3.0   4.0

Distance (mi)

headland blocked the nearby Cape Disappointment Lighthouse (the oldest in the state). Lighthouse tours ($2.50 adults, free children 17 and under) start every 20 minutes most days. The view to the south includes tree-covered McKenzie Head where you started the hike.

Return the way you came to complete the hike.

For bonus views, take a short walk on the wide dirt path that ascends McKenzie Head. The well-marked trail starts from the small parking area on the south side of Fort Canby Road. Along the way, get a glimpse of the black and white Cape Disappointment Lighthouse, and atop the hill explore a World War II coastal defense battery. Scramble to the top of the battery for the best view.

▲ LIGHTHOUSE ON CAPE DISAPPOINTMENT

DIRECTIONS

From Ilwaco, drive south on Highway 100 to Cape Disappointment State Park. At Fort Canby (about 5.5 miles from Ilwaco), turn right on Fort Canby Road. Drive about 0.2 mile and then turn right on Fort Canby. Drive 0.4 mile and find a small parking area on the left. The hiking route starts across the street from the parking area.

GPS COORDINATES: 46.285737, –124.063346 / N46° 17.1442′ W124° 3.8008′

BEST NEARBY BITES

It would be a shame to visit the Long Beach Peninsula without sampling locally gathered oysters, clams, salmon, and other seafood. There are plenty of good post-hike dining options, including **Drop Anchor Seafood** (900 Pacific Ave. S, Long Beach, 360/642-4224, www.dropanchorseafood.com, 11am-8pm daily) and the **Pickled Fish** (409 Sid Snyder Dr., Long Beach, 360/642-2344, www.pickledfisherstaurant.com, 8am-10pm Mon.-Thurs., 8am-11pm Fri.-Sun.). From the trailhead, the 5-mile drive to Ilwaco takes about 15 minutes via Highway 100. Long Beach is about 3.3 miles (9 minutes) farther north via U.S. 101 and Highway 103.

NEARBY CAMPGROUNDS

NAME	DESCRIPTION	FACILITIES	SEASON	FEE
Cape Disappointment State Park	located on the Pacific Ocean in a setting brimming with history	310 RV and tent sites, restrooms	year-round	$12-50
244 Robert Gray Drive, Ilwaco, 888/226-7688, www.washington.goingtocamp.com				
Hobuck Beach Resort	on the Makah Indian Reservation steps from the Pacific Ocean	210+ RV and tent sites, restrooms	year-round	$25-40
2726 Makah Passage, Neah Bay, 360/645-2339, www.hobuckbeachresort.com				
Mora Campground	sheltered by coastal forest on the Quillayute River and just minutes from the beach	94 RV and tent sites, restrooms	year-round	$15
Mora Road, 2 miles east of Rialto Beach, 360/565-3130, www.nps.gov/olym				
Ozette Campground	located near Lake Ozette and the Ozette Triangle trailhead	15 tent and RV sites, restrooms	year-round	$20
Hoko-Ozette Road, Ozette, Olympic National Park, 360/565-3130, www.nps.gov/olym				
Kalaloch Campground	popular campground with sites overlooking the Pacific Ocean	170 RV and tent sites, restrooms	year-round	$22
Kalaloch Campground F Road, Kalaloch, Olympic National Park, 360/962-2271, http://recreation.gov				

OLYMPIC NATIONAL PARK

Olympic National Park routinely ranks among the nation's 10 most visited national parks, and it's easy to see why. With beaches, rain forests, churning rivers, cobalt lakes, and a secluded mountain range, this is one of America's most diverse parks. Its beauty is enhanced by the surrounding Olympic National Forest and nearby protected areas like the Dungeness National Wildlife Refuge. Waterfalls, the lush Hoh and Quinault Rain Forests, and sweeping mountaintop views are available for even casual day hikers. Meanwhile, those seeking more challenging adventures have plenty of options for leaving the crowds behind and exploring deep into the wilderness.

▲ SIGNS ON DUNGENESS SPIT

▲ QUINAULT RAIN FOREST NATURE TRAIL LOOP

◄ LAKE IN GRAND VALLEY

1 **Dungeness Spit**
DISTANCE: 10.2 miles round-trip
DURATION: 5 hours
EFFORT: Moderate/strenuous

2 **Hurricane Hill**
DISTANCE: 3.4 miles round-trip
DURATION: 2 hours
EFFORT: Easy/moderate

3 **Klahhane Ridge**
DISTANCE: 5.4 miles round-trip
DURATION: 3 hours
EFFORT: Moderate

4 **Hall of Mosses and Hoh River Trail**
DISTANCE: 6.7 miles round-trip
DURATION: 3.5 hours
EFFORT: Easy/moderate

5 **Grand Valley**
DISTANCE: 9.3 miles round-trip
DURATION: 5 hours
EFFORT: Moderate/strenuous

6 **Mount Townsend**
DISTANCE: 8 miles round-trip
DURATION: 4 hours
EFFORT: Moderate/strenuous

7 **Quinault Loop**
DISTANCE: 4 miles round-trip
DURATION: 2 hours
EFFORT: Easy

8 **Staircase Rapids and Shady Lane**
DISTANCE: 4.2 miles round-trip
DURATION: 2 hours
EFFORT: Easy

9 **Mount Ellinor**
DISTANCE: 3.4 miles round-trip
DURATION: 2.5 hours
EFFORT: Moderate

10 **Lena Lake**
DISTANCE: 6.8 miles round-trip
DURATION: 3 hours
EFFORT: Moderate

▾ LENA LAKE

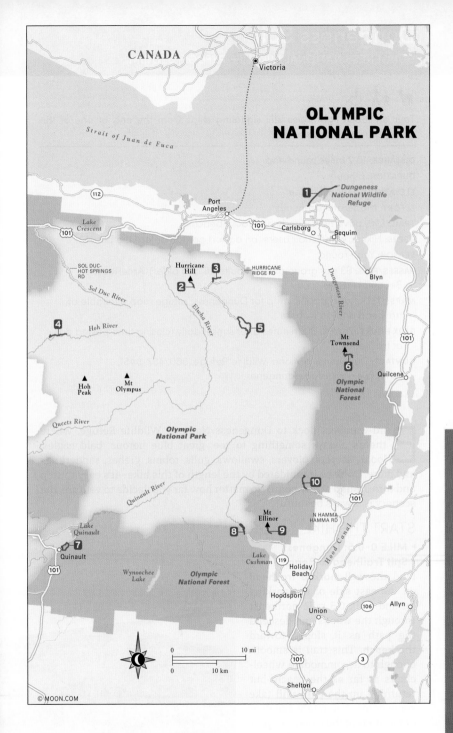

CANADA

Victoria

Strait of Juan de Fuca

OLYMPIC NATIONAL PARK

112

Lake Crescent

101

SOL DUC-
HOT SPRINGS
RD

Sol Duc River

Port Angeles

101 Carlsborg

Sequim

1 Dungeness
National Wildlife
Refuge

Hurricane
Hill **3**

2

HURRICANE
RIDGE RD

Elwha River

Blyn

Dungeness River

101

4 Hoh River

5

Mt
Townsend

6

Quilcene

Hoh
Peak

Mt
Olympus

Queets River

Olympic
National
Park

Olympic
National
Forest

101

10

Quinault River

Mt
Ellinor

N HAMMA
HAMMA RD

101

Lake
Quinault

8 **9**

7
Quinault

101

Wynoochee
Lake

Olympic
National
Forest

Lake
Cushman

119

Holiday
Beach

Hood Canal

Hoodsport

Union

106 Allyn

3

0   10 mi

0   10 km

101

Shelton

© MOON.COM

Tour an 1850s lighthouse still signaling ships from the end of one of the world's longest sand spits.

DISTANCE: 10.2 miles round-trip

DURATION: 5 hours

ELEVATION CHANGE: 130 feet

EFFORT: Moderate/strenuous

TRAIL: Dirt, pavement, sandy and rocky beach

USERS: Hikers, wheelchair users (on a short portion before the beach)

SEASON: Year-round

PASSES/FEES: $3 per group of four adults (16 and older), America the Beautiful Passes

MAPS: USGS topographic map for Dungeness; refuge map available at trailhead and on website

PARK HOURS: 7am to 30 minutes after sunset daily (closing time posted daily at trailhead)

CONTACT: Dungeness National Wildlife Refuge, 360/457-8451, www.fws.gov/refuge/dungeness

Bird-watchers flock to Dungeness National Wildlife Refuge, where there's always something to see: great blue herons, bald eagles, loons, scoters, plovers, swallows, gulls, robins, grebes, sanderlings and more. Don't be intimidated by the length of this hike—it's easy to stop and turn around at any point. No matter how far you decide to venture, the scenery is always beautiful.

START THE HIKE

▶ **MILE 0-0.5: Dungeness Spit Trailhead to Beach**

Find the **well-marked trailhead** on the east side of the parking lot and walk 0.5 mile northeast through the woods and descend the path as it slopes toward the **beach.** This trail is smooth enough to accommodate wheelchairs as far as the beach, but returning up the path will take some doing. You might see deer or raccoons in the woods on your way to trailside overlooks with

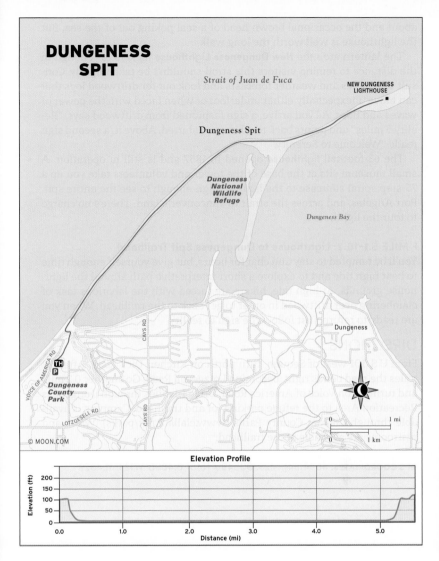

DUNGENESS SPIT

Strait of Juan de Fuca

NEW DUNGENESS LIGHTHOUSE

Dungeness Spit

Dungeness National Wildlife Refuge

Dungeness Bay

Dungeness

VOICE OF AMERICA RD

CAYS RD

TH
P

Dungeness County Park

LOTZGESELL RD

CAYS RD

© MOON.COM

0   1 mi
0   1 km

Elevation Profile

Elevation (ft)

200
150
100
50
0

0.0   1.0   2.0   3.0   4.0   5.0

Distance (mi)

telescopes to aid viewing one of the world's longest sand spits. The narrow spit, reaching nearly 5 miles into the Strait of Juan de Fuca, is formed by currents depositing sediment from rivers and coastal erosion.

On the **beach**, a **sign** states, "Birds only beyond this sign." The area hosts up to 25,000 shorebirds during their spring migration and about half that many in summer and fall. While most of the spit (and all of attached Graveyard Spit) is closed to humans, the west-side beach is open year-round.

▶ MILE 0.5–5.1: Beach to Lighthouse

Reaching the lighthouse requires 4.6 miles of **beach,** but it doesn't have to be your destination. Just a few steps on the beach will be enough to enjoy the waves lapping at your feet and the sight of sanderlings scampering about and the occasional brown head of a seal poking out of the sea. But the lighthouse is well worth the long walk.

The lantern atop the **New Dungeness Lighthouse** flickers far enough in the distance to remind visitors this stroll shouldn't be taken lightly. Consult tide tables and weather forecasts and look out for driftwood logs that can move unexpectedly either underfoot or when faced with the power of waves and tides. As you arrive, a sign fashioned from driftwood says, "Reality 5 miles" and points back to where you started. Above it, a second sign reads "Welcome to Serenity."

The 63-foot-tall **lighthouse** opened in 1857 and is still in operation. A small museum sits at the base of the tower and volunteers take you up a 75-step spiral staircase to the lantern, high enough to see the entire spit, Port Angeles, and across the strait to Vancouver Island. There's no charge to tour the lighthouse.

▶ **MILE 5.1-10.2: Lighthouse to Dungeness Spit Trailhead**
You'll be tempted to stay and chat for hours, but give yourself enough time to beat high tide and to explore a short interpretive path around the lighthouse grounds. At high tide, hikers are forced with the laborious task of clambering over driftwood in order to get back to the trailhead. When you are ready to return, just follow the sign to reality.

DIRECTIONS

From U.S. 101 west of Sequim, turn north on Kitchen-Dick Road. After 3.2 miles the road bends right, becoming Lotzgesell Road. Go another 0.2 mile and turn left on Voice of America Road. Drive 1.1 miles through Dungeness Recreation Area to the refuge parking lot and trailhead. Camping is available through Clallam County Parks (www.clallam.net/parks). Water and restrooms are available at the trailhead.

GPS COORDINATES: 48.141341, –123.190549 / N48° 8.4805′ W123° 11.4329′

BEST NEARBY BITES

After hiking along the Salish Sea, get a taste of its bounty at **Salty Girls Sequim Seafood Co.** (210 W. Washington St., 360/775-3787, www.saltygirlsseafood.com, hours vary). The oyster bar has local beer on tap and a menu that includes oysters (raw or baked), steamed clams, and Dungeness crab from Olympic Peninsula suppliers. From the trailhead, the 7-mile drive southeast takes about 15 minutes via Sequim-Dungeness Way.

Hurricane Hill

OLYMPIC NATIONAL PARK, HURRICANE RIDGE

🦌 ✳ 🚶 ♿

Get serious bang for your buck on this easy hike with mile-high views of the Strait of Juan de Fuca, British Columbia, and Cascade and Olympic peaks.

DISTANCE: 3.4 miles round-trip
DURATION: 2 hours
ELEVATION CHANGE: 700 feet
EFFORT: Easy/moderate
TRAIL: Dirt, pavement
USERS: Hikers, wheelchair users
SEASON: June-October, snowshoeing in winter
PASSES/FEES: 7-day national park pass, Olympic Annual Pass, America the Beautiful Passes
MAPS: Green Trails Map 134S for Elwha North-Hurricane Ridge
CONTACT: Olympic National Park Wilderness Information Center, 360/565-3130, www.nps.gov/olym

This is a perfect hike for people of all ages, and as a result it's often crowded, which takes a toll on the trail and makes parking difficult. The park is in the middle of a **rehabilitation project,** so check availability before you go. During construction, the hike starts at **Picnic Area B,** with a 0.3-mile serpentine path through the trees to reach the main trail.

START THE HIKE

▸ **MILE 0-0.4: Parking Lot to Hurricane Hill Path**
You'll start getting views of the Bailey Range before you even open your car door. At the primary parking lot, signs point the way to the wide, **paved path**. From here, there's hardly a step that doesn't have a good view. Purple bells-of-Scotland and other wildflowers add color. Mountain goats and even bears sometimes meander across surrounding slopes. Rabbits, grouse, deer, and marmots make

◂ VIEW FROM HURRICANE HILL

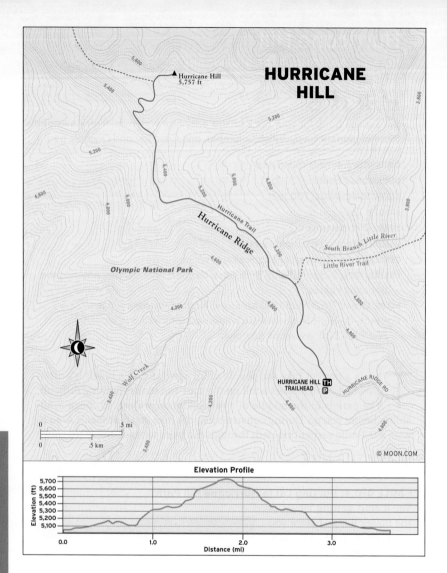

more frequent appearances. After 0.4 mile, pass a **turnoff** for the **Little River Trail**.

▶ MILE 0.4-1.5: Hurricane Hill Path to Junction

In another 0.7 mile, find yourself looking up at the steepest section of the trail. Don't worry—sweeping **switchbacks** make easy work of the 200-foot climb over the next 0.4 mile.

▶ MILE 1.5-1.7: Junction to Hurricane Hill Viewpoint

After climbing you'll reach a **junction;** keep straight and follow the path as it bends right, offering several hilltop paths over the next 0.2 mile. Finally, you'll be 5,761 feet above the Strait of Juan de Fuca, enjoying a 360-degree panorama that includes Port Angeles, Vancouver Island, and the peaks of

▲ MOUNTAIN GOATS ON HURRICANE HILL

the Cascades, Olympics, and British Columbia. Take some selfies and explore a battered USGS benchmark on the rocks nearby.

If you can pull yourself away from the view, make your way back to your car the same way you came.

DIRECTIONS

From U.S. 101 in Port Angeles, turn south on Race Street and drive about 1.8 miles (the road changing to Mt. Angeles Road along the way) to the Olympic National Park visitors center. Bear right just beyond the visitors center onto Hurricane Ridge Road and drive 18 miles to Hurricane Ridge. Drive through the parking lot and continue 1.3 miles to the trailhead. (In 2020, the hike will start at Picnic Area B, 1.2 miles beyond the Hurricane Ridge parking lot.) Toilets are located at the trailhead.

GPS COORDINATES: 47.976311, -123.517537 / N47° 58.5787' W123° 31.0522'

BEST NEARBY BREWS

Near the Port Angeles ferry terminal, **Barhop Brewing** (124 W. Railroad Ave., 360/797-1818, hours vary) serves rotating house beers and artisan pizza cooked in its stone oven. The brewer describes the beer as "aggressive California-style ales, with a Northwest twist, using fresh Northwest ingredients." Can't beat that. From the trailhead, the 21-mile drive north takes less than 45 minutes via Hurricane Ridge Road and U.S. 101.

Hurricane Hill

Climb steep slopes adorned with wildflowers to a ridge overlooking the Strait of Juan de Fuca, Canada, and the Olympics.

DISTANCE: 5.4 miles round-trip

DURATION: 3 hours

ELEVATION CHANGE: 1,700 feet

EFFORT: Moderate

TRAIL: Dirt trail, exposed slopes, rock

USERS: Hikers

SEASON: Mid-June-October

PASSES/FEES: 7-day national park pass, Olympic Annual Pass, America the Beautiful Passes

MAPS: Green Trails Map 134S for Elwha North-Hurricane Ridge

CONTACT: Olympic National Park Wilderness Information Center, 360/565-3130, www.nps.gov/olym

START THE HIKE

▶ **MILE 0-0.6: Switchback Trailhead to Trail Intersection**

The **Switchback Trail**'s name gives away what's in store as you depart the tiny roadside parking area next to a cascading creek. This trailhead, with a sign clearly marking the trail, is one of four in the park with trails leading to skyscraping Klahhane Ridge. This is the shortest trail, but it's also the steepest. You may spot bears, deer, mountain goats, and marmots, but keep your distance. An **intersection** appears at a switchback 0.6 mile into the hike.

▶ **MILE 0.6-1.6: Trail Intersection to Klahhane Ridge**

A sign points left to Hurricane Ridge (a mellower 2.5-mile hike); you can make an escape here if you wish, but you'll get more breathtaking views if you turn right and continue climbing **Klahhane Ridge.** The view improves with each step over the next 1 mile. Avalanche lilies, lupine, scarlet paintbrush, and other wildflowers color the slopes in summer. Mount

VIEW FROM KLAHHANE RIDGE ▶

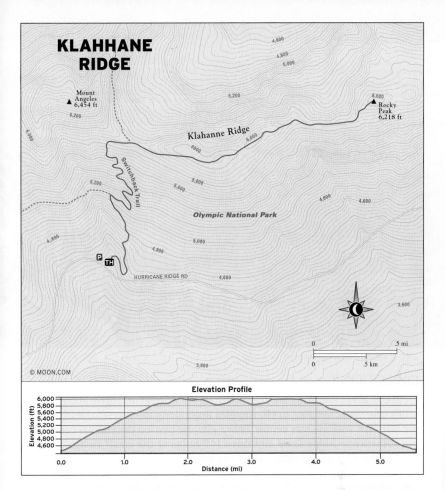

KLAHHANE RIDGE

Mount Angeles 6,454 ft

Rocky Peak 6,218 ft

Klahanne Ridge

Switchback Trail

Olympic National Park

HURRICANE RIDGE RD

© MOON.COM

0   .5 mi
0   .5 km

Elevation Profile

Elevation (ft): 6,000 / 5,800 / 5,600 / 5,400 / 5,200 / 5,000 / 4,800 / 4,600

Distance (mi): 0.0   1.0   2.0   3.0   4.0   5.0

Olympus is visible to the south, and below you can see cars and hardy cyclists ascending Hurricane Ridge Road. The climbing ends as you arrive at a **saddle** between two rocky peaks. Here, the view doubles in grandeur with the additions of the Strait of Juan de Fuca and Victoria on Vancouver Island.

▶ **MILE 1.6–2.7: Klahhane Ridge to High Point**

From the **saddle**, you can turn left to descend to Heather Park, but I recommend going right for a real treat. The thrill of strolling across the sky is likely to encourage even those with tired legs to push on a little farther.

Over the next 1.1 miles, stroll across the basalt rocks of **Klahhane Ridge,** enjoying views of Port Angeles's Ediz Hook and Sequim's Dungeness Spit reaching into the strait 6,000 feet below. You'll make a final short climb and arrive at a **high point** ideal for a break. This is a good place to turn back. Beyond this point, the trail starts descending to Lake Angeles.

For the return trip, retrace your path across the ridge and head back down the **Switchback Trail.** Your knees are likely to be less cranky about the steep descent if you use trekking poles.

▲ PORT ANGELES SEEN FROM KLAHHANE RIDGE

DIRECTIONS

From U.S. 101 in Port Angeles, turn south on Race Street and drive about 1.8 miles (the road changing to Mt. Angeles Road along the way) to the Olympic National Park visitors center. Bear right just beyond the visitors center onto Hurricane Ridge Road and drive 14.7 miles to the small Switchback Trail parking lot on the right side of the road.

GPS COORDINATES: 47.986502, –123.461159 / N47° 59.1901' W123° 27.6695

BEST NEARBY BITES

In Discovery Bay, stop at the giant wood-carved hamburger sitting in front of **Fat Smitty's** (282624 U.S. 101, 360/385-4099, www.fatsmittys. com, 10:30am-7pm daily). The Smitty Burger that headlines the menu isn't as big as the sculpture, but it is gargantuan in its own right. The most expensive wallpaper on the peninsula is courtesy of visitors who decorate dollar bills and pin them to the walls and ceiling. Every five years a Boy Scout troop removes the money (more than $26,000 in 2017), which is donated to the Scouts and other local organizations. From the trailhead, the 51-mile drive east takes about 1 hour, 15 minutes via Hurricane Ridge Road and U.S. 101.

OLYMPIC NATIONAL PARK, HOH RAIN FOREST

Wander beneath blankets of moss hanging from towering trees as you follow family-friendly trails through the Hoh Rain Forest.

BEST: Spring Hikes
DISTANCE: 6.7 miles round-trip
DURATION: 3.5 hours
ELEVATION CHANGE: 300 feet
EFFORT: Easy/moderate
TRAIL: Dirt trail, bridge crossings
USERS: Hikers, wheelchair users
SEASON: Year-round
PASSES/FEES: 7-day national park pass, Olympic Annual Pass, America the Beautiful Passes
MAPS: Green Trails Map 133S for Seven Lakes Basin-Mount Olympus
CONTACT: Hoh Rain Forest Visitor Center, www.nps.gov/olym

This route combines the very popular Hall of Mosses loop with a taste of the less traversed Hoh River Trail, the entirety of which stretches 17.3 miles to Glacier Meadows beneath Mount Olympus, the highest peak on the Olympic Peninsula. On summer afternoons, Olympic National Park uses meter lights to control traffic as visitors flock from around the globe to experience the Hoh's lush, green wonderland. Get here early to avoid the crowds.

START THE HIKE

▶ **MILE 0-0.9: Visitors Center to Hall of Mosses**
Starting from the visitors center, walk about 0.1 mile to an **intersection** and sign directing you left toward the **Hall of Mosses.** The 0.8-mile Hall of Mosses loop lives up to its name as you quickly find yourself immersed in green. Ferns and other plants cover the forest floor, trees with bizarre root formations line the path, and sheets of moss hang from branches. Make sure to make the 200-foot side trip to the **Maple Grove.**

▶ **MILE 0.9-3.8: Hall of Mosses to Hoh River Trail**
After completing the loop, return to the first intersection and continue straight for 0.1 mile to the **Hoh River Trail.** As **Mineral Creek** cascades down a moss-covered cliff on its way to the river, it creates a lovely setting and a good destination for those wanting to sample the trail. Reach the falls by walking the mostly flat, neatly groomed Hoh River Trail for 2.8 miles. Along the way, listen to chirping birds and the churning Hoh River while keeping a lookout for Roosevelt elk.

Hall of Mosses and Hoh River Trail

OLYMPIC NATIONAL PARK

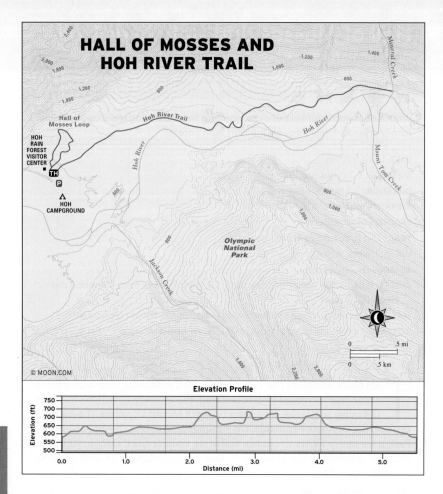

HALL OF MOSSES AND HOH RIVER TRAIL

Elevation Profile

In the final bit of this stretch, the trail undulates a bit before coming to a **bridge** crossing Mineral Creek. The falls are visible through the vegetation. On the far side of the crossing, a well-worn social trail leads up the slope to the base of the falls. However, rangers prefer visitors stay off this path to protect the undergrowth.

▶ **MILE 3.8–6.7: Hoh River Trail to Visitors Center**

From here you can continue deeper into the rain forest or turn back to return 2.9 miles to the visitors center.

▲ MINERAL CREEK FALLS

DIRECTIONS

From U.S. 101 (12 miles south of Forks and 90 miles north of Hoquiam) turn east on Upper Hoh Road and drive 18 miles to the Hoh Rain Forest Visitor Center parking lot. Restrooms and camping are available.

GPS COORDINATES: 47.860490, –123.934749 / N47° 51.6294' W123° 56.0849'

BEST NEARBY BITES

Looking out over Kalaloch Creek and the Pacific Ocean, it's hard to beat the view at **Creekside Restaurant** (157151 U.S. 101, 866/622-9928, www.thekalalochlodge.com, hours vary). The restaurant partners with local farms and businesses to produce delicious, hearty fare. Try the dry-rubbed salmon or the bacon, lettuce, tomato, and avocado sandwich. From the trailhead, the 39-mile drive southwest takes about 55 minutes via Upper Hoh Road and U.S. 101.

Hall of Mosses and Hoh River Trail

OLYMPIC NATIONAL PARK

Watch marmots play, relax beside a pristine lake, and gaze at Mount Olympus while hiking through the aptly named Grand Valley.

BEST: Wildflower Hikes
DISTANCE: 9.3 miles round-trip
DURATION: 5 hours
ELEVATION CHANGE: 2,500 feet
EFFORT: Moderate/strenuous
TRAIL: Dirt trail, log crossing, loose rock, rock steps
USERS: Hikers
SEASON: Mid-July–mid-October
PASSES/FEES: 7-day national park pass, Olympic Annual Pass, America the Beautiful Passes
MAPS: Green Trails Map 134S for Elwha North–Hurricane Ridge
CONTACT: Olympic National Park Wilderness Information Center, 360/565-3130, www.nps.gov/olym

START THE HIKE

▶ **MILE 0–0.2: Parking Lot to Badger Valley Trail**
Make your way to the eastern edge of one of the highest parking lots in the Olympics (elev. 6,100 feet). This hike starts at **Obstruction Point,** which would be a fulfilling destination for most hikes—but on this trail it's just the beginning. Admire the view of the snowcapped Olympics and the lush green valleys below before following the signs left to **Badger Valley and Deer Park.** Yes, the sign points right for a more direct trip to Grand Lake, but Badger Valley offers a gentler, more knee-friendly descent; you'll finish the loop on the other trail. In 0.2 mile, you'll reach an unmarked **intersection** on the slope beneath Obstruction Point. Turn right at the intersection to drop into the valley on the switchbacking **Badger Valley Trail.**

▶ **MILE 0.2–3.1: Badger Valley Trail to Badger Creek**
The trail is steep at first but soon mellows. After 1 mile, keep straight, passing the Elk Mountain Trail. Over the next 1.9 miles enjoy the peaceful beauty of the valley as you walk along the gurgling **Badger Creek** through sections of forest. Butterflies flutter about scarlet paintbrush, bluebells-of-Scotland, lupine, and other summer wildflowers. The grass alongside the trail sometimes grows waist-high. You may even glimpse a bear.

▶ **MILE 3.1–5.9: Badger Creek to Grand Pass Trail**
You'll cross **Badger Creek** on some stable logs before reaching the first uphill section. Climb for 0.4 mile, cross a bridge over **Grand Creek,** and

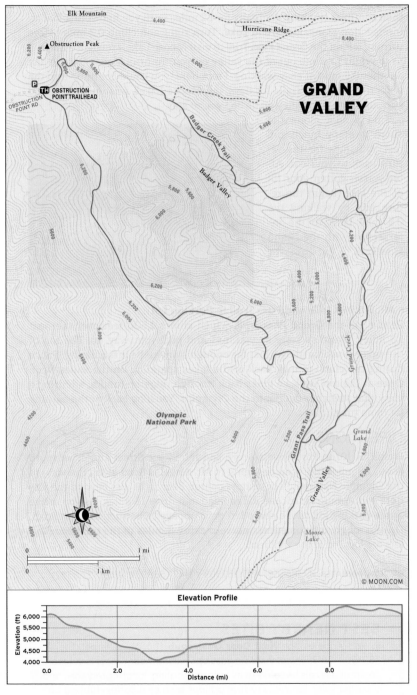

Elevation Profile

then continue climbing gradually for 1.2 miles until you find yourself at an intersection alongside **Grand Lake.** Turn right and climb 0.2 mile before turning left on the **Grand Pass Trail** to visit Moose Lake. (You'll use the trail to the right to climb out of the valley on your return.) Moose Lake is just another 0.5 mile of easy walking. From here, you could continue into the wilderness, linking trails for days, but Moose Lake's pristine waters and surrounding steep valley walls beg you to stay.

Find a spot along the shore to enjoy lunch and rest your legs for the return back to your car. After you've gotten your fill of the lake, begin the return trip by walking the 0.5 mile back to the **intersection** with the Grand Pass Trail.

GRAND LAKE ▸

▸ **MILE 5.9-9.3: Grand Pass Trail to Parking Lot**
Return via the **Grand Pass Trail,** which climbs 1,500 feet over the next 1.8 miles. Marmots stare as you huff and puff your way up. The top of the ridge is visible above, just far enough away to be intimidating. Pause during the climb to look back at the lakes sparkling on the valley floor. Once at the top, walk 1.6 miles back through ridgetop tundra, admiring a view that stretches deep into the Olympics. You'll be back at the parking lot in no time.

DIRECTIONS

From U.S. 101 in Port Angeles, turn south on Race Street and drive south about 1.8 miles (the road changing to Mt. Angeles Road along the way) to the Olympic National Park visitors center. Bear right just beyond the visitors center onto Hurricane Ridge Road and drive 18 miles. As you arrive at the parking lot, take a sharp left onto unpaved Obstruction Point Road. Drive a rough and sometimes nerve-racking 8 miles to the trailhead. Toilets are located at the trailhead.

GPS COORDINATES: 47.918386, –123.382303 / N47° 55.1032′ W123° 22.9382′

BEST NEARBY BITES
In Port Angeles, the **Next Door Gastropub** (113 W. 1st Street, Ste. A, 360/504-2613, www.nextdoorgastropub.com, hours vary) is a favorite among locals because of its outdoor seating, local ingredients, and a burger selection with creative options such as a coffee-rubbed bacon cheeseburger called Not Your Average Joe. From the trailhead, the 27-mile drive north takes less than 90 minutes via Hurricane Ridge Road and U.S. 101.

Wander upward past waterfalls, rhododendrons, and wildflowers to a peak with views of the Olympics, Cascades, and the Strait of Juan de Fuca.

DISTANCE: 8 miles round-trip

DURATION: 4 hours

ELEVATION CHANGE: 3,000 feet

EFFORT: Moderate/strenuous

TRAIL: Dirt, rock

USERS: Hikers, leashed dogs

SEASON: June–November

PASSES/FEES: None

MAPS: Green Trails Map 136 for Tyler Peak

CONTACT: Olympic National Forest, Hood Canal Ranger District, 360/765-2200, www.fs.usda.gov

Mount Townsend gives away a million-dollar view for free—unless you count the toll it takes on your legs. A view stretching from Vancouver Island to Seattle and the Cascades awaits atop the broad 6,280-foot peak. You just have to climb 3,000 feet to get there.

START THE HIKE

▶ **MILE 0–1.6: Mount Townsend Upper Trailhead to Townsend Creek**
Starting from the **upper trailhead,** follow the path at the west end of the parking lot as it climbs into the woods. The sound of Townsend Creek splashing toward the Big Quilcene River welcomes you as you approach a series of **switchbacks.** Pass hemlocks, Douglas fir, cedar, and rhododendrons (typically blooming in May and June), and maybe cross paths with a deer or smaller critters as you continue upward. After 1.5 miles, you get your first glimpse of what makes this hike special as you step from the trees and get a view of the upper slope. Cross **Townsend Creek** beneath a tiny cascade and find another stack of switchbacks in 0.1 mile.

▶ **MILE 1.6–3: Townsend Creek to Silver Lakes Trail Intersection**
In another 1.1 miles, a sign points right to continue climbing (but if you're ready for a break, take a quick 50-yard detour to the left and enjoy tiny Windy Lake). The **switchbacks** continue, passing the **intersection** with the Silver Lakes Trail in another 0.3 mile.

▶ **MILE 3–4: Silver Lakes Trail Intersection to Mount Townsend Summit**
The steepest section of trail is beyond **Silver Lakes junction**, but it doesn't last long. The trees thin and scarlet paintbrush, fireweed, and other plants add color as the next 0.7 mile puts you atop the ridge. From here the incline

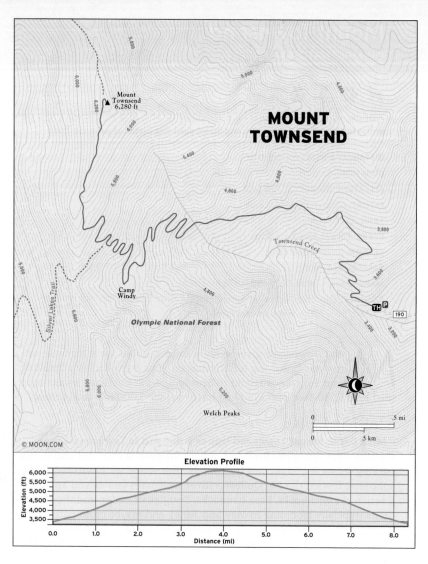

Elevation Profile

is gradual as you walk the final 0.3 mile (staying right at the **intersection** just below the high point).

The bird's-eye view is the highlight of any trip to the summit. Dungeness Spit reaching out into the Strait of Juan de Fuca, Townsend's Olympic neighbors, Seattle's glistening skyline, Puget Sound, and the Cascades all unfurl below you. Rock outcroppings give hikers plenty of places to sit and enjoy lunch or duck out of the wind. A USGS benchmark is affixed to one of the rocks.

Recharge your legs with a little break before asking them to carry you back down the same trail they just hauled you up.

▲ MOUNT TOWNSEND

DIRECTIONS

Follow U.S. 101 to Penny Creek Road (0.9 mile south of Quilcene Ranger Station and 50.5 miles north of Shelton) and turn west. Drive 1.5 miles and bear left on Big Quilcene River Road/Forest Road 27 and drive 13.5 miles (past the Mount Townsend Trail sign directing traffic to the lower trailhead) to Forest Road 27-190 and turn left. Follow the road 0.8 mile to the small trailhead parking lot. A toilet is located at the trailhead.

GPS COORDINATES: 47.85611, –123.03597 / N47° 51.3666′ W123° 2.1582′

BEST NEARBY BITES

At Quilcene's **Gear Head Deli** (294963 U.S. 101, 360/301-3244, 10am-4pm Tues.-Sat.), grab lunch for your hike or relax on the deck with a pulled pork sandwich served on a ciabatta roll. The pork is smoked in-house and topped with homemade barbecue sauce. From the trailhead, the 17-mile drive southeast takes less than 45 minutes via Big Quilcene River Road/Forest Road 27 and U.S. 101.

Combine two trails to experience the vast variety of this rain forest—giant trees, a cedar bog, waterfalls, and Lake Quinault.

BEST: Waterfall Hikes

DISTANCE: 4 miles round-trip

DURATION: 2 hours

ELEVATION CHANGE: 350 feet

EFFORT: Easy

TRAIL: Dirt; boardwalk, paved road when the lakeshore is flooded

USERS: Hikers, wheelchair users (on a short portion of Rain Forest Nature Loop), leashed dogs

SEASON: Year-round

PASSES/FEES: Northwest Forest Pass

MAPS: Green Trails Map 197 for Lake Quinault, Custom Correct Map for Quinault-Colonel Bob

CONTACT: Olympic National Park, Pacific Ranger District, 360/288-2525, www.fs.usda.gov

Along the way, keep an eye out for squirrels scampering up trees, Chinook salmon spawning in the streams during the fall, and bald eagles soaring above the lake.

START THE HIKE

▶ **MILE 0-0.3: Trailhead Kiosk to Quinault Loop Trail**

Moss and a tiny tree grow atop the **trailhead kiosk.** Take about 10 steps up the trail and come to a choice: right or left on the 0.5-mile **Rain Forest Nature Trail Loop**? Either direction works, but turning left is the most direct route for this hike—and it immediately delivers a colossal 400-year-old Douglas fir. (The Forest Service lists the first portion of the nature loop in either direction as wheelchair accessible.) After 0.1 mile, pass a trail on your left (you'll close your loop hike at this intersection) and walk 0.2 mile along the edge of a narrow gorge holding Willaby Creek. At another mossy kiosk, turn left on the **Quinault Loop Trail** (staying to the right takes you on the remainder of the nature loop and back to the trailhead).

▶ **MILE 0.3-2.2: Quinault Loop Trail to Cascade Falls**

Enjoy a quiet walk dwarfed by 15- to 20-story-tall western hemlocks, Douglas firs, western red cedars, and Sitka spruce. Pass a closed trail on the right shortly before crossing a **bridge over Willaby Creek.** In 1 mile, come to the intersection with the **Willaby Creek Trail** and continue straight. The trail can get muddy before **boardwalks** offer a cleaner (but sometimes slippery)

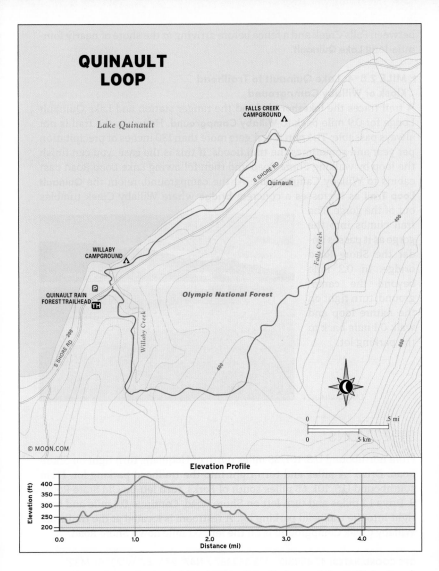

QUINAULT LOOP

Elevation Profile

route through a cedar bog. After hiking 0.6 mile beyond the Willaby Creek Trail intersection, pass a triangle kiosk and a trail on your left heading to historic Lake Quinault Lodge. (This 0.6-mile trail is a good option if you're looking for a shortcut.) Go right and cross a **bridge over Falls Creek.** In another 0.3 mile, cross the bridge at **Cascade Falls** where you're sure to be inspired to pause for a photo.

▶ **MILE 2.2-2.8: Cascade Falls to Lake Quinault**
An intersection 0.2 mile farther gives you the option to extend your trip. (Turning right on the Gatton Creek Trail delivers more forest, falls, and creeks with an option to visit the "World's Largest Sitka Spruce.") But, to head to the lakeshore, turn left and cross Falls Creek on a **wooden bridge.** In 0.4 mile, cross **South Shore Road** near the ranger station. The trail travels

between Falls Creek and a fence before arriving at the shore of nearly four-mile-long **Lake Quinault.**

▶ **MILE 2.8-4: Lake Quinault to Trailhead Kiosk or Willaby Campground**

A trail traces the **lakeshore** behind the ranger station and Lake Quinault Lodge for 0.9 mile back to **Willaby Campground.** However, the trail is not always passable: The rain forest gets more than 130 inches of precipitation per year and sometimes the trail floods. If this is the case, you can finish the loop by walking Shore Road and then following Lake Loop Road past cabins to Willaby Campground. At the campground, rejoin the **Quinault Loop Trail** as it crosses a concrete **bridge** where Willaby Creek tumbles out of the gorge. The trail climbs into the gorge as it passes under the Shore Road bridge. In 0.2 mile beyond the campground, turn right on the nature loop and walk 0.1 mile back to the parking lot.

LAKE QUINAULT ▶

DIRECTIONS

From northbound U.S. 101, 38 miles north of Hoquiam, turn right on Shore Road. Drive 1.4 miles and turn right into the trailhead parking lot. From southbound U.S. 101, 65 miles south of Forks, turn left on Old State Route 9. Drive 1.1 miles and turn left on Shore Road. Continue 0.4 mile and turn right into the trailhead parking lot. A restroom is located at the trailhead. Willaby Creek Campground is on the left, 0.1 mile down Shore Road.

GPS COORDINATES: 47.459812, –123.862387 / N47° 27.5887′ W123° 51.7432′

BEST NEARBY BITES

Nine months before President Franklin D. Roosevelt signed the bill creating Olympic National Park, he had lunch at the **Lake Quinault Lodge** (360/288-2900, www.olympicnationalparks.com, 7:30am-8pm daily). The dining room now bears Roosevelt's name. The lunch menu includes several styles of burgers and sandwiches including a smoked salmon BLT. Reservations are accepted but not required. From the trailhead, the 1-mile drive northeast takes less than 2 minutes via Shore Drive.

8

Staircase Rapids and Shady Lane
OLYMPIC NATIONAL PARK

Combine two trails into one kid-friendly hike through a mossy forest of towering trees—both upright and fallen—while visiting rumbling rapids and crossing a suspension bridge.

DISTANCE: 4.2 miles round-trip

DURATION: 2 hours

ELEVATION CHANGE: 300 feet

EFFORT: Easy

TRAIL: Wide dirt path, suspension bridge

USERS: Hikers, wheelchair users

SEASON: Year-round, but road may close for snow and add 1 mile each way to hike

PASSES/FEES: 7-day national park pass, Olympic Annual Pass, America the Beautiful Passes

MAPS: Green Trails Map 167 for Mount Steel

CONTACT: Olympic National Park, 360/565-3130, www.nps.gov/olym

START THE HIKE

▶ **MILE 0–1: Ranger Station to Shady Lane**
Start from the ranger station and, over the first 0.1 mile, cross the North Fork Skokomish River on a wide **bridge.** Once on the other side, a sign points left to **Shady Lane Trail.** The next 0.1 mile leading to the wooden bridge over Elk Creek is flat and the dirt tread is wheelchair friendly. Beyond the bridge, the trail continues to follow the North Fork Skokomish River opposite the 49-site Staircase Campground. Even on sunny days you'll find the trail is aptly named as you pass under cedars, hemlocks, and Douglas firs. Keep an eye out for elk, birds, and butterflies as you wander 0.8 mile to the trail's end at a small parking lot on Forest Road 2451 (an alternate starting point).

▶ **MILE 1–1.9: Shady Lane to River Bridge**
By the time you follow the trail back to the river **bridge,** you'll have 1.9 miles under your belt. If you're up for part two of this hike, turn left on the **Staircase Rapids Loop.**

▶ **MILE 1.9–2.3: Staircase Rapids Loop to Big Cedar**
Shortly after starting the **Staircase Rapids Loop,** pass a **spur** on the left leading to the small Elk Creek hydro plant that powers the ranger station. Continue another 0.3 mile to a sign pointing left to the **"Big Cedar."** The short side trip (about 0.1 mile round-trip) visits a fallen 14-foot-wide western red cedar. Immediately after finishing this fascinating aside, pass a

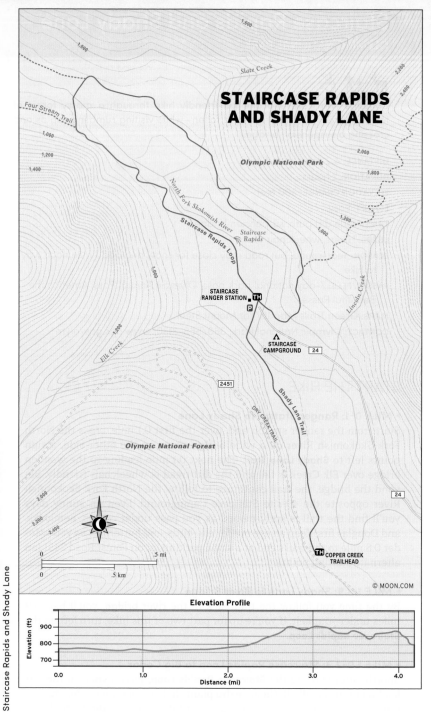

STAIRCASE RAPIDS AND SHADY LANE

Slate Creek

Four Stream Trail

Olympic National Park

North Fork Skokomish River

Staircase Rapids Loop

Staircase Rapids

STAIRCASE RANGER STATION

TH **P**

STAIRCASE CAMPGROUND

24

Lincoln Creek

Elk Creek

2451

DRY CREEK TRAIL

Shady Lane Trail

Olympic National Forest

24

TH COPPER CREEK TRAILHEAD

0   .5 mi
0   .5 km

© MOON.COM

Elevation Profile

Elevation (ft)

900
800
700

0.0   1.0   2.0   3.0   4.0

Distance (mi)

▲ SUSPENSION BRIDGE ACROSS THE NORTH FORK SKOKOMISH RIVER

viewpoint of the river and its rapids. The park classifies the path up to this point (including the Big Cedar spur) as wheelchair accessible, but I'd concur with the trail brochure's footnote: "May need assistance." Those uncomfortable rolling across this terrain can backtrack to the river.

▶ **MILE 2.3–3: Big Cedar to North Fork Skokomish River Suspension Bridge**
Spend the next 0.6 mile following the river and enjoying the moss-covered trees and boulders until you reach an **intersection** with the Four Stream Trail. Turn right to stay on the loop trail and walk 0.1 mile to a **suspension bridge** crossing the North Fork Skokomish River.

▶ **MILE 3–4.2: North Fork Skokomish River Suspension Bridge to Parking Lot**
After crossing the bridge—and snapping a few photos—stay left and, shortly after, reach the **North Fork Skokomish River Trail.** Turn right where the sign points the way back to the ranger station. This section of the loop is quieter as it travels farther from the river. Cross a couple of creeks and enjoy the lush greenery as the path meanders 1.1 miles back to Staircase's **parking lot.** Follow the parking lot's driveway downhill to return to the ranger station and campground in a short distance.

DIRECTIONS

From U.S. 101 in Hoodsport, head west on Highway 119 for 9.3 miles. At the stop sign turn left on Forest Road 24 and drive 6.6 miles to the Staircase Ranger Station and the trailhead. The driveway to the parking lot is just before the ranger station. Toilets and a campground are located at the trailhead.

GPS COORDINATES: 47.515213, –123.328773 / N47° 30.9128′ W123° 19.7264′

Mount Ellinor
OLYMPIC NATIONAL FOREST

🦌 ❀ 🐾

Let views of Rainier, the Hood Canal, and Lake Cushman inspire you upward to a mountaintop on every Olympic hiker's must-do list.

BEST: Dog-Friendly Hikes
DISTANCE: 3.4 miles round-trip
DURATION: 2.5 hours
ELEVATION CHANGE: 2,400 feet
EFFORT: Moderate
TRAIL: Dirt, log steps, rock, scree
USERS: Hikers, leashed dogs
SEASON: July-October
PASSES/FEES: Northwest Forest Pass
MAPS: Custom Correct Map for Mount Skokomish-Lake Cushman, Green Trails Map 168SX for Olympic Mountains East
CONTACT: Olympic National Forest, Hood Canal Ranger District, 360/765-2200, www.fs.usda.gov

There are three trailhead options for climbing Mount Ellinor, but don't think that starting from the upper parking lot makes this trip easy. You'll just get to the steep stuff (and some of the best views in the Olympics) a little quicker.

START THE HIKE

▶ **MILE 0-0.7: Mount Ellinor Upper Trailhead to Winter Trail Junction**
Find the **upper trailhead** on the west edge of the parking lot and quickly enter the woods. The trail climbs gradually for 0.3 mile until it **intersects** with the trail approaching from the lower lot. Turn right to continue upward. In another 0.4 mile, a sign marks the **junction** with the winter trail. Unless you have mountaineering gear and the requisite skills and the rocky upper slopes are covered with snow, the winter route isn't advised. Continue straight to stay on the **summer trail** as the climbing starts to get serious.

▶ **MILE 0.7-1.7: Winter Trail Junction to Mount Ellinor Summit**
The woods soon give way to **subalpine meadows** where daisies, purple Jeffrey's shooting stars, yarrow, and other wildflowers grow. There is no shade as you scamper up rocky steps and steep pitches. On hot summer days you'll be happy to have packed extra water, sunglasses, and a hat.

The higher you climb the more spectacular the view becomes. Lake Cushman and Hood Canal glisten in the glacier-carved landscape. Mount

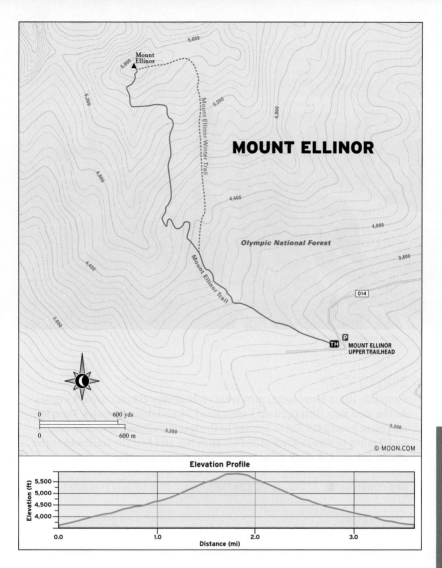

Rainier and the Cascades rise in the distance. Introduced to the Olympics in the 1920s, mountain goats have long frequented Mount Ellinor. Keep your distance if you encounter these creatures, but the likelihood of crossing paths with goats is decreasing: In 2018, federal and state agencies started moving the peninsula's estimated 725 goats to the Cascades. After 1 mile of climbing, the argillite rock of Ellinor's 5,944-foot **summit** offers numerous places to sit, have a snack, and enjoy the scenery from the edge of the Olympics.

If you can pry yourself away from the view, the route back is the same steep trail you used to get here.

▲ ATOP MOUNT ELLINOR

DIRECTIONS

From U.S. 101 in Hoodsport, turn west on Highway 119 and drive 9.3 miles. At the stop sign turn right on Forest Road 24 and drive 1.6 miles. Turn left on Forest Road 2419. Drive 5 miles to the lower trailhead and then continue 1.7 miles to Forest Road 2419-014. Turn left and find the trailhead at the end of the road. A vault toilet is located in the parking lot.

GPS COORDINATES: 47.510271, –123.247888 / N47° 30.6163′ W123° 14.8733′

BEST NEARBY DRINKS

Hoodsport has several options for a post-hike adult beverage. **The Hardware Distillery Co.** (24210 N. Highway 101, 206/300-0877, www. thehardwaredistillery.com, hours vary) serves artisan whiskey, gin, vodka, and other spirits. From the trailhead, the 18-mile drive southeast to Hoodsport takes 45 minutes via Highway 119.

Follow a beloved all-ages trail to a picturesque emerald lake surrounded by timber-covered slopes in Olympic National Forest.

DISTANCE: 6.8 miles round-trip

DURATION: 3 hours

ELEVATION CHANGE: 1,300 feet

EFFORT: Moderate

TRAIL: Dirt trail

USERS: Hikers, leashed dogs

SEASON: April–November

PASSES/FEES: Northwest Forest Pass

MAPS: Green Trails Map 168 for The Brothers

CONTACT: Olympic National Forest, Hood Canal Ranger District, 360/765-2200, www.fs.usda.gov

One of the most popular trails on the Olympic Peninsula, Lena Lake fits neatly into a lot of agendas. It's an easy first backpacking trip for the kids, while those looking for a challenge have the option of a butt-kicking extension to a higher lake. Get started early and come on a weekday if you want to avoid the crush of hikers.

START THE HIKE

▶ **MILE 0-1.9: Lena Lake Roadside Trailhead to First Bridge**

Start from the **roadside trailhead** on a wide, mostly smooth path that soon begins its gradual, switchbacking climb through second-growth forest. Listen for the sound of Lena Creek as it rolls downhill to the Hamma Hamma River. After 1.9 miles, reach a **wooden bridge** that inspires many hikers to pause and pose for pictures. The gully beneath the bridge is dry as Lena Creek flows underground in this area.

▶ **MILE 1.9-3: First Bridge to Ledge Viewpoint**

Reach a second photo-worthy **bridge** in another 0.7 mile as you close in on your destination. A **junction** 0.4 mile beyond the bridge allows the option of going left to Upper Lena Lake. Instead, turn right and in a matter of seconds find yourself standing on a **ledge** overlooking the 55-acre lake. Keep an eye out for bear, elk, deer, and a variety of birds.

▶ **MILE 3-3.4: Ledge Viewpoint to Lena Lake**

This space at the edge of the trees is an ideal and scenic destination for day hikers, but you can explore a little more by following the path along the west side of lake for another 0.4 mile (passing campsites and a pit toilet) to another **intersection**. Here you get a second chance to turn left and climb to Upper Lena Lake (note this will quickly take you into

OLYMPIC NATIONAL PARK

Lena Lake

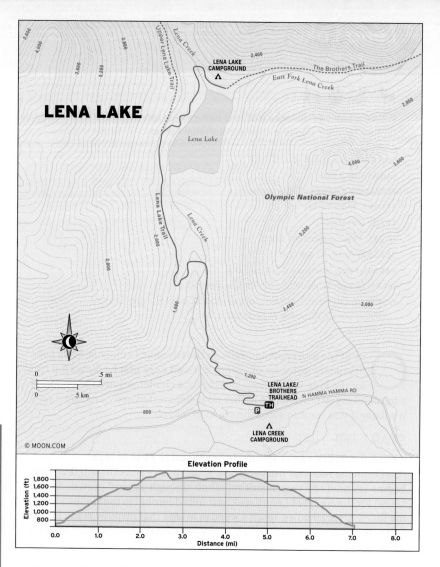

LENA LAKE

Elevation Profile

Olympic National Park, where dogs are not allowed). Go right and in a few steps you'll arrive at an appealing **rest stop** where Lena Creek cascades toward to the lake.

When it's time to leave, return to your car via the Lena Lake Trail.

DIRECTIONS

From U.S. 101 near milepost 318 (14 miles north of Hoodsport and 23 miles south of Quilcene), turn west on Hamma Hamma River Road/Forest Road 25 and drive 7.5 miles to the trailhead. A toilet is located at the trailhead.

GPS COORDINATES: 47.599739, –123.150884 / N47° 35.9843′ W123° 9.053′

▲ LENA LAKE

BEST NEARBY BREWS

Located in the small Hood Canal town of Quilcene, **101 Brewery** (294793 U.S. 101, 360/765-6485, www.101brewery.com, 7am-7pm Sun.-Thurs., 7am-8pm Fri.-Sat.) crafts four beers and offers a menu that includes pizza, burgers, pie, and ice cream. Make sure to sample Quilcene's most famous export: oysters. From the trailhead, the 30-mile drive northeast takes less than 45 minutes via Hamma Hamma Road/Forest Road 25 and U.S. 101.

Lena Lake

NEARBY CAMPGROUNDS

NAME	DESCRIPTION	FACILITIES	SEASON	FEE
Sol Duc Campground	situated in thick old-growth forest on the Sol Duc River	82 RV and tent sites, restrooms	year-round	$21

Sol Duc Hot Springs Road, Olympic National Park, 360/565-3130, www.recreation.gov

NAME	DESCRIPTION	FACILITIES	SEASON	FEE
Heart O' the Hills Campground	ideally located for adventures into northern Olympic National Park and Hurricane Ridge	105 RV and tent sites, restrooms	year-round	$20

Hurricane Ridge Road, Port Angeles, Olympic National Park, 360/565-3131, www.nps.gov/olym

NAME	DESCRIPTION	FACILITIES	SEASON	FEE
Staircase Campground	old-growth forest along the Skokomish River	49 RV and tent sites, restrooms	year-round	$20

Staircase Road, Hoodsport, Olympic National Park, 360/565-3131, www.nps.gov/olym

NAME	DESCRIPTION	FACILITIES	SEASON	FEE
Willaby Campground	steps from Lake Quinault and the Quinault Rain Forest Nature Trail Loop	21 RV and tent sites, restrooms	April-November	$25

South Shore Road, Quinault, Olympic National Forest, 360/288-0203, www.recreation.gov

NAME	DESCRIPTION	FACILITIES	SEASON	FEE
Hoh Campground	immersed in the lush greenery of the rain forest	78 RV and tent sites, restrooms	year-round	$20

Hoh Valley Road, Hoh Rain Forest, Olympic National Park, 360/565-3131, www.nps.gov/olym

SEATTLE AND VICINITY

Water or mountains? Vibrant city or the solitude of nature? The Seattle and Puget Sound area is an ideal hub for adventurers who don't want to make these tough choices. Twenty-five miles is all that separates the sound-view paths at Discovery Park from the short trail climbing to Poo Poo Point on Tiger Mountain. Whether you want to watch birds on the Nisqually Delta, explore history on Whidbey Island, or take in the majestic view from atop Oyster Dome, Puget Sound offers abundant opportunities within two hours of Seattle. And if you want to test your legs in the mountains, it's less than 40 minutes to North Bend, home of scenic local favorites such as Mailbox Peak, Mount Si, and the Rattlesnake Ledges.

▲ DECEPTION PASS BRIDGE   ▲ PARAGLIDER AT POO POO POINT

1 Oyster Dome
DISTANCE: 3.9 miles round-trip
DURATION: 2 hours
EFFORT: Easy/moderate

2 Deception Pass: Rosario Head and Lighthouse Point
DISTANCE: 3.3 miles round-trip
DURATION: 1.5 hours
EFFORT: Easy

3 Ebey's Landing
DISTANCE: 5.5 miles round-trip
DURATION: 2.5 hours
EFFORT: Easy/moderate

4 Discovery Park Loop
DISTANCE: 2.9 miles round-trip
DURATION: 1.5 hours
EFFORT: Easy

5 Poo Poo Point via Chirico Trail
DISTANCE: 3.8 miles round-trip
DURATION: 2 hours
EFFORT: Moderate

6 Rattlesnake Ledges
DISTANCE: 4.9 miles round-trip
DURATION: 2.5 hours
EFFORT: Moderate

7 Mount Si
DISTANCE: 7.6 miles round-trip
DURATION: 4 hours
EFFORT: Moderate/strenuous

8 Twin Falls
DISTANCE: 2.6 miles round-trip
DURATION: 1.5 hours
EFFORT: Easy/moderate

9 Mailbox Peak: Old-New Loop
DISTANCE: 8.2 miles round-trip
DURATION: 6 hours
EFFORT: Strenuous

10 Nisqually Estuary Boardwalk Trail
DISTANCE: 4.1 miles round-trip
DURATION: 2 hours
EFFORT: Easy

▼ VIEW FROM MOUNT SI

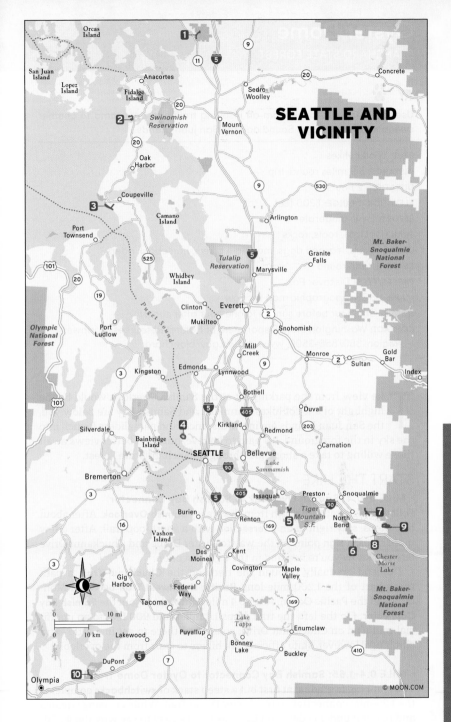

SEATTLE AND VICINITY

Orcas Island
San Juan Island
Lopez Island
Anacortes
Fidalgo Island
Swinomish Reservation
Oak Harbor
Coupeville
Camano Island
Port Townsend
Port Ludlow
Whidbey Island
Clinton
Mukilteo
Kingston
Edmonds
Silverdale
Bainbridge Island
Bremerton
Vashon Island
Gig Harbor
Tacoma
Lakewood
DuPont
Olympia

Concrete
Sedro-Woolley
Mount Vernon
Arlington
Granite Falls
Marysville
Tulalip Reservation
Everett
Snohomish
Mill Creek
Monroe
Gold Bar
Sultan
Index
Lynnwood
Bothell
Duvall
Kirkland
Redmond
Carnation
SEATTLE
Bellevue
Lake Sammamish
Issaquah
Preston
Snoqualmie
Burien
Renton
Tiger Mountain S.F.
North Bend
Des Moines
Kent
Covington
Maple Valley
Federal Way
Puyallup
Lake Tapps
Enumclaw
Bonney Lake
Buckley
Chester Morse Lake

Mt. Baker-Snoqualmie National Forest
Olympic National Forest
Puget Sound
Mt. Baker-Snoqualmie National Forest

9
11
5
20
20
20
525
101
20
19
101
3
3
16
3
5
405
90
405
5
169
18
169
410
7
5
2
530
9
2
9
203
90

0   10 mi
0   10 km

© MOON.COM

SEATTLE AND VICINITY

Use forest trails to climb from an inspiring trailhead panorama to another sweeping view of Puget Sound and the San Juan Islands.

BEST: Winter Hikes
DISTANCE: 3.9 miles round-trip
DURATION: 2 hours
ELEVATION CHANGE: 1,200 feet
EFFORT: Easy/moderate
TRAIL: Dirt trail, roots, rocks
USERS: Hikers, leashed dogs, mountain bikers, horseback riders
SEASON: Year-round
PASSES/FEES: Discover Pass
MAPS: USGS topographic map for Bow
HOURS: One hour before sunrise to one hour after sunset
CONTACT: Washington State Department of Natural Resources, Northwest Region, 360/856-3500, www.dnr.wa.gov/blanchard

The view from the parking lot at the Samish Overlook would be the highlight of a lot of hikes. Farmland and Samish Bay are below you, the San Juan Islands are in the distance, and paragliders launch into the sky in the foreground. It's hard to believe, but even better views await those willing to take a short hike through Blanchard State Forest.

START THE HIKE

▶ **MILE 0-0.4: Samish Overlook to Samish Bay Connector**
Follow the gravel path north from the grassy **Samish Overlook**. After about four steps, stay right at an **intersection** with a short loop trail. After a few more steps, a **sign** pointing the way to Oyster Dome and Chuckanut Drive lets you know you're heading in the right direction.

Descend gradually through the trees on the **Chuckanut Trail**, a path that's part of the 1,200-mile-long **Pacific Northwest Trail** between Montana and the Pacific Ocean. After 0.4 mile turn right to join the **Samish Bay Connector**. (To the left, the trail drops 1.4 miles and 900 feet to an unofficial trailhead on Chuckanut Drive; some start there to get in a little extra climbing. However, state officials ask hikers to start from the overlook.)

▶ **MILE 0.4-1.65: Samish Bay Connector to Oyster Dome Trail**
The climbing is gradual at first but a steep stack of **switchbacks** completes the 1.25-mile connection to the Oyster Dome Trail. While crossing streams and passing under cedars and Douglas firs it's easy to see why the 4,500-acre forest has a long logging history. Today timber and biomass (residual limbs and small pieces of wood) are sold by the state to help fund schools,

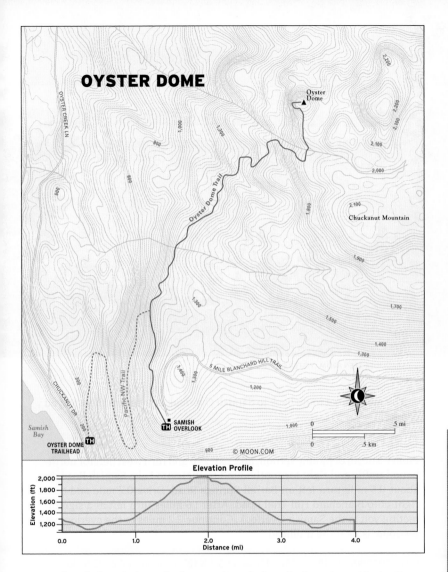

OYSTER DOME

Oyster
Dome

Chuckanut Mountain

Samish
Bay

SAMISH
OVERLOOK

OYSTER DOME
TRAILHEAD

© MOON.COM

Elevation Profile

roadwork, hospitals, and other services. Before the junction with the **Oyster Dome Trail**, pass a mangled interpretive sign explaining that a mile-high glacier creeped through this area 18,000 years ago.

▶ **MILE 1.65-1.95: Oyster Dome Trail to Oyster Dome**
Continue straight as you join the **Oyster Dome Trail**. The path is a bit vague as it approaches a creek, but it becomes clearer after you step over the stream. Finish this 0.3-mile stretch by scampering over rocks and roots and then popping out of the trees onto a **rock outcropping** with views of Puget Sound, the San Juan Islands, and the Olympics. Look for bald eagles and other birds circling overhead. Watch your step as you snap photos and stake out a place to relax; the rock is slippery when it's wet.

▲ PARAGLIDER SEEN FROM OYSTER DOME

The most direct route back to Samish Overlook is to return the way you came.

DIRECTIONS

From I-5 north of Mount Vernon, take exit 240 and turn west (left for northbound traffic and right for southbound traffic) onto Lake Samish Road. In about 0.5 mile turn left on Barrell Springs Road. Drive 0.7 mile and turn right onto Blanchard Hill Trail Road. After 1.6 miles turn left at a sign directing you to the Samish Overlook. Continue 2.2 miles to the overlook. A restroom is near the trailhead.

GPS COORDINATES: 48.609757, –122.426313 / N48° 36.5854′ W122° 25.5788′

BEST NEARBY BITES

A star of the Bellingham burger scene since it opened in 1989, **Boomer's Drive-In** (310 N. Samish Way, 360/647-2666, www.boomersdrivein.com, 11am-10pm Sun.-Thurs., 11am-11pm Fri.-Sat.) is the perfect place for a post-hike cheeseburger and shake. Let a carhop bring a quarter-pound Boomer Burger to your window or grab a seat around the circular fireplace inside the 1950s-themed diner. From the trailhead, the 16.5-mile drive north takes less than 30 minutes via I-5.

Deception Pass:
Rosario Head and Lighthouse Point

DECEPTION PASS STATE PARK

Explore the perimeter of Bowman Bay to find views of Rosario Strait, the Olympics, islands, and an iconic bridge.

DISTANCE: 3.3 miles round-trip
DURATION: 1.5 hours
ELEVATION CHANGE: 500 feet
EFFORT: Easy
TRAIL: Dirt, gravel
USERS: Hikers, leashed dogs
SEASON: Year-round
PASSES/FEES: Discover Pass
MAPS: Green Trails Map 41S for Deception Pass
PARK HOURS: 6:30am–dusk daily summer, 8am–dusk daily winter
CONTACT: Deception Pass State Park, 360/675-3767, http://parks.state.wa.us

Deception Pass draws more visitors than any other Washington state park, and it's evident why as you stroll around Bowman Bay. The boat launch parking lot accesses several short out-and-back hikes, including this scenic duo that is easily fused into one sublime, longer hike.

START THE HIKE

▶ **MILE 0–1.8: Rosario Head Loop**
Heading northwest from the parking lot, walk through the **picnic area** and past the **Civilian Conservation Corps Interpretive Center.** The center pays tribute to Franklin Roosevelt's Great Depression-era program responsible for developing so many state and national parks. Past the **picnic shelter**, find a path entering the woods. The trail bends left after an awkward section that seems destined to lead you through a campsite.

For the next 0.4 mile, walk among Douglas firs and madrone while crossing a steep hillside above the bay. The trail quickly deposits you at another picnic area at **Sharpe Cove.** Stay left, arcing along the cove, and follow a short gravel path past an access point to Rosario Beach.

The Maiden of Deception Pass welcomes visitors to **Rosario Head.** Carved from cedar in the early 1980s, the story pole depicts Ko-Kwal-al-woot, legend of the Samish Indian Nation. From the maiden, make a 0.25-mile loop around Rosario Head. Standing atop cliffs dropping sharply to Rosario Strait, enjoy a view that includes Vancouver Island, the San Juans, and the Olympics. Return the way you came (1.8 miles round-trip). The parking lot is also the starting point for part two of this hike.

Deception Pass: Rosario Head and Lighthouse Point

SEATTLE AND VICINITY

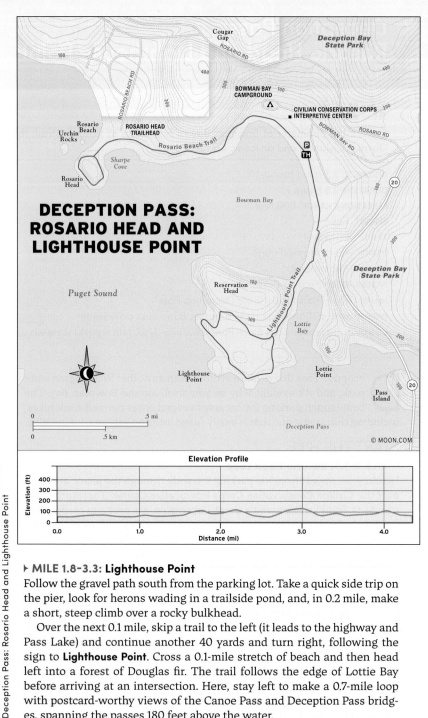

DECEPTION PASS: ROSARIO HEAD AND LIGHTHOUSE POINT

Elevation Profile

▶ **MILE 1.8-3.3: Lighthouse Point**

Follow the gravel path south from the parking lot. Take a quick side trip on the pier, look for herons wading in a trailside pond, and, in 0.2 mile, make a short, steep climb over a rocky bulkhead.

Over the next 0.1 mile, skip a trail to the left (it leads to the highway and Pass Lake) and continue another 40 yards and turn right, following the sign to **Lighthouse Point**. Cross a 0.1-mile stretch of beach and then head left into a forest of Douglas fir. The trail follows the edge of Lottie Bay before arriving at an intersection. Here, stay left to make a 0.7-mile loop with postcard-worthy views of the Canoe Pass and Deception Pass bridges, spanning the passes 180 feet above the water.

After completing the loop, return to the parking lot (a 1.5-mile round-trip) and pick your next adventure in the 3,854-acre park.

▲ THE MAIDEN OF DECEPTION PASS

DIRECTIONS

From the Clinton ferry dock on Whidbey Island, follow Highway 525 north for 22 miles and then continue straight on Highway 20 for 26 miles. Shortly after crossing the Deception Pass Bridge, turn left on Rosario Road.

From Mount Vernon, take Highway 536 west to Highway 20. (From Burlington, access Highway 20 at exit 230 on I-5). Continue straight on Highway 20 for 7 miles to a traffic circle. Take the second exit in the traffic circle and follow Highway 20 south for 4.4 miles; turn right on Rosario Road shortly after entering Deception Pass State Park.

After turning on Rosario Road, take an immediate left onto Bowman Bay Road and drive 0.4 mile to the parking area. A restroom, playground, beach access, and picnic tables are available at the trailhead. Camping is available nearby.

GPS COORDINATES: 48.416739, –122.650780 / N48° 25.0043' W122° 39.0468'

BEST NEARBY BITES

Make the 15-minute drive north to Anacortes to sample the pizza and beer menu at **Rockfish Grill** (314 Commercial Ave., Anacortes, 360/293-2544, www.anacortesrockfish.com, 11am-9pm Sun.-Thurs., 11am-10pm Fri.-Sat.). The pizza is made with local ingredients and prepared in a wood-fired oven. Anacortes Brewery crafts the beverages next door. From the trailhead, the 9-mile drive north takes about 15 minutes via Highway 20.

3

Ebey's Landing

EBEY'S LANDING NATIONAL HISTORICAL RESERVE, WHIDBEY ISLAND

Get a history lesson while admiring Admiralty Inlet, the Olympics, and Whidbey Island's prairie.

DISTANCE: 5.5 miles round-trip

DURATION: 2.5 hours

ELEVATION CHANGE: 300 feet

EFFORT: Easy/moderate

TRAIL: Dirt, sand, gravel, beach

USERS: Hikers, leashed dogs

SEASON: Year-round

PASSES/FEES: None, but Discover Pass required if you park at Ebey's Landing State Park parking lot

MAPS: USGS topographic map for Coupeville, WA

CONTACT: Ebey's Landing National Historical Reserve, 360/678-6084, www.nps.gov/ebla

Saved by local citizens from the hands of developers, Ebey's Landing became the country's first national historical reserve in 1978. Today, Ebey's offers plenty of trails amid its 17,572 acres; the following route links the Ebey's Prairie Ridge and Bluff Trails to sample the best of this Puget Sound gem.

START THE HIKE

▶ **MILE 0–0.5: Ebey's Prairie Ridge Trail Trailhead to Pratt Loop Trail Intersection**

Starting from the trailhead for **Ebey's Prairie Ridge Trail** near the historic Sunnyside Cemetery, follow the wide gravel path as it makes its way 0.3 mile along an alfalfa field to **Ebey House,** open Memorial Day through Labor Day weekends (10am-4pm Thurs.-Sun.). From the house, the trail dips to the left of a barbwire fence and descends gradually as it makes its way toward **Admiralty Inlet.**

In 0.2 mile, pass the **intersection** with the Pratt Loop Trail, continuing straight and enjoying an unobstructed view over the prairie. Occasionally the silence is broken by the thunderous jet engines at nearby Whidbey Island Naval Air Station.

▶ **MILE 0.5–1.4: Pratt Loop Trail Intersection to Bluff Trail**

After another 0.4 mile, you'll reach the **Bluff Trail** above the glistening water. Turn left and descend 0.4 mile to a bench with a view of the ferry route between Whidbey Island and Port Townsend. Drop 0.1 mile to the **parking lot** and a restroom. (Note that this parking lot off Ebey Road, the Ebey's Landing State Park parking lot, requires a Discover Pass.)

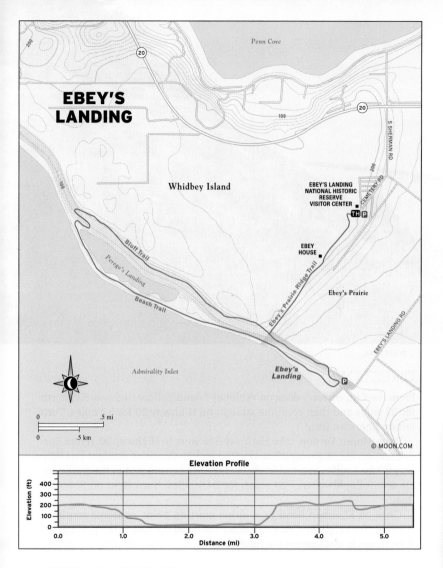

Elevation Profile

© MOON.COM

▶ **MILE 1.4-3.5: Bluff Trail to Perego's Lake**

Facing the water, turn right and stroll 1.7 miles on the rocky, driftwood-lined **beach**. Gulls and the occasional bald eagle soar overhead. Seals poke their brown heads out of the water. At the far end of **Perego's Lake,** regain the **Bluff Trail** and climb 200 feet over the next 0.3 mile to the top of the bank. (For a gentler climb, hike this loop in the opposite direction.) The view from the grassy slope looking over the lake and Puget Sound might be the best in the reserve.

▶ **MILE 3.5-5.5: Perego's Lake to Ebey's Prairie Ridge Trail**

For the next 1.1 miles, walk the edge of the bluff along the **Robert Y. Pratt Preserve** to complete the Bluff Trail Loop. Turn left on the **Ebey's Prairie Ridge Trail** and follow the familiar path 0.9 mile back to your car.

▲ BLUFF TRAIL

DIRECTIONS

From the Clinton ferry dock on Whidbey Island, follow Highway 525 north for 22 miles and then continue straight on Highway 20 for 6.2 miles. Turn left on Sherman Road.

From Mount Vernon, take Highway 536 west to Highway 20. (From Burlington, access Highway 20 at exit 230 on I-5). Continue straight on Highway 20 for 7 miles to a traffic circle. Take the second exit in the traffic circle and follow Highway 20 south for 24.5 miles. Turn right on Sherman Road.

Once on Sherman Road from either starting point, continue south for 0.3 mile. Turn right on Cemetery Road and drive 0.3 mile to the parking lot. A restroom is available at the trailhead.

GPS COORDINATES: 48.204608, –122.707119 / N48° 12.2765' W122° 42.4271'

BEST NEARBY BREWS

Less than 1.4 miles and five minutes northeast of the trailhead, **Penn Cove Taproom** (103 S. Main St., Coupeville, 360/682-5747, www.penncovebrewing.com, hours vary) has 14 taps serving local brews, including its own Madrona Way IPA. It's all about the beer here; the menu's modest food options include nachos, hot dogs, and popcorn.

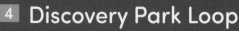

Loop through Seattle's largest park while enjoying views of Puget Sound, Mount Rainier, and the Olympics.

BEST: Brew Hikes
DISTANCE: 2.9 miles round-trip
DURATION: 1.5 hours
ELEVATION CHANGE: 300 feet
EFFORT: Easy
TRAIL: Dirt, gravel, sandy and paved paths
USERS: Hikers, leashed dogs (not allowed on beaches), bikes (paved surfaces only)
SEASON: Year-round
PASSES/FEES: None
MAPS: Free maps at visitors center or online at www.friendsofdiscoverypark.org/maps
PARK HOURS: 4am-11:30pm daily
CONTACT: Discovery Park, 206/684-4075, www.seattle.gov

START THE HIKE

The 534-acre park is Seattle's largest, and its forest, well-maintained trails, and views of Puget Sound make for an easily accessible oasis.

▶ **MILE 0-1.3: Visitors Center Parking Lot to**
Discovery Park Boulevard Intersection
Starting at the northeast corner of the **visitors center parking lot**, walk down a few steps and into the woods. In less than 0.1 mile arrive at the **intersection** where the **Loop Trail** begins and ends. Go right and take a **tunnel** under Discovery Park Boulevard.

The trail has some modest inclines but is mostly flat and wide. Pass under Douglas firs, maples, and alders, wind in and out of lush green drainages, and cross four roads in the first 1.1 miles. Upon crossing the fourth, follow signs left to stay on the loop.

In another 0.1 mile, cross **Discovery Park Boulevard**, a road that can be busy at times, and stay right at the **intersection** just past the restroom.

▶ **MILE 1.3-2: Discovery Park Boulevard Intersection to Magnolia Bluff**
The park's famous view from atop **Magnolia Bluff** unfolds before you in another 0.4 mile. As you spend the next 0.3 mile walking the **sandy trail**, watch ferries cut across Puget Sound and seaplanes soar overhead; Rainier is visible to the south. You'll be tempted to stay long enough to watch the sun set behind the Olympics. To the west, in the middle of the park, what looks like a giant golf ball is an FAA radar dome that was relocated to Fort Lawton from McChord Air Force Base in 1960.

SEATTLE AND VICINITY

Discovery Park Loop

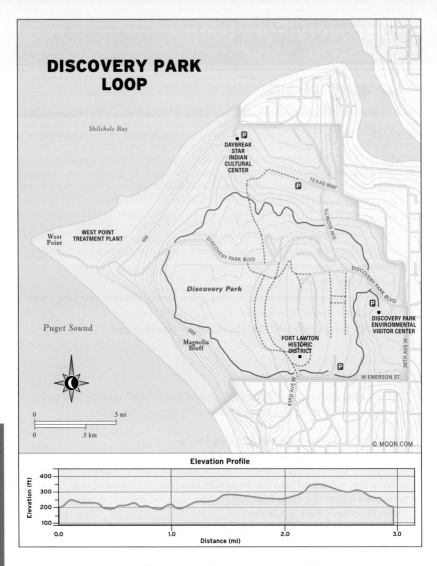

DISCOVERY PARK LOOP

Shilshole Bay

DAYBREAK STAR INDIAN CULTURAL CENTER

TEXAS WAY

ILLINOIS AVE

West Point

WEST POINT TREATMENT PLANT

100

DISCOVERY PARK BLVD

DISCOVERY PARK BLVD

Discovery Park

Puget Sound

200

Magnolia Bluff

FORT LAWTON HISTORIC DISTRICT

DISCOVERY PARK ENVIRONMENTAL VISITOR CENTER

38TH AVE W

W EMERSON ST

43RD AVE W

0   .5 mi

0   .5 km

© MOON.COM

Elevation Profile

Elevation (ft) — 400 300 200 100

0.0   1.0   2.0   3.0

Distance (mi)

▶ **MILE 2–2.9: Magnolia Bluff to Visitors Center Parking Lot**

From the bluff, the trail turns inland for a 0.4-mile jaunt to the **south parking lot** (an alternative starting point). Continue on the **Loop Trail** for 0.5 mile (passing shortcuts to the visitors center) before closing the loop. Turn right at the familiar **intersection** and make the short walk back to the parking lot.

DIRECTIONS

From I-5, take exit 167 and follow Mercer Street toward Seattle Center. After 1.6 miles veer right on Elliott Avenue. Travel 1.9 miles as Elliott Avenue becomes 15th Avenue, and then take the Emerson/Nickerson exit. Stay right and follow Nickerson Street 0.2 mile to a stop sign; turn left on Emerson Street. In 0.5 mile turn right on Gilman Avenue. Continue 1.1 miles as

▲ PUGET SOUND

Gilman becomes Government Way and then Discovery Park Boulevard. In the park, take the first left to the visitors center and the east parking lot. Restrooms are available in the building (8:30am-5pm Tues.-Sun.), behind the building, and along the trail.

Additional parking is available in the south parking lot. Get there by returning to the intersection of Government Way and 36th Avenue and turning right on 36th. Turn right on Emerson Street after 0.3 mile, then drive west 0.4 mile and turn right to enter the park. Drive 0.2 mile to the south parking lot.

King County Metro's Route 33 ends at the park. Exit at Government Way and 36th Avenue and make the 0.1-mile walk to the visitors center trailhead. Route 24 stops at Emerson Street and Magnolia Boulevard, 0.1 mile from where the loop trail passes the south parking lot.

GPS COORDINATES: 47.658218, -122.406216 / N47° 39.4931' W122° 24.373'

BEST NEARBY BREWS

Post-hike brews are easy to find in Seattle. Local favorites like the **Pike Brewing Company** (1415 1st Ave., 206/622-6044, www.pikebrewing. com, 11am-midnight Sun.-Thurs., 11am-1am Fri.-Sat.) and **Old Stove Brewing** (1901 Western Ave., Pike Place Market, 206/602-6120, www. oldstove.com, hours vary) are less than 8 miles southeast and about 20 minutes away via 15th and Elliott Avenues. Even closer is the **Fremont Brewing Company** (1050 N. 34th St., 206/420-2407, www.fremontbrewing.com, 11am-9pm daily), just 3.8 miles and 13 minutes east via Nickerson Street.

Poo Poo Point via Chirico Trail

TIGER MOUNTAIN STATE FOREST, ISSAQUAH

Make the climb from a paraglider landing strip to the launching pad while enjoying views of Mount Rainier, Mount Baker, and Lake Sammamish.

DISTANCE: 3.8 miles round-trip

DURATION: 2 hours

ELEVATION CHANGE: 1,700 feet

EFFORT: Moderate

TRAIL: Dirt trail, rocks

USERS: Hikers, leashed dogs, paragliders

SEASON: Year-round

PASSES/FEES: None

MAPS: Green Trails Map 204S for Tiger Mountain

CONTACT: Washington State Department of Natural Resources, 360/825-1631, www.dnr.wa.gov

START THE HIKE

▸ **MILE 0-0.9: Parking Lot to Chirico Trail**

The trail starts at the north end of the **gravel parking lot**. In the first few steps, you'll encounter a **wooden sculpture** of a winged lion. The popular hike to Poo Poo Point starts at a paragliding landing strip (at the parking lot) and climbs all the way up to the launching pad. The trail was built by Marc Chirico, owner of Seattle Paragliding (11206 Issaquah-Hobart Rd. SE, Issaquah, 206/387-3477, www.seattleparagliding.com), which will fly you down for $225-250.

From the winged lion, pass under the **Chirico Trail** sign and follow the trail for 0.1 mile before it turns into the woods, passes through a gate, and starts climbing. After 0.7 mile of climbing along **Yah-er Wall,** Poo Poo Point's steep, fern-lined face, you'll arrive at a log bench that tempts hikers to pause to catch their breath. If you skip this one, don't worry—there's another one in 0.1 mile. Stay left at each bench to continue climbing the Chirico Trail.

▸ **MILE 0.9-1.9: Chirico Trail to Poo Poo Point Launch Site**

The ascent continues over the next 0.6 mile past Douglas fir, western hemlock, and purple foxglove before hitting an **intersection;** turn left here to stay on Chirico. In 40 yards you'll hit another **intersection;** keep left yet again. After another 0.2 mile you'll arrive at a **clearing,** used as the south paragliding launch site. The views of Puget Sound and Mount Rainier to the south are this trail's first big reward. You might glimpse an eagle soaring overhead. Stay left here and catch the trail at the edge of the clearing for the final 0.2-mile uphill push to the main **Poo Poo Point launch site.**

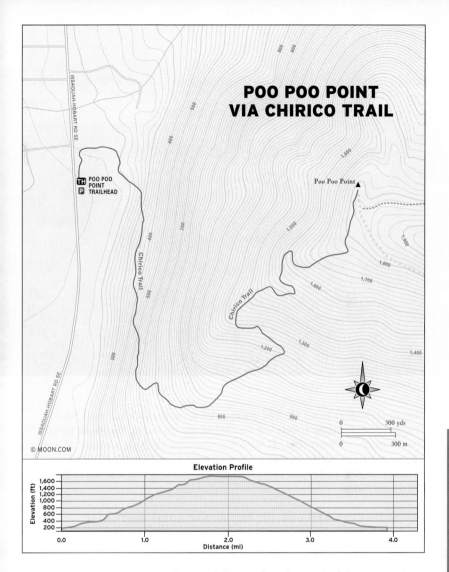

POO POO POINT
VIA CHIRICO TRAIL

Elevation Profile

At Poo Poo Point, watch paragliders unfurl their colorful canopies before they soar off to become part of the scenery, which includes neighboring Squak and Cougar Mountains, Issaquah, Lake Sammamish, and, on particularly clear days, Mount Baker. Note that the point's amusing name has nothing to do with what jumping off the side of the mountain might scare out of you, or the scat from bear, deer, and other animals you might see along the way. Rather, the name refers to the sound made by old steam whistles when loggers worked the forest.

If you don't fly down, simply retrace your path to the trailhead.

DIRECTIONS

From Seattle, follow I-90 east to exit 17 in Issaquah. Turn right and merge onto Front Street North and then continue 2.8 miles as the road becomes

▲ PARAGLIDER AT POO POO POINT

Issaquah-Hobart Road SE. The parking lot is on the left just past Seattle Paragliding. Portable toilets are located at the trailhead. **Trailhead Direct** (www.trailheaddirect.com, $1.50-2.75), operated by King County Metro Transit, offers shuttle service to the trailhead from Seattle's Mount Baker Transit Center, Bellevue's Eastgate Freeway Station, and the North Bend Park and Ride.

GPS COORDINATES: 47.500216, –122.022128 / N47° 30.013' W122° 1.3277'

BEST NEARBY BITES

Signs on the windows at Issaquah's **XXX Root Beer Drive-in** (98 NE Gilman Blvd., Issaquah, 425/392-1266, www.triplexrootbeer.com, 11am-9pm daily, cash or check only) read "Warning: Nothing that you eat or drink here is good for you!" But after a day of hiking, it's easy to justify a burger and a huge root beer served in a frosted mug. And the 1950s-diner vibes—think classic-car memorabilia and a jukebox playing Elvis tunes—transport you to a time when the world was blissfully unaware of trans fat. From the trailhead, the 3-mile drive north takes 9 minutes via Front Street.

Reach a trio of rock outcroppings high above Rattlesnake Lake and the Cedar River Watershed via a moderate climb up one of Washington's most popular trails.

BEST: Brew Hikes

DISTANCE: 4.9 miles round-trip

DURATION: 2.5 hours

ELEVATION CHANGE: 1,600 feet

EFFORT: Moderate

TRAIL: Dirt single track

USERS: Hikers, leashed dogs

SEASON: Year-round

PASSES/FEES: None

MAPS: Green Trails Map 205S for Rattlesnake Mountain/Upper Snoqualmie Valley, USGS topographic map for North Bend

CONTACT: Washington State Department of Natural Resources, 360/825-1631, www.dnr.wa.gov

START THE HIKE

▶ **MILE 0-1: Parking Lot to Rattlesnake Lake Viewpoint**

Slip past the gate at the northwest edge of the parking lot to start your hike on the **Rattlesnake Ledge Trail.** Listen to the greetings of chirping birds and croaking frogs while following a wide gravel path along the perimeter of Rattlesnake Lake.

After 0.25 mile, you'll have access to portable toilets. A large **kiosk** displays a map of the trail. Notice a sign warning of steep cliffs; this isn't to be taken lightly, as people have fallen to their deaths here. The trail is often accessible in winter, but hikers should check conditions before attempting during cold months. From the kiosk, the trail climbs through a forest of western hemlock, cedar, and Douglas fir, passing a bench in 0.75 mile that offers a view through the trees of **Rattlesnake Lake.**

▶ **MILE 1-2: Rattlesnake Lake Viewpoint to Lower Ledge**

After admiring the view, continue on the trail, which skirts the **Cedar River Watershed** (the source of Seattle's water). The gurgle of this stream not visible from the trail lures some hikers off the path, but don't follow their lead; signs warn that hikers can be prosecuted for wandering off-trail.

After 1 mile, you'll reach a **sign** that directs you along the Rattlesnake Mountain Trail to East Peak. The sign signals your arrival at the first ledge. Turn right and continue about 50 yards to the **lower ledge** (Rattlesnake Ledge), which offers views of the Cedar River Watershed, Rattlesnake

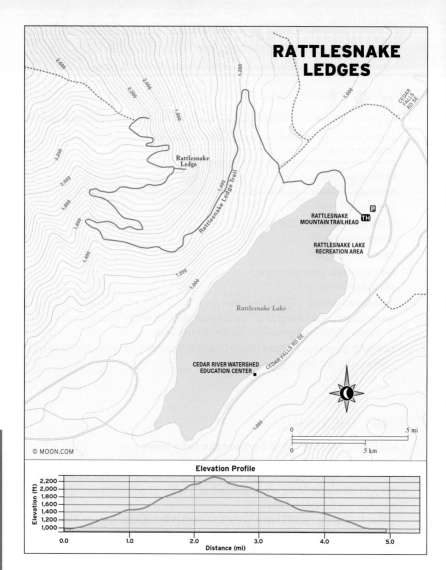

Elevation Profile

Lake, the Cascades, and North Bend. This is as far as most people go, making this rocky outcrop crowded on most sunny days.

▶ MILE 2-2.45: East Peak to Middle and Upper Ledges

The upper ledges offer more solitude—and arguably even better views—for just a bit more work. Turn left at the sign for the lower ledge and continue another 0.2 mile through the forest until you reach an unsigned spur trail at a switchback. This short trail leads to the **middle ledge**. Continue up another 0.25 mile to find the unsigned spur to the **upper ledge**. The spur is easy to find on the right at a switchback. The views seem a little more exclusive the higher you go, even though they're separated by only about five minutes of hiking. From the upper ledge, you can see the throng of hikers 300 feet below on the lower ledge. And here's a fun trick to make

▲ MIDDLE LEDGE OF RATTLESNAKE MOUNTAIN

the view even more special: Get up early and hike by headlamp to the upper ledge to watch the sun rise over the foothills—and then scoot down to the middle ledge to watch it rise again.

When you're finished enjoying the scenery, return the way you came.

DIRECTIONS

From Seattle, follow I-90 east to North Bend and take exit 32. Turn right on 436th Avenue SE. Drive 2.8 miles, continuing straight as the road becomes Cedar Falls Road SE. The parking lot will be on the right. Portable toilets are available at the parking lot and about 0.25 mile into the hike.

GPS COORDINATES: 47.434701, –121.768716 / N47° 26.0821' W121° 46.123'

BEST NEARBY BREWS

A short drive from the trailhead, the **Snoqualmie Brewery and Taproom** (8032 Falls Ave. SE, Snoqualmie, www.fallsbrew.com, 425/831-2357, summer 11am-9pm Sun.-Tues., 11am-10pm Wed.-Sat., winter noon-9pm Mon.-Thurs., 11am-10pm Fri.-Sat.) has a menu that ranges from creative (Black Frog Nitro Stout ice cream float) to Canadian (poutine with beer-battered fries). However, it's best known for its brewers' greatest hits: Copperhead Pale Ale, Haystack Hefeweizen, Steam Train Porter, and many more. From the trailhead, the 8.5-mile drive northwest takes about 20 minutes via 436th Avenue and Highway 202.

MOUNT SI NATURAL RESOURCES CONSERVATION AREA,
NORTH BEND

Seattle's StairMaster, Mount Si is a popular workout destination for hikers looking for a challenge that rewards with views of the Cascades, Olympics, and Snoqualmie Valley.

DISTANCE: 7.6 miles round-trip
DURATION: 4 hours
ELEVATION CHANGE: 3,200 feet
EFFORT: Moderate/strenuous
TRAIL: Dirt single track, large boulders
USERS: Hikers, leashed dogs
SEASON: April–November, but conditions often suitable for winter hiking
PASSES/FEES: Discover Pass
MAPS: Green Trails Map 206S for Mount Si
CONTACT: Washington State Department of Natural Resources, www.dnr.wa.gov/mountsi

START THE HIKE

▸ **MILE 0-1.8: Mount Si Trail Trailhead to Snag Flats**
At the north end of the parking lot, the Mount Si Trail starts with a flat, 0.1-mile gravel section that crosses a **bridge** before unleashing what makes this trail so famous: oodles of uphill. You'll ascend 600 feet in the next 0.7 mile before reaching the first of two **intersections** with the Talus Loop Trail. Keep left to stay on the Mount Si Trail, ascending another 750 feet in 0.9 mile before reaching the second intersection with the Talus Loop. Keep left again. (If the Mount Si Trail is proving too much, the Talus Loop is a convenient way to switch to an easier hike—3.7 miles round-trip with 1,400 feet of climbing.) Just past the second Talus Loop junction, Mount Si gives you a rare break with a level 0.1-mile section known as **Snag Flats.** Here you can see standing dead trees (snags), remnants of a 1910 fire. An interpretive sign on a short wooden boardwalk tells the story of a 350-year-old, 175-foot-tall Douglas fir damaged in the fire.

▸ **MILE 1.8-3.8: Snag Flats to Mount Si Viewpoint**
From Snag Flats, the trail dishes out its toughest section: 1,800 feet of elevation gain over 2 miles. There's not much in the way of views along the majority of this section—mostly ferns, hemlocks, cedars, and other flora. You might catch a glimpse of deer and there have been occasional bear and cougar sightings. At the end of this challenging stretch, step out of the trees and onto a **boulder field**. Take a few more steps and Si's famous view unfurls before you.

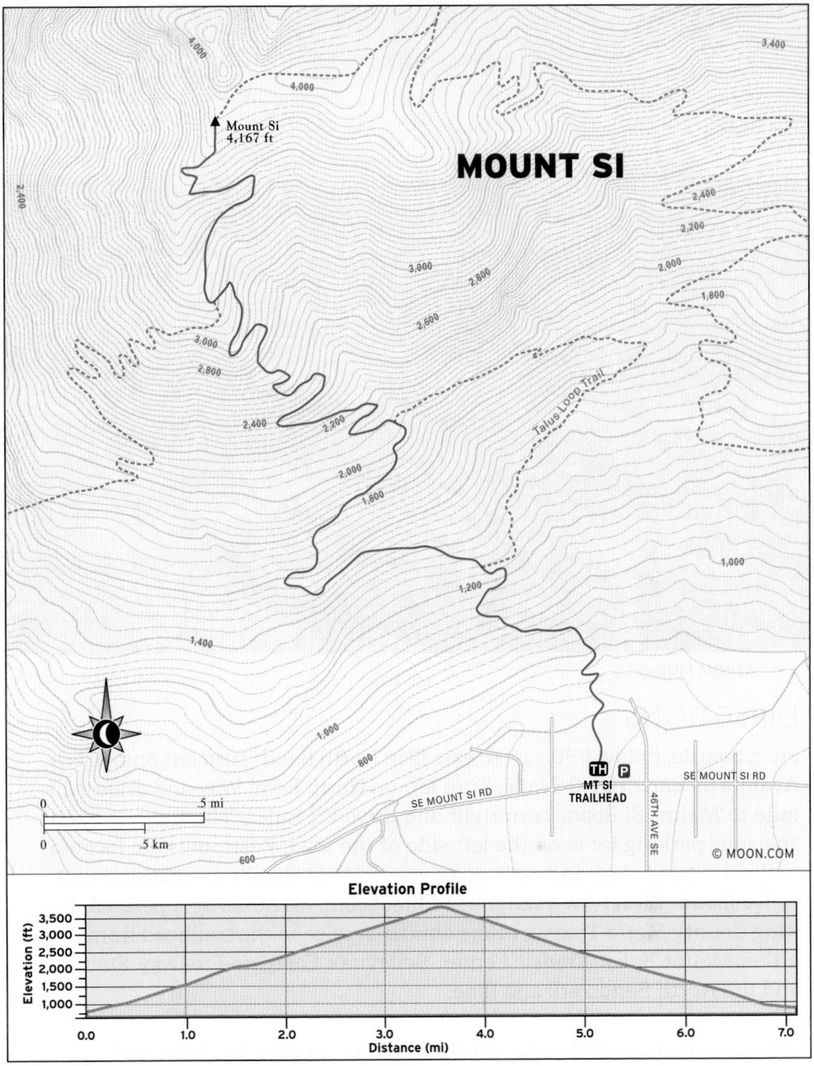

MOUNT SI

Mount Si
4,167 ft

Talus Loop Trail

MT SI
TRAILHEAD

SE MOUNT SI RD

SE MOUNT SI RD

46TH AVE SE

© MOON.COM

0   .5 mi
0   .5 km

Elevation Profile

Elevation (ft)

3,500
3,000
2,500
2,000
1,500
1,000

0.0   1.0   2.0   3.0   4.0   5.0   6.0   7.0
Distance (mi)

While snapping some pictures and enjoying a snack, you may find yourself intrigued by the rock feature above known as the Haystack. This is Si's summit but attempting it shouldn't be taken lightly; hikers have died falling from this slope. Good footwear is essential. Reaching the top requires hiking around to the northeast side of the Haystack and then scrambling up a steep slope. Watch your step and stay alert for rocks knocked loose by people (or possibly even mountain goats) higher on the slope. Keep in mind that the view atop Haystack isn't much different from that at the main viewpoint.

After enjoying the view and resting your legs, return the way you came.

▲ VIEW FROM MOUNT SI

DIRECTIONS

From Seattle, follow I-90 east to exit 32 in North Bend. Turn left onto 436th Avenue SE and drive 0.5 mile. Turn left on North Bend Way and drive 0.25 mile to Mount Si Road. Turn right and drive 2.3 miles. The trailhead and spacious parking lot is on the left side of the road. Restrooms are located at the trailhead. Arriving early gives you the best chance at a parking spot.

Trailhead Direct (www.trailheaddirect.com, $1.50-2.75), operated by King County Metro Transit, offers shuttle service to the trailhead from Seattle's Mount Baker Transit Center, Bellevue's Eastgate Freeway Station, and the North Bend Park and Ride.

GPS COORDINATES: 47.488020, –121.723229/ N47° 29.2812' W121° 43.3937'

BEST NEARBY BITES

You might recognize Mount Si from the opening credits of the 1990s TV cult classic *Twin Peaks*, so it seems fitting to cap your hike with a visit to **Twede's Café** (137 W. North Bend Way, North Bend, 425/831-5511, www.twedescafe.com, 8am-8pm daily). Pick something from the extensive burger menu, or channel your inner Dale Cooper and order a slice of cherry pie and a "damn fine cup of coffee." From the trailhead, the 4-mile drive west takes about 10 minutes via Mount Si Road and North Bend Way.

Twin Falls

OLALLIE STATE PARK, NORTH BEND

Walk a gentle path along the South Fork of the Snoqualmie River to views of Twin Falls.

BEST: Waterfall Hikes
DISTANCE: 2.6 miles round trip
DURATION: 1.5 hours
ELEVATION CHANGE: 600 feet
EFFORT: Easy/moderate
TRAIL: Dirt single track, wooden bridges, stairways
USERS: Hikers, leashed dogs
SEASON: Year-round
PASSES/FEES: Discover Pass
MAPS: Green Trails Map 205S for Rattlesnake Mountain.
PARK HOURS: 6:30am-dusk daily summer, 8am-dusk daily winter
CONTACT: Olallie State Park, 425/455-7010, http://parks.state.wa.us

START THE HIKE

▸ **MILE 0-0.2: Parking Lot to South Fork Snoqualmie River**
At the southern end of the parking lot in Olallie State Park, find the well-marked **Twin Falls Trail** and start with a gentle 0.2-mile stretch along the **South Fork Snoqualmie River.** From the rumbling of the river and the sound of the water plunging over the falls to the occasional groan of a semitruck on nearby I-90, not a single step of this hike is quiet in spring and early summer.

▸ **MILE 0.2-0.4: South Fork Snoqualmie River to Switchbacks**
Ferns, vine maples, and salmonberry shrubs (*Olallie* is Chinook jargon for salmonberry) line parts of the trail. Various spots offer opportunities to get a little closer to the river and maybe catch a glimpse of a cutthroat trout. After 0.2 mile, the trail turns away from the river and climbs briefly using a few **switchbacks**. As you gain a little elevation an impressive carpet of sword ferns covers the forest floor.

▸ **MILE 0.4-1.1: Switchbacks to Lower Falls Spur**
Continue 0.3 mile to a series of benches that provide the first glimpse of the 135-foot **lower falls**. This spot alone is worth the trip, but keep going for more dynamic views. In 0.4 mile, reach a **staircase** that drops to a wooden platform with an up-close, top-to-bottom view of the lower falls. The falls' name comes from the Twin Falls Gorge it plunges through.

▲ LOWER TWIN FALLS

▶ **MILE 1.1–1.3: Lower Falls Spur to Twin Falls Upper Falls**
To see more cascading water, continue 0.1 mile beyond the top of the stair-case, to a **bridge** that passes over the river and has views of the top of the lower falls and the bottom of the upper falls. The second **switchback** 0.1 mile beyond the bridge offers the best view of the **upper falls**.

This is an ideal place to turn around. Return the way you came.

DIRECTIONS

From Seattle, follow I-90 east to exit 34. Turn right on 468th Avenue SE and travel 0.5 mile to SE 159th Street. Turn left and follow SE 159th Street until it ends in the small trailhead parking lot. Signs mark the way to the trailhead. Toilets are located at the trailhead.

GPS COORDINATES: 47.453099, –121.705347 / N47° 27.1859 W121° 42.3208

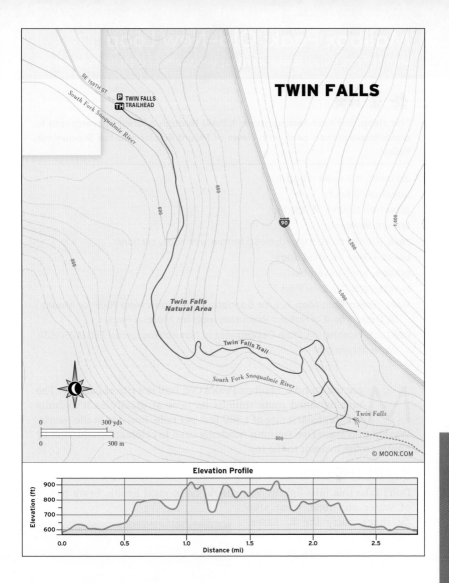

TWIN FALLS

Twin Falls Natural Area

Twin Falls Trail

South Fork Snoqualmie River

Twin Falls

© MOON.COM

Elevation Profile

BEST NEARBY BITES

Since it opened in 1998, the **North Bend Bar & Grill** (145 E. North Bend Way, North Bend, 425/888-1243, www.northbendbarandgrill.com, 8am-midnight daily) has established itself as a popular après-hike/ski/run/bike destination. It's easy to see why after you cap a hike with a draft beer and one-third-pound bacon Trail Burger served on a freshly baked bun. From the trailhead, the 5.5-mile drive northwest takes about 10 minutes via I-90 and Cedar Falls Way.

Mailbox Peak: Old-New Loop

MIDDLE FORK SNOQUALMIE NATURAL RESOURCES CONSERVATION AREA

✿ 🐾 🚍

This steep, fortitude-testing ascent travels through a forest of evergreens to a mailbox-adorned peak with views of Mount Rainier and the Snoqualmie Valley.

DISTANCE: 8.2 miles round-trip

DURATION: 6 hours

ELEVATION CHANGE: 4,000 feet

EFFORT: Strenuous

TRAIL: Gravel road, rugged, steep terrain with rocky sections

USERS: Hikers, leashed dogs

SEASON: April–November

PASSES/FEES: Discover Pass

MAPS: Green Trails Map 206 for Bandera, Green Trails Map 206S for Mount Si, Department of Natural Resources map for Mailbox Peak

CONTACT: Washington State Department of Natural Resources, 360/825-1631, www.dnr.wa.gov

More than a hike, Mailbox Peak's Old Trail is a rite of passage. The unmaintained route thumbs its nose at gravity as it assaults the thighs at a rate of 1,300 feet per mile. Recruits at the nearby Washington State Fire Training Academy used to celebrate graduation by hauling a fire hydrant to the top.

START THE HIKE

Don't take this hike lightly: You should be in good health, bring plenty of water and food, wear sturdy shoes, carry the 10 Essentials, and arrive early. Not only do the parking lots fill quickly on weekend mornings, but it's also best to give yourself as much time as possible. Take the challenge seriously and Mailbox will deliver an immense sense of accomplishment.

▸ **MILE 0-0.3: Upper Parking Lot to New Trail**

Slip past the white gate at the end of the upper parking lot and follow a dirt road gently

THE MAILBOX ON MAILBOX PEAK ▸

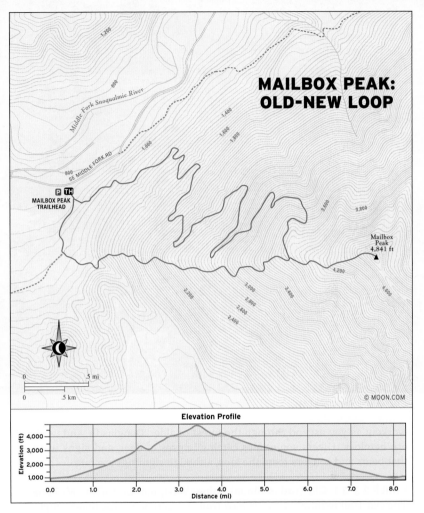

Elevation Profile

upward. After 100 yards, take note of a trailhead on your left for the New Trail, which adds 2.5 miles to your hike (each way) but is significantly less steep than the Old Trail. To take on the famous **Old Trail** (which this hike follows), keep walking up the dirt road.

At 0.3 mile, you'll find one last warning. A sign bolted to a wooden **kiosk** cautions that what lies beyond is "steep, wet, unmaintained, difficult, challenging" and the site of frequent search and rescue missions. Still game? Then follow the path as it plunges into the woods and let the workout begin.

▶ **MILE 0.3–2.3: New Trail to Old Trail**
The next 0.2 mile of mellow ascent near a gurgling creek might lure you into thinking the route isn't as tough as you've heard. Those thoughts fall away quickly as the trail morphs into a ladder of roots and rocks. Let the **white diamond markers** posted on trees guide you as the trail refuses to relent for the next 1.8 miles. There are no views to distract you from the

▲ DESCENDING MAILBOX PEAK

workout as you ascend through the forest of alder, Douglas fir, and western hemlock. Hikers sometimes catch glimpses of deer, and signs warn that bears and cougars roam the area, although sightings are rare.

▶ **MILE 2.3–3.1: Old Trail to Mount Rainer Viewpoint and White Mailbox**
The Old Trail reunites with the **New Trail** just in time for the hike's toughest stretch: a 1,000-foot climb over 0.8 mile. A few **switchbacks** lead to a rocky **stairway** that cuts upward to an **open ridge,** where the destination finally comes into view. The final push up the ridge is the steepest yet. The challenge is rewarded with a sweeping view and one of the Northwest's most famous summit accoutrements, a large white **mailbox** that once stashed a summit register. It's now stuffed with surprises: letters, toys, and, if you're lucky, chocolate and whiskey.

▶ **MILE 3.1–8.2: Mount Rainer Viewpoint and**
White Mailbox to Upper Parking Lot
After refueling, taking in the views of Rainier and the Snoqualmie Valley, and snapping a selfie with the mailbox, return the way you came 0.8 mile to the **intersection** with the Old and New Trails, staying mindful of how your tired legs handle the steep descent. Stay on the longer yet gentler **New Trail** for the entire descent to give your knees and ankles a break. The path sweeps back and forth as its drops past evergreens, blossoming

trillium, and occasional salmonberry bushes on a 4.3-mile journey back to the parking lot. You'll cross two wooden bridges on the way down; after the second you're in the homestretch and it's safe to start celebrating your accomplishment.

DIRECTIONS

From Seattle, take exit 34 on I-90 and turn north onto 468th Avenue SE. After 0.6 mile, turn right on Southeast Middle Fork Road. Continue 2.6 miles, staying left at the junction with Dorothy Road, to a small parking area. Turn right and follow a short driveway to a larger parking lot if the gate is open. The gate closes at dusk and the upper parking lot is closed Monday-Thursday.

Trailhead Direct (www.trailheaddirect.com, $1.50-2.75), operated by King County Metro Transit, offers shuttle service to the trailhead from Seattle's Mount Baker Transit Center, Bellevue's Eastgate Freeway Station, and the North Bend Park and Ride.

GPS COORDINATES: 47.466669, –121.673748 / N47° 28.000′ W121° 40.255′

BEST NEARBY BITES

Let North Bend's mayor cook you a cheeseburger at **Scott's Dairy Freeze** (234 E. North Bend Way, North Bend, 425/888-2301, 8am-9pm Mon.-Sat., 8am-8pm Sun.). Mayor Ken Hearing owns the nearly 70-year-old burger stand and often works the grill. Bagging Mailbox is also worthy of a milk shake, the second most popular menu item here. From the trailhead, the 6.2-mile drive northwest takes about 14 minutes via Middle Fork Road and North Bend Way.

This easy boardwalk trail on the Nisqually River Delta is a bird-watching wonderland and an ideal spot to introduce children to nature.

BEST: Winter Hikes
DISTANCE: 4.1 miles round-trip
DURATION: 2 hours
ELEVATION CHANGE: Negligible
EFFORT: Easy
TRAIL: Wooden boardwalks, dirt trail
USERS: Hikers, wheelchair users
SEASON: Year-round
PASSES/FEES: $3 adults, free children 16 and younger; America the Beautiful Passes accepted
MAPS: USGS topographic map for Nisqually, WA; free maps at visitors center and on the website
HOURS: Sunrise-sunset daily
CONTACT: Billy Frank Jr. Nisqually National Wildlife Refuge, 360/753-9467, www.fws.gov

Despite the sound of passing cars on nearby I-5, the Billy Frank Jr. Nisqually National Wildlife Refuge feels as if it's a world away from civilization. More than 275 species of birds visit the refuge each year, making it a popular destination for bird-watchers. Many believe the best time to visit is within two hours of high tide, when bird activity is at its peak.

START THE HIKE

▶ **MILE 0-1.1: Twin Barns Loop Trail to Nisqually Estuary Boardwalk Trail**
To delve into nature, head to the right of the visitors center (9am-4pm Wed.-Sun.) on the **Twin Barns Loop Trail.** You'll start by walking on a boardwalk (careful—it's slippery when wet) through a riparian forest for about 0.6 mile. Along the way, interpretive signs help visitors understand the habitat they're experiencing at the mouth of the Nisqually River. The trail passes a beaver dam and under a green, leafy canopy to an overlook of the Nisqually River. From here, turn left on a wide dirt path—the **Nisqually Estuary Trail**—and walk northwest about 0.6 mile to the **Nisqually Estuary Boardwalk Trail.**

▶ **MILE 1.2-2.2: Nisqually Estuary Boardwalk Trail to Estuary Observation Areas**
Continue on the elevated boardwalk for 1 mile, observing the estuary from several observation areas. Take a seat on one of the benches and watch

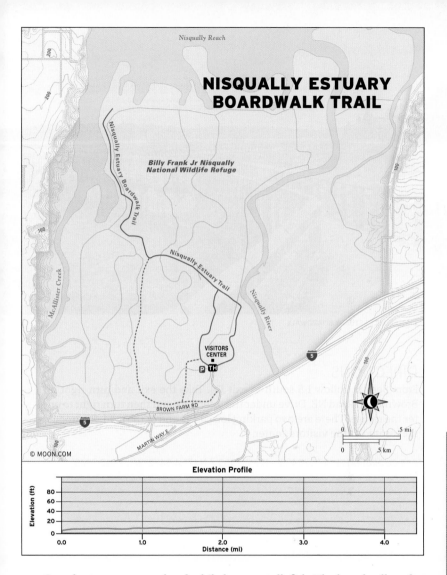

NISQUALLY ESTUARY BOARDWALK TRAIL

Nisqually Reach

Billy Frank Jr Nisqually
National Wildlife Refuge

Nisqually Estuary Boardwalk Trail

Nisqually Estuary Trail

McAllister Creek

Nisqually River

VISITORS
CENTER

P TH

BROWN FARM RD

MARTIN WAY E

© MOON.COM

0   .5 mi
0   .5 km

Elevation Profile

Elevation (ft)

80
60
40
20
0

0.0   1.0   2.0   3.0   4.0

Distance (mi)

Canada geese soar overhead while herons stalk fish. The boardwalk ends at a **covered area** with a telescope that can be used to observe wildlife or gaze up Puget Sound to Anderson and Ketron Islands, the Narrows bridges, and a sliver of Chambers Bay Golf Course. Note: The last 700 feet of the boardwalk closes October 15-January 25 for waterfowl hunting season.

▶ **MILE 2.2-4.1: Estuary Observation Area to Visitors Center**

Return the way you came. After 1.5 miles, you'll pass a gathering place with picnic tables and portable toilets in front of two large barns. Turn right off of the dirt path here, heading southeast on the **Twin Barns Loop** boardwalk to finish the hike. The final 0.4 mile of boardwalk cuts through the wetland. Listen for birds chirping in the willows as the trail returns you to the visitors center.

▲ NISQUALLY ESTUARY BOARDWALK

DIRECTIONS

From Seattle, follow I-5 south to exit 114. Take the exit and turn right on Brown Farm Road NE. Drive under the interstate and then turn right to enter the refuge. There are two parking lots at the end of the road. Restrooms are located at the visitors center.

GPS COORDINATES: 47.072453, –122.712959 / N47° 4.3472′ W122° 42.7775′

BEST NEARBY BREWS

In DuPont, just outside Joint Base Lewis-McChord, the **FOB Brewing Company** (2750 Williamson Pl. NW, Ste. 100, 253/507-4667, www.fob-brewingcompany.com, 3pm-11pm Tues.-Sun.) is decorated with military memorabilia and is staffed by workers in military gear. Even the beer pays tribute to the troops with names like SNAFU, 1000 Yard Stare, and Charlie Don't Surf (a reference to one of Robert Duvall's famous lines in the 1979 film *Apocalypse Now*). From the trailhead, the 7-mile drive northeast takes less than 15 minutes via I-5 and DuPont-Steilacoom Road.

NEARBY CAMPGROUNDS

NAME	DESCRIPTION	FACILITIES	SEASON	FEE
Larrabee State Park	on the edge of Samish Bay beneath Chuckanut Mountain	77 RV and tent sites, restrooms	year-round	$12-50

245 Chuckanut Drive, Bellingham 888/226-7688, www.washington.goingtocamp.com

NAME	DESCRIPTION	FACILITIES	SEASON	FEE
Deception Pass State Park	three campgrounds in a popular state park	211 RV and tent sites, restrooms	year-round	$12-50

41229 State Route 20, Oak Harbor, Fidalgo and Whidbey Islands, 888/226-7688, www.washington.goingtocamp.com

NAME	DESCRIPTION	FACILITIES	SEASON	FEE
Fort Ebey State Park	the site of a World War II coastal defense fort on Whidbey Island	50 RV and tent sites, restrooms	March–October	$12-50

400 Hill Valley Drive, Coupeville, 888/226-7688, www.washington.goingtocamp.com

NAME	DESCRIPTION	FACILITIES	SEASON	FEE
Dash Point State Park	a popular destination on Puget Sound for everybody from beachcombers to skim-boarders	141 RV and tent sites, restrooms	year-round	$12-50

5700 SW Dash Point Road, Federal Way, 888/226-7688, www.washington.goingtocamp.com

NAME	DESCRIPTION	FACILITIES	SEASON	FEE
Tinkham Campground	a forested campground on the South Fork Snoqualmie River	47 RV and tent sites, restrooms	early May–mid-September	$16.37-18.19

Tinkham Road, North Bend, Mount Baker-Snoqualmie National Forest, 877/444-6777, www.recreation.gov

NORTH CASCADES

Blanketed by evergreens, glaciers, and craggy peaks, the North Cascades is home to some of the nation's most breathtaking wilderness. A set of volcanoes—Mount Baker and Glacier Peak—and deep valleys stoke a spirit of adventure. Find ice caves, waterfalls, historic fire lookouts, and sweeping panoramas that include Puget Sound, the Olympics, and Canada. Marvel at beauty both natural and man-made (like the reservoirs created by massive dams on the Skagit River). Enjoy one of the few national parks that doesn't charge an entrance fee. Cross paths with mule deer, whistling marmots, and other creatures as you explore some of the Northwest's most stunning alpine terrain.

▲ ICE CAVE AT THE BASE OF BIG FOUR MOUNTAIN   ▲ CEDAR BERRIES

◀ STONE ARCH ON CHAIN LAKES LOOP TRAIL

1 **Winchester Mountain**
DISTANCE: 3.6 miles round-trip
DURATION: 2 hours
EFFORT: Moderate

2 **Skyline Divide**
DISTANCE: 6.8 miles round-trip
DURATION: 3.5 hours
EFFORT: Moderate

3 **Table Mountain**
DISTANCE: 3 miles round-trip
DURATION: 1.5 hours
EFFORT: Easy/moderate

4 **Chain Lakes Loop**
DISTANCE: 7.5 miles round-trip
DURATION: 4 hours
EFFORT: Moderate

5 **Thunder Knob**
DISTANCE: 3.6 miles round-trip
DURATION: 2 hours
EFFORT: Easy/moderate

6 **Cascade Pass**
DISTANCE: 7.4 miles round-trip
DURATION: 4 hours
EFFORT: Moderate

7 **Maple Pass Loop**
DISTANCE: 6.8 miles round-trip
DURATION: 4 hours
EFFORT: Moderate

8 **Cedar Falls**
DISTANCE: 3.5 miles round-trip
DURATION: 1.5 hours
EFFORT: Easy

9 **Green Mountain**
DISTANCE: 8.4 miles round-trip
DURATION: 5 hours
EFFORT: Moderate/strenuous

10 **Mount Pilchuck**
DISTANCE: 5.4 miles round-trip
DURATION: 3 hours
EFFORT: Moderate

11 **Lake Twenty-Two**
DISTANCE: 6.2 miles round-trip
DURATION: 3.5 hours
EFFORT: Moderate

12 **Big Four Ice Caves**
DISTANCE: 2.4 miles round-trip
DURATION: 1.5 hours
EFFORT: Easy

▼ LAKE ON MAPLE PASS LOOP

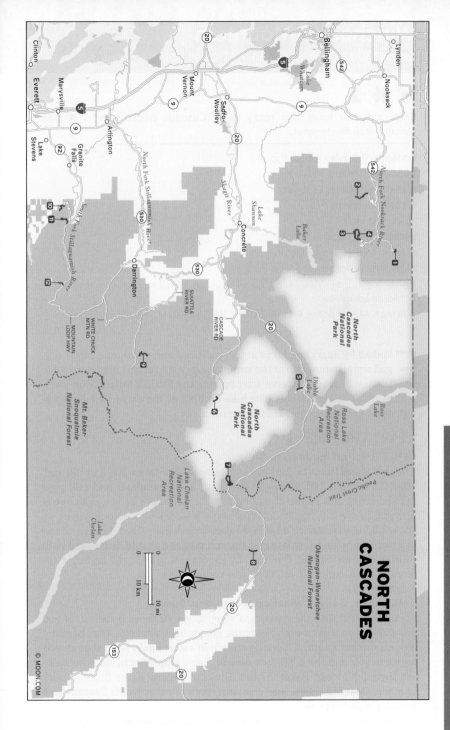

NORTH CASCADES

Bellingham
Lynden
Nooksack
Lake Whatcom
North Fork Nooksack River
Mount Vernon
Sedro-Woolley
Skagit River
Lake Shannon
Baker Lake
Concrete
North Cascades National Park
Ross Lake
Ross Lake National Recreation Area
Diablo Lake
Everett
Marysville
Arlington
Granite Falls
Lake Stevens
Clinton
North Fork Stillaguamish River
South Fork Stillaguamish River
Darrington
SUIATTLE RIVER RD
CASCADE RIVER RD
WHITE CHUCK MTN RD
MOUNTAIN LOOP HWY
North Cascades National Park
Lake Chelan National Recreation Area
Lake Chelan
Mt. Baker-Snoqualmie National Forest
Okanogan-Wenatchee National Forest
Pacific Crest Trail

0   10 km
0   10 mi

© MOON.COM

1

Winchester Mountain

MOUNT BAKER–SNOQUALMIE NATIONAL FOREST

Gaze out over lakes and rocky North Cascade peaks from a historic mountaintop fire lookout.

DISTANCE: 3.6 miles round-trip

DURATION: 2 hours

ELEVATION CHANGE: 1,350 feet

EFFORT: Moderate

TRAIL: Dirt, rock

USERS: Hikers, leashed dogs

SEASON: Mid-July–mid-October

PASSES/FEES: Northwest Forest Pass

MAPS: Green Trails Map 14 for Mount Shuksan; USGS topographic map for Mount Larrabee

CONTACT: Mount Baker Ranger District, 360/599-2714, www.fs.usda.gov

Flanked by sparkling lakes at the trailhead and surrounded by a rugged alpine panorama at the summit, every step of this hike is a visible feast, which you deserve after braving the final 2.5 suspension-pummeling miles to Twin Lakes. The hike is uphill all the way to the fire lookout, but it's a breeze compared to the drive.

START THE HIKE

▶ MILE 0-1: Parking Area to Gully

The trail starts from the parking area between the lakes. Head uphill and, after 0.2 mile, go left at the intersection. In late summer and fall, pass huckleberries and plants changing to their fall colors as you **switchback** upward. Snow can linger on Winchester's slopes well into summer, so snow hiking experience might be necessary. A **gully** 0.8 mile beyond the intersection holds snow late into the summer and should be crossed with caution (and an ice axe). Don't be shy about turning back and finding a different trail to explore if you don't feel comfortable.

▶ MILE 1-1.8: Gully to Winchester Mountain Summit

Spend the next 0.4 mile crossing a steep slope. At times it feels as if you are walking on a shelf high above the glistening west lake. After bending around the mountain, a 0.4-mile stretch of **switchbacks** is all that stands between you and the 6,521-foot **summit.** From atop Winchester, the scenery includes Mount Baker, Mount Shuksan, Yellow Aster Butte, Mount Larabee, Goat Mountain, and a smorgasbord of other North Cascade and British Columbia peaks.

The view is especially striking when all the **lookout** windows are propped open and the structure accents rather than blocks the vista. Built in 1935, the Forest Service long ago stopped using the building and

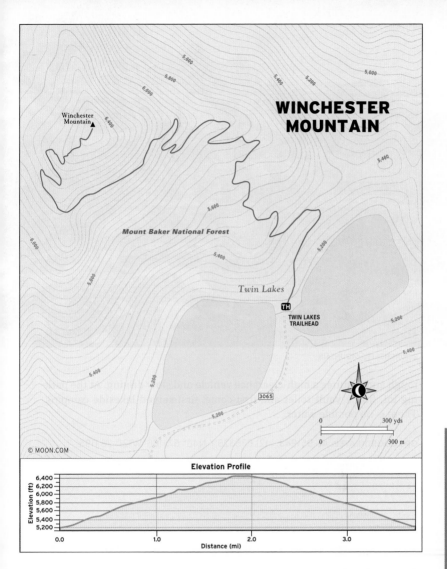

Elevation Profile

scheduled it for demolition in the 1980s. Volunteers saved and restored the lookout. They continue to maintain the structure, which is available for camping on a first-come, first-served basis. Bears frequent the area, so make sure to secure all food and scented items. Even if you can't stay overnight, you'll want to spend some time on Winchester absorbing the tranquility and the endless view.

When you're ready to go, use the same trail to return to Twin Lakes.

DIRECTIONS

From I-5 in Bellingham, take exit 255 and head east on Highway 542 for 46 miles to Forest Road 3065/Twin Lakes Road, on the east side of a state Department of Transportation facility. Turn left and drive 7 miles to Twin Lakes. The 2.5 miles beyond the Yellow Aster Butte trailhead is especially

▲ WINCHESTER MOUNTAIN

rough and requires a high-clearance vehicle and slow driving. At the parking lot, find a vault toilet and first-come, first-served lakeside camping. There is no potable water.

GPS COORDINATES: 48.951943, –121.635325 / N48° 57.1166′ W121° 38.1195′

BEST NEARBY BITES

La Fiamma Wood Fire Pizza (200 E. Chestnut St., Bellingham, 360/647-0060, www.lafiamma.com, hours vary) has been messing with perfection for two decades, and the result is one of the Northwest's most intriguing pizza menus. In addition to traditional offerings, try the eggs Benedict pizza or pizza topped with mashed potatoes (the Spuddy), shrimp (Finn) or mango chutney (Major Grigio). A walk-up window called the Pye Hole sells pizza by the slice. From the trailhead, the 56-mile drive west takes 1 hour, 45 minutes via Highway 542.

Walk among wildflowers on a ridge that brings you face-to-face with Mount Baker while delivering views stretching from Puget Sound to Canada.

BEST: Wildflower Hikes
DISTANCE: 6.8 miles round-trip
DURATION: 3.5 hours
ELEVATION CHANGE: 2,500 feet
EFFORT: Moderate
TRAIL: Dirt, rock
USERS: Hikers, leashed dogs, pack llamas
SEASON: July-October
PASSES/FEES: Northwest Forest Pass
MAPS: Green Trails Map 13 for Mount Baker, USGS topographic map for Mount Baker, USGS topographic map for Bearpaw Mountain
CONTACT: Mount Baker Ranger District, 360/599-2714, www.fs.usda.gov

The ability to adjust the dial on the difficulty is just one of the things that makes this hike special. And popular. In fact, even hiking as little as 3.8 miles round-trip is far enough for the North Cascades' rugged beauty to knock your merino socks off.

START THE HIKE

▸ **MILE 0-1.9: Skyline Divide Trailhead to Ridge**
Starting from the busy trailhead, walk a few steps up the road and turn left into the forest. Climb among the firs on well-trodden trail. After 1.9 miles, enter the **Mount Baker Wilderness,** emerge from the evergreens, and try to keep your eyes from popping out of your head like a smitten cartoon character. Colorful fields of lupine, heather, daisies, asters, and other wildflowers carpet the ridge running above deep valleys. Mount Shuksan rises to the east and the glaciated slopes of Mount Baker dominate the view to the south. You don't have to go any farther to feel as if this was worth the trip. But the trail along the ridge urges you to continue with promises of more soul-stirring views.

▸ **MILE 1.9-2.5: Ridge to Second Knoll Fork**
Turning left takes you on a 0.25-mile side trip to the top of a knoll, but turning right allows you to wander the rolling ridge toward Mount Baker and Hadley Glacier. Turn right and in 0.4 mile reach a **fork** beneath the second knoll. Go right to skirt the knoll or left to crest it using a rougher trail. The paths reconnect on the other side. Cross the west slope of another knoll 0.2 mile farther.

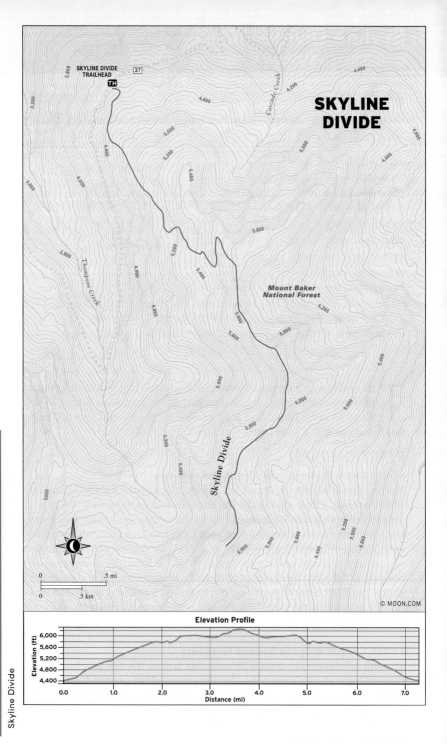

SKYLINE DIVIDE TRAILHEAD

37

SKYLINE DIVIDE

Mount Baker National Forest

Skyline Divide

Thompson Creek

Cascade Creek

0   .5 mi

0   .5 km

© MOON.COM

Elevation Profile

Elevation (ft)

6,000
5,600
5,200
4,800
4,400

0.0   1.0   2.0   3.0   4.0   5.0   6.0   7.0

Distance (mi)

▲ SKYLINE DIVIDE TRAIL

▶ **MILE 2.5–3.4: Second Knoll Fork to Skyline Divide Ridge**
Go 0.5 mile more to a **fork** where the path on the left descends to Dead-horse Camp. Stay right to continue your walk across the sky. Climb 0.4 mile to a **broad spot** on the ridge (6,300 feet)—a perfect place to snap sel-fies, enjoy a picnic lunch, and let your gaze wander from Puget Sound to British Columbia while identifying peaks like Table, Winchester, and Yellow Aster Butte.

Be on the lookout for mountain goats, bears, and other wildlife in the area. Looking to the north, the trail you followed to get here traces the ridgetop. You'll return on this path back to your car.

DIRECTIONS

From I-5 in Bellingham, take exit 255 and head east on Highway 542 for 34.3 miles to Forest Road 39/Glacier Creek Road in Glacier. Turn right and then take an immediate left onto Forest Road 37. Follow this unpaved road for 12.6 miles to the trailhead. A vault toilet is located at the trailhead.

GPS COORDINATES: 48.88035, –121.86502 / N48° 52.821′ W121° 51.9012′

BEST NEARBY BITES

Chairlift seats hang outside and snowboards are mounted above the bar at **Chair 9 Woodstone Pizza and Bar** (10459 Mount Baker Hwy., Glacier, 360/599-2511, www.chair9.com, noon-close Mon.-Thurs., 11am-close Fri.-Sun.). The name and décor pay homage to Mount Baker's legendary skiing and snowboarding scene, but the thin-crust pizza and beer from Bellingham's Kulshan Brewing Company hit the spot year-round. From the trailhead, the 13-mile drive northwest takes about 15 minutes via Forest Road 37 and Highway 542.

3

Table Mountain

MOUNT BAKER-SNOQUALMIE NATIONAL FOREST

Scale the steep wall of Table Mountain and take in views of the Chain Lakes and the icy peaks of Baker and Shuksan.

DISTANCE: 3 miles round-trip

DURATION: 1.5 hours

ELEVATION CHANGE: 700 feet

EFFORT: Easy/moderate

TRAIL: Dirt, rock, potential late-season snow

USERS: Hikers

SEASON: July-mid-October

PASSES/FEES: Northwest Forest Pass

MAPS: Green Trails Map 14 for Mount Shuksan, USGS topographic map for Shuksan Arm

CONTACT: Mount Baker Ranger District, 360/599-2714, www.fs.usda.gov

Towering above Artist Point, Table Mountain is both alluring and intimidating. It might look like you should have packed rock-climbing shoes, but it is a nontechnical walk when it's free of snow. But that's not to say there aren't potential hazards.

START THE HIKE

▶ **MILE 0-0.5: Parking Lot to Table Mountain Trail**

After taking in the already stunning views from the boot-shaped parking lot, find the trailhead where the laces would be (on the north side of the lot). Start by walking about 100 yards on the **Chain Lakes Trail.** To get to the even better views, turn right on the **Table Mountain Trail;** in 0.2 mile, you'll begin the steep ascent. The trail hugs the side of the cliff and uses **rock steps** as it ascends almost 400 feet in 0.3 mile. Watch out for rocks kicked loose by hikers higher on the trail and holler "rock" to warn others should you knock a piece loose.

TABLE MOUNTAIN ▶

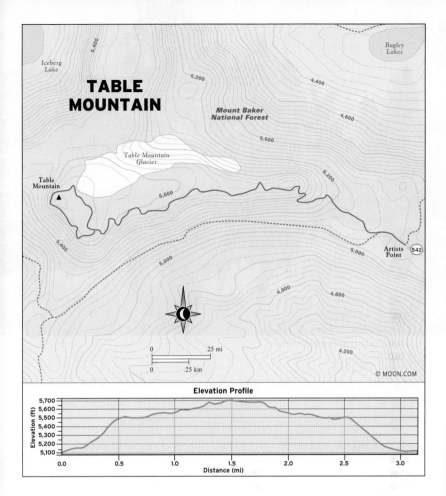

Elevation Profile

> ▶ **MILE 0.5-1.5: Table Mountain Trail to Table Mountain Summit**

On top of the **mesa-like peak**, a short spur to the right offers views of the Heather Meadows area and surrounding peaks. Turn left at this intersection and walk along the mostly flat plateau that formed when an ancient lava flow pooled into a lake of molten rock. Follow the path for 1 mile along the **south rim**, passing trees, patches of snow, and pools of water. On the west side of Table Mountain (its highest point at 5,746 feet), enjoy the bird's-eye view of the Chain Lakes and a 360-degree panorama of the North Cascades including Baker and Shuksan. Look for mountain goats, birds, and other wildlife.

> ▶ **MILE 1.5-3: Table Mountain Summit to Parking Lot**

Maps show a steep route descending to the Chain Lakes Trail, but it is treacherous, rarely used, and not recommended. Instead, when you've finished exploring the plateau, retrace your steps. If conditions don't allow or you aren't comfortable scaling Table Mountain, you can hike around it on the Chain Lakes Trail or make the easy 1.2-mile walk to Huntoon Point on the Artist Ridge Trail.

▲ A SMALL LAKE ATOP TABLE MOUNTAIN

DIRECTIONS

From I-5 in Bellingham, take exit 255 and head east on Highway 542 for 57 miles to the highway's terminus at Artist Point and the trailhead. Toilets are in the parking lot.

GPS COORDINATES: 48.846538, -121.693351 / N48° 50.7923' W121° 41.6011'

BEST NEARBY BITES

Milano's (9990 Mount Baker Hwy., Glacier, 360/599-2863, www.milanosrestaurantbar.com, 4pm-9pm Fri.-Sat., 4pm-8pm Thurs. and Sun., closed Mon.-Wed.) and its linguine topped with mussels, clams, and prawns draw a crowd. Bar Veneto shares the building and offers build-your-own tacos and gin, rum, vodka, and brandy from the owner's distillery, Paraty Spirits. From the trailhead, the 24-mile drive northwest takes 50 minutes via Highway 542.

4

Chain Lakes Loop
MOUNT BAKER-SNOQUALMIE NATIONAL FOREST

Visit a collection of alpine lakes while climbing ridges to views of Mount Baker and Mount Shuksan.

BEST: Summer Hikes
DISTANCE: 7.5 miles round-trip
DURATION: 4 hours
ELEVATION CHANGE: 1,800 feet
EFFORT: Moderate
TRAIL: Dirt, rocks, scree slopes
USERS: Hikers, leashed dogs
SEASON: Late July-mid-October
PASSES/FEES: Northwest Forest Pass
MAPS: Green Trails Map 14 for Mount Shuksan
CONTACT: Mount Baker Ranger District, 360/599-2714, www.fs.usda.gov

This stunning loop linking shimmering lakes, mountain views, and alpine meadows is only free of snow during the summer, so arrive at sunrise if you want to beat the crowds.

START THE HIKE

▶ **MILE 0-0.8: Bagley Lakes Trailhead to Bagley Lake**
There are several trailhead choices for this hike along the final stretch of the Mount Baker Highway, but for a grand loop on the **Chain Lakes Trail,** start at the **Bagley Lakes Trailhead** near the ski area. In the first 100 yards beyond the kiosk, stay right and cross a small dam on **Bagley Creek.** The trail bends left and spends a flat 0.7 mile tracing the shoreline of the first **Bagley Lake** and following the creek to the **second lake.** Look for sandpipers and ouzels around the water.

▶ **MILE 0.8-2.5: Bagley Lake to Herman Saddle**
At the outlet of the small second lake, an arched **stone bridge** crosses the creek and offers a stunning photo op with Table Mountain in the background. (It's also an opportunity to abbreviate the hike with a kid- and creaky-knee-friendly 1.5-mile loop.) Go straight past the bridge to continue along the lake, and in 0.2 mile the climbing begins. Marmots watch from the rocks as you ascend the open slope for 1.5 miles to Herman Saddle between Mazama Dome and Table Mountain. The view gets more majestic the higher you climb until, at the **saddle,** you can catch your breath and admire Mount Baker and Mount Shuksan, the Bagley Lakes, and, to the west, the next lakes you'll visit on this loop.

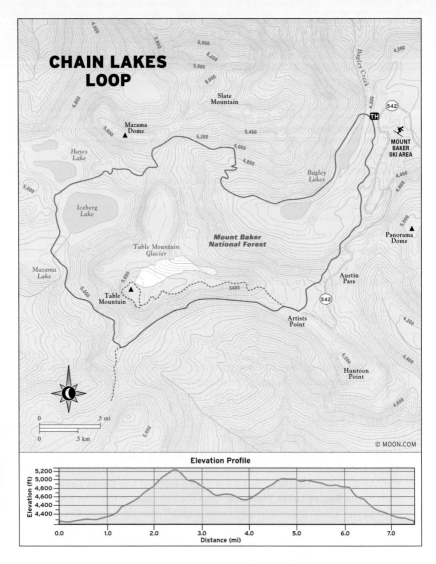

CHAIN LAKES
LOOP

Elevation Profile

MILE 2.5-3.4: **Herman Saddle to Hayes Lake Spur Trail**

Descend 500 feet in 0.7 mile on the west side of the saddle. Follow the path over a strip of land between **Hayes and Iceberg Lakes.** The peaceful alpine lakes invite visitors to stay, take a quick dip, and relax for a while. In 0.2 mile, pass the Hayes Lake Trail (a flat, 0.9-mile loop around Hayes Lake that also visits Arbuthnot Lake) and a short, well-marked spur (on the left) leading to a pit toilet overlooking Iceberg Lake.

MILE 3.4-5.7: **Hayes Lake Spur Trail to Artist Point**

Continue south along the west side of Iceberg Lake, passing tiny **Mazama Lake** (another options for a chilly swim) after 0.4 mile. Spend the next 0.8 mile ascending until you reach the **intersection** with the Ptarmigan Trail at a gap between Table Mountain and Ptarmigan Perch. Go left to stay on

Chain Lakes Loop

▲ CHAIN LAKES LOOP

the loop and walk 1.1 miles along the south slope of Table Mountain to **Artist Point,** enjoying views of the Swift Creek valley and Mount Baker along the way.

▶ **MILE 5.7–7.5: Artist Point to Wild Goose Trail**
At Artist Point is a large parking lot that will likely be packed with cars; the point's views of the North Cascades make it one of the most scenic summer driving destinations in the Northwest. Cross the lot and find the **Wild Goose Trail** next to the toilets. Take this trail, which crosses the highway and then descends—sharply at times, on log steps linked with cables—for 1 mile to the **Austin Pass Picnic Area** and the **Heather Meadows Visitor Center.** Should snow and ice make the trail unsafe, the shoulder of the road offers a more gradual descent. From the picnic area, follow the Wild Goose Trail 0.7 mile to complete the loop.

DIRECTIONS
From I-5 in Bellingham, take exit 255 and head east for 54 miles on Highway 542 to the Bagley Lakes Loop trailhead just above the Heather Meadows base area at Mount Baker Ski Area. Toilets are located at the trailhead.

GPS COORDINATES: 48.861551, –121.682533 / N48° 34.7448' W120° 28.7034'

BEST NEARBY BITES
Graham's Restaurant (9989 Mount Baker Hwy., 360/599-1933, noon-9pm Mon.-Fri., 8am-9pm Sat.-Sun.) pays tribute to Mount Baker's history as a filming location, with pictures of actors Clark Gable and Robert De Niro adorning the walls of the century-old building: Gable's *Call of the Wild* (1935) and De Niro's *The Deer Hunter* (1978) filmed scenes at Heather Meadows. According to locals, though, the real star at Graham's is the bacon meatloaf sandwich. From the trailhead, the 22-mile drive northwest takes 42 minutes via Highway 542.

Admire man-made Diablo Lake from an overlook at the end of a short trail starting from a popular campground.

DISTANCE: 3.6 miles round-trip
DURATION: 2 hours
ELEVATION CHANGE: 600 feet
EFFORT: Easy/moderate
TRAIL: Dirt, rocks, pavement (in campground)
USERS: Hikers, leashed dogs
SEASON: Year-round
PASSES/FEES: None
MAPS: Green Trails Map 48 for Diablo
CONTACT: North Cascades Visitor Center, 206/386-4495 (mid-May–September); North Cascades National Park, 360/854-7200, www.nps.gov/noca

The family-friendly hike to a bluff overlooking Diablo Lake might be short, but a visit to this part of Ross Lake National Recreation Area doesn't have to be. The campground is a popular hub for those exploring this stunning landscape. From paddling and fishing on Diablo Lake to hiking and mountaineering, there is plenty to do.

START THE HIKE

▶ **MILE 0-0.5: Parking Lot to Highway 20 Bridge Viewpoint**

From the parking lot on the north side of the highway, walk the paved **driveway** into the **north campground**, making your way to the walk-in campsites and the clearly marked trailhead. The trail is immaculately maintained but not until after you make your way through an area reconfigured by prior flooding. Signs point the way and bridges cross channels carved by the creek. Walk toward campsite No. 11, crossing a bridge, then continue as the trail surface becomes smoother while traveling under hemlocks and Douglas firs and past moss-covered boulders. The trail climbs gently and 0.5 mile from the highway an opening in the trees frames a view of the Highway 20 bridge over the Thunder Arm of Diablo Lake.

▶ **MILE 0.5-1.3: Highway 20 Bridge Viewpoint
to Colonial Peak Viewpoint**

Benches dot the next 0.4 mile, which brings you to a **clearing** with views of the steep, tree-covered slopes above the lake. Look south to see Colonial Peak and the glacier feeding Colonial Creek. Listen for woodpeckers as you pass a marsh in another 0.4 mile, and then continue upward under lodgepole pine to the top of the knob. This area is one of the best in the park for bird-watching. Get going early before the area is bustling with

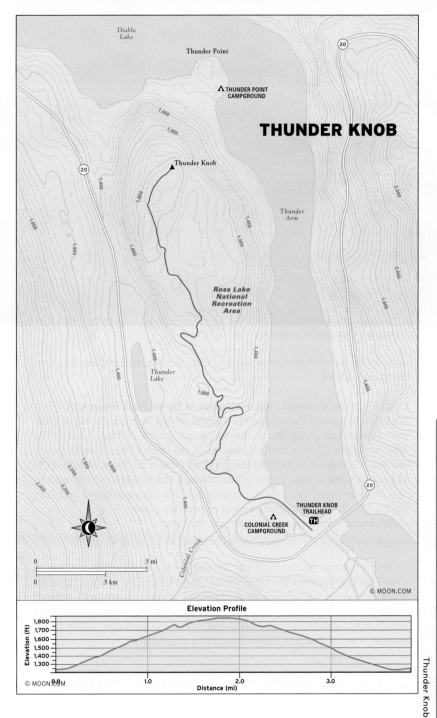

Diablo
Lake

Thunder Point

⊼ THUNDER POINT
CAMPGROUND

1,400

1,600

THUNDER KNOB

▲ Thunder Knob

Thunder
Arm

1,400

1,600

1,600

20

1,400

1,600

1,800

**Ross Lake
National
Recreation
Area**

1,600

Thunder
Lake

1,400

1,600

1,600

2,200

2,600

1,800

1,600

20

1,400

THUNDER KNOB
TRAILHEAD
TH

⊼
COLONIAL CREEK
CAMPGROUND

Colonial Creek

2,400

2,200

2,000

1,800

1,600

20

0   .5 mi

0   .5 km

© MOON.COM

Elevation Profile

Elevation (ft): 1,800 / 1,700 / 1,600 / 1,500 / 1,400 / 1,300

Distance (mi): 0.0 / 1.0 / 2.0 / 3.0

© MOON.COM

activity for the best chance to see thrushes, red-breasted nuthatches, warblers, and others.

▶ MILE 1.3–1.8: Colonial Peak Viewpoint to Davis Peak Viewpoint

It's 0.4 mile beyond the wetland to a **bench** with a westward view of 7,051-foot Davis Peak rising above the turquoise waters of Diablo Lake. The trail continues 0.1 mile to the north end of the knob where another bench awaits. While most of the soul-invigorating view is the work of nature, Diablo is part of a series of man-made lakes on the Skagit River. Formed by the 389-foot-high Diablo Dam, the reservoir sits between Gorge and Ross Lakes. The three dams produce most of Seattle's power.

To return to the campground retrace your route.

DIRECTIONS

From Burlington, follow Highway 20 east for about 70 miles to Colonial Creek Campground on Thunder Arm of Diablo Lake. The trailhead is in the campground on the left side of the highway. If the campground is closed or no parking is available, there is a parking area along Highway 20 near the campground entrance. Toilets and water are available in the campground. Part of Colonial Creek Campground is located on the south side of the highway.

GPS COORDINATES: 48.690350, –121.097972 / N48° 41.421′ W121° 5.8783′

Switchback your way through an old-growth forest to a mountain pass with views of the rocky and glaciated spires of the North Cascades.

DISTANCE: 7.4 miles round-trip
DURATION: 4 hours
ELEVATION CHANGE: 1,800 feet
EFFORT: Moderate
TRAIL: Dirt path
USERS: Hikers
SEASON: July–mid-October
PASSES/FEES: None
MAPS: Green Trails Map 80 for Cascade Pass
CONTACT: North Cascades National Park Wilderness Information Center, 360/854-7245, www.nps.gov/noca

START THE HIKE

▶ **MILE 0-2.4: Loop Parking Lot to Switchbacks**
The trail starts on the north side of the loop **parking lot,** but before you even get out of the car it is obvious this is a special place. Johannesburg Mountain rises sharply above the parking lot with glaciers clinging to its rocky cliffs. Ice and rock sometimes crash down the slopes, the rumble echoing through the basin.

Five steps into the hike, the path folds back 180 degrees for a taste of what's to come: thirty-four **switchbacks** in 2.4 miles. Think of them as your friend—they make a steep climb comparatively easy.

▶ **MILE 2.4-3.7: Switchbacks to Cascade Pass**
Making a game out of this daunting stretch can also make the trek easier. Feel free to use mine: at each switchback, name an athlete who wore the corresponding jersey number (1, Warren Moon; 2, Derek Jeter,

CASCADE PASS TRAIL ▶

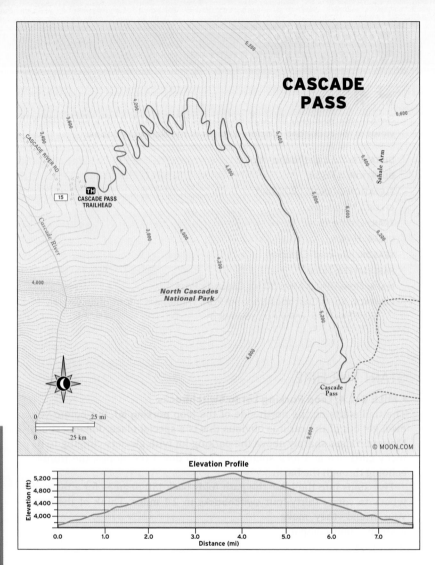

CASCADE PASS

North Cascades National Park

Cascade Pass

Elevation Profile

© MOON.COM

etc.). Before you know it, you will be making the **1.3-mile traverse** from Switchback 34 to the pass. It's during this traverse that you trade the dense woods for views of Johannesburg, Eldorado, Mix-up and other peaks.

At the **pass**, rest on one of the granite slabs arranged in a semicircle and check out the USGS benchmark disc. A path leads to a vault toilet. When gazing down into Pelton Basin, take in the effects of the last ice age, when massive continental glaciers covered much of the North Cascades. At 5,392 feet above sea level, Cascade Pass was used by Native Americans for generations to cross the North Cascades. Archaeologists have found stone tools and cooking hearths here dating back 9,000 years. Today, this area is one of the most easily accessed high-country adventures in the North Cascades.

Once you've had your fill of alpine views, return the way you came.

▲ PEAKS ABOVE CASCADE PASS

DIRECTIONS

From Burlington, follow Highway 20 east for about 57 miles to Marble-mount. When the highway bends left in town, continue straight and cross a steel bridge over the Skagit River on Cascade River Road. Follow the road for 19 miles to the Cascade Pass Trailhead parking lot. A vault toilet is at the trailhead.

GPS COORDINATES: 48.475443, –121.075064 / N48° 28.5266′ W121° 4.5038′

Maple Pass Loop

OKANOGAN-WENATCHEE NATIONAL FOREST, RAINY PASS

Hike one of the North Cascades' classic trails through old-growth forest to ridge-top meadows above a glittering alpine lake.

BEST: Fall Hikes

DISTANCE: 6.8 miles round-trip

DURATION: 4 hours

ELEVATION CHANGE: 2,100 feet

EFFORT: Moderate

TRAIL: Dirt, rock

USERS: Hikers, wheelchair users (paved path to Rainy Lake), leashed dogs

SEASON: July–October

PASSES/FEES: Northwest Forest Pass

MAPS: Green Trails Map 49 for Mount Logan, Green Trails Map 50 for Washington Pass

CONTACT: Okanogan-Wenatchee National Forest, 509/996-4000, www.fs.usda.gov

START THE HIKE

▶ **MILE 0-1.4: Rainy Pass Trailhead to Lake Ann Trail Junction**
Starting at the **Rainy Pass Trailhead**, near where the Pacific Crest Trail makes its final highway crossing before the Canadian border, find the paved **Rainy Lake Trail** running behind the trailhead kiosk just south of the parking/picnic area loop. Look for the well-marked Maple Pass Trail behind the **kiosk** and start climbing. Take solace in knowing the climbing is more gradual heading this direction.

The **Maple Pass Trail** ascends through an old-growth forest of firs and hemlocks and, in late summer and fall, allows glimpses of the colorful foliage that lies ahead. Pass avalanche chutes with larger doses of color and a small waterfall before arriving at the **junction** with the Lake Ann Trail at 1.3 miles. The trail to the left reaches the lake in 0.6 mile, but stay right on the **Maple Pass Loop** and you'll get views of the lake in about 0.1 mile.

MAPLE PASS TRAIL ▶

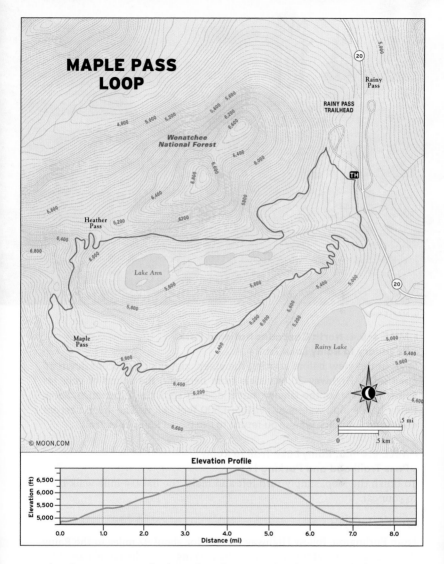

MAPLE PASS LOOP

Wenatchee National Forest

Rainy Pass

RAINY PASS TRAILHEAD

Heather Pass

Lake Ann

Maple Pass

Rainy Lake

© MOON.COM

0   .5 mi

0   .5 km

Elevation Profile

The shimmering pool adorned with a tiny island continually lures your gaze as you make your way toward the ridge high above.

▶ MILE 1.4–4: Lake Ann Trail Junction to North Cascades National Park Boundary

One mile past the Lake Ann spur, a sign bolted to a tree welcomes you to **Heather Pass.** Keep straight and in 0.9 mile reach a marker indicating the boundary of **North Cascades National Park.** Most of the climbing is behind you at this point. Spend the next 0.7 mile strolling through ridge-top **meadows**, portions of which are roped off to prevent visitors from trampling fragile vegetation.

▲ MAPLE PASS

▶ **MILE 4-6.4: North Cascades National Park Boundary to Rainy Lake Trail**

Soak in the view before starting the steep, zigzagging descent down an **open slope.** Highway 20 is visible from here and the sound of vehicles sometimes breaks the silence, but it doesn't spoil the experience. Soon, Rainy Lake's blue waters are visible 1,500 feet below. The steep descent ends after 2.4 miles when you return to the paved **Rainy Lake Trail.**

▶ **MILE 6.4-6.8: Rainy Lake Trail to Rainy Pass Trailhead and Parking Lot**

To finish the loop, simply turn left and make the flat 0.4-mile walk back to your car.

DIRECTIONS

From Burlington, follow Highway 20 east for about 97 miles to the Rainy Pass picnic area and turn right into the parking area. The Rainy Lake, Maple Pass, and Pacific Crest Trails converge in this area. A restroom is located near the trailhead.

GPS COORDINATES: 48.515511, -120.735769 / N48° 30.9307' W120° 44.1461'

BEST NEARBY BITES

Set on the bank of the Methow River in the Old West-themed town of Winthrop, the **Rocking Horse Bakery** (265 Riverside Ave., Winthrop, 509/996-4241, www.rockinghorsebakery.com, 7am-4pm daily) serves an array of breakfast pastries along with pizza, sandwiches, and salads. From the trailhead, the 35-mile drive west takes about 40 minutes via Highway 20.

Take an easy walk up a North Cascades valley to a place where Cedar Creek makes two sharp plunges.

BEST: Waterfall Hikes
DISTANCE: 3.5 miles round-trip
DURATION: 1.5 hours
ELEVATION CHANGE: 500 feet
EFFORT: Easy
TRAIL: Dirt, rock
USERS: Hikers, leashed dogs, mountain bikers, horseback riders
SEASON: May–early November
PASSES/FEES: Northwest Forest Pass
MAPS: Green Trails Map 50 for Washington Pass
CONTACT: Okanogan-Wenatchee National Forest, 509/996-4000, www.fs.usda.gov

Each season offers something different on the Cedar Creek Trail. Some make the long snowshoe via the closed North Cascade Highway in the winter to see the falls when they're frozen. Visit soon after the highway opens and snow is melting to find the creek thundering over the falls. Spring brings wildflowers. And autumn colors accent the journey when the falls have a smaller volume.

START THE HIKE

▶ **MILE 0-0.75: Cedar Creek Trailhead to Goat Peak Viewpoint**
The ambience improves quickly once you start hiking the **Cedar Creek Trail.** It's no surprise, really, considering the hike starts at a **gravel pit.** Starting from the **kiosk** at the southeast end of the gravel pit, the trail heads into the forest and immediately passes the Varden Lake Trail. Continue straight on the **Cedar Creek Trail** for a short bit of uphill before the trail settles into a gradually climbing valley walk. The forest of firs, spruce, and occasional cedars allows enough sunlight for wildflowers like lupine and scarlet paintbrush to grow. Look for deer and butterflies, but also be on the lookout for rattlesnakes.

Peek at peaks through the trees before, 0.75 mile into the hike, an **open spot** offers a view of the surrounding valley. Goat Peak and its rocky cliffs rise in the distance.

▶ **MILE 0.75-1.75: Goat Peak Viewpoint to Cedar Falls**
In 1 mile hear the roar of the falls cascading through a narrow canyon. The two tiers of the **falls** drop 40 and 55 feet, respectively. Exploring the area, you'll find **overlooks** with views of the falls, although there is not a

NORTH CASCADES

Cedar Falls

145

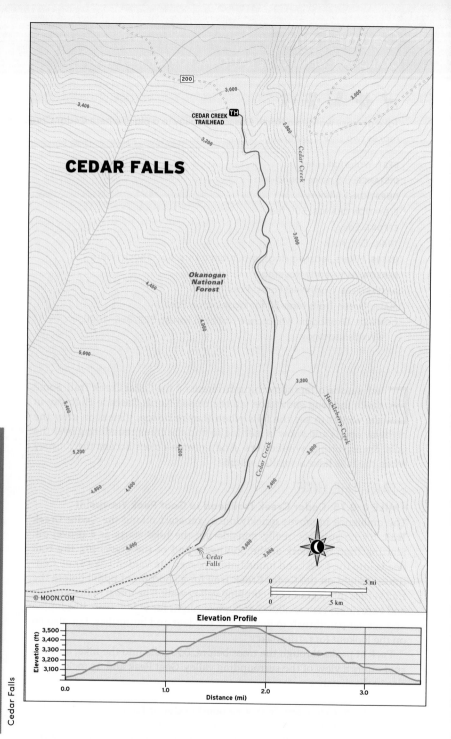

CEDAR FALLS

CEDAR CREEK TRAILHEAD

200

Okanogan National Forest

Cedar Creek

Huckleberry Creek

Cedar Falls

3,400
3,000
2,800
3,200
3,000
4,400
4,000
5,000
5,400
5,200
4,800
4,600
4,200
4,000
3,200
3,600
3,400
3,600
3,800

0   .5 mi
0   .5 km

© MOON.COM

Elevation Profile

Elevation (ft)

3,500
3,400
3,300
3,200
3,100

0.0   1.0   2.0   3.0

Distance (mi)

▲ CEDAR FALLS

viewpoint where you can squeeze both drops into one picture. Keep children and pets close and don't go near the edge of the exposed overlooks.

When you're ready to call it a day, retrace your route along Cedar Creek back to the trailhead.

DIRECTIONS

From Burlington, follow Highway 20 east for about 114 miles. Follow the Cedar Creek sign directing you to turn right on Forest Road 200. Drive 0.8 mile to the trailhead. A toilet is located at the trailhead parking area.

GPS COORDINATES: 48.57908, –120.47839 / N48° 34.7448′ W120° 28.7034′

BEST NEARBY BITES

Nearly a century old, **The Mazama Store** (50 Lost River Rd., Mazama, 509/996-2855, www.themazamastore.com, 7am-6pm daily) sells pottery, soap, jewelry, and other items made by Methow Valley residents. Its fresh pastries, pies, pizza, and soup make it a popular stop for breakfast and lunch. From the trailhead, the 7-mile drive northeast takes about 20 minutes via Highway 20.

Cedar Falls

Green Mountain

MOUNT BAKER-SNOQUALMIE NATIONAL FOREST

🐐 ❁ 🐾

Listen to whistling marmots, enjoy colorful wildflowers, and visit an old fire lookout while experiencing a far-reaching view of the North Cascades.

DISTANCE: 8.4 miles round-trip
DURATION: 5 hours
ELEVATION CHANGE: 3,300 feet
EFFORT: Moderate/strenuous
TRAIL: Dirt single track
USERS: Hikers, leashed dogs
SEASON: July–October
PASSES/FEES: Northwest Forest Pass
MAPS: Green Trails Map 80 for Cascade Pass
CONTACT: Darrington Ranger District, 360/436-1155, www.fs.usda.gov

The verdant journey along this beloved trail to one of Washington's most breathtaking views visits forest and grassy meadows. Experience for yourself how Green Mountain got its name.

START THE HIKE

▶ **MILE 0-1.5: Green Mountain Trailhead to Meadow**

The **well-marked trail** starts under a canopy of evergreens. The ascent, gradual at first, soon gets steeper. The shade won't last long, so carry plenty of water and sun protection as well as bug spray. After 1.5 miles, emerge from the trees and enter a lush **meadow** with a view of snowcapped peaks.

▶ **MILE 1.5-3: Meadow to Ponds**

The scenery only gets better as you continue. Hip-high leafy greenery lines the trail as you **switchback** upward for 1.5 miles before dropping about 100 feet to a **pair of ponds** at about 5,200 feet.

▶ **MILE 3-4.2: Ponds to Green Mountain Summit**

The trail gets steeper and the view more mesmerizing beyond the ponds as you climb 1,300 feet over the final 1.2 miles. Take your time and enjoy the columbine, glacier lilies, and bluebells

HIKERS ON GREEN MOUNTAIN ▶

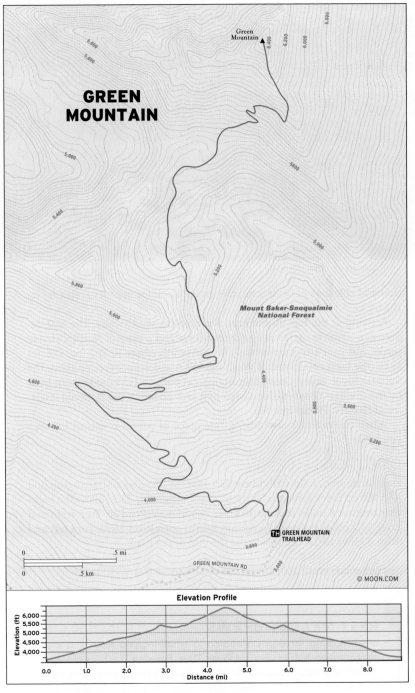

GREEN MOUNTAIN

Green Mountain

5,800
5,600
5,000
5,400
5,800
5,600
4,600
4,200
4,000

Mount Baker-Snoqualmie
National Forest

5,800
6,400
6,200
6,000
5,600
5,000
4,400
3,800
3,600
3,200
3,600
3,400

TH GREEN MOUNTAIN
TRAILHEAD

GREEN MOUNTAIN RD

0   .5 mi
0   .5 km

© MOON.COM

Elevation Profile

Elevation (ft): 6,000 / 5,500 / 5,000 / 4,500 / 4,000

Distance (mi): 0.0 1.0 2.0 3.0 4.0 5.0 6.0 7.0 8.0

Green Mountain

▲ THE SUMMIT OF GREEN MOUNTAIN

that add splashes of color amid the green. Look for marmots relaxing on the rocks.

Arriving at the **top**, all the hard work seems worthwhile. The 360-degree panorama includes deep green valleys and a bevy of North Cascade peaks. But your attention is likely to turn south where 10,520-foot Glacier Peak (the least celebrated of Washington's five volcanoes) rises above the Suiattle River valley. Green Mountain's capper is a 1933 fire lookout built by the Civilian Conservation Corps that was added to the National Register of Historic Places in 1987.

When you're finished enjoying this piece of paradise, return the way you came.

DIRECTIONS

From Arlington, follow Highway 530 east for 28 miles to Darrington and turn left on Emens Avenue North to stay on Highway 530. Follow the highway another 8 miles to Suiattle River Road/Forest Road 26. Turn right and drive 20.2 miles to Green Mountain Road/Forest Road 2680. Turn left and drive 6 miles to the trailhead near the end of the road.

GPS COORDINATES: 48.269521, –121.236484 / N48° 16.1713' W121° 14.189'

BEST NEARBY BREWS

When passing through Darrington, a small logging town and ideal recreation hub, swing by **River Time Brewing** (660 Emens Ave. E., 267/483-7411, www.rivertimebrewing.com, hours vary) and try a chicken sandwich or flatbread pizza while sampling craft beers with names like Life Changer and Another Red Headed Stranger. From the trailhead, the 30-mile drive west takes about 90 minutes via Suiattle River Road/Forest Road 26 and Highway 530.

Perched on the edge of the Cascades, a historic fire lookout gives you a place to gawk at one of Washington's best views.

DISTANCE: 5.4 miles round-trip
DURATION: 3 hours
ELEVATION CHANGE: 2,300 feet
EFFORT: Moderate
TRAIL: Dirt, log and rock steps, short scramble over granite boulders
USERS: Hikers, leashed dogs
SEASON: July–early November
PASSES/FEES: Northwest Forest Pass
MAPS: Green Trails Map 109 for Granite Falls
CONTACT: Verlot Public Service Center, 360/691-7791, www.fs.usda.gov; Darrington Ranger District, 360/436-1155; Mount Pilchuck State Park, 360/793-0420, http://parks.state.wa.us

Some days it feels like you can see the entire state from the top of Mount Pilchuck. And some days it feels like the entire state has joined you on the trail. A short hike easily accessed from Seattle and with a three-volcano view, Mount Pilchuck is one of Washington's most popular trails.

START THE HIKE

▶ **MILE 0-1: Mount Pilchuck Trailhead to Mount Pilchuck State Park**
From the trailhead, start on what was once a ski area **service road.** In about 0.1 mile step over **Rotary Creek**; in another 0.2 mile, pass a weathered sign signaling your passage into 1,903-acre **Mount Pilchuck State Park.** Walk among cedars and firs and cross a **scree slope** in another 0.7 mile.

▶ **MILE 1-1.7: Mount Pilchuck State Park to Historic Chairlift**
A historical remnant sits trailside after another 0.7 mile. A large concrete foundation once anchored a **chairlift.** From 1951 to 1980, Pilchuck was home to a ski area.

▶ **MILE 1.7-2.7: Historic Chairlift to Mount Pilchuck Summit**
From here, there's 1 mile to go. The **summit** comes into view as the path's pitch increases on **slopes** covered with granite boulders and heather. The way is typically easy to find from summer until early November, making it an attraction for novice hikers eager to bag their first mile-high peak. However, this hike isn't without hazards. Snow can linger, sections of trail are exposed, and the final 100 feet or so to the lookout requires scrambling over large **granite boulders** (an impracticality for some children and pets).

NORTH CASCADES

Mount Pilchuck

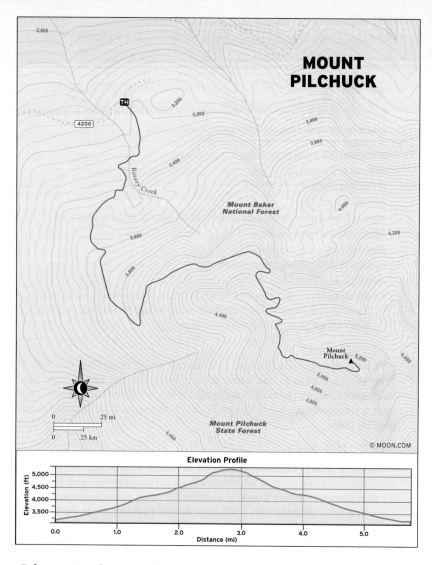

MOUNT PILCHUCK

Mount Baker National Forest

Mount Pilchuck

Mount Pilchuck State Forest

© MOON.COM

Elevation Profile

Poles, traction devices, and a willingness to turn around when conditions exceed your skill level are important.

A short scramble over the boulders and a climb up an eight-rung **ladder** places you on the deck of a historic **fire lookout** on the western edge of the Cascades. The view includes Mount Rainier, Mount Baker, Glacier Peak, and numerous other Cascade mountains. The Olympics, Puget Sound, Everett, and Seattle add to the scenery. Need help identifying what's what? Diagrams inside the lookout show the names of the surrounding peaks.

You won't want to leave this heavenly perch. Some unfurl sleeping bags and stake their claim to spots on the lookout floor. Others lie on boulders. When you do finally leave, use the same route for your descent.

▲ SUNSET ON MOUNT PILCHUCK

DIRECTIONS

From Seattle, follow I-5 north to exit 194 and follow U.S. 2 east. After 1.8 miles, follow the signs for Highway 204 and continue east toward Lake Stevens. After 2.1 miles turn left on Highway 9. In 1.6 miles turn right on Highway 92 and continue toward Granite Falls. Pass through three traffic circles as the road becomes 96th Street. At Alder Avenue turn left. This road becomes the Mountain Loop Highway.

In 10.8 miles, pass the Verlot Public Service Center on the left. Drive another mile and turn right onto Mount Pilchuck Road just after crossing a bridge. Follow the road 6.8 miles to the trailhead parking lot. The final mile of the road is not paved. A restroom is located at the trailhead.

GPS COORDINATES: 48.07029, –121.8145 / N48° 4.2174′ W121° 48.888′

Mount Pilchuck

MOUNT BAKER-SNOQUALMIE NATIONAL FOREST

Hike past waterfalls and giant cedars on your way to the striking setting of Lake Twenty-Two.

BEST: Dog-Friendly Hikes
DISTANCE: 6.2 miles round-trip
DURATION: 3.5 hours
ELEVATION CHANGE: 1,350 feet
EFFORT: Moderate
TRAIL: Dirt path, rocks, talus slopes, boardwalks
USERS: Hikers, leashed dogs
SEASON: May–October
PASSES/FEES: Northwest Forest Pass
MAPS: Green Trails Map 109 for Granite Falls
CONTACT: Mount Baker–Snoqualmie National Forest, 360/436-1155, www.fs.usda.gov; Verlot Public Service Center, 360/691-7791

The trail and lake sit in the 790-acre Lake Twenty-Two Research Natural Area, a section of Mount Baker-Snoqualmie National Forest set aside in 1947 for the study of western red cedar, western hemlock, and various plants. The giant cedars are every bit the stars of this hike alongside the lake and waterfalls.

START THE HIKE

▶ **MILE 0-1.8: Trailhead to Three Fingers and Liberty Peaks Viewpoint**
From the South Fork Stillaguamish River on the opposite side of the Mountain Loop Highway to Twenty-Two Creek, the sound of moving water is constant as you walk under an evergreen canopy. The first 0.5 mile climbs gradually before giving way to switchbacks. After 0.5 mile of switchbacks, get your first of several looks at the **cascades.** The trail keeps climbing through old-growth forest and past ferns, salmonberry, violets, and trilliums for another 0.8 mile before reaching a **talus slope** with views of Three Fingers and Liberty Peaks to the north.

▶ **MILE 1.8-2.5: Three Fingers and Liberty Peaks Viewpoint to Lake Twenty-Two**
At 0.4 mile beyond the **talus slope,** the trail relents for a gentle 0.3-mile walk along the creek to the lake. Steep slopes rise above three sides of **Lake Twenty-Two** (2,400 feet elev.), creating a microclimate that supports subalpine vegetation usually found at higher elevations.

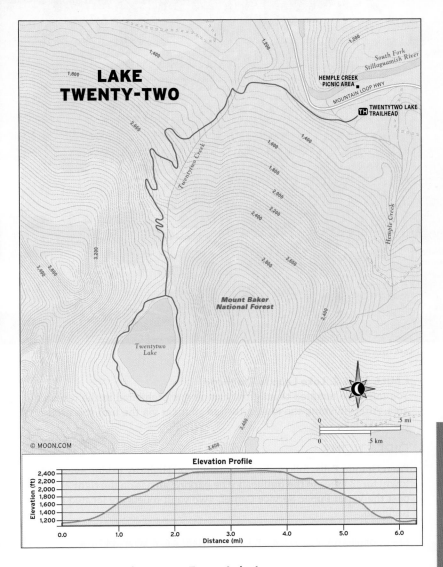

LAKE TWENTY-TWO

Twentytwo Lake

Mount Baker
National Forest

HEMPLE CREEK
PICNIC AREA

TWENTYTWO LAKE
TRAILHEAD

MOUNTAIN LOOP HWY

South Fork
Stillaguamish River

Hemple Creek

Twentytwo Creek

© MOON.COM

0   .5 mi
0   .5 km

Elevation Profile

Elevation (ft)

2,400
2,200
2,000
1,800
1,600
1,400
1,200

0.0   1.0   2.0   3.0   4.0   5.0   6.0

Distance (mi)

▶ **MILE 2.5–3.7: Lake Twenty-Two to Lake Loop**

At the lake, turn left on the **boardwalk** and take a few steps to a **bridge** crossing **Twenty-Two Creek.** This is arguably the best view at the lake, but you can gain a variety of perspectives by crossing the bridge and following the 1.2-mile **loop** around the water. Shortly into the loop, the boardwalk gives way to traditional trail.

Cross a **talus slope** before another short **boardwalk** on the lake's south side. Be aware of conditions if you hike the loop. Avalanches can crash down the rocky slopes early in the hiking season. Listen for frogs and scan the slopes for mountain goats. The clear lake is 53 feet deep and can be a good place for anglers to land rainbow trout.

▲ LAKE TWENTY-TWO

▶ MILE 3.7-6.2: Lake Loop to Trailhead

You might be tempted to stay, but camping is prohibited in the research area. After finishing the loop, return to your car via the trail you used to reach the lake.

DIRECTIONS

From Granite Falls, follow the Mountain Loop Highway (Alder Avenue in town) for 13 miles to the trailhead. The parking area is on the right 2 miles past the Verlot Public Service Center. Two vault toilets are located at the trailhead.

GPS COORDINATES: 48.077134, –121.74579 / N48° 4.628′ W121° 44.7474′

🏹 🌸 ♨ 🐾 🚶 ♿

Scope out ice caves formed by melting snow at the foot of Big Four Mountain at the end of a family-friendly trail.

DISTANCE: 2.4 miles round-tip
DURATION: 1.5 hours
ELEVATION CHANGE: 250 feet
EFFORT: Easy
TRAIL: Gravel path, paved path, boardwalk
USERS: Hikers, wheelchair users, leashed dogs
SEASON: late June-September
PASSES/FEES: Northwest Forest Pass
MAPS: Green Trails Map 110 for Silverton
CONTACT: Verlot Public Service Center, 360/691-7791, www.fs.usda.gov;
   Darrington Ranger District, 360/436-1155.

Shortly before publication, the Forest Service removed the bridge over the Stillaguamish River and it is unclear when the bridge will be replaced. Hikers can still reach the caves if they ford the river, which is often about knee deep in summertime. Contact the ranger station for current conditions.

START THE HIKE

▶ **MILE 0-0.3: Information Kiosk to Pond**
Starting on the paved path left of the information kiosk, a walk to the **Big Four Ice Caves** immerses visitors in the wonders of nature. Salmonberries, ferns, and mossy trees line the trail that turns into a wooden boardwalk after 0.1 mile. Continue to pass nurse logs and uprooted trees for another 0.2 mile before reaching the intersection with a dirt path. Turn left and get your first glimpse of **Big Four Mountain** through the trees. In short order you'll pass a pond, a good place to linger and listen to birds and perhaps glimpse a beaver.

▶ **MILE 0.3-1: Pond to Forest Edge**
Another 0.1 mile brings you to an aluminum bridge spanning the **Stillaguamish River**, followed soon after by a wooden bridge over a creek. The 0.6 mile beyond the bridge cuts through the woods before the evergreen veil is lifted and the rocky slopes of the mountain can be viewed from top to bottom. Waterfalls look like tiny icicles as they cascade over the upper reaches of the peak. At the base of the mountain's avalanche chutes, water plunges into huge piles of melting snow, helping to carve the caves that lure so many visitors.

▶ **MILE 1-1.2: Forest Edge to Big Four Ice Caves**
A boulder-lined **cul-de-sac** marks the end of the trail in 0.2 mile. Here hikers will see warnings to go no farther. A boulder is engraved with the Forest

NORTH CASCADES

Big Four Ice Caves

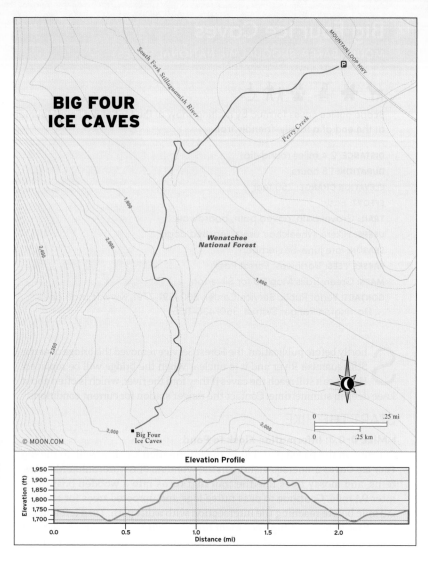

BIG FOUR ICE CAVES

South Fork Stillaguamish River

MOUNTAIN LOOP HWY

Perry Creek

Wenatchee National Forest

1,800

1,800

2,400

2,000

2,200

2,000

2,000

1,800

Big Four
Ice Caves

© MOON.COM

| 0 | .25 mi |
| 0 | .25 km |

Elevation Profile

Elevation (ft)

1,950
1,900
1,850
1,800
1,750
1,700

0.0   0.5   1.0   1.5   2.0

Distance (mi)

Service logo and a description of the hazards of getting too close to the caves. Climbing atop the caves can be just as dangerous as exploring inside. Rangers don't always patrol this area, but they warn of avalanches, fissures in the snowfield, and falling rocks. Enjoy the ice caves from a distance.

When ready, return the way you came.

DIRECTIONS

From Granite Falls, follow the Mountain Loop Highway (Alder Avenue in town) east 25.2 miles and find the sign for the trailhead parking lot on the right. It is located 0.6 mile past a turnout for the Big Four Picnic Area, which offers alternate access to the ice caves trail. Three ADA restrooms are located at the trailhead.

GPS COORDINATES: 48.06598, –121.51048 / N48° 3.9588' W121° 30.6288'

NEARBY CAMPGROUNDS

NAME	DESCRIPTION	FACILITIES	SEASON	FEES
Verlot Campground	situated on the South Fork Stillaguamish River	25 RV and tent sites, restrooms	late April-late September	$18.34

Mountain Loop Highway, Verlot, Mount Baker-Snoqualmie National Forest, 877/444-6777, www.recreation.gov

NAME	DESCRIPTION	FACILITIES	SEASON	FEES
Newhalem Campground	located near Newhalem Creek and the Skagit River	107 RV and tent sites, restrooms	mid-May-mid-September	$16

Highway 20, Newhalem, North Cascades National Park, 360/854-7200, www.recreation.gov

NAME	DESCRIPTION	FACILITIES	SEASON	FEES
Colonial Creek Campground	two large camping areas set amid old-growth forest on Diablo Lake at the base of Colonial Peak	135 RV and tent sites, restrooms	year-round	$16

Highway 20, Diablo, North Cascades National Park, 877/444-6777, www.recreation.gov

NAME	DESCRIPTION	FACILITIES	SEASON	FEES
Douglas Fir Campground	under Douglas firs, hemlocks, and cedars on the North Fork Nooksack River	26 RV and tent sites, restrooms	late May-early September	$18.54-20.39

Mount Baker Highway, Glacier, Mount Baker-Snoqualmie National Forest, 360/419-5115, www.recreation.gov

NAME	DESCRIPTION	FACILITIES	SEASON	FEES
Klipchuck Campground	set in the woods along Early Winters Creek	46 RV and tent sites, restrooms	May-October	$12

Highway 20, Mazama, Okanogan-Wenatchee National Forest, 509/996-4000

CENTRAL CASCADES

The Central Cascades might be Washington's most convenient place to wander wilderness. Alpine lakes, towering waterfalls, and rocky mountaintops are all a day hike away in this region of the Cascades traversed by I-90, U.S. 2, and Highway 410. With an abundance of entry points, visitors can easily access the Alpine Lakes Wilderness and wander among cedars, Douglas firs, and, in fall, golden larches. But that's not all: Hikers can explore historical railroad routes and walk through a 2.3-mile tunnel; climb to a fire lookout with a view stretching from Mount Rainier north to Mount Baker and from eastern Washington west to the Olympics; or splash in a frigid lake and catch glimpses of mountain goats, deer, eagles, and other wildlife.

▲ SNOW LAKE

▲ FIRE LOOKOUT ON GRANITE MOUNTAIN

◄ THE HIKE TO LAKE INGALLS

1 Wallace Falls
DISTANCE: 5.2 miles round-trip
DURATION: 2.5 hours
EFFORT: Easy/moderate

2 Lake Serene and Bridal Veil Falls
DISTANCE: 8.2 miles round-trip
DURATION: 5 hours
EFFORT: Moderate

3 Barclay Lake
DISTANCE: 4.4 miles round-trip
DURATION: 2.5 hours
EFFORT: Easy/moderate

4 Iron Goat Trail
DISTANCE: 5.9 miles round-trip
DURATION: 3.5 hours
EFFORT: Easy/moderate

5 Colchuck Lake
DISTANCE: 8.2 miles round-trip
DURATION: 4.5 hours
EFFORT: Moderate

6 Talapus and Olallie Lakes
DISTANCE: 5.6 miles round-trip
DURATION: 3 hours
EFFORT: Moderate

7 Granite Mountain
DISTANCE: 8.6 miles round-trip
DURATION: 5 hours
EFFORT: Strenuous

8 Snow Lake
DISTANCE: 6.8 miles round-trip
DURATION: 3.5 hours
EFFORT: Moderate

9 Palouse to Cascades State Park Trail: Snoqualmie Tunnel
DISTANCE: 5.2 miles round-trip
DURATION: 3 hours
EFFORT: Easy/moderate

10 Lake Ingalls
DISTANCE: 9.6 miles round-trip
DURATION: 4.5 hours
EFFORT: Moderate/strenuous

▾ TRAIL TO TALAPUS AND OLALLIE LAKES

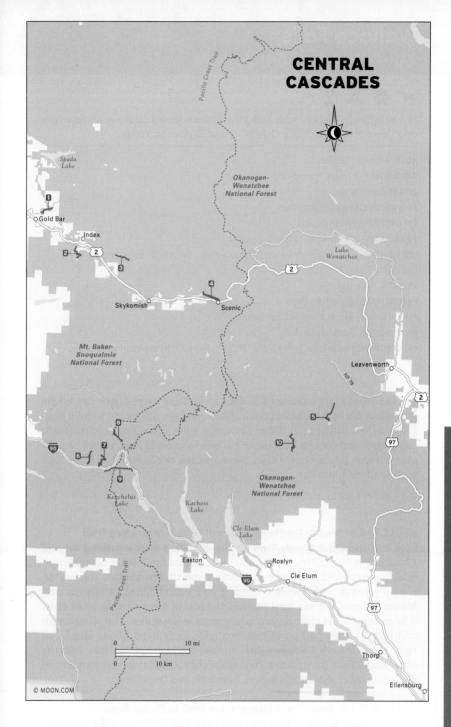

CENTRAL CASCADES

Wallace Falls

WALLACE FALLS STATE PARK, GOLD BAR

Follow a family-friendly path along the Wallace River to a series of waterfalls and views of the Cascades, Olympics, and Skykomish Valley.

BEST: Waterfall Hikes
DISTANCE: 5.2 miles round-trip
DURATION: 2.5 hours
ELEVATION CHANGE: 1,300 feet
EFFORT: Easy/moderate
TRAIL: Wide and single-track dirt paths
USERS: Hikers, wheelchair users (first 0.4 mile), leashed dogs, mountain bikers (first 0.4 mile)
SEASON: Year-round
PASSES/FEES: Discover Pass
MAPS: Green Trails Map 142 for Index
PARK HOURS: 8am–dusk daily
CONTACT: Wallace Falls State Park, 360/793-0420, http://parks.state.wa.us

n the woods just outside Gold Bar, the Wallace River draws day hikers of every ilk as it makes three dramatic plunges during its 15-mile journey to the Skykomish River. Featuring quiet lakes, old-growth forest, campsites, and cabins, 1,380-acre Wallace Falls State Park would be popular without its namesake falls. Nevertheless, the 265-foot cascade tops most visitors' to-do list.

START THE HIKE

▶ **MILE 0-0.5: Woody Trailhead to Small Falls Interpretive Trail**
Find the wide, flat **Woody Trail** on the east side of the parking lot and spend 0.3 mile walking under crackling power lines amid blackberries, huckleberries, and salmonberries. Before the trail bends into the woods, visit a **turnout** with views of Baring and Philadelphia Mountains and Mount Index. Over the next 0.1 mile the sound of the power lines gives way to that of the river as you arrive at an **intersection**. The wheelchair- and bike-friendly portion of this excursion ends here; hikers should go right, pass through a **wooden gate,** and descend toward the river. Pass the short Small Falls Interpretive Trail in another 0.1 mile, as you wander under a canopy of red cedar, western hemlock, and Douglas fir.

▶ **MILE 0.5-1.8: Small Falls Interpretive Trail to Picnic Area**
Two side trails leading to the multiuse Greg Ball Trail are on the left at 0.5 and 1 mile beyond the Small Falls spur. Continue straight both times and,

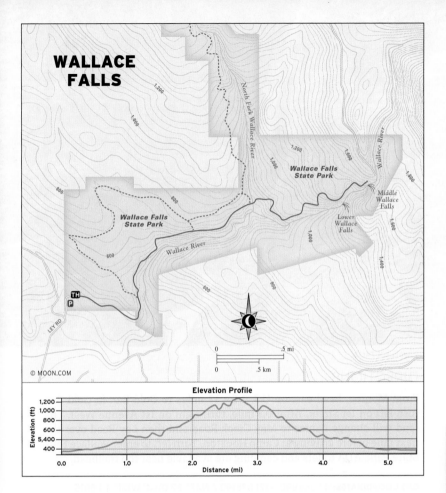

WALLACE FALLS

Wallace Falls State Park

Wallace Falls State Park

Middle Wallace Falls

Lower Wallace Falls

North Fork Wallace River

Wallace River

Wallace River

© MOON.COM

0   .5 mi

0   .5 km

Elevation Profile

after the second, descend to a **wooden bridge** spanning the North Fork Wallace River. The trail's first climbing of any significance awaits across the bridge, but don't worry: The climb is short and in 0.3 mile you'll arrive at a covered **picnic area** perfect for a break.

▶ MILE 1.8-2.6: Picnic Area to Upper Falls Overlook

The **lower falls viewing area** is 0.3 mile farther. Watch the river careen over cliffs at what's arguably the most impressive of the viewing areas. Scan the treetops and sky for bald eagles.

There's more to see, but the trail makes you work for these views. Climb (more steeply now) through the trees 0.3 mile to a view of the Skykomish Valley and the Olympics. Then continue 0.2 mile to the **upper falls overlook**.

You can extend your trip by exploring more of the park's 12 miles of trails, but retrace your steps for the most direct route back to the parking lot.

▲ WALLACE FALLS

DIRECTIONS

From Monroe, head east on U.S. 2 for 13 miles to Gold Bar. In Gold Bar, turn left on 1st Street. After 0.3 mile, turn right on 1st Avenue West. The road will change names to May Creek Road and then Ley Road over the next mile before arriving at Camp Houston. Turn left to enter Wallace Falls State Park. ADA toilets and camping are available near the trailhead.

GPS COORDINATES: 47.866990, -121.678192 / N47° 52.0194' W121° 40.6915'

BEST NEARBY BITES

For many who love to the play in the mountains along U.S. 2, the **Sultan Bakery** (711 W. Stevens Ave., Sultan, 360/793-7996, 5:15am-7pm daily) is synonymous with the region. Start your adventure with a breakfast pastry or cap it with a large sandwich built on soft, fresh bread. Or do both. From the trailhead, the 7-mile drive west takes 14 minutes via U.S. 2.

2 Lake Serene and Bridal Veil Falls

MOUNT BAKER-SNOQUALMIE NATIONAL FOREST, INDEX

Relax at the edge of a lake shimmering beneath the rocky slopes of Mount Index after visiting a massive seven-tiered waterfall.

BEST: Waterfall Hikes
DISTANCE: 8.2 miles round-trip
DURATION: 5 hours
ELEVATION CHANGE: 2,500 feet
EFFORT: Moderate
TRAIL: Dirt, steps, slippery rocks
USERS: Hikers, leashed dogs
SEASON: May-November
PASSES/FEES: Northwest Forest Pass
MAPS: Green Trails Map 142 for Index
CONTACT: Mount Baker-Snoqualmie National Forest, Skykomish Ranger District, 360/677-2414

Located just south of U.S. 2 and the confluence of the Skykomish River's north and south forks, this hike is ideal for people who love alpine lakes and giant waterfalls. In fact, one of the beauties of this trip is you don't have to venture all the way to the lake to be blown away. A round-trip to Bridal Veil Falls is 4.2 miles, a trip to the lake and back is 7.4 miles, and visiting both is 8.2 miles.

START THE HIKE

▶ **MILE 0-2.1: Old Logging Trail to Bridal Veil Falls**
From the parking lot, head south on an **old logging trail**. Pass alders, maples, Douglas firs, and hemlocks and step over creeks flowing toward the South Fork Skykomish over the next 1.7 miles. After descending some steps, turn right on the **spur for Bridal Veil Falls**. It's just 0.4 mile farther, but the way is steep and includes several sections of stairs. On warm summer days you might appreciate the spray from the falls as you arrive at the viewing areas. Other days, you might wish you packed a raincoat. Bridal Veil Creek fans out on the cliffs as it splashes down from Lake Serene. The falls drop nearly 1,300 feet over seven tiers. The entirety of the falls is too much to take in from any one spot, but you'll have no problem finding an impressive vantage point. Just be careful on the slippery rocks.

▶ **MILE 2.1-4.5: Bridal Veil Falls to Bridal Veil Falls Bridge and Lake Serene**
When you're finished marveling at the force of nature, descend 0.4 mile back to the **junction**. Turn right and, after 0.2 mile, cross the **Bridal Veil Falls bridge** to continue to Lake Serene. The most significant bit of climbing sits

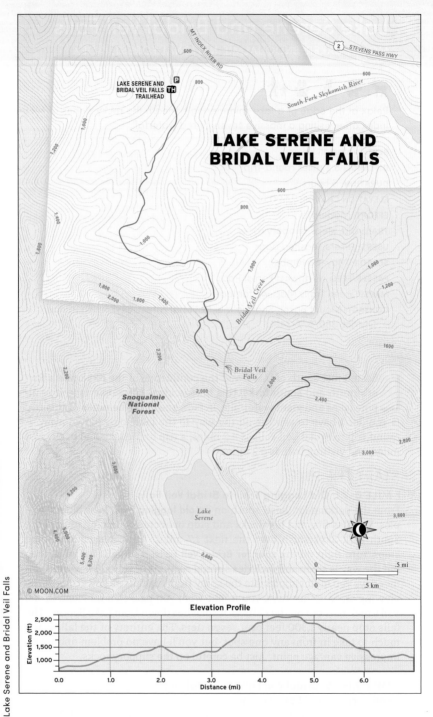

LAKE SERENE AND BRIDAL VEIL FALLS

LAKE SERENE AND BRIDAL VEIL FALLS TRAILHEAD

MT INDEX RIVER RD

STEVENS PASS HWY

South Fork Skykomish River

Bridal Veil Creek

Bridal Veil Falls

Snoqualmie National Forest

Lake Serene

© MOON.COM

0   .5 mi

0   .5 km

Elevation Profile

Elevation (ft) | Distance (mi)

2,500
2,000
1,500
1,000

0.0   1.0   2.0   3.0   4.0   5.0   6.0

▲ MOUNT INDEX

between the bridge and the lake. Spend 1.8 miles climbing **switchbacks** up 1,500 feet until the lake's stunning beauty finally comes into view.

▶ MILE 4.5-8.2: Lake Serene to Parking Lot

Lake Serene mirrors Index's sheer rock walls and invites you to stay and relax. Early in the season, when snow and ice still cling to the imposing cliffs of Mount Index, it's not uncommon for serenity to be interrupted by a loud crack as avalanches rumble down the slopes on the other side of the lake.

Despite this occasional drama, Lake Serene lives up to its name, even when it draws a crowd. Find room to sit on a shoreline boulder and do your own reflecting at the north end of the lake, where the path leads over the lake's outlet and passes a short spur trail leading to a view of the valley. When you've had your fill of serenity, ready your knees for the downhill return via the same trail.

DIRECTIONS

From Monroe, drive east for 20 miles on U.S. 2 and turn right on Mount Index Road just before a steel bridge crossing the South Fork Skykomish River. Drive 0.3 mile and turn right to access the parking lot. Vault toilets are in the parking lot.

GPS COORDINATES: 47.809189, −121.573693 / N47° 48.5513′ W121° 34.4216′

Follow a family-friendly path along a creek to Barclay Lake at the foot of Baring Mountain.

DISTANCE: 4.4 miles round-trip
DURATION: 2.5 hours
ELEVATION CHANGE: 550 feet
EFFORT: Easy/moderate
TRAIL: Single track
USERS: Hikers, leashed dogs
SEASON: April-November
PASSES/FEES: Northwest Forest Pass
MAPS: Green Trails Map 143 for Monte Cristo
CONTACT: Mount Baker-Snoqualmie National Forest, Skykomish Ranger District, 360/677-2414, www.fs.usda.gov

START THE HIKE

If solitude is what you seek, consider saving this popular hike for a weekday in mid-spring or mid-fall.

▶ **MILE 0-1.2: Parking Lot to Bridge**
Starting from the southeast end of the parking lot, the trail dives immediately into the shade provided by a forest recovering from a previous clearcut. The path has mellow ups and downs as it follows Barclay Creek to the lake, but it is friendly for legs of all ages and is popular with backpackers, anglers, and families.

Walk among the cedars, Douglas firs, and western hemlocks on a path lined by salmonberry, ferns, and moss. After 1.2 miles reach a large **footlog bridge** with a handrail. Cross the creek and find the most substantial—but still gentle—climb.

BARCLAY LAKE ▶

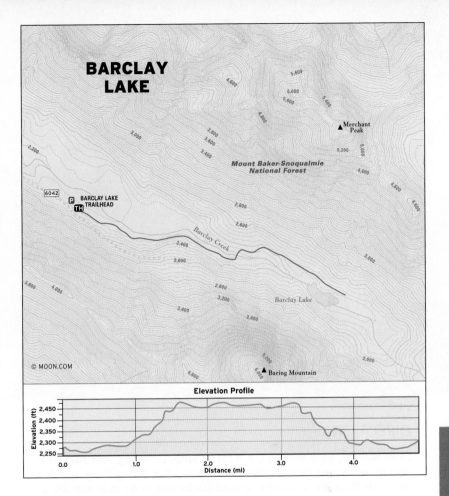

BARCLAY LAKE

Elevation Profile

> ▶ MILE 1.2–1.7: **Bridge to Barclay Lake**

The incline won't slow you much, but the view might stop you in your tracks. Just a few hundred yards past the bridge, 6,129-foot Baring Mountain comes into view through the trees on the right side of the trail. At 0.5 mile past the bridge, get your first view of the blue waters of **Barclay Lake** glistening in the sunlight.

> ▶ MILE 1.7–2.2: **Barclay Lake to Picnic Areas**

While the trail continues for another 0.5 mile along the lake to a large camping spot and a spur trail leading to a vault toilet, you need not travel that far to find a spot to stop. Any of the trailside spots accessing the lake are ideal for picnicking, taking a dip, and enjoying Baring's towering splendor. This is a good place to introduce kids to alpine lake fishing. The lake is open year-round for rainbow trout fishing.

When you're finished playing at the lake, simply retrace your steps to return to the trailhead.

▲ BARING MOUNTAIN

DIRECTIONS

From Monroe, head east on U.S. 2 for 27 miles to Baring. Just past milepost 41 and across from the Bavarian-themed Der Baring Store, turn left on 635th Place NE. Cross the railroad tracks and in 0.3 mile stay left as the road becomes Forest Road 6024. Continue 3.9 miles to the trailhead. A privy is located at the small parking area.

GPS COORDINATES: 47.792468, –121.459345 / N47°47.5481 W121°27.5607

BEST NEARBY BITES

Adam's Northwest Bistro & Brewery (104 N. Lewis St., Monroe, 360/794-4056, www.adamsnwbistro.com, hours vary) is a relaxed bistro serving local, sustainable foods. Chef Adam Hoffman left Seattle's fine-dining scene to open the restaurant, where bacon, salmon, and brisket are smoked in-house and the beer is brewed on-site. From the trailhead, the 30-mile drive northwest takes about 50 minutes via U.S. 2.

4 Iron Goat Trail

STEVENS PASS

🦌 ❀ ⚱ 🐾 🚶 ♿

Hear modern trains chugging over Stevens Pass while exploring the remnants of the old Great Northern Railway

DISTANCE: 5.9 miles round-trip
DURATION: 3.5 hours
ELEVATION CHANGE: 800 feet
EFFORT: Easy/moderate
TRAIL: Dirt, boardwalk, short paved section
USERS: Hikers, wheelchair users, leashed dogs
SEASON: Late May–November
PASSES/FEES: Northwest Forest Pass
MAPS: Green Trails Map 176 for Stevens Pass
CONTACT: Mount Baker-Snoqualmie National Forest, Skykomish Ranger District, 360/677-2414

In 1893, when the Great Northern Railway pushed its way over Stevens Pass and linked Seattle to Saint Paul, Minnesota, it was considered an epic feat of engineering. Today, thanks to an epic feat of volunteering, the remains of the route make for a riveting walking history lesson.

START THE HIKE

▶ **MILE 0-0.1: Red Caboose to Windy Crossover Trail Junction**
Starting from the **red caboose** at the **Iron Goat Trail Interpretive Site**, follow a gentle uphill grade into the woods, continuing straight past the Windy Crossover trail you'll use to finish this loop. This ADA-friendly section of the trail is unpaved (after a short, paved stretch near the parking lot) and surprisingly narrow considering its history.

▶ **MILE 0.1-0.3: Windy Crossover Trail Junction to Cement Wall**
In 0.2 mile (past the first of several white signs marked with the old rail line mileage), reach the first long, tall **cement wall** lining the trail. The walls, surreal in this natural setting, are remnants of snowsheds that covered the tracks and protected trains from avalanches. The trail is lined with ferns, wildflowers, huckleberries, and nettles and is a good place to view owls, woodpeckers, jays, and other birds, but it's the relics of the past that set this hike apart.

▶ **MILE 0.3-1.8: Cement Wall to Twin Tunnels and Railroad Tie Bridge**
In 1 mile visit an **overlook** with a view of the current railway. A few steps farther bring you to the **Twin Tunnels,** blasted through the granite in 1916. You can't walk through these tunnels, but you can step inside and read an interpretive sign. The trail skirts the tunnels and, over the next 0.2

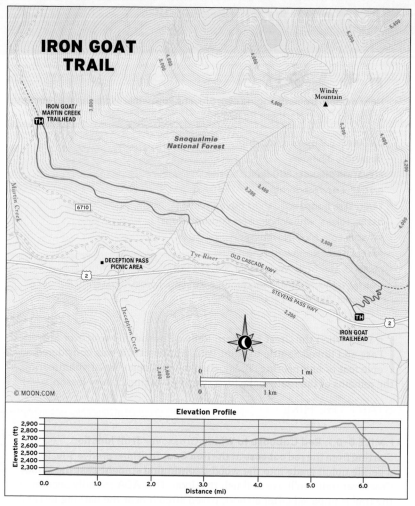

IRON GOAT TRAIL

mile, uses a **boardwalk** to pass through a narrow gulch. Cross a **bridge** made of railroad ties 0.1 mile farther. Go another 0.2 mile and you might feel a draft of cold air as you pass an adit (one of the tunnel's small ventilation shafts).

▶ **MILE 1.8-3: Railroad Tie Bridge to Martin Creek Crossover**
After 1 mile, near the Martin Creek trailhead, the ADA portion of the journey comes to an end as you turn right on the **Martin Creek Crossover** and ascend 0.2 mile to the upper portion of loop. At the mouth of **Tunnel 14,** turn right to follow a rougher, but still easily manageable dirt path. Pass salmonberries and ferns growing beneath Douglas fir and hemlock. Parts of the trail are overgrown, so take care to avoid tripping on unseen hazards.

▲ BRIDGE ON IRON GOAT TRAIL

▶ **MILE 3–4.2: Martin Creek Crossover to Reservoir**
After 1.2 miles on the upper trail pass the **Spillway Spur** on the left. The trail leads to a reservoir in a ravine below Windy Mountain.

▶ **MILE 4.2–5.9: Reservoir to Parking Lot**
Continue on the upper trail 1.2 miles to the **Windy Point Tunnel**. To finish the loop, turn right on the **Windy Crossover trail**. In a steep, switchbacking 0.5-mile stretch you'll give back all the vertical you slowly accumulated during your walk.

Turn left at the intersection toward the bottom to return to the parking lot.

DIRECTIONS

From Monroe, follow U.S. 2 east 43 miles to the Iron Goat Interpretive Site, located on the left side of the road about 9 miles east of Skykomish. Toilets, interpretive signs, and an old caboose are located at the trailhead.

GPS COORDINATES: 47.711262, –121.161761 / N47° 42.6757' W121° 9.7057'

BEST NEARBY BITES
Zeke's Drive-In (43918 U.S. 2, Gold Bar, 360/793-2287, 11am-7:30pm Mon.-Wed., 11am-8pm Thurs.-Sun.) opened in 1968 and is still a popular roadside burger stop. Menu highlights include two dozen flavors of shakes and the half-pound Honeymoon Special burger. From the trailhead, the 27-mile drive northwest takes about 30 minutes via U.S. 2.

🦌 ❀

Sample the granite grandeur of the Enchantments on a rugged trail climbing to one of the Northwest's most stunning alpine lakes.

BEST: Brew Hikes
DISTANCE: 8.2 miles round-trip
DURATION: 4.5 hours
ELEVATION CHANGE: 2,300 feet
EFFORT: Moderate
TRAIL: Roots, rocks, bridge, footlog
USERS: Hikers
SEASON: July-October
PASSES/FEES: Northwest Forest Pass; free day-use pass available at trailhead
MAPS: Green Trails Map 209S for The Enchantments
CONTACT: Okanogan-Wenatchee National Forest, Wenatchee River Ranger District, 509/548-2550, www.fs.usda.gov

As this trail dives immediately into dense forest, it's not obvious why the Enchantments are one of the most beloved hiking destinations in Washington. But it will all make sense when you reach the deep-blue water of Colchuck Lake reflecting the granite spires of Dragontail and Colchuck Peaks.

START THE HIKE

▶ **MILE 0-2.4: Stuart Lake Trail to Colchuck Lake Trail**
Each party is required to register at the trailhead kiosk and carry a free permit. Paperwork complete, follow the Stuart Lake Trail as it climbs gradually along Mountaineer Creek. Even when you can't see the creek, its burble keeps you company as you wander the thick forest and its pine trees and boulders the size of RVs. In 1.6 miles, cross the creek on a **footlog,** after which the trail steepens and the forest thins. Catch an occasional glimpse of the steep valley walls over the next 0.8 mile before arriving at a well-marked intersection; turn left on the Colchuck Lake Trail to keep climbing toward the lake.

▶ **MILE 2.4-4.1: Colchuck Lake Trail to Boulders**
In 0.1 mile use a **bridge** to cross Mountaineer Creek to a boulder field. Follow the path as it bends right and winds through the boulders, running briefly along the creek before reentering the forest and resuming the ascent. Over the next 1.6 miles the trail ascends **granite slopes** offering occasional views of the valley. The trail is rooted and rocky, adding to the challenge, but the payoff is well worth the effort.

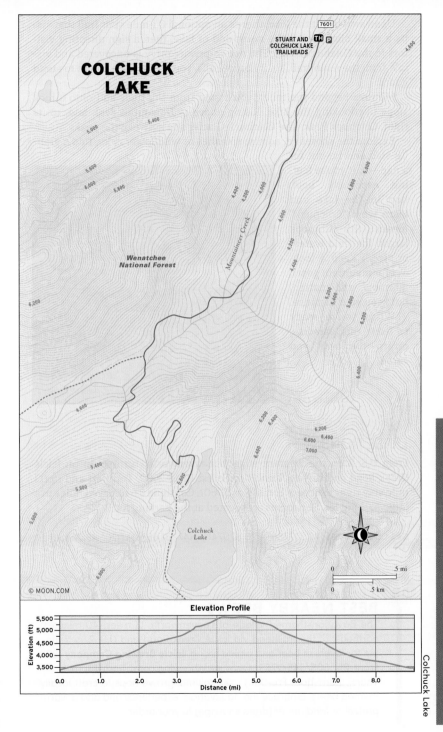

COLCHUCK
LAKE

7601

STUART AND
COLCHUCK LAKE
TRAILHEADS

TH P

Wenatchee
National Forest

Mountaineer Creek

Colchuck
Lake

0   .5 mi
0   .5 km

Elevation Profile

© MOON.COM

CENTRAL CASCADES

Colchuck Lake

177

Upon arriving at the **lake**, there's an optional 0.1-mile spur trail that visits a small blue pool at the north end of lake, then a sign directing visitors to the Colchuck toilet. The not-so-private privy is uncovered and visible from the main trail, so, if nature calls, you might ask a friend to stand guard.

Minutes beyond the toilet, you'll step from the trees and onto a rock slope overlooking the lake. Rising above is Dragontail Peak and, to its right, Colchuck Peak. The Colchuck Glacier sits between the peaks.

Explore the shoreline, admire splashes of wildflower color, find a granite slab and lie out for a nap—or, if you're feeling especially bold, hop in the lake and learn what "Colchuck" means. (It's Chinook jargon for "cold water" or "ice.") Keep a lookout for mountain goats, marmots, and marten, but keep your distance.

When you're ready to leave this paradise, return the way you came.

COLCHUCK LAKE ▶

DIRECTIONS

From U.S. 2 on the western edge of Leavenworth, turn south on Icicle Creek Road and drive 8.4 miles to Forest Road 7600. Turn left and in 0.1 mile stay right to access Forest Road 7601. Continue 3.6 unpaved miles to a large parking lot. Restrooms are located at the parking lot.

GPS COORDINATES: 47.527788, –120.820741 / N47° 31.6673' W120° 49.2445'

BEST NEARBY BREWS

The Bavarian-themed village of Leavenworth, 13 miles (40 minutes) northeast of the trailhead via Icicle Creek Road and U.S. 2, is a utopia for lovers of beer and alpine hiking. **Icicle Brewing Company** (935 Front St., 509/548-2739, www.iciclebrewing.com, 11am-10pm Sun.-Thurs., 11am-11pm Fri.-Sat.) uses Yakima-grown hops to craft locally themed beers. Embrace the "fauxvarian" experience and add a warm pretzel or *landjaeger* (dried sausage) to your order.

Take a dip in chilly Talapus or Olallie Lake at the end of a recently reconstructed family-friendly trail.

DISTANCE: 5.6 miles round-trip
DURATION: 3 hours
ELEVATION CHANGE: 1,250 feet
EFFORT: Moderate
TRAIL: New dirt paths, roots, boardwalk
USERS: Hikers, leashed dogs
SEASON: Mid-May–early November
PASSES/FEES: Northwest Forest Pass
MAPS: Green Trails Map 207 for Snoqualmie Pass
CONTACT: Mount Baker-Snoqualmie National Forest, Snoqualmie Ranger District, 425/888-1421, www.fs.usda.gov

The trail starts at the far end of the undersized parking lot, but odds are you'll start by walking a section of the dirt road if you don't arrive early on summer weekends. The shimmering lakes and relatively easy trail draw a crowd and it's not uncommon for parked cars to line the side of the road for a quarter mile or more. But as is the case with popular trails, there's good reason for the crowds.

START THE HIKE

▶ **MILE 0–0.2: Parking Lot to Talapus Lake Trail**
The **Talapus Lake Trail** is wide as it dives from the parking lot into a forest of Douglas fir. At 0.2 mile those with a keen eye and good memory might notice something is different: The Washington Trails Association, a legion of hardworking volunteers, unveiled a new section of trail here in 2017. The new route climbs gradually through the trees as it enters the Alpine Lakes Wilderness. The trail is made wide enough to handle heavy traffic while maintaining a route that's relatively easy to follow.

▶ **MILE 0.2–1.7: Talapus Lake Trail to Talapus Lake**
Walk 1.3 miles along gurgling **Talapus Creek** to an intersection with a sign pointing the way to the lakes. Go right to stay on the trail and cross a **footbridge** moments before arriving at **Talapus Lake,** 0.2 mile beyond the intersection.

▶ **MILE 1.7–2.8: Talapus Lake to Olallie Lake**
An obvious open space below the trail at 17.4-acre Talapus Lake is where most hikers stop. Hikers take turns posing for pictures on shoreline logs while others scout places to swim. The trail continues to the right of the lake and climbs gradually on rougher, root-strewn tread. After 0.8 mile

Talapus and Olallie Lakes

CENTRAL CASCADES

179

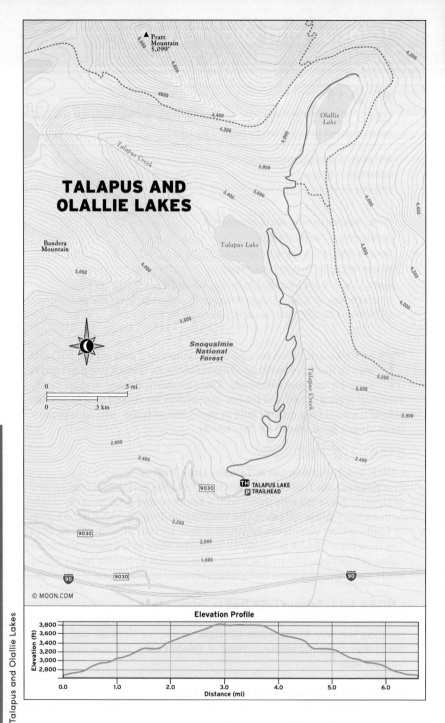

TALAPUS AND OLALLIE LAKES

Pratt Mountain
5,099'

Olallie Lake

Talapus Creek

Talapus Lake

Bandera
Mountain

Snoqualmie
National
Forest

Talapus Creek

0   .5 mi

0   .5 km

9030

TH TALAPUS LAKE
P TRAILHEAD

9030

9030

90

90

© MOON.COM

Elevation Profile

Elevation (ft)

Distance (mi)

▲ TALAPUS LAKE

reach a **signed intersection** pointing the way to Olallie and Pratt Lakes. (Pratt is an option for extending your hike by about 6 miles round-trip.)

Turn left to follow the spur trail to **Olallie Lake.** In 0.3 mile, the 13.2-acre lake comes into view through the trees. A bit farther, a trailside clearing on the right offers access to the shoreline. This is a good place for day hikers to call their destination, but the trail does continue. A side trail to a toilet is a few steps farther, and campsites are available as the trail continues to the north end of the lake. Kids can take a dip in the lakes that by late summer are warm by Alpine Lakes Wilderness standards. (To be clear, that's still pretty chilly.) Fishing is permitted at both lakes and the state Department of Fish and Wildlife sometimes stocks Talapus with rainbow trout.

However you choose to enjoy the wilderness lakes, when it's time to go retrace your steps to the trailhead.

DIRECTIONS

From Seattle, follow I-90 east to exit 45. Turn left and follow Forest Road 9030 for 0.9 mile to an intersection with Mason Lake Road. Turn right to stay on Forest Road 9030 and continue 2.3 miles to the small parking lot. A vault toilet is located at the trailhead.

GPS COORDINATES: 47.401160, –121.518412 / N47° 24.0696' W122° 31.1047'

🦌 ❀ 🐾

Test your fitness and reward yourself with a sweeping view of the Cascades from an old fire lookout.

BEST: Fall Hikes
DISTANCE: 8.6 miles round-trip
DURATION: 5 hours
ELEVATION CHANGE: 3,800 feet
EFFORT: Strenuous
TRAIL: Dirt and rock trail
USERS: Hikers, leashed dogs
SEASON: Late June–early November
PASSES/FEES: Northwest Forest Pass
MAPS: Green Trails Map 207 for Snoqualmie Pass
CONTACT: Mount Baker–Snoqualmie National Forest, Snoqualmie Ranger District, 425/888-1421, www.fs.usda.gov

A classic hike for those who like their fall colors with a side of thigh burn, the route climbs relentlessly from I-90 to one of the best views on the Snoqualmie Pass corridor.

START THE HIKE

▶ **MILE 0-1: Pratt Lake Trailhead to Granite Mountain Trail**
Starting on the north side of the parking lot, follow the **Pratt Lake Trail** as it tilts upward, making sweeping switchbacks. After 1 mile, turn right on the **Granite Mountain Trail** (the Pratt Lake Trail continues straight).

▶ **MILE 1-2.4: Granite Mountain Trail to Meadow**
Granite Mountain Trail heads northeast for 0.4 mile before the switchbacks tighten and the assault on the valley wall gets more challenging. The trail pops in and out of the trees, offering glimpses of changing leaves if you visit in the fall. These open areas are an appreciated dose of variety, but the slopes bring an element of danger in early spring when snow and ice sometime linger high on the mountain. Granite Mountain is prone to avalanches; early-season hikers should have experience, proper equipment, and the latest avalanche forecasts (www.nwac.us).

After another 1 mile of switchbacks, start reaping the reward for your work as you step out of the trees. The **meadow** yields huckleberries and views of the valley and surrounding peaks. This is also where fall colors are most dazzling.

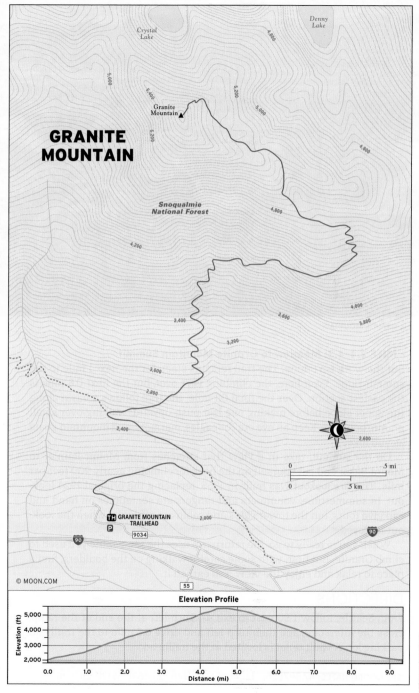

GRANITE MOUNTAIN

Crystal Lake

Denny Lake

Granite Mountain ▲

Snoqualmie National Forest

TH GRANITE MOUNTAIN TRAILHEAD
P
90
9034

90

55

0 _____ .5 mi
0 _____ .5 km

© MOON.COM

Elevation Profile

Elevation (ft)
5,000
4,000
3,000
2,000

0.0 1.0 2.0 3.0 4.0 5.0 6.0 7.0 8.0 9.0
Distance (mi)

▲ GRANITE MOUNTAIN

▶ **MILE 2.4–4.3: Meadow to Granite Mountain Summit**
But the work isn't done. The trail remains steep for the next 1 mile to the summit ridge. Even here, the climbing isn't over, but the next 0.8 mile is the easiest section. Over the final 0.1 mile, the trail follows a basin along the upper slope before making one last push upward, walking over small granite boulders. Keep an eye out for eagles, marmots, and mountain goats as you hike.

On the summit, take in a view that stretches from Mount Rainier to Mount Baker and pat yourself on the back for climbing nearly 900 feet per mile. The **fire lookout** was built in 1955, replacing the original 1924 lookout. In summertime, volunteers and rangers are sometimes on hand and can give tours, but the tower steps and cabin are off-limits when the lookout is closed.

When you're ready to go, the return trip uses the same route you used to climb Granite. But first, with some careful walking on the boulders, find a place to relax and enjoy the view. You earned it.

DIRECTIONS

From Seattle, follow I-90 east to exit 47. Turn left at the end of the ramp, cross the interstate, and then turn left and drive 0.3 mile to the trailhead parking lot. A vault toilet is located at the trailhead.

GPS COORDINATES: 47.397826, –121.486560 / N48° 23.8696′ W121° 29.1936′

Snow Lake
ALPINE LAKES WILDERNESS, SNOQUALMIE PASS

🦌 ❀ 🐾

Hike the most popular trail in the Alpine Lakes Wilderness to a lake reflecting jagged Cascade peaks.

DISTANCE: 6.8 miles round-trip
DURATION: 3.5 hours
ELEVATION CHANGE: 1,800 feet
EFFORT: Moderate
TRAIL: Rocks, dirt trail
USERS: Hikers, leashed dogs
SEASON: Late June–early November
PASSES/FEES: Northwest Forest Pass
MAPS: Green Trails Map 207 for Snoqualmie Pass
CONTACT: Mount Baker-Snoqualmie National Forest, Snoqualmie Ranger District, 425/888-1421, www.fs.usda.gov

On sunny summer weekends, the large parking lot at Alpental ski area is nearly as packed as it is on powder days in winter. There are 615 miles of trails and more than 700 lakes in the Alpine Lakes Wilderness, and none receive more visitors than Snow Lake and its namesake trail. The steep, jagged faces of Roosevelt and Chair Peaks reflect in the 152.9-acre lake, creating the setting that lures so many.

START THE HIKE

▶ **MILE 0–1.7: Alpental Parking Lot to Source Lake Spur Trail**
Start with a quick climb up crib steps across the street from the northeast corner of the Alpental parking lot, then ascend gradually while traversing a slope above the South Fork Snoqualmie River.

For 1.7 miles pass through forest and cross avalanche chutes on your way to the intersection with the **Source Lake spur trail**. It's a gentle and peaceful walk in the summer, but winter avalanches have killed snowshoers on this trail.

▶ **MILE 1.7–2.4: Source Lake Spur Trail to Snow Lake Ridge**
At the intersection, turn right for 0.7 mile of **switchbacks** climbing to a ridge above Snow Lake. A sign bolted to a ridge-top tree welcomes visitors to the wilderness area. The ridge separates the watersheds of the south and middle forks of the Snoqualmie.

▶ **MILE 2.4–3.1: Snow Lake Ridge to Snow Lake Vista**
A quick trip to the left offers a view of the lake, but going right and staying on the trail delivers a stunning vista just as quickly. The next 0.7 mile descends almost 400 feet to the lake. A spur trail to the right leads to a pit toilet with a view of Snow Lake.

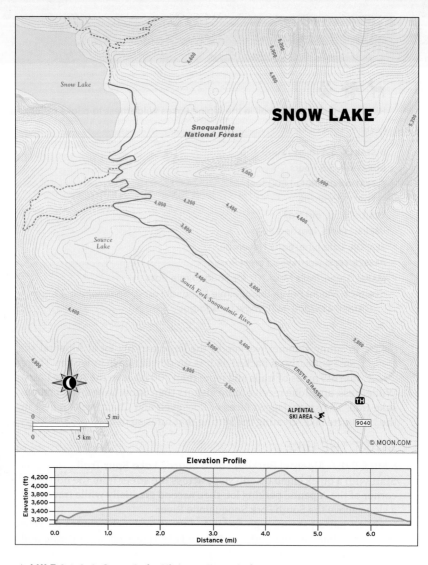

Elevation Profile

▶ MILE 3.1-3.4: Snow Lake Vista to Snow Lake

Follow the path along the edge of the lake for 0.25 mile to a large **open area** overlooking the lake. Too glorious a spot to allow any one party to claim as a campsite, this is a designated day-use area. Take a dip in the cold water if you're feeling courageous or drop a line and try to land a rainbow trout. Just know that the fishing is notoriously slow—views and mosquitoes are the only sure things at Snow Lake.

Make the return trip via the same trail you used to access this Cascade paradise.

▲ TRAIL TO SNOW LAKE

DIRECTIONS

From Seattle, follow I-90 east to Snoqualmie Pass and exit 52. Turn left on Highway 509, and in 0.2 mile continue straight on Erste Strasse. Continue 1.25 miles to the Alpental ski area parking lot. The well-marked trail starts across the road north of the parking lot. Vault toilets are located across the road from the trailhead.

GPS COORDINATES: 47.445273, –121.423740 / N47° 26.7164′ W121° 25.4244′

BEST NEARBY BITES AND BONUS

Located at the base of the Summit at Snoqualmie ski hills, **The Commonwealth** (10 Pass Life Way No. 1, Snoqualmie Pass, 425/434-0808, www.commonwealth906.com, hours vary) serves up locally sourced food. The 906 Burger is topped with white cheddar cheese, garlic aioli, and longhorn beef raised 50 miles down the road in Ellensburg. After you eat, head next door to check out Debbie Armstrong's 1984 Olympic gold medal at the **Washington State Ski & Snowboard Museum** (www.wsssm.org, free admission). From the trailhead, the 5.5-mile drive northeast takes 8 minutes via I-90.

9

Palouse to Cascades State Park Trail: Snoqualmie Tunnel

SNOQUALMIE PASS

🐾 🚶 ♿

Delve into darkness while exploring a 2.3-mile-long retired railroad tunnel running under a ski area and the Pacific Crest Trail.

DISTANCE: 5.2 miles round-trip
DURATION: 3 hours
ELEVATION CHANGE: Negligible
EFFORT: Easy/moderate
TRAIL: Wide dirt trail through a dark tunnel
USERS: Hikers, wheelchair users, leashed dogs, mountain bikers, horseback riders
SEASON: May–October
PASSES/FEES: Discover Pass
MAPS: Green Trails Map 207 for Snoqualmie Pass
PARK HOURS: 6:30am–dusk daily
CONTACT: Lake Easton State Park, 509/656-2230, http://parks.state.wa.us

There are three things you can count on when exploring the 1914 Snoqualmie Tunnel: a cool escape from the summer heat, terrible views, and a hike unlike any other in Washington.

START THE HIKE

▶ **MILE 0–0.3: Cascades State Park Trailhead to Snoqualmie Tunnel**
The Palouse to Cascades State Park Trail runs along the west side of the parking lot. Turn right (north) on the trail previously known as the John Wayne Pioneer/Iron Horse State Park trail before it was renamed in 2018. The trail uses the right-of-way of the defunct Chicago, Milwaukee, St. Paul and Pacific Railroad (commonly referred to as the Milwaukee Road).

Reach the **tunnel** from the trailhead in a matter of minutes. It's just 0.3 mile until you're standing in front of the giant opening with huge doors on either side. A cool wind blows

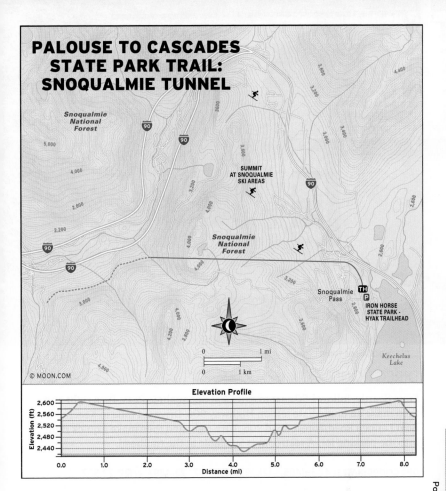

PALOUSE TO CASCADES STATE PARK TRAIL: SNOQUALMIE TUNNEL

Elevation Profile

from the tunnel. It's always chilly inside and sometimes moisture drips from the ceiling, so a jacket is a good idea.

Strong primary and secondary light sources are a must, not just so you can see where you're going, but so others can see you.

▶ **MILE 0.3-2.6: Snoqualmie Tunnel to Pacific Crest Trail Underpass**
Scan the walls with your headlamp as you walk, and notice the pinprick of light in the distance: That's the end of the tunnel 2.3 miles away and it's not as close as it looks. While there's not much to see, it's interesting to think about what's above you. You're cutting under part of the state's most popular ski area (Summit at Snoqualmie) and, toward the west end, you'll pass under the Pacific Crest Trail.

▶ **MILE 2.6-5.2: Pacific Crest Trail Underpass**
  to Cascades State Park Trailhead
When your eyes adjust to the light after emerging from the far end of the tunnel, find a picnic table and a pit toilet. Relax here for a bit before returning the way you came.

▲ THE SNOQUALMIE TUNNEL

DIRECTIONS

From Seattle, follow I-90 east to exit 54 at Snoqualmie Pass. Turn right and then make an immediate left on Highway 906. Drive 0.4 mile to Keechelus Boat Launch Road/Forest Road 906. Turn right and then make a quick right into the parking lot. A restroom is available at the trailhead.

GPS COORDINATES: 47.391495, –121.392616 / N47° 23.4897' W121° 23.557'

BEST NEARBY BREWS

Hikers at mile 2,393 of the 2,650-mile Pacific Crest Trail must think it's a mirage: a brewery just a third of a mile off the trail. **Dru Bru** (10 Pass Life Way, Snoqualmie Pass, 425/434-0700, hours vary) uses Snoqualmie Pass water and Yakima-grown hops to craft a variety of European-inspired beers, but it doesn't serve food. Visitors are welcome to bring their own or have it delivered. From the trailhead, the 3-mile drive north takes 6 minutes via Highway 906.

10

Lake Ingalls

OKANOGAN-WENATCHEE NATIONAL FOREST

🦌 ❀ ♨

Experience the striking contrast of golden larches against cobalt sky during a fall hike to an alpine pool cradled in a granite basin.

BEST: Fall Hikes

DISTANCE: 9.6 miles round-trip

DURATION: 4.5 hours

ELEVATION CHANGE: 2,700 feet

EFFORT: Moderate/strenuous

TRAIL: Dirt, scree, short scramble over boulders

USERS: Hikers

SEASON: July-October

PASSES/FEES: Northwest Forest Pass

MAPS: Green Trails Map 209 for Mount Stuart

CONTACT: Okanogan-Wenatchee National Forest, Cle Elum Ranger District, 509/852-1100, www.fs.usda.gov

Fall color zealots call it Larch Madness. It comes each autumn when these conifers create a golden spectacle so breathtaking it overshadows even the sight of a jagged peak mirrored in an alpine lake. Such is the case with the trail leading to Lake Ingalls. Even with a generous parking lot, cars line the roadside for over a mile on October weekends (summer weekends are busy, too). Arrive before sunrise for the best chance at finding a parking spot and long stretches of solitude on the trail.

START THE HIKE

▶ **MILE 0-1.6: Trailhead Kiosk to Ingalls Way Trail**

The North Fork Teanaway River cascades past the parking lot and Esmerelda Peaks rise above, setting the tone for a memorable hike. Start next to a trailhead kiosk reminding hikers that dogs aren't permitted beyond the wilderness boundary. Follow the **Esmerelda Basin Trail** above the river for 0.3 mile before turning right on **Ingalls Way Trail**. Trees and grass soon give way to scree over the next 1.3 miles as you climb to a junction. Continue straight (right leads to Longs Pass).

▶ **MILE 1.6-3.6: Ingalls Way Trail to Ingalls Pass and Alpine Lakes Wilderness**

The dirt trail follows the contour of the slope as it climbs at a gradual grade, the view of the surrounding peaks and Teanaway River basin growing more spectacular the higher you go. Finally, 1.7 miles beyond the Longs Pass junction, Mount Rainier appears to the southwest. Continue upward another 0.3 mile, a few switchbacks mitigating the steepness, to Ingalls Pass and the Alpine Lakes Wilderness.

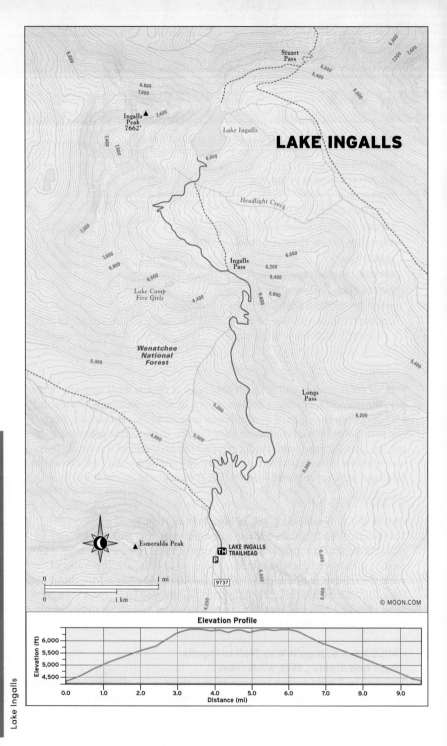

LAKE INGALLS

Stuart Pass

Ingalls Peak 7662'

Lake Ingalls

Headlight Creek

Ingalls Pass

Lake Camp Fire Girls

Wenatchee National Forest

Longs Pass

Esmeralda Peak

LAKE INGALLS TRAILHEAD

9737

© MOON.COM

0   1 mi
0   1 km

Elevation Profile

Elevation (ft)

6,000
5,500
5,000
4,500

0.0   1.0   2.0   3.0   4.0   5.0   6.0   7.0   8.0   9.0

Distance (mi)

▲ LARCHES NEAR INGALLS LAKE

▶ **MILE 3.6–4.8: Ingalls Pass and Alpine
Lakes Wilderness to Ingalls Lake**

Here, nature somehow turns the scenery dial up to 11. On the opposite side of the pass, larches dot the granite slopes of Headlight Basin and the Stuart Range's majestic namesake juts skyward in the distance. At an intersection on the pass, continue straight. The trail to the right shaves 0.25 mile off the trip to the lake but requires descending and then climbing out of the basin. Instead, take the flatter route around the basin and spend the next 1 mile snapping pictures of larches, picking your way through giant boulders, and passing campsites that will inspire you to come back and stay awhile. Mountain goats frequent the area; give them plenty of space. Wildflowers add bright patches of color in the spring and early summer.

When the trails intersect again on the opposite side of the basin, step over **Headlight Creek** and make the short 0.2-mile scramble over boulders to **Ingalls Lake.** Cradled in a basin below Ingalls Peak, the peaceful lakeside setting is the perfect place to kick back on a rocky slab and take a high-country nap.

▶ **MILE 4.8–9.6: Ingalls Lake to Trailhead Kiosk**

The return route is the same as your approach, although early birds are bound to find the descent takes longer as you constantly step aside to yield to the ascending masses. Give them a smile and be glad you set your alarm early enough to stay ahead of the madness.

DIRECTIONS

From I-90 in Cle Elum, take exit 85. Turn left on Highway 970/Sunset Highway, cross over I-90, and turn right to stay on the highway. Drive 7.6 miles and turn left (north) on Teanaway Road. After 7.3 miles the road bends right and becomes North Fork Teanaway Road. Drive another 5.8 miles

▲ LARCHES NEAR LAKE INGALLS

and, 0.1 mile beyond Twenty-Nine Pines Campground, turn right on Forest Road 9737. Continue 1.3 miles and turn left to stay on Forest Road 9737. The road ends at the trailhead after another 8.4 miles. A restroom is located on the west side of the parking lot.

GPS COORDINATES: 47.436773, –120.937097 / N47° 26.2064' W120° 56.2258'

BEST NEARBY BITES

Situated in one of Cle Elum's oldest buildings, **Beau's Pizza, Pasta and Steak** (124 E. 1st St., 509/674-9798, www.beauspizzaandpasta.com, hours vary) offers weary hikers a place to enjoy a post-hike pizza and local microbrew while sitting next to a large fireplace. From the trailhead, the 31-mile drive south takes 70 minutes via Forest Road 9737 and Highway 970.

NEARBY CAMPGROUNDS

NAME	DESCRIPTION	FACILITIES	SEASON	FEE
Lake Wenatchee State Park	on the shore of Lake Wenatchee, a short drive from Leavenworth	197 RV and tent sites, restrooms	year-round	$12-50

21588 State Route 207, Coles Corner, 888/226-7688, www.washington.goingtocamp.com

NAME	DESCRIPTION	FACILITIES	SEASON	FEE
Money Creek Campground	in old-growth forest near a popular swimming spot on the South Fork Skykomish River	25 tent and RV sites, restrooms	early May-mid-September	$18.19-22

Old Cascade Highway, Skykomish, Mount Baker-Snoqualmie National Forest, 877/444-6777, www.recreation.gov

NAME	DESCRIPTION	FACILITIES	SEASON	FEE
Kachess Campground	ideal for family camping, located on the northwest shore of Kachess Lake, offers easy access to hiking and boating adventures	148 RV and tent sites, restrooms	June-mid-September	$21

Kachess Lake Road, Easton, Okanogan-Wenatchee National Forest, 877/444-6777, www.recreation.gov

NAME	DESCRIPTION	FACILITIES	SEASON	FEE
Beckler River Campground	amid thick forest on the banks of the Beckler River	27 RV and tent sites, restrooms	late May-mid-September	$16.37-18.37

Beckler Road, Skykomish, Mount Baker-Snoqualmie National Forest, 877/444-6777, www.recreation.gov

NAME	DESCRIPTION	FACILITIES	SEASON	FEE
29 Pines Campground	on the North Fork Teanaway River	59 RV and tent sites, restrooms	year-round	Discover Pass

Teanaway Road, Cle Elum, Teanaway Community Forest, 509/925-8510, www.dnr.wa.gov/teanaway

MOUNT RAINIER

In a land of mountains, Rainier is king. Locals refer to the stately peak simply as "the mountain." On clear days, the 14,411 feet of rock and ice rises above Puget Sound like a massive billboard beckoning people to get outside and explore. The most glaciated peak in the contiguous United States is the genesis of six major rivers and it brims with recreational opportunities. Here you can test your legs and lungs with a hike to Camp Muir (10,188 feet), stroll among the ancient trees in the Grove of the Patriarchs, wander through fields of colorful wildflowers, and visit fire lookouts. All the while admire the many faces of the famous mountain as you make your way around the park.

▲ SILVER FALLS

▲ CAMP MUIR

◄ HIKERS TRAVERSE MOUNT RAINIER'S MUIR SNOWFIELD

1 Tolmie Peak
DISTANCE: 6.2 miles round-trip
DURATION: 3 hours
EFFORT: Easy/moderate

2 Spray Park
DISTANCE: 5.8 miles round-trip
DURATION: 3.5 hours
EFFORT: Moderate

3 Second Burroughs Loop
DISTANCE: 6.4 miles round-trip
DURATION: 3.5 hours
EFFORT: Moderate

4 Naches Peak Loop
DISTANCE: 3.5 miles round-trip
DURATION: 2 hours
EFFORT: Easy/moderate

5 Camp Muir
DISTANCE: 8.2 miles round-trip
DURATION: 5 hours
EFFORT: Strenuous

6 Skyline Trail Loop
DISTANCE: 5.8 miles round-trip
DURATION: 3 hours
EFFORT: Moderate

7 Grove of Patriarchs and Silver Falls
DISTANCE: 2.6 miles round-trip
DURATION: 2 hours
EFFORT: Easy

8 High Rock Lookout
DISTANCE: 3.2 miles round-trip
DURATION: 2 hours
EFFORT: Moderate

▾ EUNICE LAKE

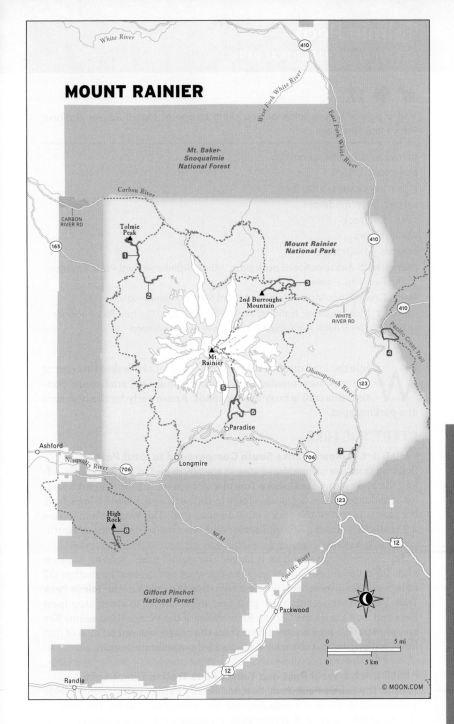

MOUNT RAINIER

1 Tolmie Peak

MOUNT RAINIER NATIONAL PARK

🐐 ❀ 🚶

Visit a pair of serene lakes as you climb to one of Mount Rainier National Park's four fire lookouts.

DISTANCE: 6.2 miles round-trip
DURATION: 3 hours
ELEVATION CHANGE: 1,100 feet
EFFORT: Easy/moderate
TRAIL: Dirt, rock
USERS: Hikers
SEASON: July–October
PASSES/FEES: 7-day national park pass, Mount Rainier Annual Pass, America the Beautiful Passes
MAPS: Green Trails Map 269SX for Mount Rainier–Wonderland
CONTACT: Mount Rainier National Park, 360/569-2211, Carbon River Ranger Station (May–Nov.), 360/829-9639, www.nps.gov/mora

While the long dirt road leading to Mowich Lake makes this part of the park less crowded than the tourist hubs at Paradise and Sunrise, this trail is busy on weekends. Arrive early for the best shot at a parking spot.

START THE HIKE

▶ **MILE 0-1.4: Mowich Lake South Campground to Ipsut Pass**
Starting from the campground area at the south end of Mowich Lake, follow the aptly named **Lakeshore Trail** along the west side of the park's largest and deepest lake. Signs also refer to the path as the **Wonderland Trail,** because it is part of the park's most famous trail. The Wonderland makes a 93-mile loop around Mount Rainier and is a dream trip for many Northwest backpackers.

Follow the Wonderland as it leaves the glacial basin holding Mowich after 0.7 mile and continues into the forest of evergreens. In another 0.7 mile, reach an intersection where a sign directs you left to the **Tolmie Peak Trail.** Before making this turn, go a few steps farther to stand atop **Ipsut Pass** and look across the Carbon River valley. If the Wonderland seems like an easy stroll so far, the steep drop from the pass gives you an idea of just how challenging it is to make the around-the-mountain circuit.

▶ **MILE 1.4-2.2: Ipsut Pass and Tolmie Peak Trail to Eunice Lake**
Back at the **Tolmie Peak Trail,** descend briefly before a short climb yields a nice reward. Here, 0.8 mile beyond the intersection, enjoy the view of the steep talus slopes of Tolmie Peak plunging to the azure waters of Eunice Lake. Meadows speckled with wildflowers and evergreens rim a lake that is often guarded by mosquitoes. Bears, deer, and smaller animals

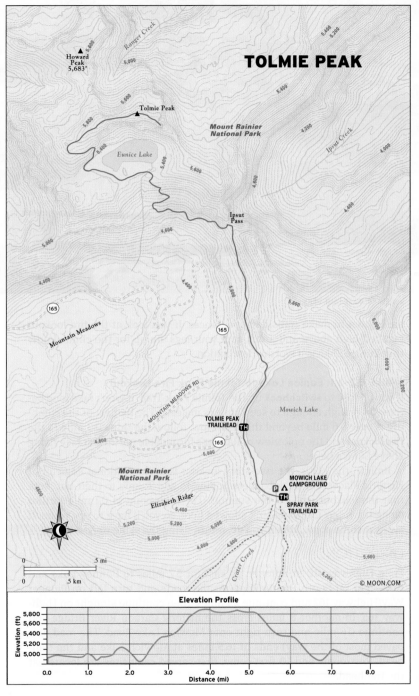

▲ VIEW FROM TOLMIE PEAK

are known to make trailside appearances. If you look at the fire lookout perched high above and aren't sure your legs are up for the climb, know that Eunice Lake is a worthy destination.

▶ MILE 2.2–3.1: Eunice Lake to Tolmie Peak Fire Lookout

If you choose to **switchback** up the Tolmie Peak Trail, it won't take long before you're high enough to see Rainier's majesty. The hardest of the climbing is over 0.6 mile beyond the lake. Now, follow the ridge 0.3 mile to the **fire lookout** and the epic view of Rainier's formidable northwest face rising above Eunice Lake.

Built in the 1930s, the two-story lookout is in the National Register of Historic Places. For peak baggers hoping to add Tolmie to their list, note that the lookout isn't on the summit. The high point is 0.1 mile farther along the ridge. Camping isn't allowed here, so you'll have to pry yourself away at some point. When you do, return using the same trails.

DIRECTIONS

From Highway 410 in Sumner, go east for 5.7 miles to Bonney Lake and turn right on South Prairie Road. At the road's end turn left on Pioneer Way/Highway 162 and continue 2.1 miles; then continue straight on Highway 165. In another 8 miles cross the historic Carbon River Bridge and continue 0.6 mile and turn right onto Mowich Lake Road. The road (unpaved most of the way) ends in 16.5 miles at Mowich Lake and the trailhead. Restrooms and 10 first-come, first-served campsites are located at the trailhead.

GPS COORDINATES: 46.933259, –121.864815 / N46° 55.9955' W121° 51.8889'

Wander vast meadows of wildflowers under the icy slopes of Mount Rainier and make a quick side trip to a 300-foot waterfall.

DISTANCE: 5.8 miles round-trip

DURATION: 3.5 hours

ELEVATION CHANGE: 1,600 feet

EFFORT: Moderate

TRAIL: Dirt

USERS: Hikers

SEASON: June-October

PASSES/FEES: 7-day national park pass, Mount Rainier Annual Pass, America the Beautiful Passes

MAPS: Green Trails Map 269SX for Mount Rainier-Wonderland

CONTACT: Mount Rainier National Park, 360/569-2211, Carbon River Ranger Station (May-Nov.), 360/829-9639, www.nps.gov/mora

One of Washington's classic wildflower hikes, Spray Park can draw a crowd. Luckily the sprawling meadows offer plenty of places to find moments of solitude even on busy days.

START THE HIKE

▶ **MILE 0-0.25: Mowich Lake South Campground to Spray Park Trail**
Starting from the campground at the south end of Mowich Lake, follow the well-marked **Wonderland Trail** south into a forest of hemlocks. The trail makes a 93-mile loop around the mountain, but you'll spend just 0.25 mile on the century-old path. (Many Wonderland Trail backpackers use the Spray Park Trail as an alternative route because of the epic views.) At the intersection head left on the **Spray Park Trail.** Douglas firs and cedars mix with the hemlocks while huckleberries and rhododendrons line the trail.

▶ **MILE 0.25-1.9: Spray Park Trail to Spray Falls Spur Trail**
In another 1.25 miles, pass the **Eagle Cliff Viewpoint** on your right. This side trip is only a few steps and has a striking view of Rainier across the Spray Creek and Mowich River drainages. Keep an eye out for deer and listen for birds as you hike. In another 0.4 mile (after passing Eagle's Roost Camp), reach another worthy side trip: the **Spray Falls Spur,** a 0.2-mile round-trip to a 300-foot cascade.

▶ **MILE 1.9-2.9: Spray Falls Spur Trail to Spray Park**
The steepest stretch is up next. The trail **switchbacks** upward for 0.5 mile until it crosses **Grant Creek.** The next 0.5 mile ascends more gradually. You'll know you've arrived at **Spray Park** as pocket meadows awash with

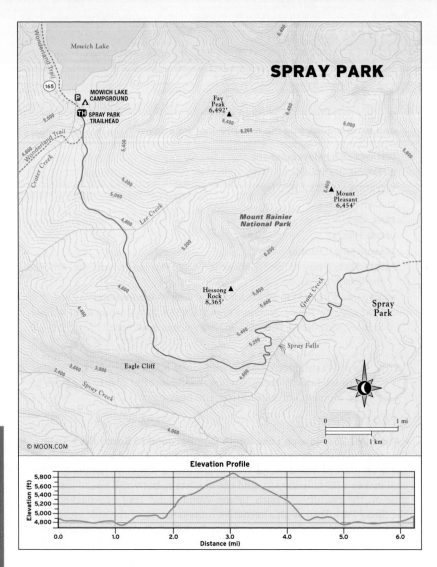

summer wildflowers start allowing views of Rainier to the south and Hessong Rock and Mount Pleasant to the north. Gazing across fields of lilies, Rainier seems so close that you could casually stroll past Observation and Echo Rocks and up to the summit. Perhaps catch a glimpse of a marmot or a bear.

You can continue wandering or stay and enjoy the heavenly setting for a while. There's no landmark designating the turnaround point. That's up to you. When you're ready, return the way you came.

DIRECTIONS

From Highway 410 in Sumner, go east for 5.7 miles to Bonney Lake and turn right on South Prairie Road. At the road's end turn left on Pioneer Way/ Highway 162 and continue 2.1 miles; then continue straight on

Highway 165. In another 8 miles cross the historic Carbon River Bridge and continue 0.6 mile and turn right onto Mowich Lake Road. The road (unpaved most of the way) ends in 16.5 miles at Mowich Lake and the trailhead. Restrooms and 10 first-come, first-served campsites are located at the trailhead.

GPS COORDINATES: 46.933259, –121.864815 / N46° 55.9955′ W121° 51.8889′

BEST NEARBY BITES

Everybody enters through a door marked VIP at **Wally's White River Drive-In** (282 Route 410, Buckley, 360/829-0871, www.wallys restaurants.com, 8am-9pm Sun.-Thurs., 8am-10pm Fri.-Sat.). The most popular menu item is the Waltimate, a three-quarter-pound burger topped with grilled onions, sautéed ham, onion rings, Swiss and American cheese, lettuce, and tomato. You might need a knife and fork. From the trailhead, the 27-mile drive northwest takes 70 minutes via Mowich Road/Highway 165.

Enjoy unobstructed views from tundra-topped mountains so close to Rainier you can hear the rumble of rockfall.

BEST: Summer Hikes

DISTANCE: 6.4 miles round-trip

DURATION: 3.5 hours

ELEVATION CHANGE: 1,400 feet

EFFORT: Moderate

TRAIL: Dirt, rock

USERS: Hikers

SEASON: July–mid-October

PASSES/FEES: 7-day national park pass, Mount Rainier Annual Pass, America the Beautiful Passes

MAPS: Green Trails Map 269SX for Mount Rainier-Wonderland

CONTACT: Mount Rainier National Park, 360/569-2211, www.nps.gov/mora

I f you're wondering how early you need to arrive to beat the crowds, well, it's in the name. Sunrise and Paradise (on the mountain's south side) are the national park's most popular destinations.

START THE HIKE

▶ **MILE 0–0.2: Sunrise Day Lodge Path to Ridge Trail**

At 6,400 feet, Sunrise is the highest you can drive on paved roads in Washington. Add in the up-close view of Mount Rainier, and it's understandable that you might need a minute to catch your breath before starting this hike. To make the classic hike to Second Burroughs, start on the paved path between the **Sunrise Day Lodge** and the comfort station. In 0.1 mile turn right at the **Sourdough Ridge Trailhead**. In another 0.1 head left at a **fork** and continue ascending to the ridge trail, where you'll turn left at another **intersection**. Look back down the steep meadow and watch cars hunting for parking spots.

▶ **MILE 0.2–1.5: Ridge Trail to Five-Way Intersection**

Pass the **Huckleberry Creek Trail** on the right in 0.4 mile before the trail descends slightly as you cross a **steep slope** and scree on your way toward **Frozen Lake**. In 0.6 mile, the trail switches back just below the small lake. Resist the urge to scamper up to the roped-off lake. The lake is the primary source of drinking water at Sunrise and access is prohibited. Stick to the trail and you'll get a good view soon enough. Stay right after the switchback and over the next 0.25 mile pass a **spur** to an overlook before passing Frozen Lake and arriving at a **five-way intersection**.

▲ SNOW ON MOUNT RAINIER

▶ **MILE 1.5–2.1: Five-Way Intersection to First Burroughs**

To ascend the Burroughs, take the **uphill trail** to the left. As you climb, look for bears, goats, marmots, and other animals below you. Be prepared for patches of snow in places where a fall could be treacherous. Snow can linger late into summer. It's often easily passable, but if you don't have an ice axe and traction, don't be shy about turning back if you don't feel safe. Check conditions before your hike by visiting or calling the White River Wilderness Information Center (located at the park's White River entrance, 360/569-6670).

In 0.6 mile, reach the top of **First Burroughs** where Rainier dominates the 360-degree view. Should you be tempted to do some *Sound of Music*-style hilltop twirling a la Julie Andrews, be careful to stay on the path. The tundra covering Burroughs is similar to that found in the Arctic and it's quite fragile.

▶ **MILE 2.1–2.9: First Burroughs to Second Burroughs and Peak**

Reach the **junction** with the Sunrise Rim Trail in 0.2 mile. You'll return on this trail but continue straight to visit **Second Burroughs.** In another 0.6 mile, arrive atop the **peak** where a rock bench awaits. Take a seat and enjoy the in-your-face view of Rainier as the sound of rockfall occasionally pierces the silence. Berkeley Park, Skyscraper Mountain, and Mount Fremont are visible to the north. The White River and Goat Island Mountain are to the southeast.

Second Burroughs Loop

MOUNT RAINIER

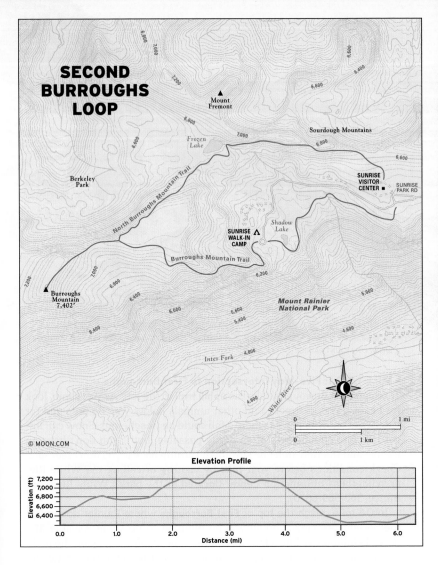

Elevation Profile

© MOON.COM

▶ MILE 2.9-3.5: **Burroughs Peak to Sunrise Rim Trail**

When ready, turn back and make a smaller loop by returning 0.6 mile to the **Sunrise Rim Trail** and turning right.

▶ MILE 3.5-5.1: **Sunrise Rim Trail to Shadow Lake**

Enjoy wildflowers and dramatic views of the White River Canyon as you descend. In 1.1 mile, pause at an **overlook** for a spectacular view of the Emmons Glacier giving life to the White River. In another 0.5 mile find a **restroom** at an intersection near Sunrise Camp and Shadow Lake. Go right here, passing short paths leading to the small lake. Summer wildflowers are especially brilliant beyond the lake.

▲ VIEW OF THE WHITE RIVER FROM BURROUGHS MOUNTAIN

▶ **MILE 5.1-6.4: Shadow Lake to Sunrise**

Over the final 1.3 miles pass the Wonderland's descent to the **White River Campground** and the scenic, kid-friendly **Silver Forest Trail** before returning to **Sunrise,** across the parking lot from where your hike began.

DIRECTIONS

From Enumclaw, follow Highway 410 east 37.2 miles to Sunrise Park Road and turn right. Four miles after the park entry station, turn right at the intersection with White River Campground Road and continue 10 miles to Sunrise. Restrooms, a cafeteria (which often serves ice cream), and a visitors center are located at the trailhead.

GPS COORDINATES: 46.914531, –121.640776 / N46° 54.8719′ W121° 38.4466′

BEST NEARBY BITES

Charlie's Café (1335 Roosevelt Ave. E., Enumclaw, 360/825-5191, 5am-2pm daily) in Enumclaw is a classic breakfast stop for those heading into the mountains and those with big appetites. In 2015, after setting the women's fastest known time by finishing the 93-mile Wonderland Trail in 22 hours, 4 minutes, and 7 seconds, Jenn Shelton of Colorado stopped at Charlie's and became the first female ever to finish the Bigfoot Challenge: an 8-ounce fried steak smothered in gravy, four eggs, hash browns, toast, and a pancake in 30 minutes or less. Feel free to order something a little lighter. From the trailhead, the 52-mile drive northwest takes 1.25 hours via Sunrise Park Road and Highway 410.

Starting from an alpine lake, enjoy sweeping views while using the Pacific Crest Trail to loop around Naches Peak.

DISTANCE: 3.5 miles round-trip

DURATION: 2 hours

ELEVATION CHANGE: 600 feet

EFFORT: Easy/moderate

TRAIL: Dirt trail

USERS: Hikers

SEASON: June–October

PASSES/FEES: 7-day national park pass, Mount Rainier Annual Pass, America the Beautiful Passes

MAPS: Green Trails Map 269SX for Mount Rainier-Wonderland

CONTACT: Mount Rainier National Park, 360/569-2211, www.nps.gov/mora

Using the Pacific Crest and Naches Peak trails, a quick loop around Naches Peak passes through colorful meadows with views of the surrounding valleys, Dewey Lake, and Rainier. Go clockwise for the most and best views of the Northwest's highest peak.

START THE HIKE

▶ **MILE 0-0.3: Parking Lot to Chinook Pass Bridge and Pacific Crest Tail**

From the parking lot, walk east toward Tipsoo Lake for about 100 yards and then turn left to follow the **Naches Loop Trail** as it climbs 0.25 mile through a stand of evergreens to the **Pacific Crest Trail.** Canada is to the left and Mexico is to the right. Turn right and reach a different kind of border in just a few steps. A **log bridge** over the highway doubles as the **Chinook Pass Entrance Arch** and sits on the boundary of Mount Rainier National Park and Wenatchee National Forest. Cross the bridge (built in 1936 and listed in the National Register of Historic Places in 1991) and follow the PCT along the north side of Naches Peak. The Rainier Fork of the American River and Highway 410 drop off to your left.

▶ **MILE 0.3-0.5: Pacific Crest Trail to William O. Douglas Wilderness**

In 0.2 mile enter the **William O. Douglas Wilderness,** named for the former U.S. Supreme Court justice who was a high school valedictorian in nearby Yakima. Scarlet paintbrush, columbine, purple aster, lupine, and other wildflowers color the slopes. An emerald pool sits trailside and snowmelt creates small seasonal cascades. Look for deer, marmots, and other creatures.

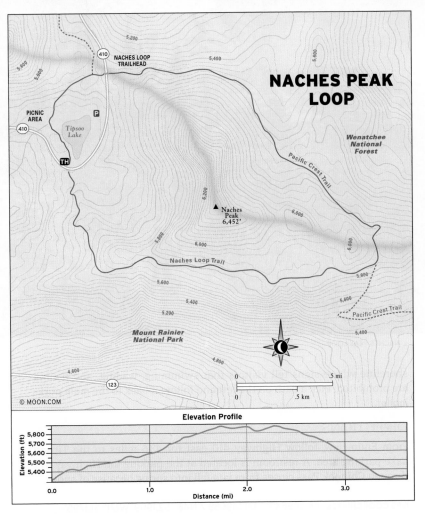

Elevation Profile

▶ **MILE 0.5–1.7: William O. Douglas Wilderness to Naches Peak Loop Trail**

An **overlook,** 1.2 miles after entering the wilderness area, offers views of Dewey Lake. A few steps farther, the PCT veers left and descends to the lake (a fun side trip if you have time), but go straight on the **Naches Peak Loop Trail.**

▶ **MILE 1.7–3.2: Naches Peak Loop Trail to Highway 410**

In 0.5 mile, find a trailside **rest spot** perfect for taking pictures of Rainier. The glaciated volcano highlights the scenery for much of the next 1 mile as you pass the Eastside Trail shortly before reaching **Highway 410.**

▶ **MILE 3.2–3.5: Highway 410 to Tipsoo Lake and Parking Lot**

Over the next 0.3 mile, cross the highway and pick up the trail again at the northwest end of a small **parking lot.** Descend to **Tipsoo Lake's** grassy

▲ NACHES PEAK LOOP

shoreline where signs tell visitors that swimming, wading, and fishing are prohibited. Pick a path on the left and follow it back to the **main parking lot.**

DIRECTIONS

From Enumclaw, follow Highway 410 east for 43.6 miles to the Tipsoo Lake parking area. A restroom is located at the parking lot. Highway 410 through Chinook Pass closes from late fall into spring because of snow.

GPS COORDINATES: 46.869848, –121.519659 / N46° 52.1909' W121° 31.1795'

BEST NEARBY BITE

About 26 miles (35 minutes) north of Chinook Pass via Highway 410, **Wapiti Woolies** (58414 Rte. 410 East, Greenwater, 360/663-2268, www.wapitiwoolies.com) is a popular stop for travelers craving ice cream. The huckleberry ice cream is popular, but Wapiti Woolies is best known for its creative winter caps.

Camp Muir

MOUNT RAINIER NATIONAL PARK

🦌 ❋ ⚐

Trek above 10,000 feet to the most popular climber's high camp on Mount Rainier and take in the majestic, surreal views.

DISTANCE: 8.2 miles round-trip

DURATION: 5 hours

ELEVATION CHANGE: 4,700 feet

EFFORT: Strenuous

TRAIL: Pavement, dirt, rocks, steep snowfield

USERS: Hikers, mountaineers

SEASON: July-September

PASSES/FEES: 7-day national park pass, Mount Rainier Annual Pass, America the Beautiful Passes

MAPS: Green Trails Map 269SX for Mount Rainier-Wonderland

CONTACT: Mount Rainier National Park, 360/569-2211, www.nps.gov/mora, www.mountrainierclimbing.blogspot.com

There's a fine line between beauty and danger, and you're more likely to find that line when you're on the icy slopes of a volcano. This is a must-tick box on most Northwest hikers' bucket lists, but calling this trip a hike requires expanding your definition of the activity.

START THE HIKE

▶ **MILE 0-1.6: Jackson Visitor Center Steps to Skyline Trail**

Starting on the steps next to the **Jackson Visitor Center,** follow the paved **Skyline Trail** as you ascend through Paradise's colorful wildflower meadows. Skirt the west side of **Alta Vista,** a small hill that temporarily blocks your view of Rainier, and in 0.7 mile reach a wide paved area on the north side of the hill. Here, the pavement gives way to dirt trail as you continue walking toward Rainier. Over the next 0.9 mile, enjoy views of surrounding peaks, distant waterfalls, and the Nisqually Glacier. Keep your distance from wildlife such as bears, mountain goats, and marmots, which often make appearances around Paradise.

▶ **MILE 1.6-2.2: Skyline Trail to Muir Snowfield**

Turn left on the **Pebble Creek Trail** and, after another 0.3 mile, pass a trail leading right to the High Skyline Trail. Go straight for 0.3 mile, hop **Pebble Creek,** and prepare for the push up the **Muir Snowfield.**

▶ **MILE 2.2-4.1: Muir Snowfield to Camp Muir**

Over the next 1.9 miles from the creek to Camp Muir, you'll climb about 3,000 feet. Take a cue from the lines of climbers following their guides: They purposely travel slow and take breaks every hour as they acclimate to the thin air and conserve energy for their summit attempts.

There is no trail on the steep snowfield flanked by glaciers. On blue-sky days, the way is obvious, and you'll share the hill with hundreds of hikers. But the weather can change without warning. It is vital to check gear, weather forecasts, and the mirror before hiking to Camp Muir. You should be fit and skilled in route finding and snow travel to make this trip.

Above a rock outcrop known as **Moon Rocks** (9,200 feet), it's worth angling right toward **Anvil Rock** (9,584 feet) for a view across the gaping crevasses of the Cowlitz and Paradise Glaciers. Then angle upward back across the snowfield to Muir.

▶ MILE 4.1-8.2: **Camp Muir to Jackson Visitor Center**

Pat yourself on the back as you arrive at the **high camp** (10,188 feet) and plop down on a rock for a snack and a 100-mile view. Some days, you look out over cloud tops and it seems as if you could walk across a carpet of white fluff all the way to the upper slopes of Mounts Adams and Hood. It's no wonder this place was called Cloud Camp before it was renamed for naturalist John Muir, who climbed the 14,411-foot peak in 1888.

The ugly, battered **black box** is a shelter for climbers staying overnight with guide services. Meanwhile, rock shelters harmoniously blending into the landscape are more classic reasons Camp Muir is listed in the National Register of Historic Places.

Enjoy your time above the clouds but give yourself plenty of time for the return trip. The descent is usually riskier than the climb.

DIRECTIONS

From Highway 7 in Elbe, continue straight on Highway 706 for 13.6 miles to Mount Rainier National Park's Nisqually Entrance. Continue 17.5 miles inside the park to the large Paradise parking lot. Restroom facilities are located at the trailhead. The Jackson Visitor Center is open daily in summer and weekends and holidays in the winter. The Paradise Inn is typically open from May to mid-October.

GPS COORDINATES: 46.786070, –121.735881 / N46° 47.1642′ W121° 44.1529′

BEST NEARBY BITES

Lhakpa Gelu Sherpa, a 15-time Mount Everest summiteer, has helped many people climb the world's highest peak. As the owner of **The Wildberry Restaurant** (37718 Rte. 706 E, Ashford, 360/569-2277, www. rainierwildberry.com, hours vary) he brings a taste of Nepal to Rainier. In addition to burgers and traditional American fare, the Himalayan Special menu includes momo (steamed dumplings) and Sherpa stew. From the trailhead, the 19-mile drive southwest takes about 35 minutes via Paradise Road and Highway 706.

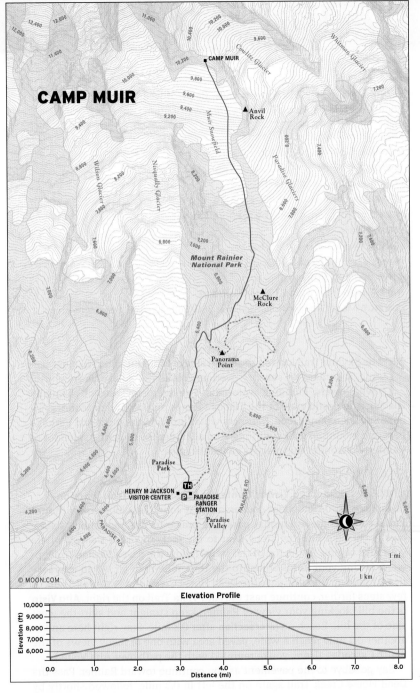

CAMP MUIR

12,400 12,600 11,000 10,200 12,000 11,400 10,000 Coulitz Glacier 9,600 Whitman Glacier

■ CAMP MUIR

9,800 7,200

9,600 ▲ Anvil Rock

9,400 9,200 8,400 Muir Snowfield 8,600

8,800 8,200 8,000 Paradise Glaciers 7,400

Wilson Glacier 7,600 Nisqually Glacier 8,200 6,000 7,800 7,200

7,000 Mount Rainier National Park 6,800

6,800 ▲ McClure Rock 6,600

6,400 ▲ Panorama Point

5,200

5,800 5,600

5,800 5,600

Paradise Park 5,800

HENRY M JACKSON **TH** PARADISE
VISITOR CENTER **P** RANGER
STATION

Paradise Valley PARADISE RD 5,200

4,200 PARADISE RD 4,600 4,800

0 ——————— 1 mi
0 ——————— 1 km

© MOON.COM

Elevation Profile

Elevation (ft): 10,000 / 9,000 / 8,000 / 7,000 / 6,000

Distance (mi): 0.0 1.0 2.0 3.0 4.0 5.0 6.0 7.0 8.0

View the Nisqually Glacier, waterfalls, fields of wildflowers, and a bevy of South Cascade peaks as Rainier towers overhead.

BEST: Wildflower Hikes
DISTANCE: 5.8 miles round-trip
DURATION: 3 hours
ELEVATION CHANGE: 1,400 feet
EFFORT: Moderate
TRAIL: Dirt, rock, pavement; be prepared for snow
USERS: Hikers
SEASON: Mid-June–mid-October
PASSES/FEES: 7-day national park pass, Mount Rainier Annual Pass, America the Beautiful Passes
MAPS: Green Trails Map 270S for Paradise
CONTACT: Mount Rainier National Park, 360/569-2211, www.nps.gov/mora

The Skyline Trail loop on the south side of Mount Rainier isn't just scenic, it borders on sensory overload. Meadows ablaze with colorful wildflowers. Plunging waterfalls. The deep crevasses of Nisqually Glacier. A majestic view of the Tatoosh Range and beyond to Mounts Adams, St. Helens, and Hood. Marmots whistling from the rocks and perhaps bear and mountain goat sightings. And all under the towering splendor of Rainier. No wonder this place is called Paradise.

START THE HIKE

▶ **MILE 0-1.0: Jackson Visitor Center to Glacier Vista Trail Junction**
In the late 1800s, eloquent conservationist John Muir lobbied for Mount Rainier to become a national park. His praise for the mountain's meadows is chiseled into the steps next to the **Jackson Visitor Center,** where your hike begins. At the top of the steps, follow the paved **Skyline Trail** upward, letting your lungs adjust to the thin, mile-high air. At an **intersection** 0.1 mile up the trail, pass the Dead Horse Creek and Waterfall Trails. A few steps farther, continue past the Alta Vista Trail on the right. **Alta Vista** is the hill blocking your view of Rainier; keep straight and skirt the west side of the hill. Reach an **intersection** after 0.3 mile. Stay right here and in another 0.3 mile reach a wide, paved area with one of many views of the South Cascades. (Here, you're reunited with the path over Alta Vista.)

Say goodbye to the pavement as you continue toward Rainier. Pass the Dead Horse Creek Trail again on the left in 0.3 mile, followed shortly by the **Glacier Vista Trail junction,** also on the left. The views of the Nisqually Glacier are spectacular from this side trail, but Skyline has glacier views, too, a little farther ahead.

▲ SKYLINE TRAIL LOOP

▶ **MILE 1.0-1.8: Glacier Vista Trail Junction to Panorama Point**
In 0.6 mile, pass the **Pebble Creek Trail** (the jumping-off point for Camp
Muir) and then ascend along a steep, rocky slope for 0.2 mile to **Panorama
Point.** Take some time here to look across Paradise to the Tatoosh Range,
the Goat Rocks, and Mounts St. Helens, Adams, and Hood.

▶ **MILE 1.8-3.2: Panorama Point to Golden Gate Trail Junction**
Continue by following the **High Skyline Trail** to the left. In 0.4 mile pass another chance to join the Pebble Creek Trail shortly before the loop reaches
its highest point (7,100 feet).

Rejoin the main **Skyline Loop** in 0.4 mile beyond the Pebble Creek intersection, then continue downward another 0.6 mile to the **intersection** with
the Golden Gate Trail on the right. Golden Gate offers a shortcut back to
the parking lot that shaves about a mile off your trip, but continue straight
to see what else Skyline has in store.

▶ **MILE 3.2-3.9: Golden Gate Trail Junction to
Stevens-Van Trump Historical Monument**
In 0.7 mile, shortly after stepping over the **Paradise River** and passing the
Paradise Glacier Trail on the left, arrive at the **Stevens-Van Trump Histori-
cal Monument**. Erected in 1921, the monument is on the site where Hazard
Stevens and P. B. Van Trump made camp before making the first document-
ed summit of Rainier on August 17, 1870. Sluiskin, their Native American
guide, reportedly waited here certain the men would perish.

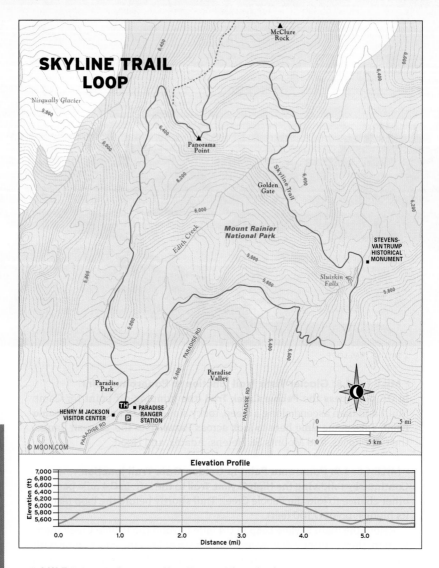

SKYLINE TRAIL LOOP

Elevation Profile

▶ **MILE 3.9–5.3: Stevens-Van Trump Historical Monument to Myrtle Falls**

Pass the Lakes Trail in 0.4 mile and then descend into the **Paradise Valley.** Spend the next 1 mile passing more side trails and wildflowers before crossing a bridge over **Myrtle Falls.** The falls viewpoint is just a few steps off the path on the left if you need one last postcard-worthy photo.

▶ **MILE 5.3–5.8: Myrtle Falls to Parking Lot**

Return to paved trail just beyond the **bridge** for the final 0.5 mile to the parking lot.

▲ SUNSET ON THE SKYLINE TRAIL LOOP

DIRECTIONS

From Highway 7 in Elbe, continue straight on Highway 706 for 13.6 miles to Mount Rainier National Park's Nisqually Entrance. Continue 17.5 miles inside the park to the large Paradise parking lot. Restroom facilities are located at the trailhead. The Jackson Visitor Center is open daily in summer and weekends and holidays in the winter. The Paradise Inn is typically open from May to mid-October.

GPS COORDINATES: 46.786070, –121.735881 / N46° 47.1642' W121° 44.1529'

BEST NEARBY BITES

Built as a service station in 1925, the **Copper Creek Inn** (35707 Rte. 706 E, Ashford, 360/569-2326, www.coppercreekinn.com, hours vary) restaurant opened in 1946 and has been a popular stop for Rainier visitors ever since. Skip to the dessert menu to find the most popular order: blackberry pie à la mode. From the trailhead, the 20-mile drive southwest takes less than 40 minutes via Paradise Road and Highway 706.

Skyline Trail Loop

MOUNT RAINIER

7

Grove of the Patriarchs and Silver Falls

MOUNT RAINIER NATIONAL PARK

Wander an easy forest path along the Ohanapecosh River to an island of giant trees and a four-story waterfall.

DISTANCE: 2.6 miles round–trip

DURATION: 2 hours

ELEVATION CHANGE: 400 feet

EFFORT: Easy

TRAIL: Dirt, bridges (one suspension bridge), boardwalk

USERS: Hikers

SEASON: May–October

PASSES/FEES: 7–day national park pass, Mount Rainier Annual Pass, America the Beautiful Passes

MAPS: Green Trails Map 269SX for Mount Rainier–Wonderland

CONTACT: Mount Rainier National Park, 360/569–2211, www.nps.gov/mora

C ombine two short and easy hikes along different parts of the Eastside Trail to a pair of awe-inspiring destinations: an island of 1,000-year-old trees and a 40-foot waterfall.

START THE HIKE

▶ **MILE 0-1.2: Eastside Trail Loop**

Find the well-marked dirt path next to the parking lot restroom and follow the wide, gently descending **Eastside Trail** under a canopy of western red cedar, western hemlock, and Douglas fir. Walking along the **river,** you can see why it received its name: Ohanapecosh is believed to be a Taidnapam Indian word meaning "standing at the edge." As in, each summer Mount Rainier visitors flock to the Ohanapecosh River to stand at the edge of something beautiful. After 0.3 mile, reach an **intersection** and then descend to the right toward a narrow **suspension bridge.** Only one person should cross at a time so the span's undulations don't knock others off-balance.

On the other side of the bridge is an **island** surrounded by channels of the Ohanapecosh and packed with old-growth timber. Pass massive root wads from trees felled by the wind and nurse logs raising the next generation of evergreens on your way to a boardwalk loop visiting the island's giants. Twin century-old Douglas firs stand proud despite rotten cores. Some trees reach 200 feet into the sky and some have a circumference of more than 40 feet. The boardwalk loops around a colossal cedar that might be the park's most photographed tree.

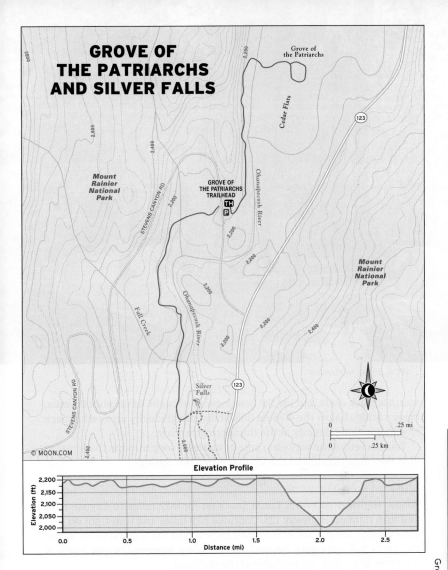

GROVE OF THE PATRIARCHS AND SILVER FALLS

Grove of the Patriarchs

Cedar Flats

123

Mount Rainier National Park

STEVENS CANYON RD

GROVE OF THE PATRIARCHS TRAILHEAD

TH
P

Ohanapecosh River

Mount Rainier National Park

Fall Creek

Ohanapecosh River

2,200

2,200

2,400

Silver Falls

123

0   .25 mi

0   .25 km

© MOON.COM

Elevation Profile

After closing the loop, cross the **suspension bridge** and return the way you came. You'll have covered a scant 1.2 miles by the time you return to the **parking lot.** Cross the road to continue to Silver Falls.

▶ **MILE 1.2-2.6: Silver Falls Loop**

Reenter the lush green forest on the west side of the road opposite the **parking lot** and notice this section of **Eastside Trail** is much less crowded. Silver Falls is a popular destination, but most visitors access it using a longer (2.8 miles) loop trail from the Ohanapecosh Campground. The river's rumblings grow louder as it tumbles over boulders and cuts through a narrow gorge. In 0.5 mile, reach an **intersection** where the Silver Falls Loop bends back toward the campground. Go left on the **loop trail** and in another 0.1 mile pass a sign directing you to the **Silver Falls Overlook.** This is

▲ GROVE OF THE PATRIARCHS

worth a quick aside, but for the best view go straight. In another 0.1 mile, cross a bridge below the 40-foot falls and climb gradually up a switchback to a spot looking directly at the thundering cascade.

You can return the way you came or make the loop through the forest to visit the campground and the Ohanapecosh Hot Springs.

DIRECTIONS

Follow Highway 410 from Enumclaw east for 40.7 miles to Cayuse Pass and turn right on Highway 123. Continue 10.9 miles and turn right on Stevens Canyon Road. Park in the small lot just past the entry station. When the lot is full, cars park beyond the lot along Stevens Canyon Road. A restroom and water are available at the trailhead.

GPS COORDINATES: 46.758121, –121.557487 / N46° 45.4873′ W121° 33.4492′

BEST NEARBY BITES

With a fence made of skis and old ski posters hanging on the walls, Packwood's **Cliff Droppers** (12968 U.S. Hwy. 12, Packwood, 360/494-2055, 11am–7pm daily) pays tribute to the nearby White Pass Ski Area while serving big burgers. Favorites include the one-third-pound bacon bleu cheese burger and the Canadian bacon-topped, two-third-pound Sasquatch burger. From the trailhead, the 13.5-mile drive southwest takes less than 25 minutes via Highway 123 and U.S. 12.

8

High Rock Lookout

GIFFORD PINCHOT NATIONAL FOREST, ASHFORD

Hike up a forested ridge to a cliffside fire lookout with views of four iconic Cascade volcanoes: Rainier, Adams, St. Helens, and Hood.

BEST: Dog-Friendly Hikes

DISTANCE: 3.2 miles round-trip

DURATION: 2 hours

ELEVATION CHANGE: 1,400 feet

EFFORT: Moderate

TRAIL: Single track; short, steep rock slope at the top

USERS: Hikers, leashed dogs

SEASON: Mid-June–October

PASSES/FEES: None

MAPS: Green Trails Map 301 for Randle, USGS topographic map for Sawtooth Ridge

CONTACT: Gifford Pinchot National Forest, Cowlitz Ranger District, www.fs.usda.gov

START THE HIKE

▶ **MILE 0-0.7: Towhead Gap Trailhead to Mount Rainier Viewpoint**
The **Towhead Gap Trail** starts from the edge of Forest Road 8440 near a sign that reads "High Rock Trail 266." The task might seem daunting as you stand at the trailhead and look north to see High Rock Lookout perched precariously atop a cliff, but try to keep in mind that you'll be rewarded mightily for your work. The skinny dirt path starts with two quick **switchbacks** in the first 0.2 mile and then straightens out to continue the ascent along the tree-covered ridge. It doesn't take long before glimpses through the cedars and Douglas firs show the tops of green foothills, hints of the dramatic views to come. Keep a look out for deer and listen for chirping birds. Bears are sometimes spotted in this area.

After 0.4 mile, the trail steepens. You'll reach the top of the first pitch in another 0.1 mile, where a strategically placed **bench** awaits. The climbing only continues from here, but your eyes will inspire your thighs as you get your first peek of Mount Rainier about a hundred yards past the bench. Not much farther, Mount Adams and Mount St. Helens make their first appearances.

▶ **MILE 0.7-1.4: Mount Rainier Viewpoint to Johnnie T. Peters Memorial**
In 0.7 mile, the lookout can be seen through a wide opening in the trees. As you continue your ascent, you'll notice a **plaque** affixed to a rocky **overlook**. The plaque pays tribute to Johnnie T. Peters, who brought materials

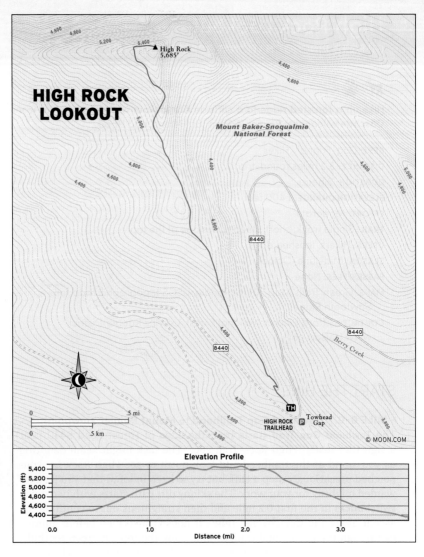

Elevation Profile

by mule from the town of Mineral to build this lookout and 10 others in 1930.

▶ **MILE 1.4-1.6: Johnnie T. Peters Memorial to High Rock Lookout**

From the **plaque,** it's less than 0.1 mile to the steep, exposed rocky **slope** that ascends to the lookout. You only need to climb about halfway up the slope for a 360-degree panorama view. Mount Rainier dominates to the north, while Adams, St. Helens, Hood, and the Goat Rocks fill out the view to the south. Far below, Cora Lake reflects the sunlight while the Nisqually River makes its way from Rainier to Puget Sound. You'll be hard-pressed to find a better view of Rainier outside of the national park.

Continue 0.1 mile to the top to see the 90-year-old **fire lookout,** though it's boarded up and no longer staffed. Watch your pets, kids, and step here.

▲ HIGH ROCK LOOKOUT

In addition to a 500-foot drop that makes many a little weak in the knees, vandalism and litter mean the threat of glass and other sharp objects hiding in the rocks.

Retrace your steps when you're ready to return to the trailhead.

DIRECTIONS

From Highway 7 in Elbe, continue east on Highway 706 for 10.1 miles through Ashford to Kernahan Road. Turn right on Kernahan Road and drive south 1.4 miles where the road turns left and becomes Skate Creek Road. Continue another 3.3 miles and turn right on Forest Road 84. There is no sign for the road approaching from this direction. Follow Forest Road 84 for 6.8 miles (staying left at the fork with Forest Road 8420) and then go right on Forest Road 8440. Continue another 2.6 miles to Towhead Gap, a level spot in the road with enough parking for a handful of vehicles. There are no toilets at the trailhead.

GPS COORDINATES: 46.666642, –121.891227 / N46° 39.9985' W121° 53.4736'

BEST NEARBY BITES

In 1969, a logging truck weigh station was moved to Elbe from neighboring Ashford. In 1985, it was converted into **Scaleburgers** (54109 Mountain Hwy. E, Elbe, 360/569-2247, 11am-7pm daily), a burger stand that quickly became a favorite of hungry hikers. Try the especially popular Overload Burger. All seating is at outdoor picnic tables, but dogs are not permitted in the dining area. From the trailhead, the 24.5-mile drive northwest takes about 45 minutes via Skate Creek Road and Highway 706.

NEARBY CAMPGROUNDS

NAME	DESCRIPTION	FACILITIES	SEASON	FEE
Ohanapecosh Campground	on the Ohanapecosh River in the southeast corner of the park	188 RV and tent sites, restrooms	late May-late September	$20

Ohanapecosh Road, Packwood, Mount Rainier National Park, 877/444-6777, www.recreation.gov

NAME	DESCRIPTION	FACILITIES	SEASON	FEE
Cougar Rock Campground	situated near the confluence of the Paradise and Nisqually Rivers	173 RV and tent sites, restrooms	late May-late September	$20

Paradise Road, Longmire, Mount Rainier National Park, 877/444-6777, www.recreation.gov

NAME	DESCRIPTION	FACILITIES	SEASON	FEE
Mowich Lake	a ring of campsites near the park's biggest lake (Mowich) and longest trail (Wonderland)	10 walk-in tent sites, restrooms	early July-early October	none

Mowich Lake Road/Highway 165, Carbonado, Mount Rainier National Park, 360/569-2211, www.nps.gov/mora

NAME	DESCRIPTION	FACILITIES	SEASON	FEE
White River Campground	near the headwaters of the White River and a short drive (or a 3.3-mile uphill hike) from Sunrise	112 RV and tent sites, restrooms	late June-late September	$20

White River Road, Mount Rainier National Park, 360/569-2211, www.nps.gov/mora

NAME	DESCRIPTION	FACILITIES	SEASON	FEE
La Wis Wis Campground	in old-growth forest and with quick access to Mount Rainier National Park and the South Cascades	100 RV and tent sites, restrooms	late May-early September	$20

Forest Road 1272, Packwood, 877/444-6777, www.recreation.gov

SOUTH CASCADES

Stretching from the Columbia River Gorge north to U.S. 12, the South Cascades is one of the quietest parts of the range despite its explosive reputation. Mount St. Helens's gaping crater and the blast zone from its 1980 eruption give visitors experiences they're hard-pressed to duplicate anywhere else. Tucked away and hard to spot from western Washington, Mount Adams is the state's second tallest (behind Rainier) and second most isolated volcano (behind Glacier Peak). A network of forest roads deliver access to lakes, views of the volcanoes and the Goat Rocks Wilderness, a subterranean adventure in a lava tube called Ape Cave, and some of Washington's most scenic terrain.

▲ MONITOR RIDGE

▲ PACKWOOD LAKE

1 Packwood Lake
DISTANCE: 8 miles round-trip
DURATION: 4 hours
EFFORT: Moderate

2 Tongue Mountain
DISTANCE: 3 miles round-trip
DURATION: 2 hours
EFFORT: Easy/moderate

3 Harry's Ridge
DISTANCE: 8 miles round-trip
DURATION: 4 hours
EFFORT: Moderate

4 Killen Creek
DISTANCE: 6.2 miles round-trip
DURATION: 3 hours
EFFORT: Moderate

5 Ape Cave
DISTANCE: 2.9 miles round-trip
DURATION: 2 hours
EFFORT: Easy

6 Monitor Ridge to Mount St. Helens Summit
DISTANCE: 10 miles round-trip
DURATION: 8 hours
EFFORT: Strenuous

7 Lava Canyon
DISTANCE: 5.8 miles round-trip
DURATION: 3 hours
EFFORT: Moderate

SUSPENSION BRIDGE IN LAVA CANYON

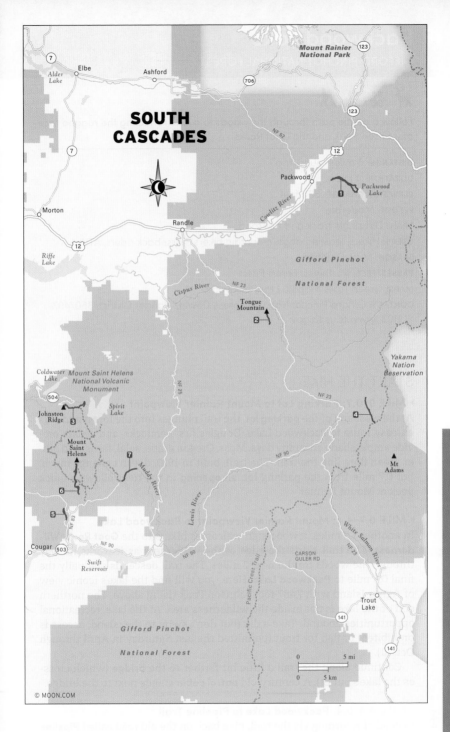

Packwood Lake
GIFFORD PINCHOT NATIONAL FOREST

Follow a gentle path through the woods to a lake reflecting the rugged face of Johnson Peak and the Goat Rocks.

DISTANCE: 8 miles round-trip
DURATION: 4 hours
ELEVATION CHANGE: 600 feet
EFFORT: Moderate
TRAIL: Dirt single track and fire road
USERS: Hikers, leashed dogs, mountain bikers, horseback riders, ATVs
SEASON: May–October
PASSES/FEES: Northwest Forest Pass
MAPS: Green Trails Map 302 for Packwood
CONTACT: Gifford Pinchot National Forest, Cowlitz Ranger District, 360/497-1103, www.fs.usda.gov

START THE HIKE

▶ **MILE 0-0.7: Parking Lot to Mount Rainier Viewpoint**
At the west end of the **parking lot,** the trail plunges into the forest and cuts an easy route to Packwood Lake. Douglas firs, hemlocks, and cedars provide ample shade on sunny days. Moss, Oregon grape, salal, ferns, and other green flora line the trail. The trail, built in 1910, doesn't change much, but 0.7 mile from the parking lot, an **opening** in the trees allows a quick peek at Mount Rainier.

▶ **MILE 0.7-4.4: Mount Rainier Viewpoint to Packwood Lake**
In another 1.3 miles, a wood sign welcomes hikers to the **Goat Rocks Wilderness.** The trail skirts the edge of the wilderness as it works its way through the woods for the next 2 miles. The trail descends gradually the final 0.3 mile to **Packwood Lake.** Here, you will find the lake's iconic view of Agnes Island with 7,487-foot Johnson Peak rising above. The northern end of the lake is not inside the wilderness area. At the lake, recreational opportunities abound. Take a dip (but don't swim to the island; access is prohibited) or fish for trout (permitted the last Saturday in April through Oct. 31).

Continue along the trail a little bit farther to the **bridge** (which crosses the lake's outlet). A century-old **patrol cabin** stands next to the bridge.

▶ **MILE 4.4-5.4: Packwood Lake to Pipeline Trail**
Instead of returning via the trail, hike back on the old road called **Pipeline Trail.** From the **historic patrol cabin,** find the road running past the dam. When hiking in this direction the road offers more to see than the upper

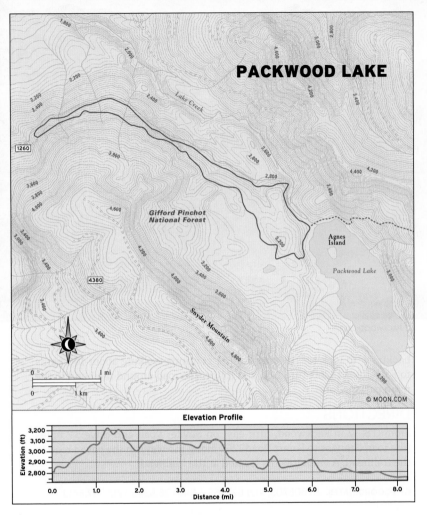

PACKWOOD LAKE

Lake Creek

1260

Gifford Pinchot
National Forest

4380

Snyder Mountain

Agnes
Island

Packwood Lake

0   1 mi

0   1 km

© MOON.COM

Elevation Profile

trail, including a section along the creek and views of Mount Rainier. At
0.3 mile a sign directs horse and foot traffic to go right and follow a trail
that travels above the edge of the **creek's ravine** for 0.7 mile before rejoin-
ing the road.

▶ MILE 5.4–5.9: Pipeline Trail to Southern Face Mount Rainier Viewpoint

Walk another 0.5 mile where, at a bend in the road, you'll get a view of the
southern face of Mount Rainier.

▶ MILE 5.9–8: Southern Face Mount Rainier Viewpoint to Parking Lot

Over the next 2.1 miles enjoy the flat, easy walk past occasional red columbine and other wildflowers. Notice the unmarked but heavily trodden
spur trail on the left that is the final 200-foot uphill push to the parking
lot. Don't worry if you miss this unmarked path: The Pipeline Trail continues a few hundred yards to the motorized trailhead. From there, either

▲ PACKWOOD LAKE

backtrack to look for the spur trail or continue walking about 100 yards to Forest Road 1260, turn left, and follow the road around the bend to the main parking lot.

DIRECTIONS

From U.S. 12 in Packwood, turn east on Snyder Road and drive 5.7 miles (the road changes to Forest Road 1260 along the way) on the paved road to the trailhead. A vault toilet is located at the trailhead.

GPS COORDINATES: 46.608709, -121.627365 / N46° 36.5225' W121° 37.6419'

BEST NEARBY BITES

The hunger you work up on the trail is quickly vanquished at Packwood's **Cruiser's Pizza** (13028 U.S. 12, 360/494-5400, 9am-9pm Mon.-Fri., 8am-10pm Sat., 8am-9pm Sun.). A large combo pizza is nearly nine pounds, with so much pepperoni, Canadian bacon, sausage, and mushrooms the servers say it barely fits in the oven. From the trailhead, the 6-mile drive southwest takes about 15 minutes via forest roads and U.S. 12.

Tongue Mountain

GIFFORD PINCHOT NATIONAL FOREST, RANDLE

🐐 ❀ 🐾 🚶

Look for mountain goats on the rocky slopes of an easily accessed peak with an unobstructed view of Mount Adams.

DISTANCE: 3 miles round-trip
DURATION: 2 hours
ELEVATION CHANGE: 1,050 feet
EFFORT: Easy/moderate
TRAIL: Dirt single track, rock
USERS: Hikers, leashed dogs, mountain bikers, motorcyclists
SEASON: May-early November
PASSES/FEES: Northwest Forest Pass
MAPS: Green Trails Map 333 for McCoy Peak
CONTACT: Gifford Pinchot National Forest, Cowlitz Ranger District, 360/497-1103, www.fs.usda.gov

START THE HIKE

▶ **MILE 0-0.9: Forest Road 2904 to Tongue Mountain Lookout Trail 294A**

The 4,838-foot peak is easily accessed from Forest Road 2904. Find the Tongue Mountain Trail 294 sign on the east side of the road, opposite the Juniper Ridge Trail. The multiuse trail undulates—worn into rolling dirt waves by years of dirt bike traffic—as it gradually climbs through the forest. Get a reprieve in 0.9 mile at an **intersection** where you'll turn right on the Tongue Mountain Lookout Trail 294A. The trail has a traditional surface and is open only to hikers.

It shouldn't be a surprise that mountain goat sightings are common on this lightly used trail. Tongue Mountain was a traditional mountain goat hunting ground for the Taidnapam Indians. Keep your distance and give these creatures plenty of space. If a goat approaches, slowly move away; if that doesn't work, try to scare it off.

▶ **MILE 0.9-1.5: Tongue Mountain Lookout Trail 294A to Tongue's Fork**

In 0.3 mile, reach a short section of tight **switchbacks** that quickly climb above the trees and deliver views of Mount St. Helens. Ferns, vine maple, and huckleberries flank the path. In another 0.25 mile find yourself at the **tongue's fork,** a saddle between the two flat summits.

This might be as far as you choose to go. Reaching the top requires a short scramble in either direction. The summit is to the left (north), atop an imposing slope. Experienced hikers might find the short climb isn't as challenging as it looks, but it shouldn't be taken lightly. The easier scramble and best views are to the right (south), on the lower peak.

SOUTH CASCADES

Tongue Mountain

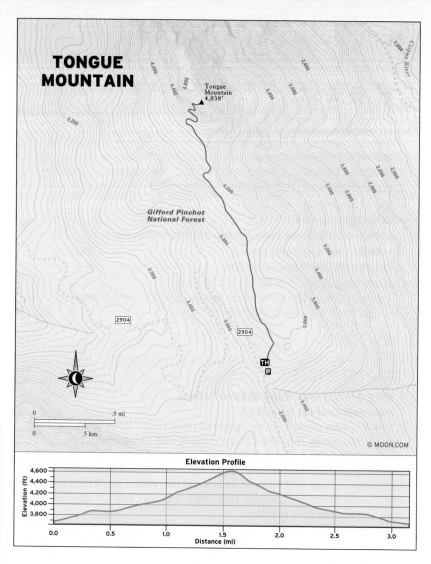

TONGUE
MOUNTAIN

Tongue
Mountain
4,838'

Gifford Pinchot
National Forest

2904

2904

TH
P

Cispus River

0   .5 mi

0   .5 km

© MOON.COM

Elevation Profile

Mount Adams is in your face, the Cispus River is far below, and Mount Rainier looms to the north. (On the actual summit, Rainier is blocked by a small stand of evergreens.)

Mug for a picture or two (some goofy hikers snap apropos tongue-out selfies) before returning the way you came.

DIRECTIONS

From U.S. 12 in Randle, go south for 1 mile on Highway 131 and then bear left on Cispus Road/Forest Road 23. After 8.1 miles turn right to stay on Cispus Road and continue 0.9 mile to a Y-intersection. Bear left to access Forest Road 29. Drive 3.8 miles on the dirt road to Forest Road 2904 and turn

▲ VIEW FROM THE SUMMIT OF TONGUE MOUNTAIN

left. After 4 rough miles, find the trailhead on the left across from the Juniper Ridge trailhead. Restrooms and water are not available.

GPS COORDINATES: 46.3967, –121.76532 / N46° 23.802' W121° 45.9192'

BEST NEARBY BITES

In Randle, the **Mt. Adams Café** (9794 U.S. 12, Randle, 360/497-5556, 7am-7pm Sun.-Thurs., 7am-8pm Fri.-Sat.) is conveniently located to deliver that Angus burger and slice of pie you started craving during the final stretch of your hike. From the trailhead, the 17-mile drive northwest takes about 35 minutes via Forest Road 23 and Highway 131.

🦌 ❀ ♿

Set your camera to panoramic mode if you're going to squeeze Mount St. Helens and Spirit Lake into one picture.

DISTANCE: 8 miles round-trip
DURATION: 4 hours
ELEVATION CHANGE: 1,000 feet
EFFORT: Moderate
TRAIL: Dirt, ash, short paved section
USERS: Hikers, wheelchair users
SEASON: Late June–mid-November
PASSES/FEES: Northwest Forest Pass (display at the observatory)
MAPS: Green Trails Map 332 for Spirit Lake
CONTACT: Johnston Ridge Observatory, 360/274-2140 (mid-May–late October), Mount St. Helens National Volcanic Monument, 360/449-7800, www.fs.usda.gov

START THE HIKE

▶ **MILE 0-0.4: Johnston Ridge Observatory to Boundary Trail**

From the **Johnston Ridge Observatory** (watching the observatory's short film about Mount St. Helens's 1980 eruption is a perfect way to start your hike), the moonscape of the blast zone unfurls between you and the volcano's gaping maw. Let the magnitude of one of North America's most destructive geological events sink in. Follow the paved, wheelchair-accessible **Eruption Trail** as it switchbacks to the top of a knoll. From here, those with a keen eye might look east and notice the destination, an old weather station atop Harry's Ridge.

Follow the paved path down the hill and past a **monument** with the names of those killed by the eruption. At 0.4 mile, as the paved trail bends back to the **parking lot** (a possible shortcut on your return trip), turn right on the **Boundary Trail,** leave the pavement, and follow the ash-covered path into the Mount Margaret Backcountry. This is where the ADA portion of the hike ends. Signs warn of a "minimum $100 fine" for straying off-trail. Shrubs and wildflowers display nature's resiliency, adding patches of color to the desolate landscape. Look for elk and black-tailed deer, which have returned to the area since the eruption.

▶ **MILE 0.4-1.8: Boundary Trail to Satan's Shortcut**

In 1.4 miles after leaving the pavement, pass an alternate route called Devil's Elbow. Erosion forced the closure of this path across steep slopes in 2018. Go straight following the detour I call **"Satan's Shortcut."**

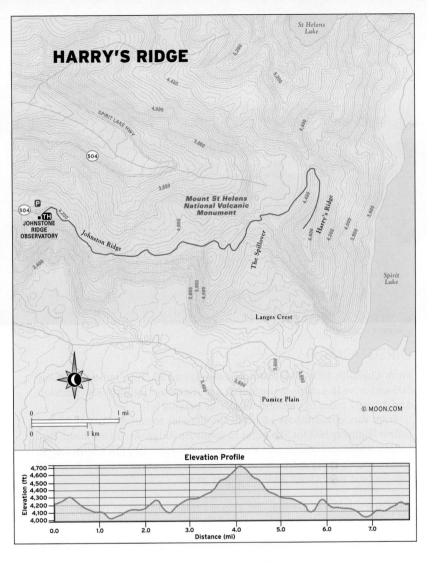

HARRY'S RIDGE

Elevation Profile

▶ **MILE 1.8-4: Satan's Shortcut to Harry's Ridge**

Half a mile farther, pass the Truman Trail (a 6.2-mile path to Windy Ridge) on your right and continue 0.9 mile to a **junction** at a saddle overlooking Spirit Lake. Turn right on **Harry's Ridge Trail** and spend the next 0.8 mile knocking out the steepest part of the journey. At the **high point**, look over massive Spirit Lake littered with logs left when the eruption blew away the once lush forest surrounding its shores. Mount St. Helens dominates the view to the south, but the glaciated peaks of Hood and Adams join the scenery.

The overwhelming sight urges you to stay for a while, but when it's time to go, travel back using the same trails.

▲ HARRY'S RIDGE TRAIL

DIRECTIONS

From Chehalis, follow I-5 south 15 miles to exit 63. Turn left on Highway 505 and drive 16.4 miles to the Spirit Lake Highway/Highway 504. Turn left and drive 37 miles to the Johnston Ridge parking lot.

From Vancouver, follow I-5 north for 48 miles to exit 49. Turn right and follow Highway 504 for 51.6 miles to Johnston Ridge. At the trailhead, find toilets, a seasonal concession stand, and an observatory ($8 adults, free 15 and younger). Entry is free for one adult with a Northwest Forest Pass and free for four adults with an interagency pass.

GPS COORDINATES: 46.276883, −122.216526 / N46° 16.613' W122° 12.9916'

BEST NEARBY BITES

The view alone is worth the stop at **Fire Mountain Grill** at 19 Mile House (15000 Spirit Lake Hwy., 360/957-1025, www.fmgrill.com, hours vary seasonally, closed winter). Overlook the North Fork Toutle River from the back porch while enjoying an elk burger and peach cobbler. From the trailhead, the 33-mile drive west takes about 40 minutes via Highway 504.

Get up close with Washington's second-tallest mountain, exploring its forests and colorful meadows and visiting the Pacific Crest Trail.

DISTANCE: 6.2 miles round-trip
DURATION: 3 hours
ELEVATION CHANGE: 1,500 feet
EFFORT: Moderate
TRAIL: Dirt, ash, rock
USERS: Hikers, leashed dogs, horseback riders
SEASON: Mid-July–October
PASSES/FEES: Northwest Forest Pass
MAPS: Green Trails Map 367S for Mount Adams
CONTACT: Gifford Pinchot National Forest, Mount Adams Ranger District, 509/395-3400, www.fs.usda.gov

Western Washington's wet climate and eastern Washington's dry weather converge in the Mount Adams Wilderness, resulting in an ecological diversity that delights visitors. On the north side of 12,276-foot Mount Adams, the Killen Creek Trail cuts through a forest of Douglas fir and pine and visits meadows made colorful by wildflowers. While Mount Adams's southern slope extends like a long ramp inviting hikers to make the nontechnical climb to the summit, its north face is steep, daunting, and best left to experienced climbers—but it makes an impressive backdrop for your adventure.

START THE HIKE

▶ **MILE 0-2.2: Registration Kiosk to Meadow**
Starting from the climber's **registration kiosk** in the parking lot, head into the woods. Going above 7,000 feet requires a Cascade Volcano Pass, available at the kiosk. You'll only get to 6,200 feet on this hike, but you'll still have to fill out a registration form at a second kiosk (a few steps down the trail as you enter the 47,122-acre wilderness). The trail climbs gradually and consistently for the first 2 miles as it passes through the woods.

The path was made by Native Americans who picked berries in the area. In season, you might have opportunities of your own to sample huckleberries. Keep an eye out for elk and deer while admiring aster, lupine, and other wildflowers. As you continue, Mount Adams comes into view, a majestic reward for your work. Expect a few short, steep sections over the next 0.2 mile before arriving at a **large meadow.**

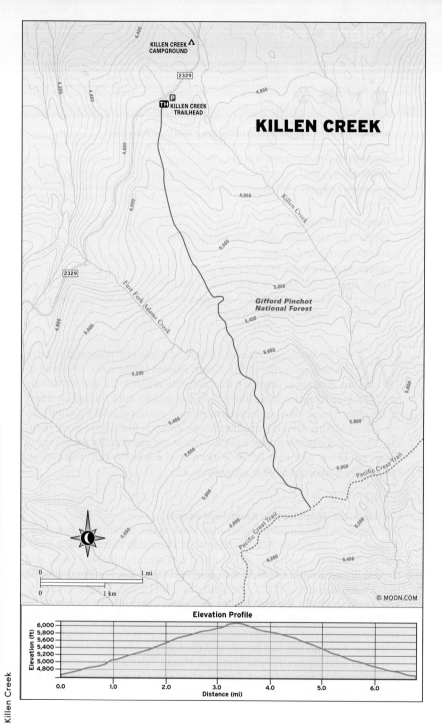

KILLEN CREEK

KILLEN CREEK CAMPGROUND

2329

TH KILLEN CREEK TRAILHEAD

Killen Creek

East Fork Adams Creek

2329

Gifford Pinchot National Forest

Pacific Crest Trail

Pacific Crest Trail

0 — 1 mi
0 — 1 km

© MOON.COM

Elevation Profile

Elevation (ft)

6,000
5,800
5,600
5,400
5,200
5,000
4,800

0.0   1.0   2.0   3.0   4.0   5.0   6.0
Distance (mi)

▲ KILLEN CREEK TRAIL

▶ **MILE 2.2–3.1: Meadow to Pacific Crest Trail Junction**
After another 0.9 mile that climbs gradually, the trail flattens and a battered placard atop a weathered post welcomes you to the 2,650-mile **Pacific Crest Trail.** Here, find a place to relax and enjoy the surroundings.
When you're ready, retrace your route.

DIRECTIONS

From U.S. 12 in Randle, go south for 1 mile on Highway 131 and then bear
left on Cispus Road/Forest Road 23. After 8.1 miles continue straight to remain on Forest Road 23 for 22.4 miles. Turn left on Forest Road 2329. Follow
Forest Road 2329 for 4.8 miles to the trailhead.

From White Salmon, go north on Highway 141 for 20.3 miles to the town
of Trout Lake and then continue straight on Mount Adams Road. In 1.3
miles continue straight on Forest Road 23. After another 23.2 miles turn
right on Forest Road 2329. Follow Forest Road 2329 for 4.8 miles to the trailhead. A vault toilet is at the trailhead.

GPS COORDINATES: 46.288471, –121.552446 / N46° 17.3083' W121° 33.1468'

Go on an underground adventure at the foot of Mount St. Helens by scrambling through one of the longest lava tubes in the United States.

DISTANCE: 2.9 miles round-trip

DURATION: 2 hours

ELEVATION CHANGE: 400 feet

EFFORT: Easy

TRAIL: Boulder fields, uneven terrain inside an unlit cave, ladder, stairs, single track

USERS: Hikers

SEASON: May–November

PASSES/FEES: Northwest Forest Pass

MAPS: Green Trails Map 332S for Mount St. Helens National Volcanic Monument

CONTACT: Mount St. Helens National Volcanic Monument, 360/449-7800, www.fs.usda.gov.

The Ape Cave formed about 1,900 years ago when Mount St. Helens erupted with glowing orange lava rather than its more common explosive eruptions. The lava flowed into and through a stream drainage for about a year. The lava cooled on the surface and sides, and when the lava stopped flowing the 13,042-foot lava tube (believed to be the third longest in the United States) was left behind.

START THE HIKE

▶ **MILE 0-0.1: Visitors Center to Cave Floor**

This underworldly hike starts on a paved path beside the **visitors center** at the north end of the parking lot. Shoe brushes are trailside to clean your boots. Cleaning your gear before and after entering the cave helps protect bats from the deadly white-nose syndrome.

At 0.1 mile, reach a set of **stairs** that descend into a large pit. You can walk down the first set of steps and still have plenty of light to appreciate the subterranean setting. But by the bottom of the second staircase you'll need a trustworthy headlamp. The Forest Service recommends carrying three sources of light and extra batteries. Sturdy shoes, warm clothing (it's 42 degrees year-round in the cave), and lightweight gloves with good grip are also a good idea. Even with gloves, however, try not to touch the slick walls. This slime is a food source for cave life and takes years to grow.

▶ **MILE 0.1-1: Cave Floor to Upper Cave and Lava Fall**

Once on the cave's floor you'll have two options. A **sign** bolted to the wall points right to the easier and shorter lower cave, a 0.75-mile, out-and-back walk that's a fun option for kids. Go left, past the stairs, to explore the

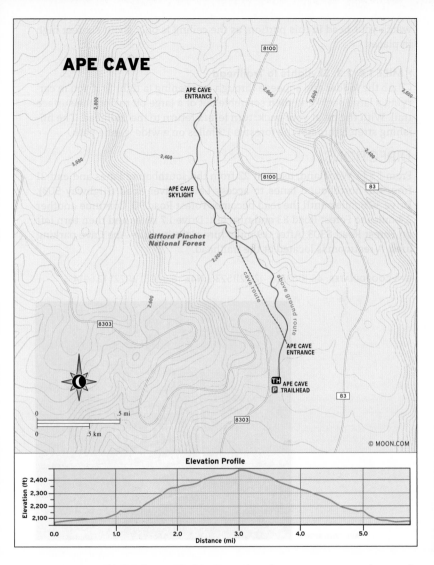

APE CAVE

APE CAVE
ENTRANCE

APE CAVE
SKYLIGHT

Gifford Pinchot
National Forest

cave route

above ground route

APE CAVE
ENTRANCE

TH APE CAVE
P TRAILHEAD

8100

8100

83

8303

8303

83

0   .5 mi

0   .5 km

© MOON.COM

Elevation Profile

Elevation (ft)

2,400
2,300
2,200
2,100

0.0   1.0   2.0   3.0   4.0   5.0

Distance (mi)

upper cave. The 88-foot-wide **Big Room** is a few steps away and a good place to appreciate this geological wonder.

Beyond the Big Room, traveling the upper cave requires a little extra work. You'll climb over 27 large **boulder piles** called breakdown. These boulders fell from the walls and ceiling after the ancient eruption subsided.

About 0.9 mile into the upper cave, reach an 8-foot-tall **"Lava Fall."** This basalt wall might require a little teamwork to scale. A notch is chiseled about halfway up the left side of the wall to help cavers.

▶ MILE 1-1.6: Lava Fall to Skylights

Another 0.4 mile brings you to the first of two **skylights** at the upper end of the lava tube. Continue 0.2 mile farther to the exit. Should you want to explore a little more, you can go another 500 feet to the end of the cave;

watch your head in this portion, as the ceiling is only about six feet high in places.

▸ MILE 1.6-2.9: Skylights to Trailhead

Climb the **ladder** and squeeze through an opening (a tight fit if you're carrying a large pack) and then scramble out of a large pit to find the surface trail. With the pit at your back, turn left to return to the trailhead. The finishing stretch through the forest is 1.3 miles on a wide, gentle path.

DIRECTIONS

From I-5 in Woodland, use exit 22 from the southbound lanes and exit 21 from the northbound lanes to access Lewis River Road (Highway 503). Drive 30.6 miles until the road becomes Forest Road 90. Continue another 3.4 miles to Forest Road 83 and turn left. Drive 1.7 miles and then turn left on Forest Road 8303. After 0.9 mile, turn right into the Ape Cave parking area. A restroom is located at the trailhead.

GPS COORDINATES: 46.108338, –122.211523 / N46° 6.5003' W122° 12.6914'

APE CAVE SIGN ▸

BEST NEARBY BITES

Woodland's **Fat Moose Bar and Grill** (1382 Lewis River Rd., 360/225-7944, www.fatmoosebarandgrill.com, 11am-10pm Mon.-Thurs., 11am-1am Fri.-Sat., 9am-8pm Sun.) can prepare a box lunch before your adventure, quell your hunger with a burger and brew, or test your alimentary limits. The Undertaker Burger is about seven inches tall and includes two pounds of hamburger, eight slices of ham, and four eggs. It's $25, but it comes with a pound of french fries and a pitcher of soda. Finish it all in less than 30 minutes and it's free. From the trailhead, the 37-mile drive southwest takes about 50 minutes via Highway 503/Lewis River Road.

6

Monitor Ridge to Mount St. Helens Summit

MOUNT ST. HELENS NATIONAL VOLCANIC MONUMENT, COUGAR

Scramble up snowfields and a rocky ridge to the crater rim of a volcano that blew its top in 1980.

DISTANCE: 10 miles round-trip

DURATION: 8 hours

ELEVATION CHANGE: 4,500 feet

EFFORT: Strenuous

TRAIL: Dirt, steep snow slopes, boulders, ash

USERS: Hikers

SEASON: Mid-May-October

PASSES/FEES: Northwest Forest Pass, climbing permit ($22 per person)

MAPS: Green Trails Map 364S for Mount St. Helens Climbing

CONTACT: Mount St. Helens National Volcanic Monument, 360/449-7800, www.fs.usda.gov

This is a challenging hike, but it's easier than it used to be. Prior to the morning of May 18, 1980, Mount St. Helens was a symmetrical stratovolcano standing 9,677 feet above sea level. But, that morning, the most disastrous eruption in U.S. history blew away the mountain's north face and shortened the summit elevation to 8,337 feet. If those facts don't do it already, the sheer magnitude of the event that created the 2-mile-wide crater is likely to blow your mind once your reach the top.

START THE HIKE

▶ **MILE 0-2.1: Ptarmigan Trailhead to Loowit Trail**

The hiking begins on the **Ptarmigan Trail** at Climber's Bivouac on the mountain's south side, but your journey needs to start in front of a computer on March 18 at 7am PDT, when permits go on sale. To limit visitor impact on the peak, climbing permits are limited to 100 per day May 15-October 31, when climbing is most popular. The first-come, first-served permits ($15 per person plus $6 per transaction) sell out within minutes at www.recreation.gov. But, often, hikers can buy passes from other hikers at www.purmit.com.

The Ptarmigan Trail starts by climbing through an evergreen forest where you might hear birds chirp and see squirrels scurrying up trees. Views are scarce at first, but after about 1.5 miles you'll get glimpses of the **rocky ridge** you're about to climb. Over the next 0.6 mile the trail steepens and offers a view of Mount Adams before it intersects with the Loowit Trail.

A pit toilet (the only one on this trip) is located near the **intersection.** The 28-mile Loowit Trail loops around the mountain. Cross the Loowit

▲ DESCENDING MOUNT ST. HELENS

Trail and soon you'll step out of the trees and find yourself staring up the steep slopes of Mount St. Helens. A **sign at 4,800 feet above sea level** reminds hikers that this is as far as you can go without one of those coveted climbing permits.

▶ MILE 2.1–4.9: Loowit Trail to Monitor Ridge

From here, pick your way up the boulders to access **Monitor Ridge.** Posts placed along the ridge help hikers navigate the next 2.8 miles to the crater rim. Sometimes, forward progress is hard to come by as ash makes the climb reminiscent of scaling an enormous sand dune.

While it's not a bad option to work your way from post to post while scrambling over boulders, many find it more comfortable to leave the rocks and make their way upward on the snowfields. With the absence of trail, enjoy the options but be sure to regularly confirm the route: It's hard to get off course during the slow uphill push, but relatively easy to do on the descent. Gaiters help keep ash and snow out of your boots. Gloves can protect your hands from abrasive surfaces. Trekking poles will help with balance and take some of the stress off your knees during the long descent. In winter, spring, and early summer, conditions might require crampons and an ice axe.

▶ MILE 4.9–5: Monitor Ridge to Mount St. Helens Summit

The final few steps to the **rim** are visually stunning. Mount Rainier and Spirit Lake come into view. And, below you, the volcano's new lava dome rises from the crater floor. It is important to keep your feet on solid ground at the summit. Cornices form on the crater rim and sometimes block the view. A short walk along the rim usually yields an opening.

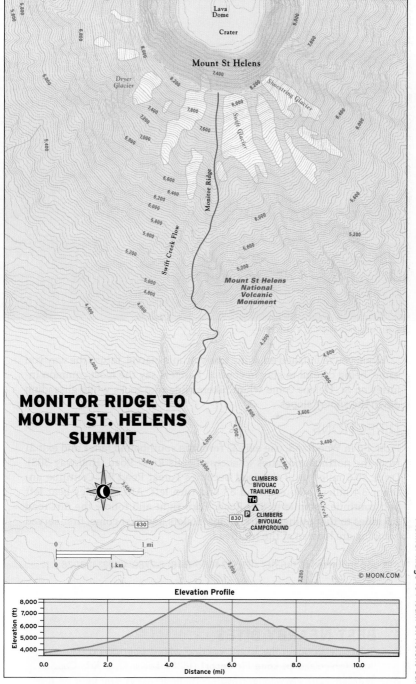

MONITOR RIDGE TO MOUNT ST. HELENS SUMMIT

Lava Dome

Crater

Mount St Helens
7,400

Dryer Glacier

Shoestring Glacier

Swift Glacier

Monitor Ridge

Swift Creek Flow

Mount St Helens National Volcanic Monument

CLIMBERS BIVOUAC TRAILHEAD
TH
P
830
CLIMBERS BIVOUAC CAMPGROUND

830

Swift Creek

0 — 1 mi
0 — 1 km

© MOON.COM

Elevation Profile

Elevation (ft)

8,000
7,000
6,000
5,000
4,000

0.0   2.0   4.0   6.0   8.0   10.0

Distance (mi)

▲ THE VIEW FROM MOUNT ST. HELENS

When you're finished enjoying this volcanic marvel, return the way you came, being careful to stay in control. Rangers say the most common injuries on St. Helens come when hikers slide into rocks while glissading down the snowy slopes.

DIRECTIONS

From I-5 in Woodland, use exit 22 from the southbound lanes and exit 21 from the northbound lanes to access Lewis River Road (Highway 503). Drive 30.6 miles until the road becomes Forest Road 90. Continue another 3.4 miles to Forest Road 83 and turn left. After 3 miles bear left and continue 0.4 mile to 830 Road. Turn right and follow the dirt road 2.5 miles to the trailhead parking lot. Toilets and first-come, first-served camping are located at the trailhead.

GPS COORDINATES: 46.146315, –122.183460 / N46° 8.7789' W122° 11.0076'

> ## BEST NEARBY BITES
>
> Celebrate bagging this iconic volcano with a beer and a thin-crust "Kick Ash" pizza at **Lone Fir Resort** (16806 Lewis River Rd., Cougar, 360/238-5210, www.lonefirresort.com, hours vary). The beer on tap comes from Northwest breweries. From the trailhead, the 14-mile drive southwest takes less than 30 minutes via Forest Road 83 and Highway 503.

7

Lava Canyon

MOUNT ST. HELENS NATIONAL VOLCANIC MONUMENT, COUGAR

🦌 ❀ ⛲ 🚶 ♿

Cross a suspension bridge and descend a 30-foot ladder while exploring a narrow canyon scoured by the 1980 eruption of Mount St. Helens.

DISTANCE: 5.8 miles round-trip
DURATION: 3 hours
ELEVATION CHANGE: 1,600 feet
EFFORT: Moderate
TRAIL: Paved trail, dirt trail, exposed sections, ladders, stairs, suspension bridge
USERS: Hikers, wheelchair users
SEASON: Late May–November
PASSES/FEES: Northwest Forest Pass
MAPS: Green Trails Map 364 for Mount St. Helens
CONTACT: Mount St. Helens National Volcanic Monument, 360/449-7800, www.fs.usda.gov

Lava Canyon Trail 184 is a three-layer hike with each level a little more challenging than the last. Start with a paved wheelchair-friendly section and work your way up to a better-watch-your-step stretch that sometimes feels like a shelf hanging on the canyon wall.

START THE HIKE

▶ **MILE 0–0.3: ADA Trailhead to Muddy River Views**
The paved **ADA trail** starts on the south side of the parking lot and descends a grade steep enough to give pause to some wheelchair users. Benches are available along the path that quickly delivers views of the **Muddy River.** Interpretive signs on this 0.3-mile section tell the story of how the river carved the canyon and how ancient lava flows created large volcanic rock formations. The 1980 Mount St. Helens eruption scoured away trees, leaving a dingy gray canyon that's since recovered its green.

▶ **MILE 0.3–0.7: Muddy River Views to Suspension Bridge**
The ADA path continues to a **waterfall viewing area,** but if you plan to hike farther turn right just before the viewing area (you'll visit it on your return) and use the **steel bridge** to cross the river. On the east side, turn left and walk down cement steps, a metal staircase, and a rocky path for 0.4 mile to a **suspension bridge** that moves with each step. Cross it back to the west side of the canyon and find an option to turn left to return to the parking area, or turn right for the hike's most challenging layer.

▶ **MILE 0.7–2.95: Suspension Bridge to Smith Creek Trail**
Turning right, descend the exposed trail hugging the edge of the canyon with a steep drop to the river on the right. In 0.5 mile the trail is interrupted

SOUTH CASCADES

Lava Canyon

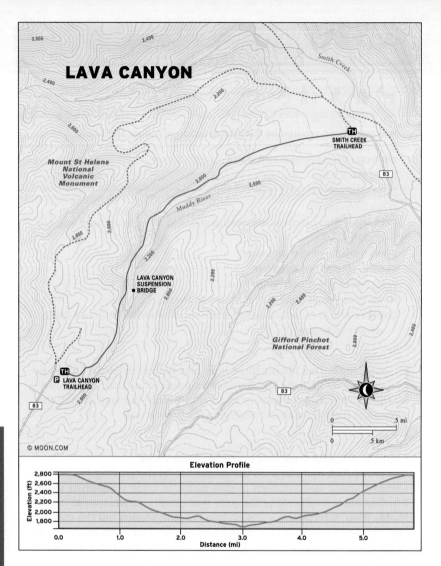

LAVA CANYON

Mount St Helens
National
Volcanic
Monument

Smith Creek

SMITH CREEK
TRAILHEAD

83

Muddy River

LAVA CANYON
SUSPENSION
BRIDGE

Gifford Pinchot
National Forest

83

LAVA CANYON
TRAILHEAD

83

© MOON.COM

0   .5 mi
0   .5 km

Elevation Profile

by a **cliff**. A 30-foot **ladder** allows you to continue into the heart of the canyon. Pass a spur trail 0.25 mile beyond the ladder. (This 0.3-mile round-trip side trail uses a ladder to ascend a rock formation called The Ship and deliver views up the canyon.) Continue 1.5 miles beyond **The Ship spur** to the **intersection** with the Smith Creek Trail. Along the way, emerge from older forest into an area with trees so small it seems like a Christmas tree farm. The intersection is where you'll turn back, but first head right a few steps on the **Smith Creek Trail** to view the confluence of Smith Creek and the Muddy River.

▸ **MILE 2.95-5.8: Smith Creek Trail to ADA Trailhead**
When you're ready to return, head back the way you came. At the **suspension bridge**, continue straight to explore the west side of the **intermediate**

▲ LOWER LAVA CANYON TRAIL

loop and visit the **waterfall viewing area.** This 0.3-mile section of the **Lava Canyon Loop** will deposit you back on the **ADA trail** for a 0.3-mile stroll back to the parking lot.

DIRECTIONS

From I-5 in Woodland, use exit 22 (southbound) and exit 21 (northbound) to access Lewis River Road (Highway 503). Drive 30.6 miles until the road becomes Forest Road 90. Continue another 3.4 miles to Forest Road 83 and turn left. After 3 miles bear right and continue 7.5 miles to the trailhead. A toilet is located at the trailhead.

GPS COORDINATES: 46.165722, –122.088385 / N46° 9.9433′ W122° 5.3031′

BEST NEARBY BITES
The Cougar Bar and Grill (16849 Lewis River Rd., 360/238-5252, 10am-9pm Mon.-Thurs., 10am-10pm Fri., 8am-10pm Sat.-Sun.) pays tribute to local soldiers past and present with framed images hanging above the bar. The Volcano Burger topped with jalapeno and chipotle mayo is popular among visitors, but the restaurant is best known for its halibut. The staff says some customers make the 130-mile round-trip drive from Portland each week just for the popular dish. From the trailhead, the 18-mile drive southwest takes about 30 minutes via Forest Road 83 and Highway 503.

NEARBY CAMPGROUNDS

NAME	DESCRIPTION	FACILITIES	SEASON	FEE
Iron Creek	situated on the Cispus River and easily accessed from Randle and Highway 12	98 RV and tent sites, restrooms	late May–early September	$20
Forest Road 25, Randle, 877/444-6777, www.recreation.gov				
Takhlakh Lake Campground	a lakeside campground with views of Mount Adams	54 tent sites, restrooms	late June–late September	$18
Takhlakh Loop Road, Randle, 877/444-6777, www.recreation.gov				
Kid Valley Campground	in the woods along North Fork Toutle River with easy access to Mount St. Helens	30 RV and tent sites, restrooms	year-round	$20-30
9360 Spirit Lake Highway, east of Toutle, 360/274-9060, www.kidvalley.com				
Lower Falls Campground	a forested camp with trails leading to the Lewis River and several waterfalls	43 RV and tent sites, restrooms	late May–late September	$15
Forest Road 90, Mount Adams, Gifford Pinchot National Forest, 509/395-3400, www.recreation.gov				
Swift Forest Camp	on the Swift Reservoir just outside Mount St. Helens National Volcanic Monument	93 tent and RV sites, restrooms	late April–September	$18
280 Road, Cougar, 360/238-5251, www.pacificcorp.com				

CENTRAL WASHINGTON

In stark contrast to the Cascades, Puget Sound, and the Pacific Ocean beaches, Central Washington adds to the breadth of the state's diversity. With topography shaped by lava flows and massive ice age floods, it is a wonderland for geology lovers. Hiking here challenges your imagination more than your legs. What was the view like from atop Badger Mountain when ancient Lake Lewis covered the Tri-Cities area? What was it like 15 million years ago when the lava flows that helped form Yakima's Cowiche Canyon covered most of the state east of the Cascades? What would Steamboat Rock look like before dams created the Banks Lake reservoir in Grand Coulee? Whether you want to cap a day of hiking with a dip in a lake or indulge your inner scientist, this region has you covered.

▲ VIEWS ON THE YAKIMA SKYLINE TRAIL ▲ STEAMBOAT ROCK

1 **Steamboat Rock**
DISTANCE: 3.2 miles round-trip
DURATION: 1.5 hours
EFFORT: Easy/moderate

2 **Ancient Lakes**
DISTANCE: 4.4 miles round-trip
DURATION: 2.5 hours
EFFORT: Easy

3 **Yakima Skyline Trail**
DISTANCE: 6 miles round-trip
DURATION: 3 hours
EFFORT: Moderate

4 **Cowiche Canyon**
DISTANCE: 5.6 miles round-trip
DURATION: 3 hours
EFFORT: Easy/moderate

5 **Badger Mountain: Trailhead Park Loop**
DISTANCE: 3 miles round-trip
DURATION: 1.5 hours
EFFORT: Easy/moderate

▾ WATERFALL AT ANCIENT LAKES

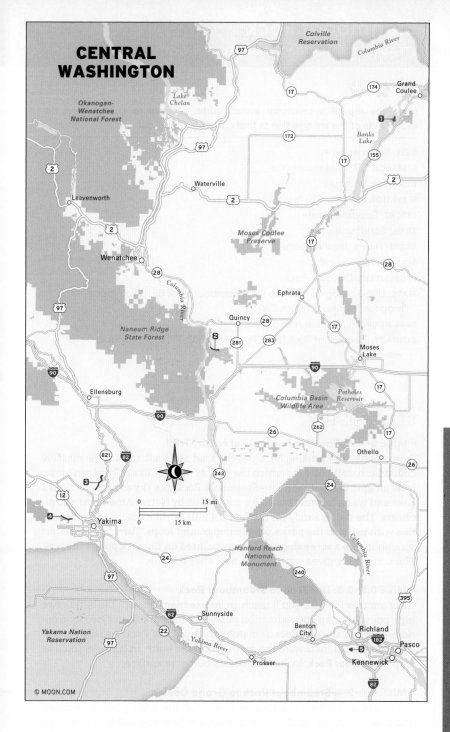

CENTRAL
WASHINGTON

Okanogan-
Wenatchee
National Forest

Colville
Reservation

Columbia River

Lake
Chelan

Grand
Coulee

Banks
Lake

Waterville

Leavenworth

Moses Coulee
Preserve

Wenatchee

Columbia River

Ephrata

Quincy

Naneum Ridge
State Forest

Moses
Lake

Ellensburg

Potholes
Reservoir

Columbia Basin
Wildlife Area

Othello

Yakima

Hanford Reach
National
Monument

Columbia River

Sunnyside

Benton
City

Richland

Pasco

Yakama Nation
Reservation

Yakima River

Prosser

Kennewick

© MOON.COM

0   15 mi

0   15 km

Steamboat Rock

STEAMBOAT ROCK STATE PARK, ELECTRIC CITY

From the top of a columnar basalt butte, attempt to comprehend the magnitude of the ice age floods that carved Grand Coulee.

BEST: Summer Hikes
DISTANCE: 3.2 miles round-trip
DURATION: 1.5 hours
ELEVATION CHANGE: 800 feet
EFFORT: Easy/moderate
TRAIL: Sand, scree, dirt
USERS: Hikers, leashed dogs
SEASON: Year-round
PASSES/FEES: Discover Pass
MAPS: USGS topographic map for Steamboat Rock SE, USGS topographic map for Steamboat Rock SW
PARK HOURS: 6:30am-sunset daily
CONTACT: Steamboat Rock State Park, 509/633-1304, http://parks.state. wa.us

START THE HIKE

▶ **MILE 0-0.5: Day-Use Parking Lot to Dirt Trail**

From the day-use **parking lot,** cross the road and walk toward the massive columnar basalt butte for which the park is named. To say "you can't miss it" is an epic understatement—Steamboat Rock juts skyward out of Banks Lake and was a landmark used for navigation by Native Americans and pioneers. The trail is sandy for the first 0.4 mile, until it reaches an **intersection** with paths to the park's other campground loops. Turn right and start scrambling up a **scree slope.** An arrow painted on the rock points the way. The scrambling gives way to a dirt trail after 0.1 mile.

▶ **MILE 0.5-0.8: Dirt Trail to Steamboat Rock**

After another 0.1 mile, you'll reach an **intersection** between the butte's two high points. A map approximation posted by the park shows two loop options here, but the trail doesn't match this depiction. For the easiest-to-follow path, turn right toward the north end of the butte. In 0.2 mile, you'll be atop **Steamboat Rock,** looking across its 600-acre surface.

▶ **MILE 0.8-2.4: Steamboat Rock to Grand Coulee**

Turn right and follow the 1.6-mile loop. Walking amid grass, sagebrush, and balsamroot, you might have moments where you feel as if you're exploring a typical patch of arid Central Washington wilderness. Then the trail runs along the rim of the butte, and you're reminded that you're in the

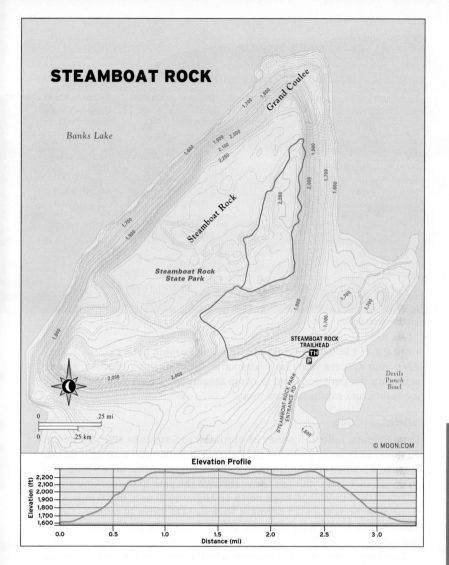

STEAMBOAT ROCK

Banks Lake

Grand Coulee

Steamboat Rock

Steamboat Rock
State Park

STEAMBOAT ROCK
TRAILHEAD

Devils
Punch
Bowl

STEAMBOAT ROCK PARK
ENTRANCE RD

0   .25 mi

0   .25 km

© MOON.COM

Elevation Profile

middle of a geological marvel. As the name implies, **Grand Coulee** is the most famous of the deep channels that ice age floods carved in eastern Washington. Steamboat Rock was an island in that ancient, diverted Columbia River bed. When the waters subsided and the Columbia returned to its usual route, the island became a massive butte. From atop the butte you can hear chatter from boats and the nearby campground as you look out over the lake toward **Northrup Canyon.** Keep an eye out for bald and golden eagles and peregrine falcons.

You may be thinking that the steep slopes of the coulee may look familiar. They made a six-second cameo in the 1984 adventure classic *Indiana Jones and the Temple of Doom*, part of a scene in which Indy and friends jumped out of a plane with nothing but an inflatable raft.

▲ STEAMBOAT ROCK

▶ **MILE 2.4–3.2: Grand Coulee to Day-Use Parking Lot**
Alas, your descent won't be so dramatic. After finishing the loop, simply return on the path you used to climb Steamboat. Watch your step on the loose rock and sandy, steep sections.

DIRECTIONS

From Ephrata, follow Highway 28 northeast to Soap Lake and turn left on Highway 17. Drive 21.3 miles to the Dry Falls Junction and turn right on U.S. 2. Drive 4.3 miles and continue straight on Highway 155. In 18.9 miles the park entrance is on your left. Drive through the park to the parking area.

From U.S. 2 in Wilbur, head north on Highway 21 and, in 0.6 mile, continue straight as the road becomes Highway 174. Drive 19 miles to Grand Coulee, then turn left on Highway 155. In 7 miles the park entrance is on the right.

Camping, restrooms with showers, a boat launch, and 56 picnic sites are located in the park.

GPS COORDINATES: 47.863779, –119.121098 / N47° 51.8267' W119° 7.2659'

COLUMBIA BASIN WILDLIFE AREA, QUINCY

Enjoy pothole lakes and a waterfall deep inside Potholes Coulee, carved out by the ice age floods.

DISTANCE: 4.4 miles round-trip
DURATION: 2.5 hours
ELEVATION CHANGE: 250 feet
EFFORT: Easy
TRAIL: Sand, dirt, road, single track
USERS: Hikers, leashed dogs, mountain bikers, horseback riders
SEASON: March–November
PASSES/FEES: Discover Pass
MAPS: USGS topographic map for Babcock Ridge
CONTACT: Columbia Basin Wildlife Area, 509/765-6641, www.wdfw.wa.gov

While many people explore this area in the summer, bring plenty of water and be prepared for intense, triple-digit heat. Consider doing this hike early in the morning, in the evening, or in the spring or fall when temperatures are a little lower.

If you hike here on a summer afternoon when triple-digit temperatures bake the shrub-steppe desert, you might be shocked to find lakes at the end of this sandy trail. Such is the wonder of Washington's channeled scablands. The setting stands in stark contrast to the forested and mountainous hikes just over an hour away in the Cascades—a reminder of the diversity that makes Washington such a fascinating place

START THE HIKE

▶ **MILE 0-0.3: Jeep Trailhead to First Trail Junction**
The hike starts on a sandy **Jeep trail** beyond the gate at the south end of the parking lot. Fat bulrushes rise from trailside wetlands as you walk along **Babcock Bench** above the Columbia River. Be sure to look up for American kestrels, hawks, and other birds. But also look down for rattlesnakes sunning along the path. After 0.3 mile, reach the first of several paths heading east along the floor of the ravine. Any of the trails will take you to Ancient Lakes, but turning left on the first keeps you closest to the wall with the added bonus of taking you past a waterfall.

▶ **MILE 0.3-1.2: First Trail Junction to Waterfall and Boulder**
In another 0.9 mile, the **waterfall** splashes over the edge of the coulee. Pass a **boulder** so large it blocks the sound of the falling water. Continue following the path east through sagebrush and perennial wildflowers such as lupine and balsamroot.

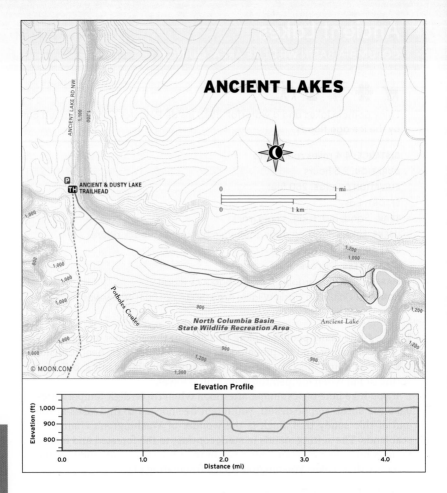

ANCIENT LAKES

ANCIENT & DUSTY LAKE
TRAILHEAD

North Columbia Basin
State Wildlife Recreation Area

Ancient Lake

Potholes Coulee

© MOON.COM

Elevation Profile

▶ MILE 1.2-2.7: Waterfall and Boulder to Lakeshore

The **lakes** come into view after another 0.3 mile. Use the faint, dusty trails to find your way to the **lakeshore** at the northeast corner of the coulee. In another 0.6 mile you'll reach the north end of the lake. Spend some time here admiring the striking view: a multilevel **waterfall** cascading down a basalt slope. Walk the vegetated horseshoe-shaped shoreline for 0.6 mile and keep a lookout for ducks and other waterfowl as the trail turns back to the west.

▶ MILE 2.7-4.4: Lakeshore to Jeep Trailhead

At the west end of the lake, turn right on a dirt path and climb uphill for 0.1 mile to rejoin the trail you used to get to the lake. You can return the way you came 1.6 miles back to the car or find another path to walk along the open canyon floor.

DIRECTIONS

From I-90 near George, take exit 149 (eastbound) or exit 151 (westbound) and follow Highway 281 north (5.5 miles from exit 249 or 4.5 miles from

▲ THE ANCIENT LAKES ARE IN A CANYON CARVED BY ICE AGE FLOODS.

exit 251). Turn left on White Trail Road at the north end of Colockum Ridge Golf Course (on the left). Drive 7.8 miles and turn left on Road 9 NW. After 2 miles the road becomes Ancient Lake Road and continues for 3.8 miles to the trailhead. A toilet is available.

GPS COORDINATES: 47.15995, -119.98061 / N47° 9.597' W119° 58.8366'

BEST NEARBY BITES

Quell your post-hike hunger in Ephrata, where you won't have any trouble finding tasty Mexican food at restaurants like **El Agave** (906 Basin St. SW, 509/717-2062, 11am-9pm Sun.-Thurs., 11am-10pm Fri.-Sat.) and **Tequila's** (222 Basin St. NW, 509/754-1306, hours vary). From the trailhead, the 11-mile drive northeast takes about 20 minutes via Ancient Lake Road and Highway 28.

3 Yakima Skyline Trail

WENAS WILDLIFE AREA, SELAH

Walk the rim of the Yakima River canyon while enjoying views of Roza Dam, two towering volcanoes, and spring wildflowers.

BEST: Brew Hikes
DISTANCE: 6 miles round-trip
DURATION: 3 hours
ELEVATION CHANGE: 1,600 feet
EFFORT: Moderate
TRAIL: Dirt road, dirt and rock trail
USERS: Hikers, leashed dogs, horseback riders, off-road vehicles
SEASON: March-November
PASSES/FEES: Discover Pass
MAPS: WDFW maps available at www.wdfw.wa.gov
CONTACT: Wenas Wildlife Area, 509/697-4503, www.wdfw.wa.gov

Yakima—"The Palm Springs of Washington" as its famous I-82 sign proclaims—gets about 200 days of sunshine annually, making it an ideal escape for vitamin D-deprived hikers from the Seattle area. The Yakima Skyline Trail is a scenic place to enjoy that sunshine in full: There is no shade, so pack plenty of water and sunscreen.

START THE HIKE

▶ **MILE 0-0.7: Buffalo Road Gate to Yakima Skyline Trail**

From the gate, where the state Department of Natural Resources hopes to soon build a small parking lot, walk **Buffalo Road** northeast for 0.7 mile. This section of the road above the Roza Canal and Yakima River is often closed to motorized vehicles to protect soils and vegetation. Enjoy the view to the southeast of the imposing Fred G. Redmon Memorial Bridges over Selah Creek Canyon. Find the **Yakima Skyline Trail** next to a battered post at a hairpin bend on Buffalo Road. The dirt and rock path climbs gradually from the north side of the road. The path can be muddy and slippery after a rain. In the spring, lupine, bitterroot, larkspur, and other wildflowers add splashes of purples and pinks to the landscape.

Wenas Wildlife Area is home to such a diverse collection of wildlife that my hiking partner and I found ourselves playing "Name that Scat." Elk, deer, bears, bighorn sheep, grouse, turkey, quail, raptors, and reptiles (stay alert for rattlesnakes) frequent the area. Check hunting regulations and plan accordingly. Wearing hunter orange is a wise move. Ornithologists frequent the area, too, in hopes of catching glimpses of Bullock's orioles, warblers, sparrows, and other birds.

CENTRAL WASHINGTON

Yakima Skyline Trail

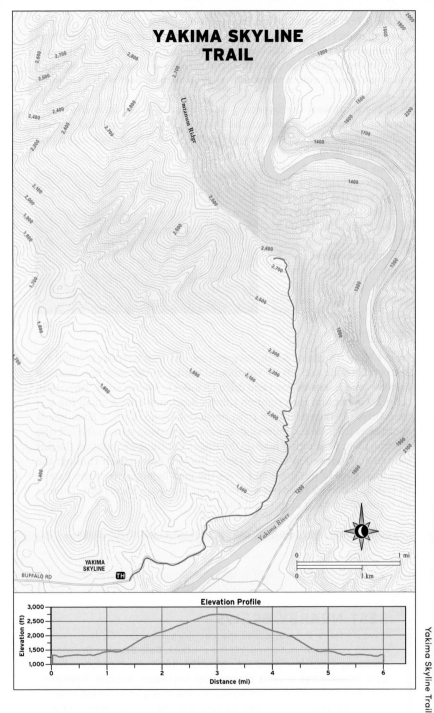

YAKIMA SKYLINE TRAIL

Umtanum Ridge

Yakima River

YAKIMA
SKYLINE

BUFFALO RD

TH

0 — 1 mi

0 — 1 km

Elevation Profile

Elevation (ft): 1,000 / 1,500 / 2,000 / 2,500 / 3,000

Distance (mi): 0 1 2 3 4 5 6

▶ **MILE 0.7–3: Yakima Skyline Trail to Canyon Rim**

The trail makes its way east for 0.5 mile before turning north and climbing the **canyon rim**. A few false summits might lure you into thinking you're closer to the scenic high point than you actually are, but after another 1.8 miles you'll reach your destination: a **hilltop hitching post** with a stunning view.

To the southwest the sweeping view includes Selah, farmland, and a sliver of Yakima visible through the Selah Gap. On clear days, the scenery includes Mount Rainier and Mount Adams. To the north, look down into the canyon holding the serpentine paths of the Yakima River and Highway 821. Below you, the 67-foot-tall Roza Dam diverts a portion of the river into the 94.8-mile Roza Canal.

From this scenic perch, return the way you came.

SUNSET ON YAKIMA
SKYLINE TRAIL ▶

DIRECTIONS

From I-82 northeast of Selah, take exit 26 and turn northwest (right for eastbound traffic and left for westbound traffic) on Highway 821. Take the first left onto Harrison Road and drive 1.9 miles to Wenas Road. Turn right, drive 2.9 miles, and turn right on Gibson Road, just after a small fire station. Drive 0.2 mile and turn right on Buffalo Road. Buffalo Road bends south after 0.5 mile and immediately passes a parking area on the left (the starting point for another hike up the ridge). Continue 1.5 miles on the dirt road to an intersection with a gate on the left. Let yourself through the gate, park beside the road, and close the gate behind you. If the gate is locked, do not block the driveway to private property on the right. There is no restroom or water at the trailhead.

GPS COORDINATES: 46.708167, –120.486566 / N46° 42.49' W120° 29.194'

BEST NEARBY BREWS

It would be a shame to visit the country's most prolific hop-producing valley without sampling the product. **Bale Breaker Brewing Company** (1801 Birchfield Rd., 509/424-4000, www.balebreaker. com, hours vary) is on a commercial hop farm. Wander through the fields, grab a pint in the taproom, and play games on the lawn. Food is not prepared on-site; visitors often have pizza delivered or bring their own food. From the trailhead, the 15-mile drive northeast takes less than 30 minutes via I-82 and Highway 24.

CENTRAL WASHINGTON   Yakima Skyline Trail

4 Cowiche Canyon

YAKIMA

Listen to singing birds while following a creek through a canyon formed by ancient lava flows.

BEST: Wildflower Hikes
DISTANCE: 5.6 miles round-trip
DURATION: 3 hours
ELEVATION CHANGE: 200 feet
EFFORT: Easy/moderate
TRAIL: Wide dirt path
USERS: Hikers, leashed dogs, mountain bikers, horseback riders (no bikes and horses when the trail is muddy)
SEASON: Year-round
PASSES/FEES: None
MAPS: Trail maps available at www.cowichecanyon.org
CONTACT: Cowiche Canyon Conservancy, 509/248-5065, www.cowichecanyon.org

START THE HIKE

▶ **MILE 0-0.6: Parking Lot East End to First Cowiche Creek Bridge**
From the small **parking lot** at the east end of the **Cowiche Canyon Trail,** follow the wide gravel path westward past an organic hop farm as it enters the canyon. In 0.6 mile, you'll reach the first of nine bridges crossing **Cowiche Creek.** The creek gives life to a lush green riparian swath cutting through the otherwise brown, arid environment. You'll walk past golden balsamroot and pink bitterroot growing amid the sagebrush. This trail is especially popular for bird-watching. Hummingbirds, turkey vultures, red-tailed hawks, wrens, Bullock's orioles, and robins are canyon regulars. Keep an eye out for rattlesnakes and other wildlife as well. Marmots are sometimes spotted playing among the rocks.

▶ **MILE 0.6-1: First Cowiche Creek Bridge to Vineyard Trail Detour (1.6 miles)**
At 0.4 mile beyond the **first bridge,** you'll reach an intersection with the **East Upland Trails.** A few steps farther (just over a bridge) is the **Vineyard Trail,** a 1.6-mile one-way digression especially alluring to wine lovers. The spur leads out of the canyon to views of Mount Rainier and Mount Adams—and the tasting room at Wilridge Estate Vineyard, Winery & Distillery (250 Ehler Rd., Yakima, 509/966-0686, www.wildridgewinery.com).

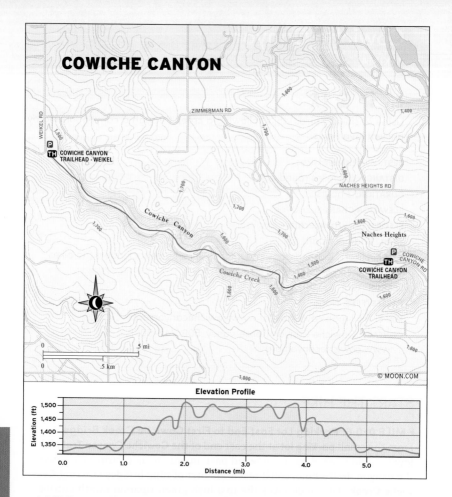

COWICHE CANYON

ZIMMERMAN RD

WEIKEL RD

COWICHE CANYON
TRAILHEAD - WEIKEL

NACHES HEIGHTS RD

Cowiche Canyon

Naches Heights

COWICHE
CANYON RD

COWICHE CANYON
TRAILHEAD

Cowiche Creek

0   .5 mi

0   .5 km

© MOON.COM

Elevation Profile

Elevation (ft)

1,500
1,450
1,400
1,350

0.0   1.0   2.0   3.0   4.0   5.0

Distance (mi)

▶ **MILE 1-1.7: First Cowiche Creek Bridge to Cowiche Canyon Floor**

If you're not detouring, continue 0.7 mile along the creek to the narrowest section of the **canyon**. About 15 million years ago, lava flowed from fissures near Pullman and covered much of eastern Washington and Oregon. The rocky canyon floor and south wall are just the tip of the basalt-berg that reaches about a mile beneath the earth's surface.

▶ **MILE 1.7-2.4: Cowiche Canyon Floor to Lone Pine Trail**

Walk another 0.7 mile past the narrow stretch to another **intersection,** this time with the **Lone Pine Trail,** which leads south (left) to a collection of short trail loops you can explore. If you don't want to investigate these trails, continue straight.

▶ **MILE 2.4-2.8: Lone Pine Trail to Weikel Road**

At 0.4 mile beyond the intersection, the trail passes a few homes as it arrives at its **west trailhead** on Weikel Road, the stopping point. Return the way you came through the canyon.

▲ COWICHE CANYON TRAIL

DIRECTIONS

From U.S. 12 in Yakima, turn southwest on Ackley Road and then make a quick left on Powerhouse Road. Drive 0.2 mile and turn right on Cowiche Canyon Road. Continue 2.2 miles to the east trailhead. A portable toilet is at the small trailhead parking lot.

GPS COORDINATES: 46.622220, -120.614727 / N46° 37.3332′ W120° 36.8836′

BEST NEARBY BITES

Miner's Drive-In (2415 S. 1st St., Yakima, 509/457-8194, 8am-2am Sun.-Thurs., 8am-3:30am Fri.-Sat.) has been a fixture in the Yakima Valley since 1948. The vast menu is highlighted by the famous Big Miner Burger, which is roughly the size of a human head. From the trailhead, the 12-mile drive southeast takes less than 20 minutes via U.S. 12 and I-82.

Badger Mountain: Trailhead Park Loop

BADGER MOUNTAIN CENTENNIAL PRESERVE, RICHLAND

Hike to a view of the Columbia River, Eastern Oregon, and the Tri-Cities without ever leaving Richland's city limits.

BEST: Dog-Friendly Hikes
DISTANCE: 3 miles round-trip
DURATION: 1.5 hours
ELEVATION CHANGE: 800 feet
EFFORT: Easy/moderate
TRAIL: Dirt, pavement, crushed rock
USERS: Hikers, leashed dogs, mountain bikers, horseback riders
SEASON: Year-round
PASSES/FEES: None
MAPS: USGS topographic map for Badger Mountain, Friends of Badger Mountain map available at www.friendsofbadger.org
CONTACT: Benton County Parks, 509/736-3053, www.co.benton.wa.us; Friends of Badger Mountain, 509/783-6558, www.friendsofbadger.org

Badger Mountain Centennial Preserve comprises more than one square mile, with eight miles of trails that attract more than 200,000 visitors per year. The Trailhead Park Loop links three trails for a direct and scenic visit to the top of Badger Mountain. On toasty summer days, early morning and evening are ideal times to hike this trail.

START THE HIKE

▶ **MILE 0-1.1: Trailhead Park Parking Lot to Skyline Trail**
Starting from the parking lot, skirt the perimeter of **Trailhead Park**'s play area before arriving at a **kiosk** with a map, a bird-viewing display, and a history of the area's geology. Leashes are available to borrow at the trailhead. A restroom is located nearby. Continue 0.1 mile, the climbing already underway, to an intersection; continue straight to follow the popular **Canyon Trail.** On warm summer evenings and mornings, you might catch some shade in the canyon before following the trail upward through the dryland grass on the opposite slope.

Keep ascending as you start to get a sense of the view that awaits. Pasco, Richland, and Kennewick are visible below. At 1,250 feet, notice the **Lake Lewis marker** and ponder the fact that thousands of years ago everything beneath you was underwater.

After 1 mile on **Canyon Trail** (and passing wildflowers like balsamroot and phlox in the spring), arrive at the **Skyline Trail** and the fence surrounding the radio towers. Turn left here, but first take time to appreciate the view. Walk past the fence and let your gaze trace the path of the Columbia

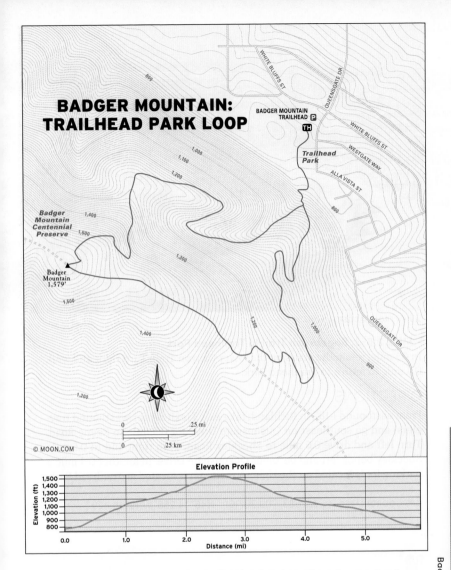

BADGER MOUNTAIN: TRAILHEAD PARK LOOP

BADGER MOUNTAIN TRAILHEAD

Trailhead Park

Badger Mountain Centennial Preserve

Badger Mountain 1,579'

WHITE BLUFFS ST

QUEENSGATE DR

WHITE BLUFFS ST

WESTGATE WAY

ALLA VISTA ST

QUEENSGATE DR

© MOON.COM

0   .25 mi

0   .25 km

Elevation Profile

River. Look across miles of fertile farmland and, on clear days, see as far as Mounts Hood, Adams, and Rainier.

▶ MILE 1.1–2.5: Skyline Trail to Sagebrush Trail

The Skyline Trail is wide and rocky in places but easily navigated as it descends over the next 0.5 mile under power lines. Turn left on the **Sagebrush Trail**. Named for the predominant trailside shrubbery, the path descends more gradually than the Canyon Trail and offers a view of the Columbia. After 0.9 mile, turn left following the direction of a "Hikers Only" sign.

▲ VIEW FROM BADGER MOUNTAIN

▶ **MILE 2.5-3: Sagebrush Trail to Trailhead Park**
In 0.1 mile, rejoin the stairs on the lower Canyon Trail. Turn right and walk 0.4 mile to return to Trailhead Park.

DIRECTIONS

From eastbound I-182 in Richland, take exit 3 (exit 3A for westbound travelers) and go southeast on Queensgate Drive for 0.5 mile to Keene Road. Turn left and drive 0.6 mile to Shockley Road. Turn right and in 0.5 mile Shockley bends left and becomes Queensgate Drive. In another 0.4 mile a parking lot is located on the right. A restroom is located at Trailhead Park.

GPS COORDINATES: 46.237583, –119.307161 / N46° 14.255' W119° 18.4297'

BEST NEARBY BREWS

The world's first industrial-size nuclear reactor was built north of Richland during World War II. Today, **Atomic Ale Brewpub & Eatery** (1015 Lee Blvd., 509/946-5465, www.atomicalebrewpub.com, 11am-9pm Sun.-Thurs., 11am-10pm Fri.-Sat.) pays tribute to this history while practicing its own science: brewing. Cap your hike with a thin-crust pizza like the spicy Reactor Core (salami, sausage, red onions, red pepper, jalapeños, and "nuclear butter") and hand-crafted beers like the Proton Pale Ale, Atomic Amber, and Plutonium Porter. From the trailhead, the 5-mile drive northeast takes about 10 minutes via I-182 and George Washington Way.

NEARBY CAMPGROUNDS

NAME	DESCRIPTION	FACILITIES	SEASON	FEE
Steamboat Rock State Park	situated on Banks Lake at the foot of Steamboat Rock and one of the most popular campgrounds east of the Cascades	174 tent and RV campsites, restrooms	year-round	$12-50

51052 Highway 155, Electric City, 888/226-7688, www.washington.goingtocamp.com

NAME	DESCRIPTION	FACILITIES	SEASON	FEE
Yakima Sportsman State Park	situated on nearly 270 acres of green in the desert and popular among anglers and bird-watchers	67 RV and tent sites, restrooms	March–October	$20-50

904 University Parkway, Yakima, 888/226-7688, www.washington.goingtocamp.com

NAME	DESCRIPTION	FACILITIES	SEASON	FEE
Big Pines Campground	the largest of the four BLM campgrounds in the Yakima Canyon	40 camper and tent sites, restrooms	year-round	$15

Canyon Road, Roza, Big Pines Recreation Site, 509/665-2100, www.recreation.gov

NAME	DESCRIPTION	FACILITIES	SEASON	FEE
Hood Park Campground	on the shore of Lake Wallula, formed by the McNary Dam on the Columbia River	67 RV and tent sites, restrooms	mid-May–early September	$24-26

123 Ice Harbor Road, Burbank, 509/547-2048, www.recreation.gov

NAME	DESCRIPTION	FACILITIES	SEASON	FEE
Quincy Lakes Unit	a wilderness area with dispersed camping for those with tents and small campers	dispersed camping, restrooms	March–October	Discover Pass

Road 3 NW, Quincy, 509/754-4624, www.wdfw.wa.gov

EASTERN WASHINGTON

From amber waves of grain to Blue Mountains majesties, Eastern Washington offers a variety of lightly visited settings. Explore nature trails and rock formations in a protected natural area minutes from Spokane, one of Washington's largest cities. Hike up Kamiak Butte in the rolling hills of the Palouse. Or head to the state's most secluded corners: To the northeast, look for bighorn sheep on the slopes above Sullivan Lake and ascend Abercrombie Mountain for a panorama that includes Idaho, British Columbia, and the Pend Oreille River. In the southeast, wander the Blue Mountains to a staffed fire lookout with views of peaks in three states.

▲ MARKER ON ABERCROMBIE MOUNTAIN

▲ ROCK FORMATION NEAR ILLER CREEK

◄ ABERCROMBIE MOUNTAIN

1 Abercrombie Mountain
DISTANCE: 7.8 miles round-trip
DURATION: 4 hours
EFFORT: Moderate

2 Sullivan Lakeshore Trail
DISTANCE: 8.4 miles round-trip
DURATION: 4 hours
EFFORT: Moderate

3 Iller Creek Conservation Area
DISTANCE: 5 miles round-trip
DURATION: 2.5 hours
EFFORT: Easy/moderate

4 Kamiak Butte
DISTANCE: 2.5 miles round-trip
DURATION: 1.5 hours
EFFORT: Easy/moderate

5 Oregon Butte
DISTANCE: 5.8 miles round-trip
DURATION: 3 hours
EFFORT: Easy/moderate

▼ SULLIVAN LAKE

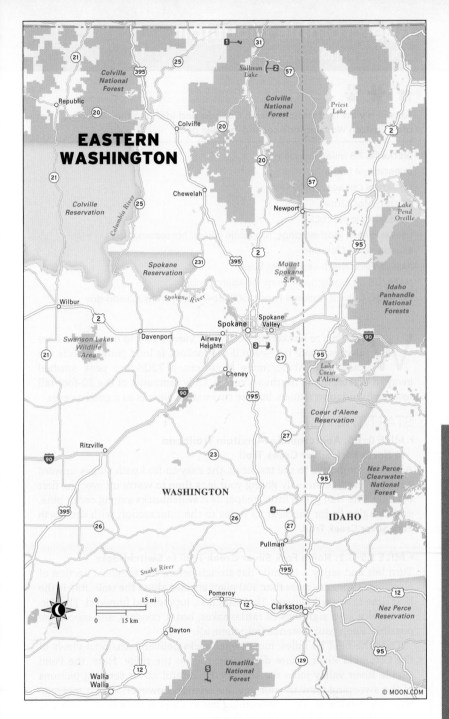

EASTERN WASHINGTON

Abercrombie Mountain

COLVILLE NATIONAL FOREST

Take in a view that stretches from Canada and Idaho to the Cascades from atop Eastern Washington's second-highest peak.

DISTANCE: 7.8 miles round-trip
DURATION: 4 hours
ELEVATION CHANGE: 2,400 feet
EFFORT: Moderate
TRAIL: Dirt, loose rock
USERS: Hikers, leashed dogs, mountain bikers, horseback riders
SEASON: June–October
PASSES/FEES: Northwest Forest Pass
MAPS: USGS topographic map for Abercrombie
CONTACT: Colville National Forest, 509/684-7000, www.fs.usda.gov

When you're hankering for a great view, hikes to fire lookouts are always a safe bet—even if the lookout is long gone. Such is the case with Abercrombie Mountain, a 7,308-foot peak stashed away in Washington's northeast corner. Only remnants of the 20-foot-tall tower's foundation remain, but the two-nation view is as a good as ever.

START THE HIKE

▶ **MILE 0-1.5: Abercrombie Mountain Trailhead to North Fork Silver Creek Trail**

After the long drive to the trailhead, the easy-to-find path slopes upward gently at first, generously giving your legs time to warm up over the first 0.4 mile. The trail gets a little steeper as it **switchbacks** among cedar, pine, and Douglas fir for the next 1.1 miles to the intersection with the **North Fork Silver Creek Trail.**

▶ **MILE 1.5-3.2: North Fork Silver Creek Trail to Switchbacks**

Turn left and enjoy a 0.3-mile flat stretch before the toughest section of climbing. There are more than 100 plant species along the trail. July is the best time to see wildflowers like bear grass, lupine, and fireweed. The Forest Service says sightings of rattlesnakes, bears, cougars, and moose are possible. Keep your distance from them all.

Over the next 1.4 miles, more **switchbacks** deliver occasional views of the Columbia River before depositing you on the ridge. Here, the Pend Oreille River valley joins the scenery. Be careful about sending pictures of the sweeping view to your envious friends, however: I got a message from my service provider welcoming me to Canada (less than 5 miles to the north) and to substantially higher rates.

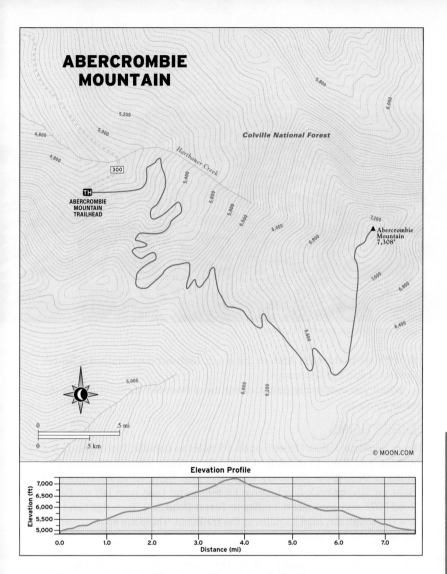

ABERCROMBIE MOUNTAIN

Colville National Forest

Harthaker Creek

ABERCROMBIE
MOUNTAIN
TRAILHEAD

Abercrombie
Mountain
7,308'

© MOON.COM

Elevation Profile

▶ **MILE 3.2-3.6: Switchbacks to Flume Creek Trail**

Put your phone on airplane mode and follow the trail up Abercrombie's south side for 0.4 mile to the intersection with the **Flume Creek Trail.** Turn left but snap a mental image of the intersection for the return trip. It can be easy to miss.

▶ **MILE 3.6-3.9: Flume Creek Trail to Abercrombie Mountain Summit**

It's just another 0.3 mile to the **summit.** Pass gnarly snags and spend the final 100 yards walking over the **loose rock** that covers the broad Selkirk peak. Note the remains of a tower, look for a battered USGS benchmark, and soak in the view. Sherlock and Hooknose Peaks are nearby. The Kettle Range is visible to the west and, on clear days, so are the Cascades. The

▲ THE PEAK OF ABERCROMBIE MOUNTAIN

Rockies are to the east. And, to the north, look out over southeast British Columbia and the Kootenays.

When you eventually pull yourself away from the view, return via the same route.

DIRECTIONS

From Spokane, follow U.S. 395 north 65 miles to Colville. Turn right on 3rd Avenue and drive 1.1 miles to Aladdin Road. Turn left and continue 25.5 miles to Deep Lake Boundary Road and turn right. After 7.3 miles turn right on Silver Creek Road. Drive 1.9 miles and then turn left on Forest Road 7078 and continue 4.3 miles to Forest Road 300. Turn right and follow the rough dirt road 3.1 miles to the trailhead. There are no restroom facilities at the trailhead.

GPS COORDINATES: 48.932052, –117.482448 / N48° 55.9231′ W117° 28.9469′

BEST NEARBY BREWS

In Colville, **Fired Up Brewing** (1235 S. Main St., 509/684-3328, hours vary) bakes pizza in an earthenware oven and brews beer using locally grown hops. The beer names are a tip of the hat to local landmarks, such as Little Pend Oreille Pale Ale and Red Dome Red; hard ciders are also on tap. From the trailhead, the 43-mile drive southwest takes 1 hour, 20 minutes via Deep Lake Boundary and Aladdin Roads.

2 # Sullivan Lakeshore Trail

COLVILLE NATIONAL FOREST, METALINE FALLS

Trace the eastern shore of Sullivan Lake on an easy trail and maybe catch a glimpse of a bighorn sheep on Hall Mountain.

DISTANCE: 8.4 miles round-trip
DURATION: 4 hours
ELEVATION CHANGE: 1,000 feet
EFFORT: Moderate
TRAIL: Dirt single track, rocky slopes
USERS: Hikers, leashed dogs
SEASON: April-November
PASSES/FEES: Northwest Forest Pass
MAPS: USGS topographic map for Metaline Falls
CONTACT: Colville National Forest, 509/446-7500, www.fs.usda.gov

From spring wildflowers to summer swims to golden fall larches to opportunities to see bears and bighorn sheep, Sullivan Lake has plenty to offer. Tucked away in the lightly traveled northeast corner of the state, this National Scenic Trail in the Colville National Forest starts at East Sullivan Campground at the north end of the lake. However, it's just as easy to start from the Noisy Creek Campground at the lake's southern end.

START THE HIKE

▶ **MILE 0-0.3: Trailhead Kiosk to Nature Loop Trail**
Starting from the **kiosk** at the small roadside parking area, the trail climbs gently and briefly. In about 100 yards, pass the 0.6-mile **Nature Loop Trail.** To take the self-guided tour and learn about a 200-year-old larch and a resilient Douglas fir, borrow the worn paper pamphlet at the trailhead kiosk (but remember to return it when you're done). About 0.25 mile beyond the nature loop, the trail crests above the campground and the **lake** comes into view. A trailside bench offers a spot to enjoy the sight of swimmers and water-skiers playing in one of Colville National Forest's largest lakes. The waters are clear and, in the summer, surprisingly warm (but still chilly).

▶ **MILE 0.3-1.6: Nature Loop Trail to Trailside Picnic Spot**
The lake will be in view for most of the rest of this hike. The trail passes under trees and undulates a bit. After 1.3 miles pass a small **clearing** between the trail and the lake. It's just big enough to pitch a tent or to have a picnic. Spots like these are scarce on the trail, which runs along the base of Hall Mountain. It's not uncommon to come across resting hikers on the narrow stretches, sitting on the trail with their legs hanging over the slope. The steep slopes of Hall Mountain above are home to a herd of bighorn sheep. Biologists are studying the herd, and signs posted at the

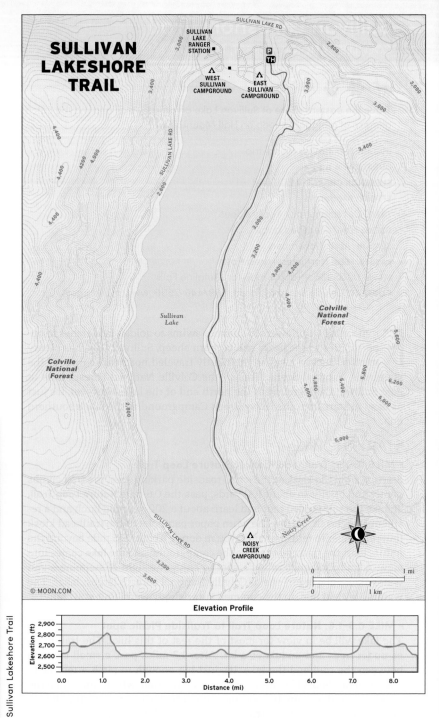

trailheads ask hikers to report sightings to the national forest or the state Department of Fish and Wildlife.

▶ **MILE 1.6–4.2: Trailside Picnic Spot to Noisy Creek Campground**

For 2.2 miles beyond the **trailside picnic spot**, cross rockslides, pass trees charred by wildfires, and listen to the sounds of small planes taking off and landing at the north end of the lake. Near a bench overlooking a bay at the south end of the lake you might find an old spur trail and option for a side trip to a closed mine. To continue to the Noisy Creek Campground, enjoy a flat 0.4 mile beyond the bluff. This section passes through the trees and offers several places to access the lake. The trail ends in a parking lot near a restroom and a popular swimming hole at **Noisy Creek Campground.**

For the return trip, simply follow the path back to your car.

DIRECTIONS

From Spokane, follow U.S. 2 north for 36 miles and turn left on Highway 211. Drive 15.2 miles to Highway 20 and turn left. Drive 31 miles along the Pend Oreille River; when the road becomes Highway 31, continue straight for 3.1 miles. Turn right on Sullivan Lake Road; just after crossing the Ione bridge, stay left to keep on Sullivan Lake Road. Drive 12.4 miles to Forest Road 22 and turn right. After 0.4 mile, turn right at the sign for the East Sullivan Lake Campground. A small trailhead parking area is on the left before the campground. There are toilets at the campground, but not at the trailhead.

GPS COORDINATES: 48.840494, -117.278366 / N48° 50.4296' W117° 16.702'

SULLIVAN LAKE ▶

BEST NEARBY BITES

The Farmhouse Café (221 E. 5th Ave., Metaline Falls, 509/446-2447, 6am-6:30pm Mon.-Fri., 7am-2pm Sat.-Sun.) in the old mining town of Metaline Falls dishes up biscuits and gravy, burgers, pie, and more. The train footage in the opening credits of the 1993 Johnny Depp film *Benny & Joon* was filmed nearby. From the trailhead, the 7.5-mile drive west takes 15 minutes via Sullivan Lake Road and Highway 31.

Stroll through a riparian setting before ascending to views of the Spokane Valley and the Palouse from a ridge crowned with granite monoliths.

DISTANCE: 5 miles round-trip
DURATION: 2.5 hours
ELEVATION CHANGE: 1,200 feet
EFFORT: Easy/moderate
TRAIL: Single track
USERS: Hikers, leashed dogs, mountain bikers, horseback riders
SEASON: Year-round
PASSES/FEES: None
MAPS: USGS topographic map for Spokane SE, www.spokanecounty.org/1406/Trail-Maps
CONTACT: Spokane County Parks, 509/447-4730, www.spokanecounty.org

The 966-acre Iller Creek/Stevens Creek Unit of the Dishman Hills Conservation Area allows visitors easy access to a forest of ponderosa pine, hemlock, and larch and wildflowers such as Oregon grape and balsamroot. It's also home to moose, elk, coyotes, and numerous bird species. One of 51 stops on the National Audubon Society's Palouse to Pines Loop, Iller Creek is a place to see red crossbills, hummingbirds, cedar waxwings, wrens, and more.

START THE HIKE

▶ **MILE 0-0.9: Parking Lot South End to Iller Creek Marker**
At the south end of the small parking area, slip past the fence and follow the trail right for a counterclockwise loop through one of the Spokane Valley's most beloved conservation projects. Start with a shaded, gradually climbing stretch along **Iller Creek** (typically dry by midsummer). As squirrels, snakes, and birds rustle the bushes, it's easy to forget you're about 5 miles from downtown Spokane. The first 0.9-mile stretch brings you to a **marker** directing you to head right. Here, the climbing gets a little steeper.

▶ **MILE 0.9-2.2: Iller Creek Marker to Rock Monolith**
In another 0.7 mile, pass the **intersection** with the Upper Valley Trail; this trail is a good option if you're looking to abbreviate your trip by about 0.7 mile, but you'll also bypass the best views. The steepest sections of the trail come during the next 0.4 mile, but you'll get a little inspiration as you step out into an **opening** and the Rocks of Sharon come into view to your left. Descend gradually over the next 0.2 mile and arrive at the first house-size **rock monolith.** (Here, a spur trail ascends to the right and visits more rock outcrops but leaves the conservation area in about 0.2 mile.)

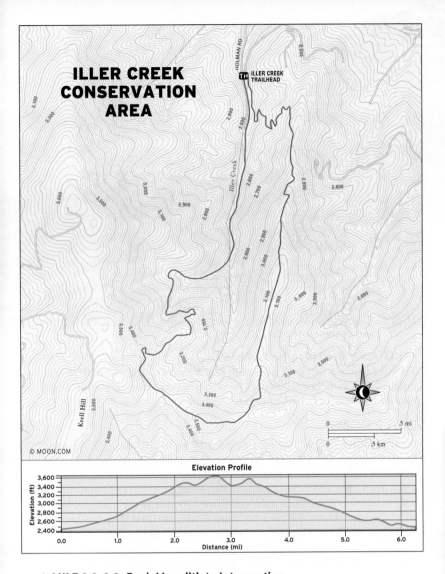

ILLER CREEK
CONSERVATION
AREA

© MOON.COM

Elevation Profile

▶ MILE 2.2-2.6: Rock Monolith to Intersection

Continue past the **spur trail,** following the sign toward the Stevens Creek Trail, and, 0.2 mile farther, keep straight at the **intersection** and climb a little higher to a sweeping view that includes Steptoe Butte rising above the Palouse. Keep going and, 0.2 mile after the Stevens Creek Trail intersection, reach another **intersection.** Continue straight as the ridge descends.

▶ MILE 2.6-4.3: Intersection to Trail Ridge

In 0.5 mile, pass the eastern **intersection** with the Upper Valley Trail. Keep following the **Iller Creek Trail** along the ridge and in a short distance reach a stretch where the forest was thinned by fire. Enjoy views of the Spokane Valley and Mount Spokane at times over the next 1.2 miles.

▲ ROCK FORMATIONS NEAR ILLER CREEK

▶ **MILE 4.3-5: Trail Ridge to Trailhead**
The hike winds down with a 0.4-mile descent on switchbacks built by volunteers. The switchbacks deposit you back in the riparian setting along Iller Creek for a flat 0.3-mile jaunt to the trailhead.

DIRECTIONS

From Spokane, follow I-90 east to exit 287 and turn south on Argonne Road. Continue for 3.5 miles as the road becomes Dishman-Mica Road then turn right on Schafer Road. In 0.9 mile the road ends at East 44th Avenue. Turn right and drive 0.2 mile to Farr Road. Turn left and continue 0.3 mile to Holman Road. Turn right and drive 0.75 mile to the trailhead located at the turn where the road becomes Rockcrest Lane. The trailhead is well marked. There is limited parking and one portable toilet.

GPS COORDINATES: 47.601881, –117.281793 / N47° 36.1129′ W117° 16.9076′

BEST NEARBY BREWS

Spokane's **Iron Goat Brewing Company** (1302 W. 2nd Ave., 509/474-0722, www.irongoatbrewing.com, 11am-close daily) is known for crafting creative beers and a vegan-friendly menu. They'll even add tofu to your thin-crust pizza. The brewery has created 150 different beers, but consider a classic like the fruity Impaler Imperial IPA. Iron Goat gets its name from Spokane's most famous trash can: Built for the 1974 world's fair, an iron goat sculpture in Riverfront Park has a built-in vacuum allowing it to eat trash. From the trailhead, the 12-mile drive northwest takes 20 minutes via I-90.

Kamiak Butte

KAMIAK BUTTE COUNTY PARK, PALOUSE

Take in sweeping views of the Palouse's fertile farmland from atop an isolated, tree-covered hill standing in contrast to its surroundings.

BEST: Spring Hikes
DISTANCE: 2.5 miles round-trip
DURATION: 1.5 hours
ELEVATION CHANGE: 750 feet
EFFORT: Easy/moderate
TRAIL: Dirt, gravel, steps
USERS: Hikers, leashed dogs
SEASON: March-November
MAPS: USGS topographic map for Albion
PARK HOURS: 7am-dusk daily
CONTACT: Whitman County Parks and Recreation, 509/397-6238, www.whitmancounty.org

START THE HIKE

▶ **MILE 0-0.5: Picnic Area Kiosk to Pine Ridge Trail**

To explore this steptoe (an isolated hill surrounded by lava flows), start from the **picnic area kiosk** by ascending a short section of **steps** to a wide path. In a few steps, pass the **Larch Shelter** on the left and, to the right, the trail you'll use to finish the loop. For the next 0.5 mile, the **Pine Ridge Trail** climbs through a forest of ponderosa pine, Douglas fir, and western larch. Keep an eye out for wildlife such as deer, porcupines, chipmunks, owls, and squirrels. The park is home to about 30 types of mammals and more than 130 bird species. Once you've switchbacked your way up the ridge, Washington State University and the University of Idaho, across the border in Moscow, are both part of the panorama.

▶ **MILE 0.5-1.5: Pine Ridge Trail to Kamiak Butte Summit**

Atop the ridge, turn right to continue on the **Pine Ridge Trail** as it climbs gradually for the next 0.9 mile. Along the way, take note of the contradicting microclimates of the butte's north- and south-facing slopes. Shade and cooler temperatures on the north side allow for dense forest and wildflowers like trillium and yellowbells. Meanwhile, more direct sunlight on the south side creates difficult growing conditions. Pass areas scarred by fire and reach an **intersection** in the woods. Continue straight for 0.1 mile to the 3,641-foot **summit**. This section is on private property and signs ask hikers to stick to the trail.

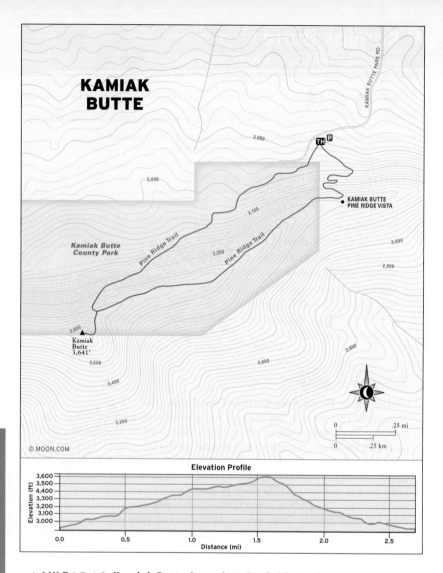

KAMIAK BUTTE

Kamiak Butte County Park

Kamiak Butte 3,641'

KAMIAK BUTTE PINE RIDGE VISTA

Pine Ridge Trail

KAMIAK BUTTE PARK RD

© MOON.COM

0   .25 mi
0   .25 km

Elevation Profile

Elevation (ft) / Distance (mi)

▶ **MILE 1.5–1.6: Kamiak Butte Summit to Backside Trail**

From the **summit**, you can create a longer loop by following the West End Primitive Trail (this adds 1.4 miles to your trip and dogs are prohibited on this section), but for the most direct descent return 0.1 mile and turn left on the **Backside Trail.** The trail passes through a narrow band of young trees reclaiming a slope cleared in the 1950s for a ski run.

▶ **MILE 1.6–2.5: Backside Trail to Larch Shelter and Trailhead**

After a 0.4-mile descent, turn right to stay on the trail. Keep right at **two intersections** over the next 0.2 mile (trails to the left lead to the campground). Continue through a spring-fed **thicket** teeming with trees and shrubs that attract birds and other animals. After 0.25 mile arrive back at the **Larch Shelter.** Turn left to return to the trailhead.

▲ WINTER ON KAMIAK BUTTE

DIRECTIONS

From Colfax follow Highway 272/Canyon Street east for 5.4 miles and turn right on Clear Creek Road. Drive 8.1 miles to Fugate Road/Road 5100 and turn right. In 0.7 mile, turn left on Kamiak Butte Park Road. Drive 0.8 mile to the trailhead near the picnic area and restrooms. Camping is available in the park.

GPS COORDINATES: 46.870298, –117.152982 / N46° 52.2179′ W117° 9.1789′

BEST NEARBY BITES

Get a taste of college life in Pullman—14 miles (20 minutes) south of the trailhead via Highway 27—by dining at a classic WSU hangout. Grab a huge burger and fries at **Cougar Cottage,** better known as **The Coug** (900 NE Colorado St., 509/332-1265, 11am-2am daily).

Oregon Butte

UMATILLA NATIONAL FOREST

🦌 🌸 🐾 🚶

Wander across the top of the Blue Mountains to a nearly 90-year-old fire lookout with a 360-degree view spanning three states.

DISTANCE: 5.8 miles round-trip
DURATION: 3 hours
ELEVATION CHANGE: 1,200 feet
EFFORT: Easy/moderate
TRAIL: Dirt
USERS: Hikers, leashed dogs, hunters, horseback riders
SEASON: June–November
PASSES/FEES: Northwest Forest Pass
MAPS: USGS topographic map for Oregon Butte, USFS map for Wenaha-Tucannon Wilderness
CONTACT: Umatilla National Forest, Pomeroy Ranger District, 509/843-1891, www.fs.usda.gov

Oregon Butte isn't in the state it's named for, but you can see it from here. The views of Idaho and Washington are pretty spectacular too. In fact, the views of the Blue Mountains start the moment you step out of your car, more than a mile above sea level. This sample panorama is a reward for a drive you might find more taxing than the hike.

START THE HIKE

▶ **MILE 0-1: Mount Misery Trailhead to West Butte**
Find the **Mount Misery Trail** at the east end of the parking lot and step immediately into 176,557-acre Wenaha-Tucannon Wilderness. Take note of the sandy trail surface. It is composed of wind-deposited silt (loess) and ash from an ancient eruption. The trail offers several day-hiking and backpacking options as it travels across hilltops and through a forest of Douglas fir, spruce, larch, and lodgepole pine. After 1 mile of gradual climbing, reach an **unmarked intersection**. Veer right to visit the top of West Butte.

▶ **MILE 1-1.8: West Butte to Mount Misery Trail**
In another 0.5 mile, pass just below the summit of **West Butte** (6,292 feet). Catch your first glimpse of your destination, the fire lookout on the neighboring peak. Enjoy the south-facing slopes that are often adorned with spring and summer wildflowers. From West Butte, descend **switchbacks** and rejoin the **Mount Misery Trail** in 0.3 mile.

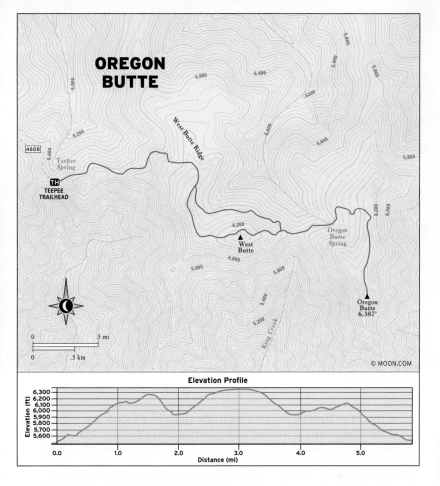

Elevation Profile

▶ MILE 1.8–2.9: **Mount Misery Trail to Sawtooth Ridge Trail and Lookout**

Descend another 0.3 mile to **Oregon Butte Spring.** The spring pumps water into a trough carved into a tamarack log. The lookout stationed atop Oregon Butte all summer relies on the spring as her water source. From here, the trail ascends 0.3 mile to an intersection with the **Sawtooth Ridge Trail.** Turn right and continue upward for 0.1 mile to the ridge. Turn south and enjoy the view as you ramble another 0.4 mile to the **lookout.**

Built in 1931, the lookout stands on the highest point (6,387 feet) in the wilderness and is staffed in the summer. Rows of peaks and valleys seem to stretch forever in every direction. Idaho's Seven Devils Range is visible to the southeast, while to the south the view includes Oregon's Wallowa and Elkhorn Mountains. The Oregon border is about 7.5 miles away. It can be chilly in late summer and fall, and mid-September snowfall isn't uncommon. Snow can also linger on the north-facing slopes into summer.

When you're ready to return, retrace your steps.

▲ OREGON BUTTE

DIRECTIONS

From U.S. 12 in Dayton, drive east on 4th Street and follow the sign toward Ski Bluewood. Go 5 miles (the street becomes Touchet Road along the way) and turn left on Hatley Gulch Road. Follow the unpaved road for 4.4 miles and turn right on Kendall Skyline Road. Drive 5.9 miles to the Kendall Monument and turn right to stay on Kendall Skyline Road. Drive 11.5 miles and then turn left on Forest Road 4608 at the Godman Guard Station. Drive 6 miles to the trailhead. A vault toilet is located at the parking area.

GPS COORDINATES: 46.11808, –117.71393 / N46° 7.0848' W117° 42.8358'

BEST NEARBY BREWS

Chief Spring's Brew Pub (148 E. Main St., Dayton, 509/382-4677, www.fireandironsbrewpub.com, hours vary) is named for co-owner and brew master Mike Spring, a local fire chief. Spring and his wife, Ann, own the pub and the neighboring pizzeria. Enjoy slices, pints, tacos, burgers, chili, and more while admiring the firehouse décor. From the trailhead, the 36-mile drive northwest takes about 1 hour, 20 minutes via Kendall Skyline Road and U.S. 12.

NEARBY CAMPGROUNDS

NAME	DESCRIPTION	FACILITIES	SEASON	FEE
Noisy Creek Campground	on the southern end of Sullivan Lake	19 RV and tent sites, restrooms	mid-May-early September	$18

Sullivan Lake Road, Ione, Colville National Forest, 877/444-6777, www.recreation.gov

NAME	DESCRIPTION	FACILITIES	SEASON	FEE
Tucannon Campground	on the Tucannon River bordering the W. T. Wooten State Wildlife Area	18 RV and tent sites, restrooms	year-round	$8

Forest Road 47, Mountain Top, Umatilla National Forest, 509/843-1891, www.fs.usda.gov

NAME	DESCRIPTION	FACILITIES	SEASON	FEE
Bowl and Pitcher Campground	one of four campgrounds in Riverside State Park; access to giant basalt formations via a suspension bridge across the Spokane River	32 tent and RV sites, restrooms	May 15-September 15	$12-50

9711 W. Charles Road, Nine Mile Falls, 888/226-7688, www.washington.goingtocamp.com

NAME	DESCRIPTION	FACILITIES	SEASON	FEE
Kamiak Butte	situated in the woods at the base of Kamiak Butte, just minutes from Pullman	8 tent sites, restrooms	year-round	$15

Road 6710, Palouse, 509/397-4622, www.whitmancounty.org

NAME	DESCRIPTION	FACILITIES	SEASON	FEE
Liberty Lake Campground	in a county park east of Spokane, just a short walk from Liberty Lake	27 RV and tent sites, restrooms	May-September	$22-40

3719 S. Zephyr Road, Liberty Lake Regional Park, 509/954-0808, www.spokanecounty.org

▲ TRAIL TO BAGBY HOT SPRINGS

OREGON

COLUMBIA RIVER GORGE

Roughly 15,000 years ago, the first of several floods—part of a larger event later dubbed the Missoula Floods—swept through the Columbia River and carved out one of the region's most iconic natural features: the Columbia River Gorge. Some 80 miles long and up to 4,000 feet deep, the river canyon cuts through the Cascades and forms the boundary between Washington and Oregon. Trails on both sides of the Gorge draw nature lovers with their dramatic beauty. The National Scenic Area comprises old-growth forests, spectacular waterfalls, and iconic bluffs and ridges, making it one of the Pacific Northwest's most popular hiking destinations, even after the 2017 Eagle Creek Fire burned nearly 50,000 acres on the Oregon side.

▲ FOOTBRIDGE ON LARCH MOUNTAIN

▲ MOUNT HOOD FROM MCCALL POINT

1 Latourell Falls Loop
DISTANCE: 3.1 miles round-trip
DURATION: 1.5 hours
EFFORT: Easy/moderate

2 Angel's Rest
DISTANCE: 4.9 miles round-trip
DURATION: 2.5 hours
EFFORT: Moderate

3 Wahkeena Falls-Multnomah Falls Loop
DISTANCE: 5.9 miles round-trip
DURATION: 3 hours
EFFORT: Moderate

4 Larch Mountain Crater Loop
DISTANCE: 7.1 miles round-trip
DURATION: 3.5 hours
EFFORT: Easy/moderate

5 Beacon Rock
DISTANCE: 2 miles round-trip
DURATION: 1 hour
EFFORT: Easy/moderate

6 Dry Creek Falls
DISTANCE: 5 miles round-trip
DURATION: 2.5 hours
EFFORT: Moderate

7 Dog Mountain
DISTANCE: 6.9 miles round-trip
DURATION: 4 hours
EFFORT: Moderate/strenuous

8 Coyote Wall (Labyrinth Loop)
DISTANCE: 6.3 miles round-trip
DURATION: 3.5 hours
EFFORT: Easy/moderate

9 Mosier Plateau
DISTANCE: 3.7 miles round-trip
DURATION: 1.5 hours
EFFORT: Easy/moderate

10 Tom McCall Point Trail
DISTANCE: 3.8 miles round-trip
DURATION: 2 hours
EFFORT: Easy/moderate

▾ VIEW FROM DOG MOUNTAIN

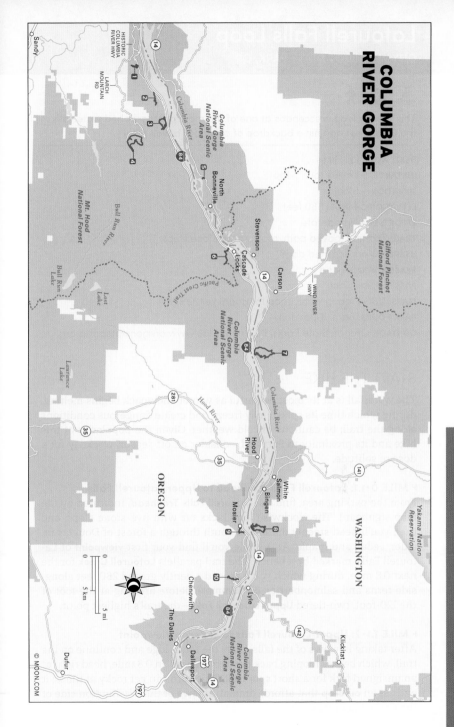

COLUMBIA RIVER GORGE

Latourell Falls Loop

GUY W. TALBOT STATE PARK, OR

This breezy loop crescendos at one of the most photographed waterfalls in the Gorge, set against a backdrop of columnar basalt pillars.

BEST: Waterfall Hikes
DISTANCE: 3.1 miles round-trip
DURATION: 1.5 hours
ELEVATION CHANGE: 880 feet
EFFORT: Easy/moderate
TRAIL: Dirt trail, paved path, roots, rocks, stone steps
USERS: Hikers, leashed dogs
SEASON: Year-round
PASSES/FEES: None
MAPS: USGS topographic map for Bridal Veil, OR-WA
PARK HOURS: 6am-10pm daily
CONTACT: Oregon State Parks, 503/695-2261, www.oregonstateparks.org

START THE HIKE

The waterfall is at its most powerful as winter snowpack begins melting, during which time its splash may freeze and create dangerous conditions along the trail; be cautious in cold weather. Given the popularity of this hike and its proximity to Portland, consider an off-season weekday for a dose of solitude.

▶ **MILE 0-1.1: Latourell Falls Trailhead to Upper Latourell Falls**
From the parking area, find the **Latourell Falls Trailhead,** indicated by the map signboard. The clockwise loop kicks off with five stone steps, and then you'll head steeply uphill and south through a forest of Douglas fir, alder, cedar, and maple. At 0.3 mile you'll find your first **viewpoint** of Latourell Falls, marked by a bench. The trail parallels **Latourell Creek** for the next 0.8 mile, during which you'll ascend a gently graded 280 feet alongside ferns and salmonberries (in summer), before arriving at the foot of the 120-foot, two-tiered **Upper Latourell Falls**—the trail's highest point.

▶ **MILE 1.1-2: Upper Latourell Falls to Outcrop Viewpoint**
After taking in views of the falls, cross the footbridge and continue on the trail, which begins looping back north from here. In 0.8 mile, head right at an unsigned fork for a short **spur trail.** This path can get rocky at times; it ends at an **outcrop** that affords dramatic views of the Washington side of the Columbia River Gorge.

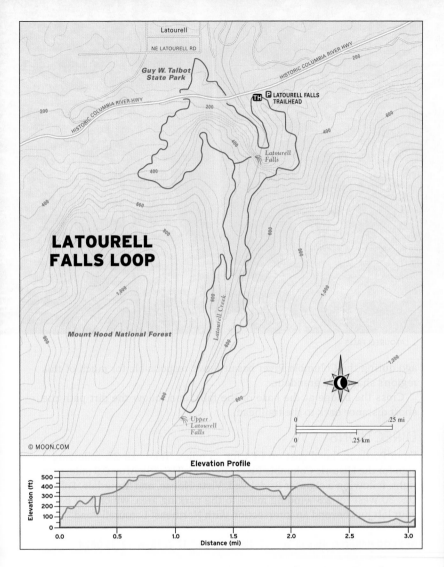

LATOURELL
FALLS LOOP

Elevation Profile

▶ MILE 2-3.1: Outcrop Viewpoint to Latourell Falls and Trailhead

Back on the main trail, you'll climb gently for the next 0.25 mile before steadily descending back toward the Columbia River. Cross the Historic Columbia River Highway in another 0.6 mile, and pick up the unmarked trail on the north side of the road. Take a sharp left onto the paved path at the first unsigned intersection almost immediately after crossing the highway. The trail descends a small stone staircase and immediately forks; turn right to head east, following a sign for the Loop Trail and Base of Lower Falls and passing some shaded picnic benches to your left. The paved path curves back south and continues under the highway, once again paralleling Latourell Creek. After 0.2 mile, you'll arrive at the misty base of photogenic **Latourell Falls,** which tumbles 200 feet amid lichen-colored columnar basalt pillars—created more than 10 million years

▲ LATOURELL FALLS

ago during the Columbia River basalt flows responsible for much of this region's shape and grandeur.

Cross the bridge at the base of the falls, and follow the dirt path the short distance back to the trailhead.

DIRECTIONS

From Portland, head east on I-84 for 25 miles. Take exit 28, following a sign for the Historic Columbia River Highway (U.S. 30). After 0.5 mile, turn right, following a sign for Bridal Veil, Vista House, and Troutdale. Follow U.S. 30 west for 2.8 winding miles to the parking area, which will be on your left just beyond an intersection with Northeast Latourell Road.

GPS COORDINATES: 45.53873, -122.21804 / N45° 32.3238' W122° 13.0824'

BEST NEARBY BREWS

Built in 1911 as the Multnomah County poor farm, today **McMenamins Edgefield** (2126 SW Halsey St., Troutdale, 503/669-8610, www.mc-menamins.com, hours vary by individual venue) is a hotel and part of the McMenamins regional chain, which is known for refurbishing historic properties while adding a modern sense of whimsy. This property hosts numerous bars and restaurants serving McMenamins' libations from its on-site brewery, winery, and distillery, not to mention a popular concert venue and two par-3 golf courses. From the trailhead, the 16-mile drive west takes 25 minutes via the Historic Columbia River Highway and I-84.

Hike through a wildfire-scarred landscape and past waterfalls to arrive at the summit of an exposed bluff offering spectacular views of the Columbia River Gorge.

DISTANCE: 4.9 miles round-trip

DURATION: 2.5 hours

ELEVATION CHANGE: 1,300 feet

EFFORT: Moderate

TRAIL: Dirt trail, rock scrambles, roots

USERS: Hikers, leashed dogs

SEASON: Year-round

PASSES/FEES: None

MAPS: USGS topographic map for Bridal Veil, OR-WA

PARK HOURS: 6am-10pm daily

CONTACT: Columbia River Gorge National Scenic Area, 541/308-1700, www.fs.usda.gov

START THE HIKE

Damaged by the Eagle Creek Fire, this trail reopened after months of restoration and has quickly regained its popularity; make this a midweek hike in the off-season if you can to avoid crowds.

▶ **MILE 0-0.6: Angel's Rest Trailhead to Upper Coopey Falls**
From the main parking area, head south to cross the Historic Columbia River Highway and find the **Angel's Rest Trailhead.** In a couple of hundred feet, you'll arrive at an unsigned, Y-shaped junction; head left to continue uphill. Here you'll see several burned tree trunks, evidence of the Eagle Creek Fire, though for the most part this early stretch comprises dense forest including ferns, old-growth trees, and white trillium blossoms in early spring. For the first 0.4 mile, you'll steadily ascend a gentle slope to arrive at the top of 150-foot **Coopey Falls.** After another 0.1 mile along the trail, you'll cross a bridge over **Coopey Creek** and, almost immediately, find a short spur trail to your left offering views of the 35-foot **Upper Coopey Falls.**

▶ **MILE 0.6-2.1: Upper Coopey Falls to Rockslide**
Back on the main trail, the hike begins to intensify, gaining 300 feet before arriving, in another 0.6 mile, at Eagle Creek Fire-devastated forest; from here to the summit, the greenery gradually gives way to downed logs, snags, and blackened tree trunks. After another 0.5 mile, you're almost entirely surrounded by toothpick-like snags littering the hillsides (much

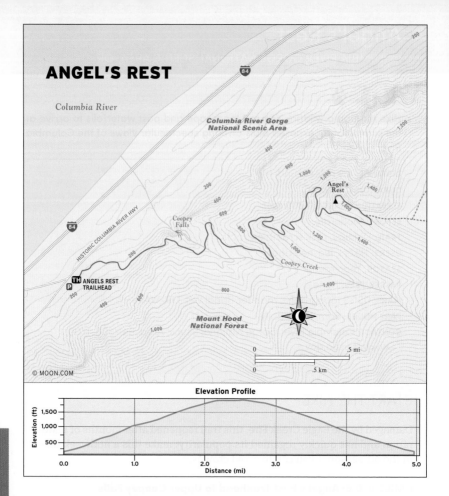

ANGEL'S REST

Columbia River

Columbia River Gorge
National Scenic Area

Angel's
Rest

Coopey
Falls

HISTORIC COLUMBIA RIVER HWY

Coopey Creek

ANGELS REST
TRAILHEAD

Mount Hood
National Forest

0   .5 mi

0   .5 km

© MOON.COM

Elevation Profile

of this area burned in a 1991 wildfire as well). As you switchback up the slopes—with the summit of Angel's Rest now visible to the east—you'll see several shortcuts filled in with rocks and spur trails blocked off with logs; stay on the established trail at all times, as there's a high risk of falling trees, uneven ground, and erosion as the area recovers. In roughly 0.4 mile, you'll arrive at a 150-foot-long rockslide that can be slippery after rainfall.

▶ **MILE 2.1–2.45: Rockslide to Angel's Rest Summit**

After another 0.25 mile of steep climbing, you'll arrive at an unsigned Y-junction. Continue straight to head north, and delicately climb a 15-foot rock scramble. As soon as you navigate this tricky stretch, you'll arrive at the **Angel's Rest summit,** featuring epic views: To the east, you'll see Beacon Rock, Hamilton Mountain, and some charred forests; to the west is the Vista House, built in 1916 as a rest stop for travelers on the Historic Columbia River Highway, on the basalt promontory of Crown Point.

Return the way you came.

▲ UPPER COOPEY FALLS

DIRECTIONS

From Portland, head east on I-84 east for 25 miles. Take exit 28, following a sign for the Historic Columbia River Highway (U.S. 30). You'll arrive at the main parking area to your right after 0.5 mile, just beyond a sign for Bridal Veil, Vista House, and Troutdale. Additional parking is also available farther west along the Historic Columbia River Highway.

GPS COORDINATES: 45.56022, -122.17264 / N45° 33.6132' W122° 10.3584'

BEST NEARBY BREWS

Choose among a well-rounded selection of balanced beers at **Migration Brewing** (18188 NE Wilkes Rd., Portland, 971/274-3770, http://migrationbrewing.com, 11am-9pm Sun.-Thurs., 11am-10pm Fri.-Sat.). Its lineup includes a mix of lagers, barrel-aged beers, and hop-forward IPAs and pale ales. From the trailhead, the 16-mile drive west takes 17 minutes via I-84.

Angel's Rest

Wahkeena Falls–
Multnomah Falls Loop

COLUMBIA RIVER GORGE NATIONAL SCENIC AREA, OR

Enjoy dense, old-growth forest and plenty of waterfalls along this loop, including iconic Multnomah Falls—the tallest in Oregon.

BEST: Waterfall Hikes

DISTANCE: 5.9 miles round-trip

DURATION: 3 hours

ELEVATION CHANGE: 1,670 feet

EFFORT: Moderate

TRAIL: Dirt trail, paved path, stream crossings, rocks, gravel

USERS: Hikers, leashed dogs

SEASON: Year-round, but trail may be icy or snowy winter–early spring

PASSES/FEES: None

MAPS: USGS topographic map for Multnomah Falls, OR-WA; free trail maps available at the U.S. Forest Service information center inside Multnomah Falls Lodge

CONTACT: Columbia River Gorge National Scenic Area, 541/308-1700, www.fs.usda.gov

The loop between Wahkeena Falls and Multnomah Falls is one of the most popular hikes in Oregon—no surprise, given that Multnomah Falls is among the state's biggest tourist draws.

START THE HIKE

Plan to share portions of this trail with scores of fellow hikers; consider saving this hike for a weekday if possible, or start before 9am.

▶ **MILE 0-0.8: Multnomah Falls Lodge to Wahkeena Falls**
From the parking lot, follow the pedestrian crosswalk south under I-84, crossing Multnomah Creek and the Historic Columbia River Highway, to the plaza in front of **Multnomah Falls Lodge,** which has a snack stand and restrooms; you can also grab a free trail map inside. Pause to appreciate views of **Multnomah Falls** from here now or at the end of the hike. From the lodge head west to begin the counterclockwise loop along the shoulder of the **Historic Columbia River Highway.** After 0.1 mile, take a slight left onto the **Return Trail.** This mostly flat dirt and gravel path parallels the highway and connects the parking areas at Multnomah and Wahkeena Falls (so you could start the hike from either end—but there's more parking at this trailhead). After 0.5 mile, you'll descend a short series of stone steps before coming to a junction; turn left to head west on the **unnamed paved path.** You'll shortly see a sign for Wahkeena Falls; proceed up the paved path, ascending through a forest of Douglas fir and hemlock. In 0.2

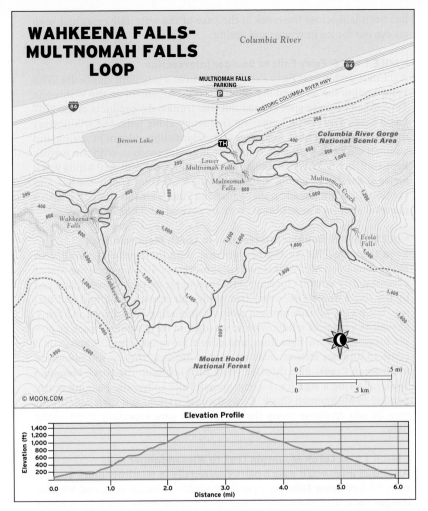

WAHKEENA FALLS-MULTNOMAH FALLS LOOP

Columbia River

MULTNOMAH FALLS PARKING

HISTORIC COLUMBIA RIVER HWY

84

84

Benson Lake

TH

Columbia River Gorge National Scenic Area

Lower Multnomah Falls

Multnomah Falls

Multnomah Creek

Wahkeena Falls

Ecola Falls

Wahkeena Creek

Mount Hood National Forest

© MOON.COM

0   .5 mi
0   .5 km

Elevation Profile

Elevation (ft): 1,400 / 1,200 / 1,000 / 800 / 600 / 400 / 200

Distance (mi): 0.0 / 1.0 / 2.0 / 3.0 / 4.0 / 5.0 / 6.0

mile, you'll emerge at the base of the upper tier of **Wahkeena Falls,** which cascades more 240 feet total and gets its name from the Yakama Nation's word for "most beautiful."

▶ **MILE 0.8-1.4: Wahkeena Falls to Lemmons Viewpoint**
The paved path switchbacks steeply uphill beyond the falls, arriving in 0.6 mile at a junction; turn right for a short spur trail to **Lemmons Viewpoint,** named for a firefighter who died nearby; it offers unfettered views of the Columbia River Gorge, including Beacon Rock and Hamilton Mountain to the east.

▶ **MILE 1.4-1.7: Lemmons Viewpoint to Fairy Falls**
Back at the junction, head south on the **Wahkeena Trail,** a dirt path that parallels **Wahkeena Creek** through a lush canyon before arriving, in 0.3 mile, at the base of **Fairy Falls.** Good news: This marks the end of the hardest part of the ascent, and the trail levels out from here. A wooden plank

has been laid across the creek at the base of the waterfall; cross and keep an eye out for ice in winter and spring.

▸ MILE 1.7–2.6: Fairy Falls to Boulder Intersection

A 0.1-mile amble past Fairy Falls brings you to a junction; ignore the Vista Point Trail to the left, and instead head right to remain on the Wahkeena Trail. You'll begin to spot burned-out tree trunks—by-products of the 2017 Eagle Creek Fire—with increasing frequency along here, but wildflowers including purple phlox, bear grass, and dandelions bloom in spring and summer along this stretch. In 0.4 mile is an intersection with the Angel's Rest Trail, but head left to remain on the Wahkeena Trail. In 0.4 mile you'll arrive at another junction; again ignore the Vista Point Trail to the left, and continue straight ahead on the Wahkeena Trail. This intersection is also a pleasant spot for a snack break, with its several boulders for sitting.

▸ MILE 2.6–3.5: Boulder Intersection to Larch Mountain Trail

Soon after you'll hit yet another junction, with the Devil's Rest Trail; veer left to remain on the Wahkeena Trail. Shortly you'll come upon the first of several minor stream crossings, and then enter an area heavily damaged by the Eagle Creek Fire; every tree along this stretch is burned and barren, but plenty of undergrowth remains, including vine maple and ferns, as well as variety of wildflowers in spring and early summer, such as purple foxglove, yellow tiger lilies, and purple fireweed. After 0.9 mile, you'll come to another stream crossing as you descend the canyon alongside **Multnomah Creek.** Shortly after you'll turn left onto the **Larch Mountain Trail,** following a sign for the Multnomah Falls Lodge and heading north, parallel to Multnomah Creek. Cross the last stream, and then watch your step as you continue along the trail, which gets especially rocky along here.

▸ MILE 3.5–4: Larch Mountain Trail to Wiesendanger Falls

After 0.25 mile, you'll pass a pair of waterfalls in relatively quick succession: 55-foot **Ecola Falls,** only partially visible from the trail, and **Wiesendanger Falls,** also cascading 55 feet into a small gorge. You'll get a better look at Wiesendanger Falls in another 0.2 mile when the trail switchbacks to its base; where the waterfall enters the creek makes a popular swimming hole in summer.

▸ MILE 4–4.7: Wiesendanger Falls to Multnomah Falls Viewpoint Spur

Another 0.1 mile past Wiesendanger Falls you'll pass **Dutchman Falls,** a series of three short waterfalls. In 0.3 mile, head left at the junction, following a sign for the **Multnomah Falls Viewpoint.** The 0.3-mile round-trip spur ends at a plaza at the top of Multnomah Falls; while you don't see much of the waterfall itself from here, it's worth the short side trip for its views of the Columbia River Gorge.

▸ MILE 4.7–5.9: Multnomah Falls Viewpoint Spur to Multnomah Falls Lodge

Back at the junction, turn left onto the Larch Mountain Trail, following the Multnomah Falls Lodge sign. You'll ascend briefly before descending via

▲ MULTNOMAH FALLS

11 paved switchbacks, crossing **Benson Bridge** near the base of **Multnomah Falls;** the 635-foot waterfall tumbles over basalt cliffs in two major steps and is among the most popular natural attractions in the Pacific Northwest, drawing more than two million visitors each year. After 1.2 miles, the trail levels out back at the Multnomah Falls Lodge.

DIRECTIONS

From Portland, head east on I-84 for 28.3 miles. Take exit 31—off to the left—and follow the signs for Multnomah Falls to arrive in the parking area.

The many parking areas near Multnomah Falls fill to capacity regularly, even on weekdays, so consider taking the **Columbia Gorge Express** (888/246-6420, http://columbiagorgeexpress.com), a shuttle between Portland and several popular destinations in the Gorge, including Multnomah Falls (US$7.50 round-trip). The shuttle departs Portland at the **Gateway Transit Center** (9900 NE Multnomah St., Portland), and the ride takes 35-45 minutes. Buses operate year-round, but check the website for the schedule because it varies seasonally.

GPS COORDINATES: 45.57769, -122.11719 / N45° 34.6614' W122° 7.0314'

> ## BEST NEARBY BITES
>
> Enjoy an upscale meal at **Multnomah Falls Lodge** (53000 E. Historic Columbia River Hwy., Bridal Veil, 503/695-2376, www.multnomah-fallslodge.com, 8am-9pm daily). Located at the base of Multnomah Falls, its on-site restaurant offers fine Northwest-inspired cuisine.

Hike into an eroded crater atop Larch Mountain—and enjoy jaw-dropping views of Mount Hood and other Cascade peaks.

DISTANCE: 7.1 miles round-trip
DURATION: 3.5 hours
ELEVATION CHANGE: 1,200 feet
EFFORT: Easy/moderate
TRAIL: Dirt trail, rocks, roots, stream crossings, paved path, stairs, roadside
USERS: Hikers, leashed dogs
SEASON: June–October
PASSES/FEES: Northwest Forest Pass
MAPS: USGS topographic map for Multnomah Falls, OR-WA
CONTACT: Columbia River Gorge National Scenic Area, 541/308-1700, www.fs.usda.gov

L arch Mountain is an extinct volcano near the western edge of the Columbia River Gorge. On this clockwise loop hike, you'll descend into a crater near the mountain's 4,055-foot peak.

START THE HIKE

▸ **MILE 0-2.1: Larch Mountain Trail to Multnomah Creek Way Trail**
Start hiking on the unsigned paved path—the **Larch Mountain Trail**—framed by two wooden posts at the northwestern edge of the parking lot. The path forks almost immediately; take the trail that heads slightly downhill to the left. It soon becomes a dirt trail and goes past a restroom. Old-growth Douglas fir and hemlock forest surrounds you. After about 0.2 mile you'll arrive at an unsigned T-shaped junction; head left to continue downhill. As you descend, vine maple, rhododendron, and summertime huckleberries flank the trail. You'll lose about 600 feet of elevation over the next 1.4 mile, at which point you'll arrive at an old roadbed and well-signed junction; cross the road to continue downhill on the Larch Mountain Trail. Enjoy the purple, bell-shaped foxglove along this stretch; it blooms in late spring and remains vibrant through midsummer. You'll come to a T-shaped junction in another 0.5 mile; head right to take the **Multnomah Creek Way Trail.**

▸ **MILE 2.1-5.2: Multnomah Creek Way Trail to Oneonta Trail**
The trail flattens out in 0.2 mile, where you'll cross **Multnomah Creek** on a wooden footbridge; this trickling creek feeds Multnomah Falls a few miles downstream. Red cedar and salmonberries grow along the trail here. Immediately after the bridge crossing, turn right to remain on the Multnomah Creek Way Trail and begin looping back south from where you came. You'll head into a marshy area, for a brief moment out from under the forest

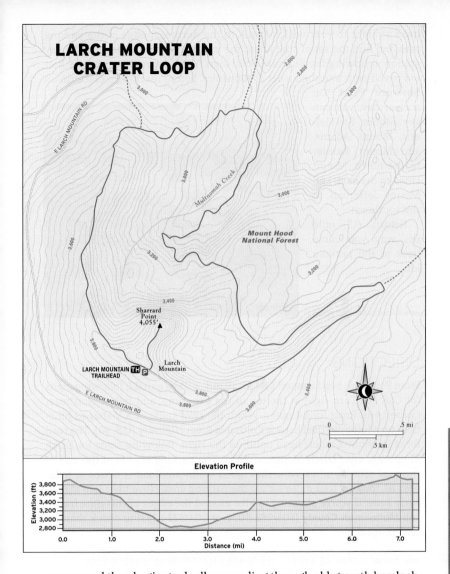

LARCH MOUNTAIN CRATER LOOP

Elevation Profile

canopy, and then begin gradually ascending through old-growth hemlock. The trail crosses numerous small, trickling streambeds over its next winding stretch, but the flow won't rise much above your boot sole. Along this stretch you'll find vibrant undergrowth and wildflowers in spring-summer, including twinflowers, noted for their Y-shaped stalks, and the three-petaled trillium. Some 2.9 miles beyond the Multnomah Creek crossing, you'll arrive at a T-shaped junction; turn right onto the **Oneonta Trail.**

▶ **MILE 5.2–7.1: Oneonta Trail to Sherrard Point and Parking Lot**
Steadily ascend the ridgeline; to your left is the **Bull Run Watershed,** the primary source of drinking water for the city of Portland. After 0.9 mile, the trail ends at **Larch Mountain Road;** turn right to head uphill, walking along its shoulder. The road ends, after 0.4 mile, at the parking area. Rather than

head straight to your vehicle, walk to the northeast edge of the parking area and find the set of stairs near the information board/day-use fee pay station, following the Sherrard Point sign. You'll ascend for 0.3 mile, first via paved path and then a set of **100 stairs,** before reaching a platform on

Sherrard Point. On a clear day, you can see Mount St. Helens, Mount Adams, and Mount Rainier to the north, Mount Hood to the east, and Mount Jefferson to the southeast.

Return 0.3 mile the way you came back to the parking lot.

VIEW FROM SHERRARD POINT ▶

DIRECTIONS

From Portland, head east on I-84 for 19 miles. Take exit 22, following signs for Corbett. Turn right at the top of the exit ramp, and follow Northeast Corbett Hill Road for 1.4 miles. When the road splits at a Y-shaped junction, turn left onto the Historic Columbia River Highway (U.S. 30). The road forks in about 2 miles; head uphill to the right, following signs for Larch Mountain, onto Larch Mountain Road. The parking area is at the end of the road after 14 miles. Note that Larch Mountain Road is closed at milepost 10, roughly four miles before the parking area, November–late May or early June. If you're planning to hike around the edges of this time frame, call **Multnomah County** (503/988-5050 or 503/823-3333) to check that the road is open.

GPS COORDINATES: 45.52948, –122.08878 / N45° 31.7688′ W122° 5.3268′

BEST NEARBY BREWS

Located at the edge of Glendoveer Golf Course, **Von Ebert Brewing Glendoveer** (14021 NE Glisan St., Portland, 503/878-8708, http://glendoveer.vonebertbrewing.com, 11am–10pm Sun.–Thurs., 11am–11pm Fri.–Sat.) serves beers brewed on-site, as well as at its other location in Portland's Pearl District, alongside classic pub fare. From the trailhead, the 30-mile drive east takes 50 minutes via Larch Mountain Road and I-84.

5 Beacon Rock

BEACON ROCK STATE PARK, WA

Follow a shelf-like path blasted into the side of a towering monolith to a sweeping view of the Columbia River Gorge.

DISTANCE: 2 miles round-trip
DURATION: 1 hour
ELEVATION CHANGE: 650 feet
EFFORT: Easy/moderate
TRAIL: Dirt, wooden bridges, paved path
USERS: Hikers
SEASON: Year-round
PASSES/FEES: Discover Pass
MAPS: Green Trails Map 429 for Bonneville Dam
PARK HOURS: 8am–dusk daily
CONTACT: Washington State Parks, 509/427-8265, http://parks.state.wa.us

Rising above the Columbia River, Beacon Rock is the core of an ancient volcano. Lewis and Clark gave the rock its name when they camped here in 1805. Hiking to its top wouldn't be possible without the considerable efforts of Henry Jonathan Biddle, a wealthy engineer and geologist from Philadelphia who developed a love for the area and purchased Beacon Rock, saving it from demolition. From 1916 to 1918, Biddle and his friend Charles Johnson built a harrowing trail up the side of the rock. They blasted a 4-foot-wide path into the cliff and spanned narrow fissures with 22 wooden bridges and more than 100 concrete slabs.

START THE HIKE

▶ **MILE 0-1: Monolith West Side to Beacon Rock**

The path starts in the woods on the west side of the monolith and after a few bends passes through a **gate.** From there, 52 easy-to-manage **switchbacks** are packed into the 1 mile it takes reach the top. Handrails line the route, giving visitors a bit of comfort as they shift their attention between views of the Columbia River, the moss and

SWITCHBACKS ▶

Beacon Rock

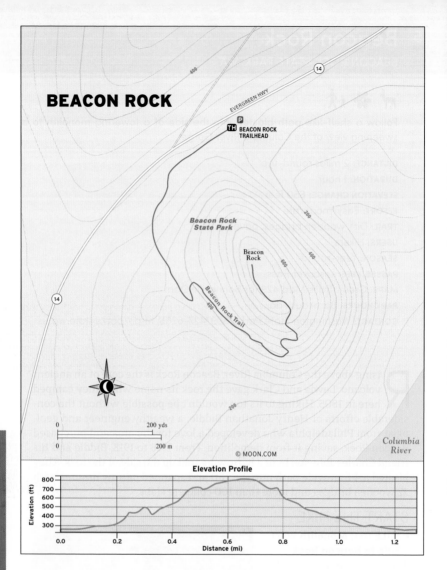

BEACON ROCK

Beacon Rock
State Park

Beacon
Rock

Beacon Rock Trail

Columbia
River

0 — 200 yds

0 — 200 m

© MOON.COM

Elevation Profile

lichen growing on the rock, and occasional wildflowers blooming in the crevices. Warblers, flycatchers, pigeons, hummingbirds, woodpeckers, and other birds frequent the area.

▶ **MILE 1-2: Beacon Rock to Monolith West Side**

Stone steps deliver you to the **top** (848 feet above sea level) and a view that stretches miles up and down the Columbia River Gorge. Ships motor up the river, and trains chug along the banks following the route the Lewis and Clark expedition pioneered two centuries ago. There's not much room at the top, so on nice days you might have to wait for an opportunity to stand at the railing and snap pictures of the Gorge.

After your turn, zigzag your way back to your car.

▲ TRAIL ALONG BEACON ROCK

DIRECTIONS

From I-205 in Vancouver, Washington, take exit 27 and merge onto Highway 14. Drive east for 28 miles. Beacon Rock and trailhead parking is on the right side of the road. Toilets are near the parking lot.

GPS COORDINATES: 45.628571, –122.022222 / N45° 37.7143' W122° 1.3333'

BEST NEARBY BITES

The riverside community of Stevenson, 8.5 miles (12 minutes) northeast of the trailhead via Highway 14, offers tasty post-hike options that include a salmon sandwich at the **Big River Grill** (192 2nd St., Stevenson, WA, 509/427-4888, www.thebigrivergrill.com, hours vary) and burgers and brews in the century-old saloon at **Clark & Lewie's Traveler's Rest Saloon & Grill** (130 SW Cascade Ave., Stevenson, WA, 509/219-0097, www.clarkandlewies.com, hours vary).

Beacon Rock

Dry Creek Falls

COLUMBIA RIVER GORGE NATIONAL SCENIC AREA, OR

Located just a couple of miles east of the Eagle Creek Fire's origin point, this trail offers some of the most gripping views of the devastation wrought by the wildfire—but it also shows signs of life, and concludes at a lovely waterfall.

DISTANCE: 5 miles round-trip

DURATION: 2.5 hours

ELEVATION CHANGE: 1,240 feet

EFFORT: Moderate

TRAIL: Dirt trail, roots, rocks, gravel roads

USERS: Hikers, leashed dogs, horseback riders

SEASON: Year-round

PASSES/FEES: Northwest Forest Pass

MAPS: USGS topographic maps for Bonneville Dam, OR-WA, and Carson, WA-OR

CONTACT: Columbia River Gorge National Scenic Area, 541/308-1700, www.fs.usda.gov

START THE HIKE

▶ **MILE 0-0.3: Bridge of the Gods Trailhead Parking to Eagle Creek Fire-Burned Forest**

From the southern edge of the **Bridge of the Gods Trailhead** parking area, walk south across the road leading to the Bridge of the Gods tollbooth, following a sign onto the **Pacific Crest Trail (PCT).** Walk 0.1 mile on the gently sloping trail, then turn right onto **Southwest Moody Avenue,** under I-84, heading uphill. After a few hundred feet, turn right onto the **unsigned gravel road,** following it for a couple of hundred feet before turning left to rejoin the **PCT.** In 0.1 mile you'll come upon Eagle Creek Fire-charred tree trunks, downed trees, and jagged snags lining the trail. But even with all the damage, signs of life are everywhere: You'll hear the occasional bird over nearby highway noise, and find ferns and raspberry bushes along the narrow trail.

▶ **MILE 0.3-1.3: Eagle Creek Fire-Burned Forest to Power Lines and PCT**

You'll gain 495 feet over the next 1 mile, steadily yet gently ascending, before arriving at a T-shaped intersection. Head right onto the **unnamed gravel road,** following a sign for the PCT, as the road curves uphill and ducks under a set of power lines. Just past the power lines, turn left, back onto the **PCT.**

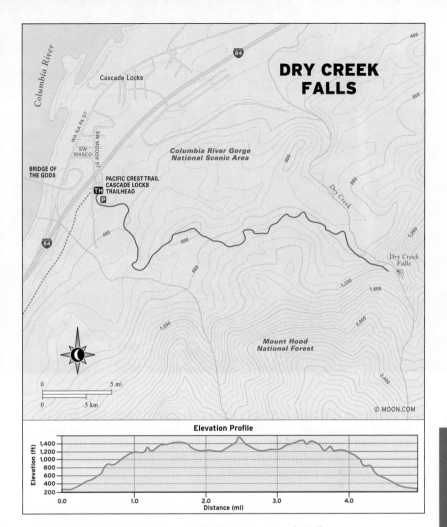

DRY CREEK FALLS

Columbia River

Cascade Locks

Columbia River Gorge
National Scenic Area

BRIDGE OF
THE GODS

PACIFIC CREST TRAIL
CASCADE LOCKS
TRAILHEAD

Dry Creek

Dry Creek
Falls

Mount Hood
National Forest

0   .5 mi
0   .5 km

© MOON.COM

Elevation Profile

▶ **MILE 1.3-2.5: Power Lines and PCT to Dry Creek Falls**

Continue your gradual ascent through a forest of Douglas fir, vine maple, and hemlock for another 0.9 mile, at which point you'll arrive at a junction; make a hard right onto the wide **Dry Creek Falls Trail** for 0.3 mile. The trail ends at the base of **Dry Creek Falls,** a 75-foot plume in the heart of a narrow basalt canyon.

Return the way you came.

DIRECTIONS

From downtown Cascade Locks, head south on Wa Na Pa Street toward the Bridge of the Gods. Turn left at a sign for the Bridge of the Gods toll bridge, and follow the road as it loops around to the east. After a few hundred feet, turn right into a parking area at a sign for the Bridge of the Gods Trailhead in Toll House Park.

If you'd rather not drive and fight for parking at this popular trailhead, the **Columbia Gorge Express** (888/246-6420, http://columbiagorgeexpress.

▲ DRY CREEK FALLS

com) stops at the Cascade Locks Justice Court, just 0.5 mile from the trail-head ($10 round-trip). The shuttle departs from Portland at the **Gate-way Transit Center** (9900 NE Multnomah St., Portland), and the ride takes roughly an hour. Buses operate year-round, but check the website for the schedule because it varies seasonally.

GPS COORDINATES: 45.66233, –121.8959 / N45° 39.7398' W121° 53.754'

BEST NEARBY BITES

Enjoy hearty pizza and pub fare—and wash it down with a refreshing craft beer—at **Cascade Locks Ale House** (500 Wa Na Pa St., Cascade Locks, 541/374-9310, http://cascadelocksalehouse.com, noon-5pm Wed., noon-9pm Thurs.-Mon.). The pub serves pizza, sandwiches, and burgers alongside a selection of craft beer from Portland and the Columbia River Gorge. From the trailhead, the 0.5-mile drive takes 5 minutes via Wa Na Pa St.

COLUMBIA RIVER GORGE

Dry Creek Falls

COLUMBIA RIVER GORGE NATIONAL SCENIC AREA, WA

Climb through colorful fields of wildflowers to a sweeping view of Mount Hood and the Columbia River Gorge.

BEST: Spring Hikes, Wildflower Hikes
DISTANCE: 6.9 miles round-trip
DURATION: 4 hours
ELEVATION CHANGE: 2,900 feet
EFFORT: Moderate/strenuous
TRAIL: Dirt, talus fields
USERS: Hikers, leashed dogs
SEASON: March–December
PASSES/FEES: Northwest Forest Pass, permit required March 31–July 1 ($1.50 per person)
MAPS: Green Trails Map 430 for Hood River, OR
CONTACT: Columbia River Gorge National Scenic Area, 541/308-1700, www.fs.usda.gov/crgnsa

Even if its slopes were barren and dusty, Dog Mountain's striking view of the Columbia River Gorge would draw a crowd. But they aren't. The upper mountain comes alive with color each spring as wildflowers bloom and hikers arrive by the busload. Springtime traffic is so heavy that in 2018 the Forest Service started requiring permits during the season, designed to encourage hikers to take public transportation and alleviate congestion at the trailhead. Permits are free for those riding the shuttle bus from Stevenson. Otherwise, buy a permit (www.recreation.gov) and arrive before sunrise for the best chance of staying ahead of the crowds.

START THE HIKE

▶ **MILE 0-0.6: Parking Lot to First Old Trail Junction**
From the 100-car parking lot, there are three options for making the 2,900-foot climb: Long but gradual (Augspurger Trail), shorter but steeper (the new Dog Mountain Trail), or even shorter and steeper (the old Dog Mountain Trail). Ascending on the new trail and returning via the Augspurger Trail makes an enjoyable loop with loads of inspiring scenery.

From the east end of the parking lot, follow the **new trail,** which tilts upward as heads east and arrives at a toilet in a matter of steps. Here, the real climbing commences, through a forest of Douglas fir. Trailside flora includes Oregon grape, snowberry, and poison oak. After 0.6 mile, pass the **old trail** on your left.

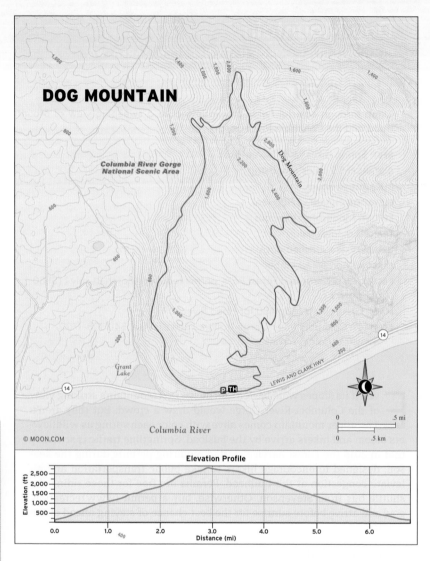

DOG MOUNTAIN

Columbia River Gorge
National Scenic Area

Dog Mountain

Grant
Lake

14

14

P TH

LEWIS AND CLARK HWY

Columbia River

© MOON.COM

0   .5 mi

0   .5 km

Elevation Profile

Elevation (ft)

2,500
2,000
1,500
1,000
500

0.0   1.0   2.0   3.0   4.0   5.0   6.0

Distance (mi)

▶ **MILE 0.6–2.1: First Old Trail Junction to Second Old Trail Junction**
After another 1.5 steep miles of hard work, pass the **upper junction with the
old trail.** Views of the Gorge and the knowledge that the old trail is even
steeper help distract you from the grind.

▶ **MILE 2.1–3: Second Old Trail Junction to**
  Columbia River Gorge Viewpoint
Push on for another steep 0.4 mile before finding yourself in vibrant **Pup-
py Dog Meadow.** Yellow balsamroot, scarlet paintbrush, purple lupine,
red columbine: The kaleidoscope of colors coupled with views of Mount
Hood and the Columbia River is so stunning some hikers choose to make
this their destination. Look for a USGS survey disc on the trail before

continuing upward 0.3 mile, then turning right on a 0.2-mile **spur** that takes you to the high point and another breathtaking view of the Gorge.

▶ MILE 3-4.1: Columbia River Gorge Viewpoint to Augspurger Trail Junction

Wherever you choose to stop climbing, you can return the way you came or take the Old Trail shortcut. But to finish the loop retrace your steps on the spur and turn right to follow the **Dog-Augspurger Tie Trail** north along the ridge for 0.9 mile. At the junction with **Augspurger Trail,** turn left (right makes a 4-mile-each-way side trip to Augspurger Mountain)

▶ MILE 4.1-6.9: Augspurger Trail Junction to Parking Lot

Descend through the forest for about 0.8 mile before reaching the first of several **talus fields.** These rocky sections are easy to navigate if you watch your step, although I have seen hikers slowed enough by these stretches during evening hikes that they found themselves not finishing until after dark.

Expect more of the same for the final 2 miles to the car, with occasional views through the evergreens to Grant Lake. After all that work to get up Dog Mountain, this comparatively gradual descent is a knee's best friend.

DIRECTIONS

From I-205 in Vancouver, Washington, take exit 27 and merge on to Highway 14. Drive east for 47 miles. The well-marked Dog Mountain parking lot is on the left side of the road. A vault toilet is located near the trailhead.

Gorge TransLink (www.gorgetranslink.com) offers shuttle service to the busy trailhead 7:30am-4:30pm on weekends March 31-July 1. The $1-each-way service from the Skamania County Fairgrounds (710 SW Rock Creek Dr., Stevenson, WA) includes a Dog Mountain hiking permit and discounts at Stevenson businesses. Leashed dogs are permitted.

GPS COORDINATES: 45.699265, –121.708174 / N45° 41.9559' W121° 42.4904'

BEST NEARBY BREWS

Brewers stir every batch of beer by hand at **Walking Man Brewing** (240 SW 1st St., Stevenson, WA, 509/427-5520, www.walkingman-beer.com, 11:30am-9pm Wed.-Sun.) in Stevenson. The old-fashioned approach has served the two-decade-old, award-winning brewery well. Pizza, burgers, and salads supplement the beer selection. From the trailhead, the 9.5-mile drive west takes about 15 minutes via Highway 14.

🦌 ❀ 🏞 🐾

Link trails to visit fields of wildflowers, views of the Columbia River, and the edge of a basalt cliff.

BEST: Brew Hikes, Dog-Friendly Hikes
DISTANCE: 6.3 miles round-trip
DURATION: 3.5 hours
ELEVATION CHANGE: 1,200 feet
EFFORT: Easy/moderate
TRAIL: Dirt, rocks, paved and dirt road
USERS: Hikers, leashed dogs, off-leash dogs (July–Nov.), mountain bikers, horseback riders (May–Sept.)
SEASON: Year-round
PASSES/FEES: Northwest Forest Pass
MAPS: Green Trails Map 432S for Columbia River Gorge East; free maps at www.fs.usda.gov/crgnsa
CONTACT: Columbia River Gorge National Scenic Area, 541/308-1700, www.fs.usda.gov/crgnsa

When your hiking route is called "the Labyrinth," it's a good idea to double-check that you packed a good map. At Coyote Wall, for good measure, you might even snap a photo of the large map on the back of the trailhead kiosk or download a map from the Forest Service website (www.fs.usda.gov/crgnsa). With the Columbia River visible most of the way it's hard to stay lost, but a multitude of paths and sparse signage make it easy to wander off course.

START THE HIKE

▶ **MILE 0-0.4: Parking Lot East End to Trail Junction**
Starting at the east end of the parking lot beneath **Coyote Wall,** it's quickly evident why **Old Highway 8** was retired. The paved road is littered with huge rocks that fell from the basalt cliff. Look for jumping fish in Locke Lake, watch trains chug along the Columbia River, and gaze into Oregon as you walk the flat road. At 0.4 mile, pass a trail you'll use to finish the loop.

▶ **MILE 0.4-1.1: Trail Junction to Labyrinth Creek**
In another 0.3 mile, turn left on **Co7** (the Labyrinth Trail) and begin heading upward. Stay right at a junction a few steps up the hill, passing through a short rocky section. Pass a **small cave** in 0.3 mile and stay left at the intersection that follows. Check out a waterfall and cross **Labyrinth Creek** over the next 0.1 mile.

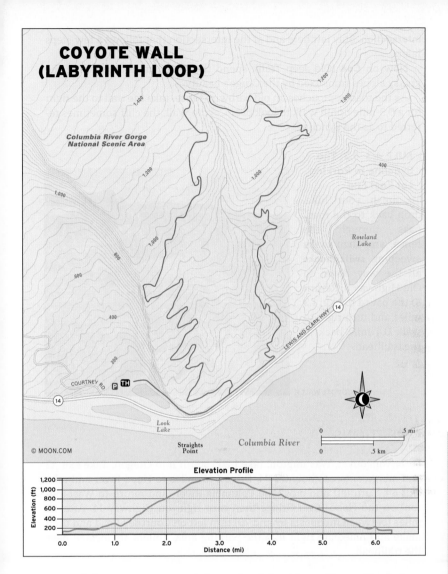

COYOTE WALL (LABYRINTH LOOP)

Columbia River Gorge
National Scenic Area

Rowland
Lake

COURTNEY RD.

LEWIS AND CLARK HWY

Look
Lake

Straights
Point

Columbia River

© MOON.COM

0   .5 mi

0   .5 km

Elevation Profile

Watch boats motor up and down the Columbia as Mount Hood rises above the panorama. In the spring, wildflowers add color to the slopes. Stay alert for rattlesnakes and poison oak.

▶ **MILE 1.1-2.5: Labyrinth Creek to Atwood Road**
Meander 0.7 mile beyond the **creek crossing** before turning left on **Co8** (Upper Labyrinth Trail) and walking another 0.7 mile (with some of the best views) to abandoned **Atwood Road.**

▶ **MILE 2.5-4.3: Atwood Road to the Syncline**
Turn left and follow the road 0.5 mile as it passes through a stand of trees, dips in and out of the Labyrinth Creek drainage, and arrives at a **three-way**

intersection. Stay left here and at the intersection that follows a few steps later.

Now on **Co4** (Old Jeep Trail), spend the next 1 mile descending the grassy slopes transfixed by the Gorge's beauty.

As the road approaches an old barbwire fence, take the trail to the right for a 0.3-mile uphill walk to look over Coyote Wall, the cliff sometimes referred to as the Syncline.

▶ **MILE 4.3–6.3: The Syncline to Parking Lot East End**
To finish your hike, drop back to the road, pass through the fence, and then make sweeping **switchbacks** all the way down to Old Highway 8. Return to the paved road in 1.3 miles and turn right to walk 0.4 mile back to the trailhead.

COYOTE WALL ▶

DIRECTIONS

From Vancouver, Washington, take I-205 south into Oregon. Take exit 22 and merge onto eastbound I-84. Drive 54.7 miles to Hood River and take exit 64. Turn left and cross the Columbia River (and return to Washington) on the Hood River Bridge then turn right on Highway 14. After 11 miles (between mileposts 69 and 70) turn left on Courtney Road and then make an immediate right into the parking area. Toilets are located near the trailhead.

GPS COORDINATES: 45.700604, –121.401706 / N45° 42.0362′ W121° 24.1024′

BEST NEARBY BREWS
Burritos and brews await in White Salmon, less than 5 miles (less than 10 minutes) west of the trailhead via Highway 14. The food and beer are locally sourced at **Everybody's Brewing** (177 E. Jewett Blvd., 509/637-2774, www.everybodysbrewing.com, 11:30am-9:30pm Sun.-Thurs., 11:30am-10pm Fri.-Sat.), where the outdoor seating area includes views of Mount Hood.

One of the newest trails in the Columbia River Gorge boasts waterfalls, wildflowers, and some of the region's best sunset views.

BEST: Winter Hikes

DISTANCE: 3.7 miles round-trip

DURATION: 1.5 hours

ELEVATION CHANGE: 560 feet

EFFORT: Easy/moderate

TRAIL: Dirt trail, gravel, roots, rocks, wooden steps

USERS: Hikers, leashed dogs

SEASON: Year-round

PASSES/FEES: None

MAPS: USGS topographic map for White Salmon, WA-OR

CONTACT: Friends of the Columbia Gorge, 541/386-5268, http://gorgefriends.org

---

This hike is a year-round gem, with bald eagles abundant in winter, more than 30 species of wildflower blooming each spring, Gorge breezes to keep you cool in summer, and fewer crowds than most Gorge hikes in the fall. Sunset views from the viewpoint on Mosier Plateau are stunning—just be sure to bring a flashlight for your return descent.

START THE HIKE

Note that ticks, rattlesnakes, and poison oak can be found along the trail, so long pants are strongly recommended, especially at the height of summer. Sensitive plants also line it, as does some private property; keep to the trail at all times.

▶ MILE 0-0.3: Parking Area to Mosier Pioneer Cemetery

From the parking area, head east for 0.2 mile along the **Historic Columbia River Highway** and cross **Mosier Bridge.** Just past the bridge you'll spot a bench on the south side of the highway, which is where the **Mosier Plateau Trail** begins. Some confusing unofficial trails converge near this early stretch, but head uphill on the well-maintained dirt trail and you'll be on the right track. In 0.1 mile, you'll arrive at **Mosier Pioneer Cemetery,** home to some of Mosier's earliest settlers.

▶ MILE 0.3-1.3: Mosier Pioneer Cemetery to Mosier Viewpoint

Continue up the gently graded trail through grassy fields, oak trees, and stands of ponderosa pine. After 0.25 mile, you'll find a **viewpoint** off to your right. Here you can see **Mosier Creek Falls** and, farther south, **Mosier Creek.** In another 0.25 mile, climb a set of wooden steps, the first of several while ascending Mosier Plateau. This stretch of trail is especially

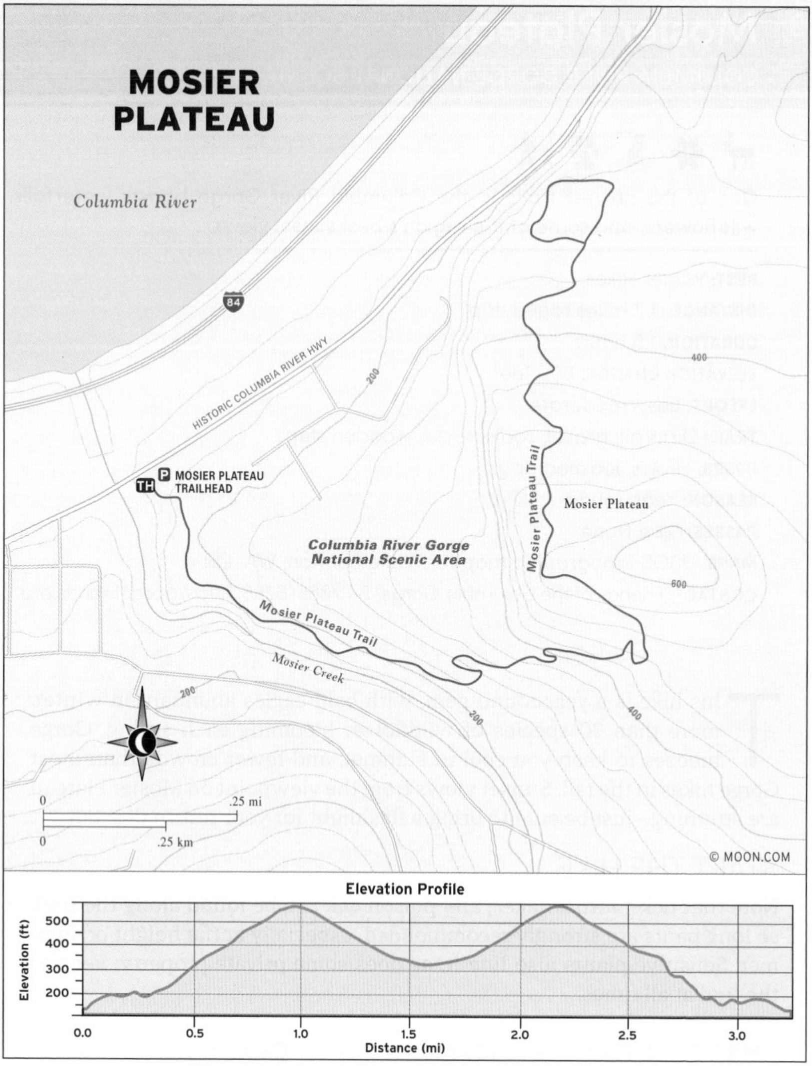

MOSIER PLATEAU

Columbia River

84

HISTORIC COLUMBIA RIVER HWY

200

TH P MOSIER PLATEAU
TRAILHEAD

400

Mosier Plateau Trail

Mosier Plateau

**Columbia River Gorge
National Scenic Area**

600

Mosier Plateau Trail

Mosier Creek

200

400

200

0 .25 mi

0 .25 km

© MOON.COM

Elevation Profile

rich with wildflowers, including bighead clover, yellow arrowleaf balsam-root, and Columbia desert parsley, noted for its reddish-purple petals. In 0.5 mile, after steadily ascending an open hillside, you'll arrive at **Mosi-er viewpoint,** just below the summit of Mosier Plateau, from which you'll have views of Mosier, Hood River, and the Columbia River Gorge that are particularly spectacular during sunset.

▶ **MILE 1.3-2: Mosier Viewpoint to Trail Loop**
Continue on the trail, heading downhill for 0.4 mile. Yellow balsamroot and purple lupine bloom along this stretch each spring. Just beyond a concrete pad, once the site of a mobile home, you'll see a sign to your left indicating the **Trail Loop.** Follow the 0.25-mile loop for river views and a quiet respite just above the highway.

▲ MOSIER VIEWPOINT

▶ **MILE 2–3.7: Trail Loop to Parking Area**
After completing the loop to rejoin the main trail, return 1.7 miles the way you came.

DIRECTIONS

From Hood River, follow I-84 east for 5.5 miles. Take exit 69, following signs for Historic Columbia River Highway (U.S. 30) and Mosier. Follow the off-ramp for about 0.2 mile; at the first intersection, turn right to head south onto U.S. 30. Follow the road as it passes through the town of Mosier. After 0.3 mile, turn left onto a gravel driveway, following a sign for public parking. The road ends in a gravel parking area between the highway and railroad tracks.

GPS COORDINATES: 45.68478, –121.39391 / N45° 41.0868′ W121° 23.6346′

BEST NEARBY BREWS

Near the banks of the Columbia River, **pFriem Family Brewers** (707 Portway Ave., Suite 101, Hood River, 541/321-0490, www.pfriembeer. com, 11am–10pm daily) delivers a lineup of outstanding beers, including a heavy-hitting Belgian dark strong ale, a piney IPA, and a crisp pilsner. From the trailhead, the 7-mile drive west takes 10 minutes via I-84.

This trail traverses celebrated wildflower-strewn meadows and an oak savanna to a hillside boasting grand views of Mount Hood and the Columbia River Gorge.

BEST: Spring Hikes, Wildflower Hikes

DISTANCE: 3.8 miles round-trip

DURATION: 2 hours

ELEVATION CHANGE: 1,080 feet

EFFORT: Easy/moderate

TRAIL: Dirt trail, rocks, roots, stone staircase

USERS: Hikers

SEASON: March-October

PASSES/FEES: None

MAPS: USGS topographic map for Lyle, WA-OR

CONTACT: The Nature Conservancy, 503/802-8100, www.nature.org

McCall Point's location between the forested western part of the Gorge and the drier prairies and highlands of eastern Oregon make this fertile ground for wildflowers. The trail is maintained by The Nature Conservancy. Arrive at the height of wildflower season, and you'll likely encounter a docent along the path; these friendly volunteers are happy to help identify plant species and offer best practices for preventing further erosion.

START THE HIKE

Keep an eye out for poison oak, ticks, and rattlesnakes on this trail.

▶ **MILE 0-0.3: Tom McCall Point Trailhead to Viewpoint**

Start hiking from the **Tom McCall Point Trailhead** at the base of the turn-around at Rowena Crest, heading south through a meadow. If you're here May-June, this meadow offers your first glimpse of why McCall Point is among the most popular wildflower hikes in the Columbia River Gorge: purple lupine, shooting stars, and yellow balsamroot mingle in the grasses, splaying out in seemingly every direction. After 0.3 mile, stop at a **viewpoint** to your right for your first vistas of the eastern edge of the Columbia River Gorge; good as these views are, they only improve from here.

▶ **MILE 0.3-1.9: Viewpoint to McCall Point Summit**

Gently ascending, you'll briefly enter an oak grove in 0.7 mile. You might catch a glimpse here of a western meadowlark, Oregon's state bird. In another 0.2 mile, you'll climb a short stone staircase through another oak

TOM MCCALL POINT TRAIL

Elevation Profile

grove. The trail opens up soon after and, in 0.3 mile, switchbacks steeply through exposed hillsides. Mount Adams to the north, and wildflowers in every direction, soon come into view. Look for fields of prairie stars, foxglove, and more. You'll reach the **McCall Point summit** in 0.4 mile. The hillside meadow is awash in yellow balsamroot, clumps of purple grass widow, and red paintbrush, and affords gorgeous Gorge views including Mount Hood to the west and Mount Adams, Rowena Plateau, and the town of Lyle to the north.

Return the way you came.

DIRECTIONS

From Hood River, follow I-84 east for 5.5 miles. Take exit 69, following signs for the Historic Columbia River Highway (U.S. 30) and Mosier.

▲ WILDFLOWERS

Follow the off-ramp and, at the first intersection, turn right to head south on U.S. 30. Follow the road as it passes through the town of Mosier and climbs into the oak savannas east of town. After 6.6 miles, turn right at a sign for the Rowena Crest Viewpoint. Follow the road for about 0.1 mile to a parking area and turnaround at Rowena Crest.

GPS COORDINATES: 45.68272, –121.30057 / N45° 40.9632' W121° 18.0342'

BEST NEARBY BREWS

Full Sail Brewery (506 Columbia St., Hood River, 541/386-2247, http://fullsailbrewing.com, 11am-9pm daily) has been churning out quality craft beer in the heart of Hood River for more than 30 years. Full Sail prides itself on sustainable practices, and its pub patio delivers sweeping views of the Columbia River. From the trailhead, the 13-mile drive west takes 20 minutes via I-84.

NEARBY CAMPGROUNDS

NAME	DESCRIPTION	FACILITIES	SEASON	FEE
Ainsworth State Park	popular campground in the Columbia River Gorge	40 full-hookup sites, 6 walk-in tent sites, restrooms	March–October	$7-26
I-84, Cascade Locks, OR, 503/793-9885, www.oregonstateparks.org				
Beacon Rock State Park	4,464-acre park on the Columbia River with scenic trails	28 RV and tent sites, restrooms	year-round	$12-50
34841 Hwy. 14, Skamania, WA, 888/226-7688, www.washington.goingtocamp.com				
Skamania County Fairgrounds	fairgrounds that sometimes hosts events (call ahead)	60 RV and tent sites, restrooms	year-round	$20-25
710 SW Rock Creek Dr., Stevenson, WA, 509/427-3980, www.skamaniacounty.org				
Wyeth Campground	former Civilian Conservation Corps campsite	13 tent and RV sites, 3 group sites, restrooms	May–September	$20-30
Wyeth Rd., Cascade Locks, OR, 541/308-1700, www.fs.usda.gov				
Memaloose State Park	campground overlooks the Columbia River	43 full-hookup sites, 66 tent sites, restrooms	March–October	$19-31
I-84, Mosier, OR, 541/478-3008, www.oregonstateparks.org				
Maryhill State Park	park has more than 4,500 feet of waterfront on the Columbia River	70 RV and tent sites, restrooms	year-round	$12-50
50 U.S. 97, Goldendale, WA, 888/226-7688, www.washington.goingtocamp.com				

OREGON COAST

The Oregon Coast is famed for its scenic, rugged terrain. Its 360 miles encompass windswept bluffs and capes, temperate rain forests, inlets and spits, waterfalls, moss-covered crags, and the peaks of the Oregon Coast Range. Hikers enjoy hundreds of miles of trails traversing the dramatic terrain, enjoying no shortage of panoramic views, from the Pacific Ocean to sweeping old-growth forests. Just be sure to bring a rain jacket—the Oregon Coast is also known for rain.

▲ CAPE SEBASTIAN

▲ HECETA HEAD LIGHTHOUSE

◀ VIEW FROM CAPE PERPETUA

1. Saddle Mountain
DISTANCE: 5.9 miles round-trip
DURATION: 3.5 hours
EFFORT: Moderate

2. Cape Falcon
DISTANCE: 5.8 miles round-trip
DURATION: 3 hours
EFFORT: Easy/moderate

3. Neahkahnie Mountain
DISTANCE: 5.9 miles round-trip
DURATION: 3 hours
EFFORT: Easy/moderate

4. Kings Mountain
DISTANCE: 5.4 miles round-trip
DURATION: 3 hours
EFFORT: Moderate

5. Cape Lookout
DISTANCE: 5.5 miles round-trip
DURATION: 2.5 hours
EFFORT: Moderate

6. Cascade Head
DISTANCE: 5.2 miles round-trip
DURATION: 2.5 hours
EFFORT: Easy/moderate

7. Drift Creek Falls
DISTANCE: 4.4 miles round-trip
DURATION: 2 hours
EFFORT: Easy/moderate

8. Cape Perpetua
DISTANCE: 5.8 miles round-trip
DURATION: 2.5 hours
EFFORT: Easy/moderate

9. Heceta Head to Hobbit Trail
DISTANCE: 5 miles round-trip
DURATION: 2.5 hours
EFFORT: Easy/moderate

10. Cape Sebastian
DISTANCE: 3.8 miles round-trip
DURATION: 2 hours
EFFORT: Easy/moderate

11. River View Trail to Redwood Nature Trail
DISTANCE: 3.3 miles round-trip
DURATION: 1.5 hours
EFFORT: Easy/moderate

▼ SADDLE MOUNTAIN TRAIL

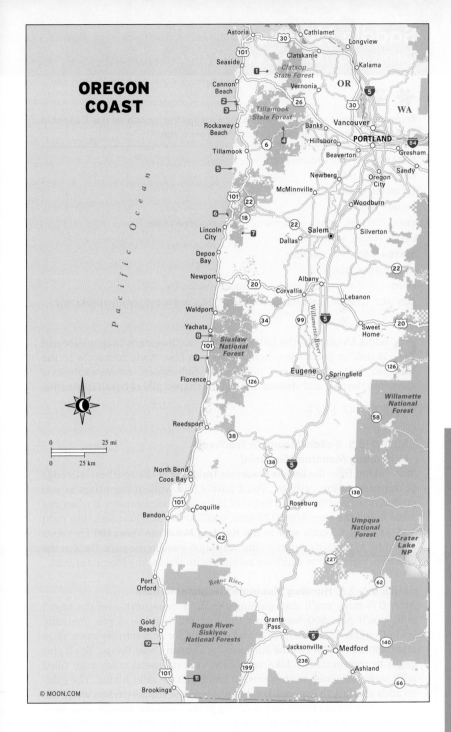

OREGON COAST

Enjoy panoramic views of the Pacific Ocean, the mouth of the Columbia River, and Cascade peaks from this mountain summit.

DISTANCE: 5.9 miles round-trip
DURATION: 3.5 hours
ELEVATION CHANGE: 1,430 feet
EFFORT: Moderate
TRAIL: Dirt trail, roots, rocks, metal mesh, wooden stairs
USERS: Hikers, leashed dogs
SEASON: March-November
PASSES/FEES: None
MAPS: USGS topographic map for Saddle Mountain, OR
CONTACT: Oregon State Parks, 503/368-5943, www.oregonstateparks.org

Saddle Mountain—the tallest point in northwestern Oregon—formed 15 million years ago when a large lava flow made contact with the sea that once covered this region. Subsequent steam explosions shattered the rock and created this saddle-shaped pile of basalt fragments.

START THE HIKE

▶ **MILE 0-0.5: Saddle Mountain Trailhead to Humbug Mountain Viewpoint**

Start hiking from the **Saddle Mountain Trailhead** at the southeastern edge of the parking lot. Early on, you'll pass a few walk-in campsites as you gradually ascend through a forest of alder, with salmonberry bushes and ferns lining the way. After 0.25 mile, you'll arrive at a junction; turn right and walk the 0.2-mile **spur** to the **Humbug Mountain Viewpoint** for views of Saddle Mountain's summit—the only such view in the park. Back at the junction, turn right to continue ascending on the Saddle Mountain Trail.

▶ **MILE 0.5-2.9: Humbug Mountain Viewpoint to Bald**

After 0.75 mile, you'll start gaining elevation in earnest; over the next 1 mile, you'll gain 600 feet—triple the first mile's gain—as you gradually trade Douglas fir, Sitka spruce, and noble fir for occasionally open skies and panoramic views of the surrounding Oregon Coast Range. You'll also begin to intermittently hike on gabion—a kind metal-mesh cage filled with rocks, designed to stop erosion and facilitate safer hiking. The gabion adds stability in dry weather, but can become slippery when wet, even with proper hiking boots and trekking poles; exercise caution after rainfall. After another 0.5 mile of steady ascent, you'll arrive at one of Saddle Mountain's famous grassy expanses, called **balds.** In spring, this area is covered in wildflowers; rosy plectritis and red paintbrush are just some of

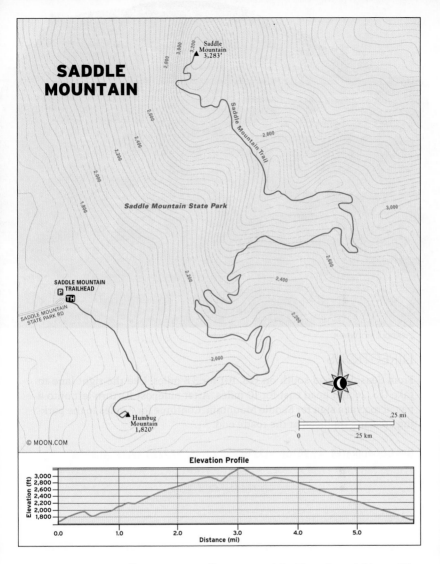

SADDLE MOUNTAIN

Saddle Mountain
3,283'

Saddle Mountain Trail

Saddle Mountain State Park

SADDLE MOUNTAIN
TRAILHEAD
P TH

SADDLE MOUNTAIN
STATE PARK RD

Humbug
Mountain
1,820'

© MOON.COM

0 .25 mi
0 .25 km

Elevation Profile

the varieties you'll encounter well into June-July. Note that picking wild-flowers is prohibited.

▶ MILE 2.9-3.2: Bald to Saddle Mountain Summit

After descending briefly to cross the saddle—from which the mountain gets its name—you'll make your final push, mostly up steep stretches of gabion; the last 0.25 mile to the **Saddle Mountain summit** entails a rugged 275-foot ascent. A few cables offer support, but this stretch becomes especially treacherous after rainfall. Still, the summit views are worth it: to the west is the Pacific Ocean; to the north the mouth of the Columbia River, Youngs Bay, and Astoria; and to the east Cascade peaks in both Oregon and Washington.

Return the way you came.

▲ SADDLE MOUNTAIN

DIRECTIONS

From Seaside, head south on U.S. 101 for 3.8 miles. Use the right lane to take U.S. 26 and head east for 10 miles. After milepost 10, turn left onto a paved road at a sign for Saddle Mountain. Continue for 7 miles to the parking area and trailhead at the road's end.

GPS COORDINATES: 45.96288, -123.68998 / N45° 57.7728′ W123° 41.3988′

BEST NEARBY BITES

Unwind with hearty fare and large portions at **Camp 18 Restaurant** (42362 U.S. 26, Elsie, 503/755-1818, www.camp18restaurant.com, 8am-8pm daily). Famous for serving massive cinnamon rolls, Camp 18 dishes out classic comfort food in a wood cabin-like interior. From the trailhead, the 15-mile drive east takes 25 minutes via U.S. 26.

Head to the top of Cape Falcon for views of nearby Neahkahnie Mountain and the Pacific Ocean, and walk through coastal rain forest to the beach.

BEST: Winter Hikes, Dog-Friendly Hikes
DISTANCE: 5.8 miles round-trip
DURATION: 3 hours
ELEVATION CHANGE: 640 feet
EFFORT: Easy/moderate
TRAIL: Dirt trail, paved path, rocks, roots, stream crossings
USERS: Hikers, leashed dogs
SEASON: Year-round
PASSES/FEES: None
MAPS: USGS topographic map for Arch Cape
CONTACT: Oregon State Parks, 503/368-3575, www.oregonstateparks.org

START THE HIKE

▶ **MILE 0-2: Cape Falcon Trailhead to Upper Blumenthal Falls**
Start hiking from the **Cape Falcon Trailhead** at the western edge of the parking area, through a forest of Douglas fir and Sitka spruce. Short Sand Creek is to your left but mostly out of sight. After 0.5 mile of mostly level hiking, you'll arrive at a T-junction; to the left, a short trail takes you down to the beach and a day-use picnic area. Ignore this spur for now, and turn right, following a sign for Cape Falcon, through a dense forest of western red cedar, western hemlock, and more Sitka spruce. In 0.3 mile, cross a small stream via logs and stones, then follow the trail as it twists and turns through the forest for another 1.1 mile, when you'll cross another stream via wooden footbridge. Keep an eye out in 350 feet for a 25-foot **spur trail** to your left, and follow it for views of **Upper Blumenthal Falls.**

▶ **MILE 2-2.7: Upper Blumenthal Falls to Cape Falcon Viewpoint**
Back on the main trail, you'll gradually ascend for the next 0.4 mile, through usually muddy stretches of trail and over webs of exposed roots, before arriving at an unsigned intersection with the Oregon Coast Trail. Take a left to continue west on the Cape Falcon Trail toward the headland, hiking through a veritable hallway of salal, a native shrub that can grow six feet or taller. After 0.3 mile, you'll arrive at a grassy, exposed **viewpoint** atop a 200-foot cliff on the southern face of **Cape Falcon.** This popular spot offers panoramic views of Neahkahnie Mountain, Short Sand Beach, Smugglers Cove—an inlet bordered by Neahkahnie Mountain to the south and Cape Falcon to the north—and the Pacific Ocean. Keep an

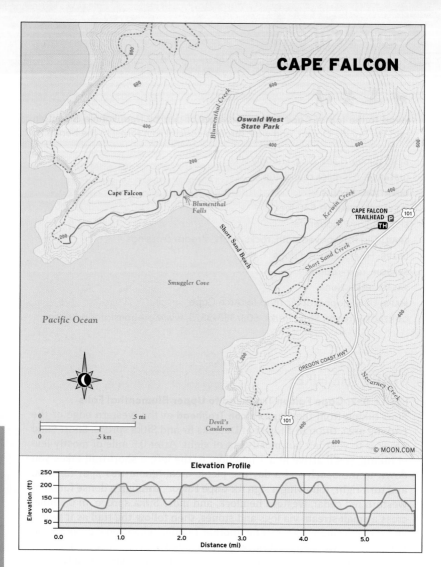

CAPE FALCON

Oswald West State Park

Cape Falcon

Blumenthal Falls

Short Sand Beach

Blumenthal Creek

Kerwin Creek

CAPE FALCON TRAILHEAD 🅿 101

Short Sand Creek

Smuggler Cove

Pacific Ocean

OREGON COAST HWY

Necarney Creek

0   .5 mi
0   .5 km

Devil's Cauldron

© MOON.COM

Elevation Profile

eye out for seals and sea lions on the rocks below, and watch for migrating gray whales offshore, especially in spring and winter.

▶ **MILE 2.7–5.1: Cape Falcon Viewpoint to Short Sand Beach**

Return the way you came, but at the first (now final) junction, continue straight for an 0.2-mile **spur** down to **Short Sand Beach,** popular with picnickers, surfers, and dogs—they're allowed to be off-leash on the beach.

▶ **MILE 5.1–5.8: Short Sand Beach to Cape Falcon Trailhead**

Back at the junction, continue east on the Cape Falcon Trail to return the way you came.

▲ TRAIL ALONG CAPE FALCON

DIRECTIONS

From Cannon Beach, head south on U.S. 101 for 9.5 miles. Turn right into the parking area at milepost 39, following a sign for the Cape Falcon Trailhead. Additional parking is available along the other side of the highway just a bit farther south along U.S. 101; take care when crossing the highway.

GPS COORDINATES: 45.76319, -123.95617 / N45° 45.7914' W123° 57.3702'

BEST NEARBY BREWS

Celebrate Oregon's public beaches with a pint at **Public Coast Brewing Co.** (264 3rd St., Cannon Beach, 503/436-0285, http://publiccoastbrewing.com, noon-9pm Sun.-Thurs., noon-10pm Fri.-Sat. summer, call for hours fall-spring), where several of the brewery's craft beers are named in honor of the state's coastline. It also offers a food menu rife with fresh, seasonal ingredients. From the trailhead, the 11-mile drive north takes 20 minutes via U.S. 101.

Cape Falcon

Enjoy sweeping coastal views from atop this 1,700-foot mountain.

DISTANCE: 5.9 miles round-trip
DURATION: 3 hours
ELEVATION CHANGE: 1,110 feet
EFFORT: Easy/moderate
TRAIL: Dirt trail, roots, rocks, rock scramble
USERS: Hikers, leashed dogs
SEASON: Year-round
PASSES/FEES: None
MAPS: USGS topographic map for Nehalem
CONTACT: Oregon State Parks, 503/368-3575, www.oregonstateparks.org

Neahkahnie Mountain was formed in the wake of Columbia River basalt lava flows some 15 million years ago and has long been a spiritually important place for the Tillamook tribe of Native Americans. Roughly translated, "Neahkahnie" means "place of the creator." The mountain is also rumored to be home to buried treasure, care of two shipwrecked sailors in the 1600s. Treasure hunters have spent the last couple hundred years searching for the loot, to no avail.

START THE HIKE

▶ **MILE 0-0.3: North Neahkahnie Mountain Trailhead to Cape Falcon and Smugglers Cove Views**

Head to the southern edge of the parking area and cross U.S. 101 to find the **North Neahkahnie Mountain Trailhead.** You'll begin ascending immediately through an open field of thick salal bushes and ferns via the **Oregon Coast Trail;** this hike takes you along a short stretch of this trail, which parallels the entire Oregon Coast. Views of Cape Falcon and Smugglers Cove open up after 0.3 mile.

FOREST ON NEAHKAHNIE MOUNTAIN ▶

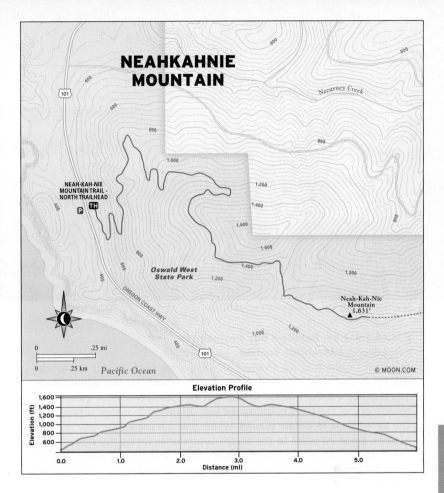

NEAHKAHNIE
MOUNTAIN

NEAH-KAH-NIE
MOUNTAIN TRAIL -
NORTH TRAILHEAD

Necarney Creek

Oswald West
State Park

OREGON COAST HWY

Neah-Kah-Nie
Mountain
1,631'

Pacific Ocean

© MOON.COM

0   .25 mi
0   .25 km

Elevation Profile

Elevation (ft)

1,600
1,400
1,200
1,000
800
600

0.0   1.0   2.0   3.0   4.0   5.0

Distance (mi)

▶ **MILE 0.3–2.9: Cape Falcon and Smugglers**
Cove Views to Nehalem Bay Viewpoint

Continue to ascend gradually through Sitka spruce thickets, salal-heavy stretches, tall ferns, and a western red cedar and western hemlock forest. In spring, you might also catch blooms of candy flower, Columbia windflower, and trillium. Exposed roots, moss-covered rocks, and soft dirt along the trail's edge can create slippery conditions, especially if it has just rained—which it often has on the Oregon Coast—so take care. In 1.25 miles, the trail levels out—you've gained about 1,000 feet in elevation so far—and starts winding toward Neahkahnie Mountain's southern face through a thick forest with little undergrowth. After another 1.3 miles, you'll arrive at a **viewpoint** just below Saddle Mountain's southern summit. From this vantage, you can gaze south into Nehalem Bay and the coastal town of Manzanita.

▲ VIEW FROM THE SUMMIT OF NEAHKAHNIE MOUNTAIN

▶ **MILE 2.9-2.95: Nehalem Bay Viewpoint to Neahkahnie Mountain Summit**

Continue on the trail for another 100 feet or so, until you hit the southern tip of this clearing and the trail heads inland. Almost immediately, you'll notice a rocky hillside to your left and possibly a spray-painted arrow on one of the trees pointing the way up the 50-foot rock scramble to the **Neahkahnie Mountain summit,** where you can see all the way to Cape Meares, some 30 miles to the south. Continue as far up the scramble as feels safe—it can be especially slippery after rainfall—and take a rest on its rocky surface for the best views, or under a tree at its base for a little shade.

Return the way you came.

DIRECTIONS

From Cannon Beach, head south on U.S. 101 for 10.8 miles. Turn right into the Neahkahnie Mountain gravel parking area past milepost 40. Take care crossing the highway to the trailhead.

GPS COORDINATES: 45.74759, –123.96185 / N45° 44.8554' W123° 57.711'

BEST NEARBY BITES

Bread and Ocean (154 Laneda Ave., Manzanita, 503/368-5823, www.breadandocean.net, 7:30am-3pm Wed., 7:30am-3pm and 5pm-8pm Thurs.-Sat., 8am-3pm Sun.) is a cozy café that serves light breakfast fare, sandwiches, soups, and pastries, as well as filling comfort food for dinner. From the trailhead, the 3-mile drive south takes 5 minutes via U.S. 101.

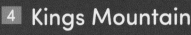

4 Kings Mountain

TILLAMOOK STATE FOREST

On this thigh-busting hike you'll start gaining elevation early and won't stop until the summit—but you'll earn views encompassing everything from the ocean to the Cascades.

DISTANCE: 5.4 miles round-trip
DURATION: 3 hours
ELEVATION CHANGE: 2,370 feet
EFFORT: Moderate
TRAIL: Dirt trail, roots, rocks
USERS: Hikers, leashed dogs
SEASON: March-November
PASSES/FEES: None
MAPS: USGS topographic map for Jordan Creek, OR
CONTACT: Oregon Department of Forestry, 503/357-2191, www.oregon.gov/odf

START THE HIKE

Trekking poles and hiking shoes with proper tread are recommended for this trail.

▶ **MILE 0-0.2: Kings Mountain Trailhead to Wilson River Trail Junction**
Start hiking from the **Kings Mountain Trailhead** at the eastern edge of the parking lot, located near an informational signboard. Stroll along this mostly flat stretch through an alder forest flanked by four- and five-foot-high sword ferns for the first 0.2 mile, at which point you'll arrive at a four-way intersection with the Wilson River Trail. Continue straight ahead on the Kings Mountain Trail, following a pointer uphill for the Kings Mountain Summit. From here you'll start ascending and, save for a few short, flat-ish stretches, continue gaining until the summit. Enjoy the lush forest, rich with alder and Douglas fir; it wasn't always this verdant. Beginning in 1933, a series of wildfires scorched 335,000 acres of old-growth forest in the Oregon Coast Range. This inspired the planting of more than 70 million seedlings and, in 1973, the creation of Tillamook State Forest.

▶ **MILE 0.2-2.1: Wilson River Trail Junction to Viewpoint**
About 0.8 mile past the trail junction, the somewhat gentle grade steepens and becomes a real thigh-burner; you'll more than double the elevation you gained in the first mile between here and the summit. In another 1.1 miles, you'll reach a T-junction; follow the 50-foot spur to your left for a **viewpoint** with sweeping vistas of the northern Oregon Coast Range.

Kings Mountain

OREGON COAST

▸ **MILE 2.1-2.3: Viewpoint to Picnic Table**

Back at the junction, continue uphill on the occasionally rocky trail. You'll pass a **picnic table**—installed by a Boy Scout troop—in about 0.2 mile. Views are limited here, but this makes a fine lunch spot, and an ideal place to catch your breath before the final push. Just past the picnic table, you'll walk through open meadows, which are covered with paintbrush, bear grass, larkspur, phlox, and other wildflowers April-June.

▸ **MILE 2.3-2.7: Picnic Table to Kings Mountain Summit**

Over the final 0.4 mile, you'll gain 625 feet, traversing steep, rocky stretches and exposed roots on narrow sections. The **Kings Mountain Summit** is denoted by a sign and trail register. From here you can see Tillamook Bay and the Pacific Ocean to the west and Mount Hood and Mount Adams to the east. The trail continues on from here, but this is your turnaround point.

Return the way you came.

VIEW FROM KINGS MOUNTAIN ▸

DIRECTIONS

From Tillamook, head east on Highway 6 for 25 miles. Just past milepost 25, turn left into the parking lot at a sign for the Kings Mountain Trailhead.

GPS COORDINATES: 45.59712, –123.50629 / N45° 35.8272′ W123° 30.3774′

BEST NEARBY BITES AND BREWS

Try some of the state's best wild ales at **de Garde Brewing** (114 Ivy Ave., Tillamook, 503/815-1635, www.degardebrewing.com, 3pm-7pm Thurs.-Fri., noon-7pm Sat., 11am-5pm Sun.), which has garnered acclaim and awards for using natural, open-air yeast strains in each recipe—no two batches taste exactly alike. From the trailhead, the 25-mile drive west takes 30 minutes via Highway 6. If you're more in the mood for a scoop of house-made ice cream—and cheese samples—head 2 miles north of the brewery on U.S. 101 to find the iconic **Tillamook Creamery** (4165 U.S. 101, Tillamook, 503/815-1300, www.tillamook.com, 8am-8pm daily early June-early Nov., 8am-6pm Mon.-Fri. and 8am-8pm Sat.-Sun. early Nov.-early June).

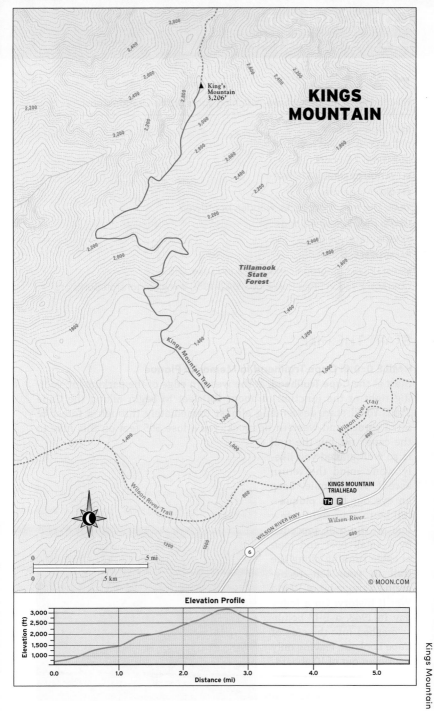

KINGS MOUNTAIN

Tillamook State Forest

King's Mountain 3,206'

Kings Mountain Trail

Wilson River Trail

KINGS MOUNTAIN TRIALHEAD

Wilson River Trail

WILSON RIVER HWY

Wilson River

6

0   .5 mi
0   .5 km

© MOON.COM

Elevation Profile

Elevation (ft) — 3,000 / 2,500 / 2,000 / 1,500 / 1,000

Distance (mi) — 0.0 / 1.0 / 2.0 / 3.0 / 4.0 / 5.0

Hike to one of the best whale-watching spots on the Oregon Coast.

BEST: Spring Hikes

DISTANCE: 5.5 miles round-trip

DURATION: 2.5 hours

ELEVATION CHANGE: 1,370 feet

EFFORT: Moderate

TRAIL: Dirt trail, roots, rocks, wooden boardwalk

USERS: Hikers, leashed dogs

SEASON: Year-round

PASSES/FEES: None

MAPS: USGS topographic map for Sand Lake, OR

CONTACT: Oregon State Parks, 503/842-4981, www.oregonstateparks.org

START THE HIKE

▶ **MILE 0-0.6: Cape Trailhead to Memorial Plaque**
Start at the **Cape Trailhead,** at the western edge of the parking lot, veering right at the junction in about 100 feet to begin hiking the Cape Trail. You'll start descending almost immediately through a forest of Sitka spruce and western hemlock; you'll lose 595 feet on this hike to the cape's tip, but the trail is so well graded you likely won't mind the return ascent. At 0.6 mile, keep an eye out for a **plaque**—it'll be to your right a few feet off the trail, preceded by a small post and metal cable running along the trail to your left—recognizing a tragic bit of World War II history: On a foggy day in 1943, a B-17 bomber crashed into the side of Cape Lookout, leaving only 1 survivor out of 10 aboard.

CAPE LOOKOUT ▶

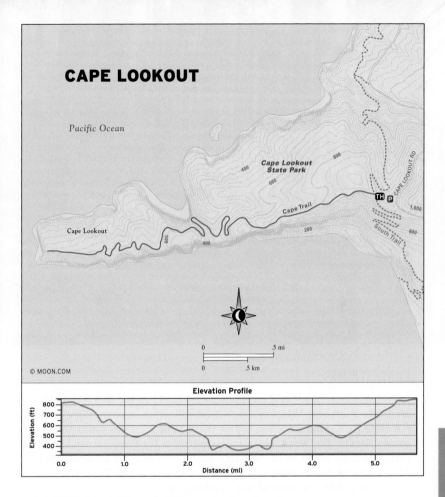

CAPE LOOKOUT

Pacific Ocean

Cape Lookout State Park

Cape Trail

Cape Lookout

South Trail

CAPE LOOKOUT RD

Elevation Profile

▶ **MILE 0.6–1.4: Memorial Plaque to Boardwalks**
In 0.4 mile, the trail switchbacks several times, offering occasional ocean views. When looking southward, keep an eye out for Cape Kiwanda and Haystack Rock near Pacific City. In another 0.4 mile, the trail becomes muddier and more slippery; short stretches of wooden boardwalk have been installed to lessen the impact, but it's tough to avoid tromping through ankle-high mud puddles here.

▶ **MILE 1.4–2.75: Boardwalks to Cape Lookout**
After another 1.1 miles, ocean views open up as you leave the forest for the final 0.25-mile stretch toward the **tip of Cape Lookout,** where you'll find a bench and 270-degree views. Take a seat and look for gray whales; they're most commonly spotted during their migration in winter and spring. On a clear day, you might also be able to see Tillamook Head, Cape Falcon, and Cascade Head.

Return the way you came.

▲ TRAIL ALONG CAPE LOOKOUT

DIRECTIONS

From Tillamook, head west on Highway 131 for 5.1 miles. At a fork in the road, take a left onto Whiskey Creek Road, following signs for Cape Lookout State Park. After 1.2 miles, follow the road as it curves south and becomes Netarts Bay Road, again following signs for Cape Lookout State Park. Continue south as the winding road becomes Cape Lookout Road. After 6.6 miles, take a right at a sign for the Cape Lookout Trail. The road ends after 250 feet in the trailhead's parking lot.

GPS COORDINATES: 45.34095, -123.9737/ N45° 20.457' W123° 58.422'

BEST NEARBY BREWS

Sip a beer in the most scenic dining room in Oregon at **Pelican Brewing Company** (33180 Cape Kiwanda Dr., Pacific City, 503/965-7007, http://pelicanbrewing.com, 10:30am-10pm Sun.-Thurs., 10:30am-11pm Fri.-Sat.). It offers more than a dozen classic and seasonal styles, all served mere feet from the Pacific Ocean. From the trailhead, the 11-mile drive south takes 15 minutes via Cape Lookout Road and Sandlake Road.

CASCADE HEAD PRESERVE

🦌 ❀

The hike to the summit of Cascade Head has it all: old-growth coastal rain forest, dazzling wildflowers, and panoramic ocean views.

DISTANCE: 5.2 miles round-trip

DURATION: 2.5 hours

ELEVATION CHANGE: 1,150 feet

EFFORT: Easy/moderate

TRAIL: Dirt trail, roots, rocks, wooden boardwalk, wooden steps, footbridges, gravel paths

USERS: Hikers

SEASON: Year-round

PASSES/FEES: None

MAPS: USGS topographic map for Neskowin; free trail map at the old trailhead 0.4 mile into the hike

CONTACT: The Nature Conservancy, 503/802-8100, www.nature.org

START THE HIKE

▶ **MILE 0-0.6: Cascade Head Trailhead to Old Cascade Head Trailhead**

Start hiking from the **Cascade Head Trailhead** next to the informational signboard at the northern edge of the parking lot. You'll immediately cross a small footbridge, the first of many, before entering a forest of ferns, salal, and Sitka spruce. After 350 feet, head straight to cross Three Rocks Road, and continue on past a sign for the Cascade Head Preserve. You'll briefly walk along wooden boardwalk. In 0.4 mile you'll emerge from the forest at a Y-shaped intersection with **Savage Road** and Ridge Road. Head left to cross Savage Road, then follow the gravel path on the road's shoulder to continue northward; several signs at this junction point the way. This stretch crosses private property, so stick to the path at all times. Follow Savage Road for 0.1 mile and, when it curves left, cross the road again, returning to the forest at a sign for the **old Cascade Head Trailhead,** where you can grab a trail map.

▶ **MILE 0.6-1.6: Old Cascade Head Trailhead to Meadow**

Cross a small footbridge and climb a set of wooden steps to begin ascending in earnest through a forest of old-growth spruce. In 0.2 mile, keep left at an unsigned, Y-shaped junction to remain on the trail. You'll gain steadily for 0.7 mile, at which point you'll arrive at a Cascade Head informational signboard and, 0.1 mile past it, a **meadow** with sweeping views of the ocean and, to the south, the mouth of the Salmon River. This is a good spot to apply sunscreen if you haven't done so already; the rest of the trail is almost entirely exposed.

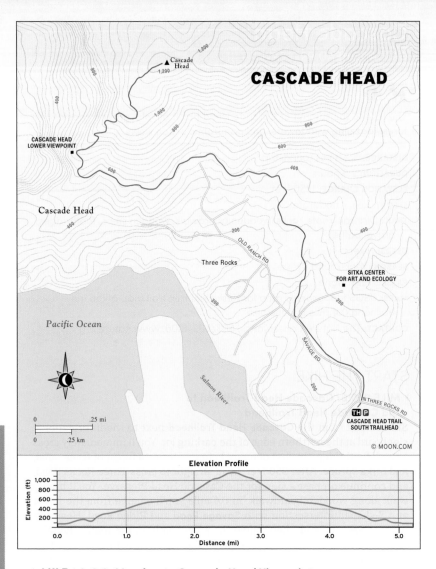

Elevation Profile

▶ MILE 1.6-2.6: Meadow to Cascade Head Viewpoint

As you switchback up the southern face of Cascade Head, take care to keep to the trail so as not to trample wildflowers, including foxglove, hairy checkermallow, Cascade Head catchfly, and the rare blue violet—a vital food source for larvae of the Oregon silverspot butterfly, a federally threatened species that emerges from its cocoon July-September. Continue ascending the uneven, occasionally rocky trail, gaining 670 feet over the final 1 mile, after which you'll arrive at a **viewpoint,** indicated by an unsigned metal post. This meadow is just below the summit of Cascade Head, but the views here are the best on the headland. Keep an eye out for elk, deer, coyote, bald eagles, owls, and various raptors. The trail continues on, connecting with a northern trailhead in about a mile, but this is a fine spot to stop, relax, and have a snack. Return the way you came.

▲ VIEW OF THE SALMON RIVER FROM CASCADE HEAD

DIRECTIONS

From Lincoln City, head north on U.S. 101 for 6.1 miles. Soon after milepost 104, take a sharp left onto North Three Rocks Road. Follow it for 2.3 miles. At the T-junction, turn left to remain on the road, following a sign for the Cascade Head Trailhead. In about 450 feet, just before a Dead End sign, turn left into the parking lot at Knight Park.

GPS COORDINATES: 45.04202, -123.99226 / N45° 2.5212' W123° 59.5356'

BEST NEARBY BREWS

Whether you're thirsting for beer, cider, mead, wine, or kombucha, you'll find it all at **Black Squid Beer House** (3001 SW U.S. 101, Lincoln City, 541/614-0733, www.blacksquidbeerhouse.com, 3pm-10pm Wed.-Thurs., 3pm-11pm Fri., 1pm-11pm Sat., 3pm-9pm Sun.). Black Squid prides itself on serving a mix of popular and hard-to-find ales and lagers from regional breweries; it offers a variety of styles, from sours and saisons to IPAs and stouts. From the trailhead, the 10-mile drive south takes 20 minutes via North Three Rocks Road and U.S. 101.

Traverse old-growth forest and a dramatic suspension bridge on your way to a waterfall.

BEST: Waterfall Hikes
DISTANCE: 4.4 miles round-trip
DURATION: 2 hours
ELEVATION CHANGE: 570 feet
EFFORT: Easy/moderate
TRAIL: Dirt trail, rocks, roots, suspension bridge
USERS: Hikers, leashed dogs
SEASON: Year-round
PASSES/FEES: Northwest Forest Pass
MAPS: USGS topographic map for Stott Mountain; U.S. Forest Service map for Drift Creek Falls, available online and at the trailhead
CONTACT: Siuslaw National Forest, 503/392-5100, www.fs.usda.gov

START THE HIKE

▶ **MILE 0-1.2: Drift Creek Falls Trailhead to Homer Creek**
Begin at the **Drift Creek Falls Trailhead,** at the eastern edge of the parking lot. You'll descend gradually through a forest of second-growth Douglas fir, vine maple, alder, ferns, and salal. Keep an eye out for white, three-petaled trillium if it's spring, and watch for nurse logs alongside the trail; you might see new shrubs, mushrooms, or trees sprouting from the decaying wood. After 0.8 mile, you'll arrive at a junction with the North Loop; head right to continue descending on the well-graded Drift Creek Falls Trail. In 0.4 mile, you'll arrive at **Homer Creek;** you wouldn't guess from this gentle trickle that most of the water cascading down Drift Creek Falls comes from this creek! Ignore another junction with the North Loop for now, crossing a bridge over the creek and continuing on the Drift Creek Falls Trail.

▶ **MILE 1.2-1.9: Homer Creek to Drift Creek Falls**
For the next 0.4 mile, the trail mostly follows Homer Creek through a forest of western red cedar and Sitka spruce, at which point you'll arrive at an impressive 240-foot **suspension bridge** spanning **Drift Creek.** From the bridge, Drift Creek Falls comes into view to your right. After crossing the bridge, descend the last 0.25 mile to the base of 75-foot-tall **Drift Creek Falls.** The falls' rock face broke away in 2010, revealing columnar basalt that formed 55 million years ago. Have a seat on one of the shaded rocks, gather energy for your return ascent, and admire the view.

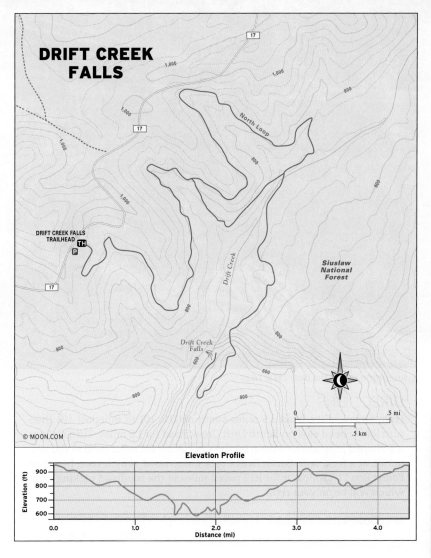

DRIFT CREEK FALLS

17

1,000

1,000

1,000

800

North Loop

1,000

17

800

1,000

800

DRIFT CREEK FALLS
TRAILHEAD **TH**
P

Drift Creek

Siuslaw
National
Forest

17

800

800

600

Drift Creek
Falls

600

800

600

© MOON.COM

| 0 | .5 mi |
| 0 | .5 km |

Elevation Profile

Elevation (ft)

900
800
700
600

0.0   1.0   2.0   3.0   4.0

Distance (mi)

▶ **MILE 1.9-4.4: Drift Creek Falls to Trailhead (via North Loop)**

Head back the way you came and cross Homer Creek. But instead of returning the way you came, on the Drift Creek Falls Trail, take a right onto the **North Loop.** You'll steadily ascend through a dense grove of old-growth Douglas fir, vine maple, huckleberry bushes, salmonberry, and ferns before reconnecting with the **Drift Creek Falls Trail** in 1 mile; turn right at the original junction you encountered on the trail, and head uphill to return to your vehicle.

▲ SUSPENSION BRIDGE AND DRIFT CREEK FALLS

DIRECTIONS

From Lincoln City, head 3.5 miles south on U.S. 101 to milepost 119, then turn left to head east on South Drift Creek Road for 1.6 miles. Turn right at a T-shaped junction to remain on the road. After 0.4 mile, head to the left, uphill, at a fork, onto South Drift Creek Camp Road, which soon becomes Forest Road 17. Follow it for 10.2 paved miles to the trailhead parking area, which will be on your right.

GPS COORDINATES: 44.93555, –123.85555 / N44° 56.133' W123° 51.333'

BEST NEARBY BREWS

Enjoy quality craft beer and creative pizzas along U.S. 101 at **Rusty Truck Brewing** (4649 U.S. 101, Lincoln City, 541/994-7729, http://rustytruckbrewing.com, brewpub 4pm-9:30pm Mon.-Thurs., 11am-11pm Sat.-Sun. summer; taproom 4pm-9:30pm Mon.-Thurs., 11am-11pm Fri.-Sat., and 11am-10pm Sun. summer, 4pm-9pm Fri., noon-10pm Sat., and noon-9pm Sun. fall-spring). The brewery regularly incorporates cherries, oranges, berries, and other fruits into classic recipes for flavorful twists. From the trailhead, the 13-mile drive west takes 30 minutes via Forest Road 17, South Drift Creek Camp Road, and U.S. 101.

Link a series of scenic trails to experience some of the region's most fascinating natural features, including what the U.S. Forest Service calls "the best view on the Oregon Coast."

BEST: Brew Hikes
DISTANCE: 5.8 miles round-trip
DURATION: 2.5 hours
ELEVATION CHANGE: 1,020 feet
EFFORT: Easy/moderate
TRAIL: Dirt trail, paved path, wooden steps, roots, rocks
USERS: Hikers, leashed dogs
SEASON: Year-round
PASSES/FEES: Northwest Forest Pass
MAPS: USGS topographic map for Yachats; U.S. Forest Service map for Cape Perpetua, available online and at the Cape Perpetua Visitor Center
PARK HOURS: Sunrise-sunset daily
CONTACT: Siuslaw National Forest, 503/392-5100, www.fs.usda.gov

START THE HIKE

▶ **MILE 0-0.8: Captain Cook Trail Loop from Cape Perpetua Visitor Center**
Head south from the **Cape Perpetua Visitor Center,** following the paved **Captain Cook Trail**—named for Captain James Cook, who first observed Cape Perpetua in 1778. You'll descend gradually through a forest of salal and western hemlock. After 0.1 mile, ignore the sign to your left for the Oregon Coast Trail, and instead head right to walk through a tunnel under U.S. 101. Make a left at the junction just after the tunnel, and then head right at the next junction in another 250 feet—following signs for Tidepools and Spouting Horn at each junction—to embark on a short loop.

The 0.4-mile **loop trail** showcases some of Cape Perpetua's most popular natural features. If the tide's low enough, you can follow an old paved path off the northern end of the loop onto a rocky stretch of shore to **tide pools,** where you might spot starfish, sea anemones, and urchins. On the southern end of the loop, you'll see **Thor's Well,** a 20-foot-deep hole in the rocky shoreline that appears to drain the Pacific Ocean once the surf washes onto the shore. South of Thor's Well is **Spouting Horn,** which puts on a geyser-like show whenever waves crash into a partially buried sea cave; at high tide, some of the water shoots upward through an opening in the cave's ceiling, looking much like a whale's spout.

Complete the counterclockwise loop and, back on the main trail, return to the visitors center the way you came.

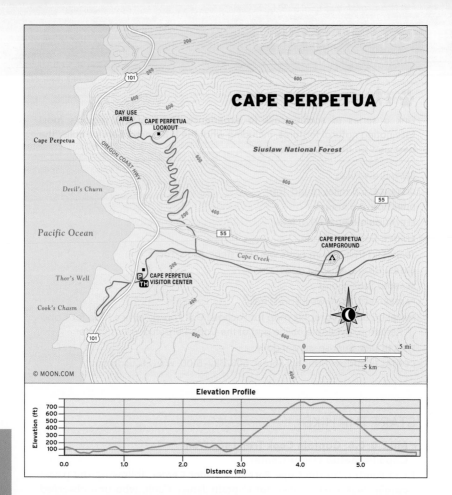

CAPE PERPETUA

Siuslaw National Forest

Pacific Ocean

Cape Perpetua

Devil's Churn

Thor's Well

Cook's Chasm

DAY USE AREA

CAPE PERPETUA LOOKOUT

OREGON COAST HWY

CAPE PERPETUA VISITOR CENTER

Cape Creek

CAPE PERPETUA CAMPGROUND

© MOON.COM

0   .5 mi

0   .5 km

Elevation Profile

Elevation (ft)

Distance (mi)

▸ **MILE 0.8–1.9: Cape Perpetua Visitor Center to Giant Spruce of Cape Perpetua**

Head north through the visitors center's plaza to find the **Giant Spruce Trail.** The 1.1-mile paved path transitions to gravel and dirt as it curves inland along **Cape Creek.** You'll notice intersections with other trails to your left along the way (including one about 0.3 mile from the visitors center for the Saint Perpetua Trail, which you'll return to), but continue straight on the mostly flat Giant Spruce Trail through a forest of Sitka spruce and vine maple to the aptly named **Giant Spruce of Cape Perpetua.** The 550-year-old Sitka spruce is 185 feet tall and 15 feet thick, and began its life as a seedling, growing atop a nurse log.

▸ **MILE 1.9–2.8: Giant Spruce of Cape Perpetua to Saint Perpetua Trailhead**

Head back in the direction from which you came. In 0.2 mile, head right at a junction toward the Cape Perpetua Campground. Cross a bridge over the creek, and stroll the 0.2-mile **loop trail** through the forest on the creek's northern shore. It concludes at a **restroom;** cross the creek again to

▲ SPOUTING HORN AT CAPE PERPETUA

reconnect with the Giant Spruce Trail, turning right to head back in the direction of the visitors center for 0.5 mile. At the junction, make a hard right onto the **Saint Perpetua Trail.**

▶ **MILE 2.8–4.1: Saint Perpetua Trailhead to Cape Perpetua Lookout**
Cross Cape Creek once more and enter the **Cape Perpetua Campground.** Make a left on the road through the campground and walk about 100 feet, then pick up the trail again to your right, ascending as it steadily switchbacks up a forested hillside, with views gradually opening up as you approach the cape's highest point. After ascending 1.25 miles, you'll arrive at an unsigned junction, some 800 feet above sea level; head left 100 feet to arrive at the **Cape Perpetua lookout,** which the Forest Service calls "the best view on the Oregon Coast." From here you can see 37 miles out to sea and 70 miles up and down the coast. There are excellent whale-watching opportunities winter-spring, as well as dazzling sunsets on clear evenings.

▶ **MILE 4.1–4.3: Whispering Spruce Trail Loop**
Continue following the trail as it curves northwest. Just past the lookout, at a Y-shaped junction, follow a sign for the Stone Shelter for a quick 0.2-mile loop on the **Whispering Spruce Trail.** On the loop you'll pass the **West Shelter,** as it's officially known. It was built by the Civilian Conservation Corps in the 1930s and sits atop a clearing that overlooks the ocean; largely protected from wind and rain, it makes a fine place for lunch. A platform at the shelter's western edge offers great ocean views. Continue clockwise on the loop, keeping right at an intersection with the Amanda Trail to remain on the Whispering Spruce Trail.

Cape Perpetua

▲ CAPE PERPETUA

▶ **MILE 4.3-5.8: Cape Perpetua Lookout to
Cape Perpetua Visitor Center**
After completing the loop, turn left to return to the Cape Perpetua look-out, then head downhill to return the way you came to the visitors center.

DIRECTIONS

From Yachats, head south on U.S. 101 for 3 miles. Past milepost 167 make a left, following signs for the Cape Perpetua Visitor Center. The road ends soon after in the parking area.

GPS COORDINATES: 44.280887, -124.108527 / N44° 16.8532' W124° 6.5116'

BEST NEARBY BREWS

The beers at **Yachats Brewing** (348 U.S. 101, Yachats, 541/547-3884, http://yachatsbrewing.com, 11:30am-9pm Sun.-Thurs., 11:30am-10pm Fri.-Sat.) reflect the region, with many named for nearby landmarks and several incorporating local fruits and malts. From the trailhead, the 3-mile drive north takes 5 minutes via U.S. 101.

Heceta Head to Hobbit Trail

HECETA HEAD LIGHTHOUSE STATE SCENIC VIEWPOINT

Make your way from one the Oregon Coast's most iconic lighthouses to a magical trail that winds its way to a beach.

DISTANCE: 5 miles round-trip
DURATION: 2.5 hours
ELEVATION CHANGE: 800 feet
EFFORT: Easy/moderate
TRAIL: Dirt trail, gravel, roots, rocks, sand, wooden steps
USERS: Hikers, leashed dogs
SEASON: Year-round
PASSES/FEES: $5 day-use fee per vehicle
MAPS: USGS topographic map for Heceta Head
CONTACT: Oregon State Parks, 541/547-3416, www.oregonstateparks.org

START THE HIKE

▶ **MILE 0-0.5: Lighthouse Trailhead to Heceta Head Lighthouse**
Head to the northern edge of the parking lot to find the **Lighthouse Trailhead,** and start ascending a gentle grade on a packed gravel path. You'll pass the old **assistant lighthouse keeper's house** after 0.3 mile—today a bed-and-breakfast—before arriving in another 0.2 mile at the **Heceta Head Lighthouse** and its attendant buildings. Rising 205 feet above the ocean, the lighthouse is among the most popular and photographed destinations on the Oregon Coast. It was first illuminated in 1894 and, as the strongest beam on the coast, can be seen more than 20 miles from land. Lighthouse tours (541/347-3416) are offered seasonally. Walk to the end of the bluff on which the lighthouse sits, and keep an eye out for migrating gray whales, shorebirds, seals, and sea lions frolicking below.

▶ **MILE 0.5-1.3: Heceta Head Lighthouse to Heceta Head**
To continue on the trail, head to the **oil house,** the easternmost building, and begin hiking steeply uphill at an interpretive panel via a few wooden steps that give way to a well-maintained dirt trail. Hike into the thick Sitka spruce forest for 0.1 mile to arrive at a **viewpoint** overlooking the lighthouse. These views will be swallowed up by the dense forest as you ascend 420 feet over the next 0.6 mile. Some 0.1 mile after you stop climbing, you'll arrive at a bench atop **Heceta Head**, overlooking a stretch of coastline to the north, including your eventual destination: Hobbit Beach.

▶ **MILE 1.3-2.5: Heceta Head to Hobbit Beach**
Slowly descend from here through a forest of Sitka spruce, salal, and shore pine. After 0.75 mile, the trail levels out with U.S. 101, off to your right,

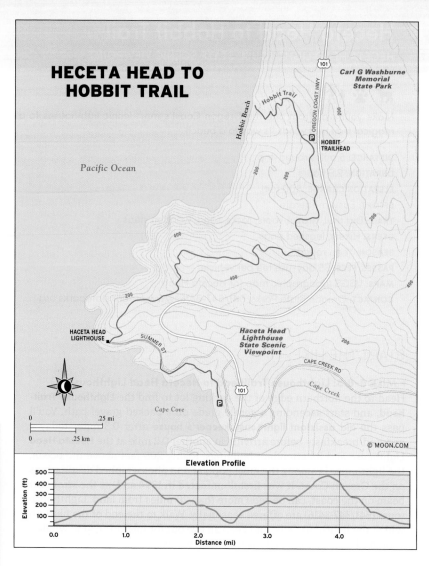

HECETA HEAD TO HOBBIT TRAIL

Carl G Washburne
Memorial
State Park

Pacific Ocean

Hobbit Trail

Hobbit Beach

HOBBIT
TRAILHEAD

HACETA HEAD
LIGHTHOUSE

SUMMER ST

Haceta Head
Lighthouse
State Scenic
Viewpoint

CAPE CREEK RD

Cape Creek

Cape Cove

0   .25 mi
0   .25 km

© MOON.COM

Elevation Profile

and you'll arrive at a junction. Continue north, straight ahead, onto the **Hobbit Beach Trail.** Twisting and turning down to the shoreline through a dense thicket of salal, rhododendron, and Sitka spruce, this enchanting trail makes you feel at times as if you're hiking through a tunnel of trees and overgrowth. After 0.3 mile, you'll pass an octopus-like tree that appears to have eight trunks stemming from one base. The trail ends 0.15 mile beyond it, at **Hobbit Beach.** You'll likely share the beach with dozens of hikers, families, and campers in high summer; otherwise, this stretch of coastline in the shadow of Heceta Head tends to be quiet.

Return the way you came.

▲ HOBBIT BEACH

DIRECTIONS

From Florence, head north on U.S. 101 for 11.4 miles. Just past a tunnel, turn right onto Cape Creek Road, following a sign for the Heceta Head Lighthouse. Continue on the road as it curves briefly to the right and then passes under U.S. 101, ending in a parking area after a few hundred feet.

GPS COORDINATES: 44.13515, –124.12296 / N44° 8.109′ W124° 7.3776′

BEST NEARBY BREWS

Popular with locals, the **Beachcomber Pub** (1355 Bay St., Florence, 541/997-6357, http://beachcomberpub.com, 7am-midnight Sun.-Thurs., 7am-1am Fri.-Sat.) pours craft beer from along the Oregon Coast and throughout the Pacific Northwest, as well as serves classic pub fare. From the trailhead, the 13-mile drive south takes 20 minutes via U.S. 101.

🦌 ❋ 🐾

Start the hike with stellar views and then descend through coastal forest to a largely inaccessible stretch of shoreline.

DISTANCE: 3.8 miles round-trip
DURATION: 2 hours
ELEVATION CHANGE: 590 feet
EFFORT: Easy/moderate
TRAIL: Dirt trail, roots, rocks
USERS: Hikers, leashed dogs
SEASON: Year-round
PASSES/FEES: None
MAPS: USGS topographic map for Cape Sebastian
CONTACT: Oregon State Parks, 541/469-2021, www.oregonstateparks.org

START THE HIKE

Long pants are recommended given some poison oak on the trail.

▶ **MILE 0–0.2: Parking Lot Viewpoint to Sitka Spruce Forest**
Before embarking on your hike, take a moment to appreciate the parking lot's vantage. This popular **viewpoint** is set more than 200 feet above the ocean, offering visibility more than 40 miles to the north—in which direction you might spy the large peak of Mount Humbug—and nearly 50 miles to the south, where Crescent City, California, is just visible. Also keep an eye out in winter and spring for migrating gray whales.

From the western edge of the parking lot, follow the paved path onto the **Oregon Coast Trail**—this is one small piece of the 382-mile trail that parallels the Oregon Coast. Views are quickly swallowed up by the hall of salal you'll enter just a few hundred feet from the trailhead. The first 0.2 mile of trail is mostly flat and heads briefly west before curving south, when you'll enter a dense forest of Sitka spruce.

▶ **MILE 0.2–1.4: Sitka Spruce Forest to Ocean View Clearings**
You'll descend gradually over next 0.7 mile, losing 275 feet of elevation along the way. Keep an eye out for purple iris, pink or purple salal, and the purple Bridges' brodiaea. The forest thins out as you make your way down a series of switchbacks, revealing ocean views. Poison oak starts to crowd the trail along this bushy stretch, so proceed cautiously. After 0.5 mile, the trail levels out, roughly 50 feet above the waterline. Several clearings along the trail here offer room to sit and enjoy ocean views.

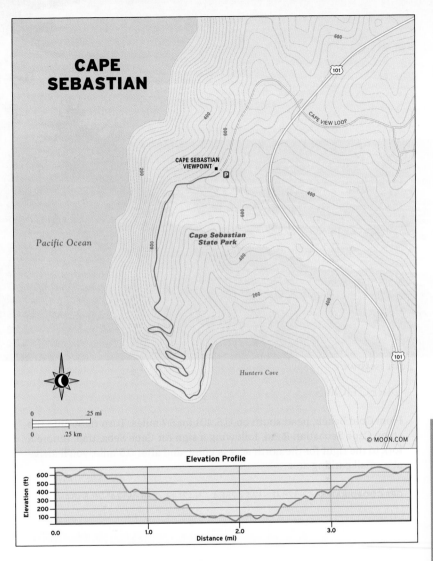

© MOON.COM

Elevation Profile

▶ MILE 1.4-1.9: Ocean View Clearings to Hunters Cove

Follow the trail another 0.4 mile to cross a small footbridge. You'll arrive at a rocky, steep slope that ends soon after at **Hunters Cove;** this last little stretch is often muddy and slick, but a series of cables provide assistance. It might be easiest to walk backward while gripping the cables on your way down. Since there's limited public access to this bit of coastline, you'll likely have it all to yourself. Enjoy a quiet stroll around the beach, assuming you're not here at high tide—when the waves leave little room to wander—and take in the ocean views, which encompass Hunters Island just offshore.

Return the way you came.

▲ CAPE SEBASTIAN

DIRECTIONS

From Gold Beach, head south on U.S. 101 for 5.7 miles. Turn right onto the steep Cape Sebastian Road, following a sign for Cape Sebastian. Ignore a fork to the right for the north access point, and after 0.5 mile, you'll arrive at a small parking area.

GPS COORDINATES: 42.32871, -124.42564 / N42° 19.7226' W124° 25.5384'

BEST NEARBY BREWS

You'll find exactly three taps at **Arch Rock Brewing Company** (28779 Hunter Creek Rd., Gold Beach, 541/247-0555, http://archrockbeer. com, 11am-6pm Tues.-Fri., 11am-5pm Sat.). But all three—a pale ale, lager, and porter—are great excuses to spend some time in the pint-sized taproom. From the trailhead, the 5-mile drive north takes 5 minutes via U.S. 101 and Hunter Creek Road.

River View Trail to Redwood Nature Trail

ALFRED A. LOEB STATE PARK AND ROGUE RIVER-SISKIYOU NATIONAL FOREST

Hike along the Chetco River and into a grove of massive redwood trees.

DISTANCE: 3.3 miles round-trip
DURATION: 1.5 hours
ELEVATION CHANGE: 590 feet
EFFORT: Easy/moderate
TRAIL: Dirt trail, rocks, roots, gravel, bark dust
USERS: Hikers, leashed dogs (Redwood Nature Trail only)
SEASON: Year-round
PASSES/FEES: None
MAPS: USGS topographic map for Mount Emily; free trail maps available at the River View Trailhead and Redwood Nature Trailhead
CONTACT: Oregon State Parks, 541/469-2021, www.oregonstateparks.org; Rogue River-Siskiyou National Forest, 541/247-3600, www.fs.usda.gov

START THE HIKE

Long pants are recommended given some poison oak on the trail.

▶ **MILE 0-0.9: River View Trailhead to Redwood Nature Trailhead**
Start hiking on the **River View Trail** from the northern edge of the parking area. This narrow trail is mostly flat and winds through a grove of Oregon myrtle; native to southwestern Oregon and northwestern California, this evergreen hardwood is noted for its beautiful colors and wide variety of grain patterns. As you head deeper into the grove, watch out for poison oak. You'll also see sword ferns, western hemlock, and vine maple, which turns vibrant shades of yellow and orange in fall. To your right are views of the **Chetco River,** which begins in the Klamath Mountains before flowing into the Pacific Ocean; a few steep spur trails head down to its rocky banks. After 0.8 mile, the trail curves left and ends at North Bank Chetco River Road. Cross the road and continue straight, heading west, past a sign for the Rogue River-Siskiyou National Forest and Redwood Nature Trail. Roughly 0.1 mile beyond the road crossing, just past a small parking area, you'll find an unsigned, Y-shaped junction.

▶ **MILE 0.9-2.4: Redwood Nature Trail Loop**
Hop onto the **Redwood Nature Trail,** turning right to begin a 1.5-mile counterclockwise loop through one of the northernmost redwood groves on Earth. You'll ascend steadily on the loop trail, gaining 390 feet, before descending. The redwoods along this trail are considered "young" at 300-800

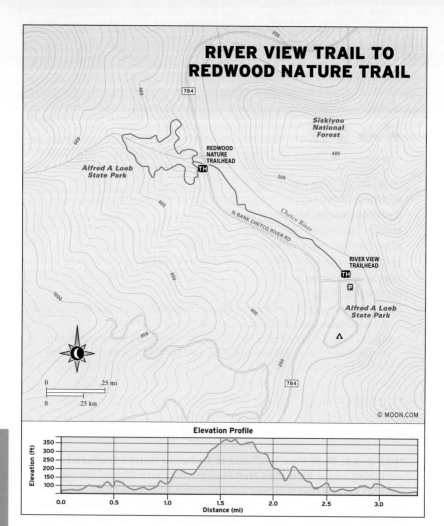

RIVER VIEW TRAIL TO REDWOOD NATURE TRAIL

Elevation Profile

years old—for context, the oldest redwood trees on record are more than 2,000 years old. Some of the redwoods here are more than 12 feet in diameter, with one of the largest being 286 feet tall; trees of this size contain enough wood to build eight two-bedroom homes. Also growing in the grove are myrtle, bigleaf maple, red alder, and Douglas fir. Keep an eye out for redwood sorrel, noted for its small pink flowers when in bloom, and the California rough-skinned newt, whose orange skin secretes a potentially deadly toxin when ingested.

▶ **MILE 2.4-3.3: Redwood Nature Trailhead to River View Trailhead**
Ignore the unsigned junction near North Bank Chetco River Road as you near the end of the trail; continue left to complete the loop. Take a right to return to the parking area, and return the way you came.

▲ REDWOOD NATURE TRAIL

DIRECTIONS

From Brookings, head east on North Bank Chetco River Road, following a sign for Loeb State Park. After 7.7 miles, turn right into Alfred A. Loeb State Park. Continue through the first intersection and, after 500 feet, turn right into a small gravel parking area with room for a half-dozen cars.

GPS COORDINATES: 42.11275, -124.18772 / N42° 6.765' W124° 11.2632'

BEST NEARBY BREWS

With 16 vegan-friendly taps, you're sure to find a few palate-pleasers at **Chetco Brewing Company** (830 Railroad St., Brookings, 541/661-5347, http://chetcobrew.com, noon-9pm Sun.-Thurs., 11:30am-10pm Fri.-Sat. summer, call for hours fall-spring). The award-winning brewery prides itself on putting inventive spins on classic styles. From the trailhead, the 9-mile drive southwest takes 15 minutes via North Bank Chetco River Road and U.S. 101.

NEARBY CAMPGROUNDS

NAME	DESCRIPTION	FACILITIES	SEASON	FEE
Saddle Mountain State Natural Area	campground at the base of Saddle Mountain	10 tent sites, restrooms	April–October	$11
Saddle Mountain State Park Rd., Cannon Beach, 503/368-5943, www.oregonstateparks.org				
Cape Lookout State Park	campground north of Cape Lookout	52 full-hookup sites, 170 tent sites, 1 electrical site with water, 13 yurts, 6 cabins, restrooms	year-round	$21-91
Cape Lookout Road, Tillamook, 503/842-4981, www.oregonstateparks.org				
Cape Perpetua Campground	quiet campground along Camp Creek	37 nonelectric sites, restrooms	March–September	$26
U.S. 101, Yachats, 541/547-4580, www.fs.usda.gov				
South Beach State Park	popular campground just south of Newport	227 electrical sites, 59 tent sites, 27 yurts, 3 group sites, restrooms	year-round	$21-78
U.S. 101, Newport, 541/867-4715, www.oregonstateparks.org				
Jessie M. Honeyman Memorial State Park	popular campground surrounded by coastal dunes	47 full-hookup sites, 121 electrical sites, 187 tent sites, 10 yurts, restrooms	year-round	$21-56
U.S. 101, Florence, 541/997-3851, www.oregonstateparks.org				
Alfred A. Loeb State Park	pastoral campground along the Chetco River	48 electrical sites, 3 log cabins, restrooms	year-round	$24-52
North Bank Chetco River Rd., Brookings, 541/469-2021, www.oregonstateparks.org				

PORTLAND AND THE WILLAMETTE VALLEY

Sixteen of Oregon's 20 largest cities sit within the Willamette Valley, making it the state's most populated region. But the area is also home to an abundance of verdant, peaceful landscapes, located conveniently close to the city centers. Portland offers easy retreats within its many green spaces, including 5,100-acre Forest Park, which hugs downtown and hosts miles of hiking trails. Near Salem, Oregon's largest state park draws crowds to its renowned waterfall hike. Elsewhere in the valley you'll find secluded hot springs and river walks, as well as summit hikes offering sweeping views of some of the region's most-beloved Cascade peaks.

▲ SAWMILL FALLS ON THE WAY TO OPAL POOL

▲ NORTH FALLS ON THE TRAIL OF TEN FALLS

1 Lower MacLeay Trail to Pittock Mansion
DISTANCE: 6.4 miles round-trip
DURATION: 3 hours
EFFORT: Easy/moderate

2 Marquam Trail to Council Crest
DISTANCE: 3.9 miles round-trip
DURATION: 2 hours
EFFORT: Easy/moderate

3 Tryon Creek State Natural Area Loop
DISTANCE: 4.5 miles round-trip
DURATION: 2 hours
EFFORT: Easy

4 Trail of Ten Falls
DISTANCE: 9.3 miles round-trip
DURATION: 4.5 hours
EFFORT: Moderate/strenuous

5 Table Rock
DISTANCE: 8.2 miles round-trip
DURATION: 4 hours
EFFORT: Moderate

6 Bagby Hot Springs
DISTANCE: 3.3 miles round-trip
DURATION: 1.5 hours
EFFORT: Easy

7 Opal Pool and Jawbone Flats Loop
DISTANCE: 8.5 miles round-trip
DURATION: 4.5 hours
EFFORT: Moderate

8 Battle Ax Mountain
DISTANCE: 6.8 miles round-trip
DURATION: 3 hours
EFFORT: Moderate

9 Marys Peak
DISTANCE: 6.9 miles round-trip
DURATION: 3.5 hours
EFFORT: Moderate

10 North Fork River Walk
DISTANCE: 7 miles round-trip
DURATION: 3.5 hours
EFFORT: Easy/moderate

▼ VIEW FROM PITTOCK MANSION

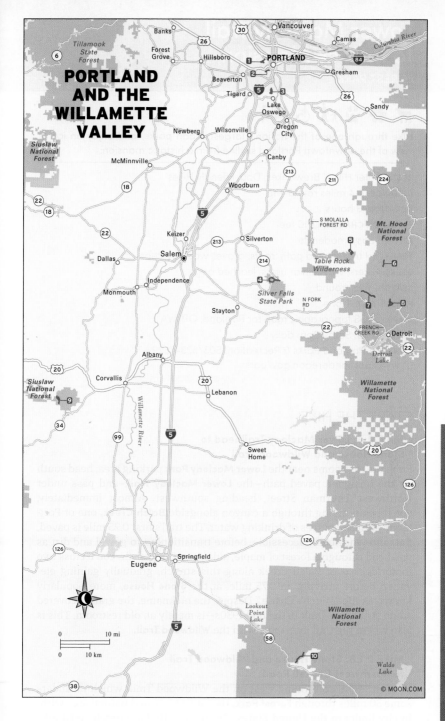

PORTLAND AND THE WILLAMETTE VALLEY

© MOON.COM

1

Lower Macleay Trail to Pittock Mansion

FOREST PARK

🦌 ❀ 🐾 🚶 ♿ 🚊

Hike through one of the nation's largest urban parks, and enjoy an iconic view of the downtown Portland skyline from a historic mansion.

BEST: Winter Hikes, Brew Hikes, Dog-Friendly Hikes
DISTANCE: 6.4 miles round-trip
DURATION: 3 hours
ELEVATION CHANGE: 1,010 feet
EFFORT: Easy/moderate
TRAIL: Dirt trail, paved path, roots, gravel, wooden steps
USERS: Hikers, wheelchiar users, leashed dogs
SEASON: Year-round
PASSES/FEES: None
MAPS: USGS topographic map for Portland, OR-WA
PARK HOURS: 5am-10pm daily
CONTACT: Portland Parks & Recreation, 503/823-7529,
www.portlandoregon.gov/parks

START THE HIKE

▶ **MILE 0-1: Lower Macleay Trailhead to
Stone House and Wildwood Trail**

From the restrooms near the **Lower Macleay Park** parking area, head south on the unsigned paved path—the **Lower Macleay Trail**—and pass under Northwest Thurman Street, heading southwest. Almost immediately, you'll begin hiking through a canyon alongside **Balch Creek,** one of Portland's earliest sources of drinking water. The trail's first 0.25 mile is paved, flat, and wheelchair-accessible, before transitioning to gravel and dirt as you head through a forest of maple, alder, and Douglas fir. You'll cross two footbridges over Balch Creek along this stretch, gradually gaining elevation before arriving, in 0.75 mile, at the **Stone House,** more popularly known as the "Witch's Castle." Despite the nickname, the graffiti-covered stone structure—built in the mid-1930s—is merely an old restroom. This is also where the trail intersects with the **Wildwood Trail.**

▶ **MILE 1-1.8: Stone House and Wildwood Trail
to Northwest Cornell Road**

Head straight, continuing west on the Wildwood Trail, which meanders some 30 miles through **Forest Park,** the largest forested natural area within city limits in the United States. On this mostly flat stretch you'll hike through a forest of Douglas fir. In roughly 0.4 mile, you'll cross a footbridge over Balch Creek. Over the next 0.4 mile, you'll ascend a series of

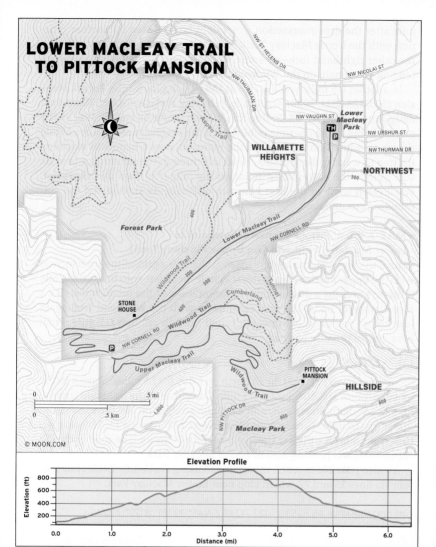

LOWER MACLEAY TRAIL TO PITTOCK MANSION

NW ST HELENS DR

NW NICOLAI ST

NW THURMAN DR

300

Aspen Trail

NW VAUGHN ST

Lower Macleay Park

TH P

NW UPSHUR ST

NW THURMAN DR

WILLAMETTE HEIGHTS

NORTHWEST

300

Forest Park

400

Lower Macleay Trail

NW CORNELL RD

Wildwood Trail

300

300

Tunnel

Cumberland

STONE HOUSE

400

Wildwood Trail

P

NW CORNELL RD

Wildwood Trail

Upper Macleay Trail

Wildwood Trail

PITTOCK MANSION

HILLSIDE

800

0   .5 mi

0   .5 km

1,000

NW PITTOCK DR

800

Macleay Park

© MOON.COM

Elevation Profile

Elevation (ft): 800, 600, 400, 200

Distance (mi): 0.0, 1.0, 2.0, 3.0, 4.0, 5.0, 6.0

switchbacks out of the canyon and follow the trail east before arriving at Northwest Cornell Road. For a fun side trip, you could turn right on the road and walk an extra 0.1 mile to visit the **Portland Audubon Wildlife Care Center,** the oldest wildlife rehab facility in Oregon. Here you can view birds and owls that have been rehabilitated.

▶ **MILE 1.8–3.4: Northwest Cornell Road to Pittock Mansion Viewpoint (via Wildwood Trail)**

Cross the road, and ascend three switchbacks. In 100 feet, you'll arrive at an intersection with the Upper Macleay Trail, but turn left to remain on the Wildwood Trail for now. After 0.5 mile of steady ascent, you'll arrive at the first of several intersections in quick succession. Long story short: Follow the signs at each to remain on the Wildwood Trail. Roughly 0.3

mile after the first intersection, you might be confused by another junction with the Upper Macleay Trail. Don't take the hard right; instead, take the other righthand fork—up some wooden steps and alongside wooden fencing—to remain on the Wildwood Trail.

In another 0.5 mile, you'll arrive at the parking lot for the **Pittock Mansion** (503/823-3623, 10am-4pm daily Feb.-May and Sept.-Dec., 10am-5pm daily June-Labor Day, $8-12, free for children under 6), built in 1914 as the private home of the onetime publisher of the *Oregonian* newspaper. While there's an admission fee to enter the mansion, now a historical museum, it's free to wander the grounds. Head left through the parking lot to walk 0.25 mile to the easternmost point on the property. From this **viewpoint,** you'll catch some of the best glimpses of Portland's skyline and the surrounding mountains.

▶ **MILE 3.4–6.4: Pittock Mansion Viewpoint to Lower Macleay Trailhead (via Upper Macleay Trail)**

Return the way you came—but when you arrive again at the intersection with the **Upper Macleay Trail** after 0.75 mile, head left onto this trail. While it doesn't present a dramatically different view of the urban forest, it's a nice change of pace. The trail reconnects with the **Wildwood Trail** again just before you cross Northwest Cornell Road in another 0.5 mile. From here, return the way you came.

DIRECTIONS

From downtown Portland, head north on I-405 for 1.5 miles. Make a left at exit 3 to follow U.S. 30 west for 0.5 mile. Use either of the right two lanes to take the Vaughn Street exit, and continue straight on Northwest Vaughn Street for 0.4 mile. Turn left onto Northwest 27th Avenue for 1 block, then turn right onto Northwest Upshur Street for 3 blocks. The road ends at a turnaround and parking area in Lower Macleay Park.

It's also possible to reach the trailhead using Portland's TriMet bus system via lines 15 and 77, which stop near Lower Macleay Park.

GPS COORDINATES: 45.53585, –122.71249 / N45° 32.151′ W122° 42.7494′

BEST NEARBY BREWS

Enjoy a pint at **Breakside Brewery** (1570 NW 22nd Ave., Portland, 503/444-7597, http://breakside.com, 11am-10pm Sun.-Thurs., 11am-11pm Fri.-Sat.). Breakside's flagship IPA has won numerous awards, but the brewery produces a well-rounded selection of flavorful crafts. From the trailhead, the 1-mile drive east takes 5 minutes via Northwest Thurman Street; you could also walk there in 20 minutes.

2

Marquam Trail to Council Crest

MARQUAM NATURE PARK

Head to one of the highest points in Portland city limits for sweeping views of downtown and nearby Cascade peaks.

DISTANCE: 3.9 miles round-trip

DURATION: 2 hours

ELEVATION CHANGE: 650 feet

EFFORT: Easy/moderate

TRAIL: Dirt trail, gravel, roadbed, roots, rocks

USERS: Hikers, leashed dogs

SEASON: Year-round

PASSES/FEES: None

MAPS: USGS topographic map for Portland, OR-WA; free trail map available at the trailhead

PARK HOURS: 5am-midnight daily

CONTACT: Portland Parks & Recreation, 503/823-7529, www.portlandoregon.gov/parks

START THE HIKE

Given this hike's accessibility and location so close to the city center, this trail is a popular after-work trek; you'll likely share it with runners and nearby residents, some of whose houses line the trail.

▶ **MILE 0-0.4: Shadyside Trail to Marquam Trail**
From the western edge of the parking lot, start hiking uphill—heading northwest—on the **Shadyside Trail,** following signs for the Marquam Trail and Council Crest. **Marquam Shelter,** to your right as you ascend, offers trail maps and interpretive information on the park through which you're hiking. After just 350 feet on the old roadbed, you'll come to a Y-shaped junction; ignore the trail heading downhill to your right, and continue uphill to the left to remain on the Shadyside Trail. Another junction, this one unsigned, arrives in another 150 feet; head left, continuing on the Shadyside Trail as it narrows and proceeds uphill. As you ascend, you'll see trillium blooms in spring, an ivy-covered forest floor, and a canopy of Douglas fir and bigleaf maple. In 0.3 mile you'll arrive at a T-junction; turn right onto the **Marquam Trail,** continuing uphill and following signs for the Council Crest summit.

▶ **MILE 0.4-1.6: Marquam Trail to Southwest Greenway Avenue**
In another 0.2 mile, head left at the T-junction to continue ascending the Marquam Trail toward the Council Crest summit; keep an eye out for barred owls, which nest in the area, amid the red cedar, western hemlock,

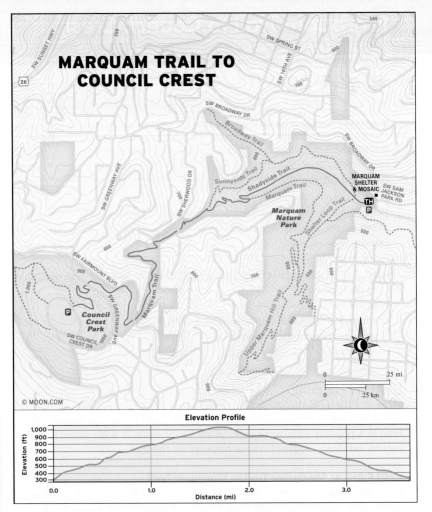

MARQUAM TRAIL TO COUNCIL CREST

Elevation Profile

and Douglas fir lining Marquam Gulch, through which you've been hiking. Cross Southwest Sherwood Drive in 0.25 mile and pick up the trail across the road. Soon after, you'll come to an unsigned junction; cross the footbridge over the dry creek bed to the left, ignoring the trail to your right. Watch here for sword ferns and Oregon grape, the official state flower. In 0.5 mile, you'll cross Southwest Fairmont Boulevard and, in another 0.2 mile, Southwest Greenway Avenue.

▸ **MILE 1.6-1.95: Southwest Greenway Avenue to Council Crest Summit**
The trail starts leveling out here, as you begin circling the summit. After 0.25 mile, you'll arrive at an unsigned junction. If you head straight, the trail soon ends at an off-leash **dog park,** just below the summit. Head right at the unsigned junction and walk a couple hundred feet to another junction, and then turn left. You'll leave the woods, cross Southwest Council Crest Drive, and continue on a paved path for about 0.1 mile to arrive at a plaza atop the **Council Crest summit**—1,073 feet above sea level. From here,

▲ MOUNT HOOD VIEW FROM THE SUMMIT OF COUNCIL CREST

you can peer into downtown Portland as well as spy the likes of Mount St. Helens, Mount Adams, and Mount Hood.

Return the way you came.

DIRECTIONS

From downtown Portland, head south on Southwest Broadway for 0.5 mile. Shortly after passing over I-405, take a right onto Southwest 6th Avenue, which becomes Southwest Terwilliger Boulevard and then Southwest Sam Jackson Park Road, for 0.5 mile. When you arrive at the U-shaped bend in the road, turn right into the parking area for Marquam Nature Park.

It's also possible to reach the trailhead using Portland's TriMet bus system via lines 8 and 68, which stop near the Marquam Trailhead.

GPS COORDINATES: 45.5028, −122.69174 / N45° 30.168' W122° 41.5044'

BEST NEARBY BREWS

Head across the Willamette River for a pint at **Hopworks Urban Brewery** (2944 SE Powell Blvd., Portland, 503/232-4677, http://hopworksbeer.com, 11:30am-10pm Sun.-Thurs., 11:30am-11pm Fri.-Sat.). Hopworks is known for using organic, sustainably raised hops and grains in its wide variety of beers. From the trailhead, the 3-mile drive east takes 10 minutes via U.S. 26.

Tryon Creek
State Natural Area Loop

TRYON CREEK STATE NATURAL AREA

Find something to love about this trail all year long, from fall foliage displays to spring wildflowers and salmon runs, at the only Oregon state park located within a major city.

BEST: Wildflower Hikes

DISTANCE: 4.5 miles round-trip

DURATION: 2 hours

ELEVATION CHANGE: 350 feet

EFFORT: Easy

TRAIL: Dirt trail, paved path, gravel, roots, rocks

USERS: Hikers, leashed dogs, horseback riders (North Horse Loop and West Horse Loop only)

SEASON: Year-round

PASSES/FEES: None

MAPS: USGS topographic map for Lake Oswego, OR; free Tryon Creek Trail Map at the Nature Center

PARK HOURS: 7am-5pm daily January and November-December, 7am-6pm daily February, 7am-7pm daily March and October, 7am-8pm daily April and September, 7am-9pm daily May-August

CONTACT: Oregon State Parks, 503/636-9886, www.oregonstateparks.org

START THE HIKE

▶ MILE 0-1.1: Nature Center to Cedar Trail

Grab a trail map from the **Nature Center** just west of the parking lot, then head south from here on the **Old Main Trail,** passing a stone amphitheater along the way, to begin this clockwise loop. In just less than 0.2 mile, make a right onto the **Big Fir Trail.** You'll enter a second-growth Douglas fir forest before arriving at another junction in about 0.1 mile; turn left to remain on the Big Fir Trail and take heart that, while this trail is junction-heavy, it's exceptionally well signed. In 0.3 mile, continue straight to remain on the trail past an intersection with the Middle Creek Trail before arriving in a couple hundred feet at another junction; turn left here to hop back on the **Old Main Trail** for several hundred feet, when you'll meet up with and turn right onto the **Red Fox Trail.** Follow this trail for 0.4 mile, crossing **Red Fox Bridge** over **Tryon Creek** and ignoring an intersection with the South Creek Trail along the way; trillium, tiger lily, and fireweed are common along this stretch in spring.

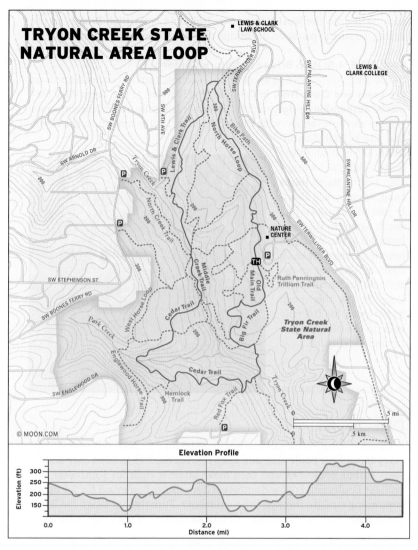

TRYON CREEK STATE NATURAL AREA LOOP

Elevation Profile

▶ **MILE 1.1–2.6: Cedar Trail to High Bridge**

Turn right onto the **Cedar Trail** and hike through the scenic cedar forest. Turn right to remain on the Cedar Trail at the junction with the Hemlock Trail, and cross **Park Creek** over **Bunk Bridge,** to begin looping back up north. Watch for a variety of wildlife in this area, including garter snakes, beavers, red foxes, coyotes, cougars, and several species of owl. In 1 mile, continue straight to remain on the Cedar Trail at a four-way intersection with the West Horse Loop—and then continue straight at another junction with this same trail in another 0.2 mile. Just past this second equestrian trail intersection—it can get confusing here—turn left onto the **Middle Creek Trail** to continue north, following the banks of Tryon Creek. The maple trees along this stretch put on dazzling foliage displays. In 0.3 mile,

379

turn right onto the **West Horse Loop Trail,** and cross **High Bridge;** in the spring, be sure to pause on the bridge to look for salmon in the creek below.

▶ **MILE 2.6–4.5: High Bridge to Nature Center**
In 100 feet, you'll arrive at another intersection; turn left to head north on the **Lewis and Clark Trail.** In 0.3 mile, you'll arrive at the **Terry Riley Memorial Suspension Bridge,** which spans a small gully. After crossing, veer right at the intersection with the 4th Avenue Trail to remain on the Lewis and Clark Trail. Continue for 0.7 mile and then make a right, following a sign for the **North Horse Loop,** which you'll shortly join to begin heading south again. In 0.5 mile, head left at the Y-shaped junction, then take a right in 100 feet to remain on the North Horse Loop. Follow this mostly flat path for 0.4 mile back to the Nature Center and parking lot.

TRYON CREEK STATE NATURAL AREA ▶

DIRECTIONS
From downtown Portland, head south on I-5 for 2.9 miles. Take exit 297, toward Terwilliger Boulevard, and keep right at the fork to head onto Southwest Barbur Boulevard, and then make another right for Southwest Terwilliger Boulevard. Follow Southwest Terwilliger Boulevard for 2.4 miles, continuing straight through the roundabout. Turn right at a sign for Tryon Creek State Park, and continue 0.2 mile to the end of the road for parking.

GPS COORDINATES: 45.44117, –122.67605 / N45° 26.4702′ W122° 40.563′

BEST NEARBY BREWS
Sasquatch Brewing (6440 SW Capitol Hwy., Portland, 503/402-1999, http://sasquatchbrewery.com, 3pm-10pm Mon.-Thurs., noon-10pm Fri.-Sat., noon-9pm Sun.) is a cozy neighborhood pub that pairs a wide-ranging beer and cider selection with a seasonal food menu. From the trailhead, the 4-mile drive north takes 10 minutes via Southwest Terwilliger Boulevard.

On this iconic Oregon trail you'll hike to 10 waterfalls in less than 10 miles.

BEST: Fall Hikes, Waterfall Hikes

DISTANCE: 9.3 miles round-trip

DURATION: 4.5 hours

ELEVATION CHANGE: 890 feet

EFFORT: Moderate/strenuous

TRAIL: Dirt trail, paved path, gravel, rocks, roots, paved staircases

USERS: Hikers, leashed dogs (Rim and Upper North Falls Trails only)

SEASON: Year-round

PASSES/FEES: $5 day-use fee per vehicle

MAPS: USGS topographic map for Drake Crossing; free trail map available at the South Falls Lodge & Café and South Falls Nature Store in the South Falls day-use area

PARK HOURS: 8am-5pm daily November-January, 8am-6pm daily February, 8am-8pm daily March, 7am-9pm daily April-August, 7am-8pm daily September, 8am-7pm daily October

CONTACT: Oregon State Parks, 503/873-8681, www.oregonstateparks.org

START THE HIKE

The renowned waterfalls along this trail are most glorious in spring, and the fall foliage is also something to see.

▶ **MILE 0-1.2: South Falls Lodge to Lower South Falls**

At the South Falls day-use area, head west on the paved path just north of the **South Falls Lodge**—built in the 1930s by the Civilian Conservation Corps and today host to a small snack bar and restrooms—following a sign for the **Canyon Trail.** In 0.1 mile, turn right onto a gravel trail, following another sign for the Canyon Trail. Here you'll see your first waterfall on this clockwise loop trail: **South Falls,** dropping 177 feet, the second-tallest falls in the park. From here continue downhill, entering the canyon where you'll spend much of this hike and ignoring an offshoot trail to your right. In 0.25 mile, you'll pass behind South Falls and drop to the base of **South Fork Silver Creek;** you'll continue straight on the Canyon Trail from here, but take a moment to step onto the footbridge to your right for some of the best views of South Falls. Back on the Canyon Trail, you'll lose about 125 feet over the next 0.75 mile, hiking through a forest of fir and vine maple that puts on a colorful show every autumn, before arriving at **Lower South Falls.** Descend the paved staircase to walk behind the 93-foot falls.

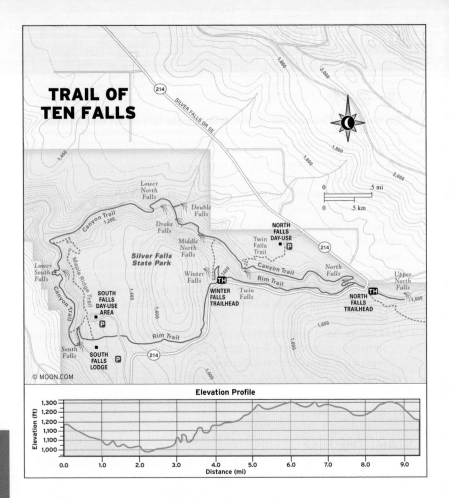

TRAIL OF TEN FALLS

Silver Falls State Park

© MOON.COM

Elevation Profile

▶ MILE 1.2–3: **Lower South Falls to Double Falls**

After a mostly flat 0.5-mile stretch you'll come to a junction; turn left and head downhill, going eastward. In another 1 mile, the 30-foot **Lower North Falls** comes into view; there's no one outstanding viewpoint for these falls, so admire them as you will and then continue another 0.1 mile, when you'll turn left for an approximately 0.2-mile round-trip jaunt to the base of 178-foot **Double Falls,** the tallest waterfall along the trail.

▶ MILE 3–5: **Double Falls to North Falls**

Back at the junction, turn left and continue on the loop, which will steadily ascend. In about 0.2 mile you'll arrive at a wooden platform overlooking the 27-foot **Drake Falls.** In another 0.2 mile you'll enjoy views of 106-foot **Middle North Falls;** you can also opt for a short spur to its base. In 0.1 mile is a junction with the Winter Trail; heading right onto the trail here would lop roughly 4 miles off your round-trip total, but continue straight to remain on the Canyon Trail. In another 0.5 mile, you'll come to another fork; head right for a view of the 31-foot **Twin Falls,** and follow the path as it rejoins the Canyon Trail. In 1 mile, you'll arrive at one of the most beautiful vantages along the whole loop, a cave-like path that takes you behind the majestic **North Falls,** which measures 136 feet tall. Have a seat on one of the benches behind the falls and enjoy.

▶ MILE 5-6.3: North Falls to Rim Trail

Continuing on, follow the trail as it curves behind the falls, ascending a staircase out of the canyon; proceed cautiously, as these steps can be slippery after rainfall and icy in winter. In 0.5 mile, you'll arrive at a T-shaped junction; turn left for an 0.8-mile round-trip spur trail to Upper North Falls, staying left again at another junction shortly on and following the **North Fork Silver Creek.** The spur ends at the base of the 65-foot **Upper North Falls.** Back at the T-shaped junction, head left onto the **Rim Trail,** which loops you back west.

▶ MILE 6.3-9.3: Rim Trail to South Falls Lodge

In 1.1 miles, you'll come upon the Winter Falls parking area; take a hard right to make the 0.5 mile out-and-back round-trip hike to the base of 134-foot **Winter Falls.** True to its name, Winter Falls is most dramatic in winter (and spring); at the height of summer, it resembles a leaky faucet. Back at the Winter Falls parking area, continue west on the Rim Trail. Along the way you'll intersect with a paved bike path; this can be confusing at various points, but don't worry: All these paths end at the South Falls day-use area where you began. In 1.2 miles, you'll arrive at a parking area with two painted lanes for pedestrians and cyclists; take the rightmost path for pedestrians to proceed onto a paved brick trail that ends, in another 0.2 mile, back at the South Falls Lodge.

DIRECTIONS

From Salem, head east on Highway 22 for 7.5 miles. Take exit 9, following a sign for Shaw and Aumsville. After looping to the south, turn right at the fork onto Shaw Highway SE, which becomes Brownell Drive Southeast and Highway 214, for 14.1 miles. After crossing a bridge and passing milepost 25, turn left at a sign for South Falls. Follow the road as it curves around toward the South Falls day-use area.

GPS COORDINATES: 44.87966, -122.65829 / N44° 52.7796' W122° 39.4974'

BEST NEARBY BREWS

It only makes sense to pair your hike with a stop at **Silver Falls Brewery** (207 Jersey St., Silverton, 503/873-3022, http://silverfallsbrewery. com, 11:30am-9pm Mon. and Wed.-Thurs., 11:30am-10pm Fri.-Sat., 11:30am-8pm Sun.). It hosts a lineup of several classic styles—including an IPA, a porter, and a hefeweizen—alongside rotating seasonal selections. From the trailhead, the 16-mile drive north takes 25 minutes via Highway 214.

🐾

Hike through a dense conifer forest to the summit of Table Rock, where you'll enjoy views of famous Cascade peaks.

DISTANCE: 8.2 miles round-trip

DURATION: 4 hours

ELEVATION CHANGE: 1,620 feet

EFFORT: Moderate

TRAIL: Dirt trail, rocks, rock scramble, roadbed, roots

USERS: Hikers, leashed dogs, horseback riders (equestrian use discouraged through the boulder field)

SEASON: June–November

PASSES/FEES: None

MAPS: USGS topographic map for Rooster Rock, OR

CONTACT: Bureau of Land Management, 503/375-5646, www.blm.gov

START THE HIKE

▶ **MILE 0-1.4: Table Rock Trailhead to Rockpile**
From the parking area, find the **Table Rock Trailhead** just north of the restroom. On this early stretch, you'll follow an old roadbed through a forest of alder and vine maple. After 0.3 mile, the trail turns right into a new-growth forest, and you'll arrive at an unsigned junction with a steep, rocky social trail; continue straight ahead on the Table Rock Trail. After another 1.1 mile, the trail again turns right, becoming faint at times as you enter a forest of hemlock and fir; follow the logs and a strategically placed rockpile.

▶ **MILE 1.4-3: Rockpile to Talus Slope**
You'll hike in basically a large U-shape over the next 0.1 mile or so, when the trail becomes more legible again. In another 1.2 miles, you'll leave the forest to scramble through a **talus slope**—which can have patches of snow on it into July—beneath an impressive display of columnar basalt on Table Rock's northern face. The informal trail through this boulder field isn't immediately obvious, so scan ahead for lighter gray rocks—a by-product of regular use—and follow this more matted, navigable path for 0.3 mile before reentering the forest.

▶ **MILE 3-4.1: Talus Slope to Table Rock Summit**
In about 0.5 mile, you'll pass a **campsite** as the trail switchbacks and steadily ascends before arriving, in another 0.6 mile, at the **Table Rock summit.** Find an open area amid the pinemat manzanita, and savor the views: From here you can see Mount Hood, Mount Jefferson, and the Three Sisters,

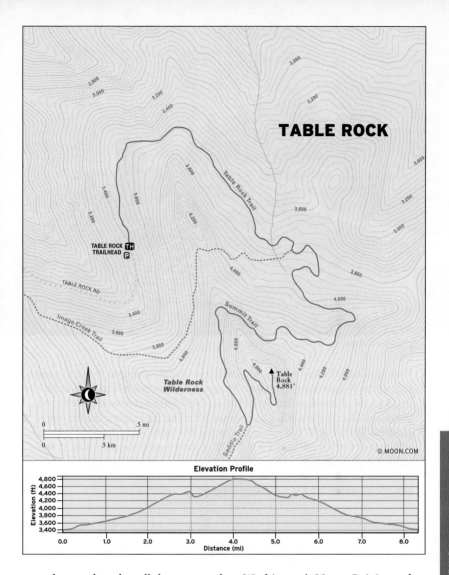

TABLE ROCK

TABLE ROCK
TRAILHEAD

TABLE ROCK RD

Image Creek Trail

Table Rock Trail

Summit Trail

Saddle Trail

Table Rock
Wilderness

Table
Rock
4,881'

0   .5 mi

0   .5 km

© MOON.COM

Elevation Profile

and, on a clear day, all the way north to Washington's Mount Rainier and south to California's Mount Shasta.

Return the way you came.

DIRECTIONS

From Oregon City, head south on Highway 213 for 9 miles, and turn left onto Union Mills Road. After 4.3 miles, turn right at a gas station to follow signs for Molalla and Woodburn on Highway 211 south. Turn left at a fork onto South Wright Road after 0.8 mile, and turn right onto South Feyrer Park Road in another 1.8 miles. Continue straight at the stop sign in 0.4 mile, when the road becomes South Dickie Prairie Road. Continue for 5.4 miles, then turn right to cross a bridge over the Molalla River, and immediately turn left onto South Molalla Forest Road. Soon after, you'll see

▲ THE FINAL APPROACH TO TABLE ROCK'S SUMMIT

your first sign for the Table Rock Trailhead. Follow the road for 11.2 miles and, at the Y-shaped fork just past milepost 11, continue left to head uphill. You'll come to another fork in 1.6 miles; head left to continue uphill onto the gravel Middle Fork Road. In another 2.7 miles, turn right onto the gravel Forest Road 7-3E-7, following a sign for the Table Rock Trailhead. Turn left at the next junction in 1.9 miles. The road ends after 2.4 miles at the trailhead parking area.

GPS COORDINATES: 44.976, –122.321 / N44° 58.56′ W122° 19.26′

BEST NEARBY BREWS
Coin Toss Brewing (14214 Fir St., Suite H, Oregon City, 503/305-6220, www.cointossbrewing.com, 3pm-8pm Tues.-Fri., noon-8pm Sat., noon-6pm Sun.) offers brews in classic styles as well as a Heritage Series in which each beer is brewed from a historical recipe. From the trailhead, the 40-mile drive north takes 1.25 hours via Highways 211 and 213.

Walk through an old-growth forest to one of the state's most popular hot springs.

BEST: Fall Hikes
DISTANCE: 3.3 miles round-trip
DURATION: 1.5 hours
ELEVATION CHANGE: 220 feet
EFFORT: Easy
TRAIL: Dirt trail
USERS: Hikers, leashed dogs, horseback riders
SEASON: June-October
PASSES/FEES: $5 fee to soak per person
MAPS: USGS topographic map for Bagby Hot Springs
CONTACT: Mount Hood National Forest, 503/630-6861, www.fs.usda.gov

START THE HIKE

Soaking at Bagby costs $5 per person. Purchase a wristband before setting out at the Ripplebrook Camp Store, which you'll pass on your way from Estacada, or at the trailhead; an attendant collects fees at the trailhead early spring-Labor Day, while a self-pay station is available Labor Day-early spring. While roads to the trail aren't maintained in winter, people with 4WD vehicles can still hike to Bagby if their vehicles can make it.

▸ **MILE 0-1.4: Bagby Hot Springs Trailhead to Wooden Bridge**
Head south from the parking area to start hiking from the **Bagby Hot Springs Trailhead** on a paved path. Almost immediately, you'll cross a footbridge over **Nohorn Creek** and continue along a dirt and gravel trail. This lush, gently graded out-and-back hike meanders through a towering old-growth forest of red cedar and Douglas fir along the **Hot Springs Fork** of the Collowash River. For a closer look at the river, you can follow a short, 50-foot spur trail off to your left after 0.6 mile. In another 0.8 mile, you'll cross a wooden bridge, near which you'll find another trail down to the riverbank. Keep an eye out for three-petaled trillium blooms in spring and vine maple—which turns vibrant shades of orange, yellow, and red—in autumn.

▸ **MILE 1.4-1.65: Wooden Bridge to Bagby Hot Springs**
While the trail continues on, you'll reach your destination in 0.25 mile: **Bagby Hot Springs.** Discovered in 1880 by local hunter Bob Bagby, the hot springs are perhaps the most popular in the state. A sign announces your arrival at the hot springs just past an old ranger cabin. The bathhouse to your right hosts one large tub, with room for up to six adults. A second

bathhouse to your left hosts three individual tubs and one large tub in an open, communal setting. To soak, open the valve to let the hot water into your tub; it comes out of the springs a little too heated for comfort—120-138°F—so add buckets of cold water, available from a nearby tub, to reach your desired temperature. The open-air, wooden structures of Bagby allow you to gaze into the surrounding forest as you soak.

Abstain from using soaps, which can pollute nearby Peggy Creek. If others are waiting (a frequent occurrence, especially on summer weekends), limit your soak to 45 minutes.

When you're ready, dry off, get dressed, and return the way you came.

DIRECTIONS

From Estacada, head south on Highway 211, which becomes Highway 224, for 25.3 miles. Just past a sign for the Ripplebrook Campground—off to the left, at whose store you can purchase a Bagby soaking wristband (503/834-2322, 10am-5pm Sun.-Thurs, 10am-8pm Fri.-Sat.)—the road forks; head right onto Forest Road 46. After 3.7 miles, turn right at a one-lane ramp, following spray-painted directions on the roadway for Bagby Hot Springs, onto Forest Road 63. Continue for 3.5 miles, then turn right onto Bagby Road/Forest Road 70. Follow the road for 7 miles and then turn left, at a sign for the Bagby Recreation Site Trailhead, into the parking lot. If you're heading here out of season, the trail is open though the roads are not maintained; call the Clackamas River Ranger District (503/630-6861) for the latest conditions before setting out.

GPS COORDINATES: 44.95404, -122.17007 / N44° 57.2424' W122° 10.2042'

BAGBY HOT SPRINGS ▸

BEST NEARBY BREWS

Fearless Brewing Company (326 Broadway St., Estacada, 503/630-2337, www.fearless.beer, 4pm-9pm Wed.-Thurs., noon-10pm Fri.-Sat., noon-9pm Sun.) offers quality craft beer at the outskirts of the Mount Hood National Forest. Its flagship is the Fearless Scottish Ale, but the brewery offers a wide variety of easy-drinking styles. From the trailhead, the 39-mile drive north takes an hour via Highways 224 and 211.

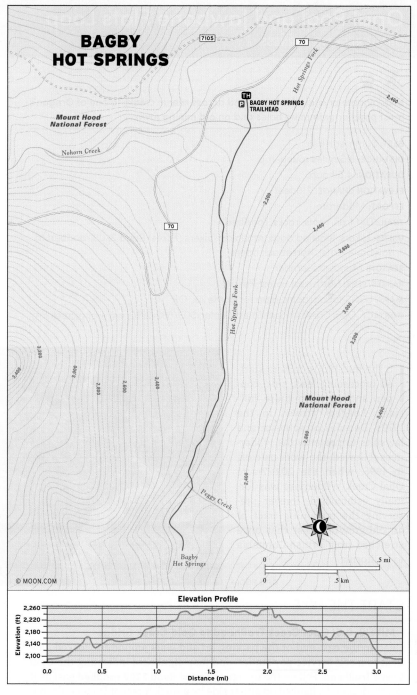

BAGBY HOT SPRINGS

7105

70

TH
🅿 **BAGBY HOT SPRINGS TRAILHEAD**

Hot Springs Fork

2,400

Mount Hood National Forest

Nohorn Creek

2,200

2,400

2,600

70

3,000

3,200

3,400
3,200
3,000
2,800
2,600
2,400

Hot Springs Fork

3,200

Mount Hood National Forest

2,600

3,400

2,600

2,400

Peggy Creek

Bagby
Hot Springs

© MOON.COM

0 _____ .5 mi
0 _____ .5 km

Elevation Profile

Elevation (ft): 2,260 / 2,220 / 2,180 / 2,140 / 2,100

Distance (mi): 0.0 / 0.5 / 1.0 / 1.5 / 2.0 / 2.5 / 3.0

Hike along a crystal-clear river and across scenic creeks to one of Oregon's most popular swimming holes and an old mining town.

BEST: Summer Hikes
DISTANCE: 8.5 miles round-trip
DURATION: 4.5 hours
ELEVATION CHANGE: 710 feet
EFFORT: Moderate
TRAIL: Dirt trail, roots, rocks, roadbed
USERS: Hikers, leashed dogs, mountain bikers (Forest Road 2209 roadbed to Jawbone Flats), horseback riders
SEASON: March–November
PASSES/FEES: Northwest Forest Pass
MAPS: USGS topographic map for Battle Ax, OR
CONTACT: Opal Creek Ancient Forest Center, 503/892-2782, www.opalcreek.org

I n the mid-1800s, miners started processing lead, zinc, copper, and silver in these hillsides. Loggers arrived in the 1970s. Decades of activism and lawsuits to preserve the wilderness followed; the work paid off in 1996, when the 20,827-acre Opal Creek Wilderness was formally established, forever preserving the remaining tract of an old-growth forest that once stretched from British Columbia to California.

OPAL POOL ▶

START THE HIKE

▶ **MILE 0–0.5: Opal Creek Trailhead to Gold Creek Bridge**
Head to the east end of the parking lot and walk around the locked gate next to a self-service pay station and map signboard indicating the **Opal Creek Trailhead.** Follow the unsigned **Forest Road 2209 roadbed** east as it gently descends, flanked on either side by a thick forest of Douglas fir that predates Columbus's arrival in North America. Along the trail you'll hear the rushing **Little North Santiam River.** You'll lose about 50 feet of elevation

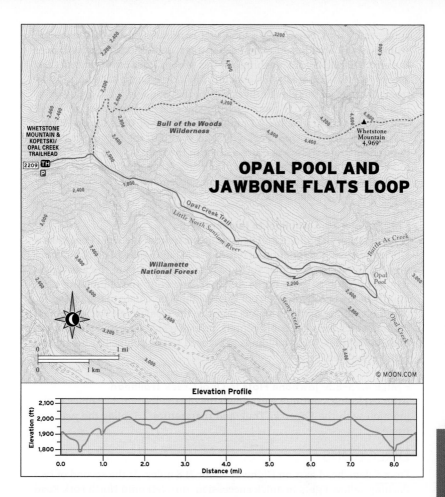

OPAL POOL AND JAWBONE FLATS LOOP

Elevation Profile

over the first 0.5 mile before crossing a bridge over **Gold Creek,** and then regain it as you head deeper into the old-growth forest.

▶ **MILE 0.5-2.4: Gold Creek Bridge to Merten Mill**

Roughly 1.7 miles past the bridge, you'll arrive at an unsigned Y-shaped junction; turn right off the roadbed to follow an unnamed **dirt trail.** You'll soon pass old tracks, axles, pipes, and other equipment; gold was found in the area in 1859, and these items were left behind when mining operations ceased in the 1950s. Just past the equipment—and after about 300 feet on the dirt trail—look for an unsigned spur to the right toward the river. Walk the 250 or so feet to a viewpoint of 30-foot **Sawmill Falls.** Back on the main trail, you'll shortly arrive at the site of **Merten Mill,** a former sawmill marked by a now-collapsed shed. As you continue east, the dirt trail reconnects with the old roadbed.

▶ **MILE 2.4-4.5: Merten Mill to Opal Pool**

In 0.3 mile, you'll reach a junction; turn right onto the **Kopetski Trail,** crossing a bridge over the river, and then turn left to proceed on the single-track trail, beginning a loop that continues east. You'll navigate stumps, small boulders, downed cedar trees, and other overgrowth over the next 0.8 mile before reaching a series of **spur trails** offering easy river access for those interested in a swim. You'll then begin ascending away from the river, as Douglas fir gives way to thousand-year-old cedar trees. In about 0.9 mile, you'll come to an unsigned Y-shaped junction. Head left onto a rocky trail some 0.1 mile to a bridge over **Opal Creek.** As you cross the bridge, the **Opal Pool** will be to your left; the remarkable clarity of its emerald waters is quite a sight in the midst of the rocky gorge. In summer, the Opal Pool is one of the region's most popular swimming holes. If you'd like to take a dip, you can descend one of the short, rocky **spur trails** to the creek bank.

▶ **MILE 4.5-4.75: Opal Pool to Jawbone Flats**
After crossing the bridge and ascending away from the Opal Pool, take a left at the unsigned junction to return to the old **roadbed** and begin looping back west. In 0.25 mile, you'll pass more remnants of the area's past mining operations, cross **Battle Ax Creek,** and enter the old mining community of **Jawbone Flats.** Most of the buildings here date to the 1930s. Today, the onetime mining camp is home to the Opal Creek Ancient Forest Center, which includes cabin rentals, private residences, and outdoor education facilities. Most buildings are closed to the public, but hikers can wander the area.

▶ **MILE 4.75-8.5: Jawbone Flats to Opal Creek Trailhead**
After exploring, continue west down the old roadbed for 1.25 miles to the junction with the Kopetski Trail, and then return 2.5 miles the way you came.

DIRECTIONS

From Salem, head east on Highway 22 for 21.8 miles. At the second of two flashing yellow lights in quick succession, turn left onto North Fork Road and follow it for 15.4 miles, when the pavement ends. Continue for 5.6 miles as the road transitions to gravel and becomes Forest Road 2209. The road ends at the trailhead parking lot.

GPS COORDINATES: 44.85986, –122.26448 / N44° 51.5916' W122° 15.8688'

BEST NEARBY BITES

Refuel with classic American comfort fare from **Poppa Al's Famous Hamburgers** (198 NE Santiam Blvd., Mill City, 503/897-2223, noon-9pm daily). The old-school restaurant serves sandwiches, soups, chili, milk shakes, and burgers, with buns baked fresh daily. From the trailhead, the 17-mile drive southeast takes just over an hour via North Fork Road and Highway 22.

Battle Ax Mountain

WILLAMETTE NATIONAL FOREST

Ascend rocky slopes and earn views of Elk Lake, Cascade peaks, and the scenic Bull of the Woods Wilderness in every direction.

DISTANCE: 6.8 miles round-trip
DURATION: 3 hours
ELEVATION CHANGE: 1,580 feet
EFFORT: Moderate
TRAIL: Dirt trail, stream crossings, rocks, roots, roadbed
USERS: Hikers, leashed dogs, horseback riders
SEASON: June-October
PASSES/FEES: None
MAPS: USGS topographic map for Mother Lode Mountain
CONTACT: Willamette National Forest, 503/854-3366, www.fs.usda.gov

START THE HIKE

▸ **MILE 0-1.2: Forest Road 4697 to Elk Lake Clearing**
From the junction with Elk Lake Campground on **Forest Road 4697,** walk 0.4 mile west up the gently graded road, turning right at a post indicating the start of **Trail #544.** On the first stretch of this counterclockwise loop trail, you'll ascend steadily northward through a forest of Douglas fir and vine maple, switchbacking twice before arriving after 0.8 mile at a small **clearing** with views of Elk Lake below.

▸ **MILE 1.2-2.4: Elk Lake Clearing to Battle Ax Mountain Trail**
In 0.5 mile, proceed cautiously through some scree. You'll encounter a bit more in another 0.3 mile as you cross a large **rockslide.** In between the rocky stretches, keep an eye out for bear grass and monkey flower, both of which bloom in spring and remain through early summer. After 0.4 mile, you'll arrive at an X-shaped junction, where you'll make a hard left onto the unsigned **Battle Ax Mountain Trail** to head uphill and begin looping back south.

▸ **MILE 2.4-3.7: Battle Ax Mountain Trail
to Battle Ax Mountain Summit**
The hike intensifies here—you still have 770 feet of elevation gain to go before the summit—as you ascend a western ridge. The forest of hemlock and pinemat manzanita gives way to narrow ledges and scree as you near the summit, which may be challenging for those with a fear of heights. Roughly 1.1 miles past the junction, you'll arrive at a clearing, and then, in 0.2 mile, the **Battle Ax Mountain summit,** marked by concrete pilings— the lone remnants of an old fire lookout. Elk Lake sits nearly 2,000 feet

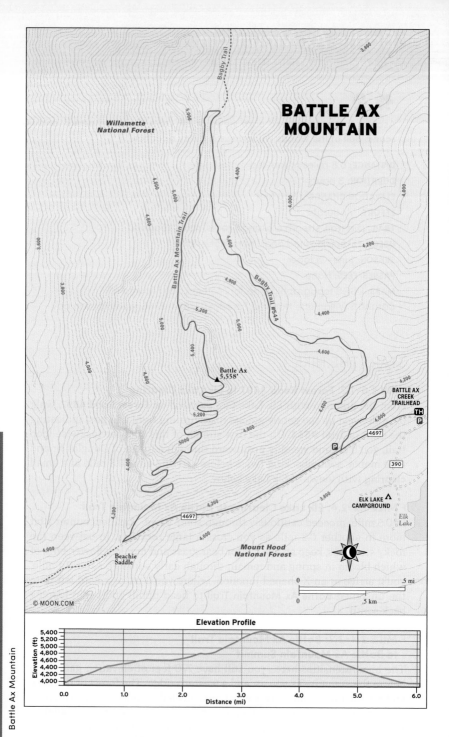

BATTLE AX MOUNTAIN

Willamette National Forest

Bagby Trail

Battle Ax Mountain Trail

Bagby Trail #544

Battle Ax 5,558'

BATTLE AX CREEK TRAILHEAD

TH
P

4697

390

ELK LAKE CAMPGROUND

Elk Lake

Mount Hood National Forest

Beachie Saddle

4697

© MOON.COM

0   .5 mi
0   .5 km

Elevation Profile

Elevation (ft)	5,400 5,200 5,000 4,800 4,600 4,400 4,200 4,000

Distance (mi): 0.0 1.0 2.0 3.0 4.0 5.0 6.0

below, and this vantage point also affords dramatic views of the Bull of the Woods Wilderness, marked by steep ridges and old-growth forest. On a clear day, Mount Jefferson, Three Fingered Jack, the Three Sisters, and several other Cascade peaks are visible.

▶ **MILE 3.7–6.8: Battle Ax Mountain Summit to Forest Road 4697**
Pick up the Battle Ax Mountain Trail just past the summit and start descending the lightly traveled path—which can appear faint at times amid the overgrowth—via switchbacks before reentering the forest. After descending gradually for 1.8 miles, you'll arrive at an unsigned junction with **Forest Road 4697;** turn left onto the old roadbed, and head steadily downhill. After 0.9 mile, you'll pass the trailhead on your left. Continue another 0.4 mile along the road to return to your vehicle.

DIRECTIONS

The final few miles to this trailhead are infamously rutted and bumpy—the potholes all seem to have potholes—so a high-clearance vehicle is strongly recommended. Whatever you do, take it slow.

From the town of Detroit, head north on Breitenbush Road, following signs for Breitenbush, Elk Lake, and Olallie Lake. Continue for 4.4 miles, then turn left onto paved Forest Road 4696. Follow the road for 0.7 mile, then turn left onto gravel Forest Road 4697. After a miserable 4.7 miles on this rutted, potholed road, turn left at a Y-junction marked only by a nondescript post. Drive another 2 mostly flat miles to a junction with Elk Lake Campground. Your best bet is to park along the road near this junction, or head downhill and park at Elk Lake Campground in 0.4 mile.

GPS COORDINATES: 44.82521, –122.125 / N44° 49.5126′ W122° 7.5′

ELK LAKE ▶

Battle Ax Mountain

BEST NEARBY BITES
Pizza? Barbecue? You can enjoy both at **Connor's BBQ** (195 Detroit Ave., Detroit, 503/913-1040, noon-9pm daily). Highlights include a giant plate of pulled pork nachos and meat-forward pies. From the trailhead, the 13-mile drive south takes 40 minutes via Forest Road 4697 and Breitenbush Road.

Hike through springtime wildflower displays to the highest point in the Oregon Coast Range for spectacular panoramic views.

DISTANCE: 6.9 miles round-trip
DURATION: 3.5 hours
ELEVATION CHANGE: 1,640 feet
EFFORT: Moderate
TRAIL: Dirt trail, roots, rocks, paved road, old roadbed
USERS: Hikers, leashed dogs, mountain bikers (East Ridge, North Ridge, and Tie Trails May 15-Oct. 15), horseback riders
SEASON: April-November
PASSES/FEES: Northwest Forest Pass
MAPS: USGS topographic map for Alsea, OR; Siuslaw National Forest website; free trail maps available at trailhead
CONTACT: Siuslaw National Forest, 541/750-7000, www.fs.usda.gov

START THE HIKE

▸ **MILE 0-2.8: East Ridge Trailhead to Summit Loop Trail**
Head to the northwest corner of the parking area—directly across the road from the restrooms—and start at the **East Ridge Trailhead.** Cross unsigned Forest Road 2005 after 0.1 mile and ascend gradually northward through lush old-growth Douglas fir forest, ferns, and clovers. You'll arrive, after 1.1 miles, at a Y-shaped junction just past a wooden bench; turn left to remain on the East Ridge Trail, continuing to ascend steadily on the pleasant grade. In 1.25 miles, you'll arrive at another junction; take a hard left to head south on the **Summit Trail** and ascend a series of short switchbacks that lead to an east-facing meadow in 0.15 mile—and your first views. To your left are the Oregon Coast Range foothills and the Willamette Valley. Cross unsigned **Marys Peak Road** in 0.2 mile, following a sign for the **Summit Loop Trail** back into the forest.

▸ **MILE 2.8-3: Summit Loop Trail to Marys Peak Summit**
In 200 feet, head left at the Y-shaped junction, following a sign for the Marys Peak summit. You'll soon leave the forest and enter a meadow teeming with grasshoppers. In another 0.2 mile, the dirt trail ends at the gravel Marys Peak Road, a fenced-in collection of radio equipment, and a picnic table on the **Marys Peak summit.** At 4,097 feet, this is the highest point in the Oregon Coast Range. The 360-degree views encompass the Pacific Ocean and Cascade peaks, from Washington's Mount Rainier in the north to Diamond Peak in southern Oregon, and Mount Hood, Mount Jefferson, the Three Sisters, Mount Bachelor, and more in between.

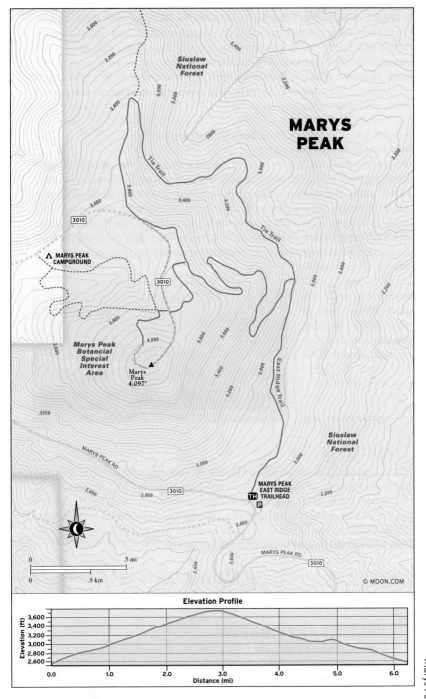

▶ MILE 3-3.6: Marys Peak Summit to Marys Peak Summit Parking Lot

Turn right from the dirt trail onto the gravel roadbed, and follow it to descend in a counterclockwise loop. Stay on the designated trail so as not to disturb the rock gardens and native vegetation on the surrounding hillside. Some 0.6 mile beyond the summit, the roadbed ends at a closed gate at the southern edge of the **Marys Peak summit parking lot,** which also affords dramatic views.

**▶ MILE 3.6-6.9: Marys Peak Summit Parking Lot
to East Ridge Trailhead**

Follow the pedestrian path around the gate, and make an immediate right onto a gravel path that soon transitions into a paved sidewalk, heading north along the eastern edge of the parking lot. Every April-June, purple penstemon, yellow glacier lily, and other wildflowers dot the hillsides here. In 300 feet, you'll see a picnic table and signboard for the **North Ridge Trail;** follow it back into the forest. In 0.7 mile, turn right onto the **Tie Trail,** beginning to loop back south, gradually descending through a forest of maple and Douglas fir. In 1.3 miles, you'll reconnect with the **East Ridge Trail** at the hike's original junction. Continue straight downhill for 1.2 miles to return the way you came.

VIEW FROM MARYS PEAK ▶

DIRECTIONS

From Corvallis, head west on U.S. 20 for 6.2 miles. Just after passing through the town of Philomath, turn left onto Highway 34, following signs for Marys Peak. After 9 miles, turn right onto Marys Peak Road. Continue for 5.4 miles, then turn right at a sign for Conner's Camp and the East Ridge Trail; the road ends in a couple hundred feet at a parking area. Note that Marys Peak Road isn't maintained in winter.

GPS COORDINATES: 44.49561, -123.54298 / N44° 29.7366′ W123° 32.5788′

BEST NEARBY BREWS

Nearby **Vinwood Taphouse** (1736 Main St., Philomath, 541/307-0457, 11am-9pm Mon.-Thurs., 11am-10pm Fri.-Sat., 11am-8pm Sun.) boasts more than two dozen taps of regional beer, wine, cider, and mead—and serves filling burgers, sandwiches, wraps, salads, and other classic American fare. From the trailhead, the 15.5-mile drive east takes 30 minutes via Marys Peak Road and Highway 34.

North Fork River Walk

WILLAMETTE NATIONAL FOREST

Walk through a bucolic forest alongside a river offering opportunities for summertime swimming and sunbathing.

DISTANCE: 7 miles round–trip
DURATION: 3.5 hours
ELEVATION CHANGE: 340 feet
EFFORT: Easy/moderate
TRAIL: Dirt trail, rocks, exposed roots, roadbed
USERS: Hikers, leashed dogs, mountain bikers, horseback riders
SEASON: Year–round
PASSES/FEES: None
MAPS: USGS topographic map for Westfir East
CONTACT: Willamette National Forest, 541/782–2283, www.fs.usda.gov

One of the many joys of this trail is the opportunities it presents for year-round recreation. Its low elevation makes it suitable for a quiet winter hike, rhododendron blooms add a splash of pink in the spring, summertime brings the chance to cool off in the river, and the vine maple dazzles with reds, oranges, and yellows in fall.

START THE HIKE

As you hike, keep an eye out for poison oak, which tends to crowd the trail, as well as cyclists; this region is a renowned mountain biking destination.

▶ MILE 0-0.7: Trailhead to Concrete Piling

Just past the Office Covered Bridge, park your car, walk to the northeast edge of the parking lot, and begin at the sign marked, simply, "**Trail.**" Follow the unmarked roadbed under a railroad bridge for just over 0.1 mile before turning right onto the **North Fork Trail.** This dirt trail is a simple out-and-back along the western side of the **North Fork of the Middle Fork of the Willamette River.** The trail soon narrows, crowded by dandelions and ferns, and the river provides an ambient soundtrack as you walk through a forest of hemlock, alder, Douglas fir, and salal, as well as rhododendron in spring. Continue straight at an unsigned junction in 0.5 mile, ignoring a trail that turns sharply left. In another 0.1 mile, you'll notice a **concrete piling** to your right. It's all that's left of an old millpond that was part of a logging operation based in the nearby town of Westfir from the 1920s to the 1980s.

▶ MILE 0.7-1.4: Concrete Piling to Spur Trail

In 0.7 mile, you'll see a slight drop-off to your right; this quick **spur trail** ends at the river's shore and offers the chance to cool off in warm weather

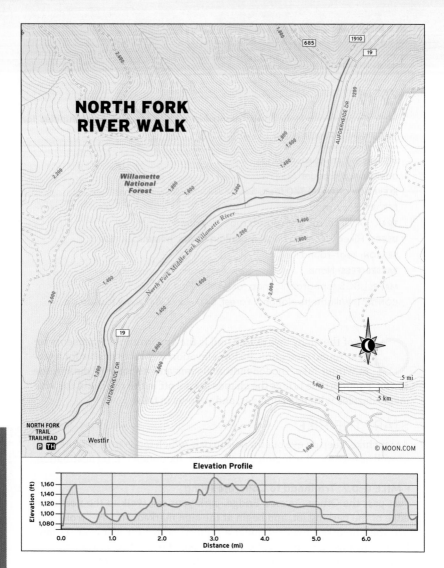

NORTH FORK RIVER WALK

Willamette National Forest

North Fork Middle Fork Willamette River

NORTH FORK TRAIL TRAILHEAD

Westfir

© MOON.COM

Elevation Profile

or, in chilly weather, cast your line for rainbow and cutthroat trout. At any time of year, you can appreciate the water's stunning clarity.

▶ MILE 1.4–3.5: Spur Trail to Forest Roads 685 and 1910

Another 1 mile farther on, keep an eye out for another short **spur trail** to your right that ends at a large, flat rock, perfect for sunbathing riverside. After another 1 mile, you'll arrive at an intersection with **Forest Roads 685 and 1910.** The trail continues on across the street, but this is a fine turn-around spot.

Relax in the shade and enjoy a snack before returning the way you came.

If you didn't do so before embarking on the trail, spend a few minutes exploring the **Office Covered Bridge** before taking off. It's the longest

▲ OFFICE COVERED BRIDGE

covered bridge in Oregon, at 180 feet. The original span was built in 1924—and subsequently replaced in the 1940s—and there's a protected pedestrian pathway through it.

DIRECTIONS

From Eugene, head east on Highway 58 for 38 miles. Turn left onto Westfir Road, following signs for Westfir and the Office Covered Bridge, for 0.5 mile. Turn left at the T-shaped junction to remain on the road for 1.8 miles, following it along the river as it becomes North Fork Road. Turn left to cross the Office Covered Bridge and enter the trailhead parking area.

GPS COORDINATES: 43.75909, -122.49601 / N43° 45.5454' W122° 29.7606'

BEST NEARBY BREWS

Unwind with a pint at **The 3 Legged Crane Pub and Brewhouse** (48329 E. 1st St., Oakridge, 541/782-2024, noon-8pm Sun.-Tues. and Thurs., noon-10pm Fri.-Sat. Nov.-Apr.; noon-9pm Sun.-Wed., noon-10pm Thurs., noon-11pm Fri.-Sat. May-Oct.). Most of its beers are casked rather than kegged, and served at specific cellar temperatures for an authentic British pub experience. From the trailhead, the 4-mile drive west takes 7 minutes via Westoak Road.

PORTLAND AND THE WILLAMETTE VALLEY

North Fork River Walk

NEARBY CAMPGROUNDS

NAME	DESCRIPTION	FACILITIES	SEASON	FEE
Silver Falls State Park	campground in Oregon's largest state park	91 tent and electrical sites, 14 cabins, restrooms	year-round	$19-53
Silver Falls Hwy. SE, Sublimity, 503/873-8681, www.oregonstateparks.org				
Bagby Campground	basic campground near the Collawash River	15 tent sites, restrooms	year-round	$18
Bagby Rd./Forest Rd. 70, Estacada, 503/668-1700, www.fs.usda.gov				
Shady Cove Campground	quiet campground along the Little North Santiam River	12 nonelectric sites, restrooms	year-round	$8
Forest Rd. 2207, Gates, 503/854-3366, www.fs.usda.gov				
Detroit Lake State Recreation Area	popular campground on Detroit Lake	267 full-hookup, electrical, and tent sites, restrooms	year-round	$19-31
Hwy. 22, Detroit, 503/854-3346, www.oregonstateparks.org				
Breitenbush Campground	quiet campground along the Breitenbush River	30 nonelectric sites, restrooms	May-September	$18
Forest Rd. 46, Detroit, 503/854-3366, www.fs.usda.gov				

MOUNT HOOD

On a clear day, Mount Hood is nearly inescapable. The state's tallest peak—at 11,250 feet—can be seen from Portland and the Willamette Valley foothills, the Columbia River Gorge, and the plains of eastern Oregon. Views of the mountain itself are spectacular, but there's no better way to experience Mount Hood's majesty than from its slopes. Its dozen glaciers remain a defining feature and its forests unfurl in every direction like a Christmas tree skirt. With panoramic views, colorful wildflower displays, old-growth forest, lakes, rivers, and waterfalls, it's no wonder Mount Hood is among the most popular destinations in northwestern Oregon, an outdoor paradise popular even after its bustling ski resorts have closed for the season.

▲ CROSSING THE SANDY RIVER ON THE RAMONA FALLS TRAIL

▲ LOST LAKE BUTTE TRAIL

1 Lost Lake Butte
DISTANCE: 4.4 miles round-trip
DURATION: 2 hours
EFFORT: Easy/moderate

2 Vista Ridge to Owl Point
DISTANCE: 5.4 miles round-trip
DURATION: 2.5 hours
EFFORT: Easy/moderate

3 Ramona Falls
DISTANCE: 8.1 miles round-trip
DURATION: 4 hours
EFFORT: Moderate

4 Salmon River
DISTANCE: 8.2 miles round-trip
DURATION: 4.5 hours
EFFORT: Moderate

5 Elk Meadows
DISTANCE: 6.9 miles round-trip
DURATION: 3.5 hours
EFFORT: Easy/moderate

▾ SANDY RIVER AND MOUNT HOOD EN ROUTE TO RAMONA FALLS

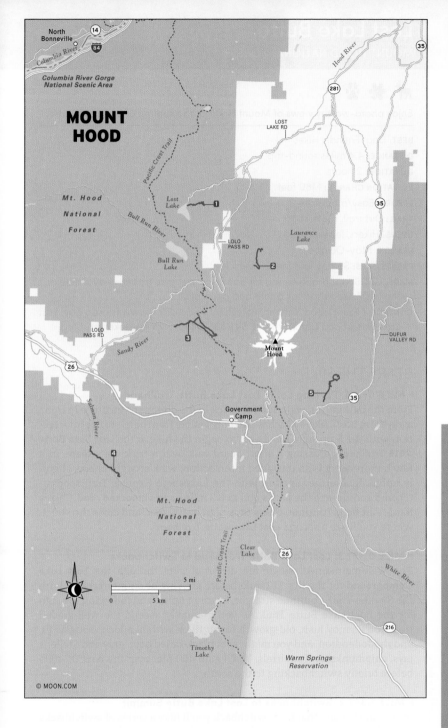

MOUNT HOOD

🦌 ✿ 🐾

Enjoy photo-worthy views of Mount Hood at the summit of Lost Lake Butte.

BEST: Dog-Friendly Hikes
DISTANCE: 4.4 miles round-trip
DURATION: 2 hours
ELEVATION CHANGE: 1,180 feet
EFFORT: Easy/moderate
TRAIL: Dirt trail, roots, rocks
USERS: Hikers, leashed dogs
SEASON: May–October
PASSES/FEES: $9 day-use fee per vehicle
MAPS: USGS topographic map for Bull Run Lake; free trail map available at the Lost Lake Resort toll booth and general store
CONTACT: Mount Hood National Forest, 503/668-1700, www.fs.usda.gov; Lost Lake Resort and Campground, 541/386-6366, www.lostlakeresort.org

START THE HIKE

▶ **MILE 0-0.4: Parking Lot to Lost Lake Butte Trailhead**

From the parking lot, walk 300 feet back in the direction you drove in from, away from Lost Lake—which is partially visible from here—to the intersection with the Stop sign. Head east to begin the hike at the **Lost Lake Butte #616 Trailhead,** crossing a short boardwalk over a trickling stream. In a few hundred feet is an unsigned intersection; walk straight ahead, slightly uphill. Ignore the junction with the Lakeshore Express Trail soon after, and continue to the path's end in 0.2 mile at an **unmarked road.** Take a hard right here, continue past a Stop sign in 100 feet, and cross the street, where you'll see a second **Lost Lake Butte Trailhead.**

▶ **MILE 0.4-1.3: Lost Lake Butte Trailhead to Switchbacks**

The well-maintained, single-file dirt trail cuts through the **Lost Lake Campground** for the first 0.2 mile before arriving at an intersection with the Skyline Trail. Continue straight, heading uphill and following the sign for the Lost Lake Butte Trail. As you gradually ascend the well-graded trail, you'll enjoy lush, old-growth forest thick with hemlock, Douglas fir, and rhododendron, and you might spot black-tailed deer, gray and Steller's jays, chipmunks, and squirrels. You'll gain 450 feet over the next 0.7 mile before briefly switchbacking to the south.

▶ **MILE 1.3-2.2: Switchbacks to Lost Lake Butte Summit**

In 0.5 mile beyond that first switchback you'll hike a series of switchbacks toward the summit. The trail flattens out in 0.4 mile, after which you'll pass some stone steps—the remnants of a **fire lookout** that once stood

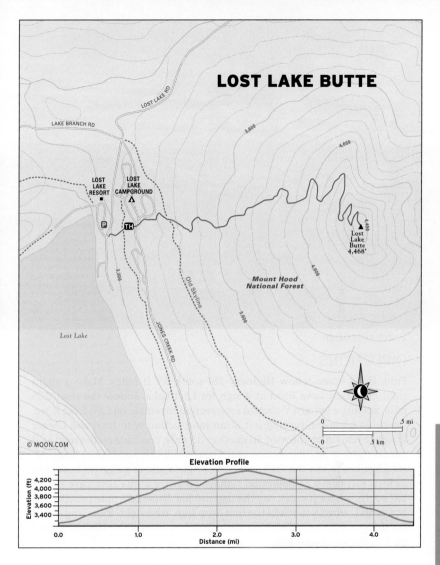

LOST LAKE BUTTE

LOST LAKE RD

LAKE BRANCH RD

3,800

4,000

LOST LAKE RESORT

LOST LAKE CAMPGROUND

P TH

3,200

Old Skyline

JONES CREEK RD

3,600

4,000

4,000

Lost Lake Butte 4,468'

Mount Hood National Forest

Lost Lake

© MOON.COM

0 — .5 mi
0 — .5 km

Elevation Profile

Elevation (ft)
4,200
4,000
3,800
3,600
3,400

0.0   1.0   2.0   3.0   4.0

Distance (mi)

here—and arrive soon after at the **Lost Lake Butte summit,** in a clearing above the Hood River Valley. Mount Hood dominates the skyline to the southeast, towering over a patchwork of clear-cuts below, and Mount Adams rises over the Columbia River Gorge to the north. For a sense of Oregon's many ecosystems, look east toward the arid Columbia Plateau—a far cry from the verdant forest surrounding you.

Return the way you came.

If you have extra time, linger at **Lost Lake** before heading out. A level path hugs the lakeshore and boasts postcard-worthy views of Mount Hood. The Lost Lake Resort's general store sells snacks and souvenirs, and visitors can rent canoes, kayaks, and fishing poles. You'll also find all manner of wildflowers blooming near the lake well into June and July.

▲ HOOD RIVER VALLEY

DIRECTIONS

From Hood River, follow Highway 281 south for 11 miles. Make a slight right onto Lost Lake Road at a sign for Lost Lake. Follow the road 0.25 mile, making a left at a Y-shaped intersection to remain on Lost Lake Road. Continue 1.3 miles, turning left at an intersection with Imai and Oleary Roads to remain on the road. In another 0.5 mile, continue on the road as it curves right, at an intersection with Carson Hill Drive and Alder Road. After 5.5 miles, follow the road as it curves right again at a sign for Lost Lake Resort. Just past a campground sign, you'll arrive at the Lost Lake Resort toll booth, where you can pay the day-use fee. Drive 0.25 mile past the toll booth and, when you reach the first Stop sign, turn right, following a sign for the general store. Continue about 300 feet toward the lakeshore, and park in the lot to your left.

GPS COORDINATES: 45.49471, –121.81803 / N45° 29.6826' W121° 49.0818'

BEST NEARBY BITES
Refuel with hearty fare at **Apple Valley BBQ** (4956 Baseline Dr., Parkdale, 541/352-3554, http://applevalleybbq.com, 11am-8pm Wed.-Sun.). The restaurant offers a full menu of barbecue classics, including a variety of sandwiches, ribs, and mac and cheese. From the trailhead, the 21-mile drive takes 45 minutes via Lost Lake Road and Highway 281.

Walk through wildflower meadows in the midst of a recovering forest, and enjoy unimpeded views of Mount Hood.

DISTANCE: 5.4 miles round-trip

DURATION: 2.5 hours

ELEVATION CHANGE: 580 feet

EFFORT: Easy/moderate

TRAIL: Dirt trail, rocks, roots

USERS: Hikers, leashed dogs

SEASON: July-October

PASSES/FEES: None; hikers must fill out and carry a self-issued wilderness permit (available along the trail)

MAPS: USGS topographic map for Mount Hood North

CONTACT: Mount Hood National Forest, 503/668-1700, www.fs.usda.gov

START THE HIKE

▶ **MILE 0-1.4: Vista Ridge Trailhead to Spur Trail**
The clearly marked **Vista Ridge Trail** starts at the southeastern edge of the parking lot. After hiking 0.2 mile through a fir forest, you'll arrive at a **wilderness permit station;** fill out a form and continue on the trail, which gets steep at times along this stretch. At a junction in another 0.25 mile, turn left to head north on the narrowing Vista Ridge Trail. It begins to flatten out as you walk through a recovering forest of fir and pine trees; here you'll see evidence of the Dollar Lake Fire, which burned more than 6,000 acres on Mount Hood's northern slopes in 2011 following a lightning strike. In 0.9 mile beyond the junction, you'll see a **spur trail** to your right; make the quick detour for your first view of Mount Hood.

▶ **MILE 1.4-2.4: Spur Trail to The Rockpile**
Back on the main trail, as you follow the ridgeline, you'll notice a handful of similar spurs; each is worth the quick side trip for improving views of Oregon's tallest peak. You'll arrive at a clearing after 0.6 mile; as the snow melts in summer, this meadow fills with purple lupine, red paintbrush, and other wildflowers. In 0.25 mile is an unsigned junction; continue straight for about 0.1 mile. A couple hundred feet on is another unsigned junction, denoted by a small rock cairn. Make a right, and walk 300 feet to **The Rockpile;** this talus slope is surrounded by huckleberry bushes at the height of summer and offers panoramic views of Mount Hood.

► **MILE 2.4-2.75: The Rockpile to Owl Point**

Return to the junction, and turn right to continue on the Vista Ridge Trail, walking through the forest of hemlock and subalpine fir. In 0.2 mile, turn right at the sign for Owl Point. Follow the trail for 0.15 mile to arrive at **Owl Point,** another jumble of talus and scree, boasting dramatic views of Mount Hood and the Hood River Valley; the best views come after careful climbing up the boulder piles before you. Hikers can sign a trail register stored in an old ammo box.

► **MILE 2.75-5.4: Owl Point to Vista Ridge Trailhead**

Head back to the junction, and return on the Vista Ridge Trail the way you came.

MOUNT HOOD ►

DIRECTIONS

From Hood River, follow Highway 281 south for 11 miles. Make a slight right onto Lost Lake Road at a sign for Lost Lake. Follow the road 0.25 mile, making a left at a Y-shaped intersection to remain on Lost Lake Road. Continue 1.3 miles, turning left at an intersection with Imai and Oleary Roads to remain on the road. In another 0.5 mile, follow the road as it curves to the right, at an intersection with Carson Hill Drive and Alder Road. After 6 miles, make a left onto Forest Road 18, following a sign for Lolo Pass; the road becomes Forest Road 16 at an intersection with Lolo Pass Road. After 4 miles, turn left to remain on Forest Road 16 at an intersection with Stump Creek Road. Continue on, uphill, for 4.5 miles, then make a hard right onto Forest Road 1650 at the intersection. Follow the gravel road uphill for 3.5 miles; the parking area is at the end of the road.

GPS COORDINATES: 45.44292, –121.72913 / N45° 26.5752′ W121° 43.7478′

BEST NEARBY BREWS

Wide-open views of Mount Hood are just the start at **Solera Brewery** (4945 Baseline Dr., Parkdale, 541/352-5500, www.solerabrewery.com, typically noon-10pm Thurs.-Tues. though hours can vary seasonally). Solera also offers a variety of small-batch beers and a solid lineup of barrel-aged offerings. From the trailhead, the 25.5-mile drive northeast takes 55 minutes via Lost Lake Road and Highway 281.

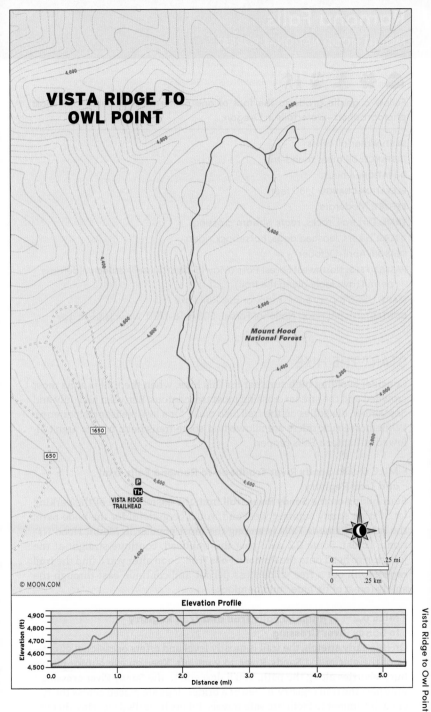

VISTA RIDGE TO OWL POINT

Mount Hood
National Forest

1650

650

VISTA RIDGE
TRAILHEAD

0   .25 mi
0   .25 km

© MOON.COM

Elevation Profile

Elevation (ft): 4,900 / 4,800 / 4,700 / 4,600 / 4,500
Distance (mi): 0.0 / 1.0 / 2.0 / 3.0 / 4.0 / 5.0

Follow a gentle grade to the foot of one of the most popular—and most photographed—waterfalls in Oregon.

BEST: Waterfall Hikes
DISTANCE: 8.1 miles round-trip
DURATION: 4 hours
ELEVATION CHANGE: 1,180 feet
EFFORT: Moderate
TRAIL: Dirt trail, rocks, roots, stream crossing
USERS: Hikers, leashed dogs, horseback riders
SEASON: April-October
PASSES/FEES: Northwest Forest Pass (May 15-Oct. 15); self-issued wilderness permit (available along the trail)
MAPS: USGS topographic map for Bull Run Lake
CONTACT: Mount Hood National Forest, 503/668-1700, www.fs.usda.gov

START THE HIKE

Consider avoiding high summer for this hike, when the trail is at its most crowded and the stream crossing most treacherous. Between mid-July and September, blackflies on the trail also make for a less pleasant experience. While horseback riders are allowed on some trails here, horses aren't allowed at Ramona Falls proper.

▶ **MILE 0-0.2: Sandy River Trailhead to Ramona Falls Trail and Trail Registry**

Start hiking on the **Sandy River Trail** from the eastern edge of the parking lot. If it's a sunny summer weekend, you'll be grateful for the wide path; the hike to Ramona Falls is among the most popular in Mount Hood National Forest. Some 0.2 mile past the trailhead, continue straight at the junction to head onto the **Ramona Falls Trail.** Soon after you'll find the **trail registry;** fill out a free wilderness permit and continue east through the shady forest of fir, alder, and hemlock.

▶ **MILE 0.2-1.2: Ramona Falls Trail and Trail Registry to Sandy River Crossing**

On this early stretch, the trail is mostly level and offers occasional glimpses of the glacier-fed Sandy River, to your left. Keep an eye out for purple huckleberries along the path. You'll descend to the **Sandy River crossing** 1 mile past the trail registry. In lieu of a bridge, logs are placed across the river each summer to facilitate safe travels; hikers have died crossing this river, so be cautious, especially early in the summer and late in the day, when currents are strongest and swiftest.

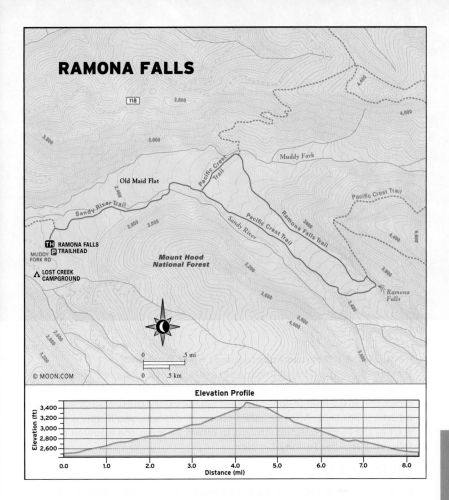

RAMONA FALLS

Elevation Profile

▶ **MILE 1.2-1.7: Sandy River Crossing to Pacific Crest Trail**

In 0.5 mile, you'll arrive at a junction; you could continue straight out-and-back for the quickest, most direct route to the waterfall—shaving 0.6 mile off the total mileage—but head left onto the **Pacific Crest Trail** for the more scenic, gradual route and to start a loop. (Horseback riders should continue straight, as horses aren't allowed on portions of the trail to the left.)

▶ **MILE 1.7-4.3: Pacific Crest Trail to Ramona Falls**

In 0.6 mile, head right at the T-shaped junction to follow the **Ramona Falls Trail** through thick pine forest. This stretch is sandy and less shady than previous sections on this hike, until the trail meets up with **Ramona Creek** in another 0.7 mile. From here, the trail parallels the creek through thick fir forest before arriving in another gently graded 1.3 miles at the 120-foot-tall **Ramona Falls,** impressive as it cascades over columns of basalt.

▲ RAMONA FALLS

▶ **MILE 4.3–8.1: Ramona Falls to Sandy River Trailhead**

From the falls, you'll begin looping back west via the unsigned Timberline Trail, through thickets of rhododendron. Proceed straight ahead at the intersection in 0.5 mile to continue west via the Pacific Crest Trail, following a Parking Lot sign. After 1.6 miles of steady descent, you'll return to the start of the loop; continue straight to return 1.7 miles the way you came, following another Parking Lot sign.

DIRECTIONS

From the town of Zigzag, turn left to head north on East Lolo Pass Road. Follow the road for 4.2 miles, and turn right onto paved Forest Road 1825, following the Trailheads and Campgrounds sign. After 0.7 mile, head right onto the Sandy River bridge. Continue 1.7 miles, and fork left onto Forest Road 100, following the Ramona Falls sign. The road ends, after a bumpy 0.4 mile, in a large gravel parking area at the end of the road.

GPS COORDINATES: 45.38676, –121.8318 / N45° 23.2056′ W121° 49.908′

BEST NEARBY BREWS

Mt. Hood Brewing Co. (87304 E. Government Camp Loop, Government Camp, 503/272-3172, http://mthoodbrewing.com, 11am–10pm daily) serves IPAs, porters, stouts, and more, brewed from pure glacial water. From the trailhead, the 17.5-mile drive south takes 25 minutes via East Lolo Pass Road and Highway 26.

Salmon River

MOUNT HOOD NATIONAL FOREST

❀ 🐾 🚶

On this hike along the Salmon River, you'll find old-growth forest, popular swimming holes (bring a swimsuit), and expansive canyon views.

DISTANCE: 8.2 miles round-trip
DURATION: 4.5 hours
ELEVATION CHANGE: 1,280 feet
EFFORT: Moderate
TRAIL: Dirt trail, rocks, roots
USERS: Hikers, leashed dogs
SEASON: April-November
PASSES/FEES: Northwest Forest Pass (May 15-Oct. 15)
MAPS: USGS topographic map for Rhododendron
CONTACT: Mount Hood National Forest, 503/668-1700, www.fs.usda.gov

START THE HIKE

▸ **MILE 0-0.4: Salmon River Trailhead to Pools**
Start at the **Salmon River Trailhead** on the east side of the road near the parking areas, hiking alongside the Salmon River. After 0.4 mile of gentle climbing through old-growth Douglas fir—you'll spend most of this hike under thick canopy—you'll pass a series of small, sun-drenched **pools** that are nice for a dip in summer. This is also a popular stretch with anglers fishing for salmon and trout.

▸ **MILE 0.4-2: Pools to Rolling Riffle Campground**
Back in the forest, you'll almost imperceptibly ascend through the forest of thick Douglas firs—some with a diameter of 6-8 feet—and alongside nurse logs, downed trees that provide nutrients for plants and habitats for small wildlife. Keep an eye out for white, three-petaled trillium blooms April-May, as well as

SALMON RIVER ▸

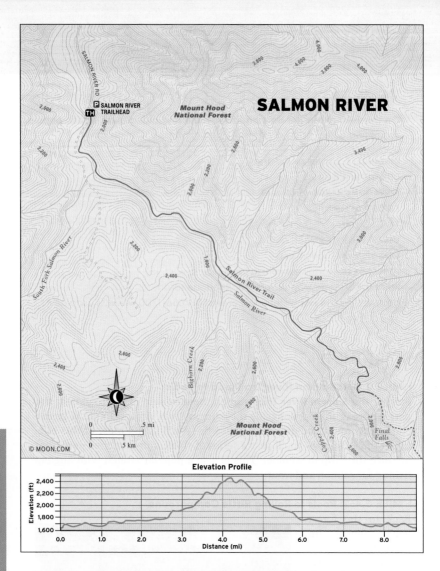

Elevation Profile

huckleberries, which are ripe for picking and snacking June-August. Some 1.2 miles past the pools, you'll pass a few backcountry campsites and, in another 0.4 mile, a few more—these are popularly known as the **Rolling Riffle Campground.** Watch for short **spur trails** along this stretch, off to your right, which lead to the riverbank. If you're hiking with children, the campground makes a good turnaround point.

▶ **MILE 2-4.1: Rolling Riffle Campground to Salmon River Canyon Viewpoint**

The trail leaves the riverside 0.5 mile past the campground. Here you'll begin ascending in earnest, gaining more than 600 feet—sometimes gradually, sometimes steeply—before arriving in 1.5 miles at an unmarked 0.1-mile **spur trail.** Turn left onto the spur to ascend briefly, and then make an

▲ SALMON RIVER CANYON VIEWPOINT

immediate right; soon after, you'll arrive at the **Salmon River Canyon view-point,** indicated by a sign that says, "Camp Under Trees Not in Meadows." The meadow boasts sweeping views of the surrounding slopes, covered in old-growth Douglas fir. The trail continues on, but this viewpoint makes a fine turnaround point.

Return the way you came.

DIRECTIONS

From the town of Sandy, follow U.S. 26 east for 17 miles. Just past a sign for the Zigzag Ranger Station, turn right to head south on East Salmon River Road for 5 miles. The parking area—on both sides of the road—comes just before a bridge.

GPS COORDINATES: 45.27786, -121.93974 / N45° 16.6716' W121° 56.3844'

BEST NEARBY BITES

Refuel—or pick something up to go for your hike—at **Wraptitude** (67441 E. U.S. 26, Welches, 503/622-0893, http://wraptitude.com, 8am-8pm Mon.-Thurs., 7am-9pm Fri.-Sat.). The café specializes in wraps but also serves burgers, sandwiches, breakfast burritos, and salads. From the trailhead, the 6.5-mile drive northwest takes 15 minutes via East Salmon River Road and U.S. 26.

One of the best wildflower hikes on Mount Hood also delivers impressive views of Oregon's tallest peak.

BEST: Wildflower Hikes
DISTANCE: 6.9 miles round-trip
DURATION: 3.5 hours
ELEVATION CHANGE: 1,090 feet
EFFORT: Easy/moderate
TRAIL: Dirt trail, rocks, roots, stream crossings
USERS: Hikers, leashed dogs, horseback riders
SEASON: June–October
PASSES/FEES: Northwest Forest Pass (May 15–Oct. 15)
MAPS: USGS topographic map for Mount Hood South
CONTACT: Mount Hood National Forest, 503/668-1700, www.fs.usda.gov

START THE HIKE

▶ **MILE 0-1.4: Elk Meadows and Sahalie Falls Trailhead to Newton Creek Crossing**

Start hiking from the **Elk Meadows and Sahalie Falls Trailhead** at the northwestern edge of the parking area to follow the **Sahalie Falls Trail,** which starts out mostly flat and heads through a hemlock and Douglas fir forest, with ripe huckleberries lining the way in summer. You'll arrive at a junction in 0.5 mile; continue straight onto the **Elk Meadows Trail,** crossing a footbridge over Clark Creek in 0.2 mile. Some 0.6 mile past Clark Creek is an intersection with the Newton Creek Trail, but continue straight to remain on the Elk Meadows Trail. In 0.1 mile you'll arrive at the **Newton Creek crossing;** logs are placed across the creek each summer, though the exact location varies year to year. Take care crossing, especially early in the season and late in the day, when currents are swifter.

▶ **MILE 1.4-2.8: Newton Creek Crossing to Perimeter Trail**

After the crossing, you'll hike through rocks and bushes before ascending a series of eight switchbacks over 1 mile, gaining 520 feet over this sometimes steep stretch. Continue straight ahead on the Elk Meadows Trail at a junction 0.2 mile past the final switchback. In another 0.2 mile you'll reach another intersection with the **Perimeter Trail.**

▶ **MILE 2.8-3.5: Perimeter Trail to Elk Meadows Shelter**

Turn left onto the Perimeter Trail for a clockwise loop around Elk Meadows. The meadows are mostly obscured by the Douglas fir and noble fir forest, but you'll catch the occasional glimpse. In 0.3 mile you'll come to

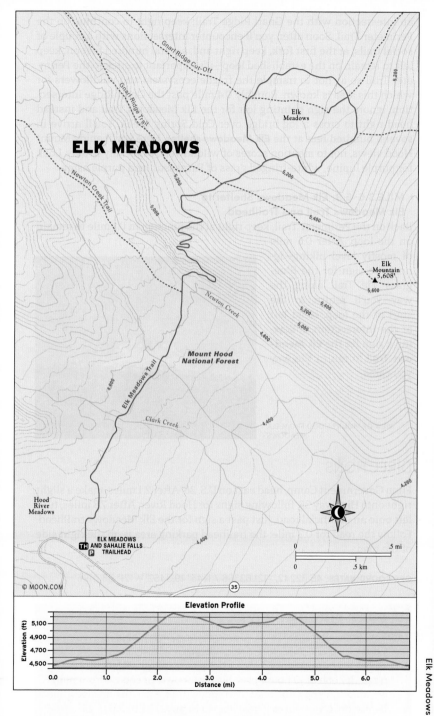

ELK MEADOWS

Elk Meadows

Gnarl Ridge Cut-Off

Gnarl Ridge Trail

Newton Creek Trail

5,200

5,000

5,200

5,400

Newton Creek

Elk
Mountain
5,608'

5,600

5,400

5,200

5,000

4,600

4,600

**Mount Hood
National Forest**

Clark Creek

4,400

4,200

4,600

Hood
River
Meadows

ELK MEADOWS
AND SAHALIE FALLS
TRAILHEAD

4,400

0   .5 mi

0   .5 km

© MOON.COM

35

Elevation Profile

Elevation (ft)

5,100
4,900
4,700
4,500

0.0   1.0   2.0   3.0   4.0   5.0   6.0

Distance (mi)

an intersection with the Gnarl Ridge Trail; keep right to continue on the Perimeter Trail. Soon after, you'll encounter intersections with a couple of social trails; at the first fork, keep right and, several hundred feet on, keep left to remain on the established loop—it's important to stick to the Perimeter Trail so as not to trample the fragile ecosystem and wildflowers for which this area is known. Roughly 0.4 mile past the Gnarl Ridge intersection, ignore the sign pointing left for the Elk Meadows Trail and instead head right to cross a log bridge over Cold Spring Creek. You'll arrive in several hundred feet at the **Elk Meadows shelter.** Here you'll enjoy Mount Hood views, not to mention scores of wildflowers, especially in July. Look for purple lupine, white-fringed grass of Parnassus, and purple aster.

▶ **MILE 3.5–6.9: Elk Meadows Shelter to Elk Meadows Trail and Trailhead**

Back on the Perimeter Trail, keep right at the junction in 0.1 mile to remain on the loop. After 0.6 mile of mostly level hiking—ignore the sign for the Bluegrass Tie Trail along the way—you'll return to the start of the loop. Head left at the intersection, following a sign for the **Elk Meadows Trail** to return the way you came.

VIEW OF MOUNT HOOD FROM ELK MEADOWS ▶

DIRECTIONS

From Government Camp, head east on U.S. 26. After 2.1 miles, make a slight right onto Highway 35, following signs for Hood River. After 7.8 miles, turn left onto an unofficial road, just past a sign for the Elk Meadows trailhead. Follow the road for 0.3 mile; the trailhead parking area is on the right side of the road.

GPS COORDINATES: 45.32242, –121.63366 / N45° 19.3452′ W121° 38.0196′

BEST NEARBY BITES

The Ratskeller (88335 E. Government Camp Loop, Government Camp, 503/272-3635, http://ratskellerpizzeria.com, 11am–10pm Sun.–Thurs., 11am–midnight Fri.–Sat.) delivers a robust selection of filling pizza. Try one of 10 house pies, build your own, or choose from burgers, salads, wraps, calzones, and sandwiches. From the trailhead, the 11-mile drive west takes 15 minutes via Highway 35 and U.S. 26.

NEARBY CAMPGROUNDS

NAME	DESCRIPTION	FACILITIES	SEASON	FEE
Tollgate Campground	quiet campground on the Zigzag River	13 tent sites, 1 group site, restrooms	May–September	$22–42
U.S. 26, Welches, 503/668-1700, www.fs.usda.gov				
Lost Creek Campground	located conveniently close to Ramona Falls and the Sandy River	5 walk-up tent sites, 8 tent and RV sites, 2 yurts, restrooms	May–September	$21–35
Forest Rd. 1825, Welches, 503/668-1700, www.fs.usda.gov				
Lost Lake Resort and Campground	popular campground at Lost Lake	148 tent and group sites, 19 yurts, 7 cabins, 1 A-frame cabin, restrooms	May–October	$29–32 tent sites, $55–65 group sites, $85–155 yurts, $88–240 cabins, $195–210 A-frame cabin
9900 Lost Lake Rd., Hood River, 541/386-6366, www.lostlakeresort.org				
Trillium Lake Campground	busy campground on Trillium Lake	52 tent and RV sites, 5 group sites, restrooms	May–September	$22–90
U.S. 26, Government Camp, 503/668-1700, www.fs.usda.gov				
Hoodview Campground	charming campground on the shore of Timothy Lake	43 tent and RV sites, restrooms	May–September	$20
Forest Rd. 57, Government Camp, 503/668-1700, www.fs.usda.gov				

BEND AND THE CENTRAL OREGON CASCADES

The high desert of Central Oregon boasts a landscape unlike anywhere else in the state. Cascade peaks stretch to the sky like an erratic EKG, their bases covered in clear mountain streams and ponderosa pine forests, before giving way to wide-open vistas, broken up only by seas of sagebrush and islands of juniper as you head east. In between, you'll find lunar lava flows, spring-fed rivers, old-growth Douglas fir, and cartoonishly blue pools. You'll find no better home base for exploring the variety of landscapes in the area than Bend, the region's largest city, with more than 90,000 residents—and, happily, dozens of craft breweries, perfect for capping off a day of hiking.

▲ FLATIRON ROCK TRAIL

▲ PATH ON TUMALO MOUNTAIN

THE MONKEY FACE ROCK FORMATION AT SMITH ROCK STATE PARK AS
◀ SEEN FROM THE MISERY RIDGE-RIVER TRAIL LOOP

1 McKenzie River Trail to Tamolitch (Blue Pool)

DISTANCE: 4.6 miles round-trip
DURATION: 2.5 hours
EFFORT: Easy

2 Little Belknap Crater

DISTANCE: 5.3 miles round-trip
DURATION: 3 hours
EFFORT: Easy/moderate

3 West Metolius River

DISTANCE: 5.7 miles round-trip
DURATION: 3 hours
EFFORT: Easy/moderate

4 Black Butte

DISTANCE: 4.8 miles round-trip
DURATION: 2.5 hours
EFFORT: Moderate

5 Tam-a-láu Trail

DISTANCE: 7.1 miles round-trip
DURATION: 3.5 hours
EFFORT: Easy/moderate

6 Misery Ridge-River Trail Loop

DISTANCE: 4.2 miles round-trip
DURATION: 2.5 hours
EFFORT: Easy/moderate

7 Tumalo Mountain

DISTANCE: 4.4 miles round-trip
DURATION: 2.5 hours
EFFORT: Moderate

8 Shevlin Park Loop

DISTANCE: 4.8 miles round-trip
DURATION: 2 hours
EFFORT: Easy

9 Flatiron Rock

DISTANCE: 6.3 miles round-trip
DURATION: 2.75 hours
EFFORT: Easy/moderate

10 Paulina Peak

DISTANCE: 4.7 miles round-trip
DURATION: 2.5 hours
EFFORT: Moderate

▾ MCKENZIE RIVER NEAR BLUE POOL

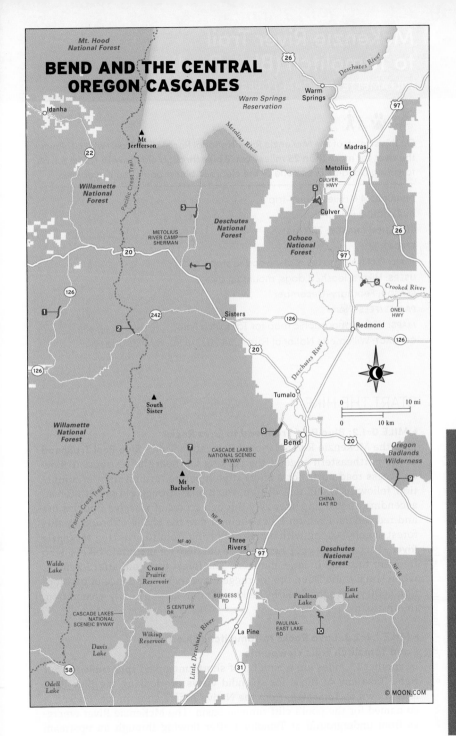

BEND AND THE CENTRAL OREGON CASCADES

Mt. Hood National Forest

Deschutes River

Warm Springs Reservation

Warm Springs

Idanha

Willamette National Forest

Mt Jerfferson

Metolius River

Deschutes National Forest

Madras

Metolius

CULVER HWY

Culver

Ochoco National Forest

METOLIUS RIVER CAMP SHERMAN

Crooked River

ONEIL HWY

Redmond

Sisters

Pacific Crest Trail

South Sister

Tumalo

Deschutes River

Bend

Oregon Badlands Wilderness

Willamette National Forest

Mt Bachelor

CASCADE LAKES NATIONAL SCENEIC BYWAY

CHINA HAT RD

NF 45

Pacific Crest Trail

NF 40

Three Rivers

Deschutes National Forest

Waldo Lake

Crane Prairie Reservoir

S CENTURY DR

CASCADE LAKES NATIONAL SCENEIC BYWAY

Wikiup Reservoir

Davis Lake

Little Deschutes River

BURGESS RD

Paulina Lake

East Lake

NF 18

La Pine

PAULINA-EAST LAKE RD

Odell Lake

© MOON.COM

0   10 mi

0   10 km

McKenzie River Trail to Tamolitch (Blue Pool)

WILLAMETTE NATIONAL FOREST

On this stretch of the McKenzie River National Recreation Trail—which follows the river for more than 25 miles—you'll hike through old-growth forest full of towering Douglas firs to one of the clearest, bluest pools you'll ever see.

DISTANCE: 4.6 miles round-trip

DURATION: 2.5 hours

ELEVATION CHANGE: 280 feet

EFFORT: Easy

TRAIL: Dirt trail, gravel, roots, wooden steps, rocks

USERS: Hikers, leashed dogs, mountain bikers

SEASON: February–December

PASSES/FEES: None

MAPS: USGS topographic map for Tamolitch Falls

CONTACT: Willamette National Forest, 541/822-3381, www.fs.usda.gov

START THE HIKE

▶ MILE 0-1.2: Blue Pool Trailhead to Lava Rocks

Find the McKenzie River National Recreation Trail's **Blue Pool Trailhead** at the northeastern edge of the parking lot, near the restroom. Follow an access road north for a short stretch before turning right at a junction, following the Blue Pool sign. You'll hike through old-growth forest, ascending almost imperceptibly through scores of massive Douglas firs and red cedars. Even on a hot summer day, the shade afforded by this forest canopy—along with a breeze flowing from the rushing **McKenzie River**—keeps hikers cool. Keep an eye out here for mountain bikers, who frequent this trail in large numbers. The forest thins out after 1.2 miles, when you'll trade Doug firs for rugged lava rocks—evidence of an eruption 1,600 years ago of nearby Belknap Crater—as you gently ascend from the riverbank.

▶ MILE 1.2-2.3: Lava Rocks to Tamolitch (Blue Pool) and Tamolitch Falls Viewpoints

In another 1.1 miles are a handful of short, unmarked **spur trails** to your right. Take any of these for splendid views overlooking the **Blue Pool,** also known as **Tamolitch,** from the Native American term for "bucket"—so named for the pool's cliff-rimmed basin. The McKenzie River emerges from underground at Tamolitch after flowing through an upstream

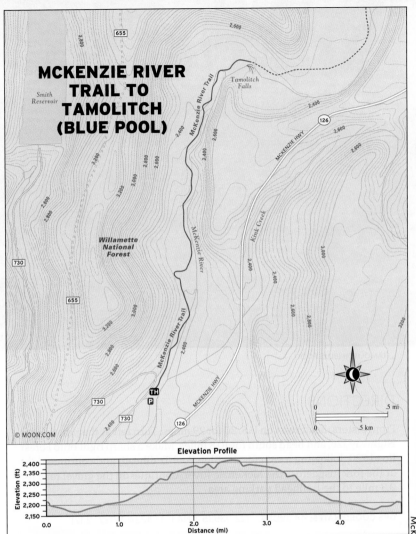

MCKENZIE RIVER TRAIL TO TAMOLITCH (BLUE POOL)

Smith Reservoir

McKenzie River Trail

Tamolitch Falls

Willamette National Forest

McKenzie River

McKenzie River Trail

Kink Creek

McKenzie Hwy

126

655

730

655

730

730

126

TH
P

© MOON.COM

0   .5 mi

0   .5 km

Elevation Profile

Elevation (ft)

2,400
2,350
2,300
2,250
2,200
2,150

0.0   1.0   2.0   3.0   4.0
Distance (mi)

lava tube, producing some of the clearest water you'll ever see. If you visit spring-early summer, you'll also enjoy views of **Tamolitch Falls,** the seasonal waterfall that partially feeds the pool, at the eastern edge of the basin. From these vantage points some 50 feet above the river, the topaz-colored water appears no deeper than a backyard pool, though it can easily be 50 feet deep or more—and the water is a chilly 37°F on average! Although you may see some hikers diving into the Blue Pool, this is dangerous—people have died doing so.

The McKenzie River National Recreation Trail continues north, but these viewpoints make a nice turnaround point. Return the way you came.

▲ TAMOLITCH (BLUE POOL)

DIRECTIONS

From Sisters, head west on U.S. 20 for 29 miles. Turn left at the junction for Highway 126, and head south for 10.8 miles. Make a sharp right onto Forest Road 730, following a sign for the Blue Pool Trailhead, and continue right at the fork just across the McKenzie River. Continue on the gravel road for 0.3 mile to the trailhead parking area.

GPS COORDINATES: 44.29054, -122.03535 / N44° 17.4324' W122° 2.121'

BEST NEARBY BREWS

Sisters's only brewery, **Three Creeks Brewing** (721 Desperado Ct., Sisters, 541/549-1963, www.threecreeksbrewing.com, 11:30am-9pm Sun.-Thurs., 11:30am-10pm Fri.-Sat.), produces roughly 50 beers each year, including year-round varietals, seasonal releases, and one-off brews. From the trailhead, the 41-mile drive east takes 45 minutes via Highway 126 and U.S. 20.

Little Belknap Crater
MOUNT WASHINGTON WILDERNESS

Hike part of the Pacific Crest Trail through centuries-old lava fields to a crater's summit boasting towering mountain views.

DISTANCE: 5.3 miles round-trip

DURATION: 3 hours

ELEVATION CHANGE: 1,020 feet

EFFORT: Easy/moderate

TRAIL: Dirt trail, sand, lava rock, rock scramble

USERS: Hikers, horseback riders, leashed dogs

SEASON: Summer-early fall

PASSES/FEES: day-use permit required Friday before Memorial Day weekend-last Friday in September, available for purchase by phone or online only (877/444-6777, www.recreation.gov, $1 processing fee)

MAPS: USGS topographic map for Mount Washington, OR

CONTACT: Mount Washington Wilderness, Willamette National Forest, 541/822-3381, www.fs.usda.gov

START THE HIKE

A sturdy pair of hiking boots is recommended given some jagged lava rocks; for this reason, although leashed dogs are allowed here, you might want to think twice about bringing your pet. Much of this hike is exposed, so you'll also want to bring plenty of water and sunscreen.

▶ **MILE 0-0.8: Pacific Crest Trail to Lava Flow**

From the parking lot, head northeast toward the sign welcoming you to the Mount Washington Wilderness. Just next to it, hop onto the **Pacific Crest Trail (PCT).** You'll soon find yourself in the first of two "islands" of forest you'll encounter on this hike, each of them surrounded by miles of lava rock. You'll emerge briefly onto lava flow at 0.4 mile, and then leave the forest behind for good in another 0.4 mile. After exiting the second forest "island," you'll see two peaks ahead: The barren slope to your left is Belknap Crater, and the smaller stump to your right is Little Belknap Crater. Most of the lava rock you're about to traverse formed after these shield volcanoes erupted more than a thousand years ago.

▶ **MILE 0.8-2.4: Lava Flow to Little Belknap Trail**

From here, you steadily ascend on the well-graded trail, gaining about 625 feet on this exposed stretch. You might notice a few gnarled whitebark pines along the way. Pause for a water break at some point, a good excuse to turn around and look back toward the trailhead, where North and

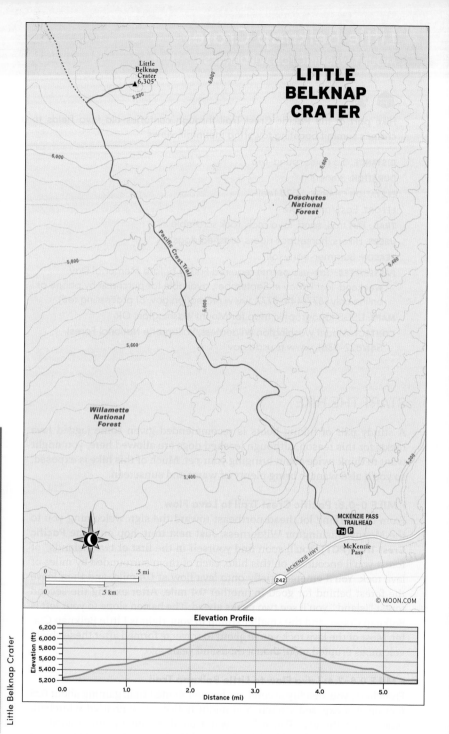

LITTLE BELKNAP CRATER

Little Belknap Crater 6,305'

Deschutes National Forest

Pacific Crest Trail

Willamette National Forest

McKenzie Pass Trailhead
TH P

McKenzie Pass

MCKENZIE HWY 242

© MOON.COM

0   .5 mi
0   .5 km

Elevation Profile

Middle Sister tower over the surrounding peaks on a clear day. In 1.6 miles, head right onto the **Little Belknap Trail.**

▸ **MILE 2.4–2.65: Little Belknap Trail to Little Belknap Crater Summit**
This 0.25-mile spur gains 100 feet along the way. You'll scramble steeply over some rocks before arriving at the **Little Belknap Crater summit.** From here, peaks seem to rise in every direction: Belknap Crater sits to the west, Mount Washington dominates views to the north, symmetrical Black Butte rises in the northeast, and Black Crater—which has a vertical notch at its summit—is visible to the southeast.

Return to the junction and take a left to head south and return the way you came.

LITTLE BELKNAP
CRATER TRAIL ▸

DIRECTIONS

From Sisters, head west on Highway 242 (McKenzie Highway) for 15.1 miles, turning right into the parking area indicated by a sign sporting a hiker symbol. This highway opens every June and usually closes by October, depending on snow levels; check with the Oregon **Department of Transportation** (800/977-6368, http://tripcheck.com) for road closures before planning your hike.

GPS COORDINATES: 44.2604, –121.81 / N44° 15.624′ W121° 48.6′

BEST NEARBY BITES, BREWS, AND A BONUS

Can't decide between coffee, beer, and pizza? You don't have to at **Hop & Brew** (523 U.S. 20, Sisters, 541/719-1295, http://hopandbrew. com, 7am-8pm Sun.-Thurs., 7am-9pm Fri.-Sat.). Grab breakfast burritos and bagel sandwiches before your hike, or unwind with pizza, sandwiches, beer, or cider afterward. From the trailhead, the 16-mile drive east takes 30 minutes via Highway 242. On the way, you might want to stop at **Dee Wright Observatory** (541/822-3381 or visit www. fs.usda.gov), located just 0.5 mile east of the trailhead parking area along Highway 242. The observatory was completed in 1935 by the Civilian Conservation Corps and affords 360-degree views of surrounding peaks; on a clear day, visitors can see Mount Washington, Mount Jefferson, the Three Sisters, Little Belknap Crater, and more.

West Metolius River

DESCHUTES NATIONAL FOREST

🐐 🌸 🐾 👫

Follow the banks of the vibrant Metolius River to a fish hatchery in the middle of a pine forest.

BEST: Dog-Friendly Hikes, Kid-Friendly Hikes
DISTANCE: 5.7 miles round-trip
DURATION: 3 hours
ELEVATION CHANGE: 270 feet
EFFORT: Easy/moderate
TRAIL: Dirt trail, roots
USERS: Hikers, leashed dogs
SEASON: Year-round
PASSES/FEES: None
MAPS: USGS topographic map for Candle Creek
CONTACT: Deschutes National Forest, 541/383-5300, www.fs.usda.gov

While wildflowers steal the show in spring and early summer, there's no bad time to hike along the Metolius, one of the largest spring-fed rivers in the United States. It remains remarkably clear year-round, and aspen groves alongside it put on colorful fall foliage displays.

START THE HIKE

▶ MILE 0-0.4: West Metolius Trailhead to Spring

Find the **West Metolius Trailhead** at the southeastern edge of the parking area near a bend in the **Metolius River.** Follow the single-track trail along the river through a forest of Douglas fir, aspen, and pine, with wildflowers blooming in mid-spring, including yellow balsamroot, western buttercup, red paintbrush, yellow monkeyflower, and purple lupine. If you're lucky, you may spy the pink- or purple-chuted Peck's penstemon; this rare wildflower grows in the forests near the town of Sisters—and nowhere else in the world. After 0.4 mile, look west to see a small **spring**—seemingly originating from the middle of the Metolius's steep riverbank—feeding into the river. Take time to admire the sapphire-colored, crystal-clear waters.

▶ MILE 0.4-2.3: Spring to Metolius Riverbank

You'll start swapping fir trees for a thick forest of old-growth ponderosa pine over the next 0.4 mile as the trail curves north, and begin gradually descending before the trail flattens out near the riverbank in another 1.5 miles—where you'll see several small islands in the middle of the Metolius. They're usually covered in wildflowers in spring, and are key habitats for local fish and bird populations.

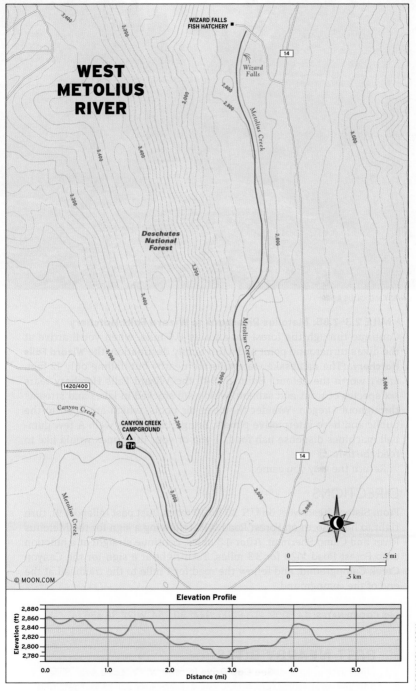

WEST METOLIUS RIVER

WIZARD FALLS FISH HATCHERY

14

Wizard Falls

Metolius Creek

Deschutes National Forest

3,400

3,200

3,000

2,800

2,600

2,800

3,000

Metolius Creek

1420/400

Canyon Creek

CANYON CREEK CAMPGROUND

P TH

Metolius Creek

3,000

14

0   .5 mi

0   .5 km

© MOON.COM

Elevation Profile

Distance (mi)	Elevation (ft)

2,880
2,860
2,840
2,820
2,800
2,780

0.0   1.0   2.0   3.0   4.0   5.0

West Metolius River

433

▲ WEST METOLIUS RIVER

▸ **MILE 2.3-2.85: Metolius Riverbank to Wizard Falls Hatchery**
Continue through the forest for another 0.5 mile, when you'll arrive at the hike's turnaround point and a fun family destination: the **Wizard Falls Hatchery.** (The namesake waterfalls are nearby but, falling only 12 feet, aren't worth the detour.) Built in 1947, the Wizard Falls Hatchery rears six species of trout and salmon, which are stocked in lakes and streams throughout Oregon. Wander the open-air pools, which are open to the public and have interpretive panels. Bring quarters, as well: A few gumball machines dispense fish food, if you or your little ones would like to feed the fish.

Return the way you came.

DIRECTIONS

From Sisters, head west on U.S. 20 for 10 miles. Just past milepost 91, turn right to head north on Forest Road 1419, following a sign for the Metolius River and Camp Sherman. After 4.8 miles, continue straight at a junction onto Forest Road 1420 for 3.3 miles. Turn right at a sign for the Canyon Creek Campground, and follow the road for 1 mile to the trailhead at the end of the campground.

GPS COORDINATES: 44.5009, -121.6411 / N44° 30.054′ W121° 38.466′

> ## BEST NEARBY BITES
> Step back in time at **Sno Cap Drive In** (380 W. Cascade Ave., Sisters, 541/549-6151, 11am-7pm daily). The classic diner serves burgers and other American fare, not to mention more than 30 flavors of homemade ice cream. From the trailhead, the 18-mile drive south takes 30 minutes via Forest Roads 1419 and 1420 and U.S. 20.

Black Butte

DESCHUTES NATIONAL FOREST

Panoramic views of nearby Cascade peaks from this symmetrical stratovolcano's summit make the unrelenting ascent worth it.

DISTANCE: 4.8 miles round-trip
DURATION: 2.5 hours
ELEVATION CHANGE: 1,560 feet
EFFORT: Moderate
TRAIL: Dirt trail, rocks, roots
USERS: Hikers, leashed dogs
SEASON: June-October
PASSES/FEES: Northwest Forest Pass (May-Sept.)
MAPS: USGS topographic map for Black Butte, OR, and Little Akawa Butte, OR
CONTACT: Deschutes National Forest, 541/383-5300, www.fs.usda.gov

START THE HIKE

Consider getting an early start on this trail if you're hiking in the summer—shade is rare after you pass through an old-growth forest early on. Bring plenty of water and sunscreen.

▶ **MILE 0-0.8: Black Butte Trailhead to Switchback**
Find the trailhead at the eastern edge of the parking area—thankfully, already about halfway up the butte—and begin ascending on the **Black Butte Trail.** On this early stretch you'll hike through an old-growth, mossy ponderosa pine forest. After 0.8 mile and 620 feet of elevation gain, you'll reach the hike's sole **switchback**—and also leave the forest behind for Black Butte's exposed southern hillside. You'll notice the Black Butte Ranch vacation resort to the south and Mount Washington to the southwest as you exit the forest.

Black Butte

BLACK BUTTE TRAIL ▶

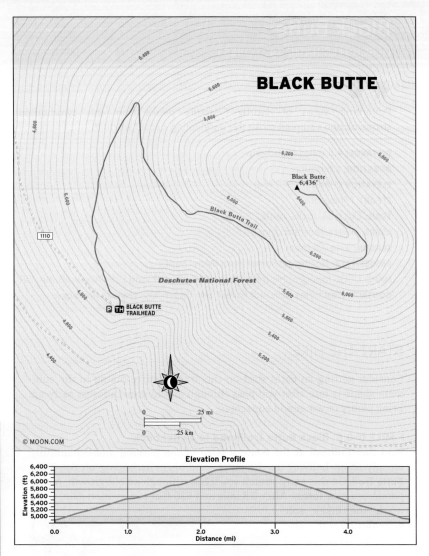

BLACK BUTTE

Black Butte 6,436'

Black Butte Trail

Deschutes National Forest

BLACK BUTTE TRAILHEAD

1110

0   .25 mi

0   .25 km

© MOON.COM

Elevation Profile

Elevation (ft)

6,400
6,200
6,000
5,800
5,600
5,400
5,200
5,000

0.0   1.0   2.0   3.0   4.0

Distance (mi)

▶ **MILE 0.8–2.4: Switchback to Black Butte Summit**

Continue hiking steadily up the trail's well-graded incline. In late spring and early summer, you may spot white Washington lilies, purple lupine, pinemat manzanita, and other wildflowers. In 1 mile, you'll start traversing scattered groves of lodgepole pine, whitebark pine, and subalpine fir. You'll gain another 425 feet over the next 0.6 mile before arriving at the **Black Butte summit,** indicated by a sign for the Black Butte Lookout Tower. To your left, on the butte's southern edge, is a **fire lookout,** built in 1995; not open to the public, it's still used to spot wildfires during summer. To your right is a **cupola** that was built in 1922, which was also used as a fire lookout until 1934. Interpretive signs near the cupola identify the many dramatic peaks before you: Broken Top, South and North Sister, Belknap

Crater, Mount Washington, Three Fingered Jack, Mount Jefferson, and—on a clear day—Mount Hood and Mount Adams to the far north.

Return the way you came.

DIRECTIONS

From Sisters, head west on U.S. 20 for 6 miles. Turn right onto Forest Road 11, just past milepost 95, following signs for Indian Ford Campground. After 3.8 miles, head left at the fork to drive uphill on Forest Road 1110. After another 4 miles, take a sharp right to stay on Forest Road 1110. From here, it's 1.2 rough and rutted miles to the trailhead at road's end. Low-clearance vehicles can handle the terrain but should proceed cautiously.

GPS COORDINATES: 44.39502, –121.64777 / N44° 23.7012′ W121° 38.8662′

BEST NEARBY BREWS

While the town of Sisters is closer, since you just hiked Black Butte, head a bit farther to Bend for a thematic pairing: Cool off with a Black Butte Porter at **Deschutes Brewery Bend Public House** (1044 NW Bond St., Bend, 541/382-9242, www.deschutesbrewery.com, 11am-10pm Sun.-Thurs., 11am-11pm Fri.-Sat.), the region's oldest brewery. From the trailhead, the 39-mile drive southeast takes an hour via U.S. 20.

Tam-a-láu Trail

THE COVE PALISADES STATE PARK

🦌 ❀ 🐾

Hike to a juniper- and sage-covered plateau overlooking the Deschutes River, Crooked River, and Lake Billy Chinook, not to mention Cascade peaks and other landforms.

DISTANCE: 7.1 miles round-trip
DURATION: 3.5 hours
ELEVATION CHANGE: 790 feet
EFFORT: Easy/moderate
TRAIL: Dirt trail, paved path, wooden steps, rocks
USERS: Hikers, leashed dogs
SEASON: March-November
PASSES/FEES: $5 day-use fee per vehicle
MAPS: Oregon State Parks map for The Cove Palisades State Park, available online and at both campground registration stations in the park
PARK HOURS: Sunrise-sunset daily
CONTACT: Oregon State Parks, 541/546-3412, www.oregonstateparks.org

START THE HIKE

Save this hike for a cool or cloudy day, and get an early start if possible, because it's quite exposed. Wear sunscreen and bring plenty of water.

▶ MILE 0-0.4: Parking Lot to Tam-a-láu Trailhead

Start your hike at the northeastern edge of the parking lot, following the Tam-a-láu Trail sign. You'll hike through a forest of juniper and pine before crossing an unnamed road in 0.4 mile. Shortly after, cross Southwest Jordan Road and pass through a small opening in the fence line to arrive at the official **Tam-a-láu Trailhead,** at the southern end of **Deschutes Campground.** (If you're camping, you can start from here and shave this opening mileage off the hike.)

VIEW FROM THE SUMMIT OF TAM-A-LÁU ▶

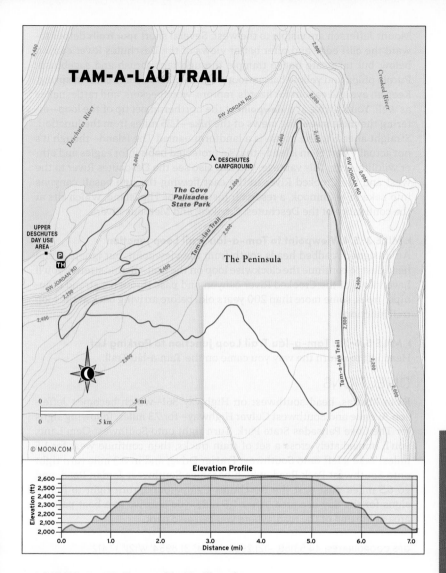

TAM-A-LÁU TRAIL

Elevation Profile

▶ **MILE 0.4-1.75: Tam-a-láu Trailhead to Tam-a-láu Trail Loop Junction**

Over the next 0.75 mile, you'll gain 450 feet as you switchback up and occasionally climb wooden stairs, with little shade. Along the way, you'll notice several boulders dotting the trail. The word "Tam-a-láu" comes from a Native American phrase that translates to "place of big rocks on the ground," and these are the namesake boulders. In 0.6 mile, you'll have gained most of the hike's elevation as you arrive at the Y-shaped junction for the **Tam-a-láu Trail Loop.**

▶ **MILE 1.75-3: Tam-a-láu Trail Loop Junction to Viewpoint**

Head left to begin a 3.6-mile clockwise loop around **The Peninsula,** as the summit of this lava plateau is known. On a clear day, the Three Sisters and

Mount Jefferson are visible to the west. Several short **spur trails** detour toward the cliff edge and offer better views of the Deschutes River canyon below, but take care not to trample through rabbitbrush and sagebrush. Purple phlox and yellow balsamroot give the plateau some color in spring. Keep an eye and ear out for lizards, raptors, woodpeckers, and rattlesnakes as well. You'll arrive at a **viewpoint** at the northernmost tip of the loop—offering the most sweeping views of the hike—1.25 miles from the junction. Straight ahead, to the north, is a landform named The Island—though it's not actually part of an island—that's a protected habitat for eagles and other wildlife. From this vantage, you can also see the Deschutes River to the west and the Crooked River to the east flowing through basalt canyons into Lake Billy Chinook, a reservoir just north of The Island, which sits at the confluence of the Deschutes, Crooked, and Metolius Rivers.

▶ **MILE 3-5.4: Viewpoint to Tam-a-láu Trail Loop Junction**
An unsigned roadbed heads south from the viewpoint, but ignore it and head east to continue the clockwise loop on the trail. On this stretch, you'll have views of the Crooked River canyon and pass through a strand of juniper trees, some more than 200 years old, before arriving back at the loop trail junction.

▶ **MILE 5.4-7.1: Tam-a-láu Trail Loop Junction to Parking Lot**
Head left to return the way you came on the Tam-a-láu Trail.

DIRECTIONS

From Madras, head southwest on Highway 361—which becomes Jefferson Avenue and Southwest Culver Highway—for 7.3 miles, following signs for The Cove Palisades State Park. Turn right onto Southwest Gem Lane; you'll immediately cross a set of train tracks, then continue west for 1.5 miles. Take a left onto Southwest Frazier Drive, and in 0.3 mile turn right onto Southwest Peck Road, which becomes Southwest Jordan Road, and go 6.5 miles. Just past the Deschutes Campground, turn right to follow signs for the day-use area. After 0.6 mile, you'll arrive at a boat parking area at the end of the road, where you can also park.

GPS COORDINATES: 44.53159, –121.2902 / N44° 31.8954′ W121° 17.412′

BEST NEARBY BITES

Enjoy fresh and healthy fare at **Great Earth Café & Market** (46 SW D St., Madras, 541/475-1500, www.greatearthcafemarket.com, 7am-6pm Mon.-Fri., 10am-3pm Sat.). It serves light breakfast items, fresh and filling sandwiches, soups, salads, and more. From the trailhead, the 15-mile drive northeast takes 30 minutes via Southwest Jordan Road and Highway 361.

Smith Rock is one of Oregon's most popular state parks for good reason, and views of its jagged formations and Cascade peaks are just some of the highlights of this hike.

BEST: Fall Hikes, Dog-Friendly Hikes

DISTANCE: 4.2 miles round-trip

DURATION: 2.5 hours

ELEVATION CHANGE: 880 feet

EFFORT: Easy/moderate

TRAIL: Dirt trail, paved path, wooden stairs, boardwalk

USERS: Hikers, leashed dogs, mountain bikers, horseback riders

SEASON: Year-round

PASSES/FEES: $5 day-use fee per vehicle

MAPS: Oregon State Parks map for Smith Rock State Park, available online and at pay stations in the park

PARK HOURS: Dawn-dusk daily

CONTACT: Oregon State Parks, 541/548-7501, www.oregonstateparks.org

Smith Rock's formations first took shape some 30 million years ago following prolonged periods of volcanic activity in the area. Basalt lava flows then poured into the region 500,000 years ago, and the Crooked River gradually eroded and sculpted the surrounding landscape—creating the rock formations you're exploring today.

START THE HIKE

▶ **MILE 0-0.5: Smith Rock Welcome Center to Crooked River Bridge**
Start hiking from the trailhead near the pay station just northeast of the **Smith Rock Welcome Center.** Follow the path, turning right at the T-shaped junction onto the **Rim Rock Trail.** In another few hundred feet, take a left at the junction to start descending on the **Canyon Trail.** You'll encounter intersections with numerous other trails on the short way down, but keep following the well-signed Canyon Trail toward the river. (You could opt to take the Chute Trail that appears to your right soon after you begin your descent, cutting 0.6 mile off the round-trip trek, but it's steeper and less scenic.) Cross over the **Crooked River bridge** at 0.5 mile.

▶ **MILE 0.5-1.8: Crooked River Bridge to Misery Ridge Summit**
At this junction, continue straight, climbing a few stone steps and beginning to ascend via the **Misery Ridge Trail,** on which you'll gain 580 feet over the next 0.6 mile, along with progressively better views of the Crooked River snaking its way through the khaki-colored canyon—and of rock

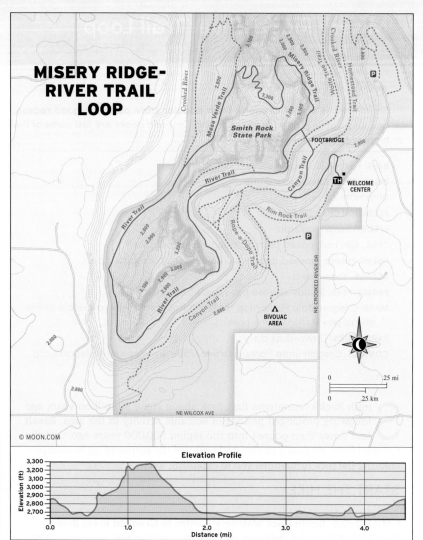

MISERY RIDGE-RIVER TRAIL LOOP

Smith Rock State Park

Crooked River

Mesa Verde Trail

Misery Ridge Trail

Wolf Tree Trail

Crooked River

Homestead Trail

FOOTBRIDGE

River Trail

River Trail

Canyon Trail

Rim Rock Trail

Rope-a-Dope Trail

TH WELCOME CENTER

NE CROOKED RIVER DR

Canyon Trail

BIVOUAC AREA

NE WILCOX AVE

© MOON.COM

0   .25 mi
0   .25 km

Elevation Profile

Elevation (ft)

3,300
3,200
3,100
3,000
2,900
2,800
2,700

0.0   1.0   2.0   3.0   4.0

Distance (mi)

climbers attempting some of the park's routes. Loose gravel dominates much of the upper Misery Ridge Trail, so watch your step. After another 0.7 mile of steady, strenuous climbing, you'll arrive at the **Misery Ridge summit.** Just left off the trail is a **viewpoint** with sweeping vistas of the surrounding rock formations and Central Oregon farmland.

▶ **MILE 1.8–2.2: Misery Ridge Summit to Monkey Face**

Head right to continue on the Misery Ridge Trail. In a few hundred feet, you'll arrive on the summit's western bluff, which has views of the Three Sisters, Broken Top, Mount Bachelor, Black Butte, and Mount Washington. On a clear day, you can see all the way north to Mount Hood. Continue on the trail for 0.3 mile, then pause to enjoy an up-close encounter with **Monkey Face,** one of Smith Rock's most iconic formations.

▶ **MILE 2.2–3.7: Monkey Face to Crooked River Bridge**

After taking a few photos, head left at the intersection onto the **Mesa Verde Trail,** following it as it drops 615 feet to the riverbank. The Mesa Verde Trail meets up with the **River Trail** after 0.4 mile. Continue straight to follow the River Trail for 1.1 miles, alongside the Crooked River and occasionally over short stretches of wooden boardwalk. Keep an eye out along this stretch for beavers, river otters, prairie falcons, and other wildlife. At the height of summer, watch out for rattlesnakes.

▶ **MILE 3.7–4.2: Crooked River Bridge to Smith Rock Trailhead**

Back at the bridge you initially crossed, head right and up the **Canyon Trail** to return the way you came.

SMITH ROCK STATE PARK ▶

DIRECTIONS

From Redmond, head north on U.S. 97 for 5.7 miles, then turn right to head east on Smith Rock Way, following signs for Smith Rock State Park. After 1.5 miles, turn left onto Northeast 17th Street. Continue for 0.5 mile before turning right at a T-shaped junction onto Northeast Wilcox Avenue. Continue for 0.5 mile, then turn left at the sign for Smith Rock State Park onto Northeast Crooked River Drive. Follow this road north for about 0.5 mile before arriving at the first of Smith Rock's numerous parking areas. The Smith Rock Welcome Center, housed in a green yurt, sits 0.1 mile past the first parking area along the western edge of Northeast Crooked River Drive, between a restroom and pay station.

GPS COORDINATES: 44.3668, –121.13617 / N44° 22.008' W121° 8.1702'

BEST NEARBY BREWS

Wild Ride Brewing (332 SW 5th St., Redmond, 541/516-8544, www. wildridebrew.com, 11am–10pm daily) pours more than a dozen beers and hosts a large outdoor seating area, several fire pits, and on-site food carts. From the trailhead, the 10-mile drive south takes 15 minutes via Northeast Smith Rock Way and U.S. 97.

If the ascent doesn't take your breath away, the views will: Mount Bachelor, Broken Top, and other peaks rise around Tumalo Mountain's open summit.

BEST: Brew Hikes
DISTANCE: 4.4 miles round-trip
DURATION: 2.5 hours
ELEVATION CHANGE: 1,340 feet
EFFORT: Moderate
TRAIL: Dirt trail, rocks, roots
USERS: Hikers, leashed dogs (May–Oct.)
SEASON: June–October
PASSES/FEES: None
MAPS: USGS topographic map for Mount Bachelor
CONTACT: Deschutes National Forest, 541/383-4000, www.fs.usda.gov

START THE HIKE

This hike is mostly shaded for the first 0.8 mile, and then not at all thereafter, so aim for a morning hike, wear sunscreen, and bring plenty of water. Note that the trail can also be quite dusty summer-early fall.

▶ **MILE 0–0.9: Tumalo Mountain Trailhead to Meadows**
You'll find the **Tumalo Mountain Trailhead** near a vault toilet at the northwestern edge of the Dutchman Flat Sno-Park parking lot. Almost immediately you'll come upon an unmarked intersection—the path that parallels the highway here is reserved for mountain bikers, so continue straight ahead to begin your steady ascent. The trail switchbacks five times over the first 0.6 mile, during which you'll gain 375 feet as you hike through a forest of ponderosa pine and mountain hemlock. In another 0.3 mile, you'll leave the forest for exposed meadows, dotted with lodgepole pine and whitebark pine. Keep an eye out for purple lupine, Davidson's penstemon, red paintbrush, and other wildflowers, which bloom well into July.

▶ **MILE 0.9–2.1: Meadows to Tumalo Mountain Summit**
In 0.25 mile, take a moment to turn around and appreciate your first views of Mount Bachelor to the west. After 0.9 mile more of steady ascent, you'll encounter a series of eight switchbacks that conclude at the **Tumalo Mountain summit.**

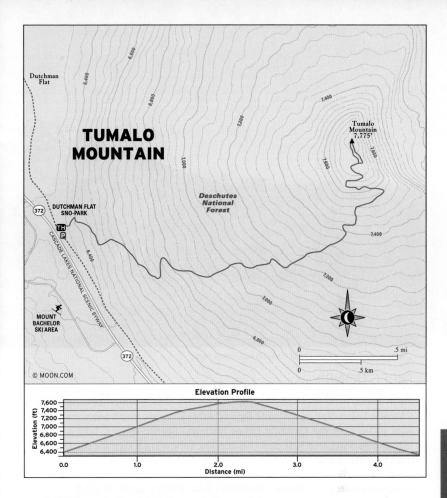

Elevation Profile

▶ MILE 2.1–2.3: Tumalo Mountain Summit Loop

Red cinder rocks denote the 0.25-mile **loop trail** around the summit that affords views in every direction. Stay within these cinder rocks, and resist the urge to follow the social trails on the northern flank; Tumalo Mountain is a protected habitat for wildflowers and wildlife, including deer and elk. Head right to start the loop and, after several hundred feet, you'll pass the concrete pilings of a long-gone **fire lookout.** From here, you can see Bend and the community of Sunriver to the east. Farther along, enjoy unimpeded views of Broken Top, as well as North and Middle Sister, at the loop's northernmost point. As you make your way back to the main trail, Mount Bachelor towers over its surroundings to the west.

▶ MILE 2.3–4.4: Tumalo Mountain Summit
to Tumalo Mountain Trailhead

Back at the junction, return 2.1 miles the way you came.

▲ MOUNT BACHELOR VIEW FROM TUMALO MOUNTAIN TRAIL

DIRECTIONS

From Bend, head west on Southwest Century Drive, which becomes the Cascade Lakes National Scenic Byway. After 17 miles, you'll see a roadside sign promoting the Cascade Lakes National Scenic Byway; take a right into the parking area just past this marker, following a sign for the Dutchman Flat Sno-Park.

GPS COORDINATES: 44.00004, –121.66371 / N44° 0.0024' W121° 39.8226'

BEST NEARBY BREWS

Enjoy more views of Cascade peaks at **Crux Fermentation Project** (50 SW Division St., Bend, 541/385-3333, www.cruxfermentation.com, 11am-10pm Sun.-Thurs., 11am-11pm Fri.-Sat. summer, call for hours fall-spring), which has a large outdoor seating area and nearly 25 taps. From the trailhead, the 21-mile drive east takes 25 minutes via the Cascade Lakes National Scenic Byway.

Hike this loop trail through a ponderosa pine forest, largely along the canyon walls above Tumalo Creek, just minutes from downtown Bend.

DISTANCE: 4.8 miles round-trip
DURATION: 2 hours
ELEVATION CHANGE: 250 feet
EFFORT: Easy
TRAIL: Dirt trail, rocks, roots
USERS: Hikers, wheelchair users, leashed dogs, mountain bikers
SEASON: March–November
PASSES/FEES: None
MAPS: Bend Parks and Recreation District map for Shevlin Park
PARK HOURS: 5am-10pm daily
CONTACT: Bend Parks and Recreation District, 541/389-7275, www.bendparksandrec.org

START THE HIKE

▶ **MILE 0-0.2: Parking Area to Shevlin Loop Trail**
Walk through the entry gate at the southern edge of the parking area. Just past the gate, turn left, following a sign for Aspen Meadow and the Tumalo Creek Trail. In 0.1 mile, head left at an unsigned junction onto the **Tumalo Creek Trail.** In another few hundred feet, continue straight at the four-way junction—you'll encounter numerous junctions on this hike, but they're typically well signed—to proceed on the **Shevlin Loop Trail,** crossing a footbridge over the creek.

▶ **MILE 0.2-2.7: Shevlin Loop Trail to Tumalo Creek**
High desert plant life abounds as you gently ascend to the canyon rim, following its mostly flat edge southwest on this clockwise loop. Continue straight at a four-way intersection in 0.8 mile to remain on the Shevlin Loop Trail, which joins with an **unnamed road** in about 0.1 mile. Head right onto the roadbed and continue for 0.25 mile, then turn right at a sign for the Shevlin Loop to return to the single-track trail. Continue on this flat stretch for 0.7 mile before heading right at a junction and then, in about 0.2 mile at a map signboard, straight, to continue on the trail. You'll ascend 75 feet over the next 0.4 mile before descending toward **Tumalo Creek** and crossing it via wooden bridge. Admire its crystal-clear waters from a shaded bench to your right.

▶ **MILE 2.7-4.3: Tumalo Creek to Fremont Road Trail**
A couple hundred feet after crossing the creek, you'll arrive at a five-way junction; veer left—but not hard left—continuing on the Shevlin Loop Trail

BEND AND THE CENTRAL OREGON CASCADES

Shevlin Park Loop

and beginning to loop back northeast. At another junction in another couple hundred feet, continue right to remain on the trail through an arid stretch of ponderosa pine. In 1.4 miles you'll arrive at a four-way intersection; here the trail crosses paths with the Historic Shevlin Railway Trail. Veer to the right just past the railway sign to remain on the loop trail. In another few hundred feet, you'll arrive at an X-shaped junction. Head right toward the **Fremont Road Trail**—which you'll reach in 0.1 mile—that bisects Shevlin Park.

▶ MILE 4.3-4.8: Fremont Road Trail to Parking Area

Closed whenever summertime fire danger is high, this paved road cuts through a forest that burned in a 2015 human-caused fire, giving hikers an up-close look at the effects of wildfire. Underbrush is rare, though stray stands of pine are flourishing. Continue north for 0.5 mile along this accessible road to return to the parking area.

DIRECTIONS

From Bend, head west on Northwest Newport Avenue, which becomes Northwest Shevlin Park Road after 1.6 miles and a handful of roundabouts. Continue on Northwest Shevlin Park Road for 2.3 miles, and turn left into the Shevlin Park parking area, just past Tumalo Creek.

GPS COORDINATES: 44.08316, –121.37791 / N44° 4.9896′ W121° 22.6746′

BRIDGE OVER TUMALO CREEK ▶

BEST NEARBY BREWS

GoodLife Brewing Company (70 SW Century Dr., Bend, 541/728-0749, www.goodlifebrewing.com, noon–10pm daily) pays tribute to the "good life" in Bend with outdoors-inspired beers, locally sourced fare, and a seasonal beer garden on the lawn. From the trailhead, the 4-mile drive southeast takes 10 minutes via Northwest Shevlin Park Road and Southwest Century Drive.

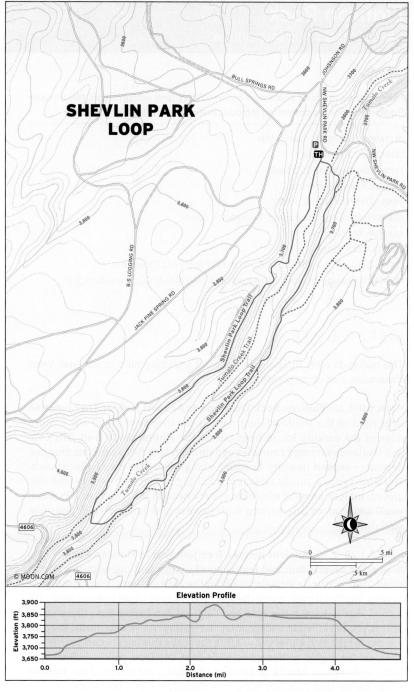

SHEVLIN PARK LOOP

BULL SPRINGS RD

JOHNSNON RD

NW SHEVLIN PARK RD

NW SHEVLIN PARK RD

Tumalo Creek

B-S LOGGING RD

JACK PINE SPRING RD

Shevlin Park Loop Trail

Tumalo Creek Trail

Shevlin Park Loop Trail

Tumalo Creek

4606

4606

© MOON.COM

0   .5 mi

0   .5 km

Elevation Profile

Elevation (ft)	Distance (mi)

3,900
3,850
3,800
3,750
3,700
3,650

0.0   1.0   2.0   3.0   4.0

OREGON BADLANDS WILDERNESS

Formed thousands of years ago by lava flows and volcanic ash, the Oregon Badlands offer a captivating introduction to the state's high desert.

DISTANCE: 6.3 miles round-trip
DURATION: 2.75 hours
ELEVATION CHANGE: 220 feet
EFFORT: Easy/moderate
TRAIL: Dirt trail, sand, rocks
USERS: Hikers, leashed dogs, horseback riders
SEASON: Year-round
PASSES/FEES: None
MAPS: BLM map for Oregon Badlands Wilderness Overview
CONTACT: Bureau of Land Management, 541/416-6700, www.blm.gov

START THE HIKE

The badlands offer little shade, so avoid a midday hike in summer, wear sunscreen, and bring plenty of water.

▸ **MILE 0-1.25: Flatiron Rock Trailhead to Ancient Juniper Trail Junction**
Veer right at the trailhead, just next to the map board near the eastern edge of the parking lot, to head out on the **Flatiron Rock Trail.** The Oregon Badlands—formed centuries ago through lava flows and volcanic ash deposits—expand in every direction along this wide, mostly flat stretch. You'll also pass a steady stream of knee-high sagebrush bushes and old-growth juniper, some of which dates back nearly 1,000 years. At 1.25 miles, you'll arrive at an intersection with the Ancient Juniper Trail. Continue straight.

▸ **MILE 1.25-2.75: Ancient Juniper Trail Junction to Flatiron Rock**
In another several hundred feet is another intersection, with the Homestead Trail; continue straight again on the Flatiron Rock Trail. You'll pass several unofficial trails along the way, and it's easy to get lost out here—it's a good idea to have a compass and GPS—so don't stray onto these spurs unless you're skilled in backcountry navigation. As you continue, keep an eye out for the rich variety of wildlife that calls this area home: prairie falcons, golden eagles, rattlesnakes, mule deer, antelope, yellow-bellied marmots, and various lizards. In another 1.5 miles, your destination—**Flatiron Rock**—comes into view, towering over the surrounding landscape.

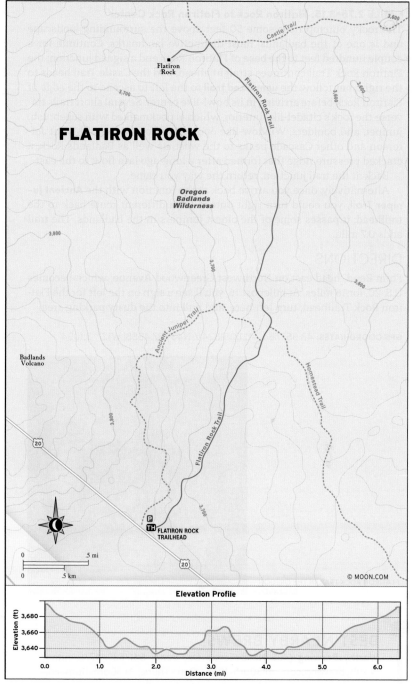

FLATIRON ROCK

Flatiron
Rock

Castle Trail

Flatiron Rock Trail

Oregon
Badlands
Wilderness

3,700

3,800

Badlands
Volcano

Ancient Juniper Trail

3,800

Homestead Trail

Flatiron Rock Trail

3,700

20

0   .5 mi
0   .5 km

P
TH FLATIRON ROCK
TRAILHEAD

20

© MOON.COM

Elevation Profile

Elevation (ft)

3,680 –
3,660 –
3,640 –

0.0   1.0   2.0   3.0   4.0   5.0   6.0
Distance (mi)

▶ **MILE 2.75–3.15: Flatiron Rock to Flatiron Rock Center**

The rocky outcrop rises some 50 feet above the surrounding landscape and is one of the badlands' most distinctive landmarks. Continue for a couple hundred feet to the base of Flatiron Rock and a signed junction; the Flatiron Rock Trail continues straight ahead, and the Castle Trail heads to the right, but follow the **unmarked trail** to the left to ascend to the edge of Flatiron Rock before arriving in its bowl-like center. Several short trails traverse the rock's citadel-like interior, which is pockmarked with sagebrush, juniper, and boulders. Window-like openings afford views of Mount Jefferson and other Cascade peaks to the west, as well as Badlands Rock, a cracked pressure ridge that formed after a long-ago lava flow, to the east.

Back at the trail junction, return the way you came.

Alternatively, once you arrive back at the junction with the **Ancient Juniper Trail,** you could turn right onto it for a different route back to the trailhead; it passes some of the oldest junipers in the badlands. The trail adds 0.7 mile.

DIRECTIONS

From Bend, head east on Northwest Greenwood Avenue, which becomes U.S. 20, for 16 miles. At milepost 16, you'll see a sign on the left for the Flatiron Rock Trailhead; turn left here, and pull into the dusty parking area.

GPS COORDINATES: 43.957764, –121.051824 / N43° 57.4658' W121° 3.1094'

FLATIRON ROCK TRAIL IN THE OREGON
BADLANDS ▶

BEST NEARBY BREWS

Worthy Brewing (495 NE Bellevue Dr., Bend, 541/639-4776, http://worthybrewing.com, 11:30am–10pm Sun.–Thurs., 11:30am–11pm Fri.–Sat.) offers a variety of hoppy beers and locally sourced food, plenty of outdoor seating, and an observatory, complete with a telescope for post-sunset stargazing. From the trailhead, the 13-mile drive west takes 15 minutes via U.S. 20.

Paulina Peak

NEWBERRY NATIONAL VOLCANIC MONUMENT,
DESCHUTES NATIONAL FOREST

Hike to the highest point within the Newberry National Volcanic Monument
and enjoy expansive views of Central Oregon's volcanic legacy.

DISTANCE: 4.7 miles round-trip

DURATION: 2.5 hours

ELEVATION CHANGE: 1,340 feet

EFFORT: Moderate

TRAIL: Dirt trail, rocky stretches, exposed roots, sand, gravel

USERS: Hikers, leashed dogs

SEASON: June–October

PASSES/FEES: $5 day-use fee or $10 three-day pass per vehicle, or Northwest
Forest Pass

MAPS: USGS topographic map for Paulina Peak

CONTACT: Deschutes National Forest, 541/383-5700, www.fs.usda.gov

This trail sits entirely within the Newberry Volcano, the largest volcano
in the Cascade Range—at 1,200 square miles, the monument's geologic
features cover an area the size of Rhode Island. Repeated eruptions over
400,000 years gave Newberry Volcano its shield-like shape, and a major
explosion 75,000 years ago left behind a caldera.

START THE HIKE

▶ **MILE 0–1.1: Crater Rim–Paulina Peak Trailhead to Viewpoint**
Start the hike on the east side of Paulina Peak Road at the **Crater Rim and
Paulina Peak Trailhead.** Two lakes sit within Newberry Volcano's caldera, and you'll catch your first glimpse of one—Paulina Lake—through the
trees after 0.6 mile of steady ascent on the **Crater Rim Trail.** Over the next
0.4 mile, you'll gain 620 feet via a few switchbacks. Look west for your
first views of the Three Sisters and Mount Bachelor. In 0.1 mile, as the trail
curves northeast, you'll arrive at a **viewpoint,** to your left. Look north for
your first glimpse of East Lake, the other lake in the caldera; northeast for
the Big Obsidian Flow, a massive lava flow of gray pumice and shiny, black
obsidian; and southeast for Paulina Peak, sitting atop the Newberry caldera's steep slopes.

▶ **MILE 1.1–2: Viewpoint to Paulina Peak Trail**
You'll trade mountain hemlock for whitebark pine in another 0.7 mile,
leaving the shade behind but gaining spectacular views of Paulina Lake
behind you. Another 0.2 mile on, a clearing to your left reveals grand
views of the Three Sisters, Mount Bachelor, and Deschutes National Forest. Shortly after, head left at the junction onto the **Paulina Peak Trail.**

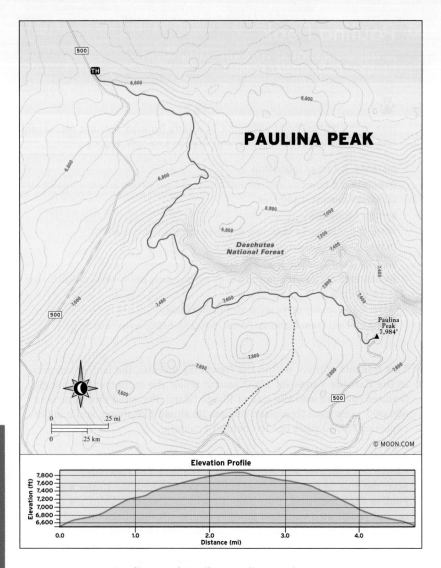

PAULINA PEAK

Deschutes
National Forest

Paulina
Peak
7,984'

© MOON.COM

Elevation Profile

▶ **MILE 2-2.35: Paulina Peak Trail to Paulina Peak**

In 0.25 mile, you'll start walking through sand and obsidian, and arrive at an unsigned Y-shaped junction; going in either direction takes you to the summit, but the right-hand trail is well graded and spares you a nerve-racking trek alongside the cliff edges. In a couple hundred feet, you'll arrive at the parking lot atop **Paulina Peak**—yes, you could have driven to this view, but where's the fun in that? At 7,984 feet, this is the highest point on Newberry Volcano. At the western edge of the parking lot, find and hike the short trail that heads up rocky terrain for slightly better views that include Broken Top and Mount Jefferson.

Return the way you came.

▲ BIG OBSIDIAN FLOW

DIRECTIONS

From Sunriver, head south on U.S. 97 for 8.7 miles. Take a left to head east onto Paulina Lake Road, following a sign for the Newberry Caldera and Paulina and East Lakes. Continue straight on this road for 11.3 miles, at which point you'll arrive at a staffed check-in station. Continue straight, and take a right after another 1.7 miles onto Paulina Peak Road, at a sign for the Paulina Lake Campground. The road turns from pavement to gravel in 0.4 mile, and trailhead parking is on the right after another 0.3 mile.

GPS COORDINATES: 43.7009, –121.2727 / N43° 42.054' W121° 16.362'

BEST NEARBY BREWS

Sunriver Brewing Company (57100 Beaver Dr., Bldg. 4, Sunriver, 541/593-3007, www.sunriverbrewingcompany.com, 11am-10pm Sun.-Thurs., 11am-11pm Fri.-Sat.) prides itself on award-winning beer, regionally sourced fare, and a family-friendly atmosphere. From the trailhead, the 24-mile drive northwest takes 30 minutes via Paulina Lake Road and U.S. 97.

Paulina Peak

NEARBY CAMPGROUNDS

NAME	DESCRIPTION	FACILITIES	SEASON	FEE
The Cove Palisades State Park	popular park with two campgrounds near Lake Billy Chinook	Crooked River Campground: 88 electrical sites, restrooms; Deschutes Campground: 82 full-hookup sites, 91 tent sites, 3 group sites, restrooms	Crooked River Campground: February-December; Deschutes Campground: May-September	$20-97

SW Jordan Road, Culver, 541/546-3412, www.oregonstateparks.org

NAME	DESCRIPTION	FACILITIES	SEASON	FEE
Creekside Campground	bustling campground near downtown Sisters	27 full-hookup sites, 33 tent sites, hiker-biker area, restrooms	April-October	$5-45

U.S. 20, Sisters, 541/323-5218, www.ci.sisters.or.us

NAME	DESCRIPTION	FACILITIES	SEASON	FEE
Tumalo State Park	campground along the Deschutes River near Bend	23 full-hookup sites, 54 tent sites, 7 yurts, 2 group camping areas, restrooms	year-round	$8-77

O. B. Riley Road, Bend, 541/388-6055, www.oregonstateparks.org

NAME	DESCRIPTION	FACILITIES	SEASON	FEE
LaPine State Park	quiet sites in a subalpine pine forest	81 full-hookup sites, 48 electrical sites, 10 log cabins, restrooms	year-round	$26-99

off U.S. 97, La Pine, 541/536-2428, www.oregonstateparks.org

NAME	DESCRIPTION	FACILITIES	SEASON	FEE
Paulina Lake Campground	popular campground along the southwest shore of Paulina Lake	68 tent and RV sites, restrooms	May-September	$18

Paulina Lake Rd., La Pine, 541/383-5300, www.fs.usda.gov

JOHN DAY RIVER BASIN

The John Day River Basin is home to some of Oregon's most diverse geologic features. At its western edge, the Ochoco National Forest hosts forested mountaintops, alpine scenery, volcanic rock formations, and high prairie expanses. Farther east along the John Day River are steep river canyons, rolling hills, and rocky terrain. But the John Day Fossil Beds National Monument, drawing more than 200,000 visitors annually, is the area's premier attraction. Volcanic eruptions and retreating glaciers scarred the landscape, which offers a glimpse into Oregon's geological past. Encompassing 14,000 acres, it holds fossils evidencing more than 40 million years of changing climates, ecosystems, and natural evolution, as well as the Painted Hills, famed for their surrealistic, colorful layers.

▲ VIEW FROM LOOKOUT MOUNTAIN

▲ WILDFLOWERS NEAR STEINS PILLAR

1 Steins Pillar
DISTANCE: 4.5 miles round-trip
DURATION: 2.25 hours
EFFORT: Easy/moderate

2 Lookout Mountain
DISTANCE: 7.7 miles round-trip
DURATION: 4 hours
EFFORT: Easy/moderate

3 Carroll Rim Trail
DISTANCE: 1.7 miles round-trip
DURATION: 1 hour
EFFORT: Easy

4 Sutton Mountain
DISTANCE: 7.5 miles round-trip
DURATION: 4 hours
EFFORT: Moderate

5 Blue Basin Overlook
DISTANCE: 3.4 miles round-trip
DURATION: 1.75 hours
EFFORT: Easy/moderate

▼ BLUE BASIN

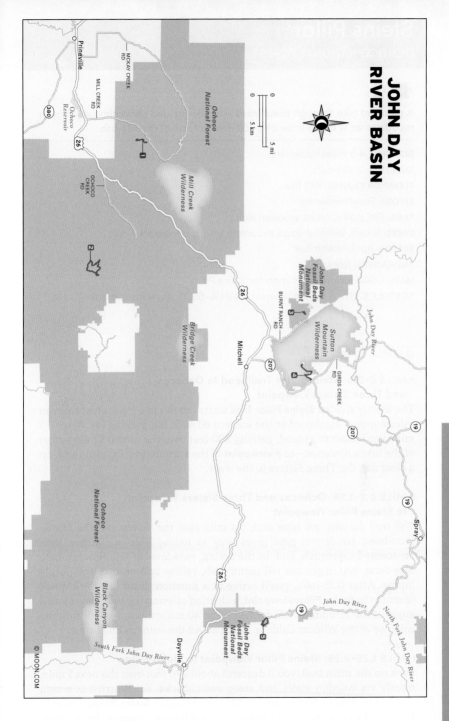

JOHN DAY
RIVER BASIN

© MOON.COM

Steins Pillar

OCHOCO NATIONAL FOREST

A pleasant hike through ponderosa pine forests and springtime wildflower meadows ends at the base of a 350-foot column of rhyolite ash.

DISTANCE: 4.5 miles round-trip
DURATION: 2.25 hours
ELEVATION CHANGE: 740 feet
EFFORT: Easy/moderate
TRAIL: Dirt paths, rocks, wooden stairs
USERS: Hikers, leashed dogs, mountain bikers, horseback riders
SEASON: April–November
PASSES/FEES: None
MAPS: USGS topographic map for Steins Pillar
CONTACT: Ochoco National Forest, 541/416-6500, www.fs.usda.gov

START THE HIKE

▶ **MILE 0-0.6: Steins Pillar Trailhead to Ochocos and Three Sisters Viewpoint**

The mostly shaded **Steins Pillar Trail** starts out flat in a pine forest from an informational signboard at the eastern edge of the parking lot. After 0.3 mile, you'll start to ascend, gaining 200 feet over the next 0.3 mile—most of the hike's elevation—to a **viewpoint** of the surrounding Ochocos and, on a clear day, the Three Sisters to the west.

▶ **MILE 0.6-1.25: Ochocos and Three Sisters Viewpoint to Steins Pillar Viewpoint**

The trail flattens out here and, 0.4 mile past the viewpoint, the cinnamon-hued ponderosa pine gives way to rolling hills of juniper, lemon-scented sagebrush, and, in the spring, meadows of wildflowers. Late May-June, you might see red paintbrush, yellow balsamroot, and purple lupine. After 0.25 mile, you'll arrive at a junction; head left for a quick jaunt to the **Steins Pillar viewpoint,** a clearing offering the best views you'll enjoy of the column, which formed some 40 million years ago during the collapse of the Wildcat Caldera, rising above the surrounding forest.

▶ **MILE 1.25-2.25: Steins Pillar Viewpoint to Steins Pillar**

Back on the main trail, you'll descend about 270 feet over the next 1 mile, mostly via wooden stairs and steep switchbacks. You'll arrive at a sign that reads "End of Maintained Trail" at the base of **Steins Pillar.** The trail peters out to gravel and rock here; take care because even in dry weather it can be slippery (the ground slopes toward the pillar's base). In sunnier months, you might see rock climbers ascending the column.

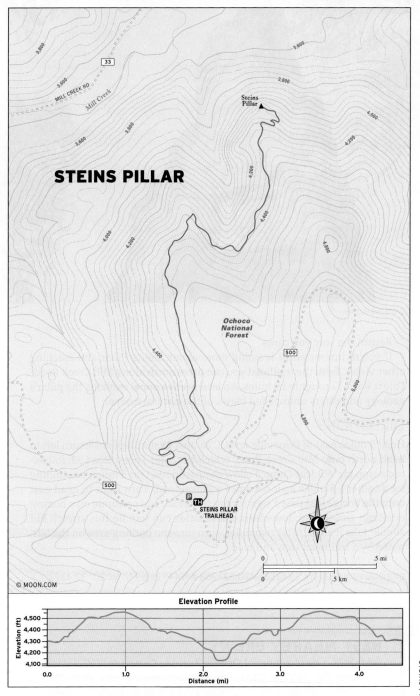

STEINS PILLAR

Steins
Pillar

MILL CREEK RD

Mill Creek

33

Ochoco
National
Forest

500

500

P TH
STEINS PILLAR
TRAILHEAD

© MOON.COM

3,800
3,800
3,800
3,600
3,800
3,800
3,600
4,200
4,200
4,400
4,000
4,200
4,800
4,400
4,400
4,600
4,800
5,000

0   .5 mi
0   .5 km

Elevation Profile

Elevation (ft)

4,500
4,400
4,300
4,200
4,100

0.0   1.0   2.0   3.0   4.0
Distance (mi)

▲ STEINS PILLAR

Return the way you came.

If you're interested in learning more about Steins Pillar and catching other views, from the trailhead you can drive north along Mill Creek Road/Forest Road 33 roughly 1.5 miles. An **interpretive panel** explains the pillar's geology and offers unimpeded views of the natural marvel.

DIRECTIONS

Head 9 miles east of Prineville on U.S. 26. Just past milepost 28, turn left to head north onto Mill Creek Road, which becomes Forest Road 33, following a sign for Wildcat Camp. Follow the paved road for 5 miles, continuing for another 1.5 miles as it becomes a gravel road. Turn right to head east onto the bridge just past a sign for the trailhead, and continue on a bumpy, one-lane gravel road; low-clearance vehicles can handle this stretch but should take it slow. After two miles, turn into the parking area on the left, noted by a trailhead sign and map.

GPS COORDINATES: 44.394962, –120.623988 / N44° 23.6977' W120° 37.4393'

BEST NEARBY BREWS

Relax with a meal or beer at **Ochoco Brewing Company** (380 N. Main St., Prineville, 541/233-0883, http://ochocobrewing.com, 11am-9pm Mon.-Sat., 11am-8pm Sun.). Ochoco prides itself on sourcing most of the ingredients for its small-batch beers and food offerings from as close to Prineville as possible. From the trailhead, the 16-mile drive west via U.S. 26 takes just under 30 minutes.

This clockwise loop trail offers something for everyone: wildflowers, Cascade peaks, alpine forests, wildlife, meadows, and vistas.

DISTANCE: 7.7 miles round-trip

DURATION: 4 hours

ELEVATION CHANGE: 1,130 feet

EFFORT: Easy/moderate

TRAIL: Dirt paths, rocky paths, minor stream crossing

USERS: Hikers, leashed dogs, mountain bikers, horseback riders

SEASON: May–November

PASSES/FEES: None

MAPS: USGS topographic maps for Lookout Mountain and Gerow Butte

CONTACT: Ochoco National Forest, 541/416-6500, www.fs.usda.gov

START THE HIKE

▶ **MILE 0-2.6: Independent Mine Trailhead to Brush Creek**

Head to the east side of the parking area to the **Independent Mine Trailhead.** Blue diamonds indicating the route to the summit are nailed to trees every hundred or so feet, just above eye level; should you sidestep a downed tree or go off-trail to avoid an early-season snow drift, keep an eye out for these blazes. Traveling southeast on the trail, you'll quickly encounter a forest rich with ponderosa pine and grand fir trees. In spring, you may hear the high-pitched call of the hermit thrush or rapid-fire drumbeat of the pileated woodpecker. After 1.2 miles and 400 feet of elevation gain, you'll find yourself in ponderosa pine and sagebrush meadows. In the late spring and early summer, a variety of wildflowers line the way, including bigleaf lupine, arrowleaf balsamroot, yellow bells, and sand lilies. You'll lose about 100 feet of elevation over the next 1.4 miles, cutting through a mix of sagebrush-covered meadows and subalpine fir forests. Keep an eye out for hummingbirds, elk, deer, and wild horses—the U.S. Forest Service estimated in 2018 that 135 wild horses call the region home.

▶ **MILE 2.6-4.5: Brush Creek to Lookout Mountain Summit**

Hop a few rocks to cross the bubbling **Brush Creek,** and then begin steadily ascending toward the summit, cutting through large swaths of fir trees broken up by frequent meadows—covered with mountain bluebells, false hellebore, and other wildflowers in spring and summer—and offering views of the Ochocos to the south. You'll arrive at an unsigned junction in another 1.3 miles; a spur trail shoots off to the left, but ignore it and continue straight, heading west on the Independent Mine Trail. As you follow the dirt trail, gradually heading north, the fir forests give way to a sagebrush-covered hillside. You'll gain 250 feet over the next 0.6 mile before arriving at a junction, and the **Lookout Mountain summit,** among the Ochocos' highest peaks.

▶ **MILE 4.5–5: Lookout Mountain Summit to Lookout Mountain Trail**
Head left on the short, unmarked trail to find the remnants of an **old stone corral,** which once formed the base of the fire lookout for which the mountain is named. On a clear day, this clearing offers the hike's best views, with the Three Sisters, Mount Bachelor, and other prominent Cascade peaks visible to the west. If the winds aren't whipping, this **viewpoint** makes a fine spot for lunch. Back at the junction, turn left to begin your descent, following the sign for the **Lookout Mountain Trail.** In another few hundred feet, you'll come to another junction—a short spur trail to the right leads to a backcountry snow shelter—but continue straight. In 0.3 mile, turn left at the junction to continue descending the Lookout Mountain Trail. (To shave a mile off the hike, you could instead continue straight here to head down the steeper, shorter, less scenic **Motherlode Trail.**)

▶ **MILE 5–7.7: Lookout Mountain Trail to Parking Area**
From here you'll steadily descend through aspen groves and pine forests as you loop back to the trailhead. After another 2.6 miles, you'll see abandoned **mining equipment** to your right. Several mines in the area opened in the early 1900s, but all had ceased operation by the 1950s; tempting as it may be, hikers should not leave the trail to explore these dilapidated structures. Just past the equipment, you'll arrive at an unsigned fork in the trail; head right to return to the parking area in a few hundred feet.

MINE SHAFT ▶

DIRECTIONS

Drive 15.5 miles east of Prineville on U.S. 26, and take a slight right onto Ochoco Creek Road at a sign for Walton Lake. Continue straight for 8.5 miles before taking a right onto Forest Road 42 for 6.5 miles. Turn right onto Forest Road 4205, following signs for Independent Mine. Take the gravel road for 1.5 miles (low-clearance vehicles should take it slow, especially over the last mile), continuing straight at the junction and ignoring signs for the Baneberry Trailhead. The road ends in the trailhead parking area.

GPS COORDINATES: 44.33934, –120.35832 / N44° 20.3604′ W120° 21.4992′

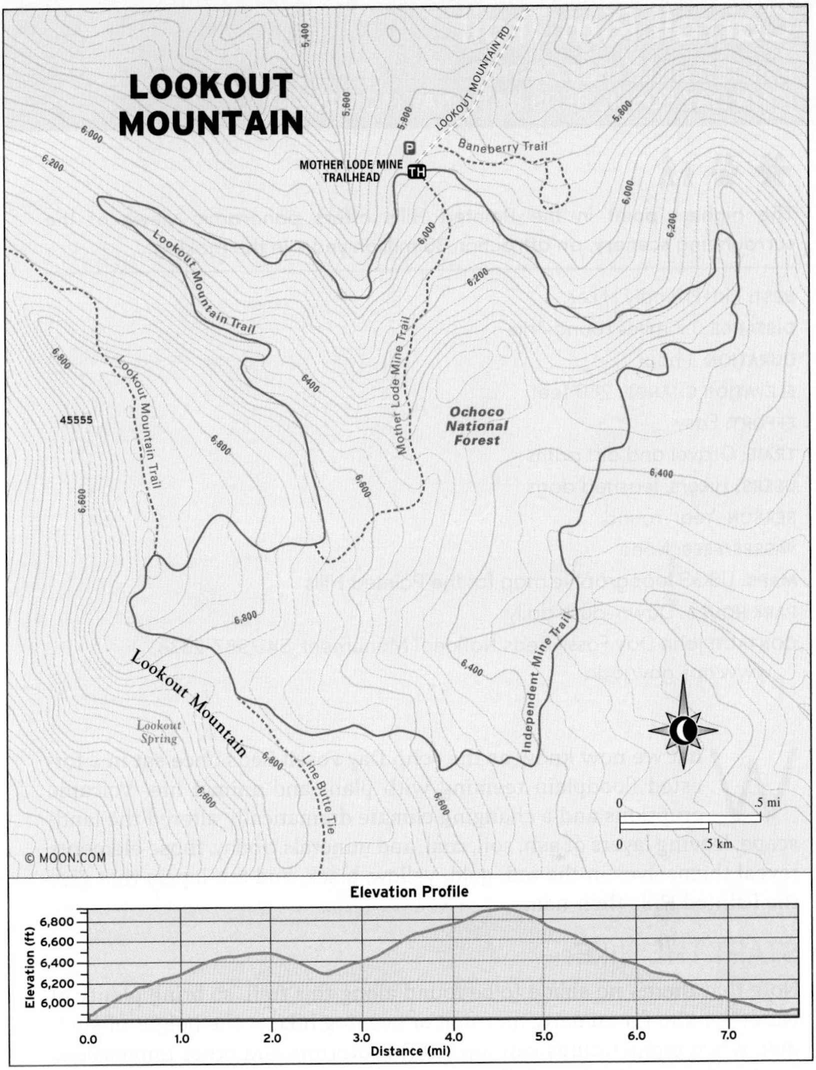

LOOKOUT
MOUNTAIN

LOOKOUT MOUNTAIN RD
Baneberry Trail

MOTHER LODE MINE
TRAILHEAD

P
TH

Lookout Mountain Trail

Mother Lode Mine Trail

Ochoco
National
Forest

45555

Lookout Mountain Trail

Lookout Mountain

Lookout
Spring

Independent Mine Trail

Line Butte Tie

© MOON.COM

6,000
6,200
6,400
6,600
6,800

5,400
5,600
5,800
6,000
6,200
6,400

0   .5 mi
0   .5 km

Elevation Profile

BEST NEARBY BITES

Dillon's Grill (142 NE 5th St., Prineville, 541/447-3203, www.dillons-grill.com, 11am-9pm Sun.-Thurs., 11am-10pm Fri.-Sat.) boasts a menu heavy on burgers and barbecue—with 13 regional craft beers and ciders on tap at any given time. From the trailhead, the 32-mile drive west takes one hour via Ochoco Creek Road and U.S. 26.

PAINTED HILLS UNIT OF THE
JOHN DAY FOSSIL BEDS NATIONAL MONUMENT

❀ 🐾 🚶

The highest point in the Painted Hills offers panoramic views of the surrounding scenery, an attraction 35 million years in the making.

BEST: Kid-Friendly Hikes
DISTANCE: 1.7 miles round-trip
DURATION: 1 hour
ELEVATION CHANGE: 260 feet
EFFORT: Easy
TRAIL: Gravel and dirt paths
USERS: Hikers, leashed dogs
SEASON: Year-round
PASSES/FEES: None
MAPS: USGS topographic map for the Painted Hills
PARK HOURS: Dawn–dusk daily
CONTACT: John Day Fossil Beds National Monument, 541/987-2333, www.nps.gov/joda

What we now know as the John Day Fossil Beds once sat in a forested floodplain teeming with plant and animal life. Volcanic eruptions and a changing climate dramatically altered the landscape, leaving layers of ash, soil, coal, and minerals. Today, those elements reveal themselves in the red, gold, yellow, black, and tan layers that give the Painted Hills their name.

START THE HIKE

Note that there's no shade to be found along this trail, so bring plenty of water—or aim for an early morning or evening hike at the height of summer, when temperatures can top 110°F. Footprints and other impressions can last for years in the soft clay, so take care not to go off-trail. Carroll Rim is the longest of the trails in the Painted Hills, but if you'd like to add more hiking to your day, four other trails in the unit, ranging 0.25-0.5 mile, are accessible via Bear Creek Road.

▶ **MILE 0-0.25: Carroll Rim Trailhead to Viewpoint**
Find the **Carroll Rim Trailhead** on the north side of Bear Creek Road from the small pullout parking area. You'll ascend steadily, slicing through an open hillside before arriving at a wooden bench and the trail's first **viewpoint** a bit less than 0.25 mile in. From here you can see the colorful hillsides to the south.

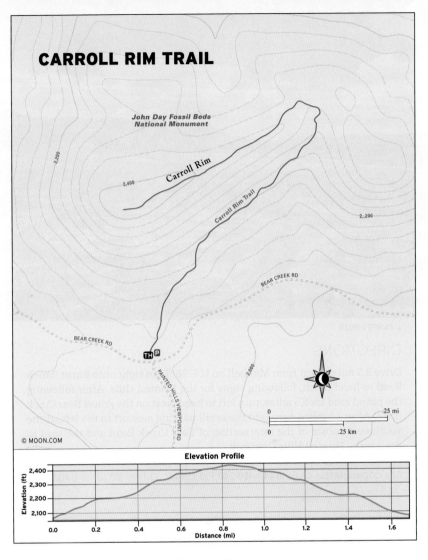

CARROLL RIM TRAIL

John Day Fossil Beds
National Monument

Carroll Rim

2,400

2,200

2,200

Carroll Rim Trail

BEAR CREEK RD

BEAR CREEK RD

TH P

PAINTED HILLS VIEWPOINT RD

2,000

© MOON.COM

0   .25 mi

0   .25 km

Elevation Profile

Elevation (ft): 2,400 / 2,300 / 2,200 / 2,100

Distance (mi): 0.0 / 0.2 / 0.4 / 0.6 / 0.8 / 1.0 / 1.2 / 1.4 / 1.6

▶ **MILE 0.25–0.85: Viewpoint to Summit**

Continue on—views keep improving as you hike uphill—and keep an eye out for yellow rabbitbrush, which typically blooms August-October, and purple bitterroot, which blooms April-May along this stretch. After gaining 200 feet over 0.3 mile, you'll hit the trail's lone **switchback** as you head west toward the summit. The trail flattens over this final 0.3-mile stretch, with sweeping views of the Painted Hills to the south and farmland to the north. Two wooden benches mark the **summit**—the end of the trail—and offer great perches from which to take in the 360-degree views. The Painted Hills' colorful slopes dominate the landscape to the south and west, lush farmlands are to the north, and Sutton Mountain rises over the hills to the east.

When you've had your fill of the vibrant palette, return the way you came.

▲ PAINTED HILLS

DIRECTIONS

Drive 3.5 miles west from Mitchell on U.S. 26. Turn right onto Burnt Ranch Road to head north, following signs for the Painted Hills. After following the paved road for 5.5 miles, turn left to head west on the gravel Bear Creek Road. After 1.1 miles, turn into the small parking area off to the left, at the southwest corner of the intersection of Bear Creek Road and the road to the nearby Painted Hills Overlook.

GPS COORDINATES: 44.651944, –120.267339 / N44° 39.1166′ W120° 16.0403′

BEST NEARBY BREWS

Tiger Town Brewing (108 Main St., Mitchell, 541/462-3663, www.tigertownbrewing.com, noon-7pm Sun.-Mon., typically noon-8pm Tues.-Thurs. and noon-9pm Fri.-Sat., though hours may vary seasonally) serves a handful of locally brewed ales and lagers alongside regional beers, ciders, and wines. The lineup changes regularly, so you'll rarely encounter the same beer twice. From the trailhead, the 10-mile drive east takes 25 minutes via Bear Creek and Burnt Ranch Roads and U.S. 26.

JOHN DAY RIVER BASIN

Carroll Rim Trail

Sutton Mountain

SUTTON MOUNTAIN WILDERNESS STUDY AREA

Not a road, not yet a trail, this rugged path to the summit of Sutton Mountain delivers sweeping views in every direction.

DISTANCE: 7.5 miles round-trip

DURATION: 4 hours

ELEVATION CHANGE: 1,670 feet

EFFORT: Moderate

TRAIL: Washed-out dirt road, rocks, cow pies

USERS: Hikers, leashed dogs, horseback riders

SEASON: Year-round

PASSES/FEES: None

MAPS: USGS topographic map for Sutton Mountain

CONTACT: Bureau of Land Management, Prineville District, 541/415-6700, www.blm.gov

Rising more than 4,500 feet, Sutton Mountain sits at the heart of a conservation effort that would protect 58,000 acres of surrounding land for public access. That proposal sits stalled in Congress, but what's here is nevertheless a worthy trail whose views justify the relentless climb.

START THE HIKE

▶ **MILE 0-1.7: Cattle Gate to Forest Departure**

A closed cattle gate, just north of the grassy parking area, marks the start of the trail—"trail" being something of a misnomer, as the entirety of this hike follows an old **unnamed roadbed.** Walk around the locked gate and follow the road, at times covered in grass, rocks, mud, or, especially at the higher elevations, dry cow pies. In 0.15 mile the path switchbacks to the left, near a privately owned **barn,** and heads southwest for 0.8 mile, gaining 460 feet in elevation along the way. You'll see plenty of ponderosa pine at these lower elevations, along with a variety of wildflowers late April-mid-June, including purple lupine and red Indian paintbrush. Since the trail offers little shade, relax while you can under the trees—and keep an eye out for rattlesnakes that might sun themselves on rocks lining the trail here. You'll climb out of a juniper and sagebrush forest after another 0.7 mile, when the trail opens to views of Horse Mountain to the east and Table Mountain to the north.

▶ **MILE 1.7-3.75: Forest Departure to Overlook**

Watch for pronghorn, elk, mule deer, and coyotes on the surrounding hillsides. After another 0.4 mile of slow but steady climbing, you'll arrive at a cattle gate. Open it—taking care to close it behind you—and continue to a second fence line just ahead. Walk through a gap in the fence and follow

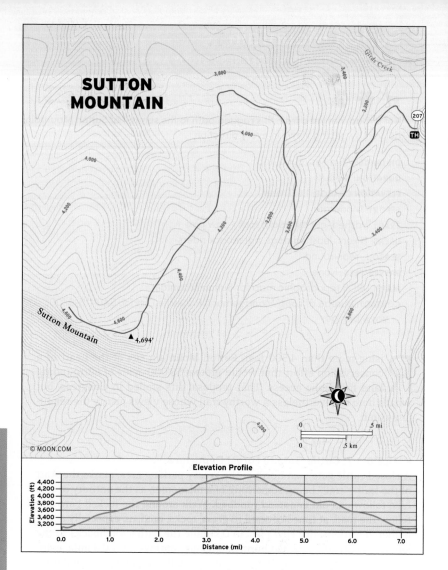

SUTTON MOUNTAIN

Elevation Profile

the roadbed uphill. The trail starts leveling out and curving around the summit in another 1.3 miles. You'll arrive at an **overlook,** just south of the summit, in 0.4 mile. The trail continues on, but this is your turnaround point. Take in the views of the Painted Hills and Ochoco Mountains.

No official trail goes to the rimrock **Sutton Mountain summit,** but if you like you can head 0.3 mile up the grassy hillside to relax in the shade of a juniper tree, look around for pink hedgehog cactus blossoms if it's spring, enjoy wide-open views of the Painted Hills and John Day River, and eye Mount Jefferson on the horizon to the west.

Return the way you came

▲ VIEW FROM SUTTON MOUNTAIN

DIRECTIONS

From Mitchell, drive 0.2 mile west on U.S. 26, and turn right to head north onto Highway 207; reset your odometer at this point, and keep an eye out at 9.5 miles. You'll see an unmarked turn to the left at a bend in the highway. (If you see a sign for Girds Creek Road, you've gone too far.) Turn left to pull into a gravel driveway; you'll immediately arrive at a barbwire gate sporting a Bureau of Land Management sign. Get out of your vehicle, open the gate—making sure to close it behind you to prevent cattle from escaping—and then turn right to head north on the washed-out road. You'll shortly arrive in a meadow with room for parking.

GPS COORDINATES: 44.664761, -120.125501 / N44° 39.8857′ W120° 7.5301′

BEST NEARBY BITES

Reward yourself with a stick-to-your-ribs meal at the **Little Pine Cafe** (100 E. Main St., Mitchell, 541/462-3532, www.mitchellstagestop.com, 7:30am-7:30pm Tues.-Fri., 11:30am-7:30pm Sat.). It claims to serve the best burgers east of the Ochocos, buoyed by more than a decade of experimentation. From the trailhead, the 10-mile drive south takes 15 minutes via Highway 207 and U.S. 26.

SHEEP ROCK UNIT OF THE
JOHN DAY FOSSIL BEDS NATIONAL MONUMENT

Hike the rim of a colorful basin deep in the heart of the John Day Fossil Beds National Monument before descending to its rocky floor.

DISTANCE: 3.4 miles round-trip

DURATION: 1.75 hours

ELEVATION CHANGE: 790 feet

EFFORT: Easy/moderate

TRAIL: Dirt and gravel paths, wooden boardwalk

USERS: Hikers, leashed dogs

SEASON: Year-round

PASSES/FEES: None

MAPS: USGS topographic maps for Picture Gorge East and Picture Gorge West

PARK HOURS: Dawn-dusk daily

CONTACT: John Day Fossil Beds National Monument, 541/987-2333, www.nps.gov/joda

The Blue Basin—really more of a blue-green—was formed nearly 30 million years ago as ash settled in the wake of nearby volcanic eruptions; the resulting rock formations became home to myriad fossils, many of which are still being discovered. Note that digging for—or removing—fossils from the area is strictly prohibited.

START THE HIKE

▸ **MILE 0-1.3: Blue Basin Overlook Trailhead to Bench**
Find the trailhead at the eastern edge of the parking lot. You'll encounter a T-shaped intersection immediately. Head left to begin a clockwise loop via the **Blue Basin Overlook Trail.** Hike up the gentle incline through sagebrush meadows for the first mile, with the outer edge of the colorful basin to your right. This trail offers little cover, so catch your breath on its only shaded **bench** 1.3 miles in, from which you can see colorful fossil beds.

▸ **MILE 1.3-1.6: Bench to John Day Fossil Beds Viewpoint**
Continue on, hiking over a short section of wooden boardwalk. In 0.25 mile, you'll arrive at the **rim of the Blue Basin,** and a junction; an easy-to-miss sign is near your feet and signals you to turn right for a short **spur trail** to a **viewpoint** of the colorful rock formations and surrounding John Day Fossil Beds.

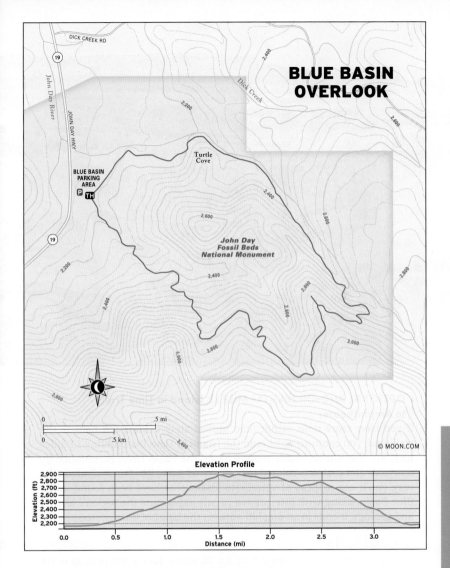

Elevation Profile

▶ MILE 1.6–3.4: John Day Fossil Beds Viewpoint to Blue Basin Overlook Trailhead

Back on the main trail, head south to continue along the basin's rim for 0.8 mile—the hike briefly enters private property, so take care not to disturb the surrounding grasslands or go off-trail here—enjoying continuous views of the colorful rocks and jagged formations. You'll descend a series of switchbacks over the next 0.8 mile to arrive at the **Blue Basin floor** and a T-shaped intersection, where the Blue Basin Overlook Trail dead-ends at the **Island in Time Trail.** Go left on the Island in Time Trail to head northwest and complete the loop back at the hike's first junction in 0.2 mile.

▲ BLUE BASIN

▶ **OPTIONAL ADD-ON HIKE (1.1 MILES): Island in Time Trail to Amphitheater**

If you have more time, rather than immediately turning left back to the trailhead, you can turn right onto the **Island in Time Trail,** adding 1.1 miles total via this out-and-back section along the basin floor, surrounded by emerald- and seafoam-colored rock. The trail gains 220 feet and, along the way, you'll see replicas of vertebrate fossils that have been found in the Blue Basin, along with interpretive panels explaining the region's history and geology. It ends in an **amphitheater** at the heart of the claystone basin.

DIRECTIONS

From Mitchell, head east on U.S. 26 for 30 miles. Take a left to head north on Highway 19 for 5.2 miles, following a sign for the Thomas Condon Visitor Center. Turn right into the parking lot for the Blue Basin trailhead.

GPS COORDINATES: 44.595616, -119.631239 / N44° 35.7370' W119° 37.8743'

NEARBY CAMPGROUNDS

NAME	DESCRIPTION	FACILITIES	SEASON	FEE
Ochoco Forest Campground	quaint campground near Lookout Mountain	5 tent and RV sites, restrooms	spring–early fall	$15
Forest Rd. 33, Prineville, 541/416-6500, www.fs.usda.gov				
Wildcat Campground	quiet campground along Mill Creek	17 tent and small RV sites, restrooms	spring–early fall	$15
Mill Creek Rd., Prineville, 541/416-6500, www.fs.usda.gov				
Ochoco Divide Campground	campground on the Ochocos' crest	25 first-come, first-served RV and tent sites, 3 accessible sites, restrooms	spring–early fall	$13
U.S. 26, Prineville, 541/416-6500, www.fs.usda.gov				
Walton Lake Campground	family-friendly campground on Walton Lake	27 tent and RV sites, 2 accessible sites, restrooms	spring–early fall	$15
Forest Rd. 22, Prineville, 877/444-6777, www.recreation.gov				
Mitchell City Park	sites in a small city park with a grassy field	4 RV sites, grass field for tents, restrooms	year-round except Labor Day weekend	$12–25
Mitchell, 541/462-3121, www.mitchelloregon.us				

CRATER LAKE NATIONAL PARK

Crater Lake is the centerpiece of Oregon's only national park, the deepest lake in North America, and one of the clearest lakes in the world. Roughly 7,700 years ago, the 12,000-foot Mount Mazama erupted in southern Oregon. The roof of its emptied magma chamber eventually collapsed, leaving behind this bowl-shaped caldera that filled over thousands of years with rainwater and snowmelt. Today, visitors come from around the world to admire the lake's dramatically blue hue—thanks to its depth and clarity—and explore the surrounding terrain, including old-growth forest, pumice fields, and waterfalls.

The park's primary southern entrance, the Annie Spring Entrance Station, is open year-round, while its northern entrance usually opens to vehicles between mid-May and late June and closes late October-early November, depending on snowfall. Check with the park and Oregon Department of Transportation (www.tripcheck.org) for the latest updates on access roads. The 33-mile Rim Drive circles Crater Lake; the West Rim Drive usually opens to vehicles between mid-May and late June, and the East Rim Drive generally opens between mid-June and late July. Snow may linger on trails well into July, and the first snowfall may arrive as early as mid-September.

▲ WITCHES CAULDRON ON WIZARD ISLAND   VIEW FROM MOUNT SCOTT

1 Boundary Springs
DISTANCE: 5.5 miles round-trip
DURATION: 2.5 hours
EFFORT: Easy/moderate

2 Cleetwood Cove and Wizard Island
DISTANCE: 4.9 miles round-trip
DURATION: 3 hours
EFFORT: Easy/moderate

3 Garfield Peak
DISTANCE: 3.4 miles round-trip
DURATION: 1.5 hours
EFFORT: Easy/moderate

4 Plaikni Falls
DISTANCE: 2.2 miles round-trip
DURATION: 1.5 hours
EFFORT: Easy

5 Mount Scott
DISTANCE: 4.6 miles round-trip
DURATION: 2.5 hours
EFFORT: Easy/moderate

BEST NEARBY BITES

- Oregon-grown ingredients take center stage at the **Crater Lake Lodge Dining Room** (565 Rim Dr., Crater Lake National Park, 541/594-2255, ext. 3200 or ext. 3201, www.travelcraterlake.com, 7am-10am, 11am-3pm, and 5pm-9:30pm daily May-Oct.). Situated on the southern lakeshore, the national park's fine-dining restaurant offers breakfast, lunch, and dinner with lovely views.

- Unwind with classic American fare at **Annie Creek Restaurant** (Mazama Village Road, Crater Lake National Park, 541/594-2255, www.travelcraterlake.com, hours vary daily May-Sept.). It serves breakfast, lunch, and dinner—including scrambles, omelets, burgers, sandwiches, and more—near the Annie Spring Entrance Station, the park's southern entry point.

- Save room for pie at **Beckie's Cafe** (56484 Hwy. 62, Prospect, 866/560-3565, www.unioncreekoregon.com, 8am-9pm daily summer, 8am-7pm Sun.-Thurs. and 8am-8pm Fri.-Sat. winter). Since 1926, Beckie's has served breakfast, lunch, dinner, and a selection of famous homemade pies—baked fresh daily. Beckie's is located just outside the park, 17 miles west of the Annie Spring Entrance Station via Highway 62.

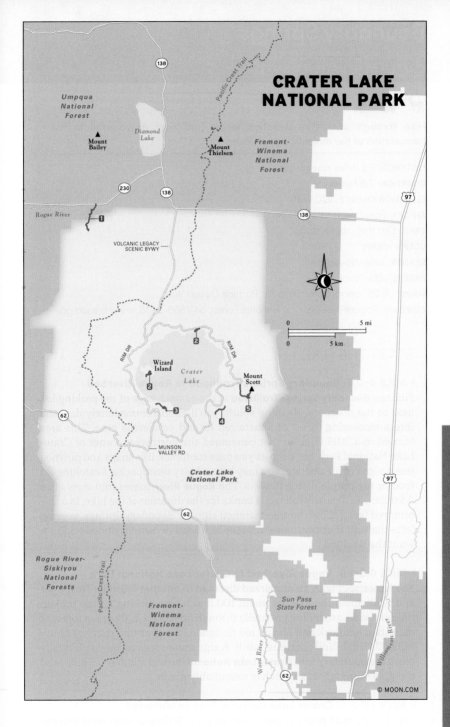

CRATER LAKE NATIONAL PARK

Boundary Springs

ROGUE RIVER-SISKIYOU NATIONAL FOREST,
CRATER LAKE NATIONAL PARK

Hike through a wildfire-scorched forest and past a waterfall to the headwaters of the majestic Rogue River.

DISTANCE: 5.5 miles round-trip

DURATION: 2.5 hours

ELEVATION CHANGE: 320 feet

EFFORT: Easy/moderate

TRAIL: Dirt trail, rocks, roots

USERS: Hikers

SEASON: June-November

PASSES/FEES: None

MAPS: USGS topographic map for Pumice Desert West

CONTACT: Rogue River-Siskiyou National Forest, 541/560-3400, www.fs.usda.gov

START THE HIKE

▶ **MILE 0-0.6: Boundary Springs Trailhead to Rogue Riverbed**

Find the **Boundary Springs Trailhead** at the eastern edge of the parking lot, next to the restroom. Heading south, you'll almost immediately descend into a recovering forest of Shasta red fir and ponderosa pine. This area burned in a 2015 wildfire that consumed the northwest corner of Crater Lake National Park, but even as you pass toothpick-like snags and downed trees, signs of life abound; you may hear a hairy woodpecker searching for food or see purple filaree flowers. The **Rogue River** comes into view after 0.5 mile; you'll mostly follow its banks for the duration of the hike. In a few hundred feet, follow the tree-fastened sign for Boundary Springs, veering left—the trail that continues straight has been decommissioned—and toward the riverbed.

▶ **MILE 0.6-1.9: Rogue Riverbed to Crater Lake National Park**

You'll intersect with an unmarked dirt road in another 0.5 mile. Turn right and walk down the road for about 100 feet before picking up the trail on its south side, ascending gradually through an increasingly green forest of mountain hemlock and Shasta red fir. Ignore the spur trail that heads uphill in 0.25 mile and continue south. A sign announces when you formally cross the boundary into **Crater Lake National Park** in another 0.5 mile, and the grade through this stretch is remarkably gentle.

▶ **MILE 1.9-2.4: Crater Lake National Park to Waterfall**

Another 0.5 mile past the park boundary, you'll drop to river level and enter a meadow where you may hear a Clark's nutcracker or yellow-rumped warbler, or see patches of yellow monkeyflower and blue lupine. You'll

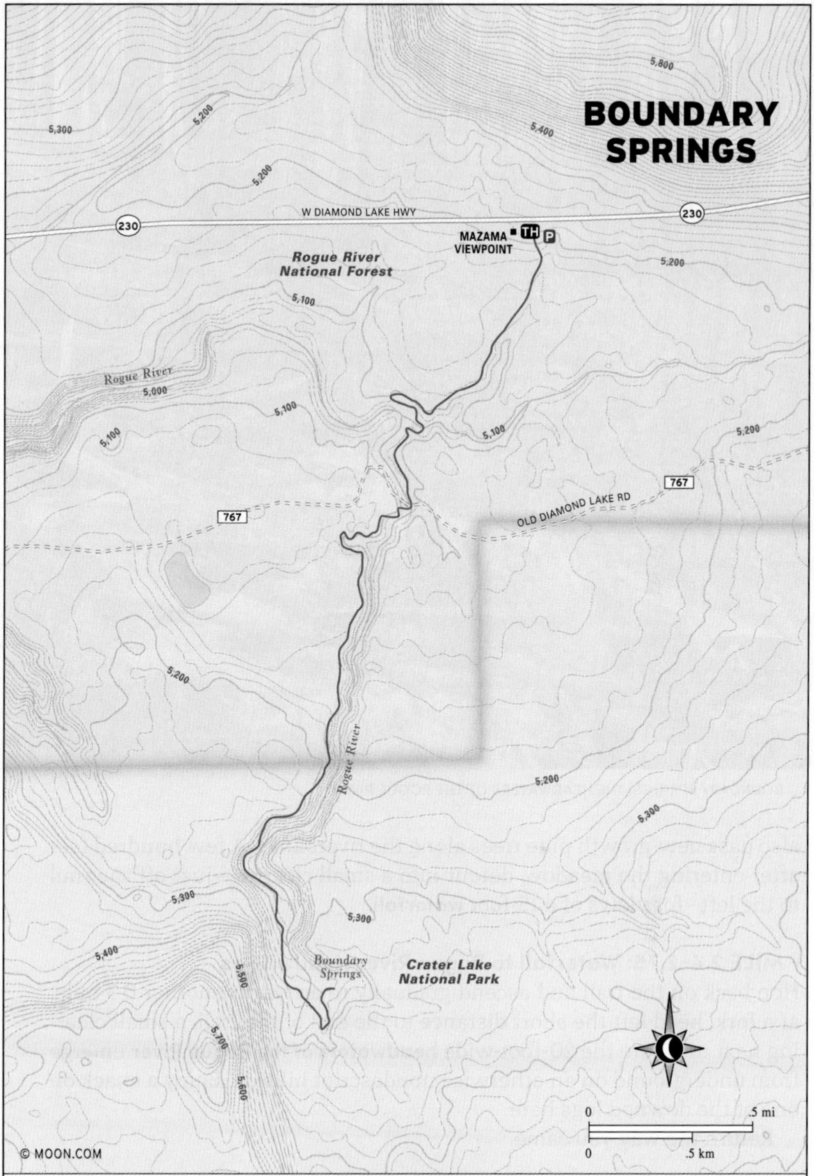

BOUNDARY SPRINGS

W DIAMOND LAKE HWY

230

230

MAZAMA VIEWPOINT
TH P

Rogue River
National Forest

5,800
5,300
5,200
5,400
5,200
5,100
5,100
5,000
Rogue River
5,100
5,100
5,200
767
767
Old Diamond Lake RD
5,200
5,200
5,200
5,200
5,300
5,300
5,200
Rogue River
5,300
5,500
5,400
5,600
5,700
Boundary
Springs
Crater Lake
National Park

0   .5 mi
0   .5 km

© MOON.COM

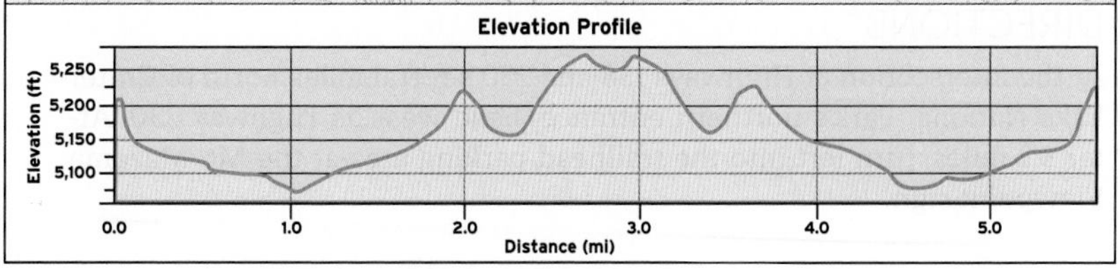

Elevation Profile

Elevation (ft)

5,250
5,200
5,150
5,100

0.0   1.0   2.0   3.0   4.0   5.0

Distance (mi)

Boundary Springs

▲ BOUNDARY SPRINGS, THE HEADWATERS OF THE ROGUE RIVER

also pass new-growth pine trees along the riverbanks. A few hundred feet after entering the meadow, detour into a small clearing—just off the trail to the left—for views of a 15-foot **waterfall.**

▶ **MILE 2.4–2.75: Waterfall to Rogue River Headwaters**

Hop back on the trail and ascend gradually to arrive, in another 0.3 mile, at a fork; head left the short distance to the end of the trail, a small clearing next to where the 20-foot-wide **headwaters of the Rogue River** emerge from underground on an otherwise nondescript hillside. Enjoy a snack on one of the downed logs here.

Return the way you came.

DIRECTIONS

At the intersection of Highways 138 and 230 several miles north of Crater Lake National Park's northern entrance, head west on Highway 230. After 5.3 miles, turn left into the trailhead parking area at the Mt. Mazama Viewpoint sign.

GPS COORDINATES: 43.09084, –122.22141 / N43° 5.4504' W122° 13.2846'

Hike the Cleetwood Cove Trail for the only safe and legal access to Crater Lake's shoreline before taking a boat out to Wizard Island to scale the mini volcano's summit.

BEST: Summer Hikes

DISTANCE: 4.9 miles round-trip (Cleetwood Cove 2.2 miles; Wizard Island 2.7 miles)

DURATION: 3 hours

ELEVATION CHANGE: Cleetwood Cove (520 feet), Wizard Island (680 feet)

EFFORT: Easy/moderate

TRAIL: Dirt trail, rocks, roots, gravel, lava rock

USERS: Hikers

SEASON: June–September

PASSES/FEES: 7-day national park pass, Crater Lake Annual Pass, America the Beautiful Passes

MAPS: USGS topographic map for Crater Lake East, free basic trail map in the Crater Lake National Park newspaper available at entry stations and at park facilities

CONTACT: Crater Lake National Park, 541/594-3000, www.nps.gov/crla

---

The Cleetwood Cove Trail is the most popular trail in Crater Lake National Park. At the end of the trail is a dock from which boat tours and shuttles launch for Wizard Island, a hikeable volcano within a volcano. Following Mount Mazama's eruption and collapse, subsequent eruptions formed numerous cinder cones within the caldera of Crater Lake. Today, Wizard Island is the only one that rises above Crater Lake's surface. Linking the hikes with a boat ride on Crater Lake is a wonderful way to spend a day in the park.

A ticket for a boat tour or shuttle boat is required to access Wizard Island. The **Wizard Island boat tour** ($55 adults, $37 children 3-12) includes an interpretive talk by a park ranger, lake cruising, and a three-hour stop at Wizard Island. Tours depart at 9:45am and 12:45pm daily in season. Including the stop on Wizard Island, the tour lasts approximately five hours total. You could also just take a **shuttle boat** ($28 adults, $18 children 3-12), bypassing the educational talk. It offers pick-up and drop-off and includes a three-hour stop on Wizard Island. Shuttles depart at 8:30am and 11:30am daily in season. The shuttle takes about half an hour to get to Wizard Island. Boats typically run June-September. Approximately half the tickets for every tour or shuttle are available in advance, online or by phone, and the other half are available 24 hours before each tour or shuttle at self-serve kiosks in the park's Crater Lake Lodge and Annie Creek Gift Shop. Any remaining tickets are sold at a booth in the parking area at the top of the Cleetwood Cove Trail. Give yourself 30 minutes for the descent to the shoreline and 45-60 minutes for the return ascent on the Cleetwood Cove Trail.

START THE HIKE

You must check in at the booth at the Cleetwood Cove parking area as well as at a second booth at the base of the trail for boat tours and shuttles. Be sure to bring plenty of water for this hike, and apply sunscreen; time on the boat alone will offer plenty of exposure, and the summit of Wizard Island is also exposed.

▶ **MILE 0-1.1: Cleetwood Cove Trailhead to Cleetwood Cove Dock**
Walk south from the Cleetwood Cove parking area after checking in, crossing Rim Drive, to arrive at the **Cleetwood Cove Trailhead.** Over the course of its 1.1 miles, you'll descend a series of nine switchbacks. The trail, wide enough for hikers to walk side-by-side, is mostly shaded, passing through a forest of lodgepole pine, Shasta red fir, and mountain hemlock, and it progressively opens up to expansive lake views. The trail ends at the **dock** and **ticket booth,** both to your left on the shore of Crater Lake. You can dive off the rocks from the lakeshore here—but note that even at the height of summer the water temperature only reaches 59°F. Check in again for your boat tour or shuttle at the ticket booth. Bathrooms are available just west of the ticket booth.

▶ **MILE 1.1-2.3: Wizard Island Dock to Summit**
Your boat tour or shuttle will drop you off at the **Wizard Island dock.** Follow the signage, heading left onto a dirt path to find the trailheads. (If you need a bathroom break, the trail to the right leads to a restroom in a few hundred feet.) You'll shortly arrive at a junction; turn right, following the Summit sign. You'll ascend steadily through a forest of western hemlock that gives way to whitebark pine, with a bed of ankle-high pinemat manzanita flanking the trail throughout. Along the way, you may spot golden-mantled ground squirrels and hear band-winged grasshoppers, which have wings that sound like a lawn sprinkler when in flight. After 1.2 miles you'll arrive at the **Wizard Island summit,** and a junction.

▶ **MILE 2.3-2.6: Witches Cauldron Loop**
Head left for an 0.3-mile clockwise loop around the crater atop Wizard Island known as the **Witches Cauldron.** The crater affords 360-degree views of Crater Lake, Mount Scott to the east, and Watchman Peak to the west. Several social trails descend to the base of the pumice-filled crater. July-August, keep an eye out for purple penstemon along the loop.

▶ **MILE 2.6-4.9: Summit to Cleetwood Cove Trailhead**
After completing the loop, return the 1.2 miles to the Wizard Island dock the way you came. If you have spare time and a towel, feel free to take a dip in Crater Lake's chilly waters while you wait for the boat to return. Back on the mainland, return to the parking area from the dock via the 1.1-mile Cleetwood Cove Trail. The ascent tests even those in good physical condition, thanks to the steady incline and steep grade of 11 percent.

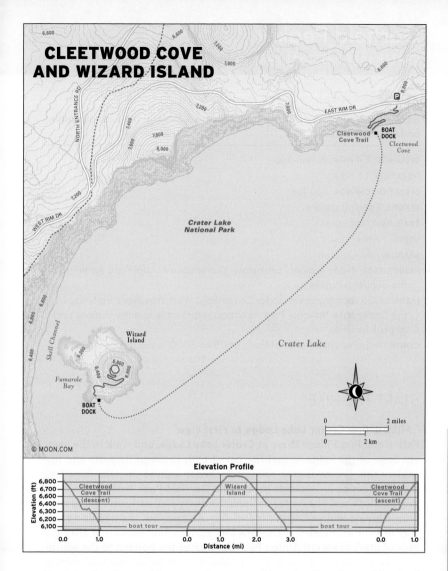

CLEETWOOD COVE AND WIZARD ISLAND

Elevation Profile

Don't be shy about taking your time; several benches line the trail for tired hikers.

DIRECTIONS

From Crater Lake National Park's northern entrance off Highway 138, drive south 8.4 miles. Turn left onto East Rim Drive, and continue 4.5 miles to the turnout for Cleetwood Cove; the parking area is north of the road. Or, from the Annie Spring Entrance Station on the park's south side, head north on Munson Valley Road for 6.5 miles. Turn left onto West Rim Drive and continue for 5.9 miles. At an intersection with the northern entry road, turn right to remain on Rim Drive for another 4.5 miles.

GPS COORDINATES: 42.97969, –122.08326 / N42° 58.7814' W122° 4.9956'

Enjoy sweeping views of Crater Lake's massive caldera, the Klamath Valley, and Cascade peaks.

DISTANCE: 3.4 miles round-trip
DURATION: 1.5 hours
ELEVATION CHANGE: 920 feet
EFFORT: Easy/moderate
TRAIL: Dirt trail, rocks
USERS: Hikers
SEASON: July–October
PASSES/FEES: 7-day national park pass, Crater Lake Annual Pass, America the Beautiful Passes
MAPS: USGS topographic map for Crater Lake West; free basic trail map in the Crater Lake National Park newspaper available at entry stations and at park facilities
CONTACT: Crater Lake National Park, 541/594-3000, www.nps.gov/crla

START THE HIKE

▶ **MILE 0-0.4: Crater Lake Lodge to First View**
Park along Rim Village Drive at **Crater Lake Lodge,** and walk to the eastern edge of the lodge to find the paved path between its patio and the caldera rim. Follow it east counterclockwise around the lake for a few hundred feet as it descends toward the **Garfield Peak Trailhead.** Mountain hemlock and Shasta red fir flank the dusty trail early on—along with purple lupine and yellow groundsel July-August—but the tree line gives way to your first views of the lake and surrounding landscape after 0.3 mile of gradual ascent. Union Peak dominates the horizon to the southwest as you arrive at the first switchback, with Mount Ashland faintly visible to its left.

▶ **MILE 0.4-1.2: First View to Ridgeline**
After continued climbing and another switchback in just under 0.2 mile, you'll start noticing less hemlock and more whitebark pine—one of the few species of tree that can survive at this elevation and withstand the region's brutal winters. As you continue on progressively rockier stretches, keep an eye out for yellow-bellied marmots and American pikas scurrying about. Continue climbing steadily for another 0.6 mile, at which point you'll arrive on a ridgeline atop the caldera.

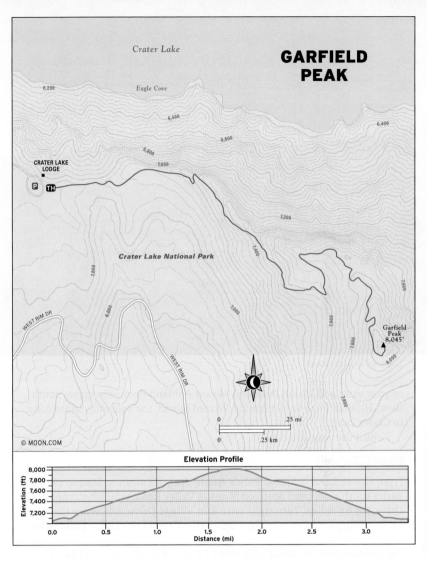

Elevation Profile

► **MILE 1.2–1.4: Ridgeline to Phantom Ship and Mount Scott Viewpoint**

At the ridgeline you'll have your first unimpeded view of Crater Lake, as well as the 168-foot-tall rock formation poking out of the water known as the Phantom Ship. Continue on another 0.25 mile for a **viewpoint** with a pair of concrete benches that let you sit and take in the Phantom Ship as well as Mount Scott, the tallest point in the park.

► **MILE 1.4–1.7: Phantom Ship and Mount Scott Viewpoint to Garfield Peak Summit**

Continue ascending the trail 0.3 mile past the benches to arrive at the **Garfield Peak summit,** where you'll be rewarded with 360-degree views, some of the best in the park. To the north, Mount Thielsen rises over Crater Lake's caldera; the Klamath Valley sits to the south; Mount Scott rises

▲ VIEW OF WIZARD ISLAND

to your east; and Union Peak and Mount Ashland dominate views southwest. Hillman Peak is just behind Wizard Island, the volcanic cinder cone in Crater Lake.

Return the way you came.

DIRECTIONS

From Crater Lake National Park's Annie Spring Entrance Station on the park's south side, head north on Munson Valley Road, which becomes Rim Drive, for 6.6 miles. Turn right onto Rim Village Drive, following the sign for Rim Village, and continue 0.4 mile to the Crater Lake Lodge parking lot.

GPS COORDINATES: 42.90947, –122.14084 / N42° 54.5682′ W122° 8.4504′

Plaikni Falls

CRATER LAKE NATIONAL PARK

This lovely forest walk features abundant wildflowers and ends at the base of a waterfall.

DISTANCE: 2.2 miles round-trip

DURATION: 1.5 hours

ELEVATION CHANGE: 140 feet

EFFORT: Easy

TRAIL: Dirt trail, gravel

USERS: Hikers, wheelchair users

SEASON: July–October

PASSES/FEES: 7-day national park pass, Crater Lake Annual Pass, America the Beautiful Passes

MAPS: USGS topographic map for Crater Lake East; free basic trail map in the Crater Lake National Park newspaper available at entry stations and at park facilities

CONTACT: Crater Lake National Park, 541/594-3000, www.nps.gov/crla

Contrary to popular belief, these falls aren't fed by Crater Lake, but by snowmelt. The name "Plaikni"—which means "from the high country"—was chosen by Klamath Native American elders.

START THE HIKE

▶ MILE 0-0.5: Plaikni Falls Trailhead to Anderson Bluffs

From the **Plaikni Falls Trailhead,** head north along the wide path of pumice and gravel. In a few hundred feet, you'll cross an old road and enter **Kerr Valley,** a glacier-carved canyon created in the ice ages. Numerous wooden benches can be found trailside if you wish to enjoy the scenery, including old-growth mountain hemlock, Shasta red fir, and summertime wildflowers such as purple lupine.

PLAIKNI FALLS TRAIL ▶

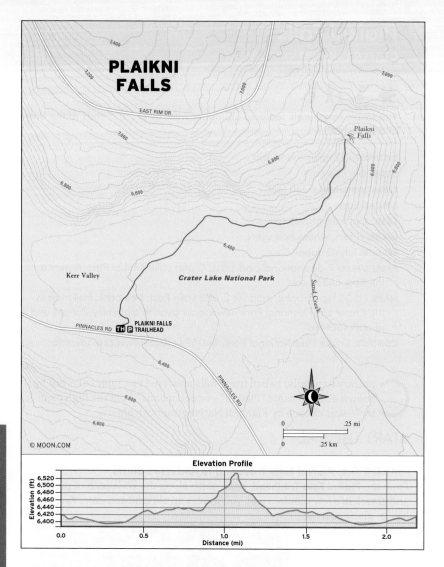

Elevation Profile

© MOON.COM

▶ MILE 0.5-0.9: Anderson Bluffs to Sand Creek

After 0.5 mile, you'll begin walking alongside the base of **Anderson Bluffs,** just behind the tree line to your left. Rock from the base of these bluffs was once extracted for use in various projects around Crater Lake National Park. In another 0.4 mile, the trail emerges from the forest into an open meadow along **Sand Creek.**

▶ MILE 0.9-1.1: Sand Creek to Plaikni Falls

From here, follow the path as it curves left, gaining 90 feet over the last 0.2 mile. (While most of the trail is accessible, this final stretch may be too steep for those in wheelchairs.) It's the longest stretch of continuous elevation gain on the trail, and it ends at a small clearing at the base of 20-foot **Plaikni Falls.** Here the spring-fed waterfall cascades over a glacier-carved

▲ PLAIKNI FALLS

cliff and feeds Sand Creek. Heed the signs in this ecologically sensitive area and stay on-trail at all times. Several varieties of wildflowers grow at the waterfall's base, including red paintbrush and arrowleaf groundsel.

Return the way you came.

DIRECTIONS

From Crater Lake National Park's Annie Spring Entrance Station on the park's south side, follow Munson Valley Road for 3.7 miles. Turn right onto East Rim Drive and follow it for 8.2 miles, then turn right onto Pinnacles Road, following a sign for Lost Creek Campground and the Pinnacles. Continue on the road for 1.1 miles. The parking area will be on the left, just past a sign indicating the trailhead.

GPS COORDINATES: 42.90187, −122.06147 / N42° 54.1122′ W122° 3.6882′

🏃 ❀

Hike to the tallest point in Crater Lake National Park—and the only place in the park where you can fit the entire lake into one photograph.

DISTANCE: 4.6 miles round-trip

DURATION: 2.5 hours

ELEVATION CHANGE: 1,150 feet

EFFORT: Easy/moderate

TRAIL: Dirt trail, sandy path, rocks, roots

USERS: Hikers

SEASON: July–October

PASSES/FEES: 7-day national park pass, Crater Lake Annual Pass, America the Beautiful Passes

MAPS: USGS topographic map for Crater Lake East; free basic trail map in the Crater Lake National Park newspaper available at entry stations and at park facilities

CONTACT: Crater Lake National Park, 541/594-3000, www.nps.gov/crla

START THE HIKE

Given its elevation, the Mount Scott Trail is among the last in the park to be completely snow-free—and the path may have some snow on it into August. Make sure to sunscreen up and bring plenty of water, as this hike is quite exposed near the summit.

▶ **MILE 0-1.1: Mount Scott Trailhead to Clearing**

Walk to the southern edge of the parking lot to find the **Mount Scott Trailhead,** and begin hiking through a mostly flat **pumice field.** Check out some of the khaki-colored, sponge-like pumice rocks along the trail—they're lighter than you think!—but be sure to put them back for others to enjoy. At 0.25 mile, you'll enter a forest of Douglas fir, lodgepole pine, and mountain hemlock—and start ascending. In another 0.5 mile, as you steadily gain elevation via a sandy, well-graded path, you'll start enjoying views of Wizard Island and Crater Lake. Keep an eye out along this stretch July-August for red paintbrush, wild onion, yellow buttercup, and other wildflowers. Also watch for black-billed magpies and blue Steller's jays, among other bird species, perched in nearby trees.

▶ **MILE 1.1-1.5: Clearing to Switchbacks**

You'll arrive in 0.35 mile at a **clearing** with views of Brown Mountain to the south and Applegate Peak—just outside the caldera—Mount Ashland, and Grizzly Peak to the southwest. The forest of hemlock starts thinning out

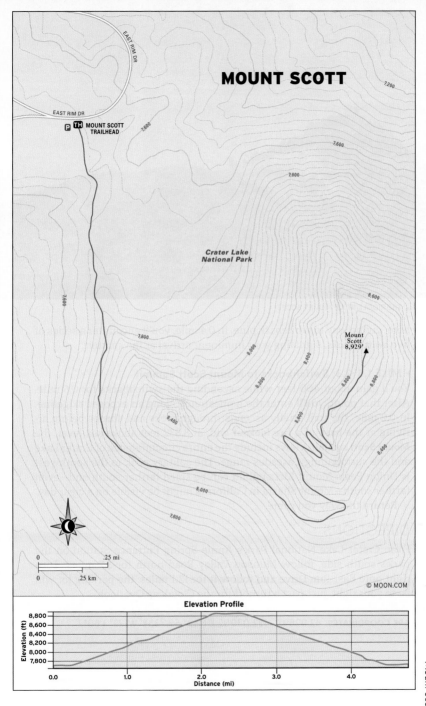

MOUNT SCOTT

EAST RIM DR

EAST RIM DR

P **TH** MOUNT SCOTT
TRAILHEAD

7,200

7,600

7,800

7,600

*Crater Lake
National Park*

8,600

7,600

7,800

8,000

Mount
Scott
8,929'

8,200

8,400

8,800

8,800

8,400

8,600

8,400

8,000

7,800

0   .25 mi

0   .25 km

© MOON.COM

Elevation Profile

Elevation (ft)				

8,800
8,600
8,400
8,200
8,000
7,800

0.0   1.0   2.0   3.0   4.0

Distance (mi)

▲ THE RIDGELINE OF MOUNT SCOTT

here, giving way to whitebark pine. In 0.4 mile, you'll encounter a series of five **switchbacks,** signaling your imminent arrival at the summit.

▶ **MILE 1.5-2.3: Switchbacks to Mount Scott Summit**
You'll gain about 400 feet while ascending the switchbacks for 0.6 mile. After that point, you'll enter the homestretch along an exposed ridgeline. In 0.2 mile, the trail briefly ascends through rocks and shrubs before arriving at the base of a **fire lookout** and, at 8,832 feet above sea level, the **Mount Scott summit.** Views include the entire circumference of Crater Lake and the surrounding Cascades range. The solitary peak to the southwest is Union Peak. Mount McLoughlin can be spied farther south and—even farther south—Mount Shasta in California might be visible on a clear day.

Return the way you came.

DIRECTIONS

From Crater Lake National Park's Annie Spring Entrance Station on the park's south side, follow Munson Valley Road north for 3.7 miles. Turn right onto East Rim Drive and follow it for 12.1 miles; the parking lot will be to your right, just past a turnoff for the Cloudcap Overlook.

GPS COORDINATES: 42.92897, -122.03002 / N42° 55.7382' W122° 1.8012'

NEARBY CAMPGROUNDS

NAME	DESCRIPTION	FACILITIES	SEASON	FEE
Mazama Campground	the only developed campground within Crater Lake National Park	214 tent, RV, and group campsites, restrooms	June–September	$21–43

Mazama Village, Crater Lake National Park, 541/594-2255 ext. 3610 or 3601, www.travelcraterlake.com

NAME	DESCRIPTION	FACILITIES	SEASON	FEE
Lost Creek Campground	tent campsites inside Crater Lake National Park	16 tent sites, restrooms	July-October	$5

Pinnacles Rd., Crater Lake National Park, 541/594-3000, www.nps.gov/crla

NAME	DESCRIPTION	FACILITIES	SEASON	FEE
Diamond Lake Campground	less than 7 miles from Crater Lake National Park's northern entrance, on the shore of Diamond Lake	238 RV and tent sites, restrooms	May–October	$16–27

Hwy. 138, Chemult, 541/498-2531, www.fs.usda.gov

NAME	DESCRIPTION	FACILITIES	SEASON	FEE
Jackson F. Kimball State Recreation Site	about 15 miles south of Crater Lake's southern entrance, at the headwaters of the Wood River	10 tent sites, restrooms	April–October	$11

Sun Mountain Rd., Chiloquin, 541/783-2471, www.oregonstateparks.org

NAME	DESCRIPTION	FACILITIES	SEASON	FEE
Union Creek Campground	17 miles west of Crater Lake National Park' southern entrance station, with access to hiking and fishing	73 RV and tent sites, 3 full-hookup sites, restrooms	May–October	$22–35

Hwy. 62, Union Creek, 541/560-3900, www.roguerec.com

ASHLAND AND THE ROGUE VALLEY

Whatever natural beauty you're seeking, chances are good you'll find it in southern Oregon's Rogue Valley and Siskiyou Mountains. Choose your own adventure, whether hiking through a colorful canyon to a waterfall, traversing rolling mountain meadows, walking a stretch of the Pacific Crest Trail, taking in sweeping views of Cascade peaks, or exploring the heart of three mountain ranges in the Cascade-Siskiyou National Monument. The city of Ashland, famous for the annual Oregon Shakespeare Festival, sits at the southern edge of the Rogue Valley—and makes a fine jumping-off point for hitting many of the region's best-loved trails.

▲ VIEW OF THE SISKIYOU MOUNTAINS FROM MOUNT ELIJAH

▲ FIRE LOOKOUT ON SODA MOUNTAIN

1 **Rainie Falls**
DISTANCE: 4.4 miles round-trip
DURATION: 2.5 hours
EFFORT: Easy/moderate

2 **Mount Elijah**
DISTANCE: 5.7 miles round-trip
DURATION: 3 hours
EFFORT: Easy/moderate

3 **Lower Table Rock**
DISTANCE: 4.8 miles round-trip
DURATION: 2.5 hours
EFFORT: Easy/moderate

4 **Grizzly Peak**
DISTANCE: 5.6 miles round-trip
DURATION: 3 hours
EFFORT: Easy/moderate

5 **Siskiyou Mountain Park**
DISTANCE: 4.9 miles round-trip
DURATION: 2 hours
EFFORT: Easy/moderate

6 **Mount Ashland (via the Pacific Crest Trail)**
DISTANCE: 8.1 miles round-trip
DURATION: 4 hours
EFFORT: Moderate

7 **Soda Mountain**
DISTANCE: 4.5 miles round-trip
DURATION: 2.5 hours
EFFORT: Easy/moderate

▼ ROGUE RIVER NEAR RAINIE FALLS

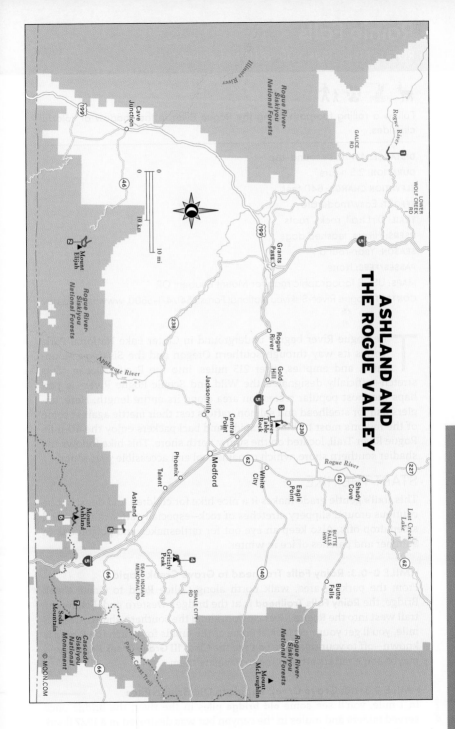

ASHLAND AND THE ROGUE VALLEY

© MOON.COM

1

Rainie Falls
ROGUE RIVER-SISKIYOU NATIONAL FOREST

🦌 ⛲ 🐾 🚶

Follow a rolling footpath along the Rogue River in the shadow of colorful cliffsides.

DISTANCE: 4.4 miles round-trip
DURATION: 2.5 hours
ELEVATION CHANGE: 640 feet
EFFORT: Easy/moderate
TRAIL: Dirt trail, rocks, roots
USERS: Hikers, leashed dogs
SEASON: Year-round
PASSES/FEES: None
MAPS: USGS topographic map for Mount Reuben, OR
CONTACT: Rogue River-Siskiyou National Forest, 541/471-6500, www.fs.usda.gov

The Rogue River begins underground in Crater Lake National Park, winds its way through southern Oregon and the Siskiyou Mountains, and empties, after 215 miles, into the Pacific Ocean. This stretch—officially designated the Wild and Scenic Rogue River—is perhaps the most popular recreation area along its entire length. Here, anglers fish for steelhead and salmon, rafters test their mettle against some of the region's most turbulent rapids, and backpackers enjoy the 40-mile Rogue River Trail, located on the sunny north shore. This hike follows the shadier southern shore, which remains cool and accessible year-round.

START THE HIKE

This trail's gentle grade makes it a nice hike for children and dogs, but be cautious around slippery stretches of rock—especially after rainfall—and steep drop-offs. Also keep an eye out for rattlesnakes and poison oak in summer and patches of ice in winter.

▶ **MILE 0-0.3: Rainy Falls Trailhead to Grave Creek Rapids**
From the parking area, walk north along Galice Road to Grave Creek Bridge; the **Rainy Falls Trailhead** is at the bridge's western end. Follow the trail west into the Rogue River canyon, along the southern shore. After 0.3 mile, you'll get your first look at some of the rapids for which the Rogue is known—off to your right you can see the Class III **Grave Creek Rapids,** and maybe some rafters attempting to navigate them.

▶ **MILE 0.3-1.3: Grave Creek Rapids to Old Bridge Piles**
In 1 mile, you'll see some **old bridge piles** in the river; the bridge once served miners and mules in the canyon but was destroyed in a 1927 flood. You'll start ascending gently but steadily here, heading into a forest of Douglas fir, oak, and madrone.

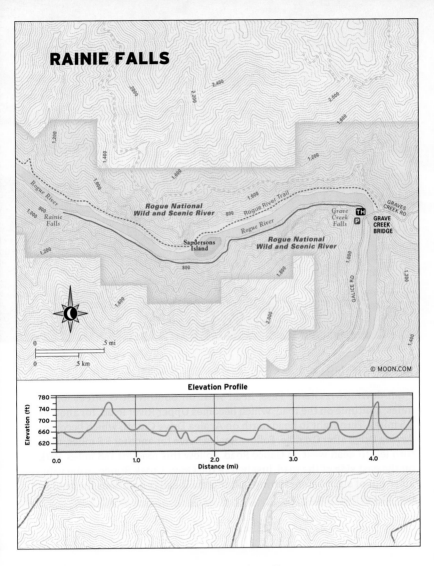

RAINIE FALLS

Elevation Profile

▶ **MILE 1.3-2.2: Old Bridge Piles to Rainie Falls**

In 0.4 mile you'll encounter some especially rocky terrain; it may be difficult to follow the trail through this stretch, especially as rainfall pools on the path—but simply continue straight ahead, looking for rocks that are a lighter shade of gray than the surrounding rubble. The path becomes clear again after a couple hundred feet. In another 0.4 mile, the trail ends in a mess of rocks at **Rainie Falls,** which, at 20 feet tall, looks less like a conventional waterfall than a series of Class V rapids—which it is. A sandy shoreline here offers a nice place to enjoy a snack. Watch for salmon and steelhead migrating upstream here; their leaps can propel the fish five feet in the air and six feet forward. Similarly, keep an eye out for great blue herons, kingfishers, ospreys, black bears, and otters, all of which feed on the fish.

Return the way you came.

▲ RAINIE FALLS

DIRECTIONS

From downtown Grants Pass, head west on Southwest G Street for 1.2 miles; continue on the road, which becomes Upper River Road, for another 2.5 miles. Turn right to head north on Azalea Drive Cutoff, which becomes Azalea Drive after 0.4 mile. Follow Azalea Drive for another 5.8 miles, then turn left to head west on Galice Road. Follow this road for 17.8 miles. Park on the east side of the road, just before the Grave Creek Bridge. Store valuables out of sight before setting out; this trailhead is notorious for vandalism and vehicle break-ins.

GPS COORDINATES: 42.64881, –123.5851 / N42° 38.9286′ W123° 35.106′

BEST NEARBY BREWS

Enjoy easy-drinking house brews and upscale pub fare on a creek-side patio at **Climate City Brewing Company** (509 SW G St., Grants Pass, 541/479-3725, http://climatecitybrewing.com, 11:30am-8pm Tues.-Thurs., 11:30am-9pm Fri.-Sun.). From the trailhead, the 28-mile drive southeast takes 40 minutes via Galice Road.

2

Mount Elijah

ROGUE RIVER-SISKIYOU NATIONAL FOREST, OREGON CAVES NATIONAL MONUMENT & PRESERVE

Ascend through forest and meadows before basking in 360-degree views from the summit of Mount Elijah.

DISTANCE: 5.7 miles round-trip

DURATION: 3 hours

ELEVATION CHANGE: 1,020 feet

EFFORT: Easy/moderate

TRAIL: Dirt trail, roots, rocks, old roadbed

USERS: Hikers, leashed dogs

SEASON: June-November

PASSES/FEES: None

MAPS: USGS topographic map for Oregon Caves; National Park Service trail map available at the Oregon Caves National Monument & Preserve

CONTACT: Rogue River-Siskiyou National Forest, 541/592-4000, www.fs.usda.gov

START THE HIKE

▶ **MILE 0-0.7: Mount Elijah-Bigelow Lakes Trailhead to Lake Mountain and Bigelow Lakes Trail**

Start from the **Mt. Elijah-Bigelow Lakes Trailhead** at the southeastern edge of the parking area, hiking on what was once part of **Forest Road 070,** flanked by maple and alder. After 0.7 mile of gently but steadily ascending—with precious little shade in the summer—you'll arrive at a junction with a map; turn left here onto the **Lake Mountain and Bigelow Lakes Trail,** heading east and uphill into a fir forest to begin a clockwise loop.

▶ **MILE 0.7-2.2: Lake Mountain and Bigelow Lakes Trail to Clearing**

About 0.3 mile past the junction, you'll begin darting in and out of meadows, ringed by fir trees and host to a variety of wildflowers in the late spring and early summer. Watch for purple fireweed, red and yellow western columbine, and red paintbrush. After another 0.3 mile, you'll notice a spur trail to your right—it goes to Bigelow Lakes—but head uphill to your left to continue on the Lake Mountain and Bigelow Lakes Trail. Continue ascending for 0.9 mile, at which point you'll emerge from the forest into a **clearing** boasting views of Bigelow Lakes, the Illinois River valley, and the Siskiyou Mountains to the northwest. The summit of Mount Elijah rises to your left, and the symmetrical, rounded peak straight ahead is Eight Dollar Mountain.

▶ **MILE 2.2-2.7: Clearing to Mount Elijah Summit**

You'll soon reenter the forest. At an intersection with the Elk Creek Trail in 0.1 mile, continue straight ahead on the Lake Mountain and Bigelow Lakes

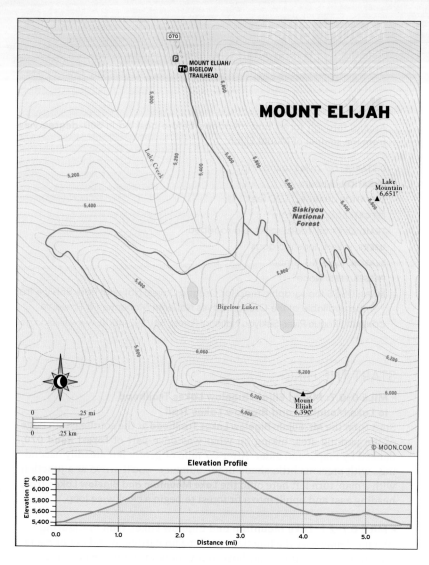

Elevation Profile

Trail. Take a right to head west at the next junction, in another 0.1 mile, following an Oregon Caves signpost. In 0.3 mile, you'll arrive at the **Mount Elijah summit,** marked by a sign and offering panoramic views. From here, you can spy Mount Shasta to the southeast and the Kalmiopsis Wilderness to the west.

▸ **MILE 2.7–5.7: Mount Elijah Summit to Mount Elijah-Bigelow Lakes Trailhead**

Once you've had your fill of views, continue west on the trail to start your descent. You'll return to the forest in another 0.4 mile and, after 0.9 mile in the woods, arrive at a Y-shaped junction. Turn right to reconnect with the old Forest Road 070 roadbed, following it 1 mile to complete the loop at the hike's original junction, and keeping left to continue on the road 0.7 mile to return the way you came.

DIRECTIONS

From the town of Cave Junction, located on U.S. 199, head east on Highway 46, following a sign for the Oregon Caves National Monument. Follow the road for 11.8 miles, at which point you'll pass Grayback Campground. RVs and trailers are not recommended on the winding roads past this point. Continue on Highway 46 another 7.9 miles to dead-end in the Oregon Caves parking lot; make a U-turn and backtrack 0.1 mile to make the tight right turn onto the paved fire access road uphill (it becomes gravel in another couple hundred feet) and continue for 3 miles. At the intersection, turn right onto Forest Road 070 to continue uphill. You'll arrive at a fork in 0.6 mile; stay right to remain on Forest Road 070, which ends in 0.8 mile at a small gravel parking area.

GPS COORDINATES: 42.101740, –123.378952 / N42° 6.1044' W123° 22.7371'

MOUNT ELIJAH SUMMIT ▶

BEST NEARBY BITES AND A BONUS

Once back in the parking lot, you might consider visiting the nearby **Oregon Caves National Monument & Preserve** (541/592-2100, www. nps.gov/orca, seasonal hours late Mar.-early Nov.), where you can take guided cave tours (standard tour $7-10, off-trail tour $45). Or go for some eats; the whole family will find something to love at **Wild River Pizza** (249 N. Redwood Hwy., Cave Junction, 541/592-3556, http:// wildriverbrewing.com, 11am-9pm Mon.-Thurs., 11am-10pm Fri.-Sat., noon-9pm Sun.). This popular restaurant serves filling pizzas, sandwiches, and broasted chicken, along with eight or more house beers at any time. From the trailhead, the 22-mile drive west takes 45 minutes via Highway 46.

Enjoy vernal pools and wildflowers in season, and 360-degree views of Mount McLoughlin and the Rogue Valley from atop Lower Table Rock's pancake-flat summit year-round.

BEST: Spring Hikes, Wildflower Hikes
DISTANCE: 4.8 miles round-trip
DURATION: 2.5 hours
ELEVATION CHANGE: 910 feet
EFFORT: Easy/moderate
TRAIL: Dirt trail, gravel path, rocks, wooden boardwalk
USERS: Hikers
SEASON: Year-round
PASSES/FEES: None
MAPS: USGS topographic map for Sams Valley
CONTACT: Bureau of Land Management, 541/618-2200, www.blm.gov

The Table Rocks—comprising Lower Table Rock and Upper Table Rock to its east—have existed in some form since a nearby shield volcano erupted 7.5 million years ago, sending lava into the present-day Rogue Valley. As millions of years passed, the Rogue River eroded much of that lava rock, leaving behind what you see today. Late winter and spring is the best time to see the vernal pools at their most impressive, and if you come in the latter season you'll also be treated to scads of wildflowers.

START THE HIKE

Watch for poison oak, ticks, and rattlesnakes along this trail in summertime.

▶ **MILE 0-1.1: Lower Table Rock Trailhead to Clearing**
Find the **Lower Table Rock Trailhead**—a signed wooden arch—next to the restroom at the southern edge of the parking lot. Head south on the trail to a junction; continue straight on the wide, gravel path to remain on the Lower Table Rock Trail as you enter an oak grove. After steadily ascending through madrone and oak trees, you'll arrive in 1.1 miles at a small **clearing** that offers the hike's first real views; to the east are Upper Table Rock and Mount McLoughlin.

▶ **MILE 1.1-1.6: Clearing to Vernal Pools**
The trail mostly levels out in 0.3 mile as you arrive at the exposed northern edge of **Lower Table Rock.** Follow the short, 0.2-mile round-trip **spur trail** to your left here, and enjoy panoramic views of Mount McLoughlin and Upper Table Rock. To the northeast, you'll see what appears to be a flat peak; that's the rim of Crater Lake. Back on the main trail, continue south,

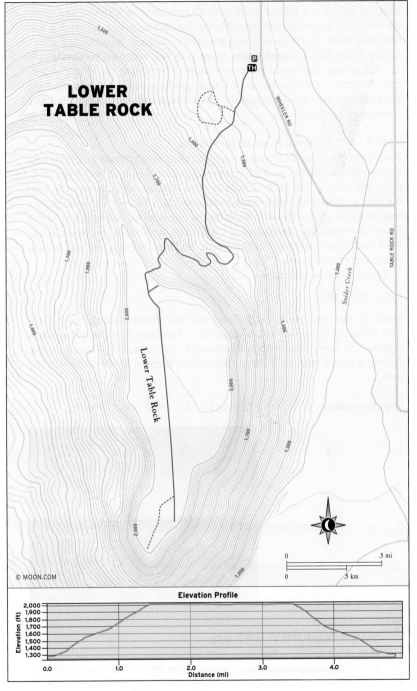

LOWER TABLE ROCK

Lower Table Rock

WHEELER RD

TABLE ROCK RD

Snider Creek

Elevation Profile

© MOON.COM

0   .5 mi

0   .5 km

keeping an eye out for the more than 75 species of wildflower that grow on the Table Rocks, including red bells, Southern Oregon buttercup, and shooting stars. You'll shortly find yourself on a short boardwalk through Lower Table Rock's **vernal pools;** these rain-fed, seasonal wetlands host several unique species of plant and animal, including the dwarf woolly meadowfoam—a five-petal plant found nowhere else on Earth—and the fairy shrimp, which swims upside down and is federally designated as a threatened species.

▶ **MILE 1.6–2.4: Vernal Pools to Viewpoints**
Soon after the boardwalk ends, you'll arrive at an unsigned junction; veer right to follow the widest and most well-maintained trail of the three options before you. The path—an old airstrip—straightens out over the next 0.8 mile as it beelines toward the southern edge of Lower Table Rock. The trail ends at an unsigned fork; going in either direction—each is just a short spur—leads to **viewpoints** of the city of Medford below you, Grizzly Peak and Mount Ashland to the south, and the Rogue River and Mount McLoughlin to the east.

Return the way you came.

DIRECTIONS

From the intersection of Biddle Road and Table Rock Road in north Medford, head north on Table Rock Road. Turn left after 7.7 miles, following a sign for the Lower Table Rock Trailhead, to head west on Wheeler Road. Follow it for 0.8 mile as it curves northwest, turning left into the parking area.

GPS COORDINATES: 42.46865, –122.94553 / N42° 28.119' W122° 56.7318'

UPPER TABLE ROCK AND
MOUNT MCLOUGHLIN ▶

BEST NEARBY BREWS

Walkabout Brewing Company (921 Mason Way, Medford, 541/734-4677, http://walkaboutbrewing.com, 3pm–8pm Mon.–Wed., 3pm–9pm Thurs.–Fri., 2pm–9pm Sat., 1pm–7pm Sun.) draws decor inspiration from the Australian Outback and serves up a variety of easy-drinking ales. From the trailhead, the 12-mile drive south takes 20 minutes via Table Rock Road.

Enjoy summertime wildflower displays and panoramic views of the Rogue Valley, Ashland, and Cascade peaks.

BEST: Brew Hikes
DISTANCE: 5.6 miles round-trip
DURATION: 3 hours
ELEVATION CHANGE: 860 feet
EFFORT: Easy/moderate
TRAIL: Dirt trail, roots, rocks
USERS: Hikers, leashed dogs, mountain bikers, horseback riders
SEASON: June-November
PASSES/FEES: None
MAPS: USGS topographic map for Grizzly Peak, OR
CONTACT: Bureau of Land Management, 541/618-2200, www.blm.gov

START THE HIKE

▶ **MILE 0-0.8: Grizzly Peak Trailhead to First Meadow**
At the southeast edge of the parking lot, next to the restroom, you'll find the trailhead, simply marked "Trail." Start heading steadily uphill on the **Grizzly Peak Trail** (despite the name, there are no grizzlies here—or anywhere in Oregon) through a forest of grand fir and Douglas fir. After 0.8 mile, you'll arrive at the hike's first meadow. Visit June-August, and you'll likely catch blooming wildflowers, including the purple Siskiyou onion and yellow Baker's violet. In the fall, you might encounter locals hunting for morel and chanterelle mushrooms.

▶ **MILE 0.8-1.5: First Meadow to Grizzly Peak Summit**
After 0.5 mile of darting in and out of meadows, you'll come to a Y-shaped junction; head right to follow the **Grizzly Peak Loop Trail** counterclockwise, west and then south. In 0.2 mile, you'll arrive at **Grizzly Peak's summit,** noted simply by a large rockpile in a shady meadow; it's underwhelming but, fortunately, better views await.

▶ **MILE 1.5-3: Grizzly Peak Summit to Viewpoint**
After another 0.2 mile, you'll come to an unsigned Y-shaped junction; to the right is a short **spur trail** to a meadow with views of Medford to the northwest. Head left to continue the loop. You'll pass through an area still bearing the scars of a 2002 wildfire that burned nearly 2,000 acres on the western slopes of Grizzly Peak. Listen for woodpeckers as you hike the scorched hillside. Roughly 1.3 miles farther on, you'll arrive at what might be the hike's best **viewpoint.** Just after reaching the top of the rocky

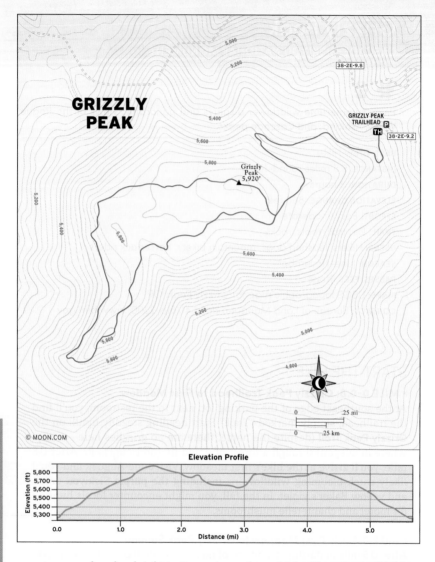

outcrop, make a hard right to its western edge, which offers views of Ashland, Emigrant Lake, and the Rogue Valley to the west; Mount Shasta and Pilot Rock to the south; and Mount McLoughlin and Diamond Peak to the north.

▶ MILE 3-5.6: Viewpoint to Grizzly Peak Trailhead

The trail begins to loop back northward from here; in 0.6 mile, you'll arrive at a Y-shaped junction. Head left, following the sign for the **Grizzly Peak Trail,** walking another 0.7 to complete the loop and reconnect with the original trail. Continue straight to head 1.3 miles downhill the way you came.

▲ VIEW FROM GRIZZLY PEAK

DIRECTIONS

From Ashland, head east on East Main Street for 2.9 miles. At road's end, turn right and then quickly left at the intersection to merge onto Highway 66. After 0.2 mile, turn left onto Dead Indian Memorial Road. Continue for 6.7 miles, and take a left at a sign for the Grizzly Peak Trail—the route is well-signed along the way—onto Shale City Road. After 3 miles, turn left onto the gravel Forest Road 38-2E-9.2. You'll come to a four-way junction after 0.8 mile; continue straight to head uphill, remaining on Forest Road 38-2E-9.2. The road ends, in another 0.9 mile, at the trailhead.

GPS COORDINATES: 42.272, –122.6063 / N42° 16.32' W122° 36.378'

BEST NEARBY BREWS

Good luck deciding among the 40 house beers at **Caldera Brewing Company** (590 Clover Ln., Ashland, 541/482-4677, http://calderabrewing.com, 11am-9pm daily). Its offerings run the gamut of styles, and the brewery displays thousands of beer bottles from around the world. From the trailhead, the 12-mile drive west takes 25 minutes via Dead Indian Memorial Road.

Grizzly Peak

Explore a network of trails boasting Rogue Valley views, just minutes from downtown Ashland.

DISTANCE: 4.9 miles round-trip
DURATION: 2 hours
ELEVATION CHANGE: 1,060 feet
EFFORT: Easy/moderate
TRAIL: Dirt trail, roots, rocks, old roadbed
USERS: Hikers, leashed dogs, mountain bikers (White Rabbit Trail only), horseback riders (White Rabbit Trail only)
SEASON: Year-round
PASSES/FEES: None
MAPS: USGS topographic map for Ashland, OR
CONTACT: Ashland Parks and Recreation, 541/488-5340, www.ashland.or.us

START THE HIKE

▸ MILE 0-0.6: Parking Area to Trailhead
From the Park Street parking area, walk uphill 0.2 mile. You'll soon trade pavement for gravel and pass a locked gate via a pedestrian pathway on either side. After another 0.4 mile of ascent, you'll arrive at a trail junction with paths veering off in seemingly every direction. Locate the map board and find the unsigned trail immediately behind it; this is the **Mike Uhtoff Trail.**

▸ MILE 0.6-1.1: Trailhead to Clearing
Start hiking west on the Mike Uhtoff Trail, heading uphill via switchbacks through a ponderosa pine forest for 0.5 mile to arrive at an unsigned Y-shaped junction. Continue uphill, to the left, to remain on the Mike Uhtoff Trail, and then pause in a **clearing** shortly after to enjoy your first views of the Rogue Valley.

▸ MILE 1.1-2.3: Clearing to Queen of Hearts Loop
Continue uphill and to the left again at a T-shaped junction in 0.2 mile to remain on the Mike Uhtoff Trail. Steadily ascend for another 0.5 mile to arrive at another junction. Head straight, remaining on the Mike Uhtoff Trail, but take a moment to rest on a bench, to your right, overlooking the city of Ashland. At this point you've ascended 715 feet, and the trail mostly flattens out from here as it traverses a fir forest. You'll arrive at an odd junction in another 0.5 mile; a sign for the Uhtoff Trail points back the way you just came, but turn left here for a partial jaunt on the (unsigned) **Queen of Hearts Loop.**

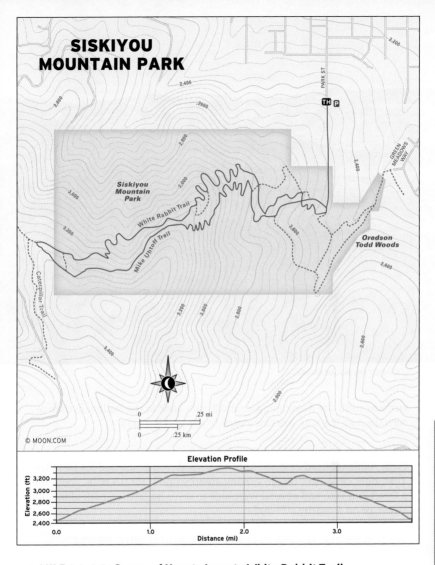

SISKIYOU MOUNTAIN PARK

Siskiyou Mountain Park

White Rabbit Trail

Mike Uhtoff Trail

Caterpillar Trail

Oredson Todd Woods

PARK ST

GREEN MEADOWS WAY

TH P

2,200
2,400
2,600
2,800
3,000
3,200
3,400
2,600
2,800
3,200
3,400
2,000
2,400
2,600

0   .25 mi
0   .25 km

© MOON.COM

Elevation Profile

Elevation (ft)

3,200
3,000
2,800
2,600
2,400

0.0   1.0   2.0   3.0

Distance (mi)

▶ MILE 2.3–2.5: Queen of Hearts Loop to White Rabbit Trail

Meander through ponderosa pine just below an impressive boulder field. You'll pass between two minivan-sized boulders before arriving, after 0.2 mile, at a sprawling trail junction. Make a hard right to start looping back east on the **White Rabbit Trail;** this is a multiuse path, so watch out for mountain bikers along its rolling slopes.

▶ MILE 2.5–4.9: White Rabbit Trail to Parking Area

In just over 0.1 mile, you'll come to a signed Y-shaped junction with the Queen of Hearts Loop and Uhtoff Trail; turn left to continue downhill and remain on the forested White Rabbit Trail. You'll intersect with other trails along the way, but just keep following signs for the White Rabbit Trail. In about 1.4 miles, the trail widens and becomes an old roadbed with a gravel

▲ VIEW OF THE ROGUE VALLEY

surface; continue descending on it 0.3 mile back to the trailhead, then return 0.6 mile the way you came back to the parking area.

DIRECTIONS

From Ashland, head east on Highway 99/Siskiyou Boulevard for 1.8 miles. Turn right onto Park Street, driving steeply uphill for 0.5 mile. You'll see a Dead End sign and several warnings to drive no farther; park along the street, or on a nearby side street.

GPS COORDINATES: 42.17287, -122.68132 / N42° 10.3722′ W122° 40.8792′

BEST NEARBY BITES

Fuel up for your hike with a breakfast burrito at **Ruby's** (163 N. Pioneer St., Ashland, 541/488-7717, http://rubysofashland.com, 7am-7pm daily). The cozy café serves a variety of hefty breakfast burritos, as well as lunch sandwiches, coffee, espresso, and more. From the trailhead, the 2.5-mile drive northwest takes 10 minutes via Siskiyou Boulevard.

6

Mount Ashland (via the Pacific Crest Trail)

KLAMATH NATIONAL FOREST

Mount Ashland—the highest peak in the Siskiyou Mountains—is known for its popular ski resort, but just below its summit are some of the region's most breathtaking wildflower displays and views of other nearby mountain peaks.

BEST: Wildflower Hikes
DISTANCE: 8.1 miles round-trip
DURATION: 4 hours
ELEVATION CHANGE: 1,050 feet
EFFORT: Moderate
TRAIL: Dirt trail, roots, rocks, roadbed, stream crossings
USERS: Hikers, leashed dogs, horseback riders
SEASON: June-November
PASSES/FEES: None
MAPS: USGS topographic map for Mount Ashland, OR-CA
CONTACT: Klamath National Forest, 530/842-6131, www.fs.usda.gov

START THE HIKE

Don't let this hike's stats dissuade you from hiking with kids; the mostly flat, well-graded trail's elevation gain rarely feels steep and, even if young ones aren't up for the whole trek, any of the mountain's many meadows make a fine turnaround point.

▸ **MILE 0-0.6: Pacific Crest Trailhead to First Meadow**
From the parking area, cross Mount Ashland Ski Road to find the trailhead—indicated by a **Pacific Crest Trail (PCT)** marker fastened to a tree—and begin to hike through the forest of grand and red fir. After 0.6 mile, you'll arrive at the first of several meadows that dot Mount Ashland's southern slopes. In addition to views of Black Butte, Mount Eddy, and—on a clear day—Mount Shasta, you'll find wildflowers blooming here in the summer, including yellow Bigelow's sneezeweed, purple and white Henderson's horkelia, and purple larkspur.

▸ **MILE 0.6-1.5: First Meadow to Fourth and Fifth Meadows**
The next meadow comes in another 0.2 mile, and a third meadow 0.3 mile past that one. As you pass through the meadows, you'll cross several foot-wide rivulets that drain water off the mountain; the overgrowth can hide wooden planks set up for crossing, so watch your feet to keep from tripping. You'll arrive at another pair of meadows over the next 0.4 mile; look out for orange agoseris and Mount Ashland lupine—found nowhere else

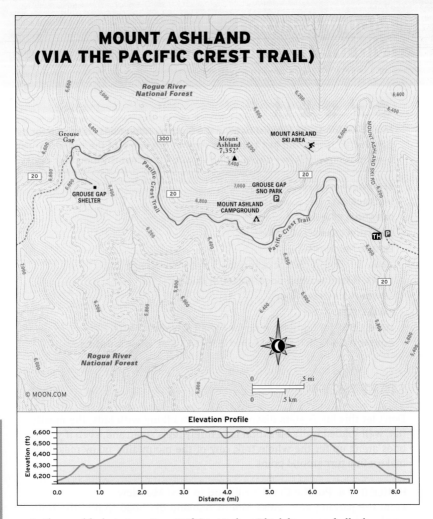

MOUNT ASHLAND
(VIA THE PACIFIC CREST TRAIL)

Elevation Profile

in the world—between June and September. Black bears and elk also roam the meadows below you, especially in the early morning and evening.

▸ **MILE 1.5-1.8: Fourth and Fifth Meadows to Grouse Gap**

In another 0.3 mile, continue straight across the unmarked Forest Road 40S15, and look to your right to spot the summit of Mount Ashland (along with a weather radar system). Soon after, the trail opens up in a grassy bowl known as **Grouse Gap;** here, the forest gives way almost entirely to meadows full of yellow buckwheat and several species of penstemon.

▸ **MILE 1.8-4.05: Grouse Gap to Grouse Gap Shelter**

In 1 mile you'll come upon a small grove of aspen trees that puts on a colorful foliage display every fall. After another 1 mile, the trail crosses Forest Road 40S30; turn left to follow the road gently downhill for 0.25 mile, then turn left into the parking area for the **Grouse Gap shelter.** The two-sided

▲ GROUSE GAP SHELTER

structure offers views of Klamath National Forest, Mount Ashland, and Mount Shasta.

Return the way you came.

DIRECTIONS

From Ashland, head south on I-5, and take exit 6, following a Mount Ashland sign. Continue on as it becomes Old Highway 99. In 1 mile, turn right at a sign for the Mount Ashland Ski Area onto Mount Ashland Ski Road. Continue for 7.2 miles, passing the milepost 7 marker before arriving at an unsigned parking area off to the right.

GPS COORDINATES: 42.07349, -122.69715 / N42° 4.4094′ W122° 41.829′

BEST NEARBY BREWS

Come for the British pub experience, including a good beer selection, at **The Black Sheep Pub & Restaurant** (51 N. Main St., Ashland, 541/482-6414, http://theblacksheep.com, 11:30am-midnight Sun.-Wed., 11:30am-1am Thurs.-Sat.). The airy pub serves up British classics, along with dramatic views of nearby peaks from its 2nd-story perch. From the trailhead, the 20-mile drive north takes about 30 minutes via Mount Ashland Ski Road and I-5.

7

Soda Mountain

SODA MOUNTAIN WILDERNESS, CASCADE-SISKIYOU NATIONAL MONUMENT

Hike through the Cascade-Siskiyou National Monument, which sits at the nexus of three distinct ecological regions: the Cascade, Klamath, and Siskiyou mountain ranges, which give this region the kind of biological diversity you won't find anywhere else in Oregon.

DISTANCE: 4.5 miles round-trip
DURATION: 2.5 hours
ELEVATION CHANGE: 710 feet
EFFORT: Easy/moderate
TRAIL: Dirt trail, rocks, roots, old roadbed
USERS: Hikers, leashed dogs, horseback riders
SEASON: June-October
PASSES/FEES: None
MAPS: USGS topographic map for Soda Mountain
CONTACT: Soda Mountain Wilderness, 541/618-2200, www.blm.gov

START THE HIKE

▶ **MILE 0-0.4: Pacific Crest Trailhead to Mount Ashland and Pilot Rock View**

At the southern edge of the parking lot, next to the restroom, you'll find the trailhead, indicated by a **Pacific Crest Trail (PCT)** marker. Begin hiking under a set of power lines through a high desert meadow that teems with summer wildflowers. Keep an eye out for western fence lizards, jackrabbits, and black-tailed deer. After 0.4 mile, views of Mount Ashland and Pilot Rock—the thumb-shaped crag rising above the tree line to the southwest—begin opening up to your right. Wildflowers dot the meadow along this stretch as well.

▶ **MILE 0.4-1.6: Mount Ashland and Pilot Rock View to Soda Mountain Lookout Road**

In 0.2 mile, you'll leave the desert to begin steadily ascending through a forest of Douglas fir, ponderosa pine, and grand fir. In 0.8 mile, you'll see a PCT signpost, to your left, and several feet past it an unsigned **connector trail** that switchbacks uphill; turn left onto the connector trail and walk 0.2 mile to the unsigned **Soda Mountain Lookout Road.**

▶ **MILE 1.6-2.25: Soda Mountain Lookout Road to Soda Mountain Summit and Fire Lookout**

Turn right onto the road and continue ascending, sometimes steeply. There's little shade along this stretch, and you'll gain 360 feet in elevation

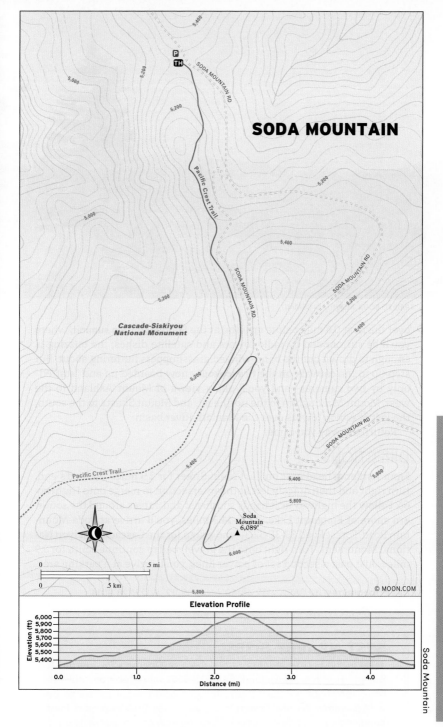

SODA MOUNTAIN

Soda Mountain Rd

Pacific Crest Trail

Cascade-Siskiyou
National Monument

Pacific Crest Trail

Soda
Mountain
6,089'

0   .5 mi
0   .5 km

© MOON.COM

Elevation Profile

▲ TRAIL TO SODA MOUNTAIN SUMMIT

over the next 0.6 mile before arriving at the **Soda Mountain summit,** where you'll be surrounded by radio towers and satellite dishes; the buzzing is enough to drown out the band-winged grasshoppers fluttering about. But step up to the catwalk on the **fire lookout**—now boarded up and "staffed" only by two cameras—and you'll enjoy views of Mount Ashland to the west, Mount McLoughlin to the northeast, and Mount Shasta to the south, the last of which towers over the Klamath River basin.

Return the way you came.

DIRECTIONS

From Ashland, head east on East Main Street for 2.9 miles. At road's end, turn right and then quickly left at the intersection to merge onto Highway 66. Follow the highway as it heads southeast and curves around the southern shore of Emigrant Lake. After 14.5 miles, you'll arrive at Soda Mountain Road/Forest Road 39-3E-32.3—and a sign for the Cascade-Siskiyou National Monument. Turn right onto the gravel road to continue south for 3.9 miles. Just past a second set of power lines, you'll arrive at a parking area.

GPS COORDINATES: 42.0852, –122.48169 / N42° 5.112′, W122° 28.9014′

BEST NEARBY BITES

Revel in the Shakespearean atmosphere of **Oberon's Restaurant & Bar** (45 N. Main St., Ashland, 541/708-6652, http://oberonsashland. com, 4pm-midnight Sun.-Thurs., 11:30am-1am Fri.-Sat.). Inspired by *A Midsummer Night's Dream,* the pub serves British comfort food amid enchanting forested decor. From the trailhead, the 22-mile drive northwest takes 45 minutes via Highway 66.

NEARBY CAMPGROUNDS

NAME	DESCRIPTION	FACILITIES	SEASON	FEE
Valley of the Rogue State Park	busy campground along the Rogue River	95 full-hookup sites, 62 tent and electrical sites, 8 yurts, restrooms	year-round	$19-53
Twin Bridges Rd., Gold Hill, 541/582-3128, www.oregonstateparks.org				
Emigrant Lake County Park	campground on the north shore of Emigrant Lake	39 tent sites, 31 RV sites, restrooms	RV sites: year-round; tent sites: March-October	$20-30
Hwy. 66, Ashland, 541/774-8183, www.jacksoncountyor.org				
Mount Ashland Campground	first-come, first-served campsites on Mount Ashland	9 tent sites, restrooms	June-October, depending on snow levels	free
Forest Rd. 20, Ashland, 530/842-6131, www.fs.usda.gov				
Schroeder Park	campground along the Rogue River	22 full-hookup sites, 22 tent sites, 2 yurts, restrooms	year-round	$20-55
Schroeder Lane, Grants Pass, 541/474-5285, www.co.josephine.or.us				
Cave Creek Campground	near Oregon Caves National Monument	17 tent sites, compostable toilets	May-September	$10
Hwy. 46, Cave Junction, 541/592-2100, www.nps.gov				

SKY LAKES WILDERNESS AND KLAMATH BASIN

Spend a few minutes on almost any trail in the Sky Lakes Wilderness, and it's easy to see how the region earned it name. It comprises three lake basins along the crest of the Cascade Range and is known for its almost unmatched water quality: Environmental Protection Agency studies in the 1980s and 1990s found that the Sky Lakes Wilderness was home to some of the most chemically pure water in the world. Just south of the Sky Lakes Wilderness, Brown Mountain straddles two worlds: Cascade forests collide with fields of lava rock, draped across the hillside like a bedsheet. Farther east, the longest linear park in Oregon hosts more than 100 miles of trails through forests, marshes, and farmland in the heart of the Klamath Basin.

▲ THE PATH TO PUCK LAKE

▲ OC&E WOODS LINE STATE TRAIL

◄ MOUNT MCLOUGHLIN AND THE BROWN MOUNTAIN LAVA FLOW TRAIL

1 **Horseshoe Lake**
DISTANCE: 6.1 miles round-trip
DURATION: 3 hours
EFFORT: Easy/moderate

2 **Brown Mountain Lava Flow**
DISTANCE: 6.1 miles round-trip
DURATION: 3 hours
EFFORT: Easy/moderate

3 **Sky Lakes Basin via Cold Springs Trail**
DISTANCE: 7.2 miles round-trip
DURATION: 3.5 hours
EFFORT: Easy/moderate

4 **Puck Lakes via Nannie Creek Trail**
DISTANCE: 5.4 miles round-trip
DURATION: 2.5 hours
EFFORT: Easy/moderate

5 **OC&E Woods Line State Trail**
DISTANCE: 4.7 miles round-trip
DURATION: 2.5 hours
EFFORT: Easy

BEST NEARBY BITES AND BREWS

Klamath Falls is the most likely staging point for hikes in the area as well as where the best nearby bites and brews are located. Most trails covered in this chapter are about an hour's drive from town, except for Brown Mountain Lava Flow, which is about a 1.75-hour drive.

- Fuel up before hitting the trail at **Green Blade Bakery** (1400 Esplanade St., 541/273-8999, http://green-blade.com, 6am-2pm Tues.-Sat.). This family-run artisan bakery sells a variety of breads and pastries, all made from scratch, and with as many locally sourced ingredients as possible.

- Morning, noon, or night, you'll always feel right at home at **The Grocery Pub** (1201 Division St., 541/851-9441, http://thegrocerypub. com, 8am-9pm Mon.-Sat., 9am-9pm Sun.). The Grocery pulls double duty as an inviting neighborhood restaurant-pub, and as a convenience store for grab-and-go snacks.

- Enjoy a slice and a pint at Klamath Falls' first brewery, **Mia & Pia's Pizzeria & Brewhouse** (3545 Summers Lane, 541/884-4880, http://miaandpiasklamathfalls.com, 11am-9:30pm Sun.-Thurs., 10:30am-10:30pm Fri.-Sat.). The family-friendly restaurant serves pizza, sandwiches, and brews both classic and eclectic.

- Housed in an old creamery, **Klamath Basin Brewing** (1320 Main St., 541/273-5222, http://kbbrewing.com, 11am-9pm Sun.-Thurs., 11am-10pm Fri.-Sat.) boasts a solid selection of classic styles. It brews its beers using geothermal energy, and each beer is named for an element of local culture.

- Bask in panoramic views of Mount McLoughlin at **Lake of the Woods Resort** (950 Harriman Rte., 541/949-8300, http://lakeofthewoodsresort.com, 8am-9pm daily May-Sept.), west of town. Its on-site restaurant serves classic American fare: omelets, sandwiches, burgers, and more. The Brown Mountain Lava Flow hike is particularly convenient to the Lake of the Woods Resort; from the trailhead, the 5-mile drive east takes less than 10 minutes via Highway 140.

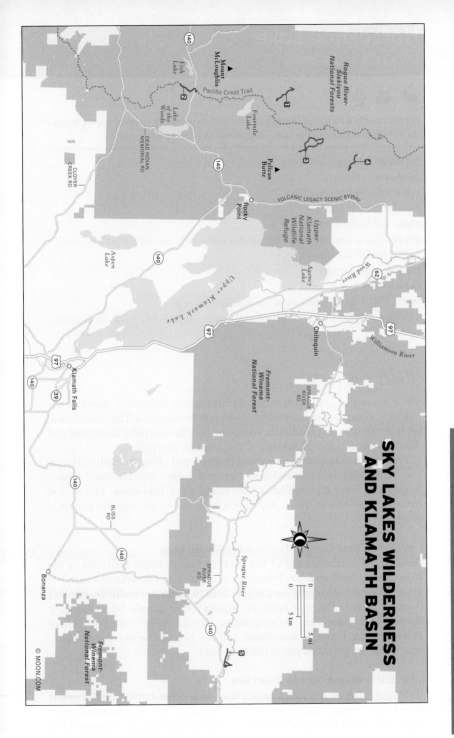

SKY LAKES WILDERNESS AND KLAMATH BASIN

© MOON.COM

Horseshoe Lake

SKY LAKES WILDERNESS

Hike through a forest of Shasta red fir and hemlock to several scenic lakes—don't forget a swimsuit in summer—in the Sky Lakes Wilderness.

DISTANCE: 6.1 miles round-trip
DURATION: 3 hours
ELEVATION CHANGE: 660 feet
EFFORT: Easy/moderate
TRAIL: Dirt trail, rocks, roots
USERS: Hikers, leashed dogs, horseback riders (horses not permitted within 200 feet of lakeshores)
SEASON: June–October
PASSES/FEES: None
MAPS: USGS topographic map for Rustler Peak, OR
CONTACT: Rogue River–Siskiyou National Forest, 541/560-3400, www.fs.usda.gov

START THE HIKE

You'll share this trail with scores of hikers and horseback riders at the height of summer, not to mention swarms of mosquitoes. The ideal time to hit the trail is in early autumn, when the mosquitoes have dissipated and the forest floor turns all manner of red, orange, and yellow.

Primitive **backcountry campsites** are dispersed along the trail to Horseshoe Lake (Rogue River-Siskiyou National Forest, 541/560-3400, www.fs.usda.gov, free) and available year-round on a first-come, first-served basis, if you'd like to turn a day hike into an overnight trip. No permit is necessary.

▶ **MILE 0-1: Blue Canyon Trailhead to Round Lake**
Head to the northern edge of the parking area to begin your hike at the **Blue Canyon Trailhead.** You'll come to a fork almost immediately; turn left onto the mostly shaded Blue Canyon Trail to begin gradually descending through a dense forest of hemlock, Shasta red fir, purple lupine (in early summer), huckleberries, and pinemat manzanita. After 1 mile, you'll arrive at **Round Lake.** If you're so inclined, you can hop on the short **spur trail** to your right, which takes you to the lakeshore.

▶ **MILE 1-2: Round Lake to Blue Lake**
Continue south on the Blue Canyon Trail. In another 1 mile, you'll arrive at **Blue Lake.** A surprising view awaits at the end of the short **spur trail** off to your right: From the shoreline you can see meadows, a thick hemlock forest, and a 300-foot cliff—and accompanying rockslide—butting up against the lake. This is also an especially popular swimming spot in summer.

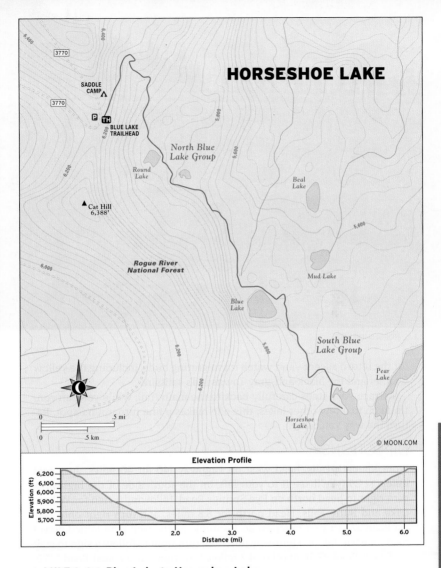

Elevation Profile

▶ MILE 2-3.1: Blue Lake to Horseshoe Lake

Back on the trail, the path splits at an unsigned Y-shaped junction 0.1 mile past Blue Lake; turn right to remain on the Blue Canyon Trail, continuing south and cutting between Blue Lake to your right and tiny, relatively unremarkable **Meadow Lake,** which remains mostly hidden, to your left. After 0.8 mile of mostly flat hiking, you'll reach **Horseshoe Lake.** It's largely obscured by the surrounding forest, so as you first spy the lake through the trees, find the faint, single-file **spur trail** off to your right for the best views, or a swim. Note that several social trails crisscross this area, so it's easy to get turned around—use GPS here to be safe and try to stick closely to the spur, which ends after about 0.2 mile at the shore, not far from the center of the horseshoe shape from which the lake gets its name. Find a log on which to sit and relax, and maybe enjoy a snack—gathering energy

▲ HORSESHOE LAKE

for the return ascent—and watch for migrating birds, including the yellow warbler and the black-and-gray Townsend's solitaire.

Retrace your steps carefully back to the main trail; while you can continue on to a few other lakes, this one makes a fine turnaround spot. Return the way you came.

DIRECTIONS

From Klamath Falls, head west on Highway 140 for 40 miles. Just past milepost 29 (you'll see it to your left, on the south side of the highway), turn right to head north on Rye Springs Road, following a sign for Willow Lake and Butte Falls. Head north for 8.8 miles, and turn right onto Forest Road 37 just past milepost 26. Continue on the well-maintained gravel road for 6.9 miles; at a four-way junction, turn right to follow a sign to stay on Forest Road 37. In another 4.2 miles, turn right onto Forest Road 3770, following a sign for the Blue Canyon Trail. You'll come to a Y-shaped junction in 4.1 miles; head left and continue uphill, following a sign for Forest Road 3770. You'll arrive at the trailhead parking area, off to the right, in another 1.1 miles.

GPS COORDINATES: 42.53037, –122.2974 / N42° 31.8222′ W122° 17.844′

Dart between thick forests and lava fields while enjoying photo-worthy views of Mount McLoughlin, southern Oregon's tallest peak at 9,493 feet.

DISTANCE: 6.1 miles round-trip

DURATION: 3 hours

ELEVATION CHANGE: 670 feet

EFFORT: Easy/moderate

TRAIL: Dirt trail, lava fields, rocks, roots, highway crossing

USERS: Hikers, leashed dogs, horseback riders

SEASON: June-November

PASSES/FEES: Free May-October, $4 Oregon State Sno-Park day-use permit per vehicle November-April

MAPS: USGS topographic map for Mount McLoughlin

CONTACT: Fremont-Winema National Forest, 541/560-3400, www.fs.usda.gov

Although this trail lies in the shadow of 7,311-foot Brown Mountain, the summit is almost never visible along this stretch. Nevertheless, you'll feel its presence: Some 2,000 years ago, the cinder cone erupted, forming the lava fields through which you'll hike.

START THE HIKE

▸ **MILE 0-0.6: Pacific Crest Access Trailhead to Highway 140**

Find the **Pacific Crest Access Trailhead** at the western edge of the parking lot near the informational signboard. Walk through lush fir forest for just over 0.2 mile before crossing a footbridge, where you'll arrive at a T-shaped junction; turn left onto the **Pacific Crest Trail,** heading south. After 0.4 mile, the mostly flat trail hits Highway 140; look both ways, cross the highway, and follow the PCT blaze, fastened to a tree. (To shorten the hike by 1.2 miles round-trip, use an unmarked turnout and parking area at the eastern edge of the metal guardrails here.)

▸ **MILE 0.6-1: Highway 140 to Lava Field**

You'll head into a forest of fir and maple before arriving, in another 0.2 mile, at an X-shaped junction. Ignore the side trails here, and continue straight ahead on the well-maintained path to arrive soon after at an intersection with the High Lakes Trail; continue straight ahead to remain on the PCT. Some 0.15 mile past this junction, you'll head into your first full-blown **lava field,** walking on crushed red cinder, lined on either side by black lava rocks. From here you'll encounter a steady diet of old lava flows, broken up by scattered forests of hemlock, Douglas fir, and Shasta red fir.

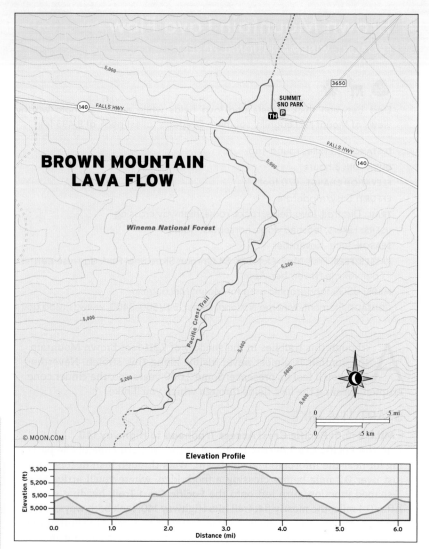

▶ MILE 1–3.05: Lava Field to Viewpoint Clearing

In 0.5 mile, as the gently ascending trail curves west, take a moment to turn around for your first view of Mount McLoughlin to the north. After 1.5 miles, soon after emerging from forested terrain, you'll descend slightly before arriving at a 50-foot stretch of lava rock sandwiched between two stands of Douglas fir; here, a small, mostly shaded **clearing** offers plenty of rocks on which to sit and enjoy a snack, with views of Mount McLoughlin. Listen for the plush toy-like squeaks of the pika, a rabbit-like mammal that lives in the alpine rocks.

While the trail continues on, this makes an ideal turnaround point. Return the way you came.

▲ BROWN MOUNTAIN LAVA FLOW WITH MOUNT MCLOUGHLIN

DIRECTIONS

From Klamath Falls, head west on Highway 140 for 36.3 miles. Roughly 0.5 mile past milepost 33 (to your left, on the south side of the highway), turn right at a sign for the Summit trailhead. Almost immediately after, turn left and drive 0.2 mile into a large parking area.

GPS COORDINATES: 42.3964, –122.285 / N42° 23.784' W122° 17.1'

Sky Lakes Basin via Cold Springs Trail

SKY LAKES WILDERNESS

There may be no finer introduction to the Sky Lakes Wilderness than this loop trail to the shores of several mountain lakes, some of which are popular swimming holes in summer.

BEST: Summer Hikes

DISTANCE: 7.2 miles round-trip

DURATION: 3.5 hours

ELEVATION CHANGE: 490 feet

EFFORT: Easy/moderate

TRAIL: Dirt trail, rocks, roots

USERS: Hikers, leashed dogs, horseback riders (horses not permitted within 200 feet of lakeshores)

SEASON: July–October

PASSES/FEES: None

MAPS: USGS topographic maps for Pelican Butte

CONTACT: Fremont-Winema National Forest, 541/883-6714, www.fs.usda.gov

START THE HIKE

Primitive **backcountry campsites** are dispersed along this trail (Fremont-Winema National Forest, 541/883-6714, www.fs.usda.gov, free) and available year-round on a first-come, first-served basis, if you'd like to turn a day hike into an overnight trip. No permit is necessary.

▶ **MILE 0–0.6: Cold Springs Trailhead to South Rock Creek Trail**

Start this loop hike from the **Cold Springs Trailhead** at the northern edge of the parking area. Almost immediately, you'll find yourself in a forest scarred by wildfire; in 2017, lightning struck this area, igniting a blaze that burned nearly 5,000 acres and left scores of burned snags, downed trees, and almost no undergrowth. After 0.6 mile of mostly level hiking through the

ISHERWOOD LAKE ▶

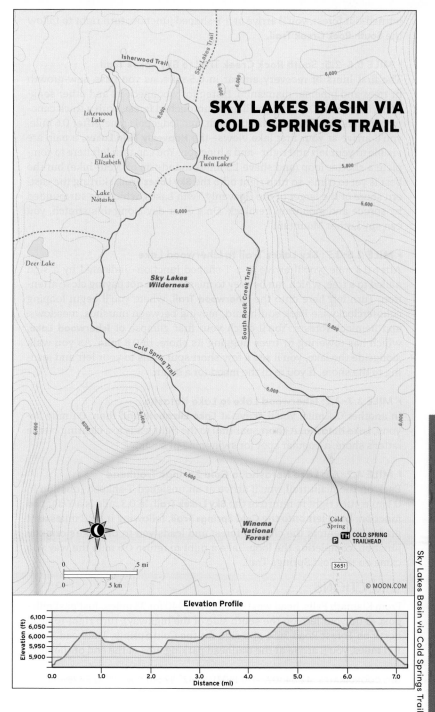

SKY LAKES BASIN VIA COLD SPRINGS TRAIL

Isherwood Trail

Sky Lakes Trail

Isherwood Lake

Lake Elizabeth

Lake Notasha

Deer Lake

Heavenly Twin Lakes

Sky Lakes Wilderness

South Rock Creek Trail

Cold Spring Trail

Winema National Forest

Cold Spring

TH COLD SPRING TRAILHEAD

P

3651

0   .5 mi
0   .5 km

© MOON.COM

Elevation Profile

Elevation (ft)

6,100
6,050
6,000
5,950
5,900

0.0   1.0   2.0   3.0   4.0   5.0   6.0   7.0
Distance (mi)

burned-out forest, you'll arrive at a Y-shaped junction; turn right to follow the **South Rock Creek Trail.**

▶ **MILE 0.6–2.5: South Rock Creek Trail to Sky Lakes Trail**
The first hints of recovery appear in 0.5 mile, as you pass new-growth fir trees and pinemat manzanita. Listen for woodpeckers and other song-birds. In another 0.8 mile, you'll enter untouched forest, with a thick cano-py of mountain hemlock, Shasta red fir, and lodgepole pine. After 0.6 mile, you'll arrive at your first lake views—the **Heavenly Twin Lakes,** a pair, are visible to your left and right—and a junction. You can turn left here to com-plete a shorter loop (and shave 1.5 miles round-trip off your hike) but the best is yet to come, so turn right onto the **Sky Lakes Trail,** skirting the east-ern shore of the larger of the Heavenly Twin Lakes, which are surrounded by spruce and mountain hemlock. On a clear day along this stretch, you can spy Luther Mountain.

▶ **MILE 2.5–3.7: Sky Lakes Trail to Isherwood Lake**
After 0.4 mile, you'll arrive at a T-shaped junction—indicated by a sign nailed to a tree, which can be easy to miss if you're not paying close atten-tion. Turn left here onto the **Isherwood Trail,** where you'll begin looping counterclockwise back southward, moving between marshes, meadows, and hemlock forests. You'll catch your first glimpse of **Isherwood Lake,** which has towering fir trees hugging its shore, in 0.8 mile. As you walk alongside the lake, you'll see a few short spur trails to your left and lead-ing to the shore, if you're in the mood for a swim.

▶ **MILE 3.7–4.2: Isherwood Lake to Lake Notasha**
In another 0.4 mile, you'll arrive at **Lake Elizabeth** and then, 0.1 mile be-yond, **Lake Notasha.** A short spur trail to the right leads to a clearing on the latter's shore, a popular spot for swimming in summer.

▶ **MILE 4.2–7.2: Lake Notasha to Cold Springs Trailhead**
Back on the main trail, you'll arrive at an unsigned T-shaped junction in 0.1 mile; turn right to return to the **Sky Lakes Trail.** In 0.3 mile is a Y-shaped junction; head left onto the **Cold Springs Trail,** following it for 2 miles as it gradually reenters the charred forest and leads you to the hike's original junction, completing the loop. Take a right to return 0.6 mile the way you came on the Cold Springs Trail.

DIRECTIONS

From Klamath Falls, head west on Highway 140 for 28 miles. Just past mile-post 41 (to your left, on the south side of the highway), turn right to head north on Forest Road 3651 at a sign for the Cold Springs Trailhead. After 10.1 miles, you'll arrive at the trailhead parking area at the end of the road.

GPS COORDINATES: 42.54302, –122.18071 / N42° 32.5812′ W122° 10.8426′

SKY LAKES WILDERNESS

Hike through a pleasant hemlock forest before arriving at Puck Lakes, a fine place to rest, snack, and—at the height of summer—go for a swim.

DISTANCE: 5.4 miles round-trip

DURATION: 2.5 hours

ELEVATION CHANGE: 680 feet

EFFORT: Easy/moderate

TRAIL: Dirt trail, rocks, roots

USERS: Hikers, leashed dogs, horseback riders (horses not permitted within 200 feet of lakeshores)

SEASON: July–October

PASSES/FEES: None

MAPS: USGS topographic maps for Pelican Butte and Devils Peak, OR

CONTACT: Fremont–Winema National Forest, 541/883-6714, www.fs.usda.gov

START THE HIKE

Primitive **backcountry campsites** are dispersed along the trail to Puck Lakes (Fremont-Winema National Forest, 541/883-6714, www.fs.usda.gov, free) and available year-round on a first-come, first-served basis, if you'd like to turn a day hike into an overnight trip. No permit is necessary.

▶ **MILE 0-1.6: Nannie Creek Trailhead to Trail High Point**

Begin hiking on the **Nannie Creek Trail** from the information signboard on the northwest edge of the parking lot. Ascend gradually via a handful of switchbacks through a forest of mountain hemlock and lodgepole pine and, after 0.6 mile, look to your left to catch views of the flat, expansive Klamath Basin to the east before you head into thick forest. Continue gently ascending for 1 mile; at this point, you've gained about 525 feet.

SKY LAKES WILDERNESS AND KLAMATH BASIN

Puck Lakes via Nannie Creek Trail

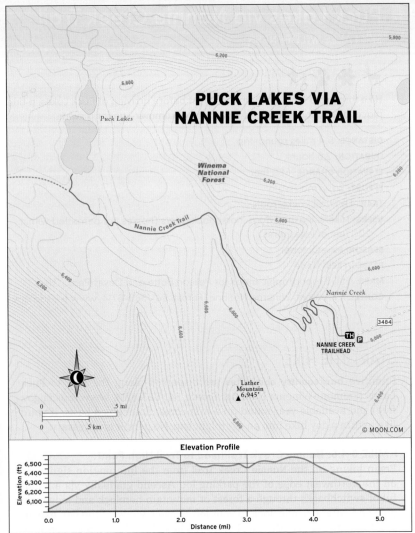

PUCK LAKES VIA NANNIE CREEK TRAIL

Puck Lakes

Winema
National
Forest

Nannie Creek Trail

Nannie Creek

3484

TH P

NANNIE CREEK
TRAILHEAD

Lather
Mountain
▲ 6,945'

© MOON.COM

0 ____ .5 mi
0 ____ .5 km

Elevation Profile

Elevation (ft): 6,500 / 6,400 / 6,300 / 6,200 / 6,100

Distance (mi): 0.0 / 1.0 / 2.0 / 3.0 / 4.0 / 5.0

▶ **MILE 1.6–2.6: Trail High Point to Unsigned Junction**

The trail levels out and then you'll start to slowly descend toward the Puck Lakes through a forest of western hemlock, new-growth fir trees, towering Shasta red fir, and huckleberry. Stay attentive or keep an eye on your GPS as you descend into the Sky Lakes Basin; with no clear signage, it's easy to miss your turnoff toward Puck Lakes, which comes after roughly 1 mile of gradual descent, when you first catch sight of the lakes through the trees to your right and arrive shortly thereafter at an unsigned junction.

▶ **MILE 2.6–2.7: Unsigned Junction to Puck Lake**

Take a right here to head north along a narrow path, which cuts through a marsh and ends, after a flat 0.1 mile, on the southern shore of 24-acre **Puck Lake,** surrounded by lodgepole pine. While you can continue meandering

▲ PUCK LAKE

along the trail to your left, heading clockwise around the larger of the two Puck Lakes, the path gets progressively fainter as it cuts between it and **Little Puck Lake** just north. And at any rate, Puck Lake is the star, famed for its clarity, and this is an ideal spot to relax, swim, and enjoy lunch. Expect to share the scene with swarms of mosquitoes in late spring and early summer—and migrating ospreys, fishing for dinner, in fall. Keep an eye out for the pink heather dotting the banks of the lake at the height of summer, as well.

Return the way you came.

DIRECTIONS

From Klamath Falls, head west on Highway 140 for 25.1 miles. Just past milepost 44, as the highway curves away from Upper Klamath Lake, turn right to head north on West Side Road, following a sign for Rocky Point, Fort Klamath, and Crater Lake National Park. After 12.2 miles, turn left onto Forest Road 3484, following a sign for the Nannie Creek Trailhead. Follow the gravel road for 4 miles; at the intersection, take a hard left to head uphill and remain on Forest Road 3484. Continue 1.5 miles to the parking lot at the end of the road.

GPS COORDINATES: 42.61382, –122.14719 / N42° 36.8292′ W122° 8.8314′

SKY LAKES WILDERNESS AND KLAMATH BASIN

Puck Lakes via Nannie Creek Trail

OC&E Woods Line State Trail

OREGON STATE PARKS

🦌 🐾 🚶

Hike along a stretch of converted railbed—part of the longest linear park in Oregon—to an abandoned rail yard along the Sprague River.

DISTANCE: 4.7 miles round-trip
DURATION: 2.5 hours
ELEVATION CHANGE: 160 feet
EFFORT: Easy
TRAIL: Dirt trail, rocks, gravel, wooden bridges, road
USERS: Hikers, leashed dogs, mountain bikers, horseback riders
SEASON: Year-round
PASSES/FEES: None
MAPS: USGS topographic maps for Beatty, OR, and Ferguson Mountain, OR
CONTACT: Oregon State Parks, 541/783-2471, www.oregonstateparks.org

On this wholly exposed hike, you'll walk along part of the OC&E Woods Line State Trail, stretching 109 miles throughout the Klamath Basin. It follows the path of an old logging railroad that served the region through much of the 20th century. Named for the Oregon, California, and Eastern Railroad, the rail lines carried as much as one million board feet of lumber per day in the early 1900s. The last of the cars ran in 1990, and it's now a rail-to-trail path.

START THE HIKE

▶ **MILE 0-1.5: OC&E Woods Line State Trailhead to Sprague River Bridge**

Find the trailhead for this section of the **OC&E Woods Line State Trail** on the east side of Godowa Springs Road. Walk through the smaller of two green gates here to begin your hike. Keep an eye out along this early stretch for sandhill cranes, bald eagles, and other birds; this region is along the Pacific Flyway, a migratory bird route that stretches from Alaska to Argentina and sees more than 350 bird species. You might also see garter snakes, antelope, badgers, and other animals. About 1.2 miles from the trailhead, the gravel path will fork; head right to continue east onto the fainter of the two paths. You'll walk through overgrowth, with expansive views of nearby sagebrush fields and marshland, before arriving in 0.25 mile at a 250-foot wooden bridge spanning the **Sprague River.**

▶ **MILE 1.5-2.2: Sprague River Bridge to Brown Cemetery**

Cross the bridge, and walk through a green gate in 0.2 mile to arrive at a T-shaped junction; turn left to head north and slightly uphill onto the **unnamed dirt road.** You'll gain roughly 100 feet over the next 0.3 mile, with views of the winding Sprague River and two-humped Saddle Mountain to the west. Turn right onto another unnamed roadbed for an 0.2-mile **spur**

OC&E WOODS LINE STATE TRAIL

FERGUSON MOUNTAIN RD

FERGUSON MOUNTAIN RD

GODOWA SPRINGS RD

Sprague Creek

TH

OC&E Woods Line State Trail

BEATTY STATION

BROWN CEMETARY

4,400

Beatty Gap

Spring Creek

140

4,400

Beatty

KLAMATH FALLS-LAKEVIEW HWY

140

0   .5 mi

0   .5 km

© MOON.COM

Elevation Profile

Elevation (ft)

4,500

4,400

4,300

0.0   1.0   2.0   3.0   4.0

Distance (mi)

to **Brown Cemetery,** the resting place of the Modoc people who once called this area home.

▶ MILE 2.2–2.8: Brown Cemetery to Ranch House and Railcar

Walk the 0.2 mile back to the main trail, and continue north for 0.3 mile as it flattens out and then descends toward an old **ranch house.** Note that this stretch of trail borders private property, so please respect the various fences and No Trespassing signs along the way. You'll encounter a sprawling unsigned junction of trails and old roads at the house; turn right onto the red cinder rock trail—it's bounded on both sides by fences—and walk several hundred feet to check out the **abandoned railcar** off to your left; this was the site of an old rail yard.

▲ THE BROWN CEMETERY

▶ **MILE 2.8–4.7: Ranch House and Railcar to
OC&E Woods Line State Trailhead**

Return to the junction, cross the gravel road, and continue straight through
the green gate with an OC&E Trail sign to begin looping back south. You'll
cross another wooden bridge over the river in 0.3 mile and, in another 0.3
mile, reconnect with the original trail; turn right to return 1.2 miles the
way you came.

DIRECTIONS

From Klamath Falls, head east on Highway 140, following a sign for Lakeview and Winnemucca, for 35.1 miles. When you arrive in the no-stoplight
hamlet of Beatty, turn left to head north on Godowa Springs Road, following a sign for Spodue Mountain. Continue for 0.7 mile until you reach the
trailhead, noted by green gates on either side of the road. There is room
for 1-3 cars to park directly in front of the gates; if there's no space available when you arrive, consider parking on the shoulder back in Beatty and
walking to the trailhead.

GPS COORDINATES: 42.45223, –121.27124 / N42° 27.1338′ W121° 16.2744′

NEARBY CAMPGROUNDS

NAME	DESCRIPTION	FACILITIES	SEASON	FEE
Fourmile Lake Campground	popular campground on the shore of Fourmile Lake	29 RV and tent sites, restrooms	May–October	$15–30
Fourmile Lake Rd., Klamath Falls, 866/201-4194, www.fs.usda.gov					
Aspen Point Campground at Lake of the Woods	popular campground on the shore of Lake of the Woods	50 RV sites, 8 double campsites, 7 tent sites, restrooms	May–October	$18–36
Forest Rd. 3704, Klamath Falls, 541/883-6714, www.fs.usda.gov					
Sunset Campground	popular campground on the shore of Lake of the Woods	64 RV and tent sites, restrooms	May–October	$18–36
Dead Indian Memorial Rd., Klamath Falls, 866/201-4194, www.fs.usda.gov					
Topsy Campground	quiet campground with views of Mount McLoughlin	13 tent sites, restrooms	May–October	$7
Topsy Grade Rd., Keno, 541/883-6916, www.blm.gov					
Odessa Campground	quiet campground offering easy boat access near the western shore of Upper Klamath Lake	6 tent sites, restrooms	year-round, with reduced services October–May	free
Forest Rd. 3639, Klamath Falls, 541/885-3400, www.fs.usda.gov					

STEENS MOUNTAIN AND ALVORD DESERT

Steens Mountain is the eighth-tallest peak in Oregon, a 50-mile-long fault-block mountain rising 9,733 feet above sea level. It formed millions of years ago when several basalt flows piled atop each other like a layer cake; over time, the basalt flows expanded and contracted, and glaciers carved Steens's most distinctive geologic feature—a series of gorges. The mountain looms over the Alvord Desert, a dry lakebed of cracked alkali beneath its eastern face; receiving only six inches of rain per year, it's the driest place in the state. With sagebrush and juniper giving way to aspen and cottonwood, wildlife from rattlesnakes to pronghorn, and canyons and gorges to explore, hikers who make it to this remote playground in southeastern Oregon will be rewarded. Prepare for the weather, as snow can fall year-round at Steens's higher elevations.

▲ ON THE BORAX LAKE HOT SPRINGS TRAIL

▲ VIEW FROM PIKE CREEK CANYON TRAIL

1 Riddle Brothers Ranch and Little Blitzen River
DISTANCE: 5.8 miles round-trip
DURATION: 2.5 hours
EFFORT: Easy/moderate

2 Big Indian Gorge
DISTANCE: 8.1 miles round-trip
DURATION: 4 hours
EFFORT: Moderate

3 Wildhorse Lake
DISTANCE: 2.8 miles round-trip
DURATION: 2 hours
EFFORT: Easy/moderate

4 Pike Creek Canyon
DISTANCE: 6.5 miles round-trip
DURATION: 3 hours
EFFORT: Moderate

5 Borax Lake Hot Springs
DISTANCE: 2 miles round-trip
DURATION: 1 hour
EFFORT: Easy

BEST NEARBY BITES, BREWS, AND A BONUS

Services around Steens Mountain are few and far between—make sure you have maps downloaded for offline use, on your phone or otherwise, as cell reception is limited. The towns of **Burns** to the north of Steens Mountain, **Frenchglen** to the west, and **Fields** to the south are your best bets for services including food and drink, as well as gas.

- Whether you're heading out from or returning to civilization, stop for a pint at **Steens Mountain Brewing Company** (353 W. Monroe St., Burns, 541/589-1159, www.steensmountainbrewingco.com, 5pm-8pm Thurs.-Fri., 3pm-8pm Sat., 2pm-6pm Sun.). The family-owned brewery uses eight varieties of heirloom hops, and each beer is inspired by a regional landmark or historical event.

- Enjoy a filling breakfast or lunch, or make reservations for a stick-to-your-ribs dinner, at **Frenchglen Hotel State Heritage Site** (39184 Hwy. 205, Frenchglen, 541/493-2825, www.frenchglenhotel.com, 7:30am-9:30am, 11:30am-2:30pm, and dinner seating 6:30pm daily mid-Mar.-Oct.). The historic hotel was built in the 1920s to host stagecoach travelers and is popular for its western-inspired decor and large porch, which affords views of Steens Mountain.

- Enjoy homecooked diner fare at **Fields Station** (22276 Fields Dr., Fields, 541/495-2275, 8am-6pm Mon.-Sat., 9am-5pm Sun.). The café serves breakfast, burgers, and sandwiches—but save room for its self-proclaimed "world famous" milk shakes. It's just 20 minutes from the Borax Lake Hot Springs trailhead.

- What better way to unwind from a hike than with a soak in hot springs? **Alvord Hot Springs** (East Steens Rd./Fields-Denio Rd., Fields, 541/589-2282, www.alvordhotsprings.com, 8am-10pm daily, $8 soaking fee pp) sit a mile below the summit of Steens Mountain, hugging the western flank of the Alvord Desert. The water comes out of the ground at 170 degrees and cools when filling the soaking pools. An on-site general store sells ice, drinks, towels, and other items. Pairing a soak here with a hike to Pike Creek Canyon is particularly convenient—it's just a few miles down the road from the trailhead.

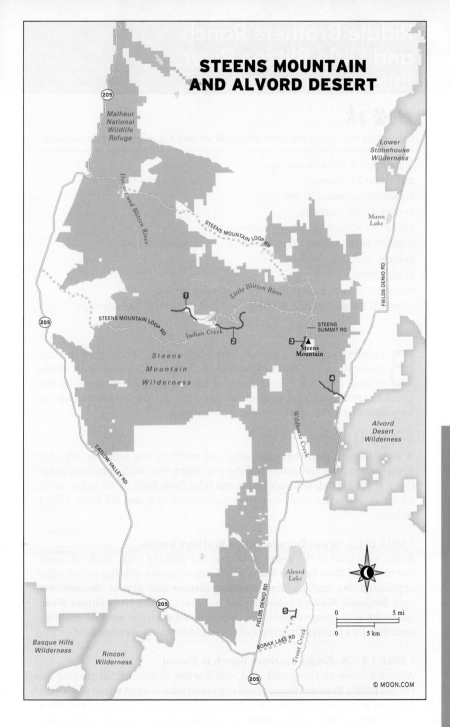

STEENS MOUNTAIN
AND ALVORD DESERT

Riddle Brothers Ranch and Little Blitzen River

STEENS MOUNTAIN WILDERNESS

Follow this trail along the Little Blitzen River and explore an old homestead.

DISTANCE: 5.8 miles round-trip
DURATION: 2.5 hours
ELEVATION CHANGE: 270 feet
EFFORT: Easy/moderate
TRAIL: Dirt trail, rocks, gravel, matted grass
USERS: Hikers, leashed dogs, mountain bikers, horseback riders
SEASON: May–November
PASSES/FEES: None
MAPS: USGS topographic map for Tombstone Canyon
CONTACT: Bureau of Land Management, 541/573-4400, www.blm.gov

Brothers Benjamin, Fredrick, and Walter Riddle each lived in their own cabins on Steens Mountain in the late 1800s and early 1900s, raising livestock. The Bureau of Land Management acquired the ranch in 1986, and today visitors can get a feel for the homesteading life by wandering around the remaining buildings.

START THE HIKE

A locked green gate regulates vehicular traffic to the property. It's only open certain days and months of the year (9am-5pm Wed.-Sun. mid-June-Oct.). If it's closed, you can begin the hike from here; if it's open, drive 1.3 miles down the road to another parking lot to shave off some hiking mileage.

▶ **MILE 0-1.3: Green Gate to Riddle Brothers Ranch**
Begin your hike at the **green gate** near the parking area. Walking down the unsigned **Cold Springs Road,** you'll pass a couple of interpretive signs explaining the region's homesteading history and almost immediately spot **Benjamin Riddle's cabin** to your right, across the **Little Blitzen River.** Although not always visible, the river is always within earshot, and this stretch offers captivating views of Steens Mountain's western face.

▶ **MILE 1.3-1.5: Riddle Brothers Ranch to Corral**
After 1.3 miles on the gravel road, you'll arrive at the official parking lot for the **Riddle Brothers Ranch.** So if the green gate is open when you arrive and you're looking to shave 2.6 miles round-trip off the hike, you can drive to this alternative starting point. A volunteer host generally lives in the **caretaker's cabin** on-site next to the parking lot June-September to take care of the property and assist hikers passing through. Just past the cabin,

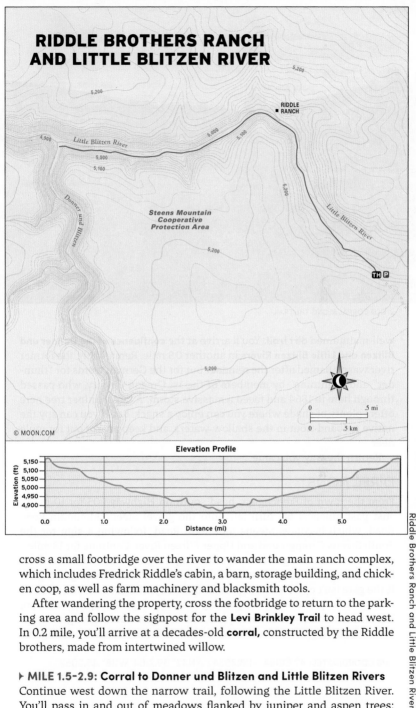

RIDDLE BROTHERS RANCH AND LITTLE BLITZEN RIVER

Elevation Profile

cross a small footbridge over the river to wander the main ranch complex, which includes Fredrick Riddle's cabin, a barn, storage building, and chicken coop, as well as farm machinery and blacksmith tools.

After wandering the property, cross the footbridge to return to the parking area and follow the signpost for the **Levi Brinkley Trail** to head west. In 0.2 mile, you'll arrive at a decades-old **corral,** constructed by the Riddle brothers, made from intertwined willow.

▶ MILE 1.5-2.9: Corral to Donner und Blitzen and Little Blitzen Rivers

Continue west down the narrow trail, following the Little Blitzen River. You'll pass in and out of meadows flanked by juniper and aspen trees; the latter puts on dazzling foliage displays every fall. After 0.5 mile, you'll arrive at an unsigned fork; take a right, toward the river and onto a

▲ OLD CORRAL ALONG THE TRAIL

well-maintained **dirt trail.** You'll arrive at the **confluence of the Donner und Blitzen and Little Blitzen Rivers** in another 0.9 mile. Remarkably, the former river wasn't named after the reindeer but for the German words for "thunder" and "lightning" by members of the 1st Oregon Cavalry, who passed through here in 1864 and faced a massive storm. A large juniper tree here offers plenty of shade where you can enjoy a snack. See if you can spy the native redband trout in the shallow waters, and keep an eye out for mule deer.

Return the way you came.

DIRECTIONS

From the town of Frenchglen, head south on Highway 205 for 10 miles. Just past milepost 68, turn left onto the gravel Steens Mountain Loop Road, which becomes Steens Mountain Road, following a sign for the South Steens Campground and Upper Blitzen River. Continue for 18 miles, and turn left onto a gravel road, following a sign for the Riddle Brothers Ranch National Historic District. In 1.2 miles you'll arrive at a green gate. If the gate isn't open, you can park in the area just right of it, and walk 1.3 miles one-way to the official parking area. If the gate is open (9am-5pm Wed.-Sun. mid-June-Oct.) and you'd like to shave some hiking mileage, continue driving down the road to the Riddle Brothers Ranch parking lot.

GPS COORDINATES: 42.66194, –118.75342 / N42° 39.7164' W118° 45.2052'

Big Indian Gorge

STEENS MOUNTAIN WILDERNESS

Explore one of the most accessible of the glacially carved gorges for which Steens Mountain is known.

DISTANCE: 8.1 miles round-trip
DURATION: 4 hours
ELEVATION CHANGE: 920 feet
EFFORT: Moderate
TRAIL: Dirt trail, rocks, roots, stream crossings
USERS: Hikers, leashed dogs, horseback riders
SEASON: June–November
PASSES/FEES: None
MAPS: USGS topographic map for Fish Lake
CONTACT: Bureau of Land Management, 541/573-4400, www.blm.gov

Roughly 10,000 years ago, several glaciers slid 10 miles down Steens's western slopes, carving several 2,000-foot gorges and leaving U-shaped valleys in their wake—including Big Indian Gorge.

START THE HIKE

This hike involves three stream crossings, each spanning 10-15 feet. Late spring-early summer, these streams may be impassable—the water can get up to calf-deep—unless you happen upon hiker-created log crossings. In late summer-early fall, however, the water flow mellows to ankle-high levels, and the crossings are easily manageable.

The first two miles of this trail are almost entirely exposed, so bring plenty of water, and load up on sunscreen, particularly if you're hiking during the height of summer. Also, keep an eye out for rattlesnakes.

▶ **MILE 0-2: Big Indian Gorge Trailhead to Big Indian Creek**
From the parking lot, follow a wide gravel path east for several hundred feet to the **Big Indian Gorge Trailhead.** You'll follow an old Jeep road, once used to shuttle supplies to ranch workers on Steens Mountain, lined by occasional boulders and juniper trees. After ascending an easy 325 feet over the first 1.9 miles, you'll arrive at **Big Indian Creek,** your first stream crossing.

▶ **MILE 2-2.7: Big Indian Creek to Log Cabin**
You'll gradually trade juniper for cottonwood and aspen over the next 0.2 mile, when you arrive at **Little Indian Creek.** After crossing the creek, head uphill and, in 0.5 mile, find a **spur trail** to your left; walk the short, scenic stretch to see the remnants of an old **log cabin.** Also keep an eye out along this spur for wild onion, buckwheat, purple lupine, and other wildflowers.

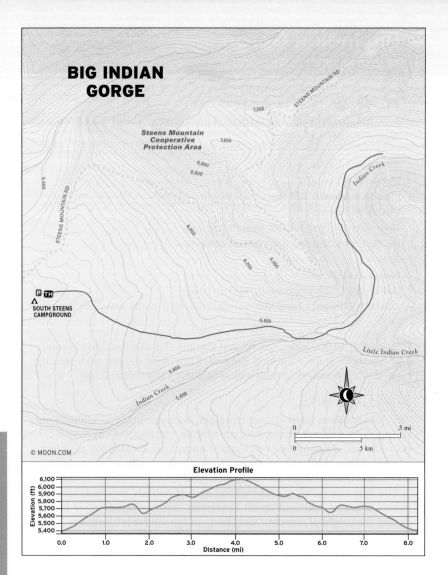

▶ MILE 2.7-3.2: Log Cabin to Big Indian Gorge

Back on the trail, continue through the forest of mountain mahogany, cottonwood, and aspen. You'll arrive after 0.5 mile at your final stream crossing, **Big Indian Creek** again. From here, sagebrush and aspen flank the trail as you gradually ascend to the foot of **Big Indian Gorge.**

▶ MILE 3.2-4.05: Big Indian Gorge to Headwall View

About 0.8 mile after the last creek crossing, you'll pass a solitary, ottoman-sized boulder—to the right of the trail—shaded by aspen trees. Enjoy a snack in the shade and continue a few hundred feet farther down the trail for a clear view of the Big Indian Gorge's headwall. Backpackers continue on another 4 miles to reach the headwall, but this is your turnaround point.
Return the way you came.

▲ THE TRAIL TO BIG INDIAN GORGE

DIRECTIONS

From the town of Frenchglen, head south on Highway 205 for 10 miles. Just past milepost 68, turn left onto the gravel Steens Mountain Loop Road for 19.3 miles, following a sign for South Steens Campground and the Upper Blitzen River. Turn right at the sign for the South Steens family camping area, and continue for 0.4 mile to the parking area at the end of the loop.

GPS COORDINATES: 42.65619, –118.72406 / N42° 39.3714' W118° 43.4436'

Descend into a glacially carved cirque and to the shore of an alpine lake near the summit of Steens Mountain.

DISTANCE: 2.8 miles round-trip

DURATION: 2 hours

ELEVATION CHANGE: 1,010 feet

EFFORT: Easy/moderate

TRAIL: Dirt trail, gravel, rocks, minor stream crossings

USERS: Hikers, leashed dogs

SEASON: July-October

PASSES/FEES: None

MAPS: USGS topographic map for Wildhorse Lake

CONTACT: Bureau of Land Management, 541/573-4400, www.blm.gov

START THE HIKE

A steady descent with scree means it's advisable to wear hiking boots with sufficient tread, bring a walking stick, and watch your step on this trail. While leashed dogs are allowed, given the rockiness it may be best to leave Fido at home.

▾ WILDHORSE LAKE

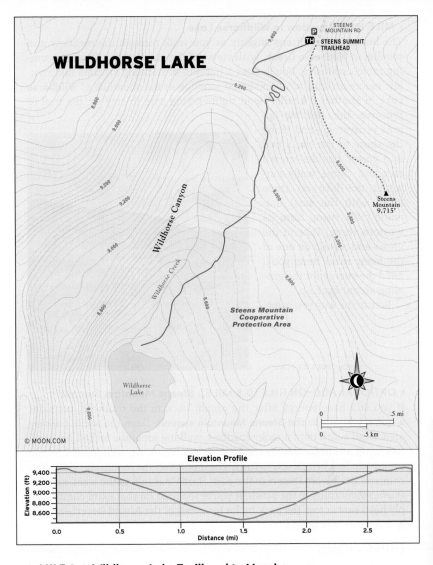

Elevation Profile

▸ MILE 0-1: Wildhorse Lake Trailhead to Meadow

Find the trailhead—marked by an unsigned metal post—on the west side of the gravel parking area to begin descending the rocky **Wildhorse Lake Trail**. In 0.2 mile, you'll arrive at an unsigned fork where you'll find a **trail register**—and your first view of Wildhorse Lake. Take a left to continue descending into the cirque—a bowl-like depression—and toward the lakeshore. You'll start traversing a series of switchbacks down a narrow, steep trail covered in loose rock. After 0.8 mile of careful descent, you'll enter a **meadow** just above Wildhorse Lake. In late spring and early summer, you may spy pink monkeyflower, purple lupine, yellow buckwheat, and other wildflowers. Keep an eye out on the surrounding cirque for mule deer and bighorn sheep.

▶ **MILE 1–1.4: Meadow to Wildhorse Lake**

The brutal grade softens slightly as you walk through the meadow and parallel to **Wildhorse Creek,** with views of the surrounding cirque becoming more expansive. You'll cross a handful of trickling streams and rivulets before arriving at an unsigned junction at the shoreline of **Wildhorse Lake** in another 0.4 mile. Head right—taking care to stay on the trail to preserve the delicate alpine ecosystem—and along the shore to the trail's end in a grassy, boulder-strewn meadow. Gorge walls surround the lake on three sides, with the most dramatic cliffs rising from its western shore. Take in the views and rest up on one of the many rocks here; you'll need the energy for the grueling ascent back up.

Return the way you came.

WILDHORSE LAKE TRAIL ▶

▶ **OPTIONAL ADD-ON HIKE (0.8 MILE): Steens Mountain Summit**

If you still have energy after the ascent back to the trailhead, consider a quick hike up to the **Steens Mountain summit.** From the same parking area, head south onto a rocky roadbed, walking around a locked gate and following a sign for the Steens Mountain summit. An additional 0.8-mile round-trip trek brings you to the highest point on the mountain; views encompass the Alvord Desert to the east, Hart Mountain to the west, and the Pueblo Mountains to the south. If you're too tired for that extra climb, simply head east across the parking lot for views of the Alvord Desert—roughly a vertical mile below.

DIRECTIONS

From the town of Frenchglen, head east onto the gravel Steens Mountain Loop Road for 3.1 miles. When you arrive at a T-shaped junction, turn left to continue on Steens Mountain Loop Road for another 22.4 miles. At the four-way intersection, follow signs for Wildhorse Lake and the Steens Mountain summit, driving an additional 2 miles. The road ends at the trailheads for Wildhorse Lake and the Steens Mountain summit.

GPS COORDINATES: 42.64146, –118.57976 / N42° 38.4876′ W118° 34.7856′

STEENS MOUNTAIN WILDERNESS

Hike into a canyon along one of the few accessible trails on Steens Mountain's sheer eastern face.

DISTANCE: 6.5 miles round-trip

DURATION: 3 hours

ELEVATION CHANGE: 1,430 feet

EFFORT: Moderate

TRAIL: Dirt trail, gravel road, rocks, stream crossings

USERS: Hikers, leashed dogs, horses

SEASON: April–November

PASSES/FEES: None, if parking along East Steens Road/Fields-Denio Road; $5 day-use fee per vehicle (payable at Alvord Hot Springs) if parking at the trailhead

MAPS: USGS topographic map for Alvord Hot Springs

CONTACT: Bureau of Land Management, 541/573-4400, www.blm.gov

START THE HIKE

▶ **MILE 0-0.7: East Steens Road/Fields-Denio Road to Pike Creek Trailhead**

If you're in a low-clearance vehicle, park at the sign for the Pike Creek Canyon trail along East Steens Road/Fields-Denio Road. On the west side of the road, you'll see a yellow cattle guard; walk across it and down the bumpy **unnamed road** through a sea of sagebrush. This section of the hike is on private property, so remain on the trail at all times. After 0.5 mile, turn left at the unsigned Y-shaped junction, and in another several hundred feet keep right, ignoring signs for Camping and Parking. In 0.15 mile you'll arrive at the end of the road, and a parking area for high-clearance vehicles noted by a juniper tree that appears to grow out of a large red boulder (those with high-clearance vehicles can drive down this road to shave 1.4 miles round-trip off the hike). Follow the unmarked trail at the northwest edge of the parking area and cross the trickling **Pike Creek** to arrive at the **Pike Creek Trailhead**.

▶ **MILE 0.7-1.75: Pike Creek Trailhead to Wooden Shed**

Roughly 0.3 mile past the creek, you'll arrive at a **trail register** at the base of the **Pike Creek Canyon**. As you enter the canyon, you'll walk across large, loose rocks, one of many such stretches from here on in, so stay mindful. As you ascend, gaining roughly 420 feet over this stretch, keep an eye out for golden eagles, bighorn sheep, pronghorn, lizards, and other wildlife. Views—both of the canyon and the Alvord Desert behind you—improve with every step. In another 0.75 mile, you'll pass a boundary sign as you officially enter the **Steens Mountain Wilderness**. This trail follows

STEENS MOUNTAIN AND ALVORD DESERT

Pike Creek Canyon

555

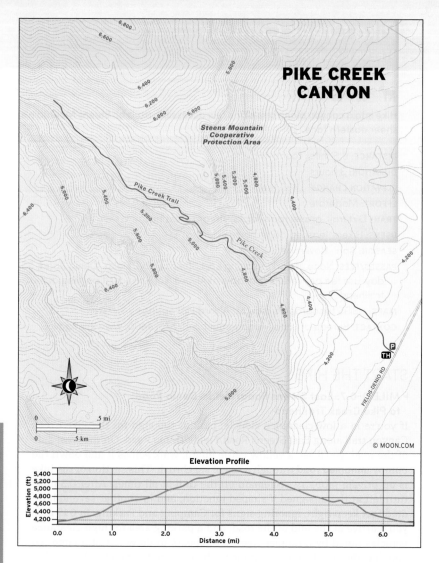

PIKE CREEK CANYON

Steens Mountain Cooperative Protection Area

Pike Creek Trail

Pike Creek

FIELDS-DENIO RD

0   .5 mi

0   .5 km

© MOON.COM

Elevation Profile

an old mining track, and just past the sign you'll see some evidence of the region's history: Behind some sagebrush to your left is a small **wooden shed,** used by miners searching for uranium in the early 1900s. Stay on the trail, and do not enter the shed.

▸ MILE 1.75-3.25: Wooden Shed to Juniper Tree Viewpoint

Past the shed, rock-hop across the trickling Pike Creek again before hiking up a few switchbacks into an open, rocky clearing. This is a nice spot to relax and enjoy a snack. Head to the clearing's northwestern edge to continue on the trail, which ascends steadily from here. You'll head up a series of switchbacks in 0.25 mile. Take time to turn around for views of Pike Creek Canyon framing the Alvord Desert below. As you gain 500 feet over the next 1.25 miles, you'll start to notice Steens's eastern face rising above

▲ VIEW ON THE PIKE CREEK CANYON TRAIL

you, its colorful canyon walls a riot of reds and oranges. Complementary yellow balsamroot and purple penstemon are just some of the wildflowers you may spy around here well into summer. After ascending a few short switchbacks, you'll arrive at a large juniper tree with several boulders beneath it—a good resting spot with views opening out to the canyon below.

The trail continues on, becoming steeper and fainter, so this is your turnaround point. Return the way you came.

If you have time, return to **Alvord Hot Springs**—where you might've bought a parking pass—for a post-hike soak. From the trailhead, the 2-mile drive southwest takes three minutes via East Steens Road/Fields-Denio Road.

DIRECTIONS

From the town of Fields, head north on East Steens Road/Fields-Denio Road. The pavement ends after 12.6 miles. Continue on the well-maintained gravel road for another 10.7 miles to the Alvord Hot Springs office and general store, where you can buy your day-use pass to park at the Pike Creek Trailhead. From here, continue north on East Steens Road/Fields-Denio Road for 2 miles until you see a yellow cattle guard on the left side of the road. If you have a low-clearance vehicle, park in the gravel parking area on the west side of the road just past the guard, near a sign for the trail. If you're in a high-clearance vehicle, you can turn left onto the rutted road and continue another 0.7 mile to reach the trailhead.

GPS COORDINATES: 42.57116, –118.52216 / N42° 34.2696' W118° 31.3296'

STEENS MOUNTAIN AND ALVORD DESERT

Pike Creek Canyon

Hike to the shores of Borax Lake—and past a series of hot springs—near the Alvord Desert.

DISTANCE: 2 miles round-trip
DURATION: 1 hour
ELEVATION CHANGE: 40 feet
EFFORT: Easy
TRAIL: Dirt trail, sandy path
USERS: Hikers
SEASON: Year-round
PASSES/FEES: None
MAPS: USGS topographic map for Borax Lake
CONTACT: The Nature Conservancy, 503/802-8100, www.nature.org

In the ice age, this valley sat buried under a lake 200 feet deep. The changing climate led to its evaporation, leaving behind only a few watery vestiges—including Borax Lake—and a bed of alkali and sodium borate. The latter is still visible on patches of trail; look for a white, snow-like substance. Tempting though it may be, forget about a soak here or even dipping a toe: The hot pools lining the trail can reach 180°F, too hot for safe contact. Borax Lake's surface temperature can reach 105°F, and arsenic levels in the lake are 25 times the critical limit for drinking water.

START THE HIKE

▶ **MILE 0-0.5: Trailhead to Borax Lake**
At the eastern edge of the parking area, walk through a pedestrian pass-through next to a locked gate and onto a wide, sandy trail. Almost immediately, you'll pass **Lower Borax Lake Reservoir** on your right; this shallow

▾ BORAX LAKE

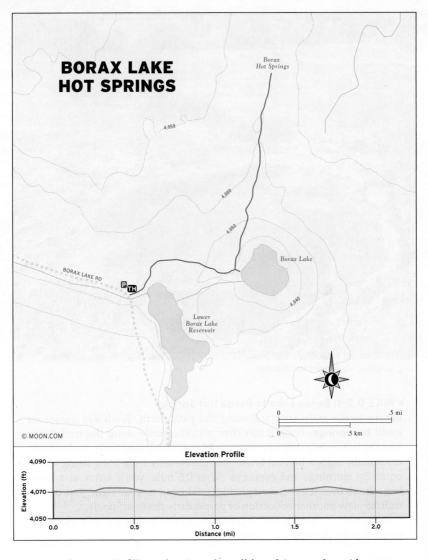

BORAX LAKE HOT SPRINGS

Borax
Hot Springs

4,050

4,060

4,050

Borax Lake

BORAX LAKE RD

P TH

4,040

Lower
Borax Lake
Reservoir

© MOON.COM

| 0 | | .5 mi |
| 0 | | .5 km |

Elevation Profile

4,090

4,070

4,050

Elevation (ft)

0.0   0.5   1.0   1.5   2.0

Distance (mi)

seasonal reservoir fills each winter but all but dries out by midsummer. In 0.4 mile, a short spur trail to your left leads to a pair of **vats** that laborers used in the late 1800s to dissolve sodium borate crusts and produce borax. A few hundred feet later, another short spur trail, this one to your right, leads you to the shore of **Borax Lake**. The 10-acre lake is fed by hot springs and sits on a bed of sodium borate deposits. It doesn't freeze in winter, so the surrounding marshland makes an ideal habitat for Canada geese, hawks, snowy plovers, herons, and other waterfowl. The most curious wildlife here is no larger than your index finger: the Borax Lake chub. The endangered minnow lives here in Borax Lake and nowhere else on Earth; it evolved with the changing climate to thrive in the increasingly warm, alkaline water.

▲ A POOL AT BORAX LAKE HOT SPRINGS

▶ **MILE 0.5-1: Borax Lake to Borax Hot Springs**

Return to the main trail, following the path north. You'll see numerous small **hot springs**—none larger than a kiddie pool—along the trail. Some hug the trail, while others are accessible via quick **spur trails,** and yet others remain hidden behind brush, noticeable only from their rising steam on chilly mornings and evenings. After 0.5 mile, you'll arrive at a fence line. Climb over it via the stepladder, and head to your right, just off the trail, to view another collection of particularly dramatic pools.

From here the path starts to get rough, so this makes a good turnaround point. Return the way you came.

DIRECTIONS

From the town of Fields, head north on East Steens Road/Fields-Denio Road. Continue straight when the road forks after 1.2 miles. In 0.5 mile, turn right onto the unmarked gravel road on the north side of the power substation. Continue on this road for 2.2 miles, and turn left onto another unmarked road, and continue for 1.8 miles to pass through an unlocked wire gate. Continue past the gate for another 0.5 mile to a parking area at a turnaround that marks the end of the road.

GPS COORDINATES: 42.32641, –118.61099 / N42° 19.5846' W118° 36.6594'

NEARBY CAMPGROUNDS

NAME	DESCRIPTION	FACILITIES	SEASON	FEE
Page Springs Campground	at the base of Steens Mountain	36 tent and RV sites, restrooms	year-round	$8
Steens Mountain Loop Rd., Frenchglen, 541/573-4400, www.blm.gov				
Jackman Park Campground	basic campground with excellent fall colors	6 tent and camper sites, restrooms	June–October	$6
Steens Mountain Loop Rd., Frenchglen, 541/573-4400, www.blm.gov				
South Steens Campground	in the heart of Steens Mountain	36 family campsites, 15 equestrian sites, restrooms	May–November	$6
Steens Mountain Loop Rd., Frenchglen, 541/573-4400, www.blm.gov				
Mann Lake Campground	no-frills campground near the Alvord Desert	5 tent sites, restrooms	year-round	free
East Steens Rd./Fields-Denio Rd., Fields, 541/573-4400, www.blm.gov				
Alvord Hot Springs	campground at the hot springs affords 24-hour access	11 tent sites, restrooms	year-round	$30
East Steens Rd./Fields-Denio Rd., Fields, 541/589-2282, www.alvordhotsprings.com				

WALLOWA MOUNTAINS AND BLUE MOUNTAINS

Northeastern Oregon is almost as rugged as the cowboys and ranchers who've called the region home for more than a century. At 9,000 feet, the Wallowa Mountains lord over the surrounding valley, dwarfing the ranches and homesteads with seemingly vertical peaks. Farther south, the arid, dusty Baker Valley still sports wagon ruts, visible some 175 years after pioneers made their way west here along the Oregon Trail. And the Elkhorn Mountains, part of the larger Blue Mountains range, host alpine lakes and forests in the shadow of granite peaks east of Baker City. Trails here offer hikers glimpses of the region's diverse natural beauty, from crystal-clear waters and summertime wildflowers to open expanses and snowcapped peaks.

▲ ANTHONY LAKE AND GUNSIGHT MOUNTAIN

▲ COVERED WAGON AT THE NATIONAL HISTORIC OREGON TRAIL INTERPRETIVE CENTER

◄ SACAJAWEA PEAK ABOVE HURRICANE CREEK

1 Hurricane Creek to Slick Rock Gorge
DISTANCE: 7.5 miles round-trip
DURATION: 3.5 hours
EFFORT: Easy/moderate

2 Iwetemlaykin State Heritage Site
DISTANCE: 2 miles round-trip
DURATION: 1 hour
EFFORT: Easy

3 Imnaha River to Blue Hole
DISTANCE: 4.6 miles round-trip
DURATION: 2.25 hours
EFFORT: Easy

4 Anthony Lake to Hoffer Lakes
DISTANCE: 3.2 miles round-trip
DURATION: 1.5 hours
EFFORT: Easy

5 National Historic Oregon Trail Interpretive Center
DISTANCE: 4.3 miles round-trip
DURATION: 2 hours
EFFORT: Easy

▾ IMNAHA RIVER

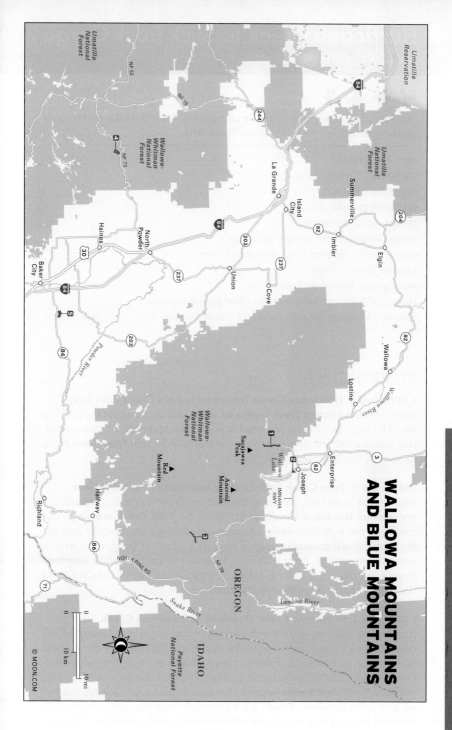

WALLOWA MOUNTAINS AND BLUE MOUNTAINS

Hurricane Creek to Slick Rock Gorge

WALLOWA–WHITMAN NATIONAL FOREST

Mountain meadows, alpine forests, unimpeded views of peaks, and crystal-clear rivers collide on the Hurricane Creek Trail.

BEST: Brew Hikes
DISTANCE: 7.5 miles round-trip
DURATION: 3.5 hours
ELEVATION CHANGE: 860 feet
EFFORT: Easy/moderate
TRAIL: Dirt trail, rocks, stream crossings
USERS: Hikers, leashed dogs, horseback riders
SEASON: June–October
PASSES/FEES: Northwest Forest Pass
MAPS: USGS topographic map for Chief Joseph Mountain
CONTACT: Wallowa-Whitman National Forest, 541/426-5546, www.fs.usda.gov

START THE HIKE

▶ **MILE 0-0.6: Hurricane Creek Trailhead to Falls Creek Falls Loop**
Begin at the **Hurricane Creek Trailhead** at the southern edge of the parking lot. In 0.1 mile, you'll see a **spur trail** to your right; make the 0.5-mile round-trip, gaining 150 feet along the way, for views of 50-foot **Falls Creek Falls,** flanked by the Wallowas' rocky peaks.

▶ **MILE 0.6-1: Falls Creek Falls Loop to Hurricane Creek Overlook**
Back on the main trail, continue heading south for 0.15 mile, hugging the eponymous **Hurricane Creek,** to arrive at the **Falls Creek crossing.** The creek can run high May-June, so step carefully; logs are typically laid out for hikers. You'll gradually ascend through a forest of Douglas fir, aspen, and ponderosa pine. After 0.25 mile, keep an eye out for a short **spur trail** to your left that ends at an **overlook** of crystal-clear Hurricane Creek and the broader basin through which it flows.

▶ **MILE 1-2.3: Hurricane Creek Overlook to Deadman Creek**
Another 0.5 mile on, you'll begin darting in and out of meadows, and Sacajawea Peak comes into view to the south; at 9,800 feet, it's the highest point in the Wallowas. In summer, these meadows are replete with wildflowers, including red paintbrush and purple phlox. Elk sightings are also possible. Roughly 0.8 mile beyond that first meadow, you'll leave the forest and cross **Deadman Creek;** it's a seasonal creek and goes dry by midsummer, but you may encounter some winter runoff before then. You can typically cross by stepping carefully on rocks in the streambed, but don't attempt the crossing if the flow is high.

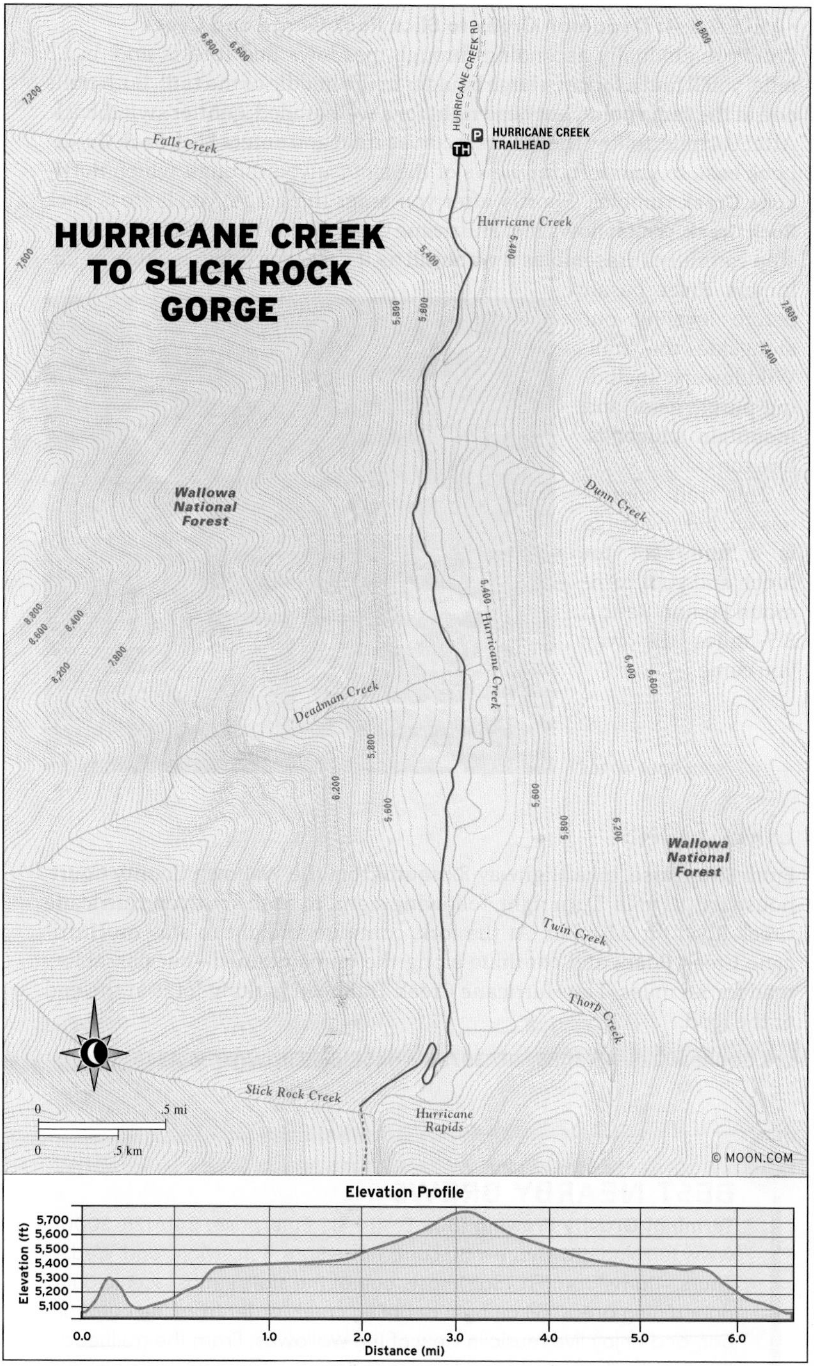

HURRICANE CREEK TO SLICK ROCK GORGE

Falls Creek

HURRICANE CREEK RD

P
TH
HURRICANE CREEK TRAILHEAD

Hurricane Creek

Dunn Creek

Wallowa National Forest

Deadman Creek

Hurricane Creek

Twin Creek

Thorp Creek

Wallowa National Forest

Slick Rock Creek

Hurricane Rapids

© MOON.COM

0   .5 mi
0   .5 km

Elevation Profile

▶ MILE 2.3-4: Deadman Creek to Slick Rock Gorge and Creek

Continue gradually ascending through meadows and forests and, in 1.3 mile, you'll find a **fork** at a large boulder in the middle of the trail. Both trails end at the same point, but head right for a well-graded, gentler switchback. After 0.4 mile, follow the trail as it curves right and enters **Slick Rock Gorge.** Look east, to your left, for views of the slot canyon through which **Hurricane Creek** rumbles. Shortly after you enter the gorge, you'll cross **Slick Rock Creek,** which flows into Hurricane Creek. It can run high in spring, so step carefully. It resembles a waterfall as it cascades down a chute of Co-

lumbia River basalt before leveling out alongside the trail. Wildflowers, including purple aster and mountain bluebells, line the trail.

The trail continues on, but the gorge is a fine spot for lunch and your turnaround point. Return 3.5 miles the way you came.

SLICK ROCK GORGE ▶

DIRECTIONS

From Enterprise, take Highway 82 south from the Wallowa County Courthouse for 0.3 mile. Turn right, following signs, to head south on Hurricane Creek Road for 5.1 miles. At the fork, continue straight to stay on Hurricane Creek Road, and continue along the unmaintained—but passable—road for 3.8 miles. The Hurricane Creek Trailhead parking lot is at the end of the road.

GPS COORDINATES: 45.31156, -117.30708 / N45° 18.6936′ W117° 18.4248′

BEST NEARBY BREWS

Terminal Gravity Brewing (803 E. 4th St., Enterprise, 541/426-3000, www.terminalgravitybrewing.com, 11am-9pm Sun.-Mon. and Wed.-Thurs., 11am-10pm Fri.-Sat.) hosts one of the state's most scenic outdoor dining areas. Sit along a bubbling creek, order from the outdoor bar, and enjoy live music in view of the Wallowas. From the trailhead, the 9-mile drive north via Hurricane Creek Road and Highway 82 takes 20 minutes.

2 Iwetemlaykin State Heritage Site

WALLOWA LAKE MANAGEMENT UNIT

This short stroll in the Wallowas is just minutes from downtown Joseph and offers dramatic views of the mountains.

DISTANCE: 2 miles round-trip
DURATION: 1 hour
ELEVATION CHANGE: 100 feet
EFFORT: Easy
TRAIL: Dirt trail, gravel paths
USERS: Hikers, leashed dogs
SEASON: Year-round
PASSES/FEES: None
MAPS: Oregon State Parks map for Iwetemlaykin State Heritage Site
CONTACT: Oregon State Parks, 541/432-4185, www.oregonstateparks.org

This area is the ancestral home of the Nez Perce people, and the park's name—Iwetemlaykin (ee-weh-TEMM-lye-kinn)—is Nez Perce for "at the edge of the lake." Their leader, Old Chief Joseph, led treaty negotiations that created a reservation for the Nez Perce people around Wallowa Lake in 1855—only to be slashed in size by 90 percent just eight years later by the U.S. government, paving the path to the Nez Perce War of 1877. The tribe surrendered, and the land was earmarked for white resettlement. Today, ranches and vacation homes dot the valley.

START THE HIKE

▶ **MILE 0-0.1: Northern Parking Area Trailhead to Ridgeline Prairie**
Walk to the trailhead—indicated by a signboard with a trail map and background information on the area—at the southern edge of the site's main parking lot, the more northerly of two. Ascend gradually on the unnamed gravel trail as it switchbacks through a grassy area before leveling off, after 0.1 mile, at an open prairie on the crest of a ridge, where you'll enjoy unimpeded views of the Wallowa Mountains to the east; the views don't let up for the duration of the hike.

▶ **MILE 0.1-0.7: Ridgeline Prairie to Knight's Pond Loop**
From atop this ridgeline prairie, follow the trail as it hugs **Silver Lake Ditch,** which joins the Wallowa River and flows into Wallowa Lake a half mile south. You'll walk past a small forest dotted with cottonwood, ponderosa pine, and Douglas fir; keep an eye out here for fox, elk, and deer. After 0.4 mile, you'll arrive at an unsigned junction. Head right for a flat, 0.2-mile loop around tranquil **Knight's Pond.** Here you might see lupine, sagebrush mariposa lily, and other wildflowers in late spring and summer.

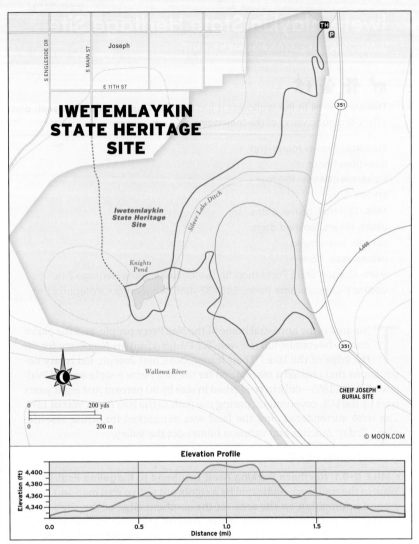

IWETEMLAYKIN
STATE HERITAGE
SITE

Iwetemlaykin
State Heritage
Site

Knights
Pond

Silver Lake Ditch

Wallowa River

CHEIF JOSEPH
BURIAL SITE

S ENGLESIDE DR

S MAIN ST

Joseph

E 11TH ST

0   200 yds
0   200 m

© MOON.COM

Elevation Profile

Elevation (ft)

4,400
4,380
4,360
4,340

0.0   0.5   1.0   1.5

Distance (mi)

▶ **MILE 0.7–1: Knight's Pond Loop to Southern Parking Area**

After completing the loop, turn right to head east, crossing a footbridge over Silver Lake Ditch, ascending the grassy hillside. Several social trails also wend up the hill, but stay on the gravel path to protect the park's fragile ecology. Traversing this hill offers the hike's best views, with no nearby houses or trees to block the imposing peaks. The mountains look especially majestic April-May, when they're still covered in snow; you can understand why they're nicknamed the "Swiss Alps of Oregon." The trail ends in 0.3 mile at the park's unmarked southern parking area.

Return the way you came.

▲ WALLOWA MOUNTAINS

▸ **OPTIONAL ADD-ON HIKE (0.2 MILE): Old Chief Joseph Gravesite**

Add 0.2-mile round-trip to your hike by visiting the **gravesite of Old Chief Joseph** before returning the way you came. His remains, originally buried elsewhere, were relocated in 1926 to a plot overlooking Wallowa Lake. From the end of the Iwetemlaykin State Heritage Site trail, turn right to walk south on the paved cycling and walking path along Highway 351, remaining on the west side of the road. In 0.1 mile, turn right at a sign for the gravesite, and follow the footpath to the grave. An interpretive panel details Old Chief Joseph's life and provides context for a dark chapter of American history.

DIRECTIONS

Drive south on Main Street through downtown Joseph, following the road for one mile as it curves to the left and becomes East 8th Street and then Highway 351. Turn right into the park's main (northern) parking lot, just 0.2 mile past South College Street, at the sign for Iwetemlaykin State Heritage Site.

GPS COORDINATES: 45.34297, -117.22349 / N45° 20.5782′ W117° 13.4094′

> ## BEST NEARBY BITES
>
> Fuel up for your hike at **Red Horse Coffee Traders** (306 N. Main St., Joseph, 541/432-3784, 7am-3pm Thurs.-Mon. summer, call for hours fall-spring), in the heart of downtown Joseph. The coffee shop serves a mix of baked goods, light breakfast and lunch fare, fair-trade coffee, and more. From the trailhead, the 1-mile drive north via Main Street and East 8th Street takes 5 minutes.

Imnaha River to Blue Hole

WILD AND SCENIC IMNAHA RIVER

Hike through an alpine forest and a landscape scarred by wildfire to Blue Hole, where the jade-hued Imnaha River emerges from a river gorge.

DISTANCE: 4.6 miles round-trip
DURATION: 2.25 hours
ELEVATION CHANGE: 230 feet
EFFORT: Easy
TRAIL: Dirt trail, rocks, gravel
USERS: Hikers, leashed dogs, horseback riders
SEASON: June–November
PASSES/FEES: Northwest Forest Pass
MAPS: USGS topographic map for Deadman Point
CONTACT: Wallowa-Whitman National Forest, 541/426-5546, www.fs.usda.gov

START THE HIKE

▶ **MILE 0-0.25: Indian Crossing Trailhead to Imnaha River Overlook**
Start at the **Indian Crossing Trailhead,** wedged between the restrooms and an informational signboard at the western edge of the parking area, following a sign for the Blue Hole and Twin Lakes onto the **South Fork Imnaha Trail.** It parallels the Imnaha River, but a shady forest of fir trees and lodgepole pine keeps it hidden—at least until you emerge, after 0.25 mile, at a small **overlook** at a break in the trees above its banks. The river originates in the Eagle Cap Wilderness and the Wallowa-Whitman National Forest and, for roughly 70 miles, follows a geologic fault line before flowing into the Snake River along the Oregon-Idaho border.

▶ **MILE 0.25-2.1: Imnaha River Overlook to Twin Lakes Trail**
From here you'll ascend gradually for the next 0.25 mile, gaining just over 100 feet along the way. The trail levels out after this initial ascent, and you'll trade forest canopy in another 0.5 mile for a sea of charred, toothpick-like snags—the result of a 1996 wildfire. The lack of tree cover on this stretch means you'll enjoy expansive views of the surrounding Imnaha River basin and Eagle Cap Wilderness. Plants and wildlife thrive here along the river. You might see goldenrod, red paintbrush, and dazzling pink fireweed in the summer. Surrounding aspen groves deliver fiery foliage displays every autumn. Keep an eye out for elk, butterflies, and birds, including Cassin's finches, yellow-rumped warblers, Steller's jays, and pileated woodpeckers. In spring, anglers enjoy fishing this stretch of the Imnaha—occasionally visible, to your left, through the snags—for Chinook salmon, Oregon's official state fish. You'll come to a fork in the trail in

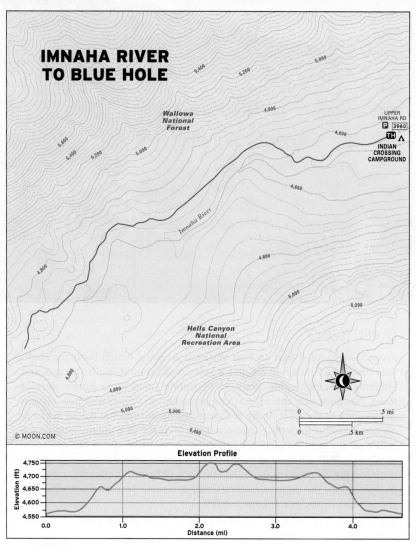

IMNAHA RIVER TO BLUE HOLE

Wallowa National Forest

UPPER IMNAHA RD

P 3960

TH Λ

INDIAN CROSSING CAMPGROUND

Imnaha River

Hells Canyon National Recreation Area

© MOON.COM

0   .5 mi

0   .5 km

Elevation Profile

another 1.1 miles; following a sign for the Blue Hole and Twin Lakes, turn left onto the **Twin Lakes Trail.**

▶ MILE 2.1–2.3: Twin Lakes Trail to Imnaha River and Blue Hole

You'll lose a bit of elevation before ending in a few hundred feet at the banks of the **Imnaha River.** Wade in during midsummer—this is a popular, if chilly, swimming hole—but exercise caution when the river runs high in spring. To your right you can see the **Blue Hole,** a teal-hued pool, emerging from a rocky, 50-foot river gorge just upstream, but you can also scramble up some rocks to the west for even better views of the pool, as well as a wider panorama of the burned-out river basin.

Return the way you came.

WALLOWA MOUNTAINS AND BLUE MOUNTAINS

Imnaha River to Blue Hole

▲ BLUE HOLE

DIRECTIONS

From Joseph, head east on East Wallowa Avenue, which becomes Highway 350, for 8.5 miles. At a sign for Salt Creek Summit, Hells Canyon, and Halfway, turn right onto Wallowa Mountain Loop Road (Forest Service Road 39)—note that this road isn't maintained in winter and may remain impassable in spring (call the Wallowa-Whitman National Forest to check on conditions if in doubt)—and continue on it for 30.5 miles. Roughly 0.5 mile past the sign for Blackhorse Campground, turn right onto Forest Service Road 3960. The paved road becomes gravel after 8.5 miles. Continue onto the gravel road for 0.3 mile, and turn right into a parking area, just past a sign for the Indian Crossing Campground (if you cross a bridge over the Imnaha River, you've gone too far).

GPS COORDINATES: 45.11223, –117.01518 / N45° 6.7338' W117° 0.9108'

BEST NEARBY BREWS

The Blue Hole trailhead is in a remote area of the Wallowas, so the closest options are in Joseph, and **Embers Brew House Restaurant and Pub** (204 N. Main St., Joseph, 541/432-2739, 11am-9pm daily) makes a satisfying stop if you're returning through the town. Embers offers a hearty selection of regional craft beer, burgers, pizzas, and outdoor seating with views of the surrounding mountain peaks. From the trailhead, the 38-mile drive northwest takes 1.75 hours via Wallowa Mountain Loop Road and Highway 350.

Anthony Lake to Hoffer Lakes

WALLOWA-WHITMAN NATIONAL FOREST

Hike past alpine lakes, through wildflower meadows, and in the shadow of granite peaks—all in just a few miles.

DISTANCE: 3.2 miles round-trip
DURATION: 1.5 hours
ELEVATION CHANGE: 490 feet
EFFORT: Easy
TRAIL: Gravel and dirt paths, rocks
USERS: Hikers, leashed dogs
SEASON: June–October
PASSES/FEES: $4 per vehicle
MAPS: USGS topographic map for Anthony Lakes
CONTACT: Wallowa-Whitman National Forest, 541/523-6391, www.fs.usda.gov

START THE HIKE

▶ MILE 0-0.5: Parking Area to Hoffer Lakes Trail

From the parking area, head south into the forest from the unsigned trailhead to shortly arrive at the shore of **Anthony Lake** and an unsigned junction. Enjoy the first of many dramatic views along this trail; visible from here are, from east to west, Gunsight Mountain, Angell Peak, and Lees Peak. Turn left onto the **Anthony Lake Shoreline Trail** to begin the hike's clockwise loop. Follow the shoreline as it cuts through subalpine fir forests and summertime wildflowers including purple asters and pink heather. After 0.3 mile, you'll cross a stone boat dock and, in a couple hundred feet, turn right onto a wide gravel path. After a mostly flat 0.2 mile, turn left onto the **Hoffer Lakes Trail.**

▶ MILE 0.5-1.4: Hoffer Lakes Trail to Hoffer Lakes

Soon after, you'll encounter a faint, unsigned Y-shaped junction. Keep left again to remain on the Hoffer Lakes Trail. Follow the rocky trail along **Parker Creek,** ascending steadily and gaining 320 feet before arriving, after 0.6 mile, at a signed junction announcing your arrival at **Hoffer Lakes.** Walk the short distance to the shore of the smaller of the two lakes for dramatic views, with Lees Peak towering above it. Then take the quick jaunt east from the junction on the 0.25-mile round-trip **spur trail.** This flat path brings you to the larger of the two Hoffer Lakes, which butts up against granite crags. You may see false hellebore and red paintbrush blooming along this trail.

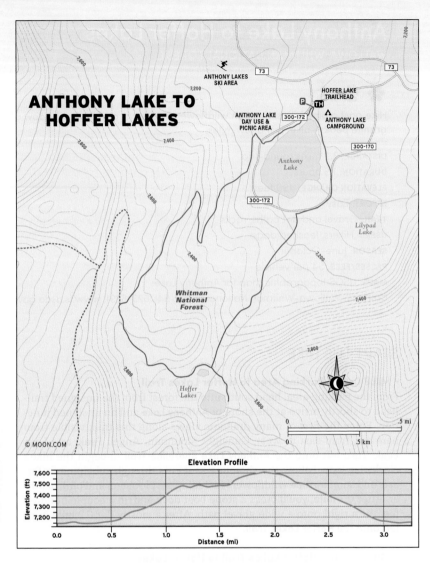

ANTHONY LAKE TO HOFFER LAKES

ANTHONY LAKES SKI AREA

73

73

HOFFER LAKE TRAILHEAD

ANTHONY LAKE DAY USE & PICNIC AREA

P **TH**

300-172

ANTHONY LAKE CAMPGROUND

7,600

7,200

7,400

7,800

300-170

Anthony Lake

300-172

Lilypad Lake

7,600

7,400

7,200

7,400

Whitman National Forest

7,800

7,600

Hoffer Lakes

7,600

0   .5 mi

0   .5 km

© MOON.COM

Elevation Profile

7,600
7,500
7,400
7,300
7,200

Elevation (ft)

0.0   0.5   1.0   1.5   2.0   2.5   3.0

Distance (mi)

▶ **MILE 1.4-1.9: Hoffer Lakes to Forest Road 5185**

Back at the junction, follow the Hoffer Lakes Trail as it heads west, following the smaller lake's shoreline before gently yet steadily ascending into open alpine meadows. These fields are littered with purple monkeyflower, northern mule-ears, bigleaf lupine, and other wildflowers late spring-early summer. You'll arrive at the unsigned **Forest Road 5185** in 0.5 mile. Turn right onto the road to start looping northeast. Lees Peak and Gunsight Mountain occasionally peek through the trees to your right.

▶ **MILE 1.9-3.2: Forest Road 5185 to Parking Area**

In 1 mile, you'll arrive at a Y-junction; head right onto the hard-packed dirt road as it curves south, back toward Anthony Lake, and continue on as it becomes gravel. After about 350 feet, you'll arrive at an unsigned

T-junction; to your left is the road to the guard station and trailhead parking area, but continue 150 feet straight ahead, and look to the left for an unsigned trail that leads to day-use sites and reconnects with the **Anthony Lake Shoreline Trail.** In summer, the purple blossoms of Jeffrey's shooting star line this stretch. You'll also pass a **gazebo,** built in the 1930s by the Civilian Conservation Corps, off to your left. Several other unmarked paths crisscross the day-use area here—you can follow any of them east and, in about 0.2 mile, you'll complete the loop, arriving back at the original junction. Turn left to return to the parking area.

DIRECTIONS

From La Grande, head east on I-84 for 23.3 miles. Take exit 285, and continue west on River Lane for 4 miles. Turn left onto Ellis Road, continuing on it for 0.7 mile. Turn right onto Anthony Lakes Highway, which becomes Forest Road 73 after 7.7 miles at a Y-shaped junction; follow the road as it curves to the right and, after another 7.9 curvy miles, turn left at a fork to follow a sign for Anthony Lake Campground. You'll soon pass the Anthony Lake Guard Station on the right. A small parking area is to your left, just across the road from a restroom.

GPS COORDINATES: 44.96147, –118.23091/ N44° 57.6882′ W118° 13.8546′

ONE OF THE HOFFER LAKES ▶

National Historic Oregon Trail Interpretive Center

BAKER CITY, VALE DISTRICT

Walk amid wagon ruts left in the Baker Valley by Oregon Trail pioneers.

BEST: Kid-Friendly Hikes

DISTANCE: 4.3 miles round-trip

DURATION: 2 hours

ELEVATION CHANGE: 480 feet

EFFORT: Easy

TRAIL: Dirt trail, paved path, gravel

USERS: Hikers, wheelchair users, leashed dogs

SEASON: Year-round

PASSES/FEES: $5-8 adults, $3.50-4.50 seniors, free for children 15 and younger

MAPS: Free trail map at the Historic Oregon Trail Interpretive Center

PARK HOURS: 9am-6pm daily Memorial Day weekend-October, subject to seasonal changes

CONTACT: Bureau of Land Management, 541/523-1843, www.blm.gov

L ocated atop Flagstaff Hill, the National Historic Oregon Trail Interpretive Center is a museum with interpretive panels, exhibits, and movies documenting the historic westward journey, as well as several miles of interpretive hiking trails.

START THE HIKE

▶ **MILE 0-0.9: Replica Wagon Train to Oregon Trail Ruts Loop**
Find the **replica wagon train** at the southern edge of the parking lot to begin this clockwise loop hike, following the wide, unmarked path known as the **Ascent Trail;** it's the steepest trail on the property and so much more fun to descend. The paved path soon transitions to gravel as you hike down toward the valley floor, passing all manner of vegetation—including sagebrush, bluebunch wheatgrass, buttercup, and fleabane—and views of the Blue Mountains open up. There's little shade along this westward route, so you'll appreciate the covered bench after 0.9 mile, at a four-way intersection. Take a left here onto the **Oregon Trail Ruts Loop,** where you'll find **Oregon Trail ruts** and a **covered wagon replica.**

▶ **MILE 0.9-2.3: Oregon Trail Ruts Loop to Rocky Outcrop Viewpoint**
After 0.1 mile, turn left onto the 0.7-mile round-trip **Auburn Burnt River Spur Trail,** an out-and-back gravel trail that takes you to the site of an **old wagon road** likely used by miners in the 1860s. Back on the Oregon Trail Ruts Loop, continue west for 0.1 mile, then take a left at the signed junction onto the gravel **Eagle Valley Railroad Grade Loop Trail.** In 0.5 mile,

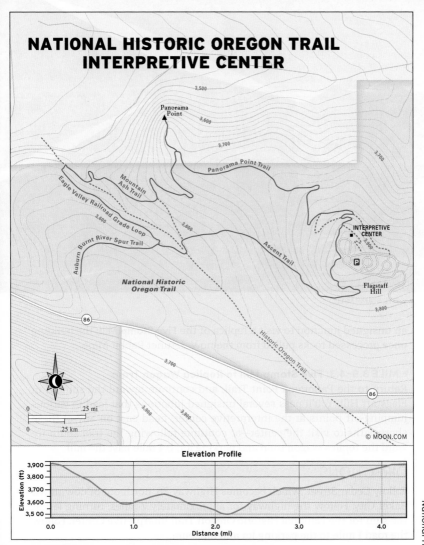

NATIONAL HISTORIC OREGON TRAIL INTERPRETIVE CENTER

Panorama Point

3,500

3,600

3,700

3,700

Panorama Point Trail

Mountain Ash Trail

Eagle Valley Railroad Grade Loop

INTERPRETIVE CENTER

3,900

Auburn Burnt River Spur Trail

3,600

3,600

Ascent Trail

P

National Historic Oregon Trail

Flagstaff Hill

3,800

86

3,700

Historic Oregon Trail

86

3,900

3,900

0   .25 mi

0   .25 km

© MOON.COM

Elevation Profile

Elevation (ft): 3,900 / 3,800 / 3,700 / 3,600 / 3,500

Distance (mi): 0.0 / 1.0 / 2.0 / 3.0 / 4.0

you'll come to a **rocky outcrop** that offers 360-degree views of Flagstaff Hill behind you, wagon ruts cutting through the southern hillside, and Baker Valley and the Blue Mountains to the west. From here, you'll gradually ascend back to the museum and summit of Flagstaff Hill.

▶ **MILE 2.3-3.9: Rocky Outcrop Viewpoint to Five Stamp Mill**

In 0.25 mile, you'll arrive at an unsigned T-shaped junction; take a left onto the paved **Mountain Ash Trail.** Head left again in 0.4 mile at a junction for the 0.25-mile round-trip **Panorama Point spur trail.** In addition to covered benches, the point offers views of the broader Baker Valley. Back at the junction, follow the sign to head back east via the **Panorama Point Trail** for a gentle ascent to the summit of Flagstaff Hill. After 0.7 mile, turn left at

▲ FIVE STAMP MILL

an unsigned junction to visit a replica of the **Five Stamp Mill;** the building once processed rocks pulled from the now-defunct Rabbit Mine.

▶ **MILE 3.9-4.3: Five Stamp Mill to Replica Wagon Train**
Return to the Panorama Point Trail, and continue toward the summit of Flagstaff Hill. You'll pass several unsigned junctions that lead to various jumping-off points at the interpretive center; head east on any of these short paths to visit the center—or continue following the trail south toward the replica wagon train and parking lot, 0.4 mile past the mill.

DIRECTIONS

Follow Cedar Street, which becomes Highway 86, north out of downtown Baker City. Follow the highway for approximately 7 miles, turning left at the sign for the National Historic Oregon Trail Interpretive Center. Follow the road 1 mile to the parking lot and museum.

GPS COORDINATES: 44.813538, –117.728864 / N44° 48.8123' W117° 43.7318'

BEST NEARBY BITES AND BREWS
No trip to Baker City is complete without a stop at **Barley Brown's Beer** (www.barleybrownsbeer.com). Grab lunch, dinner, and beer in the **restaurant** (2190 Main St., Baker City, 541/523-4266, www.barleybrownsbeer.com, 4pm-10pm Mon.-Sat.), or sample an expanded selection of Barley Brown's award-winning beers across the street in the **taproom** (2200 Main St., Baker City, 541/523-2337, 2pm-close daily). From the trailhead, the 8.5-mile drive southwest takes 15 minutes via Highway 86.

NEARBY CAMPGROUNDS

NAME	DESCRIPTION	FACILITIES	SEASON	FEE
Wallowa Lake State Park	popular campground on the southern edge of Wallowa Lake	121 full-hookup sites, 88 tent sites, 2 yurts, restrooms	year-round	$20-75
Marina Lane, Joseph, 541/432-4185, http://oregonstateparks.org				
Hurricane Creek Campground	popular campground alongside Hurricane Creek	3 tent-trailer sites, 5 tent sites, restrooms	summer-fall	$6
Hurricane Creek Rd., Enterprise, 541/426-5546, www.fs.usda.gov				
Minam State Recreation Area	quiet campground along the Wallowa River	22 tent sites, restrooms	spring-fall	$10
Hwy. 82, Minam, 800/551-6949, http://oregonstateparks.org				
Catherine Creek State Park	remote campground along a rushing river	20 tent sites, restrooms	April-October	$10
Hwy. 203, Union, 541/983-2277, http://oregonstateparks.org				
Anthony Lake Campground	alpine campground in the Elkhorn Mountains	37 tent and trailer sites, restrooms	July-September	$10-50
Forest Rd. 73, North Powder, 541/894-2332, www.anthonylakes.com				

HIKING TIPS

Safety

BEFORE YOU GO

All too often, when hikers find themselves in distress, the trouble didn't start on the trail. It started in their living room. It's the seemingly tiny mistakes made at home that can compound into significant problems in the wilderness. Forgetting to let somebody know where you're going. Not checking the weather or time of nightfall. Forgetting to pack rain gear, food, water, or extra batteries. Maybe even (and, yes, at least one of us has done this) forgetting your entire day pack. You have a map and compass, but do you know how to use them? Were you honest about your limitations and fitness level (your current fitness level) when you selected the hike?

Safe and fun hikes start during the preparation process. Here's what you need to get ready for your day hike:

The 10 Essentials

Since 1974, when it was formalized by the Seattle-based outdoor group The Mountaineers, the 10 Essentials has been widely regarded as the standard list of gear hikers and climbers need to stay safe and respond to an emergency when traveling in the backcountry.

1. Extra food: Pack more than you think you'll need.

2. Extra water: Carry more than you think you'll need or, if there are water sources along your route, carry a water purification system.

3. First aid: In a waterproof bag, carry a first-aid kit with items to care for yourself and those depending on you (including pets). Don't forget insect repellent, foot care, and medications.

4. Emergency shelter: Take a lightweight bivy, waterproof tarp, or an oversized and durable plastic bag.

5. Insulation: Pack extra clothes for warmth and protection from the elements.

6. Illumination: A headlamp and/or flashlight and extra batteries.

7. Fire: A stove, waterproof matches, or lighter and tinder.

8. Sun protection: Bring a hat and sunglasses and always use sunscreen (even on overcast days).

9. Navigation: Start with a map and compass. Consider carrying a GPS device (more resistant to weather than phones), an altimeter, and a personal locator beacon (capable of sending an emergency signal from outside cell coverage). Bring battery backup for electronic devices. While your phone is a wonderful tool, don't treat it as a lifeline: Phones are fragile, and cell coverage in the backcountry is not a given.

10. Repair kit and tools: A multipurpose tool, knife, duct tape, zip ties, safety pins, and a sewing kit are great for solving problems on the trail.

HIKING APPS

Whether you want to identify a bird or a mountain, need help finding your way, or just need directions and the weather forecast, your phone can help. There are numerous apps that can enhance your outdoor excursion. Here are some of our favorites:

- **CAIRN** (www.cairnme.com, Android, IOS, free with in-app purchases) shares your location with friends and family of your choosing and alerts them if you're overdue. The app also helps find cell coverage, records your route, and offers topographical maps to download for offline use.

- **DARK SKY WEATHER** (www.darksky.net, Android, free with in-app purchases; IOS, $3.99) and **WEATHER UNDERGROUND** (www.wunderground.com, Andriod, IOS, free with in-app purchases) are good choices for staying abreast of weather forecasts in the area you're hiking.

- **FIRST AID - AMERICAN RED CROSS** (www.redcross.org, Android, IOS, free) helps diagnose and treat common injuries and ailments you might face on the trail. Videos and written directions offer expert advice on dealing with sprains, heat stroke, hypothermia, and more.

- **GAIAGPS** (www.gaiagps.com, Android, IOS, free with in-app purchases) lets you navigate the wilderness, record your hike, download maps, check weather forecasts, and search for trails.

- **MERLIN BIRD ID** (www.merlin.allaboutbirds.org, Android, IOS, free) helps you identify more than 3,000 bird species by snapping a photo or answering questions. The app then gives you in-depth info on the bird and even lets you listen to birdsongs.

- **PEAKFINDER AR** (www.peakfinder.org, Android, IOS, $4.99) and **PEAKVISOR** (www.peakvisor.com, Andriod, $4.49, IOS, free with in-app purchases) are excellent apps for identifying peaks. Just point your phone's camera at the mountain in question: The apps use augmented reality to overlay a rendering of the peak so you can determine its name.

- **ALLTRAILS** (www.alltrails.com, Andriod, IOS, free with in-app purchases) and **WTA TRAILBLAZER** (www.wta.org, Andriod, IOS, free) are valuable tools for hikers, complete with hiking suggestions and trip reports with details about current trail and road conditions.

Hiking Prep

With the right gear and preparation, you're ready to hit the trail.

Tell a friend: If you get lost or need help, will rescuers know to look for you? It's vital to make sure a friend or family member knows where you are going and understands your itinerary.

Check the forecast: Be prepared for what the weather is supposed to be like, but remember the weather is unpredictable. So, also be ready for sudden and dramatic changes. Check with a ranger station or land manager before your trip to confirm the trail is open, whether you can reach the trailhead (or get close enough to walk). And don't forget to check the avalanche forecast.

Go old school with directions: Siri is wealth of information, but she doesn't seem to hike much. Ask for "directions to Mailbox Peak," and she'll confidently guide you to the wrong place. Same goes for other trailheads around the Northwest. Avoid this problem by researching directions before you go.

Check yourself before you wreck yourself: A mountaintop, five miles from your car, is a bad place to come to the realization that your athletic glory days are behind you. Be honest about your fitness level and how much stress your joints can handle before they turn on you. If it's been a while since you hiked, start slow. And don't worry—the Northwest (and this book) is loaded with dazzling day hikes for every level.

Double-check: Make sure your gear is in working order and double-check that you have everything you need before pulling out of the driveway.

Get trailhead-ready: Opportunistic burglars love trailheads. Lock your car and never leave valuables inside. If you routinely keep stuff in your car, consider leaving those items at home. And if you do leave items in your car, make sure they're out of sight. And don't forget to hang your parking pass.

On the Trail

WEATHER

For hikers, meteorologists are also stylists. They're talking about rain, snow, and high-pressure systems, but what we hear are guidelines for how to dress. After all, almost every day is perfect for hiking if you have the right gear. The Northwest might be famous for rain, but don't let gloomy forecasts get you down. Heading out in the rain can be a good way to avoid crowds. Plus, most rainy days have windows free of precipitation. To really dial in your forecast, head to www.weather.gov, where you can click on a location on a map and NOAA will serve up a personalized prediction.

Be sure to know what time the sun will set, especially in late summer and early fall when it's not uncommon for hikers to be surprised when darkness arrives earlier than they expected. In winter and early spring, check avalanche conditions on the Northwest Avalanche Center website (www.nwac.us).

Check for road closures and mountain pass conditions at www.tripcheck.com in Oregon and www.wsdot.com in Washington. Both link to numerous webcams that help you better understand what you'll face during your drive.

WILDLIFE

Whether it's a squirrel scurrying up a tree or a black bear foraging in a trailside huckleberry bush, wildlife encounters are an exciting and inevitable part of hiking in the Pacific Northwest. These encounters are usually peaceful if hikers keep their distance, but there's a reason these animals are called wildlife. They are wild and unpredictable. You don't know what they will do if they are startled or feel cornered, and you don't want to find out.

Give the animals plenty of space and never feed them. Feeding animals conditions them to associate humans with food. This can be unsafe for people and the animals. Rangers at Mount Rainier National Park have reported warning people to stop feeding animals out of their car windows only to see animals killed while jumping in front of cars, presumably in the pursuit of food.

Bears

If you stumble across a bear while hiking in the Northwest, it's likely a black bear. However, grizzly bears can be found in the North Cascades and northeastern Washington. Look for fresh scat, tracks, and clawed trees as you hike. Making noise by clapping your hands or talking loudly is often enough to keep bears away. Bears are attracted to scents like perfume, deodorant, and even toothpaste. If you're camping, hang everything that smells (except your hiking partner) at least 10 feet off the ground and at least 100 yards outside of camp.

If you stumble across a black bear, stop and try to stay calm as you assess the situation. If the bear doesn't notice you, slowly back away. If the bear approaches you, don't throw anything and avoid direct eye contact, which the bear could interpret as a threat. Instead, stand up, wave your hands, and talk to it in a low voice. If you are in a group, stand shoulder-to-shoulder and wave your arms to appear intimidating. If the bear charges you, fight the urge to run (bears can run 35 mph, about 7 mph faster than Usain Bolt). Stand your ground. It's likely bluff-charging. If the bear attacks, fight back.

If your encounter is with a grizzly, WDFW suggests a different approach. First, you'll need to know the difference between the bears; a dish face and shoulder hump are the most obvious sign you're dealing with a grizzly. Grizzlies have smaller ears than black bears and claws that can be twice as long. Don't try to tell them apart by their color. Black bears can be brown or cinnamon colored, and grizzly coats can be so brown they appear black. If you can't avoid the grizzly, try to distract it by dropping a coat or another nonfood item and look for a tree you can climb at least 12 feet off the ground. If you can't find a tree and the bear attacks, curl up on the ground and protect your head and neck with your arms. Don't get up until you're certain the bear is gone.

Cougars

Cougars are solitary creatures who usually want nothing to do with humans. If you happen across one of these massive cats, they're likely to scram quicker than you can process what you saw. Attacks are rare. The best way to avoid cougars is to hike in a group, make noise to avoid surprising these beasts, and stay away from animal carcasses. Cougars might be saving these dead animals for their next meal.

If you encounter a cougar, do not run. Instead, keep eye contact and make yourself look as big as possible. Open your jacket, wave your arms, shout, and throw rocks to convince the animal you are a predator, not prey. Pick up small children. Assess the situation and back away slowly if it is safe to do so. If it attacks, fight back.

Mountain Goats

Mountain goats meandering across rocky slopes are a sight to behold, but get too close and they can be dangerous. Try to stay at least 50 yards away from these peaceful-looking creatures. Mountain goats have an insatiable appetite for salt and might follow you in hope of tasting your sweat and urine or scoring a snack. Never feed them. If a goat won't leave you alone, try to scare it off by hollering, waving your arms, and throwing small rocks. They might look harmless, but if a mountain goat charges you it can be deadly.

Rattlesnakes

They slither, they're venomous, and they'll get your adrenaline pumping, but rattlesnakes aren't likely to bite if you give them plenty of space. Found east of the Cascades, rattlesnakes are most active in late spring and summer and usually shake their rattles to warn you of their presence. Don't let them scare you off the trail. Be mindful of where you step—especially when crossing scree fields, logs, and rocks—and where you put your hands (don't reach under rocks). Keep pets and kids close. And wear hiking boots to protect your feet. Rattlesnake bites are rare, but if you end up on the unlucky side of the odds, here's what the Red Cross recommends: Call 9-1-1, gently wash the wound, and keep it lower than your heart. Stay calm and, unless necessary, avoid walking.

Ticks

Ticks hang out on grass and leaves and will latch on to a human or animal if given the chance. Don't be a good host. Wearing a long-sleeve shirt, pants, and lightweight gaiters (or tucking your pants into your socks) makes it hard for these bugs to attach to you. Avoiding overgrown trails and wearing insect repellent with DEET also helps avoid these pests.

Ticks burrow into your skin and, like tiny eight-legged vampires, they want to drink your blood. If a tick attaches to you, use tweezers and grasp the bug as close to your skin as possible and slowly pull it out. Wash the bite area and apply an antibiotic ointment. You can save the tick so your doctor can test it for Lyme disease. Remember to also inspect your pet for ticks. The Red Cross warns against myths regarding removing ticks. Do not try to remove ticks by burning them or applying petroleum jelly or nail polish.

Hazardous Plants

Learning to identify and avoid poison ivy and poison oak is a good way to avoid an itchy situation. Both grow as shrubs or vines with green leaves that turn red in the fall. Poison ivy leaves have three leaflets while poison oak leaves vary in shape. Both can cause an itchy rash that will spoil your hike.

Wearing pants and a long-sleeve shirt will protect your skin. Avoid overgrown trails. If you come in contact with these plants, wash your skin. The oil emitted by the plants can linger on your gear, clothes and pets, so they'll need to be washed too. Anti-itch cream, an ice pack, and a cool shower can give you some relief.

HIKING WITH DOGS

Your dog probably loves playing in the outdoors as much as you, but just like you and your human hiking companions, things can go wrong if you aren't prepared. Here are some recommendations for making sure everything goes smoothly for you and your best friend:

- **KNOW THE RULES:** Don't leave the house before finding a destination where dogs are allowed. They are permitted in many areas, but some places (like national parks and wildlife refuges) don't allow pets.
- **FIRST-AID UPGRADE:** Make sure your first-aid kit has items than can help tend to an injured dog. Duct tape, vet wrap, wound closure strips, and antibiotic ointment are a good idea. Ask your vet about carrying an antihistamine in case of bee sting. Apply canine sunscreen to exposed skin (and don't forget the nose).
- **PAY ATTENTION TO YOUR DOG:** If your dog is panting excessively, drooling, or unsteady on its feet, it's probably overheated. Blue, purple, or bright red gums are also a sign the dog needs to cool off. Get the dog in the shade, off hot surfaces such as rocks and asphalt, and get it water to drink. Put wet towels behind its neck and on its paws, groin, and armpits.
- **FLEA AND TICK PROTECTION:** A flea and tick collar or medication helps keep these pests away. But a tick puller (or tweezers) is a good addition to your first-aid kit.
- **REIGN IT IN:** Always keep your dog on a leash, no matter how well trained it is. A leash can keep your dog from unwanted encounters with wildlife and hikers who might not love dogs as much as you. Ask before letting your dog interact with another hiker's pet.
- **GEAR UP:** Doggy jackets, booties, and sunglasses can keep your pet safe and comfortable. Plus, they're super adorable. A body harness is likely to be most comfortable for your dog. Buy one with pockets so they can carry their own food, water, and doggy doo.

▾ A LUCKY DOG GETS A RIDE

Wildfire

The biggest summer bummer for Northwest hikers in recent years has been wildfires. Local forest fires coupled with smoke blowing in from fires in California and British Columbia have led to a lousy air quality and poor visibility on many popular trails. Visit www.airnow.com to view the air-quality index. Be sure to check the forecast and call or visit a ranger station in the area where you plan to hike to determine if your plans are safe. Don't be shy about changing plans. You can always return at another time. Wildfires are unpredictable.

PROTECT THE ENVIRONMENT

Whether you're looking for inspiring views, a challenging workout, a few hours of solitude, or memories that last a lifetime, the trails of the Pacific Northwest will take care of you. All they need in return is for you to take care of them. Here are some tips for minimizing your impact:

Dirt won't hurt: Too often, hikers walk around the perimeter of trail-blocking puddles, but this often tramples vegetation and creates wide spots in the trails. Hiking through the puddle is usually the best move.

Don't cut switchbacks: It's horrible for the trail and vegetation. Even if you aren't traipsing through vegetation, these shortcuts can change the way water flows in the area and erode the slope and the trail.

Leave nothing, take nothing: Be prepared to pack out all your trash. Bonus points for collecting garbage you find along the way. Don't collect rocks, pick flowers, or take anything else. If you need a souvenir, take a picture. Don't carve initials or anniversary dates in trees or benches. It's not romantic. It's vandalism.

Be a super pooper: If you can't make it back to a trailhead or to a pit toilet, dig a hole at least six inches deep and at least 200 feet from the trail and the nearest water source. Cover the hole when you are done, but don't bury toilet paper. Pack it out. Or use natural TP like grass, leaves, or pinecones. And never bury your business in the snow. Snow melts. Pack it out.

Don't feed the animals: Feeding animals trains them to associate people with food. You don't want bears seeing you as walking beef jerky, so give other hikers the same courtesy.

Be considerate: In a 2017 interview, Ben Lawhon, educational director at Leave No Trace, told me speakers blasting music don't keep bears away (a common excuse). They are just giving users a false sense of security and spoiling the serenity for others. And it might unnecessarily scare other wildlife, he said.

Yield like a boss: Always yield to horses and uphill hikers. Don't step off the trail, if possible.

Volunteer: Several organizations give hikers the chance to give back to the trails that give them so much. Washington Trails Association (www.wta.org) is one of the largest trail volunteer organizations in the country. Call your favorite park or check www.volunteer.gov for more opportunities.

PASSES, PERMITS, AND FEES

At popular Northwest trailheads, it's somewhat common to see cars with a collection of parking passes spread out on their dashboards. For some

BEERS MADE BY WALKING

Beer enthusiast Eric Steen believes in the connection between the great outdoors and good beer. So in 2011, he founded **Beers Made By Walking** (www.beersmadebywalking.com) to bring together those seemingly disparate worlds. Every spring and summer, Steen plans a series of interpretive hikes throughout the United States, where hikers and local brewers learn about the medicinal and edible characteristics of plants they encounter.

Following the hike, the brewers turn those ideas into new beers and hold tasting events to show off the finished products. Since the first Beers Made By Walking event, these brewers have developed ales and lagers with, for example, stinging nettles, huckleberries, pine needles, sagebrush, prickly pear cactus fruit, and dozens of other ingredients. Each beer release generally raises money for conservation efforts and local nonprofits.

Beers Made By Walking is present throughout the Pacific Northwest, with events in Seattle, Carnation, Bellingham, Portland, Bend, Eugene, and Corvallis. Hikes are usually free and open to the public, and end-of-season celebrations vary by city; Seattle breweries generally cap each season with a ticketed event where patrons can try hike-inspired beers, while Portland-area brewers have, in recent years, held tapping events at participating breweries. Check the website in spring to see the upcoming list of cities, sign up for a hike, and stay up-to-date on tasting events.

hikers, it's confusing determining who manages the land they're parking on and which pass to use. It's easier just to lay out everything in the glovebox. Generally, you'll be covered if you have passes for state, national forest, and national park land. Here's what you need to legally park at the trailheads for every hike in this book.

A **Northwest Forest Pass** (discovernw.org, $5 per day, $30 annual pass) is required at developed Forest Service recreation sites in Washington and Oregon. Passes are available at Forest Service offices, through hundreds of vendors, and online at www.store.usgs.gov/forest-pass.

An **Oregon State Parks Permit** ($5 per day, $30 annual pass, $50 two-year pass when not camping at that park) is required at the 25 Oregon state parks that charge a day-use fee; it can be purchased online and at kiosks within the parks.

A **Discover Pass** (866/320-9933, www.discoverpass.wa.gov, $10 per day, $30 annual pass) is required on Washington state land managed by Washington State Parks, the Washington Department of Natural Resources, and the Washington Department of Fish and Wildlife. Twenty-eight state parks have automated pay stations. Passes are available at state park headquarters, regional offices, and more than 600 vendors and retail stores (find a complete list on the website). Passes are available online, by phone, and as an add-on option when renewing your Washington vehicle license. If you purchase a one-day pass on your phone and

HIKING WITH CHILDREN

It's you and nature vs. Netflix and the Xbox in a battle to capture your kids' imagination, and the odds aren't in your favor. Not only does it take significantly more energy to ready the little ones for an excursion, but it can also be intimidating. But if you want to pass along your love of the outdoors, the sooner you start hiking the better. Here are some tips for keeping it fun (and safe):

- **PLAN:** Your hands are going to be full on hike day, so ready maps, driving directions, gear, food, water, and pass information the night before.
- **START EASY AND INTERESTING:** The joy of testing your toughness on hard trails is usually lost on kids. Choose something you know will be easy on their little legs. And pick something with ponds, big trees, beaches, or other things that will hold their attention.
- **GO AT THEIR PACE:** Give yourself plenty of time to finish the hike. Those puddles, flowers, and ladybugs you didn't even notice are mesmerizing to kids.
- **GEAR UP:** On short, easy trails, tennis shoes are usually fine hiking footwear for kids. But making sure the youngsters are dressed appropriately for the conditions can be the difference between misery and an outing that launches a lifelong love for the outdoors. A comfortable child-carrier backpack is ideal for babies and toddlers who might need to split time between riding and walking.
- **PLAY GAMES:** Don't give kids a chance for their attention to wane. Play games like I Spy, or count squirrels, birds, or mushrooms for an added layer of entertainment.
- **PACK PLENTY OF SNACKS AND WATER:** Take snack breaks along the way and maybe even save a special snack for the halfway point.
- **GO WITH FRIENDS:** No matter how old, hiking with friends enhances the adventure. Plus, having another parent around means extra help

can't print it, you can write the transaction number on a piece of paper and display it on your dash. A processing fee of $1.50-5 applies to some pass purchases.

A **Makah Recreational Use Pass** (www.makah.com, $10 annual pass) is required on the Makah Reservation. Those heading to classic coastal hikes such as Shi Shi Beach and Cape Flattery should stop in Neah Bay for a pass. Permits are good for the calendar year in which they are purchased. Buy passes at Hobuck Beach Resort, the Makah Cultural and Research Center, Makah Marina, Makah Mini Mart, Makah Tribal Center, and Washburn's General Store.

National Parks
There's no entrance fee at North Cascades National Park, but have your credit card ready if you're visiting the Northwest's other national parks. At Mount Rainier and Olympic, entry is $30 per private vehicle (with a seating capacity of 15 or less) and good for seven consecutive days. Motorcycles

in dealing with emotional meltdowns and diaper blowouts. Looking for a kid-friendly hiking group? Hike it Baby (www.hikeitbaby.com), founded in Portland in 2013, is an excellent resource for finding family hiking meetups.

- **TEACH:** Use the outing to start teaching your kids about nature and trail and environmental etiquette.

BEST HIKES WITH KIDS:

- **HOLE-IN-THE-WALL:** Skip rocks and explore tide pools on a 1.5-mile-each-way walk along the Pacific to a sea arch (page 43).
- **BIG FOUR ICE CAVES:** On a mostly flat 2.4-mile forest walk, pass nurse logs and salmonberry plants, cross a bridge spanning the Stillaguamish River, and view caves formed in the snow at the base of Big Four Mountain. It's not safe to go near or inside the caves (page 157).
- **GROVE OF THE PATRIARCHS AND SILVER FALLS:** From the trailhead, it's 1.2 miles round-trip to the giant trees at the Grove of the Patriarchs, and kids will love crossing the Ohanapecosh River on a suspension bridge. You can easily extend this trip to thundering Silver Falls by walking 1.4 miles south (page 220).
- **WEST METOLIUS RIVER:** Follow a mostly flat footpath to the Wizard Falls Hatchery, which rears six species of trout and salmon and hosts open-air ponds and interpretive panels. For a quarter you can buy fish food out of on-site gumball machines (page 432).
- **CARROLL RIM TRAIL:** Your kids will get a kick out of this short hike to a summit offering expansive views of the surrounding Painted Hills (page 466).
- **NATIONAL HISTORIC OREGON TRAIL INTERPRETIVE CENTER:** Walk in the dusty footsteps of Oregon Trail pioneers, and head inside the interpretive center afterward for displays, movies, and more (page 578).

are $25 and walkers and cyclists are $15 each. Both parks offer an annual pass for $55.

At **Crater Lake National Park,** it's $30 per vehicle in summer (May 22-Oct. 31), $20 per vehicle in winter (Nov. 1-May 21); $25 per motorcycle in summer (May 22-Oct. 31), $20 per motorcycle in winter (Nov. 1-May 21); $15 per cyclist or pedestrian; and $55 for an annual pass. Non-annual passes are good for seven days.

Purchase passes in advance at www.yourpassnow.com.

America the Beautiful Passes

A must for outdoor lovers, America the Beautiful Passes (888/275-8747, www.nps.gov) cover entry and amenity fees on lands managed by six federal agencies: the National Park Service (national parks), U.S. Forest Service (national forests and grasslands), U.S. Fish and Wildlife Service (national wildlife refuges), Bureau of Land Management, Bureau of Reclamation, and U.S. Army Corps of Engineers. You have several options:

Annual Pass: Buy this $80 pass at a federal recreation site, by phone at 888/275-8747, or online at store.usgs.gov/pass.

Military Pass: Free for current U.S. military members and dependents; obtain a pass by showing a Common Access Card or military ID at a federal recreation site.

4th Grade Pass: Kids and their families get free access to federal recreation lands during the student's fourth-grade year. Fourth-grade teachers and those at organizations serving fourth-graders (youth group leaders, camp directors, etc.) are also eligible. Visit www.everykidinapark.gov for details.

Senior Pass: U.S. citizens and permanent residents 62 and older may buy a lifetime interagency pass for $80 or an annual pass for $20. Passes may be purchased online at www.store.usgs.gov/pass, through the mail, or, to avoid a $10 processing fee, in person at a federal recreation site. Note that Golden Age Passports are no longer sold but are still honored.

Access Pass: Free to U.S. citizens and permanent residents with permanent disabilities. Documentation of permanent disability is required. Passes are available at federal recreation sites and by mail; ordering by mail requires a $10 processing fee.

Volunteer Pass: Once you volunteer 250 hours with federal agencies participating in the Interagency Pass Program, you're eligible for a free pass. Contact your local federal recreation site for specifics. Find volunteer opportunities at www.volunteer.gov.

RESOURCES

CITY AND COUNTY PARKS

SEATTLE PARKS AND RECREATION
100 Dexter Ave. E
Seattle, WA 98109
206/684-4075
www.seattle.gov

DISCOVERY PARK
3801 Discovery Park Blvd.
Seattle, WA 98199
206/386-4236
www.seattle.gov

WHITMAN COUNTY PARKS & RECREATION
400 N. Main St.
Colfax, WA 99111
509/397-4622
www.whitmancounty.org

PORTLAND PARKS & RECREATION
1120 SW 5th Ave.
Portland, OR 97204
503/823-7529
www.portlandoregon.gov

BEND PARKS AND RECREATION DISTRICT
799 SW Columbia St.
Bend, OR 97702
541/389-7275
www.bendparksandrec.org

CITY OF ASHLAND PARKS DIVISION
1195 E. Main St.
Ashland, OR 97520
541/488-5340
www.ashland.or.us
www.whitmancounty.org

STATE PARKS AND FORESTS

WASHINGTON STATE PARKS
PO Box 42650
Olympia, WA 98504
360/902-8844
www.parks.wa.gov

DECEPTION PASS STATE PARK
41020 State Route 20
Oak Harbor, WA 98277
360/675-3767
www.parks.wa.gov

OLALLIE STATE PARK
51350 SE Homestead Valley Rd.
North Bend, WA 98045
425/455-7010
www.parks.wa.gov

WALLACE FALLS STATE PARK
14503 Wallace Lake Rd.
Gold Bar, WA 98251
360/793-0420
www.parks.wa.gov

CAPE DISAPPOINTMENT STATE PARK
244 Robert Gray Dr.
Ilwaco, WA 98624
360/642-3078
www.parks.wa.gov

BEACON ROCK STATE PARK
34841 SR 14
Skamania, WA 98648
509/427-8265
www.parks.wa.gov

MOUNT PILCHUCK STATE PARK
Granite Falls, WA 98252
360/793-0420
www.parks.wa.gov

PALOUSE FALLS STATE PARK
Starbuck, WA 99143
509/646-9218
www.parks.wa.gov

PALOUSE TO CASCADES STATE PARK TRAIL
150 Lake Easton State Park Rd.
Easton, WA 98925
509/656-2230
www.parks.wa.gov

STEAMBOAT ROCK STATE PARK
51052 Highway 155
Electric City, WA 99123
509/633-1304
www.parks.wa.gov

WASHINGTON STATE DEPARTMENT OF NATURAL RESOURCES
1111 Washington St. SE
Olympia WA 98504
360/902-1000
www.dnr.wa.gov

OREGON STATE PARKS
725 Summer St. NE, Suite C
Salem, OR 97301
503/986-0707
www.oregonstateparks.org

OSWALD WEST STATE PARK
U.S. 101
Manzanita, OR 97102
503/368-3575
www.oregonstateparks.org

CAPE LOOKOUT STATE PARK
13000 Whiskey Creek Rd.
Tillamook, OR 97141
503/842-4981
www.oregonstateparks.org

TILLAMOOK STATE FOREST
45500 Wilson River Hwy.
Tillamook, OR 97141
866/930-4646
www.oregon.gov/ODF

HECETA HEAD LIGHTHOUSE STATE SCENIC VIEWPOINT
93111 U.S. 101
Florence, OR 97439
541/547-3416
www.oregonstateparks.org

ALFRED A. LOEB STATE PARK
99917 North Bank Chetco River Rd.
Brookings, OR 97415
541/469-2021
www.oregonstateparks.org

TRYON CREEK STATE NATURAL AREA
11321 SW Terwilliger Blvd.
Portland, OR 97219
503/636-9886
www.oregonstateparks.org

SILVER FALLS STATE PARK
20024 Silver Falls Hwy. SE
Sublimity, OR 97385
503/873-8681
www.oregonstateparks.org

GUY W. TALBOT STATE PARK
U.S. 30 (Historic Columbia River Highway)
Corbett, OR 97019
503/695-2261
www.oregonstateparks.org

THE COVE PALISADES STATE PARK
7300 Jordan Rd.
Culver, OR 97734
541/546-3412
www.oregonstateparks.org

SMITH ROCK STATE PARK
9241 NE Crooked River Dr.
Terrebonne, OR 97760
541/548-7501
www.oregonstateparks.org

NATIONAL PARKS AND MONUMENTS

NORTH CASCADES NATIONAL PARK
810 State Route 20
Sedro-Woolley, WA 98284
360/854-7200
www.nps.gov/noca

MOUNT RAINIER NATIONAL PARK
55210 238th Ave. E
Ashford, WA 98304
360/569-2211
www.nps.gov/mora

OLYMPIC NATIONAL PARK
600 E. Park Ave.
Port Angeles, WA 98362
360/565-3130
www.nps.gov/olym

MOUNT ST. HELENS NATIONAL VOLCANIC MONUMENT
42218 NE Yale Bridge Rd.
Amboy, WA 98601
360/449-7800
www.fs.usda.gov

EBEY'S LANDING NATIONAL HISTORIC RESERVE
162 Cemetery Rd.
PO Box 774
Coupeville, WA 98239
360/678-6084
www.nps.gov/ebla

CRATER LAKE NATIONAL PARK
PO Box 7
Crater Lake, OR 97604
541/594-3000
www.nps.gov/crla

OREGON CAVES NATIONAL MONUMENT & PRESERVE
19000 Caves Hwy.
Cave Junction, OR 97523
541/592-2100
www.nps.gov/orca

JOHN DAY FOSSIL BEDS NATIONAL MONUMENT
32651 Highway 19
Kimberly, OR 97848
541/987-2333
www.nps.gov/joda

NATIONAL FORESTS

U.S. FOREST SERVICE—PACIFIC NORTHWEST REGION
1220 SW 3rd Ave.
Portland, OR 97204
503/808-2468
www.fs.usda.gov/r6

COLVILLE NATIONAL FOREST
765 S. Main St.
Colville, WA 99114
509/684-7000
www.fs.usda.gov/colville

GIFFORD PINCHOT NATIONAL FOREST
1501 E. Evergreen Blvd.
Vancouver, WA 98661
360/891-5000
www.fs.usda.gov/giffordpinchot

MOUNT BAKER-SNOQUALMIE NATIONAL FOREST
2930 Wetmore Ave., Suite 3A
Everett, WA 98201
425/783-6000
www.fs.usda.gov/mbs

OKANOGAN-WENATCHEE NATIONAL FOREST
215 Melody Lane
Wenatchee, WA 98801
509/664-9200
www.fs.usda.gov/okawen

OLYMPIC NATIONAL FOREST
1835 Black Lake Blvd. SW
Olympia, WA 98512
360/956-2402
www.fs.usda.gov/olympic

UMATILLA NATIONAL FOREST
72510 Coyote Rd.
Pendleton, OR 97801
541/278-3716
www.fs.usda.gov/umatilla

SIUSLAW NATIONAL FOREST
3200 SW Jefferson Way
Corvallis, OR 97331
541/750-7000
www.fs.usda.gov/siuslaw

SIUSLAW NATIONAL FOREST—CAPE PERPETUA VISITOR CENTER
2400 U.S. 101
Yachats, OR 97498
541/547-3289
www.fs.usda.gov/siuslaw

ROGUE RIVER-SISKIYOU NATIONAL FOREST
3040 Biddle Rd.
Medford, OR 97504
541/618-2200
www.fs.usda.gov/rogue-siskiyou

COLUMBIA RIVER GORGE NATIONAL SCENIC AREA
902 Wasco Ave., Suite 200
Hood River, OR 97031
541/308-1700
www.fs.usda.gov/crgnsa

MOUNT HOOD NATIONAL FOREST
16400 Champion Way
Sandy, OR 97055
503/668-1700
www.fs.usda.gov/mthood

WILLAMETTE NATIONAL FOREST
3106 Pierce Parkway, Suite D
Springfield, OR 97477
541/225-6300
www.fs.usda.gov/willamette

DESCHUTES NATIONAL FOREST
63095 Deschutes Market Rd.
Bend, OR 97701
541/383-5300
www.fs.usda.gov/deschutes

OCHOCO NATIONAL FOREST
3160 NE 3rd St.
Prineville, OR 97754
541/416-6500
www.fs.usda.gov/ochoco

KLAMATH NATIONAL FOREST
1711 S. Main St.
Yreka, CA 96097
530/842-6131
www.fs.usda.gov/klamath

FREMONT-WINEMA NATIONAL FOREST
1301 S. G St.
Lakeview, OR 97630
541/947-2151
www.fs.usda.gov/fremont-winema

WALLOWA-WHITMAN NATIONAL FOREST
1550 Dewey Ave., Suite A
Baker City, OR 97814
541/523-6391
www.fs.usda.gov/wallowa-whitman

OTHER RESOURCES
BUREAU OF LAND MANAGEMENT OREGON-WASHINGTON
1220 SW 3rd Ave.
Portland, OR 97204
503/808-6001
www.blm.gov

WASHINGTON STATE DEPARTMENT OF FISH AND WILDLIFE
1111 Washington St. SE
Olympia WA 98501
360/902-2200
www.wdfw.wa.gov

WASHINGTON TRAILS ASSOCIATION
www.wta.org

WASHINGTON STATE FERRIES
310 Maple Park Ave. SE
PO Box 47300
Olympia, WA 98504
888/808-7977
206/464-6400
www.wsdot.wa.gov/ferries

WASHINGTON PASS CONDITIONS
www.wsdot.com

THE MOUNTAINEERS
www.mountaineers.org

THE NATURE CONSERVANCY—OREGON
821 SE 14th Ave.
Portland, OR 97214
503/802-8100
www.nature.org

FRIENDS OF THE COLUMBIA GORGE
www.gorgefriends.org

TRAILKEEPERS OF OREGON
www.trailkeepersoforegon.org

OREGON DEPARTMENT OF TRANSPORTATION TRIPCHECK TRIP-PLANNING TOOL
www.tripcheck.com

CRATER LAKE HOSPITALITY
www.travelcraterlake.com

OREGON NATURAL DESERT ASSOCIATION
www.onda.org

OREGON WILD
www.oregonwild.org

TRAVEL OREGON
www.traveloregon.com

NATIONAL WEATHER SERVICE
www.weather.gov

NORTHWEST AVALANCHE CENTER
www.nwac.us

AIRNOW AIR QUALITY INDEX
www.airnow.gov

TIDES AND CURRENTS
www.tidesandcurrents.noaa.gov

INDEX

INDEX

PHOTO CREDITS

Page 1 © Craig Hill; page 2-3 © Matt Wastradowski; page 6 © Craig Hill; page 7 © Matt Wastradowski (top), © Craig Hill (bottom); page 8 © Matt Wastradowski (top), © Craig Hill (middle), © Kristen Hill (bottom); Page 9 © Craig Hill (top), ©Matt Wastradowski (bottom); page 10 © Hotshotsworldwide | Dreamstime.com (top), © Crux Fermentation Project (bottom); page 11 © Matt Wastradowski; page 13 © Craig Hill; page 16 © Craig Hill; page 17 © Ravina Schneider; page 19 © Craig Hill; page 20 © Jake Martinez/Icicle Brewing (left), © Devyn Sullivan for Everybody's Brewing (right); page 21 ©Crux Fermentation; page 22 © Matt Wastradowski; page 23 © Craig Hill; page 24 © Craig Hill; page 27 © Kan1234 | Dreamstime.com

Washington
All photos by Craig Hill except: page 36 © Victoria Ditkovsky | Dreamstime.com; page 45 © Pierre Leclerc | Dreamstime.com; page 112 ©Kristen Hill; page 153 © Kristen Hill; page 205 © Kristen Hill; page 248 ©Kristen Hill; page 264 © Kristen Hill

Oregon
All photos by Matt Wastradowski except: page 296 © Craig Hill; page 311 © Craig Hill; page 313 © Leslie Clemens | Dreamstime.com; page 322 © Craig Hill; page 476 © Donna Nonemountry | Dreamstime.com

Background
© Craig Hill

  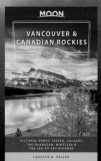

MOON NATIONAL PARKS

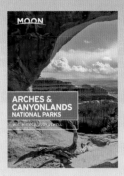

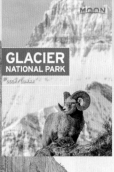

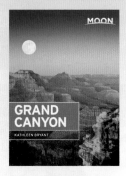

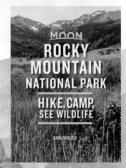

In these books:

- Full coverage of gateway cities and towns
- Itineraries from one day to multiple weeks
- Advice on where to stay (or camp) in and around the parks

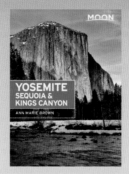

TRAILS AT A GLANCE

PAGE	HIKE NAME	DISTANCE	DURATION
WASHINGTON: WASHINGTON COAST			
34	Cape Flattery	1.5 mi rt	1 hr
37	Point of Arches via Shi Shi Beach	9 mi rt	4.5 hr
40	Ozette Triangle	9.3 mi rt	4.5 hr
43	Hole-in-the-Wall	3 mi rt	1.5 hr
46	North Head Trail	3.8 mi rt	2 hr
WASHINGTON: OLYMPIC NATIONAL PARK			
54	Dungeness Spit	10.2 mi rt	5 hr
57	Hurricane Hill	3.4 mi rt	2 hr
60	Klahhane Ridge	5.4 mi rt	3 hr
63	Hall of Mosses and Hoh River Trail	6.7 mi rt	3.5 hr
66	Grand Valley	9.3 mi rt	5 hr
69	Mount Townsend	8 mi rt	4 hr
72	Quinault Loop	4 mi rt	2 hr
75	Staircase Rapids and Shady Lane	4.2 mi rt	2 hr
78	Mount Ellinor	3.4 mi rt	2.5 hr
81	Lena Lake	6.8 mi rt	3 hr
WASHINGTON: SEATTLE AND VICINITY			
88	Oyster Dome	3.9 mi rt	2 hr
91	Deception Pass: Rosario Head and Lighthouse Point	3.3 mi rt	1.5 hr
94	Ebey's Landing	5.5 mi rt	2.5 hr
97	Discovery Park Loop	2.9 mi rt	1.5 hr
100	Poo Poo Point via Chirico Trail	3.8 mi rt	2 hr
103	Rattlesnake Ledges	4.9 mi rt	2.5 hr
106	Mount Si	7.6 mi rt	4 hr
109	Twin Falls	2.6 mi rt	1.5 hr
112	Mailbox Peak: Old-New Loop	8.2 mi rt	6 hr
116	Nisqually Estuary Boardwalk Trail	4.1 mi rt	2 hr

DIFFICULTY	SEASONAL ACCESS	WILDLIFE	WATER-FALLS	DOG-FRIENDLY
Easy	Year-round	X		X
Moderate	Year-round	X		
Moderate/strenuous	Year-round	X		
Easy	Year-round	X		X
Easy	Year-round	X		X
Moderate/strenuous	Year-round	X		
Easy/moderate	June-Oct.	X		
Moderate	Mid-June to Oct.	X	X	
Easy/moderate	Year-round	X	X	
Moderate/strenuous	Mid-July to mid-Oct.	X		
Moderate/strenuous	June-Nov.	X	X	X
Easy	Year-round	X	X	X
Easy	Year-round	X		
Moderate	July-Oct.	X		X
Moderate	Apr.-Nov.	X	X	X
Easy/moderate	Year-round	X		X
Easy	Year-round	X		X
Easy/moderate	Year-round	X		X
Easy	Year-round	X		X
Moderate	Year-round	X		X
Moderate	Year-round	X		X
Moderate/strenuous	Apr.-Nov.	X		X
Easy/moderate	Year-round	X	X	X
Strenuous	Apr.-Nov.			X
Easy	Year-round	X		

PAGE	HIKE NAME	DISTANCE	DURATION
WASHINGTON: NORTH CASCADES			
124	Winchester Mountain	3.6 mi rt	2 hr
127	Skyline Divide	6.8 mi rt	3.5 hr
130	Table Mountain	3 mi rt	1.5 hr
133	Chain Lakes Loop	7.5 mi rt	4 hr
136	Thunder Knob	3.6 mi rt	2 hr
139	Cascade Pass	7.4 mi rt	4 hr
142	Maple Pass Loop	6.8 mi rt	4 hr
145	Cedar Falls	3.5 mi rt	1.5 hr
148	Green Mountain	8.4 mi rt	5 hr
151	Mount Pilchuck	5.4 mi rt	3 hr
154	Lake Twenty-Two	6.2 mi rt	3.5 hr
157	Big Four Ice Caves	2.4 mi rt	1.5 hr
WASHINGTON: CENTRAL CASCADES			
164	Wallace Falls	5.2 mi rt	2.5 hr
167	Lake Serene and Bridal Veil Falls	8.2 mi rt	5 hr
170	Barclay Lake	4.4 mi rt	2.5 hr
173	Iron Goat Trail	5.9 mi rt	3.5 hr
176	Colchuck Lake	8.2 mi rt	4.5 hr
179	Talapus and Olallie Lakes	5.6 mi rt	3 hr
182	Granite Mountain	8.6 mi rt	5 hr
185	Snow Lake	6.8 mi rt	3.5 hr
188	Palouse to Cascades State Park Trail: Snoqualmie Tunnel	5.2 mi rt	3 hr
191	Lake Ingalls	9.6 mi rt	4.5 hr

DIFFICULTY	SEASONAL ACCESS	WILDLIFE	WATER-FALLS	DOG-FRIENDLY
Moderate	Mid-July to mid-Oct.	X		X
Moderate	July-Oct.	X		X
Easy/moderate	July to mid-Oct.	X		
Moderate	Late July to mid-Oct.	X		X
Easy/moderate	Year-round	X		X
Moderate	July to mid-Oct.	X		
Moderate	July-Oct.	X	X	X
Easy	May-early Nov.	X	X	X
Moderate/strenuous	July-Oct.	X		X
Moderate	July-early Nov.	X		X
Moderate	May-Oct.	X	X	X
Easy	June-Sept.	X	X	X
Easy/moderate	Year-round	X	X	X
Moderate	May-Nov.	X	X	X
Easy/moderate	Apr.-Nov.	X		X
Easy/moderate	May-Nov.	X	X	X
Moderate	July-Oct.	X		
Moderate	Mid-May to early Nov.	X		X
Strenuous	Late June-early Nov.	X		X
Moderate	Late June-early Nov.	X		X
Easy/moderate	May-Oct.			X
Moderate/strenuous	July-Oct.	X	X	

TRAILS AT A GLANCE (continued)

PAGE	HIKE NAME	DISTANCE	DURATION
WASHINGTON: MOUNT RAINIER			
200	Tolmie Peak	6.2 mi rt	3 hr
203	Spray Park	5.8 mi rt	3.5 hr
206	Second Burroughs Loop	6.4 mi rt	3.5 hr
210	Naches Peak Loop	3.5 mi rt	2 hr
213	Camp Muir	8.2 mi rt	5 hr
216	Skyline Trail Loop	5.8 mi rt	3 hr
220	Grove of the Patriarchs and Silver Falls	2.6 mi rt	2 hr
223	High Rock Lookout	3.2 mi rt	2 hr
WASHINGTON: SOUTH CASCADES			
230	Packwood Lake	8 mi rt	4 hr
233	Tongue Mountain	3 mi rt	2 hr
236	Harry's Ridge	8 mi rt	4 hr
239	Killen Creek	6.2 mi rt	3 hr
242	Ape Cave	2.9 mi rt	2 hr
245	Monitor Ridge to Mount St. Helens Summit	10 mi rt	8 hr
249	Lava Canyon	5.8 mi rt	3 hr
WASHINGTON: CENTRAL WASHINGTON			
256	Steamboat Rock	3.2 mi rt	1.5 hr
259	Ancient Lakes	4.4 mi rt	2.5 hr
262	Yakima Skyline Trail	6 mi rt	3 hr
265	Cowiche Canyon	5.6 mi rt	3 hr
268	Badger Mountain: Trailhead Park Loop	3 mi rt	1.5 hr

DIFFICULTY	SEASONAL ACCESS	WILDLIFE	WATER-FALLS	DOG-FRIENDLY
Easy/moderate	July-Oct.	X		
Moderate	June-Oct.	X	X	
Moderate	July to mid-Oct.	X		
Easy/moderate	June-Oct.	X		
Strenuous	July-Sept.	X	X	
Moderate	Mid-June to mid-Oct.	X	X	
Easy	May-Oct.		X	
Moderate	Mid-June to Oct.	X		X
Moderate	May-Oct.	X		X
Easy/moderate	May-early Nov.	X		X
Moderate	Late June to mid-Nov.	X		
Moderate	Mid-July to Oct.	X		X
Easy	May-Nov.	X		
Strenuous	Mid-May to Oct.	X		
Moderate	Late May-Nov.	X	X	
Easy/moderate	Year-round	X		X
Easy	Mar.-Nov.	X	X	X
Moderate	Mar.-Nov.	X		X
Easy/moderate	Year-round	X		X
Easy/moderate	Year-round	X		X

PAGE	HIKE NAME	DISTANCE	DURATION
WASHINGTON: EASTERN WASHINGTON			
276	Abercrombie Mountain	7.8 mi rt	4 hr
279	Sullivan Lakeshore Trail	8.4 mi rt	4 hr
282	Iller Creek Conservation Area	5 mi rt	2.5 hr
285	Kamiak Butte	2.5 mi rt	1.5 hr
288	Oregon Butte	5.8 mi rt	3 hr
COLUMBIA RIVER GORGE			
298	Latourell Falls Loop	3.1 mi rt	1.5 hr
301	Angel's Rest	4.9 mi rt	2.5 hr
304	Wahkeena Falls-Multnomah Falls Loop	5.9 mi rt	3 hr
308	Larch Mountain Crater Loop	7.1 mi rt	3.5 hr
311	Beacon Rock	2 mi rt	1 hr
314	Dry Creek Falls	5 mi rt	2.5 hr
317	Dog Mountain	6.9 mi rt	4 hr
320	Coyote Wall (Labyrinth Loop)	6.3 mi rt	3.5 hr
323	Mosier Plateau	3.7 mi rt	1.5 hr
326	Tom McCall Point Trail	3.8 mi rt	2 hr
OREGON: OREGON COAST			
334	Saddle Mountain	5.9 mi rt	3.5 hr
337	Cape Falcon	5.8 mi rt	3 hr
340	Neahkahnie Mountain	5.9 mi rt	3 hr
343	Kings Mountain	5.4 mi rt	3 hr
346	Cape Lookout	5.5 mi rt	2.5 hr
349	Cascade Head	5.2 mi rt	2.5 hr
352	Drift Creek Falls	4.4 mi rt	2 hr
355	Cape Perpetua	5.8 mi rt	2.5 hr
359	Heceta Head to Hobbit Trail	5 mi rt	2.5 hr
362	Cape Sebastian	3.8 mi rt	2 hr
365	River View Trail to Redwood Nature Trail	3.3 mi rt	1.5 hr

DIFFICULTY	SEASONAL ACCESS	WILDLIFE	WATER-FALLS	DOG-FRIENDLY
Moderate	June-Oct.	X		X
Moderate	Apr.-Nov.	X		X
Easy/moderate	Year-round	X		X
Easy/moderate	Mar.-Nov.	X		X
Easy/moderate	June-Nov.	X		X
Easy/moderate	Year-round		X	X
Moderate	Year-round		X	X
Moderate	Year-round		X	X
Easy/moderate	June-Oct.			X
Easy/moderate	Year-round	X		X
Moderate	Year-round		X	X
Moderate/strenuous	Mar.-Dec.	X		X
Easy/moderate	Year-round	X	X	X
Easy/moderate	Year-round	X	X	X
Easy/moderate	Mar.-Oct.	X		
Moderate	Mar.-Nov.			X
Easy/moderate	Year-round	X	X	X
Easy/moderate	Year-round			X
Moderate	Mar.-Nov.			X
Moderate	Year-round	X		X
Easy/moderate	Year-round	X		
Easy/moderate	Year-round		X	X
Easy/moderate	Year-round			X
Easy/moderate	Year-round	X		X
Easy/moderate	Year-round	X		X
Easy/moderate	Year-round	X		X

PAGE	HIKE NAME	DISTANCE	DURATION
OREGON: PORTLAND AND THE WILLAMETTE VALLEY			
372	Lower Macleay Trail to Pittock Mansion	6.4 mi rt	3 hr
375	Marquam Trail to Council Crest	3.9 mi rt	2 hr
378	Tryon Creek State Natural Area Loop	4.5 mi rt	2 hr
381	Trail of Ten Falls	9.3 mi rt	4.5 hr
384	Table Rock	8.2 mi rt	4 hr
387	Bagby Hot Springs	3.3 mi rt	1.5 hr
390	Opal Pool and Jawbone Flats Loop	8.5 mi rt	4.5 hr
393	Battle Ax Mountain	6.8 mi rt	3 hr
396	Marys Peak	6.9 mi rt	3.5 hr
399	North Fork River Walk	7 mi rt	3.5 hr
OREGON: MOUNT HOOD			
406	Lost Lake Butte	4.4 mi rt	2 hr
409	Vista Ridge to Owl Point	5.4 mi rt	2.5 hr
412	Ramona Falls	8.1 mi rt	4 hr
415	Salmon River	8.2 mi rt	4.5 hr
418	Elk Meadows	6.9 mi rt	3.5 hr
OREGON: BEND AND THE CENTRAL OREGON CASCADES			
426	McKenzie River Trail to Tamolitch (Blue Pool)	4.6 mi rt	2.5 hr
429	Little Belknap Crater	5.3 mi rt	3 hr
432	West Metolius River	5.7 mi rt	3 hr
435	Black Butte	4.8 mi rt	2.5 hr
438	Tam-a-láu Trail	7.1 mi rt	3.5 hr
441	Misery Ridge-River Trail Loop	4.2 mi rt	2.5 hr
444	Tumalo Mountain	4.4 mi rt	2.5 hr
447	Shevlin Park Loop	4.8 mi rt	2 hr
450	Flatiron Rock	6.3 mi rt	2.75 hr
453	Paulina Peak	4.7 mi rt	2.5 hr

DIFFICULTY	SEASONAL ACCESS	WILDLIFE	WATER-FALLS	DOG-FRIENDLY
Easy/moderate	Year-round	X		X
Easy/moderate	Year-round			X
Easy	Year-round	X		X
Moderate/strenuous	Year-round		X	X
Moderate	June-Nov.			X
Easy	June-Oct.			X
Moderate	Mar.-Nov.		X	X
Moderate	June-Oct.			X
Moderate	Apr.-Nov.			X
Easy/moderate	Year-round			X
Easy/moderate	May-Oct.	X		X
Easy/moderate	July-Oct.	X		X
Moderate	Apr.-Oct.		X	X
Moderate	Apr.-Nov.			X
Easy/moderate	June-Oct.			X
Easy	Feb.-Dec.		X	X
Easy/moderate	Summer-early fall			X
Easy/moderate	Year-round	X		X
Moderate	June-Oct.			X
Easy/moderate	Mar.-Nov.	X		X
Easy/moderate	Year-round	X		X
Moderate	June-Oct.	X		X
Easy	Mar.-Nov.			X
Easy/moderate	Year-round	X		X
Moderate	June-Oct.			X

TRAILS AT A GLANCE (continued)

PAGE	HIKE NAME	DISTANCE	DURATION
OREGON: JOHN DAY RIVER BASIN			
460	Steins Pillar	4.5 mi rt	2.25 hr
463	Lookout Mountain	7.7 mi rt	4 hr
466	Carroll Rim Trail	1.7 mi rt	1 hr
469	Sutton Mountain	7.5 mi rt	4 hr
472	Blue Basin Overlook	3.4 mi rt	1.75 hr
OREGON: CRATER LAKE NATIONAL PARK			
480	Boundary Springs	5.5 mi rt	2.5 hr
483	Cleetwood Cove and Wizard Island	4.9 mi rt	3 hr
486	Garfield Peak	3.4 mi rt	1.5 hr
489	Plaikni Falls	2.2 mi rt	1.5 hr
492	Mount Scott	4.6 mi rt	2.5 hr
OREGON: ASHLAND AND THE ROGUE VALLEY			
500	Rainie Falls	4.4 mi rt	2.5 hr
503	Mount Elijah	5.7 mi rt	3 hr
506	Lower Table Rock	4.8 mi rt	2.5 hr
509	Grizzly Peak	5.6 mi rt	3 hr
512	Siskiyou Mountain Park	4.9 mi rt	2 hr
515	Mount Ashland (via the Pacific Crest Trail)	8.1 mi rt	4 hr
518	Soda Mountain	4.5 mi rt	2.5 hr
OREGON: SKY LAKES WILDERNESS AND KLAMATH BASIN			
526	Horseshoe Lake	6.1 mi rt	3 hr
529	Brown Mountain Lava Flow	6.1 mi rt	3 hr
532	Sky Lakes Basin via Cold Springs Trail	7.2 mi rt	3.5 hr
535	Puck Lakes via Nannie Creek Trail	5.4 mi rt	2.5 hr
538	OC&E Woods Line State Trail	4.7 mi rt	2.5 hr

DIFFICULTY	SEASONAL ACCESS	WILDLIFE	WATER-FALLS	DOG-FRIENDLY
Easy/moderate	Apr.-Nov.			X
Easy/moderate	May-Nov.	X		X
Easy	Year-round			X
Moderate	Year-round	X		X
Easy/moderate	Year-round			X
Easy/moderate	June-Nov.	X	X	
Easy/moderate	June-Sept.	X		
Easy/moderate	July-Oct.	X		
Easy	July-Oct.		X	
Easy/moderate	July-Oct.	X		
Easy/moderate	Year-round	X	X	X
Easy/moderate	June-Nov.			X
Easy/moderate	Year-round	X		
Easy/moderate	June-Nov.			X
Easy/moderate	Year-round	X		X
Moderate	June-Nov.	X		X
Easy/moderate	June-Oct.	X		X
Easy/moderate	June-Oct.	X		X
Easy/moderate	June-Nov.	X		X
Easy/moderate	July-Oct.			X
Easy/moderate	July-Oct.	X		X
Easy	Year-round	X		X

TRAILS AT A GLANCE (continued)

PAGE	HIKE NAME	DISTANCE	DURATION
OREGON: STEENS MOUNTAIN AND ALVORD DESERT			
546	Riddle Brothers Ranch and Little Blitzen River	5.8 mi rt	2.5 hr
549	Big Indian Gorge	8.1 mi rt	4 hr
552	Wildhorse Lake	2.8 mi rt	2 hr
555	Pike Creek Canyon	6.5 mi rt	3 hr
558	Borax Lake Hot Springs	2 mi rt	1 hr
OREGON: WALLOWA MOUNTAINS AND BLUE MOUNTAINS			
566	Hurricane Creek to Slick Rock Gorge	7.5 mi rt	3.5 hr
569	Iwetemlaykin State Heritage Site	2 mi rt	1 hr
572	Imnaha River to Blue Hole	4.6 mi rt	2.25 hr
575	Anthony Lake to Hoffer Lakes	3.2 mi rt	1.5 hr
578	National Historic Oregon Trail Interpretive Center	4.3 mi rt	2 hr